Frommer's

Walt Disney World®*

& Orlando

2004

D0815701

Here's what the critics say about Frommer's:

"Amazingly easy to use. Very portable, very complete."
—*Booklist*

"Detailed, accurate, and easy-to-read information for all price ranges."
—*Glamour Magazine*

"Hotel information is close to encyclopedic."
—*Des Moines Sunday Register*

"Frommer's Guides have a way of giving you a real feel for a place."
—*Knight Ridder Newspapers*

Wiley Publishing, Inc.

* Walt Disney World® is officially known as Walt Disney World Resort®.

Published by:

Wiley Publishing, Inc.

111 River St.
Hoboken, NJ 07030

ISBN 0-7645-3723-7
ISSN 1082-2615

Editor: Naomi P. Kraus
Production Editor: Donna Wright
Cartographer: John Decamillis
Photo Editor: Richard Fox
Production by Wiley Indianapolis Composition Services

For information on our other products and services or to obtain technical support, please contact our Customer Care Department within the U.S. at 800-762-2974, outside the U.S. at 317-572-3993 or fax 317-572-4002.

Wiley also publishes its books in a variety of electronic formats. Some content that appears in print may not be available in electronic formats.

Manufactured in the United States of America

5 4 3 2 1

Contents

9 Shopping 287

10 Walt Disney World & Orlando After Dark 294

11 Side Trips from Orlando 310

Appendix A: Orlando in Depth 352

Appendix B: Useful Toll-Free Numbers & Websites 358

Index 361

List of Maps

About the Authors

Jim and Cynthia Tunstall have racked up plenty of time waiting in Walt Disney World lines. They were there when the Magic Kingdom opened in 1971, and in the more than 3 decades since that watershed moment they've sampled virtually everything that's part of an Orlando vacation. Their many insider experiences allow them to separate the good from the bad and the ugly, and they give you the best ways to cut through the lines, the crowds, and the theme park PR in order to find the things that are right for you.

Based 90 minutes from WDW, they've written five other Orlando and Florida books, including *Walt Disney World & Orlando For Dummies* and *Florida For Dummies*. They also are contributors to *Frommer's Florida* and *Frommer's Florida from $70 a Day*.

Acknowledgments

Angie Ranck and Katie Wilmeth of the Orlando/Orange County Convention & Visitors Bureau; Sandra Robert, Gary Buchanan, and Karen Haynes of the Walt Disney World staff; Camille Dudley at Universal Orlando; and Kjerstin Dillon with SeaWorld are perennial troopers who make sure we survive our time in the trenches.

Our grandsons, Jake and Andy Tourigny, give us a youthful perspective and the energy to attack the theme parks time after time.

And Naomi Kraus, lord high czarina and our editor at Frommer's, has soft hands but always manages to save us, in a literary sense, from wearing the emperor's clothes.

An Invitation to the Reader

In researching this book, we discovered many wonderful places—hotels, restaurants, shops, and more. We're sure you'll find others. Please tell us about them, so we can share the information with your fellow travelers in upcoming editions. If you were disappointed with a recommendation, we'd love to know that, too. Please write to:

Frommer's Walt Disney World & Orlando 2004
Wiley Publishing, Inc. • 111 River St. • Hoboken, NJ 07030

An Additional Note

Please be advised that travel information is subject to change at any time—and this is especially true of prices. We therefore suggest that you write or call ahead for confirmation when making your travel plans. The authors, editors, and publisher cannot be held responsible for the experiences of readers while traveling. Your safety is important to us, however, so we encourage you to stay alert and be aware of your surroundings. Keep a close eye on cameras, purses, and wallets, all favorite targets of thieves and pickpockets.

Other Great Guides for Your Trip:

Frommer's Florida

Frommer's Portable Tampa & St. Petersburg

Frommer's Best-Loved Florida's Driving Tours

Frommer's Irreverent Guide to Walt Disney World®

The Unofficial Guide to Walt Disney World®

*Mini Mickey: The Pocket Sized Unofficial Guide
to Walt Disney World®*

The Unofficial Disney Companion

Beyond Disney: The Unofficial Guide

Frommer's Star Ratings, Icons & Abbreviations

Every hotel, restaurant, and attraction listing in this guide has been ranked for quality, value, service, amenities, and special features using a **star-rating system.** In country, state, and regional guides, we also rate towns and regions to help you narrow down your choices and budget your time accordingly. Hotels and restaurants are rated on a scale of zero (recommended) to three stars (exceptional). Attractions, shopping, nightlife, towns, and regions are rated according to the following scale: zero stars (recommended), one star (highly recommended), two stars (very highly recommended), and three stars (must-see).

In addition to the star-rating system, we also use **seven feature icons** that point you to the great deals, in-the-know advice, and unique experiences that separate travelers from tourists. Throughout the book, look for:

Finds	Special finds—those places only insiders know about
Fun Fact	Fun facts—details that make travelers more informed and their trips more fun
Kids	Best bets for kids, and advice for the whole family
Moments	Special moments—those experiences that memories are made of
Overrated	Places or experiences not worth your time or money
Tips	Insider tips—great ways to save time and money
Value	Great values—where to get the best deals

The following **abbreviations** are used for credit cards:

AE	American Express	DISC	Discover	V	Visa
DC	Diners Club	MC	MasterCard		

Frommers.com

Now that you have the guidebook to a great trip, visit our website at **www.frommers.com** for travel information on more than 3,000 destinations. With features updated regularly, we give you instant access to the most current trip-planning information available. At Frommers.com, you'll also find the best prices on airfares, accommodations, and car rentals—and you can even book travel online through our travel booking partners. At Frommers.com, you'll also find the following:

- Online updates to our most popular guidebooks
- Vacation sweepstakes and contest giveaways
- Newsletter highlighting the hottest travel trends
- Online travel message boards with featured travel discussions

What's New in
Walt Disney World & Orlando

Little has stood in the way of Walt Disney World's explosive growth since it opened its first Florida theme park in 1971. But the September 11, 2001, terrorist attacks on the World Trade Center and the Pentagon, coupled with a still struggling economy, have had a lingering impact on Orlando tourism. While the tourist culture has climbed back slowly, Disney, Universal, the smaller attractions, and the area's hotels and restaurants are in an economic slump that continues to keep business off by 25% or more.

Disney and the wannabes have countered declining revenues and attendance with reduced operating hours. Some attractions and restaurants close seasonally, and some shows have fewer daily performances or are dark certain days of the week. And in the 20 months following the attacks, all three of the major players—Disney, Universal, and SeaWorld—hiked single-day admission prices twice. As of June 1, 2003, Disney charges $52 per adult and $42 per child, 3 to 9; Universal and SeaWorld charge $51.95 for adults and $42.95 for kids.

On a broader scale, heightened security remains in effect. And you can expect beefed up security at some hotels, the theme parks, and other public places.

Here's a summary of the things that have changed in the year since this Frommer's guide was last revised.

PLANNING YOUR TRIP The area's "other" airport, **Orlando Sanford International,** continues to grow slowly, becoming an alternative landing zone for mainly international travelers. Its big sister, **Orlando International Airport,** however, is still the overwhelming choice of most visitors.

Motorists who haven't been to Orlando in the last year will also find something new: Exit numbers have changed on all of the state's interstates, including I-4 from Daytona Beach through Orlando to Tampa. You'll find the new exit numbers in the directions to the accommodations, restaurants, theme parks, and other attractions in chapters 5 through 8. If you have Web access, you can view the new changes at **www11.myflorida. com/trafficoperations/exitnumb. htm**, then click "I-4."

WHERE TO STAY The moderately priced and Polynesian-themed **Royal Pacific** resort (✆ **800/232-7827** or 407/363-8000; www.universalorlando. com), the third Loews hotel at Universal Orlando, opened in June 2002, adding 1,000 rooms to Universal's capacity. Shortly after the new resort opened, Universal confirmed plans for two more hotels, but their names and themes haven't been announced.

Disney's long-delayed **Pop Century Resort** will open half of its 5,760 rooms in December 2003. No word on when the rest of the rooms will follow. Much like the All-Star resorts, the inexpensive Pop Century will have themes, in this case decade-long capsules of the 20th century.

For those who want to be near but not on Universal's property, the business-oriented **Crowne Plaza Orlando-Universal** (© 866/864-8627 or 407/355-0550; www.crowneplaza.com/universalfla) debuted in mid-June 2002 with 400 rooms and rates around $100 double.

For complete details on these and other lodging options in Orlando, see chapter 5, "Where to Stay."

WHERE TO DINE Tchoup-Chop (© 800/232-7827 or 407/363-8000; www.universalorlando.com) is the most noteworthy new arrival in town. Emeril Lagasse's second Orlando property is the signature restaurant at Universal's new Royal Pacific resort and features Pan-Asian cuisine.

Across town at Walt Disney World, character-dining aficionados will find a new reservations policy at **Cinderella's Royal Table** (© 407/939-3463; www.disneyworld.com). Guests wishing to make a Priority Seating reservation must leave a nonrefundable credit-card deposit of $10 for adults and $5 for kids. You can thank a New York state veterinarian and his followers for that. They used to jam the phone lines at the 7am opening bell and lock up all of the reservations, then offer them on an Internet site, in the process, blocking out other hopefuls.

Note: Don't plan on lighting up during dinner. Florida voters passed a constitutional amendment in 2002 that bans smoking in public work places, including restaurants and bars that serve food. Stand-alone bars that serve virtually no food and designated smoking rooms in hotels are exempted.

See chapter 6, "Where to Dine," for the complete menu on Orlando restaurants.

EXPLORING WALT DISNEY WORLD The economy has kept growth at a minimum at Disney, but that's not to say that Orlando's biggest

magnet lacked some christenings in the last 12 months.

- In addition to raising its **single-day admission** prices, Disney has also increased the admission for DisneyQuest, Typhoon Lagoon, and Blizzard Beach to $31 adults, $25 kids. The Mouse also increased the **parking** fee at its theme parks to $7 for a car or pickup truck, and raised the price of most multiday and special event passes. And Cirque du Soleil in Downtown Disney bumped its adult admission prices to $72 and $82, a jump of $5 and $15, respectively.

- Construction on **Epcot's Mission: Space** (© 407/824-4321; www.disneyworld.com), a motion simulator similar to the ones NASA uses to train astronauts, is expected to open just about the time this guide reaches bookstores.

- At **Disney–MGM Studios** (© 407/824-4321; www.disneyworld.com), the **Star Tours** ride is getting a retrofitted film that will include scenes from *Episode II: Attack of the Clones,* but the work may not be done until 2004. The park's **The Hunchback of Notre Dame** musical closed its run in September 2002.

- **Primeval Whirl** is the newest ride to debut at **Animal Kingdom** (© 407/824-4321; www.disneyworld.com). The carnival-style twin roller coaster with spinning, rider-controlled cars opened in May 2002.

- The news isn't so good at **River Country.** The smallest of Disney's three water parks, normally closed during the winter for refurbishment, didn't reopen in spring 2002 and its future at this point appears to be uncertain.

- Newly installed Web terminals at eight Magic Kingdom locations give guests 25-cent-per-minute access to their **e-mail** and the **Internet.** There are plans to add 60 more in the other theme parks, resorts, and restaurants.

- Disney's sports-and-recreation department has added 30-minute **horse-drawn carriage rides** for $30 at Fort Wilderness (© **407/824-4321;** www.disneyworld.com).

See chapter 7, "Exploring Walt Disney World," for complete details on all of Disney's latest improvements, events, and rides.

EXPLORING UNIVERSAL ORLANDO About the time this guidebook is published, Universal Studios Florida plans to open two new attractions:

Shrek 4-D (© **800/837-2273** or 407/363-8000; www.universalorlando. com) will be a 15-minute show that can be seen, heard, felt, and smelled thanks to film, motion simulators, OgreVision glasses, and other special effects, including water spritzers. Shrek replaces Alfred Hitchcock: The Art of Making Movies.

Jimmy Neutron's Nicktoon Blast (© 800/837-2273 or 407/363-8000; www.universalorlando.com) lets you sign aboard a spinning, careening adventure that includes a battle against Yokians—evil, egg-shaped aliens. This attraction replaces the Funtastic World of Hanna-Barbera.

Universal Studios Florida has also **closed Kongfrontation,** which opened with the park in 1990. It will be will be replaced in spring 2004 with the $40 million **Revenge of the Mummy,** an indoor roller coaster based on *The Mummy.*

Universal also moved **Halloween Horror Nights** to Islands of Adventure and boosted daily **parking** fees to $8 for cars and pickups.

AT SEAWORLD & ELSEWHERE IN ORLANDO SeaWorld (© **800/ 327-2424** or 407/351-3600; www.

seaworld.com) is diving deeper into the restaurant pool with **Dine with Shamu,** a reservations-only seafood buffet served poolside with Shamu as a special guest. The park also opened **Sharks Underwater Grill,** where diners can dig into Florida and Caribbean treats while watching denizens of the deep swim by.

Gatorland's new **Adventure Tours** program (© **800/393-5297** or 407/ 855-5496; www.gatorland.com) lets up to five guests become a Trainer for a Day. The $190 experience puts you side by side with trainers and includes a chance to wrangle an alligator (minimum age 12).

Cypress Gardens, one of Orlando's oldest attractions, closed its doors in 2003 after 64 years of continuous operation, a victim of the country's economic downturn and waning attendance. For more on the happenings and activities outside of Mickeyville, see chapter 8, "Exploring Beyond Disney: Universal Orlando, SeaWorld & Other Attractions."

SHOPPING Mall at Millenia (© **407/363-3555;** www.mallat millenia.com) opened in October 2002. The 1.3-million-square-foot shoppers' paradise near Universal Orlando is home to such high-end retailers as Bloomingdale's, Neiman Marcus, Cartier, and Louis Vuitton.

See chapter 9, "Shopping," for more on buying opportunities in Orlando.

NIGHTLIFE The on-again, off-again story of **Dolly Parton's Dixie Stampede** appears to be on again, with the alcohol-free, country-and-cowpoke-themed dinner show hoping to open by the time this guide is in bookstores.

For more on the hottest nightspots in Orlando, see chapter 10, "Walt Disney World & Orlando After Dark."

1

The Best of
Walt Disney World & Orlando

In 1971, when our daughter Chris was barely 1 and we were, well, *a lot* younger, we joined the crazed herd that stampeded to Orlando for the Magic Kingdom's grand opening. Six years earlier, no Floridian could have imagined such a place. But Walter Elias Disney did. Where others saw little but cow patties and orange groves, where the day's tourism maestros couldn't conceive beyond water-skiing shows and alligator wrestling, Uncle Walt dreamed of "Disneyland East."

In a covert operation that would have made the CIA proud, Disney started buying central Florida real estate under names that gave no clue that Mickey was his backer. By the time the *Orlando Sentinel*, the local newspaper, caught wind of it, the Wizard of Diz had options on a parcel twice the size of Manhattan.

Sadly, though, Walt Disney never saw his dream come true. He died of lung cancer in 1966, and when he died, so did his vision. Had he lived, Disney probably wouldn't have allowed his World to become what it has: a mega-commercial vacation version of New Year's Eve in Times Square. To the newer generations, including our grandsons, Jake and Andy, that means utopia, and we'd be lying if we didn't admit it touches us when we see the magic in their eyes. We also look at it as an enigma: Someday, it *will* run out of gas. (Won't it?)

Maybe not entirely, but it sure hit a speed bump in 2001 and 2002. (We'll tell you how much of one later, in "By the Numbers.") Even so, to the millions who made the pilgrimage last year, it remains, as one British journalist called it, a national shrine. It is that—and a very crowded one most of the time.

Speed bumps aside, Disney's Florida legacy is still growing. As the new millennium takes root, it includes four theme parks, a dozen smaller attractions, two nightclub districts, tens of thousands of hotel rooms, timeshare holdings, scores of eateries, and two cruise ships. Universal Orlando and SeaWorld add four theme parks, and, with the help of smaller fry, the rest of Orlando antes up 80 lesser attractions, an avalanche of restaurants, and enough hotel rooms to boost central Florida's total to more than 110,000.

When does Orlando cry "uncle?"

Well, Disney and Universal may not, but others do. Peripheral motels, restaurants, dinner shows, and attractions are here one week and gone the next. The big blow in 2001 was the closing of Church Street Station, a dining-and-club district that was the prototype for Downtown Disney, Pleasure Island, and Universal's CityWalk (see chapter 10, "Walt Disney World & Orlando After Dark"). Even in good times, the theme-park players see attendance rise and fall. And those revenue lapses often cause a negative side effect—price hikes—for those of us spending our hard-earned dollars in the parks, which are very expensive. All seven major parks charge about $52 per adult and $42 to $43 per child ages 3 to 9— per day! And that's only the tip of things. *Amusement Business,* an industry trade journal, says a typical family of four spends about $250 a day for admission, parking, a fast-food lunch, and two T-shirts. That's without a room and other meals. Still, cost and speed bumps aside, the numbers grow in a stable economy. The reason is simple: This is fantasyland, and there's so much to do in only one location—enough that a 2-week stay and deep pockets won't allow you the time to hit all of the parks and attractions.

That's why we're here. Over the years, the two of us have explored the parks, dined at Orlando's restaurants, and snooped in area hotels and motels so that we can give you an inside track on America's No. 1 young and young-at-heart landing zone. With this book, you'll have the necessary tools to plan ahead. There's more than enough information to make you a savvy shopper. Our job: to make your vacation easy to arrange and as enjoyable as possible so you'll be able to relax while you're here. At the same time, we're going to give you options to make your vacation affordable. We've noted some of the best deals in this corner of the planet and ways to keep expenses to a minimum while having maximum fun. And Orlando tourism gurus will make sure you have a steady stream of new things to see. If you don't believe that, check out the "What's New in Walt Disney World & Orlando" section for a look at what has opened in the past year or so.

Fun Fact **By the Numbers**

Central Florida's tourist economy was already reeling when terrorists attacked the World Trade Center and the Pentagon , on September 11, 2001. Theme-park attendance tumbled immediately. In a typical year, the four Disney parks entertain more than 43 million paying customers, while Universal Orlando's two parks add 15 million and SeaWorld chips in another 5 million. But attendance at most of the parks sagged in 2002, according to *Amusement Business*, a trade journal. Only one, Universal's Islands of Adventure, saw an increase in attendance, which the magazine attributed to the transfer of Halloween Horror Nights from Universal Studios Florida to Islands of Adventure. On the flip side, Disney's Epcot was the hardest hit, falling 15% in 2001 and another 8% in 2002. Here are *Amusement Business'* 2002 attendance estimates and each park's rank nationally:

- No. 1: Magic Kingdom, 14 million, down 5%
- No. 3: Epcot, 8.3 million, down 8%
- No. 4: Disney–MGM Studios, 8 million, down 4%
- No. 5: Animal Kingdom, 7.3 million, down 6%
- No. 6: Universal Studios Florida, 6.9 million, down 6%
- No. 7: Islands of Adventure, 6.1 million, up 10%
- No. 8: SeaWorld Florida, 5 million, down 2%

While attendance has recovered some since the fourth quarter of 2002, analysts say it may be a year or more before numbers return to those of the parks' heydays. In the meantime, Disney's share of the attendance pie has fallen from 75% in 1998 to 68% in 2002. Universal, meanwhile, has climbed from 16% to 23% during the same period. Is Mickey hearing footsteps?

Last year's economic downturn generally means more savings on rooms, meals, and fun things to see and do. And, if you have some energy left after touring the usual daytime venues, there's still a lot of Orlando that most tourists never see—one far from fairy-tale castles and whale shows—places where singles and seniors find plenty of R- and PG-rated as well as laid-back entertainment. (We'll tell you more about it in chapter 10, "Walt Disney World & Orlando After Dark.")

Despite the growth in after-hours venues, however, Orlando remains a place primarily for kids. Many hotels, some with whimsical themes, have video arcades and other kid-pleasing features, and just about every restaurant in town has a children's menu.

But no matter what their age, in this city, visitors are the real VIPs. The major players are vying for your business, as they engage in an ongoing high-stakes game of do-unto-others. The innovative Disney–MGM Studios theme park, with its movie-magic motif, was countered a year after it opened by Universal Studios Florida, which brought in Steven Spielberg as a creative consultant. The late, great Church Street Station, a single-admission entertainment complex, was followed closely by Disney's Pleasure Island, Downtown Disney, and City-Walk at Universal. What's Wet 'n Wild in town? In addition to that same-name Universal water park, Disney has two splash zones of its own and provides free transportation to them for its vast numbers of hotel guests. Busch Gardens in nearby Tampa has an animal park. So, *voilà!* Disney came back with an entire Animal Kingdom.

Make no mistake: In this war, *you* are the prize, and the stakes, like roller coasters, will continue to rise.

1 The Best Orlando Experiences

From Cinderella Castle to Space Mountain, everybody loves the Magic Kingdom, but here are some other great things to try at Disney and Universal, and in the greater Orlando area:

- **Spend a day at Epcot.** You can travel around the world in an afternoon at the World Showcase pavilions, get your thrills riding Body Wars and Test Track in Future World, then have a different look into the future at Innoventions, where space-age products and interactive games await you. And, what better way to cap your day than watching the gala IllumiNations fireworks, laser lights, and fountain show!

- **Visit Disney–MGM Studios.** More grown-up than the Magic Kingdom, it still has lots of great activities for kids and movie buffs. Don't miss Tower of Terror, Rock 'n Roller Coaster, and Fantasmic!—the innovative, after-dark mix of live action, waterworks, fireworks, and laser lights that rivals IllumiNations.

- **Check Out Gatorland.** Located between Orlando and Kissimmee,

---

Fun Fact **Water World**

The large moat surrounding the "Fantasmic!" stage at Disney–MGM Studios contains 1.9 million gallons of water. More than 80,000 gallons of that is needed every minute to create the three mist screens used to project video portions of the show.

Chills & Thrills

If you're a speed freak who lives for the ups and downs of a good ride, here are the top stomach churners and G-force generators in Orlando (see chapters 7, "Exploring Walt Disney World," and 8, "Exploring Beyond Disney: Universal Orlando, SeaWorld & Other Attractions," for more information):

- **Incredible Hulk Coaster** (Islands of Adventure). You'll blast from 0 to 40 mph in 2 seconds, spin upside down more than 100 feet from the ground, and execute seven rollovers and two deep drops on this glow-in-the-dark roller coaster. Can you say, "Pass the Dramamine, puhleeze?"
- **Rock 'n Roller Coaster** (Disney–MGM Studios). You'll launch from 0 to 60 mph in 2.8 seconds and go right into the first inversion as 120 speakers in your "stretch limo" mainline Aerosmith at (yeeeow!) 32,000 watts right into your ears.
- **Dueling Dragons** (Islands of Adventure). Your legs dangle as you do five inversions at 55 to 60 mph and—get this!—three times come within 12 inches of the other roller coaster.
- **Summit Plummet** (Disney's Blizzard Beach). This one starts slow, with a lift ride (even in Florida's 100° dog days) to the 120-foot summit. But it finishes with the world's fastest body slide, a test of your courage and swimsuit as it virtually goes straight down and has you moving sans vehicle at 60 mph by the end.
- **Twilight Zone Tower of Terror** (Disney–MGM Studios). The free-fall experiences (there are several scenarios) are more than thrilling—they're scary. Once your legs stop shaking, *some of you* will want to ride again.
- **The Amazing Adventures of Spider-Man** (Islands of Adventure). 3-D doesn't get any better than this chase-the-bad-guys ride where you twist, spin, and soar before a simulated 400-foot drop that feels an awful lot like the real thing. It's sure to get your Spidey senses tingling.
- **Kraken** (SeaWorld). This floorless, open-sided coaster uses speed (up to 65 mph), steep climbs, deep drops, and seven loops to create a stomach-churning ride that lasts far too long for some folks.

this throwback park is a great way to spend a half day at less than half the price of the theme parks. In addition to passive exhibits, make sure to see the Gator Jumparoo, which has been the signature show since the park opened in 1949. And, if you have deep pockets, consider becoming a Trainer for a Day.

- **Experience Universal Orlando.** Universal Studios Florida and its sister, Islands of Adventure, combine cutting-edge, high-tech special effects with great creativity. Not-to-be-missed attractions include Back to the Future, Terminator 2: 3-D Battle Across Time, Men in Black Alien Attack, Jimmy Neutron's Nicktoon Blast, Dueling Dragons,

Orlando Theme Parks

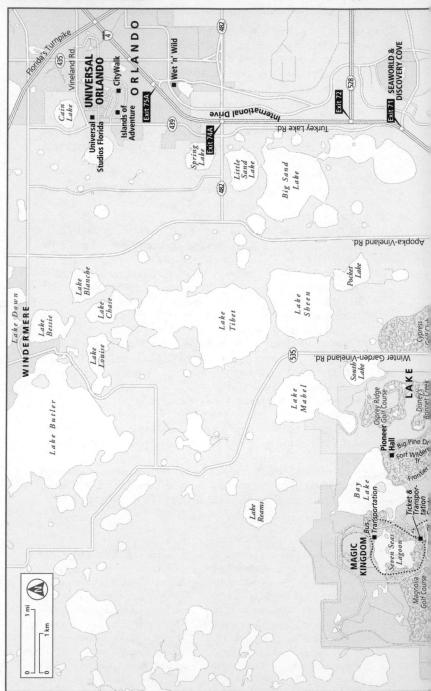

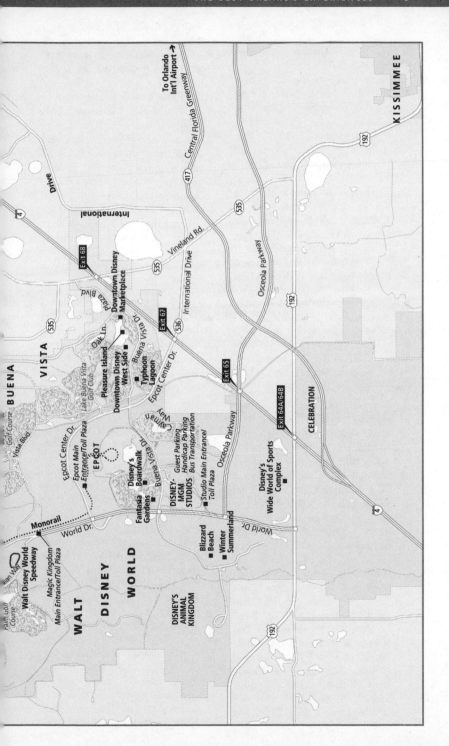

the Incredible Hulk Coaster, The Amazing Adventures of Spider-Man, and Dudley Do-Right's Ripsaw Falls.

- **Pamper Yourself at a Spa.** Orlando's business and upscale travelers have spawned a small but growing stable of places to don a robe and get rejuvenated. Our favorites are **Disney's Grand Floridian Resort & Spa** (© **407/ 934-7639** or 407/824-3000), **The Spa at the Wyndham Palace Resort** (© **800/996-3426** or 407/827-2727), the **Greenhouse Spa at Universal's Portofino Bay Hotel** (© **888/322-55541** or 407/503-1000), and **Canyon Ranch Spa Club at the Gaylord Palms** (© **877/677-9352** or 407/ 586-0000). See chapter 5, "Accommodations," to learn more about these spas and the resorts that host them.

- **Explore Eco-Entertainment at SeaWorld and Discovery Cove.** With the opening of Journey to Atlantis and Kraken, SeaWorld added a little zip to its park, but it's still better to come here looking for what this place best offers— hands-on encounters with critters and up-close views of animals ranging from polar bears to killer whales. Its newer sister, Discovery Cove, gives you a chance to swim with dolphins (alas, it will cost you $229) as part of its package.

2 The Best Hotel Bets

Get all of the information you'll need about these and other central Florida hotels and motels in chapter 5, "Where to Stay." But here are the high points:

- **Best for Families:** All Disney properties cater to families, with special menus for kids, video-game arcades, free transportation to the parks, many recreational facilities, and, in some cases, character meals. Camping at woodsy **Fort Wilderness** (© **407/934-7639** or 407/824-2900) makes for a special family experience. If bunk beds and a geyser going off in the lobby sound good, check into the **Wilderness Lodge** (© **407/934- 7639** or 407/938-4300). On the No-Mickey Front, **Holiday Inn Family Suites** (© **877/387-5437** or 407/387-5437), **Holiday Inn Nikki Bird Resort** (© **800/ 206-2747** or 407/396-7300), and **Holiday Inn Sunspree Resort Lake Buena Vista** (© **800/ 366-6299** or 407/239-4500) offer Kid Suites, kids' clubs, and more.

- **Best Moderately Priced Hotels:** Disney's **Port Orleans Resort** (© **407/934-7639** or 407/934- 5000) has dual Southern charm in its French Quarter and Riverside areas, and the pool has a water slide that curves out of a faux dragon's mouth. In the free world, **Hawthorn Suites Lake Buena Vista** (© **800/936-9417** or 407/ 581-5457) combines a location near to but sheltered from Disney with trimmings such as large rooms, free American breakfasts, and weekday social hours.

- **Best Inexpensive Hotels:** That's easy: Disney's **All-Star Movies Resort** (© **407/934-7639** or 407/939-7000), **All-Star Music Resort** (© **407/934-7639** or 407/939-6000), and **All-Star Sports Resort** (© **407/934-7639** or 407/939-5000). If you're going to stay on WDW property, you can't beat 'em under any circum-stances, although they would be significantly overpriced outside of the realm. The **Hampton Inn Maingate West** (© **800/936-9417** or 407/396-5457) is one of the nicest, most modern of the inexpensive properties in the Kissimmee area, and it's only 1½ miles west of Disney. On the north end, Winter Park's **Best Western Mount Vernon Inn** delivers hospitality Southern-style without airs and with a low price (ⓒ **800/992-3379** or 407/647-1166), but it's 25 to 30 miles from the theme parks.

- **Best Budget Motel:** The **Ramada Disney Eastgate** (ⓒ **888/298-2054** or 407/396-1111) has clean rooms, is located close to Disney, and there's a restaurant right next door. All these things make it a good budget choice. But if price is your lone consideration, it's hard to beat the nearby **Econo Lodge Maingate Resort** (ⓒ **800/356-6935,** 407/390-9063, or 407/396-2000), where rates are as low as $39 double.

- **Best for Business Travelers:** The **Renaissance Orlando Resort at SeaWorld** (ⓒ **800/327-6677** or 407/351-5555), **Gaylord Palms** (ⓒ **877/677-9352** or 407/586-0000), **Marriott's Orlando World Center** (ⓒ **800/621-0638** or 407/239-4200), and the **Peabody Orlando** (ⓒ **800/732-2639** or 407/352-4000) offer full concierge service, 24-hour room service, fine restaurants, spacious lounges, and an extensive array of business services.

- **Best for a Romantic Getaway:** The 1,500-acre grounds of the **Hyatt Regency Grand Cypress Resort** (ⓒ **800/233-1234** or 407/239-1234) are a veritable botanical garden surrounding a swan-inhabited lake. Couples enjoy stunning accommodations, great service, and first-rate restaurants. You should also consider the luxurious condos and backyard waterways (with wildlife ranging from mallards to soft-shelled

turtles) at the adjoining **Villas of Grand Cypress** (ⓒ **800/835-7377** or 407/239-4700). Another option: the **Grand Floridian,** listed next.

- **Best Location: Disney's Grand Floridian Resort & Spa** (ⓒ **407/934-7639** or 407/824-3000), **Polynesian Resort** (ⓒ **407/934-7639** or 407/824-2000), and **Contemporary Resort** (ⓒ **407/934-7639** or 407/824-1000) are on Seven Seas Lagoon or Bay Lake. They're also on the WDW monorail route, providing quick and easy access to the parks. The **Portofino Bay Hotel** (ⓒ **888/322-5541** or 407/503-1000) and the **Hard Rock Hotel** (ⓒ **888/232-7827** or 407/363-8000) are within walking distance of Universal Studios Florida, Islands of Adventure, and CityWalk, and there's also boat service to the dock at CityWalk.

- **Best Service:** The elegant **Peabody Orlando** (ⓒ **800/732-2639** or 407/352-4000) offers attentive pampering from one of the most delightful staffs we've found in O-Town. The folks at the **Gaylord Palms** (ⓒ **877/677-9352** or 407/586-0000) also make it their business to treat you as if you were best friends.

- **Best Pools:** All of the Walt Disney World resorts have terrific swimming pools, usually Olympic-size and based on themes. But arguably the best is shared by **Disney's Beach Club Resort** (ⓒ **407/934-7639** or 407/934-8000) and **Disney's Yacht Club Resort** (ⓒ **407/934-7639** or 407/934-7000). Storm Along Bay, a 3-acre free-form pool and water park, stretches between them. Outside the Disney complex, arguably the best resort pool in O-Town lies at the **Hyatt Regency Grand Cypress Resort** (ⓒ **800/233-1234**

⌐Fun Fact From All Sides

In order to produce the 13-minute IllumiNations spectacular each night at Epcot, Disney uses 68 fireworks firing positions and more than 1,100 shells.

---

or 407/239-1234). It's a half-acre lagoon-like water-world pool that flows through rock grottoes, is spanned by a rope bridge, and has 12 waterfalls and two steep water slides.

- **Best Health Club:** The **Walt Disney World Dolphin** (© 800/ 227-1500 or 407/934-4000) has

a fully equipped Body by Jake club, complete with a weight room overlooking a lake. It contains a full complement of equipment; offers aerobics classes throughout the day, plus personal training, massage, and body wraps; and has saunas and a large whirlpool.

3 The Best Dining Bets

While Orlando can't compete with U.S. destinations such as New York or San Francisco, it has everything on the restaurant front from fast fooderies to 5-Diamond winners. Look for more details on these and other eateries in chapter 6, "Where to Dine."

- **Best for Kids:** Kids adore the meals with Disney characters offered at many **Walt Disney World** resorts and theme parks. (For the scoop, see Disney character meals, p. 162). They also love the eclectic atmosphere and visuals in the jungle-themed **Rainforest Cafe** at Downtown Disney Marketplace (© 407/827-8500) and Animal Kingdom (© 407/ 938-9100). Monkey business is strongly encouraged.
- **Best Character Meal:** It doesn't get any better than **Chef Mickey's** breakfasts and dinners at the Contemporary Resort. These "events" have their respective namesake and other characters (© 407/939-3463), but a word of warning: They also attract *up to 1,600 guests* each morning.
- **Best Spot for a Romantic Dinner:** **Victoria & Albert's** takes the prize. Dinner is an intimate six-course

meal with a maid and butler serving you in plush Victorian–style surroundings (© 407/939-3463).

- **Best Spot for a Business Lunch:** **Hemingway's** (© 407/239-3854), an upscale Key West–style restaurant at the Hyatt Regency Grand Cypress Resort, is generally kidfree, and its quiet dining areas are perfect for business powwows.
- **Best View:** **Arthur's 27** (© 407/ 827-3450) has a dandy view of sunsets and Magic Kingdom fireworks, but we recommend skipping the overpriced meal in favor of a stool at the neighboring **Top of the Palace Lounge,** both on the 27th floor of the Wyndham Palace Resort in Lake Buena Vista. Outside the parks, **Manuel's on the 28th** (© 407/246-6580), so named because it's on the 28th floor of a downtown bank building, has equally gorgeous views of sunsets and the downtown skyline.
- **Best Wine List:** See for yourself why **Maison & Jardin** (© 407/ 862-4410) in Altamonte Springs has been honored by *Wine Spectator* magazine for its cellar.
- **Best Value:** At **Romano's Macaroni Grill** (© 407/239-6676),

the ambience and the northern Italian cuisine score very high, and prices are low, low, low.

- **Best (if pricey) Diner Cuisine:** The **B-Line Diner** in the Peabody Orlando hotel (℃ **407/345-4460**) serves meat loaf and mashed potatoes (as well as belly-busting omelets and other homey foods) that would make most mothers proud.

- **Best Oriental Cuisine: Little Saigon** (℃ **407/423-8539**) has palate-pleasing Vietnamese cuisine in a no-frills neighborhood setting. On the pricier side, **Ming Court** (℃ **407/351-9988**) offers a menu that's tasty and diverse enough to make it one of Orlando's most popular Chinese restaurants.

- **Best California Cuisine:** Twin filets marinated in Ybor Gold beer, anyone? Find it at **Pebbles** in Lake Buena Vista (℃ **407/827-1111**), a mini, local chain with a following to match its reputation.

- **Best Barbecue:** Hands down, follow your nose to **Bubbalou's Bodacious BBQ** (℃ **407/628-1212**) after catching a whiff of the tangy hickory smoke. It tastes as good as it smells.

- **Best Italian Cuisine:** We'd have to call it a toss-up between **Enzo's on the Lake** in Longwood (℃ **407/834-9872**) on the pricey side and **Pacino's Italian Ristorante** in Kissimmee (℃ **407/396-8022**) in the more affordable class.

- **Best Seafood:** While this region doesn't have a stellar seafood restaurant, it has one very good one: **Fulton's Crab House** (℃ **407/934-2628**), which offers a creative menu and a rich wine list.

- **Best Tapas: Cafe Tu Tu Tango** (℃ **407/248-2222**) takes the tapas concept to another dimension with items ranging from Cajun egg rolls with blackened chicken to alligator bites.

- **Best Steak House:** At the **Yachtsman Steakhouse** at Disney's Yacht Club Resort (℃ **407/939-3463**), the aged steaks, chops, and seafood are grilled over a wood fire.

- **Best Vegetarian/Sushi Dining:** The **California Grill** at Disney's Contemporary Resort (℃ **407/939-3463** or 407/824-1576) has a rotating menu that, depending on when you visit, might feature mesquite-roasted tofu, summer vegetable risotto, or Dungeness crab rolls. On the sushi side of things, **Ran-Getsu of Tokyo** (℃ **407/345-0044**) has exotic fare such as *chirashi, tekka-don,* and *una-ju.*

- **Best Late-Night Dining:** The trendy **B-Line Diner** (℃ **407/345-4460**) at the Peabody Orlando is open around the clock for eclectic fare ranging from steaks to falafel sandwiches to grits and eggs.

- **Best Spot for a Celebration: Emeril's** at Universal's CityWalk (℃ **407/224-2424**) is a great choice for a high-end special occasion. For the pure party factor, you can't beat **Jimmy Buffett's Margaritaville** (℃ **407/224-2155**) at CityWalk.

- **Best Outdoor Dining:** The terrace at **Artist Point** (℃ **407/939-3463**), the premier restaurant at Disney's Wilderness Lodge, overlooks a lake, waterfall, and scenery evocative of America's national parks. And the **Rose & Crown** at Epcot (℃ **407/939-3463**) delivers a front-row seat for the Illumi-Nations fireworks display.

- **Best People-Watching:** The upstairs patio at **Bongo's Cuban Cafe,** Downtown Disney West Side (℃ **407/828-0999**), is where it's at, even if the food isn't.

- **Best Afternoon Tea: The Peabody Orlando** (℃ **407/345-4550**) hosts

Tips **Orlando's Best Online Sites**

Given Orlando's enormous popularity, it should come as no surprise that hundreds of websites are devoted to it. They have a lot of information about everything from Walt Disney World history to getting around town.

There are several sites written by Disney fans, employees, and self-proclaimed experts. Our favorite (**www.hiddenmickeys.org**) is about **Hidden Mickeys,** a park tradition (see chapter 7, "Exploring Walt Disney World"). These subtle Disney images can be found scattered throughout the realm, though they sometimes are in the eye, or imagination, of the beholder. **Deb's Unofficial Walt Disney World Information Guide (http://wdwig.com)** is another crowd pleaser if you are a diehard Disney fan. And you should definitely take a look at Disney's official site, **www.disneyworld.com**, if you're planning a pilgrimage to the Land of the Mouse.

If a trip to one of Universal Orlando's theme parks or CityWalk is on your dance card, then stop at **www.universalorlando.com**. You can order tickets, make reservations, and find out about special events, among other things on the site. And fish fans can get in the know about SeaWorld at **www.seaworld.com** and Discovery Cove at **www.discoverycove.com**.

If you're seeking general information about the city, accommodations, dining, nightlife, or special events, head over to the Orlando/Orange County Convention & Visitors Bureau site at **www.orlandoinfo.com**. *Orlando Weekly* (**www.orlandoweekly.com**) offers cutting-edge reviews and recommendations for arts, movies, music, restaurants, and much more from Orlando's premiere alternative weekly. Links at the site include dining, arts and culture, shopping, and news.

teas weekdays from 3 to 4:30pm in the lobby outside Dux, its signature eatery. As you sip your tea and munch on a pastry, you're entertained by the frolicking of the Peabody's resident ducks in a nearby fountain.

- **Best Sunday Brunch: Atlantis** at the Renaissance Orlando Resort at SeaWorld (© 407/351-5555) serves a champagne brunch in its atrium. Themes change monthly, but the menu usually features such treats as quail, duck, lamb chops, Cornish hen, clams, mussels, snapper, sea bass, sushi, and more.

- **Best Special Sunday Brunch:** The **House of Blues** (© 407/ 934-2583), at Disney's West Side, has a down-home gospel brunch featuring live foot-stomping music and an array of Southern/Creole vittles that includes greens, red beans and rice, jambalaya, catfish, shrimp, and beef. The food is so-so—the same quality of a dinner show, which this is, morning-style. But the entertainment makes it a certifiable winner. Reservations aren't accepted for parties under six, so arrive early for the 10:30am or 1pm show.

2

Planning Your Trip to Walt Disney World & Orlando

Talk about overload! Central Florida has so many hotels, restaurants, attractions, and package plans that you might have an anxiety attack if you don't do a little advance planning. That's why we've filled this chapter with things you need to know before you go. In addition to the information contained in the following pages, you'll find more tips in chapters 5 through 8—those covering the area's best hotels, restaurants, theme parks, and smaller attractions.

1 Visitor Information

As soon as you decide to go to Orlando, contact the **Orlando/Orange County Convention & Visitors Bureau,** 8723 International Dr., Suite 101, Orlando, FL 32819 (© **407/363-5872;** www. orlandoinfo.com). Staffers can answer questions, assist you with reservations, help you find discounts, and send maps and brochures, such as the *Official Visitors Guide, African-American Visitors Guide, Area Guide to Restaurants, Unexpected Orlando,* and *Official Accommodations Guide.* The free packet should land in 3 weeks and include a "Magicard," which is good for $500 in discounts on rooms, car rentals, attractions, and more.

If you don't require a human voice, you can get all of the above by calling © **800/643-9492** or 800/551-0181.

For general information about **Walt Disney World,** including vacation brochures and videos or to ask questions, write to Walt Disney World, Box 10000, Lake Buena Vista, FL 32830-1000; call © **407/824-2222,** 407/824-4321, or 407/934-7639, or, on the Internet, go to **www.disneyworld. com.** If you don't mind waiting a couple of days for a response, e-mail questions to wdw.guest.communications@ Disney.com.

For information about **Universal Studios Florida, CityWalk,** and **Islands of Adventure,** call © **800/837-2273** or 407/363-8000, or write to **Universal Orlando,** 1000 Universal Studios Plaza, Orlando, FL 32819. On the Internet, visit **www.universal orlando.com.**

You also can visit the **Kissimmee–St. Cloud Convention & Visitors Bureau,** 1925 E. Irlo Bronson Memorial Hwy. (U.S. 192), Kissimmee, FL 34744; or write to P.O. Box 422007, Kissimmee, FL 34742-2007 (© **800/327-9159** or 407/847-5000; www. floridakiss.com). The folks there will send a packet of maps, brochures, coupon books, and the *Kissimmee–St. Cloud Vacation Guide,* which details accommodations and attractions.

For information on the **International Drive** area, call © **407/248-9590** or on the Internet go to **www. InternationalDriveOrlando.com.** The staff has information about rooms, restaurants, attractions, shops, and the I-Ride Trolley.

For information about places to stay, eat, and visit north of the Orlando metro area, contact the **Winter Park Chamber of Commerce,**

Walt Disney World & Orlando—Red Alert Checklist

- From the *literally red*-alert news desk: Once you arrive, you'll see a lot of folks sporting a boiled-lobster complexion. They ignored the No. 1 survival rule for an Orlando vacation: **Use sunscreen!** From early spring through late fall, Florida's sun can deliver a dangerous burn, including sun poisoning, if you're not protected with a 25- or higher-rated sunscreen. (We've even seen it happen on winter days.) You can also protect yourself by wearing wide-brimmed hats, airy clothes, and sunglasses. Also, to avoid dehydration, remember to drink plenty of fluids. Don't forget to pack a pair of comfortable walking shoes for those days spent pounding the theme-park pavement. And if you have children in tow, remember that they need protection as much or more than you.
- Don't get shut out at dinnertime. You can make same-day or day-before reservations in most Orlando eateries, but there are some exceptions to the rule, including Emeril's (p. 149) and Victoria and Albert's (p. 140). In fact, any Disney restaurant—especially those serving character meals—can have a waiting list a mile long in peak periods. So take our advice and use Walt Disney World's version of a reservation, **priority seating (✆ 407/939-3463)**, which lets you stake a claim to a table 30 or more days in advance.
- Many visitors come with their hearts set on (and days planned around) specific attractions, hotels, or restaurants. But some dreams don't come true. Disney has **reduced the park hours**, limited the days certain shows are staged, and continues to temporarily close some restaurants and attractions to cut expenses in response to the weakened economy. Universal, SeaWorld, and smaller players have taken similar steps. Before you promise your family or yourself anything,

150 New York Ave., P.O. Box 280, Winter Park, FL 32790 (✆ **407/644-8281;** www.winterparkcc.org).

ONLINE INFORMATION

The websites we listed above are good for a ton of other information. Disney's **www.disneyworld.com** has theme park maps, current ticket prices, directions, park hours on specific days, ride and show information, thumbnails about WDW restaurants, resort prices, information about special events, indoor and outdoor recreation options, the Disney Cruise Line, an online booking service, and more.

Deb's Unofficial Walt Disney World Information Guide (http://wdwig.com) is an excellent information source, arguably the best unofficial Disney guide on the Internet as well as in the galaxy, though it's one that at times isn't entirely objective for those of you who may be cynics. Disney doesn't own it, but it's run and written mainly by fans, so you have to factor out (or in, if you prefer) their exuberance while digesting the many tips this site offers. The no-nonsense, text-driven site includes comprehensive insider information on tickets, restaurant menus, the Disney Cruise Line, and other valuable tips. Some sections are aimed at travelers with special needs, and include tips for touring the Disney parks if you're physically challenged, elderly, or towing kids.

make sure your dreams can come true by calling or checking the websites provided throughout this book. Also note that in the best of times, theme park rides break down or have to be shut down for routine maintenance (though you don't get a break on ticket prices when your favorite rides or shows are dark). Some of the websites listed earlier in this chapter, including Deb's Unofficial Walt Disney World Information Guide, have **"rehab"** schedules and update them almost daily.

- If you purchased traveler's checks, have you recorded the check numbers and stored the documentation separately from the checks?
- Did you pack your camera and an extra set of camera batteries, and purchase enough film? If you packed film in your checked baggage, did you invest in protective pouches to shield film from airport X-rays? You may be **best advised** to buy your film in a local discount store, such as Wal-Mart, or a drugstore, such as Walgreens, after you arrive.
- Do you have a safe, accessible place to store cash?
- Did you bring ID cards, such as AAA and AARP cards, student IDs, and so forth, that could entitle you to discounts?
- Speaking of identification, did you bring a photo ID? That's very important since September 11, 2001.
- Did you bring emergency drug prescriptions and extra glasses and/or contact lenses?
- Do you have your credit-card pin numbers?
- If you have an E-ticket, do you have documentation?
- Did you leave a copy of your itinerary with someone at home?

The sites built by Universal Orlando, **www.universalorlando.com**, and SeaWorld, **www.seaworld.com**, offer ride descriptions, details, ticket prices, and information not directly related to the theme parks. But both lack the thoroughness of Deb's and the Disney sites.

The city's newspaper, the *Orlando Sentinel*, produces an online site at **www.orlandosentinel.com**. It has a variety of entertainment information. If you go to another Sentinel-produced website, **www.go2orlando.com**, you'll find the focus on attractions, accommodations, restaurants, discounts, and other things important to visitors. Also visit **www.insidecentralflorida.com** for information about dining, clubs, performances, theme parks, sports, and special events.

2 Money

CREDIT CARDS

Credit cards are a safe way to carry money, they provide a convenient record of all your expenses, and they generally offer good exchange rates. You can also withdraw cash advances (though you'll start paying hefty interest on the advance the moment you receive the cash) from your credit cards at banks or ATMs, provided you know your PIN. If you've forgotten yours, or didn't even know you had one, call the

What Things Cost in Orlando	U.S.$	U.K.£
As of this writing,	1.55	1
Taxi from airport to Disney's Animal Kingdom Lodge area (up to 4 people)	51.00	32.85
Double room (excluding suites) at Disney's Grand Floridian Beach Resort & Spa (very expensive)	339.00–840.00	218.38–541.09
Double room at Marriott's Orlando World Center (expensive)	189.00–410.00	121.75–264.10
Double room (excluding suites) at Disney's Coronado Springs Resort (moderate)	133.00–209.00	85.67–134.85
Double room at Disney's All-Star Music Resort (inexpensive)	77.00–124.00	49.60–79.88
Six-course fixed-price dinner for one at Victoria & Albert's, not including tip or wine pairing (very expensive)	85.00–115.00	54.75–74.09
All-you-can-eat buffet dinner at Akershus in Epcot, not including tip or wine (moderate)	20.00	12.90
Bottle of American beer (non-resort restaurant)	2.95	1.90
Coca-Cola (non-resort restaurant)	1.50	0.97
Roll of ASA 100 Kodak film, 36 exposures, purchased at Walt Disney World	9.75	6.28
Adult 4-day Park Hopper admission (unlimited theme park access) to Walt Disney World	208.00	131.19
Child 4-day Park Hopper admission to Walt Disney World	167.00	107.74
Adult 2-day 2-park Universal Orlando Pass	94.95	61.17
Child 2-day 2-park Universal Orlando Pass	81.95	52.80
Adult 1-day, 1-park admission to Walt Disney World	52.00	33.55
Child 1-day, 1-park admission to Walt Disney World	42.00	27.10
Adult 1-day, 1-park admission to Universal Orlando	51.95	33.52
Child 1-day, 1-park admission to Universal Orlando	42.95	27.71
Adult 1-day, 1-park admission to SeaWorld	51.95	33.52
Child 1-day, 1-park admission to SeaWorld	42.95	27.71
Admission to Discovery Cove with dolphin swim	229.00	147.51
Adult admission to Gatorland	17.93	11.55
Child admission to Gatorland	8.48	5.46
Adult admission to Orlando Science Center	10.00	6.44
Child admission to Orlando Science Center	7.50	4.83

number on the back of your credit card and ask the bank to send it to you. It usually takes 5 to 7 business days, though some banks will provide the number over the phone if you tell them your mother's maiden name or some other personal information.

Disney parks, resorts, shops, and restaurants (but not most fast-food outlets) accept five major credit cards: American Express, Diners Club, Discover, MasterCard, and Visa. The Disney Visa Card is also welcome. Additionally, some WDW resorts offer a debit card that can be used in park shops and restaurants, but you must settle up upon checkout, which means most of you will be nauseated by another wait in line. We recommend against it unless you don't have one of the credit cards above or traveler's checks.

You can also buy **Disney dollars** (currency with the images of Mickey, Minnie, and so on) in $1, $5, and $10 denominations. They're good at WDW shops, restaurants, and resorts, as well as Disney stores everywhere. But we don't recommend buying them either because you'll have to cash in leftover bills for real currency upon leaving WDW, which means still another line, or keep them as a souvenir. Also, watch out if you have a refund coming. Some things, such as strollers, wheelchairs, and lockers, require a deposit, and, as a marketing ploy, Disney staffers frequently try to slip Mickey money into your hand instead of the real thing.

You can cash traveler's or personal checks of $25 or less (drawn on U.S.

banks, if you have a driver's license and major credit card), and exchange foreign currency at **SunTrust** Bank, 1675 Buena Vista Dr., across from Downtown Disney Marketplace. The bank also has an ATM. It's open weekdays from 9am to 4pm, and until 6pm on Thursday (© **407/828-6106**).

ATMS

The easiest and best way to get cash away from home is from an ATM (automated teller machine). The **Cirrus** (© **800/424-7787**; www.mastercard.com) and **PLUS** (© **800/843-7587**; www.visa.com) networks span the globe; look at the back of your bank card to see which network you're on, then call or check online for ATM locations at your destination. Be sure you know your personal identification number (PIN) before you leave home and be sure to find out your daily withdrawal limit before you depart.

ATMs are on Main Street in the Magic Kingdom and at the entrances to Epcot, Disney–MGM Studios, and Animal Kingdom. They're also at Pleasure Island; in Downtown Disney Marketplace; at Disney resorts; and in the Crossroads Shopping Center.

There also are ATMs near Guest Services at Universal Studios Florida, Islands of Adventure, and SeaWorld.

Inside the entrance of most of the theme parks, you'll find park maps listing all ATMs operating that day. If this isn't the case when you visit, look for the maps at Guest Relations or Guest Services near the entrances, or at most inside-the-park shops.

Tips **Online Ticketing**

The theme parks have jumped head first into a trend that allows online booking of tickets, hotel rooms, vacation packages, and more. Disney's site is at **www.disneyworld.com**. Universal Orlando's Web address is **www.universalorlando.com**. SeaWorld's site is at **www.seaworld.com**. All three offer discounts for online ticket purchases. In SeaWorld's case, that usually includes single-day tickets.

Outside the parks, most malls have at least one ATM and they're in some convenience stores, such as 7-Elevens and Circle Ks, as well as in grocery stores and drugstores. But there frequently is an extra charge for using non-bank ATMs. Depending on your institution, those charges can range from $1 to $3.50 per transaction—the average is $2.75 across Florida.

Be *very* careful when using ATMs, especially at night and in areas that are not well lit and heavily traveled. Don't let the land of Mickey lull you into a false sense of security. Goofy and Pluto won't mug you, but some of their estranged neighbors might. This is a big city, and its crime rate is the same as others. When entering your ATM PIN, make sure you shield the keyboard from others in line. And if you're using a drive-thru, keep your doors locked.

TRAVELER'S CHECKS

Traveler's checks are something of an anachronism from the days before the ATM made cash accessible at any time. Traveler's checks used to be the only sound alternative to traveling with dangerously large amounts of cash. They were as reliable as currency, but, unlike cash, could be replaced if lost or stolen.

These days, traveler's checks seem less necessary because most cities have 24-hour ATMs that allow you to withdraw small amounts of cash as needed. However, keep in mind that you will likely be charged an ATM withdrawal fee if the bank is not your own, so if you're withdrawing money every day, you might be better off with traveler's checks—provided that you don't mind showing identification every time you want to cash one.

You can get traveler's checks at almost any bank. **American Express** offers denominations of $20, $50, $100, $500, and (for cardholders only) $1,000. You'll pay a service charge ranging from 1% to 4%. You can also get American Express traveler's checks over the phone by calling ✆ **800/221-7282;** Amex gold and platinum cardholders who use this number are exempt from the fee.

Visa offers traveler's checks at Citibank locations nationwide, as well as at several other banks. The service charge ranges between 1.5% and 2%; checks come in denominations of $20, $50, $100, $500, and $1,000. Call ✆ **800/732-1322** for information. **MasterCard** also offers traveler's checks. Call ✆ **800/223-9920** for a location near you.

For tips and telephone numbers to call if your wallet is stolen or lost, go to "Lost & Found" in the Fast Facts section of chapter 4.

3 When to Go

This is theme-park central, and its busiest seasons are whenever kids are out of school, including late May to just past Labor Day, long holiday weekends, the winter holidays (mid-Dec to early Jan), and spring break (late Mar to Apr). And don't forget that kids in other hemispheres have different holiday periods. Obviously, the whole experience is best when the crowds are thinnest and the weather is the most temperate. Hotel rooms are also priced lower during off-season, but that season doesn't follow the traditional winter/summer patterns of most areas.

Peak-season rates can go into effect during large conventions and special events. Even something as remote as Bike Week in Daytona Beach (about an hour by car northeast) can raise prices, including during the off-season. These kinds of events especially impact moderate-priced properties outside

> **Tips** **Weather Wise**
>
> Florida has winter and summer rainy spells. They don't necessarily ruin a vacation, but you can save a bit by bringing a lightweight poncho with you from home. The theme parks love to see you get soaked and will in turn soak you for $5 or $6 for a throwaway that's about as sturdy as plastic wrap (and sells for $1.95 in discount stores). Speaking of rainy days, don't let them spoil your fun. The crowds are thinner on these days and there are plenty of indoor attractions to enjoy. The flip side: Many of the major outdoor thrill rides at Disney, Universal, and SeaWorld are closed during rain and lightning storms.

Central Florida Average Temperatures

	Jan	Feb	Mar	Apr	May	June	July	Aug	Sept	Oct	Nov	Dec
High °F	71.7	72.9	78.3	83.6	88.3	90.6	91.7	91.6	89.7	84.4	78.2	73.1
°C	22.0	22.7	25.7	28.7	31.3	32.5	33.2	33.1	32.0	29.1	25.7	22.8
Low °F	49.3	50.0	55.3	60.3	66.2	71.2	73.0	73.4	72.5	65.4	56.8	50.9
°C	9.6	10.0	12.5	15.7	19.0	21.8	22.7	23.0	22.5	18.6	13.8	10.5

Walt Disney World. **Best times:** The week after Labor Day until the week before Thanksgiving, the week after Thanksgiving until mid-December, and the 6 weeks before and after school spring vacations. **Worst times:** During the December holidays and summer, when out-of-state visitors take advantage of school breaks and some locals haul their families to the parks (smart locals take advantage of discounts in Florida residents' months, usually May and November). Packed parking lots are the norm during the week before and after Christmas, and summer brings a double whammy: Crowds are very large and the weather is oppressively hot and humid. *Think about pulling your kids out of school* for a few days around an off-season weekend to avoid long lines. (You probably can keep them in their schools' good graces by asking teachers to let them write a report on an educational element of the vacation. Epcot has a ton of science and technology exhibits.) Even during these periods, though, the number of international visitors guarantees you won't be alone.

Note: If you're taking advantage of a land/cruise package (see "Disney [& Other] Cruise Packages," later in this chapter), make sure you take into account hurricane season, which runs June 1 to November 30. Inland, the worst may be a ton of rain and enough wind to wipe the smile off your face. But on the coasts or at sea, these storms can be very dangerous. Also, don't take tornadoes and lightning—two particularly active summer curses—too lightly.

ORLANDO AREA CALENDAR OF EVENTS

January

- **Capital One Florida Citrus Bowl.** New Year's Day kicks off with this football game in downtown Orlando. It pits the second-ranked teams from the Southeastern and Big Ten conferences against each other. Tickets are $55 before November 1 and $65 thereafter. Call © **800/297-2695** or 407/ 423-2476 for information or **Ticketmaster** at © **877/803-7073** or 407/839-3900 for tickets (on the Internet, visit **www.fc sports.com**). A free downtown parade is held a few days before the game and features marching bands and some floats.

- **Walt Disney World Marathon.** About 90% of the 16,000 runners finish this 26.2-mile "sprint" through the resort area and parks. It's open to all, including runners with disabilities. Some Disney packages include the $75 entry fee in the price. The registration deadline is usually in early November, and pre-registration is required. There's also a 13.1-mile mini-marathon ($45) and 100-yard through 5K runs ($25–$30) for families and young kids. Call ℂ **407/939-7810** or go to **www. disneysports.com**. The races are the second week in January.

- **Zora Neale Hurston Festival.** This 4-day celebration in Eatonville, the first incorporated African-American town in America, highlights the life and works of the author and is usually held the last weekend in January. Eatonville is 25 miles north of the theme parks. Admission is $5 to $12 for adults, $3 for kids under 17. Additional fees are charged for lectures or seminars. Call ℂ **407/ 647-3307.**

February

- **Atlanta Braves.** The Braves have been holding spring training at Disney's Wide World of Sports Complex since 1998. There are 15 home games during the 1-month season. (The team arrives in mid-February; games begin in early March.) Tickets are $12 to $20. You can get more information at ℂ **407/828-3267** or www.disney sports.com. To purchase tickets, call Ticketmaster at ℂ **877/803-7073** or 407/839-3900. You can also get online information at

www.atlantabraves.com or **www. majorleaguebaseball.com/spring training**.

- **Houston Astros.** The Astros train at Osceola County Stadium, 1000 Bill Beck Blvd., Kissimmee. Tickets are $8 to $15. Get them through Ticketmaster at ℂ **877/ 803-7073** or 407/839-3900. For information, check the Astros' website at **www.astros.com**.

- **Mardi Gras at Universal Orlando.** Floats, stilt walkers, and beads thrown to the crowd add to the fun of this event, which is included in park admission. Special entertainment also enhances the festivities. A separate ticket, the same as the daily admission ($49.95 adults), is charged. It runs from mid-February to mid-March. This is a party with plenty of booze flowing, so it's probably not a good experience for kids. For information, call ℂ **800/ 837-2273** or 407/363-8000, or go online to **www.universalorlando. com**.

- **Silver Spurs Rodeo.** It features real yippee-I-O cowboys in calf roping, bull riding, barrel racing, and more. The rodeo is a celebration of the area's rural pre-Disney roots and a nice escape from tourist central. It's held at the Silver Spurs Arena, 1875 E. Irlo Bronson Memorial Hwy. (U.S. 192), Kissimmee, on the third weekend in February. Call ℂ **407/847-4052** or visit **www.silverspurs rodeo.com** for details. Tickets are $13 and $17 for adults, $7 for kids 12 and younger.

March

- **Bike Week.** More than 500,000 motorcyclists descend on Daytona Beach in early March for this hell-raising event. People-watching and some street activities are free. Prices vary for the main events including the motorcycle races at

Daytona International Speedway. Because Daytona is only 50 miles northeast of Orlando, many bikers base themselves in O-Town and roar down the highway daily to Bike Week. But unless you're into bikers, bikinis, boozing, and occasional brawls, this is a good one to skip. If you must, call ✆ **800/854-1234** or 386/255-0981, or go to **www.officialbike week.com**.

• **Bay Hill Invitational.** Hosted by Arnold Palmer and featuring Orlando-based golfers such as Tiger Woods, this PGA Tour event is held at the Bay Hill Club, 9000 Bay Hill Blvd. Daily admission Tuesday through Friday is $25 to $35; week-long tickets are $60 for grounds access; $80 for clubhouse access. Call ✆ **866/764-4843** or 407/876-7774, or check out **www. bayhillinvitational.bizland.com**. March 15 to 21, 2004.

• **Sidewalk Art Festival.** Held in Winter Park's Central Park, this 3-day exhibition draws artists from all over North America during the third full weekend in March. The festival is consistently named one of the best in the nation by *Sunshine Artist* magazine. Admission is free, though you may have to pay for parking. Call ✆ **407/672-6390** or 407/644-8281, or go to **www.wpsaf.org** for details.

April

• **Orlando Rays Baseball Season.** This Tampa Bay Devil Rays farm team plays its Southern League (Class AA) games at the Disney Wide World of Sports complex from April to early September. Admission is $5 to $8. For general information, call ✆ **407/939-4263** or check online at **www. orlandorays.com**. You also can buy tickets through Ticketmaster (✆ **877/803-7073** or 407/839-3900).

May

• **Orlando International Fringe Festival.** Over 100 diverse acts from around the world participate in this eclectic event, held for 10 days in May at various venues in downtown Orlando. Entertainers perform drama, comedy, political satire, and experimental theater. Everything performed on outdoor stages, from sword swallowing to *Hamlet,* is available free to Fringe attendees after they purchase a festival button for about $10. Tickets for indoor events vary, but most are under $10. Call ✆ **407/648-0077** or surf the Web to **www. orlandofringe.com** for details.

• **Epcot International Flower and Garden Festival.** This 6-week-long event showcases gardens, topiary characters, floral displays, speakers,

---

⒡ Fun Fact Commercial Dealings

Money really can't buy love. After the 1998 Super Bowl, Denver Broncos' coach, Mike Shanahan, made news by declining a $30,000 offer to say the catch phrase, "I'm going to Disney World." Shanahan, apparently a Universal man, said, "I don't care how much they pay me."

But he may be in the minority. Since 1987, Disney has paid a fortune to athletes, fresh off mega-stardom, for the words: "I'm going to Disney World" or "I'm going to Disneyland." Those who have appeared in the commercials include Brandi Chastain and the rest of the world-champ U.S. women's soccer team in 1999 and Barry Bonds after his 73 home-run season in 2001.

and seminars. The festival is free with regular park admission ($50 adults, $40 kids 3 to 9). For more information, call ℂ **407/824-4321** or visit **www.disneyworld.com**.

June

- **Gay Weekend.** The first weekend in June attracts tens of thousands of gays and lesbians to central Florida for what amounts, with add-ons, to a week of festivities. It grew out of "Gay Day," held unofficially at Disney World since the early 1990s and drawing some 100,000 people who revitalized Orlando's economy to the tune of $100 million. Special events at Universal and SeaWorld also cater to gays and lesbians. Look for online information on discounts, packages, hosts, and more at **www.gayday.com** or **www.gaydays.com**. Also, see "Gay & Lesbian Travel," later in this chapter.
- **Florida Film Festival.** The Enzian Theater has been showcasing American independent and foreign films for more than a decade. In 2001 this was named one of the top 10 such events in the world by *The Ultimate Film Festival Survival Guide*. Call **407/629-1088** or 407/629-0054, or look up **www.floridafilmfestival.com**.

July

- **Independence Day.** Disney's Star-Spangled Spectacular brings bands, singers, dancers, and unbelievable fireworks displays to all the Disney parks, which stay open later than normal. Call ℂ **407/824-4321** for details or surf over to **www.disneyworld.com**. SeaWorld features a dazzling laser/fireworks spectacular; call ℂ **407/351-3600** for details (www.seaworld.com). There's also a free fireworks display in downtown Orlando at Lake Eola Park. For information, call ℂ **407/246-2827**. Other fireworks events are listed in the local newspaper, the *Orlando Sentinel.*

September

- **Night of Joy.** The first weekend in September, the Magic Kingdom hosts a festival of contemporary Christian music featuring top artists. This is a very popular event, so obtain tickets early. Performers also make an appearance at Long's Christian Bookstore in College Park, about 20 minutes north of Disney. Admission to the concert is $35.95 per night (8pm–1am). Use of Magic Kingdom attractions is included. Call ℂ **407/824-4321** for concert details; for information about the free appearance at Long's, call ℂ **407/422-6934**. Universal has gone head-to-head with Disney on this one, scheduling its **Rock the Universe** concert the same weekend (ℂ **800/837-2273**. Tickets are $19.95 plus the cost of a 1-day park ticket ($51.95 adults, $42.95 kids).

October

- **Orlando Magic Basketball.** The NBA team plays half of its 82-game regular season between October and April at the TD Waterhouse Centre, 600 W. Amelia St. Ticket prices range from $16 to $150. A few tickets, usually single seats, are often available the day before games involving lesser-known NBA challengers. Call ℂ **407/896-2442** for details, **877/803-7073** or 407/839-3900 for tickets. Online go to **www.nba.com/magic**.
- **Halloween Horror Nights.** Universal Orlando's Islands of Adventure (ℂ **800/837-2273** or 407/363-8000; www.universalorlando.com) transforms its grounds for 20 or more nights into haunted attractions with live bands, a psychopath's maze, special shows, and hundreds of ghouls and goblins

roaming the streets. The studio essentially closes at dusk, reopening in a new macabre form from 7pm to midnight or later. Full admission ($51.95 adults) is charged for this event, geared to grown-ups (liquor flows freely, and the frightfulness is *truly* that). Guests can't wear costumes so Universal employees can spot their peers.

- **Mickey's Not-So-Scary Halloween Party.** The Magic Kingdom (© **407/934-7639;** www. disneyworld.com) invites you to join Mickey and his pals for a far-from-frightening time. In this one, you can come in costume and trick-or-treat through the Magic Kingdom from 7pm to midnight on any of 8 or so nights. The alcohol-free party includes parades, live music, and storytelling. The climax is a bewitching fireworks spectacular ($27.95 adults, $22.95 kids 3–9).

- **Walt Disney World Golf Classic.** Top PGA tour players compete at WDW golf courses from October 23 through October 26. Many tour professionals, including Tiger Woods, call Orlando home, so there's usually plenty of first-rate talent on display. Daily ticket prices range from $15 to $35. Tickets for the 4-day event run about $50. For information, contact Walt Disney World Golf Sales, P.O. Box 10000, Lake Buena Vista, FL 32830 (© **407/824-2250;** www.disneyworld.com). You also can get tickets through Ticketmaster (© **877/803-7073** or 407/ 839-3900).

- **Biketoberfest.** Held at the end of October, this event isn't as large as its March sister, Bike Week. But it is another celebration of motorcycles, with concerts, special events, and thousands of leather-wearing bikers flaunting their machines,

among other things. (See our criticism of Bike Week earlier, under March.) For information, contact the Daytona Beach Area Convention & Visitors Bureau at © **800/ 854-1234** or go online to **www. biketoberfest.com.**

- **Epcot International Food & Wine Festival.** Here's your chance to sip and savor the food and beverages of 25 cultures. More than 60 wineries from across the United States participate. Events include wine tastings for adults, seminars, food, dinners, concerts, and celebrity-chef cooking demonstrations. Tickets for the dinner-and-concert series or wine tastings are $79 to $125 including gratuity. The event also features 25 food-and-wine marketplaces where appetizer-size portions of dishes ranging from pizza to octopus on purple potato salad sell for under $5 each. Park admission ($52 adults) is also required. Call © **407/824-4321** for details or check out **www.disneyworld.com.** This festival runs for approximately 4 weeks from mid-October to mid-November.

November

- **ABC Super Soap Weekend.** Thirty-something daytime soap celebs are on hand for parades, parties, Q&As, music, and more in a wild weekend catering to fans and fanatics. The events are included with Disney–MGM Studios admission ($52 adults, $40 kids 3–9). Call © **407/397-6808** or surf over to **www.disney world.com** for details. First week in November.

- **Walt Disney World Festival of the Masters.** One of the largest art shows in the South takes place at Downtown Disney Marketplace for 3 days during the second weekend in November. The exhibition features top artists, photographers, and craftspeople, all winners of juried shows throughout the country. Free admission. Call © 407/ 824-4321 or visit www.disney-world.com.

December

- **Christmas at Walt Disney World.** During the Mickster's holiday festivities, Main Street in the Magic Kingdom is lavishly decked out with lights and holly, and carolers greet visitors. An 80-foot tree is illuminated by thousands of colored lights. Epcot, Disney–MGM Studios, and Animal Kingdom also offer special embellishments and entertainment throughout the holiday season, as do all of the Disney resorts. Some holiday highlights include **Mickey's Very Merry Christmas Party,** an after-dark (7pm–midnight) ticketed event ($33.95 adults, $23.95 kids 3–9). This takes place on select nights at the Magic Kingdom and offers a parade, fireworks, special shows, and admission to certain rides. You also get cookies, cocoa, and a souvenir photo. The best part? Shorter lines for the rides. The not-so-best part? Fewer rides are open. The **Osborne Family Christmas Lights** came to Disney–MGM Studios in 1995 when the

Arkansas family ran into trouble with their hometown authorities over their multimillion-light display. In a twinkle, Disney moved the whole shebang to Florida. **Holidays Around the World** and the **Candlelight Procession** at Epcot feature hundreds of carolers, celebrity narrators telling the Christmas story, a 450-voice choir, and a 50-piece orchestra in a very moving display. Fireworks are included. Regular admission ($52 adults, $42 kids 3–9) is required. Call © **407/824-4321** for details on all of the above or go to **www.disneyworld.com**. The holiday fun lasts from mid-December to early January.

- **Macy's Thanksgiving Parade.** *That's not a typo!* Universal and Macy's (the latter a tenant at the brand new Mall at Millenia, see p. 292) teamed up for the first time in December 2002 to offer a smaller version of **Macy's Thanksgiving Day Parade.** The Universal version runs from mid-December to early January, featuring 16 floats and giant balloons used in the New York City parade; and word is it will make return engagements (© **800/837-2273** or 407/363-8000; www.universalorlando.com). Park admission ($51.95 for adults,

---

Fun Fact Disney Fairy Tale

It's a story even Disney couldn't make up. The Osbornes of Arkansas apparently took to heart the old hymn that says, "You can't be a beacon if your light don't shine." Their Christmas-light collection of 2-million-plus blinkers, twinklers, and strands was so bright that neighbors complained. (Imagine it next to your bedroom window!) There were rumors that even air traffic was disrupted and the flow of the faithful in cars caused mile-long backups. The neighbors, finally seeing the light, went to court in what became a nationally known battle. Disney came to the rescue, and, in 1995, moved the entire thing to Orlando, adding a million or so bulbs. The display is now known as the Osborne Family Christmas Lights. No complaints from air traffic or neighbors—yet.

$42.95 for kids 3–9) is required. Mid-December to early January.

- **Walt Disney World New Year's Eve Celebration.** For 1 night a year, the Magic Kingdom is open until the wee hours for a massive fireworks explosion. Other New Year's festivities in WDW include a big bash at Pleasure Island featuring music headliners, a special Hoop-Dee-Doo Musical Revue at Fort Wilderness, and guest performances by well-known musical groups at Disney–MGM Studios and Epcot. Call ℂ **407/824-4321** for details or visit **www.disney world.com**. December 31.

4 Insurance, Health & Safety

TRAVEL INSURANCE AT A GLANCE

Check your existing insurance policies and credit card coverage before you buy travel insurance. You may already be covered for lost luggage, cancelled tickets, or medical expenses. The cost of travel insurance varies widely, depending on the cost and length of your trip, your age, health, and the type of trip you're taking.

TRIP-CANCELLATION INSUR-ANCE

Trip-cancellation insurance helps you get your money back if you have to back out of a trip, if you have to go home early, or if your travel supplier goes bankrupt. Allowed reasons for cancellation can range from sickness to natural disasters to the State Department declaring your destination unsafe for travel. (Insurers usually won't cover vague fears, though, as many travelers discovered who tried to cancel their trips in October 2001 because they were wary of flying.) In this unstable world, trip-cancellation insurance is a good buy if you're getting tickets well in advance—who knows what the state of the world, or of your airline, will be in 9 months? Insurance policy details vary, so read the fine print—and especially make sure that your airline or cruise line is on the list of carriers covered in case of bankruptcy. For information, contact one of the following insurers: **Access America** (ℂ **866/807-3982;** www. accessamerica.com); **Travel Guard International** (ℂ **800/826-4919;** www.travelguard.com); **Travel Insured International** (ℂ **800/243-3174;** www.travelinsured.com); and **Travelex Insurance Services** (ℂ **888/457-4602;** www.travelex-insurance.com).

MEDICAL INSURANCE Most health insurance policies cover you if you get sick away from home—but check, particularly if you're insured by an HMO. If you require additional medical insurance, try **MEDEX International** (ℂ **800/527-0218** or 410/453-6300; www.medexassist.com) or **Travel Assistance International** (ℂ **800/821-2828;** www.travelassist ance.com; for general information on services, call the company's Worldwide Assistance Services, Inc., at ℂ **800/ 777-8710**).

LOST-LUGGAGE INSURANCE On domestic flights, checked baggage is covered up to $2,500 per ticketed passenger. On international flights (including U.S. portions of international trips), baggage is limited to approximately $9.07 per pound, up to approximately $635 per checked bag. If you plan to check items more valuable than the standard liability, see if your valuables are covered by your homeowner's policy, get baggage insurance as part of your comprehensive travel-insurance package, or buy Travel Guard's "BagTrak" product. Don't buy insurance at the airport, as it's usually overpriced. Be sure to take

---

Tips   Quick ID

Tie a colorful ribbon or piece of yarn around your luggage handle, or slap a distinctive sticker on the side of your bag. This makes it less likely that someone will mistakenly appropriate it. And if your luggage gets lost, it will be easier to find.

---

any valuables or irreplaceable items with you in your carry-on luggage, as many valuables (including books, money, and electronics) aren't covered by airline policies.

If your luggage is lost, immediately file a lost-luggage claim at the airport, detailing the luggage contents. For most airlines, you must report delayed, damaged, or lost baggage within 4 hours of arrival. The airlines are required to deliver luggage, once found, directly to your house or destination free of charge.

CAR-RENTAL INSURANCE (LOSS/DAMAGE WAIVER OR COLLISION DAMAGE WAIVER)

Car-rental insurance costs about $20 a day. If you hold a private auto insurance policy, you probably are covered in the U.S., but not abroad, for loss or damage to the car, and liability in case a passenger is injured. The credit card you used to rent the car also may provide some coverage.

Car-rental insurance probably does not cover liability if you caused the accident. Check your own auto insurance policy, the rental company policy, and your credit card coverage for the extent of coverage: Is your destination covered? Are other drivers covered? How much liability is covered if a passenger is injured? (If you rely on your credit card for coverage, you may want to bring a second credit card with you, as damages may be charged to your card, and you may find yourself stranded with no money.)

THE HEALTHY TRAVELER

Limit your exposure to the sun, especially during the first few days of your trip and, thereafter, from 11am to 2pm. Use a sunscreen with a high protection factor and apply it liberally. Remember that children need more protection than adults.

WHAT TO DO IF YOU GET SICK AWAY FROM HOME

If you worry about getting sick away from home, consider purchasing **medical travel insurance** and carry your ID card in your purse or wallet. In most cases, your existing health plan will provide the coverage you need. See "Travel Insurance at a Glance," above, for more information.

If you suffer from a chronic illness, consult your doctor before your departure. For conditions like epilepsy, diabetes, or heart problems, wear a **Medic Alert Identification Tag** (© 800/825-3785; www.medic alert.org), which will immediately alert doctors to your condition and give them access to your records through Medic Alert's 24-hour hot line.

Pack **prescription medications** in your carry-on luggage, and carry prescription medications in their original containers, with pharmacy labels— otherwise, they won't make it through airport security. Also bring along copies of your prescriptions in case you lose your pills or run out. Don't forget an extra pair of contact lenses or prescription glasses.

5 Specialized Travel Resources

TRAVELERS WITH DISABILITIES

There's no reason for those of you with disabilities to miss most of the fun that Orlando and the theme parks have to offer—as long as you engage in a little advance planning.

ACCOMMODATIONS   Every hotel and motel in Florida is required by law to have a special room or rooms equipped for wheelchairs. A few have wheel-in showers. Walt Disney World's **Coronado Springs Resort** (© 407/934-7639 or 407/939-1000; www.disneyworld.com), which opened in 1997, has 99 rooms designed to accommodate guests with disabilities. Make your special needs known when making reservations. For other information about special Disney rooms, call © 407/939-7807.

If you don't mind staying 15 minutes from Disney, **Yvonne's Property Management** (© 877/714-1144 or 863/424-0795; www.villasinorlando.com) is a rental agent for, among other things, some handicapped-accessible homes that have multiple-bedrooms, multiple-baths including accessible showers, full kitchens, and pools outfitted with lifts. Most cost less than $200 a night and are located in Davenport.

Medical Travel Inc. (© 800/778-7953; www.medicaltravel.org) is another source of rentals, scooters and vans, and medical equipment, and can satisfy other needs of disabled travelers, including those with terminal illnesses, and their families.

TRANSPORTATION   Public buses in Orlando have hydraulic lifts and restraining belts for wheelchairs. They serve Universal Orlando, SeaWorld, the shopping areas, and downtown Orlando. When staying at Disney, shuttle buses from your hotel may accommodate wheelchairs.

If you need to rent a wheelchair or electric scooter for your visit, **Walker Medical & Mobility Products** offers delivery to your room, and there's a model for guests who weigh up to 375 pounds. These products fit into Disney's transports and monorails as well as rental cars. Get more information by calling © **888/726-6837** or 407/331-9500, or on the Internet go to **www.walkermobility.com**.   **CARE Medical Equipment** (© **800/741-2282** or 407/856-2273; www.caremedicalequipment.com) offers similar services.

Amtrak (© **800/872-7245**; www.amtrak.com) provides redcap service, wheelchair assistance, and special seats if you give 72 hours notice. Travelers with disabilities are also entitled to a 15% discount off the lowest available adult coach fare. Documentation from a doctor or an ID card proving your disability is required. Amtrak also provides wheelchair-accessible sleeping accommodations on long-distance trains. Service dogs are permitted aboard and travel free. TDD/TTY service is also available at © **800/523-6590,** or you can write to P.O. Box 7717, Itasca, IL 60143.

Greyhound (© **800/752-4841**; www.greyhound.com) allows a passenger with disabilities to travel with a companion for a single fare, and if you call 48 hours in advance, they'll arrange help along the way. The bus line also allows service animals.

THEME PARKS   Many attractions at the parks, especially the newer ones, are designed to be accessible to a wide variety of guests. People with wheelchairs and their parties are often given preferential treatment so they can avoid lines.

The available assistance is outlined in the guide maps you get as you enter the parks. All of the theme parks offer some parking close to the entrances for those with disabilities. Let the parking booth attendant know your needs, and you'll be directed to the appropriate spot. Wheelchair and electric cart rentals are available at most major attractions, but you'll be most comfortable in your chair or cart from home if you can bring it. Keep in mind, however, that wheelchairs wider than 24.5 inches may be difficult to navigate through some attractions. And crowds may make it tough for any guest.

At Walt Disney World: Disney's many services are detailed in each theme park's *Guidebook for Guests with Disabilities.* Although the resort will no longer mail them to you prior to your visit, you can pick one up at Guest Relations near the front entrances to the parks. Also, you can call (C) **407/824-4321** or 407/824-2222 for answers to any questions regarding special needs. If you want to see one in advance and have a computer, go to the main WDW website, **www.disneyworld.com**, then click "FAQ" on the main page. When that loads, click "Guests with Disabilities FAQ" on the left side, then scroll down and click the desired park. *Note:* When we tried the site, it loaded the guidebooks in a type size that, in our opinion, required bionic eyes. But the box that appears at the bottom-left of that page gives you a chance to increase the type-size percent (we recommend at least 150%). Examples of services are as follows:

- Almost all Disney resorts have rooms for those with disabilities.

- Braille guidebooks are available at City Hall in the Magic Kingdom and Guest Relations in the other parks (a $25 refundable deposit is required).
- Service animals are allowed in all parks and on some rides.
- All parks have special parking lots near the entrances.
- Assisted listening devices are available to amplify the audio at selected attractions at WDW parks. Also, at some attractions, hearing-impaired guests can use handheld wireless receivers that allow them to read captions about the attractions. Both services are free but require a $25 refundable deposit.
- Wheelchairs and electric carts can be rented at all of the parks.
- Downtown Disney West Side, with crowded shops and bars, may be hard to navigate in a wheelchair. The movie theater is, however, wheelchair accessible.
- For information about Telecommunications Devices for the Deaf (TDDs) or sign-language interpreters at Disney World live shows, call (C) **407/827-5141.**

At Universal Studios Florida and Islands of Adventure: Guests with disabilities should go to Guest Services, located just inside the main entrances, for a *Disabled Guest Guidebook,* a TDD, or other special assistance. Wheelchair and electric cart rentals are available in the concourse area of the parking garage. Universal also provides audio descriptions on cassette for visually impaired guests and has sign-language guides and

---

Tips **Phone Warning!!!**

Orlando is too big for its britches. **Even local calls** require extra digits. Callers in the city's 407 area code—and other parts of Orange County— have to dial 10 digits, even when calling across the street: **407** plus the 7-digit local number.

scripts for its shows (advance notice is required; ℂ 800/837-2273 or 407/363-8000 for details). You also can learn more on the Internet at **www.universalorlando.com**. From the main page, click either on Islands of Adventure or Universal Studios Florida, then scroll down on the left side to "ADA page."

At SeaWorld: The park has a guide for guests with disabilities, although most of its attractions are easily accessible to those in wheelchairs. SeaWorld also provides a Braille guide for the visually impaired and a very brief synopsis of its shows for the hearing impaired. For information, call ℂ **407/351-3600**.

OTHER RESOURCES You also can get information online at the **Orlando/Orange County Convention & Visitors Bureau's** website, **www.orlandoinfo.com**. Scroll down the left side of the main page and click "special needs."

Many travel agencies offer customized tours and itineraries for travelers with disabilities. **Flying Wheels Travel** (ℂ **507/451-5005**; www.flyingwheelstravel.com) offers escorted tours and cruises that emphasize sports and private tours in minivans with lifts. **Accessible Journeys** (ℂ **800/846-4537** or 610/521-0339; www.disabilitytravel.com) caters specifically to slow walkers and wheelchair travelers and their families and friends.

Organizations that offer assistance to disabled travelers include the **Moss Rehab Hospital** (www.mossresourcenet.org), which provides a library of accessible-travel resources online; the **Society for Accessible Travel and Hospitality** (ℂ **212/447-7284**; www.sath.org; annual membership fees: $45 adults, $30 seniors and students), which offers a wealth of travel resources for all types of disabilities and informed recommendations on destinations, access guides, travel agents, tour operators, vehicle rentals,

and companion services; and the **American Foundation for the Blind** (ℂ **800/232-5463**; www.afb.org), which provides information on traveling with Seeing Eye dogs.

For more information specifically targeted to travelers with disabilities, the community website **iCan** (www.icanonline.net/channels/travel/index.cfm) has destination guides and several regular columns on accessible travel.

SENIOR TRAVEL

Mention the fact that you're a senior citizen when you make your travel reservations. Although all of the major U.S. airlines except America West have cancelled their senior discount and coupon book programs, many hotels still offer discounts for seniors. In most cities, people over the age of 60 qualify for reduced admission to theaters, museums, and other attractions, as well as discounted fares on public transportation.

You can order a copy of the *Mature Traveler Guide,* which contains local discounts mainly on rooms but also on attractions and activities, from the **Orlando/Orange County Convention & Visitors Bureau,** 8723 International Dr., Suite 101 (southeast corner of I-Drive and Austrian Row), Orlando, FL 32819 (ℂ **800/643-9492** or 800/551-0181; www.orlandoinfo.com). You can also find it online at the CVB's website (click the "senior" link under "other areas" on the left side of the home page).

Seniors 55 and older no longer get special savings through the **Magic Kingdom Club Gold Card.** And its replacement, the **Disney Club,** is also being phased out. Disney stopped selling new memberships at the end of 2002 and benefits on existing ones will stop December 31, 2003. Word at press time was that the club will be replaced by a Disney/VISA credit card that lets cardholders accumulate points that can be redeemed for discounts.

Members of **AARP** (formerly known as the American Association of Retired Persons), 601 E St. NW, Washington, DC 20049 (© **800/424-3410** or 202/434-2277; www.aarp.org), get discounts on hotels, airfares, and car rentals. AARP offers members a wide range of benefits, including *Modern Maturity* magazine and a monthly newsletter. Anyone over 50 can join.

Amtrak (© **800/872-7245;** www.amtrak.com) offers a 15% discount on the lowest available coach fare (with certain travel restrictions) to people 62 and over.

Many reliable agencies and organizations target the 50-plus market. **Elderhostel** (© **877/426-8056;** www.elderhostel.org) arranges study programs for those aged 55 and over (and a spouse or companion of any age) in the U.S. and in more than 80 countries around the world. Most courses last 5 to 7 days in the U.S. (2–4 weeks abroad), and many include airfare, accommodations in university dormitories or modest inns, meals, and tuition.

Recommended publications offering travel resources and discounts for seniors include: the quarterly magazine *Travel 50 & Beyond* (www.travel50andbeyond.com); *Travel Unlimited: Uncommon Adventures for the Mature Traveler* (Avalon); *101 Tips for Mature Travelers,* available from Grand Circle Travel (© **800/221-2610** or 617/350-7500; www.gct.com); *The 50+ Traveler's Guidebook* (St. Martin's Press); and *Unbelievably Good Deals and Great Adventures That You Absolutely Can't Get Unless You're Over 50* (McGraw Hill).

FAMILY TRAVEL

If you have enough trouble getting your kids out of the house in the morning, dragging them thousands of miles away may seem like an insurmountable challenge. But family travel can be immensely rewarding, giving you new ways of seeing the world through smaller pairs of eyes.

No city in the world is geared more to family travel than Orlando. In addition to its theme parks, Orlando's recreational facilities provide loads of opportunities for family fun. Most restaurants have low-priced ($4–$7) children's menus plus fun distractions such as placemats to color while younger diners wait for their vittles. Many hotels have children's activity centers (see chapter 5, "Where to Stay," for details).

Keep an eye out for coupons discounting meals and attractions. The Calendar section in Friday's *Orlando Sentinel* newspaper often contains coupons and good deals. Many restaurants, especially those in tourist areas, offer great discounts that are yours for the clipping. Check the information you receive from the Orlando/Orange County Convention & Visitors Bureau (see "Visitor Information" earlier in this chapter), including free or cheap things to do. Additionally, many hotel lobbies and attractions have free coupon books for the taking.

Some theme parks offer parent-swap programs in which one parent can ride without the children, then switch off and let the other parent ride without returning to the end of the line. Inquire at Guest Services or Guest Relations, near the park entrances.

Here are more suggestions for making traveling with children easier:

- **Are Your Kids Old Enough?** Do you really want to bring an infant or toddler to an overcrowded, usually overheated world that he or she may be too young to appreciate? Our younger grandson, Andy, is 5 and just able to appreciate some of the parks' offerings. But the thrill rides frighten him, as did some of the costume-wearing characters

Moments Kid-Friendly Tours

SeaWorld earns its reputation as an education-friendly park with a variety of small-group tours. One of the most interesting is the **Polar Expedition Guided Tour.** This hour-long trek gives kids a chance to come face-to-face with a penguin and get a behind-the-scenes look at polar bears and beluga whales. **To the Rescue,** another hour-long tour, lets guests see some of the park's rescue and rehabilitation work with several species, including manatees and sea turtles. Both cost $8.95 per person, plus park admission (© **800/406-2244;** www.seaworld.com). Both tours are kid-friendly, though the latter may appeal more to the older ones. Both are on a first-come, first-served basis, so reserve your place at the Guided Tour Information desk when you enter the park. In June, July, and August, **Camp SeaWorld** has 200 classes including sleep-over programs and family courses (© **800/406-2244;** www.seaworld.com).

At Walt Disney World, the kid-friendliest tour is the **Family Magic Tour,** an interactive scavenger hunt that costs $25 per person, plus admission (© **407/939-8687;** www.disneyworld.com).

when he was a tad younger. Younger kids may need a nap when you want to see Festival of the Lion King at Disney's Animal Kingdom. And they're dead weight if you have to carry them from Jaws to Catastrophe Canyon at Universal Studios Florida. And when it comes to thrill-ride central—Islands of Adventure—well, the young and short will find slim pickings. When all is said and done, it comes down to one question: Will the whole family enjoy a trip that's going to cost you the GNP of a developing nation?

- **Planning Ahead** Make reservations for "character breakfasts" at Disney (see chapter 6, "Where to Dine") when you make hotel reservations. Also, in any park, check the daily schedule for character appearances (all of the major ones post them on maps or boards near the entrances) and make sure the kids know when they're going to get to meet their heroes. It's often the highlight of

their day. (Be wary, however, of promising specific characters, as schedules and character line-ups can change.) Advance planning will help you avoid running after every character you see. The "in" thing is getting character autographs. Take our advice: Buy an autograph book at home instead of paying theme-park prices.

- **Packing** Although your home may be toddler-proof, hotel accommodations aren't. Bring blank plugs to cover outlets and whatever else is necessary to prevent an accident from occurring in your room. Locals can spot tourists by their bright red, just-toasted sunburn; both parents and children should heed this reminder: *Don't forget to use sunscreen.* If you forget to bring it, it's available at convenience stores and drugstores. Some theme-park shops also carry it; *buy a 25 SPF rating* or higher. Young children should be slathered, even if they're

Tips Kids & Flying

Delta, Walt Disney World's official airline, has stopped allowing families with children to board first on its Orlando flights. It's fairer to the other passengers and better for the kids, who won't be cooped up as long.

in a stroller, and be sure to pack a wide-brim hat for infants and toddlers. Adults and children should also drink plenty of water to avoid dehydration.

- **Accommodations**   Kids under 12, and in many cases under 18, stay free in their parent's room in most hotels, but to be certain, ask when you book your room. Most places have pools and other recreational facilities to give you a little no-extra-cost downtime. If you want to skip a rental car and aren't staying at Disney, International Drive and Lake Buena Vista are the places to be. Hotels often offer family discounts, and some provide free or moderate-cost shuttle service to the homes of the Mouse, the Whale, and the Kong. I-Drive also has a self-serving trolley.

- **Ground Rules**   Set up firm rules before leaving home on things like bedtime and souvenirs. Your kids are going to be on an adrenaline high here—you may be, too—so don't let giddiness seize your senses.

- **At the Parks**   Getting lost is as easy as remembering your name. For adults and older kids, arrange a lost-and-found meeting place as soon as you land, and if you become separated, head there immediately. Attach a nametag to younger kids and find a park employee if they become lost.

- **Read the Signs**   Most rides explain **height restrictions,** if any, or identify those that may unsettle youngsters. Save yourself and your kids some grief before you get in line and are disappointed. Make

these rules firm—a trip down a darkened tunnel or scary loop-de-loop can make your child cranky all day and maybe scared of rides for a long while after. (The ride listings in chapter 7, "Exploring Walt Disney World," and chapter 8, "Exploring Beyond Disney: Universal Orlando, SeaWorld & Other Attractions," note any minimum heights; so do the guide maps you can get in the parks.)

- **Take a Break**   The Disney parks, Universal Orlando, and SeaWorld have stylized play areas offering parents and kids a break. Schedule time to use them. Many of these kid zones include water toys, and some parks have major water-related attractions, so you'd be smart to pack a change of clothes. Rent a locker ($7 or less) and store spare duds until you need them. During summer, the Florida humidity can keep you feeling soggy all day, so you'll appreciate the fresh clothing even if you don't go near the water.

- **Show Time**   Schedule an inside air-conditioned show two or three times a day, especially mid-afternoons in the summer. You may even get your littlest tikes to nap in the darkened theater. For all shows, arrive at least 20 minutes early to avoid the bad seats, but not so early that the kids go nuts waiting (most waits are outside).

- **Snack Times**   When dreaming of your vacation, you probably don't envision hours spent standing in lines, waiting and waiting. It helps to store some lightweight snacks in a fanny pack or back-pack, especially when traveling with small children. This may save you some headaches and will certainly save you some money over park prices.

- **Bring Your Own?** Unless you're particularly attached to your stroller, or it's specially designed for triplets, it's better to use one provided by the parks (about $6 or $7). That way you avoid hauling yours to and from the car or on and off the trams, trains, or monorails. For infants and toddlers, you may want to bring a snugly sling or backpack-type carrier for use in traveling to and from parking lots and while you're in line for attractions.
- **Recommended Reading** *The Unofficial Guide to Walt Disney World with Kids* is a good source of additional information.

You can find good family-oriented vacation advice on the Internet from sites like the **Family Travel Network** (www.familytravelnetwork.com); **Traveling Internationally with Your Kids** (www.travelwithyourkids.com), a comprehensive site offering sound advice for long-distance and international travel with children; and **Family Travel Files** (www.thefamilytravel files.com), which offers an online magazine and a directory of off-the-beaten-path tours and tour operators for families.

We've listed some additional tips for tackling the theme parks in the section "Making Your Visit More Enjoyable," in chapter 7.

GAY & LESBIAN TRAVEL

The popularity of Orlando with gay and lesbian travelers is confirmed by the expansion of the June "Gay Day" celebration at Disney World into a weeklong event that includes Universal Orlando and SeaWorld. Park-goers are supposed to wear red on Gay Day

to signify their support of the gay and lesbian community. You can get information on the event at **www.gay day.com** or **www.gaydays.com**.

For information about events for that week or throughout the year, contact **Gay, Lesbian & Bisexual Community Services of Central Florida,** 934 N. Mills Ave., Orlando, FL 32803 (© 407/228-8272; www.glbcc.org). Welcome packets usually include the latest issue of the *Triangle,* a quarterly newsletter dedicated to gay and lesbian issues, and a calendar of events pertaining to the gay and lesbian community. Though not a tourist-specific packet, it includes information and ads for local gay and lesbian clubs. **In the Company of Women** (© 407/331-3466; www.companyofwomen.com) and **Gay Orlando Network** (www.gayorlando. com) are two other planning resources for travelers. *Watermark* (© 407/481-2243; www.watermarkonline.com) is another gay-friendly publication; it can be found in many bookstores.

Orlando is a Southern town, but the entertainment industry and the theme parks have helped in the building of a strong gay and lesbian community. Same-sex dancing won't draw any unwelcome attention at most of the clubs at WDW's Pleasure Island, especially the large, crowded Mannequins. Many of Universal's City-Walk establishments are similarly gender blind. The tenor of crowds can change, however, depending on what tour is in town, so respect your own intuition.

The International Gay & Lesbian Travel Association (IGLTA) (© 800/448-8550 or 954/776-2626; www.igl ta.org) is the trade association for the gay and lesbian travel industry, and offers an online directory of gay- and lesbian-friendly travel businesses; go to their website and click on "Members."

Many agencies offer tours and travel itineraries specifically for gay and lesbian travelers. **Above and**

Beyond Tours (*©* 800/397-2681; www.abovebeyondtours.com) is the exclusive gay and lesbian tour operator for United Airlines. **Now, Voyager** (*©* 800/255-6951; www.nowvoyager. com) is a well-known San Francisco–based gay-owned-and-operated travel service.

The following travel guides are available at most travel bookstores and gay and lesbian bookstores, or you can order them from **Giovanni's Room** bookstore, 1145 Pine St., Philadelphia, PA 19107 (*©* 215/923-2960; www.giovannisroom.com): *Out and About* (*©* 800/929-2268 or 415/644-8044; www.outandabout.com), which offers guidebooks and a newsletter 10 times a year packed with solid information on the global gay and lesbian scene; and *Gay Travel A to Z: The World of Gay & Lesbian Travel Options at Your Fingertips* by Marianne Ferrari (Ferrari Publications; Box 35575, Phoenix, AZ 85069), a very good gay and lesbian guidebook series.

TRAVELING WITH PETS

Many of us wouldn't dream of going on vacation without our pets. And these days, more and more lodgings and restaurants are going the pet-friendly route. Many hotel and motel chains, such as Best Western, Motel 6, Holiday Inn, and Four Seasons-Regent Hotels, welcome pets. Policies vary, however, so call ahead to find out the rules.

None of the Disney resorts allow animals (except service dogs) to stay on-premises or have their own kennels, but resort guests are welcome to board their animals overnight in kennel facilities at the Ticket & Transportation Center. Universal Orlando & SeaWorld will board small animals during the day only.

An excellent resource is **www.pets welcome.com**, which dispenses medical tips, names of animal-friendly lodgings and campgrounds, and lists of kennels and veterinarians. Also check out *The Portable Petswelcome.com: The Complete Guide to Traveling with Your Pet* (Howell Book House), which features the best selection of pet travel information anywhere. Another resource is *Pets-R-Permitted Hotel, Motel & Kennel Directory: The Travel Resource for Pet Owners Who Travel* (Annenberg Communications).

Another valuable source is **www.dogfriendly.com**, which has Orlando and Orlando area links that include accommodations, eateries, attractions, and parks that welcome our canine companions.

If you plan to fly with your pet, the FAA has compiled a list of all requirements for transporting live animals at **http://airconsumer.ost.dot.gov/air consumer/publications/animals. htm**. You may be able to carry your pet on board a plane if it's small enough to put inside a carrier that can slip under the seat. Pets usually count as one piece of carry-on luggage. Note that summer may not be the best time to fly with your pet: Many airlines will not check pets as baggage in the hot summer months. The ASPCA

Tips **The Peripatetic Pet**

It is illegal in Florida to leave your pet inside a parked car, windows rolled down or not. The sweltering heat can easily kill an animal in only a few minutes. All of the major theme parks have kennel facilities—use them.

Make sure your pet is wearing a name tag with the name and phone number of a contact person who can take the call if your pet gets lost while you're away from home.

discourages travelers from checking pets as luggage at any time, as storage conditions on planes are loosely monitored, and fatal accidents are not unprecedented. Your other option is to ship your pet with a professional carrier, which can be expensive. Ask your veterinarian whether you should sedate your pet on a plane ride or give it anti-nausea medication. Never give your pet sedatives used by humans.

6 Planning Your Trip Online

SURFING FOR AIRFARES

The "big three" online travel agencies, **Expedia.com**, **Travelocity.com**, and **Orbitz.com**, sell most of the air tickets bought on the Internet. (Canadian travelers should try expedia.ca and Travelocity.ca; U.K. residents can go to expedia.co.uk and opodo.co.uk.) Each has different business deals with the airlines, and may offer different fares on the same flights, so it's wise to shop around. Expedia and Travelocity will also send you **e-mail notification** when a cheap fare to your favorite destination becomes available. Of the smaller travel agency websites, **Side-Step** (www.sidestep.com) has gotten the best reviews from Frommer's authors. It's a browser add-on that purports to "search 140 sites at once," but in reality only beats competitors' fares as often as other sites do.

Also remember to check **airline websites,** especially those for low-fare carriers such as Southwest, JetBlue, AirTran, WestJet, or Ryanair, whose fares are often misreported or simply missing from travel agency websites. Even with major airlines, you can often shave a few bucks from a fare by booking directly through the airline and avoiding a travel agency's transaction fee. But you'll get these discounts only by **booking online:** Most airlines now offer online-only fares that even their phone agents know nothing about. For the websites of airlines that fly to and from your destination, go to "Getting There," later in this chapter.

Great **last-minute deals** are available through free weekly e-mail services provided directly by the airlines. Most of these are announced on Tuesday or Wednesday and must be purchased online. Most are only valid for travel that weekend, but some (such as Southwest's) can be booked weeks or months in advance. Sign up for weekly e-mail alerts at airline websites or check mega-sites that compile comprehensive lists of last-minute specials, such as **Smarter Living** (www.smarterliving.com). For last-minute trips, **site59.com** in the U.S. and **last minute.com** in Europe often have better deals than the major sites.

If you're willing to give up some control over your flight details, use an **opaque fare service** like **Priceline** (www.priceline.com; www.priceline.co.uk for Europeans) or **Hotwire** (www.hotwire.com). Both offer rock-bottom prices in exchange for travel on a "mystery airline" at a mysterious time of day, often with a mysterious change of planes en route. The mystery airlines are all major, well-known carriers—and the possibility of being sent from Philadelphia to Chicago via Tampa is remote; the airlines' routing computers have gotten a lot better than they used to be. But your chances of getting a 6am or 11pm flight are pretty high. Hotwire tells you flight prices before you buy; Priceline usually has better deals than Hotwire, but you have to play their "name our price" game. If you're new at this, the helpful folks at **BiddingForTravel** (www.biddingfortravel.com) do a good job of demystifying Priceline's prices. Priceline and Hotwire are great for flights within North America and between the U.S. and Europe. But for flights to other

Frommers.com: The Complete Travel Resource

For an excellent travel-planning resource, we highly recommend **Frommers.com** (www.frommers.com). We're a little biased, of course, but we guarantee that you'll find the travel tips, reviews, monthly vacation giveaways, and online-booking capabilities thoroughly indispensable. Among the special features are our popular **Message Boards,** where Frommer's readers post queries and share advice (sometimes even our authors show up to answer questions); **Frommers.com Newsletter,** for the latest travel bargains and insider travel secrets; and **Frommer's Destinations Section,** where you'll get expert travel tips, hotel and dining recommendations, and advice on the sights to see for more than 3,000 destinations around the globe. When your research is done, the **Online Reservations System** (www.frommers.com/book_a_trip) takes you to Frommer's preferred online partners for booking your vacation at affordable prices.

parts of the world, consolidators will almost always beat their fares.

For much more about airfares and savvy air-travel tips and advice, pick up a copy of *Frommer's Fly Safe, Fly Smart* (Wiley Publishing, Inc.).

SURFING FOR HOTELS

Shopping online for hotels is much easier in the U.S., Canada, and certain parts of Europe than it is in the rest of the world. If you try to book a Chinese hotel online, for instance, you'll probably overpay. Also, many smaller hotels and B&Bs—especially outside the U.S.—don't show up on websites at all. Of the "big three" sites, **Expedia** may be the best choice, thanks to its long list of special deals. **Travelocity** runs a close second. Hotel specialist sites **hotels.com** and **hoteldiscounts.com** are also reliable. An excellent free program, **Travel Axe** (www.travelaxe.net), can help you search multiple hotel sites at once, even ones you may never have heard of.

Priceline and Hotwire are even better for hotels than for airfares; with both, you're allowed to pick the neighborhood and quality level of your hotel before offering up your money. Priceline's hotel product even covers Europe and Asia, though it's much better at getting five-star lodging for three-star prices than at finding anything at the bottom of the scale. *Note:* Hotwire overrates its hotels by one star—what Hotwire calls a four-star is a three-star anywhere else.

SURFING FOR RENTAL CARS

For booking rental cars online, the best deals are usually found at rental-car company websites, although all the major online travel agencies also offer rental-car reservations services. Priceline and Hotwire work well for rental cars, too; the only "mystery" is which major rental company you get, and for most travelers the difference between Hertz, Avis, and Budget is negligible.

7 The 21st-Century Traveler

INTERNET ACCESS AWAY FROM HOME

Travelers have any number of ways to check their e-mail and access the

Internet on the road. Of course, using your own laptop—or even a PDA (personal desk assistant) or electronic organizer with a modem—gives you the most flexibility. But even if you don't have a computer, you can still access your e-mail and even your office computer from cybercafes.

WITHOUT YOUR OWN COMPUTER

It's hard nowadays to find a city that *doesn't* have a few cybercafes. Although there's no definitive directory for cybercafes—these are independent businesses, after all—three places to start looking are at **www.cyber captive.com**, **www.netcafeguide.com**, and **www.cybercafe.com**.

To retrieve your e-mail, ask your **Internet service provider (ISP)** if it has a Web-based interface tied to your existing e-mail account. If your ISP doesn't have such an interface, you can use the free **mail2web** service (www.mail2web.com) to view (but not reply to) your home e-mail. For more flexibility, you may want to open a free, Web-based e-mail account with **Yahoo! Mail** (mail.yahoo.com).

(Microsoft's Hotmail is another popular option, but Hotmail has severe spam problems.) Your home ISP may be able to forward your e-mail to the Web-based account automatically.

WITH YOUR OWN COMPUTER

Major ISPs have **local access numbers** around the world, allowing you to go online by simply placing a local call. Check your ISP's website or call its toll-free number and ask how you can use your current account away from home, and how much it will cost.

If you're traveling outside the reach of your ISP, the **iPass** network has dial-up numbers in most countries. You'll have to sign up with an iPass provider, who will then tell you how to set up your computer for your destination(s). For a list of iPass providers, go to www.ipass.com and click on "Individuals." One solid provider is **i2roam** (www.i2roam.com; ✆ **866/811-6209** or 920/235-0475).

 Online Traveler's Toolbox

- **Visa ATM Locator** (www.visa.com), for locations of PLUS ATMs worldwide, or **MasterCard ATM Locator** (www.mastercard.com), for locations of Cirrus ATMs worldwide.
- **Foreign Languages for Travelers** (www.travlang.com). Learn basic terms in more than 70 languages and click on any underlined phrase to hear what it sounds like.
- **Intellicast** (www.intellicast.com) and **Weather.com** (www.weather.com). These sites give weather forecasts for all 50 states and for cities around the world.
- **Mapquest** (www.mapquest.com). This best of the mapping sites lets you choose a specific address or destination, and in seconds, it will return a map and detailed directions.
- **Universal Currency Converter** (www.xe.com/ucc). See what your dollar or pound is worth in more than 100 other countries.
- **Travel Warnings** (http://travel.state.gov/travel_warnings.html, www.fco.gov.uk/travel, www.voyage.gc.ca, www.dfat.gov.au/consular/advice). These sites report on places where health concerns or unrest might threaten American, British, Canadian, and Australian travelers. Generally, U.S. warnings are the most paranoid; Australian warnings are the most relaxed.

Wherever you go, bring a **connection kit** of the right power and phone adapters, a spare phone cord, and a spare Ethernet network cable.

Most business-class hotels throughout the world offer dataports for laptop modems, and a few thousand hotels in the U.S. and Europe now offer high-speed Internet access using an Ethernet network cable. You'll have to bring your own cables either way, so **call your hotel in advance** to find out what the options are.

Many business-class hotels in the U.S. also offer a form of computer-free Web browsing through the room TV set.

USING A CELLPHONE

Just because your cellphone works at home doesn't mean it'll work elsewhere in the country (thanks to our nation's fragmented cellphone system). It's a good bet that your phone will work in a major city such as Orlando. But take a look at your wireless company's coverage map on its website before heading out—T-Mobile, Sprint, and Nextel are particularly weak in rural areas. If you need to stay in touch at a destination where you know your phone won't work, **rent** a phone that does from **InTouch USA** (© 800/872-7626; www.intouchglobal.com) or a rental car location, but beware that you'll pay $1 a minute or more for airtime.

If you're not from the U.S., you'll be appalled at the poor reach of our **GSM (Global System for Mobiles) wireless network,** which is used by much of the rest of the world (see below). Your phone will probably work in most major U.S. cities; it definitely won't work in many rural areas. (To see where GSM phones work in the U.S., check out **www.t-mobile. com/coverage/national_popup.asp**.) And you may or may not be able to send SMS (text messaging) home—something Americans tend not to do anyway, for various cultural and technological reasons. (International budget travelers like to send text messages home because it's much cheaper than making international calls.) Assume nothing—call your wireless provider and get the full scoop. In a worst-case scenario, you can always rent a phone; InTouch USA delivers to hotels.

8 Getting There

BY PLANE
THE MAJOR AIRLINES

There are 35 scheduled airlines and nearly as many charter companies serving the more than 30 million passengers who land in Orlando in a normal year. **Delta** (© 800/221-1212; www.delta.com) runs nearly 25% of the flights into Orlando International Airport. It offers service from about 150 cities.

Others include **Air Canada** (© 888/247-2262; www.aircanada.ca); **America West** (© 800/235-9292; www. americawest.com); **American** (© 800/433-7300; www.americanair.com); **British Airways** (© 800/247-9297; www.british-airways.com); **Continental** (© 800/525-0280; www.continental. com); **Northwest** (© 800/225-2525; www.nwa.com); and **US Airways** (© 800/428-4322; www.usairways. com).

Several so-called no-frills airlines— low fares but few niceties—fly to Florida. The biggest is **Southwest Airlines** (© 800/435-9792; www.south west.com), which has flights from many U.S. cities to Orlando and Tampa. **Spirit Air** (© 800/772-7117; www.spiritair.com) is another no-frills choice. **JetBlue Airways** (© 800/538-2583; www.jetblue.com) is a highly rated low-cost carrier that operates out

> **Tips Unclogged**
>
> If you're flying with a cold or sinus problems, use a decongestant 10 minutes before ascent and descent, to minimize pressure buildup in the inner ear.

of a number of U.S. cities, but offers direct flights to Orlando only out of New York City.

ORLANDO'S AIRPORT

Orlando International Airport (© 407/825-2001; www.state.fl.us/goaa) offers direct or nonstop service from 60 U.S. cities and two dozen international destinations, serving more than 30 million passengers most years. It's a thoroughly modern and user-friendly facility with restaurants, shops, a 446-room on-premises Hyatt Regency Hotel, and centrally located information kiosks. All major car-rental companies are located at or near the airport; see "Getting Around" in chapter 4 and appendix B ("Useful Toll-Free Numbers & Websites") for more information about car rentals.

AN ALTERNATIVE Orlando Sanford International Airport (© 407/585-4000; www.orlandosanfordairport.com) is much smaller than the main airport, but it has grown a bit in recent years, thanks mainly to a small fleet of international carriers including Air 2000, Britannia, and Aeropostal. The airport has Avis, Alamo, Dollar, and Hertz rental-car desks on site and shuttles to Budget and Enterprise. Mears Transportation shuttles (see below) also serve it.

AIRPORT TRANSPORTATION Orlando International is 25 miles east of Walt Disney World and 20 miles south of downtown. At rush hour (7–9am and 4–6pm), the drive can be a torturous hour or more; at other times, it's about 30 to 40 minutes. **Mears Transportation Group** (© 407/423-5566; www.mearstransportation.com) has vans that shuttle passengers from the airport (you catch them at ground level) to Disney resorts and official hotels, as well as most other Orlando properties. Their air-conditioned vehicles operate around the clock, departing every 15 to 25 minutes in either direction. Rates vary by destination. Round-trip for adults is $24 ($17 for kids) between the airport and downtown Orlando or International Drive, and $28 ($20 for kids) for Walt Disney World/Lake Buena Vista or West U.S. 192.

QuickTransportation/Orlando (© 888/784-2522 or 407/354-2456; www.quicktransportation.com) is a bit more personal. Their folks greet you at baggage claim with a sign bearing your name. They're more expensive than Mears, but they're coming for you. And they're only going to *your* resort. This is a good option for four or more people. Rates run from $80 (up to seven people, round-trip) to I-Drive/Universal Studios and $130 for the Disney empire.

Tiffany Towncar (© 888/838-2161 or 407/251-5431; www.tiffanytowncar.com) offers an $80 round-trip rate for up to five people from Orlando International to Disney ($65–$70 to International Dr. or Universal).

DRIVING TO WALT DISNEY WORLD To get from the airport to the attractions, take the **North** exit out of the airport to **Highway 528 West.** Follow signs to I-4; it takes about 30 to 40 minutes to get to Walt Disney World if the traffic isn't too heavy (double or worse in rush hour or when there's an accident). When you get to I-4, follow the signs **west** toward the attractions.

Note: It's always a good idea when you make reservations to ask about transportation options between the airport and your hotel. Also be sure to ask how far you have to travel to pick up and drop off a rental car. Some lots are miles from the airport, adding to the time you'll spend waiting in line and catching shuttles.

GETTING THROUGH THE AIRPORT

With the federalization of airport security, security procedures at U.S. airports are more stable and consistent than ever. Generally, you'll be fine if you arrive at the airport **1 hour** before a domestic flight and **2 hours** before an international flight; if you show up late, tell an airline employee, and she'll probably whisk you to the front of the line.

Bring a **current, government-issued photo ID** such as a driver's license or passport, and if you've got an E-ticket, print out the **official confirmation page;** you'll need to show your confirmation at the security checkpoint, and your ID at the ticket counter or the gate. (Children under 18 do not need photo IDs for domestic flights, but the adults checking in with them do.)

Security lines are getting shorter than they were during 2001 and 2002, but some doozies remain. If you have trouble standing for long periods of time, tell an airline employee; the airline will provide a wheelchair. Speed up security by **not wearing metal objects** such as big belt buckles or clanky earrings. If you've got metallic body parts, a note from your doctor can prevent a long chat with the security screeners. Keep in mind that only **ticketed passengers** are allowed past security, except for folks escorting disabled passengers or children.

Federalization has stabilized **what you can carry on** and **what you can't.** The general rule is that sharp things are out, nail clippers are okay, and food and beverages must be passed through the X-ray machine—but security screeners can't make you drink from your coffee cup. Bring food in your carry-on rather than checking it, as explosive-detection machines used on checked luggage have been known to mistake food (especially chocolate, for some reason) for bombs. Travelers in the U.S. are allowed one carry-on bag, plus a "personal item" such as a purse, briefcase, or laptop bag. Carry-on hoarders can stuff all sorts of things into a laptop bag; as long as it has a laptop in it, it's still considered a personal item. The Transportation Security Administration (TSA) has issued a list of restricted items; check its website (www.tsa.gov/public/index.jsp) for details.

In 2003, the TSA will be phasing out **gate check-in** at all U.S. airports. Passengers with E-tickets and without checked bags can still beat the ticket-counter lines by using **electronic kiosks** or even **online check-in.** Ask your airline which alternatives are available, and if you're using a kiosk, bring the credit card you used to book the ticket. If you're checking bags, you will still be able to use most airlines' kiosks; again, call your airline for up-to-date information. **Curbside check-in** is also a good way to avoid lines, although a few airlines still ban curbside check-in entirely; call before you go.

At press time, the TSA is also recommending that you **not lock your checked luggage** so screeners can search it by hand if necessary. The agency says to use plastic "zip ties" instead, which can be bought at hardware stores and can be easily cut off.

FLYING FOR LESS: TIPS FOR GETTING THE BEST AIRFARE

There's no shortage of discounted and promotional fares to Florida. November, December, and January (excluding

Travel in the Age of Bankruptcy

At press time, two major U.S. airlines were struggling in bankruptcy court, and most of the rest weren't doing very well either. To protect yourself, **buy your tickets with a credit card,** as the Fair Credit Billing Act guarantees that you can get your money back from the credit card company if a travel supplier goes under (and if you request the refund within 60 days of the bankruptcy). **Travel insurance** can also help, but make sure it covers against "carrier default" for your specific travel provider. And be aware that if a U.S. airline goes bust mid-trip, a 2001 federal law requires other carriers to take you to your destination (albeit on a space-available basis) for a fee of no more than $25, provided you rebook within 60 days of the cancellation.

holidays) often bring fare wars that can result in savings of 50% or more, but, in a sagging economy, specials may be available more often. Watch for ads in your local newspaper and on TV, call the airlines, or check out their websites. Here are some ways to keep your airfare costs down:

- Passengers who can book their tickets **long in advance,** who can **stay over Saturday night,** or who **fly midweek** or **at less-trafficked hours** will pay a fraction of the full fare. If your schedule is flexible, say so, and ask if you can secure a cheaper fare by changing your flight plans.
- No-frills airlines have reduced their price advantage, but some **charter** flights still go to Florida, especially during the winter season and particularly from Canada. They often cost less than regularly scheduled flights, but they're very complicated. It's best to go to a good travel agent and ask him or her to find one for you.
- Search **the Internet** for cheap fares (see "Planning Your Trip Online," earlier in this chapter).
- **Consolidators,** also known as bucket shops, are great sources for international tickets, although they usually can't beat the Internet on fares within North America. Start by looking in Sunday newspaper

travel sections; U.S. travelers should focus on the *New York Times, Los Angeles Times,* and *Miami Herald. Beware:* Bucket shop tickets are usually nonrefundable or rigged with stiff cancellation penalties, often as high as 50% to 75% of the ticket price, and some put you on charter airlines with questionable safety records. Several reliable consolidators are worldwide and available on the Net. **FlyCheap** (© **800/FLY-CHEAP;** www.1800flycheap.com) is owned by package-holiday megalith MyTravel and therefore has especially good access to fares for sunny destinations.

- Join **frequent-flier clubs.** Accrue enough miles, and you'll be rewarded with free flights and elite status. It's free, and you'll get the best choice of seats, faster response to phone inquiries, and prompter service if your luggage is stolen, your flight is canceled or delayed, or if you want to change your seat. You don't need to fly to build frequent-flier miles—**frequent-flier credit cards** can provide thousands of miles for doing your everyday shopping.
- For many more tips about air travel, including a rundown of the major frequent-flier credit cards, pick up a copy of *Frommer's Fly Safe, Fly Smart* (Wiley Publishing, Inc.).

Flying with Film & Video

Never pack film—developed or undeveloped—in checked bags, as the new, more powerful scanners in U.S. airports can fog film. The film you carry with you can be damaged by scanners as well. X-ray damage is cumulative; the slower the film, and the more times you put it through a scanner, the more likely the damage. Film under 800 ASA is usually safe for up to five scans. If you're taking your film through additional scans, U.S. regulations permit you to demand hand inspections. Keep in mind that airports are not the only places where your camera may be scanned: Highly trafficked attractions are X-raying visitors' bags with increasing frequency.

Most photo supply stores sell protective pouches designed to block damaging X-rays. The pouches fit both film and loaded cameras. They should protect your film in checked baggage, but they also may raise alarms and result in a hand inspection.

An organization called **Film Safety for Traveling on Planes, FSTOP** (© 888/301-2665; www.f-stop.org), can provide additional tips for traveling with film and equipment.

Carry-on scanners will not damage **videotape** in video cameras, but the magnetic fields emitted by the walk-through security gateways and handheld inspection wands will. Always place your loaded camcorder on the screening conveyor belt or have it hand-inspected. Be sure your batteries are charged, as you will probably be required to turn the device on to ensure that it's what it appears to be.

BY CAR

Orlando is 436 miles from Atlanta; 1,312 miles from Boston; 1,120 miles from Chicago; 1,009 miles from Cleveland; 1,170 miles from Dallas; 1,114 miles from Detroit; 1,088 miles from New York City; and 1,282 miles from Toronto.

• From Atlanta, take I-75 south to the Florida Turnpike to I-4 west.
• From points northeast, take I-95 south to Daytona Beach and I-4 west.
• From Chicago, take I-65 south to Nashville, then I-24 south to I-75, then south on the Florida Turnpike to I-4 west.
• From Cleveland, take I-77 south to Columbia, S.C., and then I-26 east to I-95 south to I-4 west.
• From Dallas, take I-20 east to I-49, south to I-10, east to I-75, then south on the Florida Turnpike to I-4 west.
• From Detroit, take I-75 south to the Florida Turnpike, then exit on I-4 west.
• From Toronto, take Canadian Route 401 south to Queen Elizabeth Way, then south to I-90 (New York State Thruway), east to I-87 (New York State Thruway), south to I-95 over the George Washington Bridge, then south on I-95 to I-4 west.

AAA (© 800/222-1134; www.aaa.com) and some other auto club members should call their local offices for maps and optimum driving directions.

BY TRAIN

Amtrak trains (© 800/872-7245; www.amtrak.com) pull into stations at 1400 Sligh Blvd. in downtown

Orlando (23 miles from Walt Disney World), and 111 Dakin Ave. in Kissimmee (15 miles from WDW). There are also stops in Winter Park, 10 miles north of downtown Orlando, at 150 W. Morse Blvd.; and in Sanford, 23 miles northeast of downtown Orlando, 800 Persimmon Ave., which is also the end terminal for the Auto Train (see below).

FARES As with airline fares, you sometimes can get discounts if you book far in advance. There may be some restrictions on travel dates for discounted fares, mostly around very busy holiday times. Amtrak also offers money-saving packages—including accommodations (some at WDW resorts), car rentals, tours, and train fare (℡ **800/321-8684**).

AMTRAK'S AUTO TRAIN This option offers the convenience of bringing your car to Florida without having to drive it all the way. It begins in Lorton, VA—about a 4-hour drive from New York, 2 hours from Philadelphia—and ends at Sanford, 23 miles northeast of Orlando. (There are no stops in between.) Reserve early for the lowest prices. Fares begin at $394 ($716 with a berth) for two passengers and an auto. Call ℡ **800/872-7245** for details.

9 Packages for the Independent Traveler

The number and diversity of package tours to Orlando is staggering. But you can save money if you're willing to do the research. Start by looking in the travel section of your local Sunday newspaper and checking the ads in the back of travel magazines such as *Travel & Leisure* and *Condé Nast Traveler*. Also, stop at a sizable travel agency and pick up brochures from several companies. Go over them at home and compare offerings to find the optimum package for your trip. You should also obtain the *Walt Disney World Vacations* brochure (see details at the beginning of this chapter), which lists WDW packages. Disney's array of choices can include airfare, accommodations on or off Disney property, theme-park passes, a rental car, meals, a Disney cruise, and/or a stay at Disney's beach resorts in Vero Beach or Hilton Head, SC. And unlike the main Disney number, the number to call for a Disney vacation package is *free:* ℡ **800/828-0228** (the alternate number, 407/828-8101, is a toll call). Some packages are tied to a season, while others are for special-interest vacationers, including golfers, honeymooners, or spa aficionados.

The **Disney Club**—which offered members 10% to 30% discounts at WDW parks, resorts, and restaurants, as well savings on packages, merchandise, and car rentals—**is being phased out.** Disney stopped selling new memberships at the end of 2002, and benefits for existing members cease December 31, 2003. It's expected to be replaced by a Disney/VISA credit card that lets cardholders accumulate points that can be redeemed for discounts.

Although not on the same scale as Disney's options, Universal Orlando packages have improved greatly with the addition of the new Islands of

> ### *Tips* Package Deals
>
> Since opening in 1971, Disney hasn't offered a lot in the way of discounts. It filled parks, resorts, and restaurants without them. But depressed tourism after September 11, 2001, has humbled WDW and made Mickey a bit more willing to offer deals. Be sure to press Disney reservationists or your travel agent for the best deal they can find.

Adventure theme park, the CityWalk food-and-club district, and the Portofino Bay, Hard Rock, and Royal Pacific hotels. The options include lodging, VIP access to Universal's theme parks, and discounts to other non-Disney attractions. Some include round-trip airfare. Contact **Universal Studios Vacations** at © **888/322-5537** or 407/224-7000, or online go to **www.universalorlando.com**.

SeaWorld also offers 2- and 3-night packages that include rooms at a handful of hotels, car rental, and tickets to SeaWorld. Call © **800/423-8368** or 407/351-3600, or go online at **www.seaworld.com**.

One good source of package deals is the airlines themselves. **Delta** has them in several price ranges. They may include round-trip airfare, accommodations, rental car or round-trip airport transfers, unlimited admission to Disney parks, and other features. In packages utilizing WDW resorts, you get all of the advantages given to guests at these properties (see chapter 5, "Where to Stay," for details). There are three price options: standard, ultimate, and preferred. Prices vary widely depending on the resort you choose, your departure point, and the time of year. Delta also has Orlando packages that don't include tickets to Disney parks. You can learn more by calling © **800/872-7786** or heading over to **www.deltavacations.com**.

Other major airlines offering air/land packages include **American**

Airlines Vacations (© **800/321-2121;** www.aavacations.com), **Delta Vacations** (© **800/221-6666;** www.deltavacations.com), **Continental Airlines Vacations** (© **800/301-3800;** www.coolvacations.com), and **United Vacations** (© **888/854-3899;** www.unitedvacations.com).

Several big **online travel agencies**— Expedia, Travelocity, Orbitz, Site59, and Lastminute.com—also do a brisk business in packages. If you're unsure about the pedigree of a smaller packager, check with the Better Business Bureau in the city where the company is based, or go online at www.bbb.org. If a packager won't tell you where it's based, don't fly with them.

Touraine Travel (© **800/967-5583;** www.tourainetravel.com) is a source of packages to Disney, Universal Orlando, and SeaWorld.

For linksters, **Golf Getaways** (© **800/800-4028;** www.golfgetaways.com) and **Golfpac Vacations** (© **800/327-0878;** www.golfpacinc.com) offer play-and-stay packages.

Before you invest in a package tour, get some answers. Ask about the **accommodations choices** and prices for each. Then look up the hotels' reviews in a Frommer's guide and check their rates for your specific dates of travel online.

Finally, look for **hidden expenses.** Ask whether airport departure fees and taxes, for example, are included in the total cost.

(Moments A Mickey Mouse Affair: Getting Married at Walt Disney World

Want to fly up the aisle on Aladdin's magic carpet? Arrive in a glass coach pulled by six white horses? Or take the plunge, literally and figuratively, on the Twilight Zone Tower of Terror?

If you've always dreamed of a fairy-tale wedding, Disney is happy to oblige for a price (often a large one). Recognizing WDW's popularity as a honeymoon destination—each year, more honeymooners head here than to any other spot in America—Disney, in 1995, cut out the middleman and officially went into the wedding business. And, oh, what big business it is!

Disney's first move was building a multimillion-dollar nondenominational chapel in the middle of the Seven Seas Lagoon. Its next step was letting the world know the Disney wedding chapel was open for business. The first nuptials were televised live on the Lifetime television network. (Construction was still in progress at the chapel, so the bride and groom wore white hard hats.) About 1,700 couples were married that first year. Now, about 2,500 twosomes mix matrimony with Disney magic each year at the pavilion, which resembles a Victorian summerhouse, and more choose this destination for honeymoons.

An intimate gathering for two starts at about $3,400 including a 4-night honeymoon at Disney's Wilderness Lodge with a daylight ceremony at the lodge or the Polynesian, Boardwalk, or Yacht Club resorts. The average Disney wedding costs $25,000 and has 100 guests (Prince Charming not included). A la carte add-ons range from $250 for a white-dove fly-over and $2,200 to arrive in Cinderella's glass coach to $42,000 or more to rent the Magic Kingdom for a reception (not including ceremony, food, and other doodads). If you can imagine it, Disney probably will do it—if your pockets are deep enough.

For details, call (C) **407/828-3400** ((C) 800/370-6009 for honeymoons only) or go to **www.disneyweddings.com** on the Internet.

10 Disney Cruise Packages

There's hardly a Florida tourist market that WDW hasn't tried to tap. Ocean-going vacations are no exception. The Disney Cruise Line launched the *Magic* and *Wonder* in 1998 and 1999, respectively.

The *Magic* is Art Deco in style, with Mickey in the three-level lobby and a *Beauty and the Beast* mural in its top restaurant, Lumiere's. The *Wonder*'s decor is Art Nouveau. Ariel commands its lobby, and its featured eatery, Triton's, sports a mural from *The Little Mermaid.*

Subtle differences aside, these are nearly identical twins. Both are 83,000 tons with 12 decks, 875 cabins, and room for 2,400 guests. There are some adults-only areas but no casinos. Both ships have extensive kids' and teens' programs—they're broken into four age groups—and state-of-the-art computer equipment. There

> *Tips* **As the Stomach Turns**
>
> Nothing spoils a cruise like a storm—or worse. In the first case, consider avoiding hurricane season (June 1 to Nov 30, though the peak is July to mid Oct). These fickle storms can spoil your fun and upset your tummy. Even if you avoid the season, pack anti–motion-sickness pills or patches.
>
> **Speaking of spoiling a cruise,** several cruise ships, including the Disney *Magic,* had outbreaks of a virus that caused stomach flu-like symptoms in the fall of 2002. That's no ill reflection on one line: Cruise ships are closed environments, and sometimes a passenger brings the illness on . . . and sometimes the line doesn't clean itself well enough. For an Internet rating by the **Centers for Disease Control,** go to **www2.cdc.gov/nceh/vsp/vsp main.asp.** Note, however, that the site is often weeks out of date.

are also nurseries for 3-month-old to 3-year-old passengers.

Restaurants, shows, and other onboard activities are very family oriented. One of the unique features is a dine-around option that lets you move among main restaurants (each ship has four) from night to night while keeping the same servers.

The 3-day voyages visit Nassau and Castaway Cay, a WDW island; 4-day voyages add Freeport. There also are 7-day eastern Caribbean (St. Thomas, St. Maarten, and Castaway Cay) and 7-day western Caribbean (Key West, Grand Cayman, Cozumel, and Castaway Cay) itineraries.

Seven-day land-sea packages include 3 or 4 days afloat, with the rest of the week at a WDW resort. Prices at press time ranged from $829 to $4,999 per adult, $399 to $1,199 for kids 3 to 12, and $139 for kids under 3, depending

on your choice of stateroom and resort. Packages are available that add round-trip air and unlimited admission to WDW parks, Pleasure Island, and other attractions. Cruise-only options for 3 nights are $439 to $2,749 for adults, $229 to $799 for kids 3 to 12, and $99 for those under 3; 4-night cruises are $539 to $3,149 for adults, $329 to $899 for kids 3 to 12, and $99 for kids under 3. Disney's 7-night cruises sell for $829 to $4,999 for adults, $399 to $1,199 for kids 3 to 12, and $139 for kids under 3.

Cruises depart from Port Canaveral, about an hour east of Orlando by car. If you buy the package, transportation to and from Orlando is included. You can get discounted fares if you book well in advance and go during non-peak periods. For information, call © 800/951-3532 or go to **www.disney cruise.com.**

11 Recommended Reading

The best Walt Disney World & Orlando guidebook on the planet (yes, this one) covers almost everything most travelers need and want to know. But there are a few areas where we bow to the expertise of less-than-mainstream or special-interest books. So here are a few additional books that may be available in your local library or bookstore.

• *Team Rodent: How Disney Devours the World* (Carl Hiaasen, 1998, Ballantine Books) shares an insider's perspective of how Walt Disney and his cartoon tagalongs forever changed the face of central Florida, in some cases in the worst way (traffic jams, over-commercialization, and a service economy). This book is dripping with cynicism, but Hiaasen right-fully blames Orlando's over-growth on Mickey and Uncle Walt.

- **National Audubon Society Field Guide to Florida** (second edition, Audubon Society) is a dandy back-pocket guide that delivers a wonderful education on the state's flora and fauna, parks and pre-serves, land, weather, natural phe-nomena, and much more. Plus, it's dripping with pictures to help newcomers and natives alike tell a yellow-bellied slider from a cooter.

- **How It Feels to Be Colored Me** (1928), **Mules and Men** (1935), **Their Eyes Were Watching God** (1937), **The Florida Negro** (1938), and other books and essays by Zora Neale Hurston chronicle life and racism in Florida, including Eatonville, the town just north of Orlando where she grew up. If you're a Hurston fan, don't miss the listing for the January festival in her honor in the Calendar of Events on p. 21.

- **Vegetarian Walt Disney World and Greater Orlando** (2000, Veg-etarian World Guides) is the most comprehensive and enterprising guide around for vegetarians, veg-ans, or mainstream diners looking for a break from carnivore menus. Susan Shumaker and Than Saffel review 275 restaurants and hotels, more than half of which are on Disney soil. They also give tips about what to eat going to and from Orlando as well as the dos and don'ts of ethnic dining in cen-tral Florida. There's also a section on kids' dining.

- **Weird Florida** (Eliot Kleinberg, Longstreet, 1998) presents some of Florida's oddest oddities in a lit-erary version of *Ripley's Believe It or Not!* Stories include the man who stole 370 dirty diapers, the tasteless "sport" of dwarf tossing, and the evangelist who hired a hit man to kill his mistress' husband. Kleinberg's take on Florida: "Any time you jam descendants of slaves, rednecks, con artists, car-petbaggers, drug smugglers, fugi-tives, UFO abductees, strippers, alligators, and political refugees into a flat peninsula surrounded by water but with hardly a drop to drink anymore, you get a pretty weird place."

3

For International Visitors

Whether it's your first visit or your tenth, a trip to the United States may require an additional degree of planning. This chapter will provide you with essential information, helpful tips, and advice for the more common problems that some visitors encounter.

1 Preparing for Your Trip

VISITOR INFORMATION ABROAD

There are several **Orlando Tourism Offices** outside the United States. You can get information from the following sources:

- **Argentina** ✆ **0800-999-1749;** www.orlandoinfo.com/argentina
- **Belgium** ✆ **32-2/705-7897;** www.orlandoinfo.com
- **Brazil** ✆ **0800/556652;** www.orlandoinfo.com/brasil
- **Canada** ✆ **1-800-646-2079;** www.orlandokissimmee.com/canada
- **Germany** ✆ **0800-100-7325;** www.orlandoinfo.com/de
- **Japan** ✆ **3-3501-7245;** www.orlandoinfo.com/japan
- **Latin America** ✆ **407-363-5872;** www.orlandoinfo.com/latinoamerica
- **Mexico** ✆ **01-800/800-4636;** www.orlandoinfo.com/mexico
- **Spain** ✆ **407/363-5872;** www.orlandoinfo.com/espana
- **United Kingdom** ✆ **0800-018-6760;** www.orlandoinfo.com/uk

ENTRY REQUIREMENTS

Check at any U.S. embassy or consulate for current information and requirements. You can also obtain a visa application and other information online at the **U.S. State Department**'s website, at **www.travel.state.gov**.

VISAS The U.S. State Department has a **Visa Waiver Program** allowing citizens of certain countries to enter the United States without a visa for stays of up to 90 days. At press time these included Andorra, Australia, Austria, Belgium, Brunei, Denmark, Finland, France, Germany, Iceland, Ireland, Italy, Japan, Liechtenstein, Luxembourg, Monaco, the Netherlands, New Zealand, Norway, Portugal, San Marino, Singapore, Slovenia, Spain, Sweden, Switzerland, the United Kingdom, and Uruguay. Citizens of these countries need only a valid passport and a round-trip air or cruise ticket in their possession upon arrival. If they first enter the United States, they may also visit Mexico, Canada, Bermuda, and/or the Caribbean islands and return to the United States without a visa. Further information is available from any U.S. embassy or consulate. Canadian citizens may enter the United States without visas; they need only proof of residence.

Citizens of all other countries must have (1) a valid passport that expires at least 6 months later than the scheduled end of their visit to the United States, and (2) a tourist visa, which

Tips **Walt Disney World Services for International Visitors**

Walt Disney World welcomes millions of international guests every year and offers a phone service that provides information in many languages (© 407/824-2222). Here are other services in Disney theme parks and resorts:

- Personal translator units are available at the Magic Kingdom, Epcot, and Disney–MGM Studios in French, German, and Spanish to translate the narration at 13 shows and attractions.
- Detailed guidebooks and maps to the four major parks in Spanish, French, German, Portuguese, and Japanese are available at five International Information Centers (marked by an "i" on handout guide maps) in the theme parks and Downtown Disney.
- Currency exchanges (see "Money," later in this chapter).
- Most theme park restaurants that have table or counter service have menus written in Spanish, French, German, Portuguese, and Japanese.
- Theme park cast members who speak foreign languages wear a gold badge with the flag of that country on their nametags.
- World Key Terminals at Epcot offer basic information about the park and assistance with dining reservations in Spanish.
- Resort phones equipped with software that expedites international calls by allowing guests to dial direct to international destinations.
- There's also online help at **www.disneyworld.com**. Once you're on the website, go to the bottom of the screen and click "International Sites."

may be obtained without charge from any U.S. consulate.

To obtain a visa, the traveler must submit a completed application form (either in person or by mail) with a 1½-inch-square photo, and must demonstrate binding ties to a residence abroad. Usually you can obtain a visa at once or within 24 hours, but it may take longer during the summer rush from June through August. If you cannot go in person, contact the nearest U.S. embassy or consulate for instructions on applying by mail. Your travel agent or airline office may also be able to provide you with visa applications and instructions. The U.S. consulate or embassy that issues your visa will determine whether you will be issued a multiple- or single-entry

visa and any restrictions regarding the length of your stay.

British subjects can obtain up-to-date passport and visa information by calling the **U.S. Embassy Visa Information Line** (© 0891/200-290) or the **London Passport Office** (© 0990/210-410 for recorded information), or they can find the visa information on the U.S. Embassy Great Britain website at **www.passport.gov.uk**.

Irish citizens can obtain up-to-date passport and visa information through the **Embassy of USA Dublin,** 42 Elgin Rd., Dublin 4, Ireland (© 353/1-668-8777) or by checking the visa page on the website at www.usembassy.ie.

Australian citizens can obtain up-to-date passport and visa information by calling the **U.S. Embassy Canberra,** Moonah Place, Yarralumla, ACT 2600 (© **02/6214-5600**) or by checking the website's visa page at **www.usis-australia.gov/consular/ niv.html.**

Citizens of **New Zealand** can obtain up-to-date passport and visa information by calling the **U.S. Embassy New Zealand,** 29 Fitzherbert Terr., Thorndon, Wellington, New Zealand (© **644/472-2068**) or get the information directly from the website at **http://usembassy.org.nz.**

MEDICAL REQUIREMENTS

Unless you're arriving from an area known to be suffering from an **epidemic** (particularly cholera or yellow fever), inoculations or vaccinations are not required for entry into the United States. If you have a medical condition that requires **syringe-administered medications,** carry a valid signed prescription from your physician—the Federal Aviation Administration (FAA) no longer allows airline passengers to pack syringes in their carry-on baggage without documented proof of medical need. If you have a disease that requires treatment with **narcotics,** you should also carry documented proof with you—smuggling narcotics aboard a plane is a serious offense that carries severe penalties in the U.S.

Requirements for **HIV-positive visitors** entering the United States are vague and change frequently. According to the latest publication of *HIV and Immigrants: A Manual for AIDS Service Providers,* the Immigration and Naturalization Service (INS) doesn't require a medical exam for entry into the United States, but INS officials may stop individuals because they look sick or because they are carrying AIDS/HIV medicine.

If an HIV-positive non-citizen applies for a non-immigrant visa, the question on the application regarding communicable diseases is tricky no matter which way it's answered. If the applicant checks "no," INS may deny the visa on the grounds that the applicant committed fraud. If the applicant checks "yes" or if INS suspects the person is HIV-positive, it will deny the visa unless the applicant asks for a special waiver for visitors. This waiver is for people visiting the United States for a short time, for instance, to attend a conference, to visit close relatives, or to receive medical treatment. It can be a confusing situation. For up-to-the-minute information, contact **AIDS Info/**(© **800/448-0440** or 301/519-6616 outside the U.S.; www.aidsinfo. nih.gov) or the **Gay Men's Health Crisis** (© **212/367-1000;** www.gmhc. org).

DRIVER'S LICENSES Foreign driver's licenses are mostly recognized in the U.S., although you may want to get an international license if your home license is not written in English.

PASSPORT INFORMATION

Safeguard your passport in an inconspicuous, inaccessible place like a money belt. Make a copy of the critical pages, including the passport number, and store it in a safe place, separate from the passport itself. If

---

⌜Tips⌟ Welcome to America

Members of the Web world can get gobs of information from **USA Tourist** (**www.usatourist.com**) in English, German, French, Spanish, and Japanese. The site has Orlando and Walt Disney World information, hotels, details about the attractions, and tips. The **Orlando/Orange County Convention & Visitors Bureau** (**www.orlandoinfo.com**) has information in English, German, Japanese, Spanish, and Portuguese.

you lose your passport, visit the nearest consulate of your native country as soon as possible for a replacement. Passport applications are downloadable from the Internet sites listed below.

Note that the **International Civil Aviation Organization (ICAO)** has recommended a policy requiring that *every* individual who travels by air have a passport. In response, many countries are now requiring that children must be issued their own passport to travel internationally, where before those under 16 or so may have been allowed to travel on a parent or guardian's passport.

FOR RESIDENTS OF CANADA

You can pick up a passport application at one of 28 regional passport offices or most travel agencies. As of December 11, 2001, Canadian children who travel must have their own passport. However, if you hold a valid Canadian passport issued before December 11, 2001, that bears the name of your child, the passport remains valid for you and your child until it expires. Passports cost C$85 for those 16 years and older (valid 5 years), C$35 for children 3 to 15 (valid 5 years), and C$20 for children under 3 (valid for 3 years). Applications, which must be accompanied by two identical passport-sized photographs and proof of Canadian citizenship, are available at travel agencies throughout Canada or from the central **Passport Office,** Department of Foreign Affairs and International Trade, Ottawa, ON K1A 0G3 (© **800/567-6868;** www. dfait-maeci.gc.ca/passport). Processing takes 5 to 10 days if you apply in person, or about 3 weeks by mail.

FOR RESIDENTS OF THE UNITED KINGDOM

As a member of the European Union, you need only an identity card, not a passport, to travel to other EU countries. However, if you already possess a passport, it's always useful to carry it. To pick up an application for a standard 10-year passport (5-yr. passport for children under 16), visit your nearest passport office, major post office, or travel agency. You can also contact the **United Kingdom Passport Service** at © **0870/521-0410** or search its website at **www. ukpa.gov.uk**. Passports are £30 for adults and £16 for children under 16. Processing takes about 2 weeks.

FOR RESIDENTS OF IRELAND

You can apply for a 10-year passport, costing €57, at the **Passport Office,** Setanta Centre, Molesworth Street, Dublin 2 (© **01/671-1633;** www.irl gov.ie/iveagh). Those under age 18 and over 65 must apply for a €12, 3-year passport. You can also apply at 1A South Mall, Cork (© **021/272-525**) or over the counter at most main post offices.

FOR RESIDENTS OF AUSTRALIA

You can pick up an application from your local post office or any branch of Passports Australia, but you must schedule an interview at the passport office to present your application materials. Call the **Australian Passport Information Service** at © **131-232,** or visit the government website at **www.passports.gov.au**. Passports for adults are A$144 and for those under 18 are A$72.

FOR RESIDENTS OF NEW ZEALAND

You can pick up a passport application at any New Zealand Passports Office or download it from their website. Contact the **Passports Office** at © **0800/ 225-050** or © 04/474-8100 (both in New Zealand), or log on to **www.pass ports.govt.nz**. Passports for adults are NZ$80 and for children under 16 NZ$40.

CUSTOMS
WHAT YOU CAN BRING IN

Every visitor more than 21 years of age may bring in, free of duty, the following: (1) 1 liter of wine or hard liquor; (2) 200 cigarettes, 100 cigars (but not from Cuba), or 3 pounds of smoking tobacco; and (3) $100 worth of gifts. These exemptions are offered to travelers who spend at least 72 hours in the United States and who have not claimed them within the preceding 6 months. It is altogether forbidden to bring into the country foodstuffs (particularly fruit, cooked meats, and canned goods) and plants (vegetables, seeds, tropical plants, and the like). Foreign tourists may bring in or take out up to $10,000 in U.S. or foreign currency with no formalities; larger sums must be declared to U.S. Customs on entering or leaving, which includes filing form CM 4790. For more specific information regarding U.S. Customs, contact your nearest U.S. embassy or consulate, or the **U.S. Customs** office (© **202/927-1770;** www.customs.ustreas.gov).

WHAT YOU CAN TAKE HOME

U.K. citizens returning from a non-EU country have a customs allowance of: 200 cigarettes; 50 cigars; 250 grams of smoking tobacco; 2 liters of still table wine; 1 liter of spirits or strong liqueurs (over 22% volume); 2 liters of fortified wine, sparkling wine, or other liqueurs; 60cc of perfume; 250cc of toilet water; and £145 worth of all other goods, including gifts and souvenirs. People under 17 cannot have the tobacco or alcohol allowance. For more information, contact HM Customs & Excise at © **0845/010-9000** (from outside the U.K., 020/8929-0152), or consult their website at **www.hmce.gov.uk**.

For a clear summary of **Canadian** rules, request the booklet *I Declare,* issued by the **Canada Customs and Revenue Agency** (© **800/461-9999** in Canada, or 204/983-3500; www.ccra-adrc.gc.ca). Canada allows its citizens a C$750 exemption, and you're allowed to bring back duty-free one carton of cigarettes, one can of tobacco, 40 imperial ounces of liquor, and 50 cigars. In addition, you're allowed to mail gifts to Canada valued at less than C$60 a day, provided they're unsolicited and don't contain alcohol or tobacco (write on the package "Unsolicited gift, under $60 value"). All valuables should be declared on the Y-38 form before departure from Canada, including serial numbers of valuables you already own, such as expensive foreign cameras. *Note:* The C$750 exemption can only be used once a year and only after an absence of 7 days.

The duty-free allowance in **Australia** is A$400 or, for those under 18, A$200. Citizens age 18 and over can bring in 250 cigarettes or 250 grams of loose tobacco, and 1,125 milliliters of alcohol. If you're returning with valuables you already own, such as foreign-made cameras, you should file form B263. A helpful brochure available from Australian consulates or Customs offices is *Know Before You Go.* For more information, call the **Australian Customs Service** at © **1300/363-263,** or log on to **www.customs.gov.au**.

The duty-free allowance for **New Zealand** is NZ$700. Citizens over 17 can bring in 200 cigarettes, 50 cigars, or 250 grams of tobacco (or a mixture of all three if their combined weight doesn't exceed 250g); plus 4.5 liters of wine and beer, or 1.125 liters of liquor. New Zealand currency does not carry import or export restrictions. Fill out a certificate of export, listing the valuables you are taking out of the country; that way, you can bring them back without paying duty. Most questions are answered in a free pamphlet available at New Zealand consulates and Customs offices: *New Zealand Customs Guide for Travellers,*

Notice no. 4. For more information, contact **New Zealand Customs,** The Customhouse, 17–21 Whitmore St., Box 2218, Wellington (© **0800/428-786** or 04/473-6099; www.customs. govt.nz).

HEALTH INSURANCE

Although it's not required of travelers, health insurance is highly recommended. Unlike many European countries, the United States does not usually offer free or low-cost medical care to its citizens or visitors. Doctors and hospitals are expensive, and in most cases will require advance payment or proof of coverage before they render their services. Policies can cover everything from the loss or theft of your baggage and trip cancellation to the guarantee of bail in case you're arrested. Good policies will also cover the costs of an accident, repatriation, or death. See "Insurance, Health & Safety" in chapter 2 for more information. Packages such as **Europ Assistance's "Worldwide Healthcare Plan"** are sold by European automobile clubs and travel agencies at attractive rates. **Worldwide Assistance Services,** Inc. (© **800/821-2828;** www.worldwideassistance.com) is the agent for Europ Assistance in the United States.

Though lack of health insurance may prevent you from being admitted to a hospital in nonemergencies, don't worry about being left on a street corner to die: The American way is to fix you now and bill the living daylights out of you later.

If you get sick or are injured, there are basic first-aid centers in all of the theme parks. There's also a 24-hour toll-free number for the **Poison Control Center** (© **800/282-3171**). Disney and many other resorts have in-room medical service 24 hours a day through **Centra Care** by calling © **407/238-2000.**

Doctors on Call Service (© **407/399-3627**) is a group that makes house and room calls in most of the Orlando area. **Centra Care** has several walk-in clinics listed in the Yellow Pages, including ones on International Drive (© **407/370-4881**) and at Lake Buena Vista, near Disney (© **407/934-2273**). Prescriptions can be filled at pharmacies such as **Walgreen's** and **Eckerd Drugs,** which have some stores that are open 24 hours a day, all are listed in the Yellow Pages. Many discount stores, such as **Kmart** and **Target,** also have pharmacies.

INSURANCE FOR BRITISH TRAVELERS Most big travel agents offer their own insurance and will probably try to sell you their package when you book a holiday. Think before you sign. **Britain's Consumers' Association** recommends that you insist on seeing the policy and reading the fine print before buying travel insurance. **The Association of British Insurers** (© **020/7600-3333;** www.abi.org.uk) gives advice by phone and publishes *Holiday Insurance,* a free guide to policy provisions and prices. You might also shop around for better deals: Try **Columbus Direct** (© **020/7375-0011;** www.columbusdirect.net).

INSURANCE FOR CANADIAN TRAVELERS Canadians should check with their provincial health plan

---

(Tips) Flight Hazard

Never take an already-opened bottle of perfume or nail polish remover onto an airplane with you. The cabin pressure—especially during a long flight—will cause the liquid to evaporate, and may damage your luggage. The smell won't make you popular with your fellow travelers either.

offices or call **Health Canada** (© 613/957-2991; www.hc-sc.gc.ca) to find out the extent of their coverage and what documentation and receipts they must take home in case they are treated in the United States.

MONEY

CURRENCY The U.S. monetary system is very simple: The most common **bills** are the $1 (colloquially, a "buck"), $5, $10, and $20 denominations. There are also $2 bills (seldom encountered), $50 bills, and $100 bills (the last two are usually not welcome as payment for small purchases). All the paper money was recently redesigned, making the famous faces adorning them disproportionately large. The old-style bills are still legal tender.

There are seven denominations of coins: 1¢ (1 cent, or a penny); 5¢ (5 cents, or a nickel); 10¢ (10 cents, or a dime); 25¢ (25 cents, or a quarter); 50¢ (50 cents, or a half dollar); the new gold "Sacagawea" coin worth $1; and, prized by collectors, the rare, older silver dollar.

Note: The "foreign-exchange bureaus" so common in Europe are rare even at airports in the United States, and nonexistent outside major cities. It's best not to change foreign money (or traveler's checks denominated in a currency other than U.S. dollars) at a small-town bank, or even a branch in a big city; in fact, leave any currency other than U.S. dollars at home—it may prove a greater nuisance to you than it's worth.

If you must, you can exchange foreign currency at **Guest Relations** windows at all four Disney parks, or at **City Hall** in the Magic Kingdom and **Earth Station** at Epcot. Currency can also be exchanged at Walt Disney World resorts and at the **SunBank** across from Downtown Disney Marketplace. There are also currency exchanges at Guest Services at Universal Orlando and SeaWorld.

TRAVELER'S CHECKS Though traveler's checks are widely accepted, make sure that they're denominated in U.S. dollars, as foreign-currency checks are often difficult to exchange. The three traveler's checks that are most widely recognized—and least likely to be denied—are **Visa, American Express,** and **Thomas Cook.** Be sure to record the numbers of the checks, and keep that information in a separate place in case they get lost or stolen. Most businesses are pretty good about taking traveler's checks, but you're better off cashing them in at a bank (in small amounts, of course) and paying in cash. *Remember:* You'll need identification, such as a driver's license or passport, to exchange a traveler's check.

CREDIT CARDS & ATMS Credit cards are the most widely used form of payment in the United States: **Visa** (Barclaycard in Britain); **MasterCard** (EuroCard in Europe, Access in Britain, Chargex in Canada); **American Express; Diners Club; Discover;** and **Carte Blanche.** There are, however, a handful of stores and restaurants that do not take credit cards, so be sure to ask in advance. Most businesses display a sticker near their entrance to let you know which cards they accept. (*Note:* Businesses may require a minimum purchase, usually around $10, to use a credit card. And some require photo ID if you're paying by credit card.)

You can save yourself trouble by using plastic rather than cash or traveler's checks in most hotels, motels, restaurants, and retail stores. American Express, Diners Club, Discover, MasterCard, and Visa are accepted for admission to the Disney parks and all restaurants therein. They're also accepted at Universal Orlando and SeaWorld.

You'll find **automated teller machines (ATMs)** in most tourist areas

---

Fun Fact Boooommmmm, Boooommmmm

You may find yourself occasionally awakened by window-rattling double booms. Don't worry; it's not part of the rumored American crime culture. It's the space shuttle landing at Kennedy Space Center. The twin sonic booms are produced as the shuttle reenters the atmosphere. The loud, thunderous sound can be heard from Cape Canaveral on the coast throughout the Orlando area and all the way to the Gulf Coast. When skies are clear, night launches are really spectacular to see. You can view a launch schedule at **www.ksc.nasa.gov**.

---

as well as downtown. Some ATMs let you draw U.S. currency against your bank and credit cards. Check with your bank before leaving home, and remember that you will need your personal identification number (PIN) to do so. Most accept Visa, MasterCard, and American Express, as well as ATM cards from other U.S. banks. Expect to be charged up to $3.60 per transaction, however, if you're not using your own bank's ATM. (See "Money" in chapter 2, "Planning Your Trip to Walt Disney World & Orlando," for ATM locations.)

SAFETY

Walt Disney World and Orlando are safe in general, and the theme parks are even safer, but there are some general precautions you can take to minimize your chances of being the victim of a crime.

GENERAL SAFETY U.S. urban areas tend to be less safe than those in Europe or Japan. Stay alert. Orlando isn't a high-crime area, but visitors should exercise caution. Street signs in downtown Orlando help steer visitors away from less-desirable neighborhoods. It's wise to ask the local tourist office or your car-rental agency if you're in doubt about which neighborhoods are safe. Avoid deserted areas, especially at night. Don't go into city parks at night unless there's an event that attracts crowds. Don't carry valuables with you on the street or

display flashy cameras or electronic equipment. If you're using a pricey camera, stow it in a plain bag when you're not taking pictures. Keep money, credit cards, passports, and your driver's license in a money belt and wear it at all times. Keep only the day's spending money in your wallet and keep it in a front pocket. Sling your purse strap over your head and across your chest, not just over a shoulder. And, if you have an emergency, report it as quickly as possible by calling © **911,** which is the emergency police, ambulance, and fire number throughout Florida. Here are a few other pointers to make sure you don't get ripped off:

- Watch out for the few unsavory waiters or room clerks who pad your bills with bogus taxes or unordered services. Check and double-check those bills. Also check to see if they have added an automatic gratuity.
- Make sure cashiers keep the currency you hand them in view until you receive your change.
- Don't let strangers break large bills for you. Find a reputable currency exchanger at an airport or a bank.
- It's smart not to use your hotel room's telephone for calls; they charge ridiculously high rates. They think of it as a profit center; we think of it as legalized robbery!

Remember also that hotels are open to the public, and in a large hotel, security may not be able to screen everyone entering. Even if you're staying at a resort on Disney property, always lock your room door, even if you're simply going to get ice, and take your key or key card with you. And when you're inside, confirm the identity of anyone knocking before opening the door, even if it is hotel staff. If you requested some assistance from the front desk, call to confirm that someone associated with the hotel has been sent.

Always park in well-lighted areas and be on the lookout for suspicious characters hanging out in the parking lots or hallways. If you have concerns about someone lurking in the parking lot, head toward the hotel lobby or a public area, such as a restaurant or bar, before going to your room. Immediately report the person to the hotel staff.

DRIVING

SPEED LIMITS Obey posted speed limits. On highways and interstates, they're usually 55 or 65 mph but as high as 70 in some rural areas. In residential areas, 30 or 35 mph usually is the case. *Note:* The corridor between the attractions and downtown Orlando is a speed trap. Fines for speeding start at $157. They double in construction areas and school zones.

SEAT BELTS Seat belts are required for all passengers. Children under 3 must ride strapped into a car seat, and police will issue tickets to parents who don't put their children in restraints while driving. Car-rental agencies will provide car seats; some do it for free.

AIR BAG SAFETY Children, in or out of car seats, should ride only in the back seats of cars that are equipped with air bags. Air bags have been linked to the deaths of several young passengers in the U.S. Air bags are a standard feature on most new-model cars.

DRINKING & DRIVING Don't. Florida's rules are strict and strictly enforced. If you're planning to drink alcohol, especially after an exhausting day in the theme parks, designate a sober driver or find an alternative means of transportation. Some clubs provide free soft drinks to designated drivers. If you don't obey the law, you may wind up in a Florida jail.

DEFENSIVE DRIVING Drive with extra care in tourist-heavy areas. It's not uncommon for drivers to make sudden turns or to slow down unexpectedly when reading road signs. People often come to near stops on the highway while attempting to decipher the Disney signs, which can be confusing. The tourist areas in Orlando pack a double traffic whammy: Workers are in a hurry to get to their jobs, and tourists are scurrying to the fun. Assume all other drivers have no idea where they're going—which is often close to the truth—and you'll do fine. One of the best things to remember: Keep a safe distance between you and the car ahead of you. And, while it may sound like common sense, don't read a map while driving. Get your copilot to do it, use this book to determine your exit in advance, or call ahead to your destination to find out which exit you should take. Stay in the far right lane, the slow lane, when you begin to get near your exit.

DRIVING IN THE RAIN Watch for a hazardous condition where oil on the road creates slick patches when the road gets wet. Rainstorms in Florida are intense and frequent; they're almost a daily occurrence in summer. Exercise extreme caution and drive in the far right lane when driving much slower than the speed limit. Don't pull off onto the shoulder of the road. If visibility is especially poor, pull off at the first exit and wait out the storm; they seldom last more than an hour. Florida law requires drivers to turn on their headlights whenever they turn on their windshield wipers.

Size Conversion Chart

Women's Clothing

American	4	6	8	10	12	14	16
French	34	36	38	40	42	44	46
British	6	8	10	12	14	16	18

Women's Shoes

American	5	6	7	8	9	10
French	36	37	38	39	40	41
British	4	5	6	7	8	9

Men's Suits

American	34	36	38	40	42	44	46	48
French	44	46	48	50	52	54	56	58
British	34	36	38	40	42	44	46	48

Men's Shirts

American	14½	15	15½	16	16½	17	17½
French	37	38	39	41	42	43	44
British	14½	15	15½	16	16½	17	17½

Men's Shoes

American	7	8	9	10	11	12	13
French	39½	41	42	43	44½	46	47
British	6	7	8	9	10	11	12

IF YOU GET LOST Exit numbers continue to change and signs continue to be confusing. On interstates or Orlando's toll roads, don't try a U-turn across the grassy median. Go to the next exit and reenter the highway by accessing the on-ramp near where you get off. Avoid pulling over to ask directions from people on the street. Instead, stop at a convenience store or gas station and ask the clerk.

SAFETY WHILE DRIVING Question your rental agency about personal safety or ask for a brochure on traveler safety tips when you pick up your car. Obtain written directions from the agency or a map with the route marked in red, showing how to get to your destination. And, if possible, arrive and depart during daylight hours.

If you drive off a highway and end up in a dodgy-looking neighborhood, leave the area as quickly as possible. If you have an accident, even on the highway, stay in your car with the doors locked until you assess the situation or until the police arrive. If you're bumped from behind on the street or are involved in a minor accident with no injuries, and the situation appears to be suspicious, motion to the other driver to follow you. Never get out of your car in such situations. Go directly to the nearest police precinct, well-lighted service station, or 24-hour store. You may want to look into renting a cellphone on a short-term basis. One recommended wireless rental company is **InTouch USA** (© 800/872-7626; www.intouchusa.com).

If you see someone on the road indicating a need for help, don't stop. Take note of the location, drive to a public area (if at night, make sure it's well lighted), and telephone the police by dialing © **911.**

Park in well-lighted, well-traveled areas whenever possible. Keep your doors locked, whether you're inside the car or not. Look around before you get out and never leave packages or valuables in sight. Although theme park lots are patrolled, it's best to secure valuables at all times. For extra caution, lock any electronic equipment in the lockers available near all park entrances.

If someone tries to rob you or steal your car, don't resist. Report the incident to the police immediately.

2 Getting to & Around the U.S.

AIRLINE DISCOUNTS   The smart traveler can find numerous ways to reduce the price of a plane ticket simply by taking time to shop around. For example, overseas visitors can take advantage of the APEX (Advance Purchase Excursion) reductions offered by all major U.S. and European carriers. For more money-saving airline advice, see "Getting There" in chapter 2. For the best rates, compare fares and be flexible with the dates and times of travel.

IMMIGRATION & CUSTOMS CLEARANCE   Visitors arriving by air, no matter what the port of entry, should cultivate patience and resignation before setting foot on U.S. soil. Getting through immigration control can take as long as 2 hours on some days, especially on summer weekends, so be sure to carry this guidebook or something else to read. This is especially true in the aftermath of the September 11, 2001, terrorist attacks, when security clearances have been considerably beefed up at U.S. airports.

People traveling by air from Canada, Bermuda, and certain countries in the Caribbean can sometimes clear Customs and Immigration at the point of departure, which is much quicker.

BY PLANE   British Airways (© **0345/222-111** from within the U.K.; www.british-airways.com) offers direct flights from London to Orlando, as does **Virgin Atlantic** (© **0129/374-774;** www.virgin-atlantic.com). You can also try **Continental** (© **0293/776-446;** www. continental.com).

Canadian readers can book flights with **Air Canada** (© **800/776-3000;** www.aircanada.ca), which offers service from Toronto and Montreal to Orlando. Other airlines that fly to Florida from Canada include **US Airways** (© **800/428-4322;** www.usairways.com); **Delta** (© **800/361-6770;** www.delta.com); **American** (© **800/624-6262;** www.aa.com); and **Northwest** (© **800/225-2525;** www.nwa.com).

Some large airlines (for example, Northwest and Delta) offer travelers on transatlantic or transpacific flights special discount tickets under the name **Visit USA,** allowing mostly one-way travel from one U.S. destination to another at very low prices. These discount tickets are not on sale in the United States and must be purchased abroad in conjunction with an international ticket. This system is the best, easiest, and fastest way to see the United States at low cost. You should obtain information well in advance from your travel agent or the office of the airline concerned, because the conditions attached to these discount tickets can be changed without advance notice.

BY CAR   You're going to need a car to get around Orlando unless you're committed to staying at Disney, riding shuttles, or paying a premium for cabs. Relying on public transportation is futile, except downtown.

To rent a car, you need a major credit card and a driver's license (sometimes a hefty cash deposit can be used instead of a credit card). You

---

> **Tips The Plane Truth**
>
> Airplane cabins are notoriously dry; if you wear contact lenses, either remove them or bring plenty of eyedrops with you on the plane. Cabins are also infamous for being cramped, so try to take a walk in the aisle every hour or so to stretch out the kinks.

---

must also be at least 25 years old. Some companies rent to younger people but add a daily surcharge, which can run as high as $20 per day. There are two gas (petrol) options when renting a car: returning it with a full tank or bringing it back empty and paying the rental company's rate up front. Refueling on your own is the more cost-effective option; but if you have an early flight home, you may not want to waste the time to refuel on the way to the airport. All of the major car-rental companies are represented in Florida (see appendix B, "Useful Toll-Free Numbers & Websites," for the contact information for these companies).

BY RV   If you wish to rent a motor home in Orlando, contact **Cruise America,** 2915 N. Orange Blossom Trail, Kissimmee, FL 34744 (© **407/ 931-1409;** www.cruiseamerica.com).

BY MOTORCYCLE   The increasing popularity of Bike Week and a growing number of weekend road warriors have sparked an increase in places specializing in motorcycle rental. The Harley Davidson, in all shapes and sizes, is the most popular. You must be at least 21 and sometimes 25 years of age, have a motorcycle license, and a major credit card. Rental fees start at about $650 for 1 week or $150 per day including helmets, locks, and a brief orientation. You can rent bikes at **American V Twin,** 5101 International Dr. (© **888/ 268-8946** or 407/903-0058; www.am vtwin.com) and **Iron Horse Rentals,** 4380 L. B. McLeod Rd. (© **800/946- 4743** or 407/426-7091; www.hog ride.com). But plan ahead, months in advance if you're going to be here during Bike Week, late February to early March, or BiketoberFest in mid-October. Both are in Daytona Beach, but a lot of their visitors stay in Orlando.

BY TRAIN   International visitors (excluding Canada) can buy a **USA Railpass,** good for 15 or 30 days of unlimited travel on Amtrak (© **800/ USA-RAIL;** www.amtrak.com). The pass is available through many foreign travel agents. Prices in 2003 for a 15-day East Coast pass were $210 off-peak, $260 peak; a 30-day pass costs $265 off-peak, $320 peak. (National passes are more expensive.) With a foreign passport, you can also buy passes at some Amtrak offices in the United States, including locations in San Francisco, Los Angeles, Chicago, New York, Miami, Boston, and Washington, D.C. Reservations are generally required and should be made for each part of your trip as early as possible.

BY BUS   Although bus travel is often the most economical form of public transit for short hops between U.S. cities, it can also be slow and uncomfortable—certainly not an option for everyone (particularly when Amtrak, which is far more luxurious, offers similar rates). **Greyhound** (© **800/231-2222**), the sole nationwide bus line, offers an **International Ameripass** that must be purchased before coming to the United States, or by phone through the Greyhound International Office at the Port Authority Bus Terminal in New York City (© **212/971-0492**). The pass

---

Tips Dial Alert!

If you're making a local call within Orlando's 407 area code, you *must* dial the area code followed by the number you wish to call—a total of 10 digits.

---

can be obtained from foreign travel agents and costs less than the domestic version. The pass comes in various lengths, but the 30-day version runs $424. You can get more info on the pass at **www.greyhound.com**, or by calling ☎ **212/971-0492** (14:00 to 21:00 GMT) or ☎ **402/330-8552**

(all other times). In addition, special rates are available for senior citizens and students.

For further information about travel to Florida, see "Getting There" in chapter 2, "Planning Your Trip to Walt Disney World & Orlando."

 FAST FACTS: For the International Traveler

Automobile Organizations Auto clubs supply maps, routes, guidebooks, and emergency road service. The **American Automobile Association (AAA)** is the major auto club in the United States. If you belong to an auto club in your home country, inquire about AAA reciprocity before you leave. You may be able to join AAA even if you're not a member of a reciprocal club; to inquire, call AAA (☎ **800/222-1234**). AAA is actually an organization of regional auto clubs; so look under "AAA Automobile Club" in the White Pages of the telephone directory. AAA has a nationwide emergency road service telephone number for members (☎ **800/222-4357**).

Business Hours Banks are open from 9am to 4pm weekdays. Drive-through lanes are open until 6pm Friday. There's usually 24-hour access to the automated teller machines (ATMs) at most banks and other outlets. A few drive-through branches in central Florida are open until noon on Saturday. Generally, offices are open from 9am to 5pm weekdays. Stores are open 6 days a week, with many open on Sunday, too; malls and factory outlets usually are open until 9pm Monday through Saturday and from noon to 6pm Sunday.

Climate See "When to Go" in chapter 2.

Currency & Exchange See "Money" in the section "Preparing for Your Trip," earlier in this chapter.

Drinking Laws The legal age for buying and consuming alcoholic beverages is 21; proof of age is required and often requested at bars, nightclubs, and restaurants, so it's always a good idea to bring a photo ID when you go out. Beer and wine often can be purchased in supermarkets.

Do not carry open containers of alcohol in your car or any public area that isn't zoned for alcohol consumption. The police can fine you. And nothing will ruin your trip faster than getting a citation for DUI ("driving under the Influence"), so don't even think about driving while intoxicated. Also see "Liquor Laws" under "Fast Facts" in chapter 4.

Electricity Like Canada, the United States uses 110 to 120 volts, 60 cycles, compared to 220 to 240 volts, 50 cycles in most of Europe and Australia.

In addition to a 100-volt converter (bring one with you; they're hard to find in the U.S.), small appliances of non-American manufacture, such as hair dryers or shavers, require a plug adapter having two flat, parallel pins.

Embassies & Consulates All embassies are located in Washington, D.C. Some consulates are located in major cities, and most nations have a mission to the United Nations in New York City. International visitors can obtain telephone numbers for their embassies and consulates by calling "Information" in Washington, D.C. (© **202/555-1212**).

The **Canadian consulate** closest to Orlando is at 200 S. Biscayne Blvd., Suite 1600, Miami (© **305/579-1600**). The **British consulate** is located at 200 S. Orange Ave., Orlando (© **407/426-7855**). Other consulate offices in Orlando are the **Consulate of Mexico**, 100 W. Washington St., Orlando (© **407/422-0514**); **Consulate of the Netherlands**, 400 S. Orange Ave., Orlando (© **407/425-8000**); and **French-American Institute of Orlando**, 522 E. Washington St. (© **407/839-0581**). These consulates operate with small staffs, and many keep abbreviated business hours. Don't be surprised if you get an answering machine.

Emergencies Call (© **911** to report a fire, contact the police, or get an ambulance. This call is free from all public telephones and should be the first call made in case of any serious medical emergency or accident.

The Florida Tourism Industry Marketing Corporation, the state tourism promotions board, sponsors a **help line** (© **800/647-9284**). With operators speaking over 100 languages, it can provide general directions and can help with lost travel papers and credit cards, minor medical emergencies, accidents, money transfer, airline confirmation, and much more.

Gasoline (Petrol) Petrol is known as gasoline (or "gas") in the U.S. and is sold at service stations and convenience stores. One U.S. gallon equals 3.75 liters, and 1.2 U.S. gallons equal 1 Imperial gallon. There usually are three grades (and price levels) of gasoline available at most gas stations, and you'll notice that their names change from company to company. The ones with the highest octane are the most expensive. If you have a rental car, use the least expensive, "regular" unleaded gas. Gas prices average $1.25 a gallon, but can be 20¢ or 30¢ a gallon higher in the main tourist areas.

Holidays Banks, government offices, post offices, and some stores, restaurants, and museums are closed on legal national holidays: January 1 (New Year's Day); third Monday in January (Martin Luther King, Jr., Day); third Monday in February (Presidents' Day); last Monday in May (Memorial Day); July 4 (Independence Day); first Monday in September (Labor Day); second Monday in October (Columbus Day); November 11 (Veterans' Day/Armistice Day); fourth Thursday in November (Thanksgiving Day); and December 25 (Christmas). However, you won't find theme parks, accommodations, and most restaurants closed on these days.

Languages Major hotels may have multilingual employees. Unless your language is very obscure, they usually can supply a translator on request. In central Florida, many people speak Spanish, French, German, and Dutch. A few others are growing in frequency, including Chinese and Japanese.

Legal Aid As an international tourist, you'll probably never become involved with the American legal system. If you are stopped for a minor infraction, such as speeding or some other traffic violation, never attempt to pay the fine directly to a police officer; you may be arrested on the much more serious charge of attempted bribery. Pay fines to the clerk of the court (℡ 407/836-6000 in Orlando or ℡ 407/343-3530 in Kissimmee). If you're accused of a more serious offense, it's wise to say and do nothing before consulting a lawyer. Under U.S. law, an arrested person is allowed one telephone call to a party of his or her choice. Call your embassy or consulate.

Mail If you want to receive mail on your vacation and you aren't sure of your address, your mail can be sent to you, in your name, c/o General Delivery at the main post office of the city or region where you expect to be. The post office nearest Disney and Universal (℡ 800/275-8777) is at 10450 Turkey Lake Rd. The ZIP Code is 32819. You must pick up your mail in person and produce proof of identity (driver's license, passport, and so on).

Often found at intersections, mailboxes are blue with a white American eagle logo and carry the inscription U.S. MAIL. Make sure you see this inscription; overnight delivery companies also often have drop-off boxes along the road. Don't forget to add the five-figure postal code, or ZIP Code, after the two-letter abbreviation of the state to which the mail is addressed (FL for Florida, NY for New York, and so on).

Within the U.S., it costs 22¢ to mail a standard-size postcard and 37¢ to send letters weighing up to 1 ounce (that's about five pages of 8½-by-11-inch paper), plus 23¢ for each additional ounce. A postcard to Mexico costs 50¢, a 1-ounce letter 35¢; a postcard to Canada costs 50¢, a 1-ounce letter 60¢; a postcard to Europe, Australia, New Zealand, the Far East, South America, or elsewhere costs 70¢; a letter is 80¢ for each ounce.

Measurements The United States doesn't use the metric system. For a full explanation of the American system of measurements, please see "Metric Conversions" on the inside front cover of this guide.

Newspapers & Magazines National newspapers include the *New York Times, USA Today,* and the *Wall Street Journal.* National newsweeklies include *Newsweek, Time,* and *U.S. News & World Report.* You'll be able to find the *Miami Herald* in many cities around Florida. Most of these publications are available in bookstores and some major hotels. The best buy for local coverage, including entertainment, is the *Orlando Sentinel.*

Much harder to find are newspapers from the United Kingdom. Since 1997, the *London Daily Mail* is printed in Orlando for distribution along the East Coast. Because of the time difference, British travelers can actually pick up a paper at the airport and read the next day's newspaper on the way home.

Radio & Television There are five coast-to-coast television broadcast networks—ABC, CBS, NBC, Fox, and PBS (the Public Broadcasting System)—in America. These, plus two newer, smaller networks (UPN and WB) are available in Orlando, as are cable networks such as HBO, ESPN, and the Disney Channel. (Options on hotel TVs may be limited, so ask.) At Disney resorts, there also are Arabic, German, and Japanese channels.

You'll also find a wide choice of radio stations, broadcasting talk shows, and/or music, punctuated by news broadcasts and frequent commercials.

Most central Florida cable networks carry at least two Spanish-language stations, and there are numerous Spanish-language radio stations.

Smoking If you're a smoker, light up where and when you can. Smoking is prohibited in many of Florida's public places. While some bars have smoking areas and most hotels have smoking rooms, many are eliminating them. You're still permitted to inhale in most outdoor areas, but the Disney parks restrict where. *Note:* Don't expect to light up over dinner. In 2002, Florida voters approved a constitutional amendment that bans smoking in public work places, including restaurants and bars that serve food. Stand-alone bars that serve virtually no food and designated smoking rooms in hotels are exempt.

Taxes In the United States, there isn't a VAT (value-added tax) or other indirect tax assessed on most things at a national level. Every state, city, and county has the right to levy its own tax on purchases including hotel bills, restaurant checks, and airline tickets. In Florida, the state sales tax is 6%. Hotel tax in Orlando pushes the total to 11%; the total is 12% in Kissimmee.

Telephone, Telegraph & Fax Pay phones can be found in most restaurants, hotels, gas stations, and stores. Local calls in the United States usually cost 25¢ to 50¢. Pay phones don't accept pennies, and few will take anything larger than a quarter.

Most long-distance and international calls can be dialed directly from any phone. For direct overseas calls, dial 011 first, then the country code (Australia, 61; Republic of Ireland, 353; New Zealand, 64; United Kingdom, 44), followed by the city code, and then the number you wish to call. To place a call to Canada, the Caribbean, or another U.S. state, dial 1, followed by the area code and the seven-digit number.

For "collect" (reversed-charge) calls and for "person-to-person" calls, dial 0 (zero, not the letter "O"), followed by the area code and number you want. An operator will then come on the line, and you should specify that you're calling collect, or person-to-person, or both. If your operator-assisted call is international, ask for the overseas operator.

Because the telephone system in the U.S. is privately operated, long-distance rates can vary widely. Calling from your hotel room is convenient, but, generally, hotel surcharges on long-distance and local calls are astronomical. You're usually better off using a public pay telephone. Hotels sometimes charge a fee if you use your telephone credit card or call a toll-free number (with an 800, 877, or 888 area code), so ask about surcharges before you dial.

Prepaid calling cards don't come with the best per-minute rates in town, but they probably are fairer than the ones charged by your hotel. Calling cards are becoming increasingly popular and are sold in many convenience stores and drugstores. They usually can be purchased in $5 or $10 increments. Be sure to check for an expiration date before purchasing the card.

For local directory assistance ("Information"), dial 𝄐 411; for long-distance information in Canada or the United States, dial 1, then the appropriate area code and 𝄐 555-1212. There are three kinds of directories in the U.S. The White Pages list household numbers and business subscribers in alphabetical order. The Blue and Red Pages have government numbers. The Yellow Pages list all local services and businesses; they often include maps listing ZIP Codes and public transportation routes.

Most telegraph and telex services in the U.S. are provided by **Western Union.** You can dictate a telegram over the phone by calling ℂ **800/325-6000,** or use the number to check on the nearest location to wire money or have it sent to you.

It's also easy to send a fax. Most hotels have fax service. If yours doesn't, small copy shops found in most neighborhoods provide fax service. **Kinko's** is a prominent local chain that also provides fax service. There's a Kinko's (ℂ **407/363-2831**) at 9800 International Dr. in Orlando. Other branches are listed in the White Pages of the telephone directory. Faxes are sent for a small fee—usually around $2 or less per page. If you make arrangements, some places will also receive faxes for you and call you when anything arrives.

Time The United States is divided into six time zones. From east to west, they are: Eastern Standard Time (EST), Central Standard Time (CST), Mountain Standard Time (MST), Pacific Standard Time (PST), Alaska Standard Time (AST), and Hawaii Standard Time (HST). **Orlando,** like most of Florida, is on **Eastern Standard Time.** When it's noon in Orlando, it's 7am in Honolulu, 8am in Anchorage, 9am in Vancouver and Los Angeles, 11am in Winnipeg and New Orleans, and 6pm in London.

Daylight savings time is in effect from the first Sunday in April through 2am on the last Sunday in October. Daylight savings time moves the clock 1 hour ahead of standard time (7pm becomes 8pm and so on).

Tipping Gratuities are so ingrained in the American way of life that the annual income tax of tip-earning service personnel is based on how much they should have received in light of their employers' gross revenues. Accordingly, they may have to pay tax on a tip you didn't actually give them. Service in the United States generally tends to be good, and gratuities are increasingly being added automatically to some services, particularly those in restaurants, so check the bill closely before adding a gratuity—service is seldom good enough to double a tip.

The amount you leave should depend on the service you have received. Good service warrants the following tips: bartenders, 15%; cab drivers, 15%; checkroom attendants, $1 per garment (unless there's a charge, then no tip); hairdressers, 15%; parking valets, $1; redcaps (in airports), at least $1 per piece; and restaurant and nightclub servers, 15%. In hotels, tip bellhops at least $1 per bag ($2–$3 if you have a lot of luggage), and tip the chamber staff $1 to $2 per day (more if you've left a disaster area for them to clean up, or if you're traveling with kids).

Toilets International visitors often complain that public toilets or "restrooms" are hard to find in most U.S. cities. True, there are none on the streets, but you can usually find one in a bar, restaurant, hotel, museum, department store, convenience store, attraction, or service station—and it'll probably be clean. Note, however, that some establishments, including restaurants and bars in heavily visited areas, may display a notice that their toilets are for the use of patrons only. You can ignore this sign, or, better yet, avoid arguments by paying for a cup of coffee or a soft drink, which will qualify you as a patron. Within the theme parks, restrooms will be clearly marked on the park maps. Don't panic if you find the flushing handle is missing. Many new toilets are installed with lasers that trigger the flush automatically when you leave the stall.

4

Getting to Know Walt Disney World & Orlando

When Disney christened its Magic Kingdom theme park in 1971, Orlando was still a slow-lane Southern town. Beyond the budding tourist attraction, there wasn't much to its 'burbs except orange trees, palmetto stands, and cow patties.

But Uncle Walt and Mickey quickly changed that, blazing a pioneering trail that, during the last 34 years, has spawned a crush of over-development. Walt Disney World has grown into four major theme parks, two nighttime entertainment districts, 20 resorts and timeshare properties, nine partner hotels, two full-fledged water parks, and loads more. Those are Disney's ways of trying to keep your tourist dollars from straying to Universal Orlando, SeaWorld, or its other competitors.

No one pretends Mickey isn't the Big Cheese. At least initially, the Magic Kingdom and its offspring are what summon the masses. But all of that unrelenting cheerfulness, days of $2.50 sodas, and the solar-fried musk of sweaty patrons make it a small world, after all. Besides, you're cheating yourself if you don't spend some time away from Walt Disney's world. Enjoy the action-packed fun at Universal Studios Florida, Islands of Adventure, and Universal's nightclub and restaurant district, CityWalk. But don't overlook some of the less frazzled things to do in O-Town. SeaWorld is a laid-back park where the crowds aren't so horrid, and Gatorland is a throwback tourist attraction where the admission won't bust your bank. Last, but not least, everyone should spend at least 1 night away from the parks altogether. So get thee around town to eat and enjoy some "alternative" nightlife—not just the kind imagineered by Disney.

1 Orientation

VISITOR INFORMATION

Once you're here, you can stop at the **Orlando/Orange County Convention & Visitors Bureau,** 8723 International Dr., Suite 101, Orlando (© **407/363-5872;** www.orlandoinfo.com). Folks working at the bureau will answer questions and give you maps, brochures, and coupons good for discounts or freebies. It's worth a visit even if you take our advice in chapter 2, "Planning Your Trip to Walt Disney World & Orlando," and send for them before arriving. The bureau sells discount tickets to several attractions (savings on single-day passes to Universal and SeaWorld are $3 or less; only Disney's 4-day or longer passes are discounted). The bureau's multilingual staff will make dinner reservations and hotel referrals for you. The bureau is open daily from 8am to 8pm, except Christmas. From I-4, take Exit 74A east 2 blocks, turn south on International Drive and continue 1 mile. The center is on the left, at the corner of I-Drive and Austrian Row.

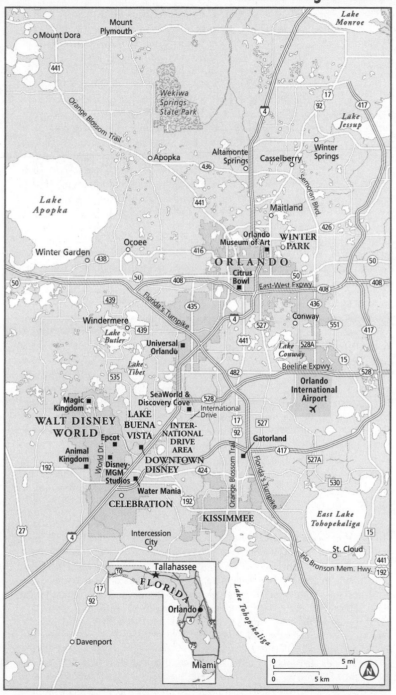

The **Kissimmee–St. Cloud Convention & Visitors Bureau** is located at 1925 E. Irlo Bronson Memorial Highway/U.S. 192, Kissimmee (© **800/327-9159** or 407/847-5000; www.floridakiss.com). It offers maps, brochures, and discount coupons, too. From I-4, take Exit 64A/U.S. 192 east about 12 miles to Bill Beck Blvd., then go left into the bureau's parking lot.

If you're driving from the north on I-75, you can stop at the **Disney Welcome Center** in Ocala, Fla. (exit 350 at Hwy. 200), about 90 miles north of Orlando (© **352/854-0770**). The center sells tickets and Mickey ears, helps plan your park itinerary, and makes hotel reservations. Hours are from 9am to 6pm daily (until 7pm June, July, and Aug). But don't come looking for cut-rate tickets. Disney really doesn't do many discounts, though you can save a few bucks if you buy multiday park-hopper passes (see chapter 7, "Exploring Walt Disney World").

Five tourism centers around Florida have statewide information. They're located 4 miles north of Jennings on I-75 south; 3 miles north of Campbellton on Highway 231; 7 miles north of Yulee on I-95; 16 miles west of Pensacola on I-10 east; and at the capitol in Tallahassee.

Finally, nearly all hotel lobbies and many restaurants, highway rest stops, and attractions have racks containing brochures for various activities. If this guidebook doesn't convince you of a game plan, these handouts might help you make up your mind. The brochures often include discount coupons.

INFORMATION (& MORE) AT THE AIRPORT

Passengers arriving at or departing from Orlando International Airport can stroll over to one of two Disney shops. The **Magic of Disney** (© **407/825-2301**) is in the main terminal, third level, right behind the Northwest Airlines ticket desk. **Disney Earport** (© **407/825-2339**) is in the main terminal, across from the Hyatt Regency. They sell WDW multiday tickets, make dinner show and hotel reservations at Disney resorts, and provide brochures and assistance. They're open daily, usually from 7am to 8pm; but don't use these airport stores to buy things unless you're on your way home and forgot to buy that must-have Pooh doll for Auntie Arugula. Chances are you'll find a better selection and (possibly) cheaper prices elsewhere in town.

The **Universal Studios Stores** (© **407/825-2473**), usually open daily from 7am to 8pm, sell park tickets at two locations: Airside A, main terminal, and Airside B, Delta side before security, both on the third level. **SeaWorld** stores, at Airside A and B, are open from 7am to 8pm (© **407/825-2614**).

CITY LAYOUT

Orlando's major artery is Interstate 4. Locals call it **I-4** or that *#@$*%^#!!* It runs diagonally across the state from Tampa to Daytona Beach. Exits from I-4 take you to all of the Disney properties, Universal, SeaWorld, International Drive, U.S. 192, Kissimmee, Lake Buena Vista, downtown Orlando, and Winter Park. Most exits are well marked, but construction is common and exit numbers have been recently changed (see **www11.myflorida.com/trafficoperations/exit numb/i_4.htm** for more information). If you get directions by exit number, always ask the name of the road, too, to avoid getting lost. (Cellphone users can dial © **511** to get a report of I-4 delays.)

The **Florida Turnpike,** a toll road, crosses I-4 and links with I-75 to the north and Miami to the south. **U.S. 192/Irlo Bronson Memorial Highway** is a major east–west artery that reaches from Kissimmee to U.S. 27, crossing I-4 near World Drive, the main Walt Disney World entrance road. Construction on 192, planned to last at least through 2003, creates backups as bad as the ones on

---

Fun Fact **Crash & Burn**

Talk about culture clash. The rocking Race Rock Café on International Drive, known for parking NASCAR racers in its lobby and having mini-racers streaking across the ceiling, was once the home of a short-lived opera-theme restaurant with live performances. It lasted until, well, the fat lady sang (ouch).

I-4 during rush hour (7–9am and 4–6pm daily). Farther north, the **BeeLine Expressway** (Hwy. 528), also a toll road, goes east from I-4 past Orlando International Airport to Cape Canaveral and Kennedy Space Center. The **East–West Expressway** (also known as Hwy. 408) is a toll road that can be helpful in bypassing surface traffic in the downtown area.

If you're jockeying between Disney and Universal, one of the lesser traffic evils is **Apopka–Vineland Road.** It tends to be less cluttered than I-4 or International Drive. Follow it north from Lake Buena Vista and the northeast side of Mickeyville to Sand Lake Road, then go right/east to Turkey Lake Road, then left/north to Universal Orlando.

I-4 and Highway 535 roughly bound **Walt Disney World** to the east (the latter is also a northern boundary) and U.S. 192/Irlo Bronson Memorial Highway bounds it to the south. World Drive is WDW's main north–south artery. Epcot Center Drive (Hwy. 536/the south end of International Dr.) and Buena Vista Drive cut across the complex in a more or less east–west direction; the two roads cross at Bonnet Creek Parkway. Despite a reasonably good highway system and explicit signs, it's easy to get lost or miss a turn here—we do at least once every trip. Again, pay attention and drive carefully. Don't panic or pull across several lanes of traffic to make an exit, especially once you're on Disney property. All roads lead to the parks, and you'll soon find another sign directing you to the same place. It may take a bit longer, but Goofy will still be there.

Clever landscaping hides the fact that many parts of WDW are very close together. (The way some roads twist and turn, it makes us wonder if Disney didn't make things purposely convoluted so visitors would drive past other attractions to whet their appetites and line Mickey's pockets.)

ORLANDO NEIGHBORHOODS IN BRIEF

Walt Disney World The empire, its big and little parks, resorts, restaurants, shops, and assorted trimmings, are scattered across 30,500 acres. The surprising thing to some folks: WDW isn't in Orlando. It's southwest of the city, off I-4 on U.S. 192 west. Stay here and learn that convenience has its price; accommodations run as much as double what they do in nearby Kissimmee.

Lake Buena Vista This is Disney's next-door neighbor. It's where you'll find "official" (though not Disney-owned) hotels. It's close to Downtown Disney and Pleasure Island. This charming area has manicured lawns, tree-lined thoroughfares, and free transportation throughout the realm, though it may take a while to get where you want to go.

Celebration Imagine living in a Disney world. This is an attempt to re-create a squeaky-clean Mickey magic town. Located on 4,900 acres, Celebration has thousands of residents living in gingerbread homes and apartments. The homes start at about $200,000. Celebration's downtown area is, however, designed for tourists. It's architecturally interesting and offers shops, restaurants, theaters, and a hotel. If you're a yuppie, particularly one with reasonably deep pockets, this may be your dream world. Think of an upscale Main Street, U.S.A. (If that doesn't appeal to you, steer clear. It can drive non-yuppies and yesteryear haters nuts.)

Downtown Disney This is more Disney dessert than an actual neighborhood, and, simply put, it's what WDW has taken to calling its two nighttime entertainment areas, Pleasure Island and Disney's West Side, as well as its shopping complex, Downtown Disney Marketplace. We consider this area a part of WDW/Lake Buena Vista.

Kissimmee This once-sleepy city is closer to Disney than Orlando. It's just a few miles from Mickey and has some of the least expensive offerings in the area, but it also has a distinctly tacky side with budget motel chains and every fast-food joint known to civilization. The town centers on U.S. 192/Irlo Bronson Memorial Highway, which, as we mentioned earlier, has traffic problems created by perpetual road construction.

International Drive Area (Hwy. 536) Can you say tourist mecca? Known as **I-Drive,** it extends 7 to 10 miles north of the Disney parks between Highway 535 and the Florida Turnpike. From bungee jumping and ice-skating to dozens of theme restaurants and T-shirt

shops, this is *the* tourist strip in central Florida. It also has numerous hotels and shopping areas, it's home to the Orange County Convention Center, and it offers easy access to SeaWorld and Universal Orlando. The central and northern sections are already packed, but developers somehow manage to shoehorn more in, year after year. The south end is less cluttered and easier to navigate.

Downtown Orlando No, not Downtown Disney, which isn't *really* downtown. To get to the real thing, you have to travel on I-4 east (it feels more like north, but the road signs say otherwise). This is where you will find less tourist-focused nightlife and attractions, including the Orlando Science Center, a multimillion-dollar complex. Scores of clubs and restaurants are located in the heart of the city, which is one of the fastest growing in the country. Dozens of antique shops line "Antique Row" on Orange Avenue near Lake Ivanhoe.

Winter Park Just north of downtown Orlando, Winter Park is the place many of central Florida's old-money families call home (and new money ones come to shop). It's home to Park Avenue, a collection of upscale shops and restaurants along a cobblestone street that's frequented by the lunch and dinner crowds. With the main attractions being shopping, dining, and small museums, this part of the 'burbs is not a good place for most kids or thrill-ride junkies. But it is a good place to relax and escape the WDW, Universal, and I-Drive crowds—if you have the wheels to get here.

2 Getting Around

In a city that thrives on its attractions, you won't find it difficult to get around—especially if you have a car. Don't count on the city bus system to get you where you want to go. (Okay, it may get you there or somewhere near there, but not quickly.) If you're traveling outside the tourist areas, avoid the periods from 7 to

9am and from 4 to 6pm like the plague, which they are. Rush hours are bad anywhere, but the commuter traffic here is complicated by tourist traffic and, given that this is a 365-day-a-year town, it doesn't get better on weekends. Most of the parks don't open until 9am or so and they usually stay open at least until dusk, so you won't miss much by leaving a little later. (The exception is Animal Kingdom, where the critters move around early, then hide; see "Animal Kingdom" in chapter 7, "Exploring Walt Disney World.")

International Drive has two alternate means of transportation—pedestrian and trolley power. We don't recommend the former because, though there are plenty of sidewalks, you may be taking your life in your hands if you try to cross this busy road. The **I-Ride Trolley** (© 407/248-9590; www.iridetrolley.com) is a safer bet. It makes 54 stops between the Belz Factory Outlets on the north end of the drive and SeaWorld to the south. The trolley runs every 15 minutes, from 8am to 10:30pm, and costs 75¢ for adults and 25¢ for seniors; kids under 12 ride free; exact change is required. There's an unlimited 1-day pass available for $2 per person. Due to I-Drive's high traffic volume, this is a great way to avoid bumper-to-bumper driving.

The good news if you are driving is that road signs have become more accurate than they were a few years back. But to make sure you're heading the right way, follow the directions we supply for the various attractions and hotels later in this book. Also, call your destination before leaving and ask whether new construction or other temporary roadblocks might be in your way. Most attractions give directions as a voice-mail option when you call the main number, but you can also ask for an operator to get clarification.

Some hotels (usually not the inexpensive ones) offer transportation to and from some theme parks and other tourist destinations; however, some of them charge you for this service. It's not difficult getting around town, but it can be expensive, so ask when booking your room.

BY DISNEY TRANSPORTATION SYSTEM

If you're going to stay at Disney and spend a majority of your time visiting its parks and attractions, your best bet may be to use the thorough and free transportation network that runs throughout Mickey's realm.

Guests at Disney resorts and "official" hotels get unlimited transportation via bus, monorail, ferry, and water taxi to all of Disney's major parks from 2 hours prior to opening until 2 hours after closing. There also is service to the hotels, Downtown Disney, Typhoon Lagoon, Blizzard Beach, Pleasure Island, and other resort areas. Disney properties offer transportation to other area attractions as well, but you'll have to pay extra.

The system has several advantages. It's free, possibly saving you on car rental, insurance, and gas. You also don't have to pay for parking ($7 per day at the theme parks). You may avoid a wait to enter the parking lots and, if your party wants to split up, you can board a transport to different areas.

The disadvantages? You're at the mercy of Disney's schedule. Sometimes you have to take a ferry to catch a bus to get on the monorail to reach your hotel. The system makes a complete circuit, but it's not necessarily the most direct path for you. It can take an hour or more to get somewhere that's right across the lagoon from you. This is especially true if you stay at the Disney resorts that lie in the outer reaches, such as Fort Wilderness. If you decide to forego a rental in favor of the transportation system, you'll also be limited to the areas the system serves, which means you're stuck in pricey Mickeyville.

If you have time before locking in your trip, call ℂ **407/824-4321** and ask the information specialist for a **Disney World Transportation Guide Map.** (It shows where various resorts are in relation to the attractions you want to visit.) Disney may refuse to mail one to you, but you can use the maps in this guide, pick up a guide map when you land, or view a more generic map and download it at **www.disneyworld.com** (you'll need Adobe Acrobat Reader). When you get on the website, click "Reservations & Info," then "Transportation," then "View and Download Some Maps."

The best rule when using Disney transportation: Ask the driver or someone at your hotel's front desk to help you take the most direct route. Keep asking questions along the way. Unlike missing a highway exit, missing a bus stop means you may reach your pension before your destination.

BY CAR

To rent or not to rent—that's the question. First, think about your vacation plans. If you're going to stay happily immersed in everything Disney, or if you're going to lock into International Drive or Universal, you might do just as well without your own wheels. If you're staying at a Disney property, the question to ask yourself is how, exactly, will you get to the parks? If the Magic Kingdom is accessible only by taking a bus, switching to the monorail, and then catching a ferry, you may want to opt for a car (more so if you want to get to Universal Orlando, SeaWorld, or downtown Orlando). The least expensive properties, the All-Star resorts, are among the farthest from the Disney parks. Wait times between buses can be considerable—if not unendurable.

During peak hours in the busiest seasons, you may have trouble getting a seat on the bus, so keep that in mind if you're traveling with seniors or with companions with disabilities. Also, if you're hauling children and strollers, consider the frustration factor of loading and unloading strollers and kiddy paraphernalia on and off buses, ferries, and trams (although, as in earlier chapters, we suggest you rent strollers at the park).

A car may drastically cut the commute time between the parks and hotels not directly on the monorail routes, so decide how much your time is worth and how much the car will cost plus the $7 per day theme-park parking charge before making a decision about renting.

In general, if you're going to spend all of your time at Disney and you're laid-back enough to go with the flow of traffic within the transportation network, there's no sense renting a car that will sit in the parking lot.

But if you're on an extended stay—a week or more—you'll probably want a car for at least a day or two to venture beyond the tourist areas. You can discover downtown Orlando, visit museums, or tour the Space Coast; it'll be good for your soul. The tourist hot spots are kind of like Las Vegas: You can't spend too

---

⎛Fun Fact⎞ What's in a Name?

Known for going to great lengths to protect its image and name—even removing unofficial Disney pictures from murals on the wall of a day-care center—Disney finally lost at its own game. Originally dubbed "Wild Animal Kingdom," WDW's newest park was renamed after complaints that the moniker too closely mirrored television's *Wild Kingdom*.

> ### (Tips Look Both Ways
>
> We don't recommend foot travel anywhere in Orlando, but occasionally you'll have to walk across a parking lot or street. *Be careful.* Orlando is the most dangerous large city in the country for pedestrians, according to the 2002 Mean Streets study. Wide roads designed to move traffic quickly and a shortage of sidewalks, streetlights, and crosswalks are to blame.

much time in a world of bright lights and make-believe without needing a good dose of reality.

All of the major car-rental companies are represented in Orlando and maintain desks at or near the airport. Many agencies provide discount coupons in publications targeted at tourists. When you're planning your trip and poring over all those brochures, keep watch for discounts on car rentals. You may also want to ask your travel agent if he or she has a recommendation, or whether a discount is included in packages. Also, it never hurts to ask about specials.

See appendix B, "Useful Toll-Free Numbers & Websites," in the back of this book for contact information.

BY BUS

Stops for the **Lynx** bus system (© 407/841-2279; www.golynx.com) are marked with a "paw" print. It will get you to Disney, Universal, and I-Drive ($1 adults, 25¢ kids 8–18), but it's generally not tourist-friendly.

Mears Transportation (© 407/423-5566; www.mearstransportation.com) operates buses to all major attractions, including Kennedy Space Center, Universal Studios, SeaWorld, and Busch Gardens (yes, in Tampa), among others. Call for rates.

BY MOTORCYCLE

The increasing popularity of Bike Week and a growing number of weekend road warriors have sparked an increase in places specializing in motorcycle rental. The Harley Davidson, in all shapes and sizes, is the most popular. You must be at least 21 and sometimes 25 years of age, have a motorcycle license, and a major credit card. Rental fees start at about $650 for 1 week or $150 per day including helmets, locks, and a brief orientation. You can rent bikes at **American V Twin,** 5101 International Dr. (© 888/268-8946 or 407/903-0058; www.amv twin.com), and **Iron Horse Rentals,** 4380 L. B. McLeod Rd. (© 800/946-4743 or 407/426-7091; www.hogride.com). But plan ahead, months in advance if you're going to be here during Bike Week, late February to early March, or BiketoberFest in mid-October. Both are in Daytona Beach, but a lot of their visitors stay in Orlando.

BY TAXI

Taxis line up in front of major hotels and a few smaller properties. The front desk will be happy to hail one for you. You also can call **Yellow Cab** (© 407/699-9999) and **Ace Metro** (© 407/855-0564) on your own. Rates run as high as $3.25 for the first mile, $1.75 per mile thereafter, though sometimes you can get a flat rate. In general, cabs are economical only if you have four or five people aboard.

FAST FACTS: Walt Disney World & Orlando

Ambulances See "Emergencies," below.

American Express There's an American Express Travel Service Office at Epcot's main gate (© **407/827-7500**). The one nearest to Universal is at **A Time to Travel**, 7512 Dr. Phillips Blvd. (© **407/345-1181**).

Babysitters Some Orlando hotels, including higher-end ones at Disney (see Animal Kingdom Lodge, Wilderness Lodge, the Beach Club, Board-walk, Contemporary, Grand Floridian, and Polynesian resorts in chapter 5) offer supervised evening babysitting services, and several have good child-care facilities with counselor-supervised activity programs. Disney programs usually run $8 per child per hour and include dinner and games or activities. Babysitting rates elsewhere usually run $10 to $15 per hour per child; some offer discounts for the second, third, or fourth child. Disney and some other hotels offer in-room sitters through a company called **Kid's Night Out** (© **407/827-5444**).

Business Hours Theme park hours vary, depending on the time of year. Most open at 9am and stay open at least until 6 or 7pm (sometimes as late as 9pm during summer and holidays). Office hours for central Florida businesses are generally Monday through Friday from 9am to 5pm. Bars are usually open until 2am. "Rave" and other after-hours clubs stay open until the wee hours. After-hours clubs don't serve alcohol.

Car Rentals See "Getting Around," in this chapter, and appendix B, "Useful Toll-Free Numbers & Websites."

Climate See "When to Go," in chapter 2.

Crime See "Safety," below.

Doctors & Dentists There are basic first-aid centers in all of the major parks. There's also a 24-hour toll-free number for the **Poison Control Center:** © **800/282-3171**.

Disney offers in-room medical service 24 hours a day by calling © **407/238-2000**. **Doctors on Call Service** (© **407/399-3627**) is a group that makes house and room calls in most of the Orlando area. **Centra-Care** has several walk-in clinics listed in the Yellow Pages, including ones on International Drive (© **407/370-4881**) and at Lake Buena Vista near Disney (© **407/934-2273**).

To find a dentist, contact **Dental Referral Service** (© **800/235-4111; www.dentalreferral.com**). Folks there can tell you the nearest dentist who meets your needs. Phones are manned weekdays from 10am to 7pm EST. Check the Yellow Pages for local 24-hour emergency services.

Emergencies Dial © **911** to contact the police or fire department, or to call an ambulance. For less urgent requests, call © **800/647-9284,** a number sponsored by the **Florida Tourism Industry Marketing Corporation,** the state tourism promotion board. With operators speaking over 100 languages, this source can provide directions and help with lost credit cards, medical emergencies, accidents, money transfers, airline confirmation, and much more.

Hospitals **Sand Lake Hospital,** 9400 Turkey Lake Rd. (© **407/351-8550**), is about 2 miles south of Sand Lake Road. From the WDW area, take I-4 east to the Sand Lake Road exit and make a left on Turkey Lake Road. The hospital is 2 miles (up on your right). **Celebration Health** (© 407/303-4000), located in the town of Celebration, is at 400 Celebration Place. From I-4, take the U.S. 192 exit. At the first traffic light, turn right onto Celebration Avenue. At the first stop sign, take another right.

Internet Access You will find a few local cybercafes listed at **www.cybercafes.com** or **www.netcafeguide.com/mapindex.htm**.

Kennels The major theme parks offer animal boarding usually for about $6 per day. Disney's kennels are at Fort Wilderness, Epcot, the Magic Kingdom, Animal Kingdom, and Disney–MGM Studios (© **407/824-6568**). Resort guests can board their pets overnight for $9 ($11 for those not staying at Disney) at the Transportation and Ticket Center's kennel on Seven Seas Drive near the Polynesian Resort. SeaWorld and Universal also offer kennels where you can leave your animals during the day but not at night. A current vaccine record is a must at all kennels.

DogFriendly.com (© 530/672-5316; www.dogfriendly.com) is a dandy source of information about canine-friendly places. It lists hotels, parks, and even restaurants that welcome well-behaved critters.

Remember: Don't leave your pet in the car—even with a window cracked—while you enjoy the park. Many pets have perished this way in the hot Florida sun, and you may be charged with animal cruelty.

Liquor Laws The minimum drinking age in Florida is 21. No liquor is served in the Magic Kingdom at Walt Disney World. However, drinks are available at the other Disney parks and are quite evident at Universal parks (more so at its Mardi Gras days and Halloween Horror Nights).

Lockers You can rent lockers at all Disney, Universal Orlando, and SeaWorld parks. The cost varies but averages $7 a day, including a $2 refundable deposit. Many other attractions, such as the water parks, also offer lockers, sometimes at a lower fee. Inquire at a Guest Services desk. For safety purposes, it's better to keep valuables, such as camera equipment, in a locker rather than in your car.

Lost Children Every theme park has a designated spot for adults to be reunited with lost children (or lost spouses). Ask where it is when you enter any park (or consult the free park guide maps) and instruct your children to ask park personnel to take them there if they get separated from you. Point out what park personnel look like. Young children should have nametags that include their parents' names, the name of the hotel where they're staying, and a contact number back home in the very rare case that parents can't be located.

Lost & Found Be sure to tell all of your credit-card companies the minute you discover your wallet has been lost or stolen while in Orlando and file a report at the nearest police precinct. Your credit-card company or insurer may require a police report number or record of the loss. Most credit-card companies have an emergency toll-free number to call if your card is lost or stolen; they may be able to wire you a cash advance immediately or deliver an emergency credit card in a day or two. Visa's U.S. emergency number is © **800/847-2911** or 410/581-9994. American Express cardholders and traveler's check holders should call © **800/221-7282**. MasterCard holders should call (℃ **800/307-7309** or 636/722-7111. For other credit cards, call the toll-free number directory at (℃ **800/555-1212.**

If you need emergency cash over the weekend when all banks and American Express offices are closed, you can have money wired to you via **Western Union** ((℃ **800/325-6000;** www.westernunion.com).

Identity theft or fraud are potential complications of losing your wallet, especially if you've lost your driver's license along with your cash and credit cards. Notify the major credit-reporting bureaus immediately; placing a fraud alert on your records may protect you against liability for criminal activity. The three major U.S. credit-reporting agencies are **Equifax** ((℃ **800/766-0008;** www.equifax.com), **Experian** ((℃ **888/397-3742;** www. experian.com), and **TransUnion** ((℃ **800/680-7289;** www.transunion.com). Finally, if you've lost all forms of photo ID, call your airline and explain the situation; they might allow you to board the plane if you have a copy of your passport or birth certificate and a copy of the police report you've filed.

Newspapers & Magazines The *Orlando Sentinel* is the major local newspaper, but you can also purchase the Sunday editions of other papers (most notably, the *New York Times*) in some hotel gift shops or bookstores such as Barnes & Noble or Borders. Don't count on finding daily editions of West Coast papers, such as the *Los Angeles Times,* without making special arrangements. The Friday edition of the *Sentinel* includes extensive entertainment and dining listings as does the *Sentinel's* website, **www.orlandosentinel.com.** *Orlando Weekly* is a free, alternative paper that has a lot of entertainment and art listings focused on events outside tourist areas.

Pharmacies **Walgreens,** 1003 W. Vine St. (Hwy. 192), just east of Bermuda Avenue ((℃ **407/847-4222**), operates a 24-hour pharmacy. There's an **Eckerd Drugs** at 12125 Apopka–Vineland Rd. ((℃ **407/238-9333**) that's open until 7pm (5pm Sun). **Turner Drugs,** 12500 Apopka–Vineland Rd. ((℃ **407/ 828-8125**) will deliver medications to the Disney resorts for a $5 delivery charge (a doctor first must fax the store your prescription). You can find other pharmacies in the Yellow Pages.

Photography Two-hour film processing is available at all major parks. Look for the PHOTO EXPRESS sign. You can also buy film in all of the theme parks. But you'll save money on both if you use discount stores in the free world, including Walgreens, Eckerd, Kmart, and Target. They often provide coupons for half-off photo processing, which could save you a significant amount of money. They're listed in the Yellow Pages under "Photo Finishing."

Post Office The post office most convenient to Disney and Universal is at 10450 Turkey Lake Rd. ((℃ **800/275-8777**). It's open Monday through Friday from 9am to 5pm, Saturday from 9am to noon. You can buy stamps and mail letters at most hotels.

Safety Don't let the aura of Mickey, Minnie, Donald, and Daisy allow you to relax your guard; Orlando has a crime rate that's comparable to that of other large U.S. cities. Stay alert and remain aware of your surroundings. It's a good idea to keep your valuables in a safe-deposit box (inquire at your hotel's front desk), although many hotels today are equipped with in-room safes. Keep a close eye on your valuables when you're in public places—restaurants, theaters, even airport terminals. Renting a locker is always preferable to leaving your valuables in the trunk of your car, even in the theme-park lots. Be cautious, even when in the parks, and avoid carrying large amounts of cash in a backpack or fanny pack, which could be easily accessed while you're standing in line for a ride or show.

If you're renting a car, carefully read the safety instructions that the rental company provides. Never stop for any reason in a suspicious or an unpopulated area, and remember that children should never ride in the front seat of a car equipped with air bags.

Special Diets Kosher, salt-free, and other dietary needs can be arranged at sit-down restaurants inside the Disney parks and resorts with 24-hour or longer notice. Call © **407/939-3463.**

Taxes Florida's 6% sales tax is charged on all goods except most grocery store items and medicines. Additionally, hotels add another 5% or 6% to your bill for a total of 11% or 12%.

Telephone Because of its growth spurt, Orlando has had to go to 10-digit dialing. If you're making a local call in Orlando's 407 area code region, even across the street, *you must dial the 407 area code followed by the number you wish to call,* for a total of 10 digits.

Time Orlando is in the **Eastern Standard Time** zone, which is 1 hour later than Chicago and 3 hours later than Los Angeles. Call © **407/646-3131** for the correct time and temperature.

Tourist Information See "Orientation," in this chapter.

Weather Look for the "Weather Channel" on Time Warner Cable, the local cable provider. Most hotels carry basic cable. The *Orlando Sentinel* also includes a daily forecast. A local 24-hour news station, Channel 13, offers weather forecasts several times an hour. You can also get weather information from the National Weather Service by calling © **321/255-0212.** (They answer as National Weather Service in Melbourne, FL, but after that you get an option to punch in 412 from a touch-tone phone, which plugs you into the Orlando forecast.) Also check with the Weather Channel online at **www.weatherchannel.com.**

5

Where to Stay

The Orlando area has more than 110,000 rooms including scores of places located in or near the major-league tourist draws: Walt Disney World, Universal Orlando, SeaWorld, and the rest of International Drive.

Beautifully landscaped grounds are the rule at properties in WDW, neighboring Lake Buena Vista, Universal Orlando, and on the southern portions of I-Drive. But heavier traffic and, at times, higher prices come with them. No matter what your budget or crowd tolerance, there's something for everyone. If you're looking for an inexpensive or moderately priced motel, check out the options in Kissimmee and, to a lesser degree, on the northern end of International Drive. We also provide a few bed-and-breakfast listings, for those who don't want to stay in the resorts or mainstream areas.

Once you've decided on a date for your Orlando vacation, book your accommodations as soon as possible, especially if you want to stay at Disney or Universal. Advance reservations are a necessity if you're hunting modest or primo rooms in this area. In addition to the individual listings in this chapter, there are several places to find discounts. **HotelKingdom.com** (*C* **877/766-6787** or 407/294-9600; www.hotelkingdom.com) is a good source of room or vacation rental bargains. Another good place to look is the **Orlando/Orange County Convention & Visitors Bureau** (*C* **800/643-9492;** www.orlandoinfo.com). You can also use the Kissimmee–St. Cloud site (**www.floridakiss.com**) or call *C* **800/333-5477.**

HOW TO CHOOSE A HOTEL & SAVE MONEY

All of the rates cited in the following pages are "rack rates." That means they're typical prices listed in the hotel brochures or the ones hotel clerks give by rote over the telephone. You almost always can negotiate a better price through package deals, by assuring the clerks they can do better, or by mentioning you belong to one of several organizations that get a discount. So, if you're a member of groups such as AARP, AAA, or labor unions, step right up and mention it. Even your credit card might get you a **5% to 10% discount** at larger chains. (Disney and the other lodging players have been a little more willing to cut rates since occupancy fell drastically in September 2001, but that bonus may disappear when hotels and motels begin filling again.) Any discount you get will help ease the impact of local resort taxes, which aren't included in the quoted rates. *These taxes add 11% to 12% depending on where you're staying.*

The **average, undiscounted hotel rate** for the Orlando area is about $110 per night double, and that rate in good times climbs 5% a year. The lowest rates at WDW are those at the All-Star resorts, which, depending on the season, run from $77 to $124. They're pricier than comparable rooms in the outside world; they're tiny, basic, and tacky, too, but they *are on Disney soil.*

WDW's 2003 value seasons or lowest rates are available from January 1 to February 12, August 25 to October 1 (except Labor Day weekend), and November 2 to December 19. Regular season rates are available from April 27 to August 23 and October 2 to November 1. Peak rates—read, the "high ones"—stretch from February 13 to April 26 and during the holiday season, December 20 through December 31. While the actual dates will shift a little, the same periods should apply in 2004.

Value Staying for Less

Although many folks participate in the airlines' frequent-flyer programs, not many take advantage of the major hotel chains' frequent-stay clubs. Even if you don't stay in a hotel for more than your yearly vacation, you may be able to realize savings by joining its program.

Like the airlines' scheme, some hotels let you build points for staying at a participating property, dining in its restaurant, or using some other service. Although programs vary, points can be traded for free nights, discounted rates, special perks, or, in some cases, frequent-flier miles. And the price to join is right—it's free. And just joining a hotel club may make you eligible for discounts, give you express check-in and checkout privileges, and provide free breakfasts, local calls, or a morning newspaper.

Here are a few frequent-stay programs that offer perks to travelers:

- **Six Continents Hotels Priority Club** (© 800/272-9273; www.priority club.com) covers the Inter-Continental Resorts, Crowne Plaza hotels and resorts, Holiday Inns, and Staybridge Suites. Priority Club members get express check-in, access to discounted rates at select hotels, and other perks. Freebies vary according to hotel but often include breakfast, local phone calls, and/or parking.

- **Choice Hotels International Guest Privileges** program (© 888/770-6800; www.guestprivileges.com) covers Sleep, Quality, Comfort, and Clarion properties. Participants receive perks such as express check-in, special rates, room upgrades based on availability, extended checkout times, and free local calls and newspapers.

- **Hyatt Hotel's Gold Passport** program (© 800/304-9288; www.gold passport.com) gives members a private reservation phone number and express check-in, complimentary newspapers, and access to the hotel's fitness center. You'll also receive special offers and discounted rates from select Hyatt properties.

- **Hilton Honors Worldwide** program (© 800/548-8690; www.hilton hhonors.com) covers Hilton, Conrad, DoubleTree, Embassy Suites, Hampton Inn, and Homewood Suites properties. It offers expedited check-in, a dedicated reservation line, late checkout, and a free daily newspaper.

Other frequent-stay programs include **Starwood Hotels Preferred Guest** (© 888/625-4988; www.starwood.com/preferredguest) and **Marriott Rewards** (© 801/468-4000; www.marriottrewards.com).

If you're not renting a car or staying at a Walt Disney World or Universal resort, be sure to ask when booking your room if the hotel or motel offers **transportation to the theme parks** and, if so, whether there's a charge. Some hotels and motels offer free service with their own shuttles. Others use Mears Transportation (see "Getting Around" in chapter 4). Rates are as high as $15 per person round-trip (some hotels make these arrangements for you; others require you to do it). On the other hand, if you have a car or pickup, expect to pay $7 or $8 a day to park it at Disney, Universal, and SeaWorld.

If you stay at a WDW resort or one of Disney's "official" hotels, transportation is complimentary within WDW. For more information on this and the other advantages of staying at Disney properties, see "The Perks of Staying with Mickey," a little later in this chapter. (We'll also tell you the downside of going to bed with The Mouse.)

In or out of Walt Disney World, if you book your hotel as part of a **package** (see "Packages for the Independent Traveler" in chapter 2 for more details), you'll likely enjoy some kind of savings. Call the **Walt Disney Travel Company** at © **800/828-0228** to book resort packages or hotel rooms at WDW.

Outside Disney, you'll probably be quoted a rate better than the rack rates contained in the following listings. Even then, try to bargain, especially with privately owned hotels. When it comes to big chains, discounts are a bit more elusive. When dealing on a national level, you'll find some discounts; on the local level, clerks usually lack incentives to fill rooms, but try anyway. Also, no matter what your landing zone, try again when you arrive. But we don't recommend coming without a reservation, and taking chances on your negotiating skills and room availability. This works in some places (and we give you some local options later in this chapter), but Orlando is a year-round destination. It has a heavy convention and business trade, and school lets out during varying times of the year in other nations. If you come without a reservation, you may face leftovers.

Ask about discounts for students, government employees, seniors, military, firefighters, police, AFL-CIO, corporate clients, and, again, AARP or AAA. *Note:* Disney has stopped selling memberships in the **Disney Club,** which offered 10% to 30% discounts at WDW parks, resorts, and restaurants, as well as savings on merchandise (current cards are good until Dec 2003). The club is expected to be replaced by a Disney/Visa credit card that lets cardholders accumulate points that can be redeemed for discounts.

Special discounts and packages may also be featured on hotel websites, especially those of the larger chains. If you don't have a computer, ask a friend who does, or go to a local Internet cafe or your public library if it offers Internet access.

In the "Amenities" section of the accommodations descriptions that follow, we mention **concierge levels** where available. In these hotels within a hotel, guests pay more to enjoy a luxurious private lounge (sometimes with great views), free continental or full breakfasts, hot and cold hors d'oeuvres served at cocktail hour, and/or late-night cordials and pastries. Rooms are usually on higher floors, and guests are pampered with special services (including private registration and checkout, a personal concierge, and nightly bed turndown) and amenities (such as upgraded toiletries, bathroom scales, terry robes, hair dryers, and more). Ask for specifics when you reserve a room.

You'll also find counselor-supervised **child care** or **activity centers** at some hotels. Very popular in Orlando, these can be marvelous, creatively run facilities that might offer movies, video games, arts and crafts, storytelling, puppet shows, indoor and outdoor activities, and more. Some provide meals and/or have beds

---

Tips **Tight Squeeze**

An average hotel or motel room in Orlando has 325 to 400 square feet and beds for four; hardly a castle, but most travelers find that adequate for a short stay. We've made a special note in the listings of properties where the rooms are substantially larger or smaller than average.

---

where a child can sleep while you're out on the town. Check individual hotel listings for these facilities.

RESERVATION SERVICES

Many of the Kissimmee hotels listed under "Places to Stay in the Kissimmee Area," found later in this chapter, can be booked through the **Kissimmee–St. Cloud Convention & Visitors Bureau** (© 800/333-5477; www.floridakiss. com). The same goes for Orlando and the **Orlando/Orange County Convention & Visitors Bureau** (© 800/643-9492; www.orlandoinfo.com).

Florida Hotel Network (© 800/293-2419; www.floridahotels.com), **Central Reservation Service** (© 800/555-7555 or 407/740-6442; www.crshotels. com), and **Hotels.com** (© 800/246-8357; www.hotels.com) are three other services that can help with room reservations and other kinds of reservations in central Florida. You can also book Disney World hotels direct by calling © 407/934-7639 or visiting **www.disneyworld.com;** Universal Orlando's properties can be booked by calling © 800/837-2273 or 407/363-8000, or surfing over to **www.universalorlando.com**.

HOW TO USE THIS CHAPTER

The hotels listed in this chapter are divided by location and price category. As you might expect, many of the inexpensive properties are the farthest from the action and/or have the most spartan accommodations.

Keep in mind, however, that this isn't one of the world's best bargain destinations. Unlike other Florida tourist areas, there are few under-$60 motels that meet the standards demanded for listing in this book. That's why we've raised the price bar. The ones in our **inexpensive** category charge an average of less than $90 per night for a double room. Those offering $90 to $180 rooms make up the **moderate** category; $180 to $250 rooms are listed as **expensive;** and anything over $250 is listed as **very expensive.** Any included extras (such as breakfast) are listed for each property. Orlando has peak and off-seasons, often with complicated boundaries. Even remote things such as Bike Week in Daytona Beach or the International Sweet Potato Growers convention in Orlando can raise off-season prices. These especially impact moderately priced properties outside WDW.

Keep in mind that rates are per night double unless otherwise noted, and they don't include hotel taxes of 11% to 12%. Also, most Orlando hotels and motels let **kids under 12 (and usually under 18) stay free** with a parent or guardian if you don't exceed maximum room occupancy. But to be safe, ask when booking a room.

1 The Perks of Staying with Mickey

The decision on whether to bunk with The Mouse is one of the first you'll have to make when planning an Orlando vacation. In the sections "Places to Stay in

Walt Disney World" and "'Official Hotels in Lake Buena Vista'" of this chapter, you'll find information on the 29 hotels, resorts, villas, timeshares, and campsites that are owned by Disney or are "official" hotels—those that are privately owned but have earned Disney's seal of approval. All 29, including two that should open before this book is revised again, are in WDW or nearby Lake Buena Vista.

In addition to their proximity to the theme parks, there are other advantages to staying at a Disney property or one of the "official" hotels. The following amenities are included at all Disney resorts, and **some** are offered by the "official" hotels, but be sure to ask when booking:

- Unlimited **free** transportation on the Walt Disney World Transportation System's buses, monorails, ferries, or water taxis to and from the four WDW parks, from 2 hours prior to opening until 2 hours after closing. **Free** transportation also is provided to and from Downtown Disney and Pleasure Island, Downtown Disney Marketplace, Typhoon Lagoon, Blizzard Beach, and the WDW resorts. Three of them—the Polynesian, Grand Floridian, and Contemporary resorts—are on the Disney monorail system. This included service can save money you might otherwise spend on a rental car, parking, and shuttles. It also means you're guaranteed admission to all of the parks, even during peak times when parking lots sometimes fill up.
- Reduced-price children's menus in most restaurants.
- Character breakfasts and/or dinners at some restaurants.
- The Extra Magic Hour (see the box "A Restored Perk," below).
- TVs equipped with the Disney Channel, nightly bedtime stories (Channel 22, 7–10pm), and WDW information stations.
- A guest services desk where you can buy tickets to all Disney parks and attractions and get information without standing in long lines at the parks.
- Playing privileges, **preferred tee times,** and, in some cases, free transport to Disney golf courses. (See "Hitting the Links" in chapter 8.)
- WDW has some of the **best swimming pools** in Orlando and recently has built new ones or remodeled old ones as zero-entry or zero-grade pools, meaning there's a gradual slope into the water on at least one side rather than only a step down. These include pools at the Grand Floridian, Animal Kingdom, and Polynesian resorts.
- Mears shuttle service access for trips to non-Disney parks and attractions (fees vary).
- On-premises National car-rental discounts (also available at the Walt Disney World Swan and Dolphin, but not at the other "official" hotels).
- The ability to purchase reduced-price Ultimate Parkhopper passes for the length of your stay. (Available at all "official" hotels as well.) The passes can offer some significant savings.
- Disney's refillable mug program lets you buy—for $8 to $11, depending on your resort—a bottomless mug for soda, coffee, tea, and/or cocoa. The offer is for the length of your stay, but it isn't transferable to the theme parks and you can only use it at the property at which it is bought, with two exceptions: Mugs are transferable between the Beach Club and Yacht Club resorts and among the three All-Star resorts.

But there are also **disadvantages** to climbing into Mickey's bed:

- The complimentary **Walt Disney World Transportation System** can be *excruciatingly slow.* Sometimes you have to take a ferry to catch a bus to get on the monorail to reach your hotel. The system makes a circuit, but may

---

Tips   A Restored Perk

Sagging attendance and revenues in 2001 caused Disney to eliminate "Surprise Mornings," a perk that let WDW resort guests into the theme parks 60 to 90 minutes before the other paying customers. But in October 2002, WDW launched its **Extra Magic Hour,** which lets resort guests into the parks an hour before other guests. At press time, the schedule was: Magic Kingdom, Sunday and Thursday; Animal Kingdom, Monday and Friday; Disney–MGM Studios, Tuesday and Saturday; and Epcot, Wednesday.

---

not necessarily take the most direct path for you. It can take an hour or more to get to a place that's right across the lagoon from you.

- Resort rates are about **20% to 30% higher** than comparable hotels and motels away from the parks.
- Without a car or another means to get off the property, you'll be a POD (prisoner of Disney) and WDW's stiff prices for meals, trinkets, and more.
- If you don't spend a little time away from the Wizard of Diz, you'll miss the real Florida.
- Mickey, MICKEY, MICKEY . . . eek! The mouse can get old after a few days, unless you take a break.

WALT DISNEY WORLD CENTRAL RESERVATIONS OFFICE & WALT DISNEY TRAVEL COMPANY

To book a room or package at Disney's resorts, campgrounds, and "official" hotels, call the **Walt Disney World Travel Company** at © 800/828-0228. You also can contact **Central Reservation Operations** (CRO), P.O. Box 10000, Lake Buena Vista, FL 32830-1000 (© 407/934-7639).

CRO and the Travel Company can recommend accommodations suited to your price range and specific needs, such as being near a particular park, facilities that offer supervised child-care centers, or a pool large enough to swim laps. But the folks who answer the phones usually don't volunteer information about a better deal or a special *unless you ask.*

Be sure to inquire about Disney's numerous package plans, which can include meals, tickets, recreation, and other features. The right package can save you money and time; but having a comprehensive game plan first is helpful in computing the cost of your vacation in advance.

CRO and the Travel Company can give you information about various theme-park ticket options, the airlines, and car rentals. They can also make dinner-show reservations for you at the resort of your choice.

OTHER SOURCES FOR PACKAGES

In addition to the Disney sources above, there are several other travel companies that offer packages utilizing Disney resorts. These include **Delta Vacations** (© 800/872-7786; www.deltavacations.com), **American Airlines Vacations** (© 800/321-2121; http://aavacations.com), and **American Express Vacations** (© 800/346-3607; http://travel.americanexpress.com/travel/personal). See "Packages for the Independent Traveler" in chapter 2 for more options. Give each a call, ask for brochures, and compare offerings to find the best package for you.

Tips **Internet Access**

WDW has installed phones with large touch screens and Internet capabilities at 65 locations in the theme parks, resorts, and elsewhere. For 25¢ a minute (4-min. minimum), you can use them to check e-mail, surf the Web, and make dining reservations from places such as the Magic Kingdom's Pirates of the Caribbean or Splash Mountain.

On a slightly smaller scale than Disney, **Universal Orlando** offers several travel packages that can include resort stays, VIP access to the parks, discounts to other Orlando attractions, and cruises. Airfare and car rentals are also available. You can book a package by calling (**800/711-0080** or 407/224-7000. On the Internet, visit **www.universalstudiosvacations.com**.

HOTEL UPS & DOWNS

There seemed to be no end to Orlando's hotel boom a few years ago. About 4,000 new rooms were added every year through 2000. Disney alone has 29 resorts, timeshares, and "official" hotels with more than 27,000 rooms and 784 campsites at Fort Wilderness. That's about 25% of the area's roster. But America's bruised economy and the September 11, 2001, terrorist attacks dealt the Mouse a major setback that lingers on. Disney's planned Pop Century resort would have added a whopping 5,760 rooms beginning in the spring of 2002, but its opening was delayed. Half those rooms are now set to open in December 2003; no word on when the rest will follow.

Still, Orlando's tourist-based economy is slowly recovering. Two major properties—the 1,000-room Royal Pacific Resort at Universal Orlando and the 450-room Crowne Plaza Orlando–Universal—have opened since this book's 2003 edition was published. And others, such as the Omni Orlando Resort and the Ritz-Carlton, are on the horizon.

2 Places to Stay in Walt Disney World

The resorts in this part are either Disney-owned or they're "official" Disney hotels that get some of the same perks. All are on the Disney Transportation System, which means those of you who don't mind being entombed in Mouseville can do without a car.

If you decide Disney is your destination, come up with a short list of preferred places to stay, then call **Walt Disney World Travel Company** ((**800/828-0228**) or WDW **Central Reservations** ((**407/934-7639**) for rates. Web wanderers can get information at **www.disneyworld.com**.

Those who come by auto will find large signs along all of the major roads on Disney property pointing the way to the various resorts. You'll find these hotels listed on the map, "Walt Disney World & Lake Buena Vista Accommodations," on p. 88.

Individual resorts don't have their own **golf courses,** but WDW has 99 holes situated along the northern end of the property (see "Hitting the Links" in chapter 8.). The same goes for kennels; resort guests can board their pets overnight at the Transportation & Ticket Center on Seven Seas Drive, near Disney's Polynesian Resort.

Prices in the following listings reflect the range available at each resort when this guide was published. Rates vary depending on season and room location, but the numbers should help you determine which places fit your budget.

VERY EXPENSIVE

Disney's Beach Club Resort ✦   This property tries to mimic a luxurious Victorian Cape Cod resort, though the Victorian gem in this world is the Grand Floridian (see below). The Beach Club is close enough to Epcot to allow health-and-fitness types to walk to the park, but most of us get enough of a workout inside the parks without having to walk to them. Stormalong Bay, a huge free-form swimming pool and water park, sprawls over 3 acres between this resort and its sister, the Yacht Club (later in this chapter). It features a 150-foot serpentine water slide. Room views range from the pool to (ugh!) the parking lot, but you'll pay a lot more to see the pool. Some rooms have balconies. The Beach Club also offers the chance to charter a reproduction of a 1930s mahogany runabout to **cruise Crescent Lake** or see Epcot's IllumiNations fireworks display (from $80.18 plus tax for up to seven people for a 30-min. cruise to $179.24 plus tax for 60 min. to catch the fireworks show, ✆ **407/824-2621** or 407/939-7529).

1800 Epcot Resorts Blvd. (off Buena Vista Dr.; P.O. Box 10000), Lake Buena Vista, FL 32830-0100. ✆ 407/934-7639 or 407/934-8000. Fax 407/934-3850. www.disneyworld.com. 583 units. $289–$660 double; $495–$2,110 suite. Extra person $25. Children 17 and under stay free in parent's room. AE, DC, DISC, MC, V. Free self-parking, $6 valet. Take I-4 east to Exit 67, Hwy. 536/Epcot Center Dr. Follow signs to WDW, then to the resort. Pets $9 a night. **Amenities:** 2 restaurants (seafood, steaks), grill, 4 lounges; 2 outdoor heated pools, kids' pool; 2 lighted tennis courts; Jacuzzi; watersports equipment; children's club; video arcade; WDW Transportation System, transportation for a fee to non-Disney theme parks; business center; salon; 24-hr. room service; babysitting; guest laundry; nonsmoking rooms. *In room:* A/C, TV, dataport, minibar, fridge ($10 a night), hair dryer, iron, safe.

Disney's Boardwalk Inn ✦✦✦   Romantics usually appreciate staying at (or at least visiting) Disney's plush 1940s-style "seaside" resort, which is set on 45 acres along Crescent Lake, close to Epcot. It's a dandy place to recapture a little bit of yesterday, whether that means kicking back in a rocker overlooking a village green or prowling the shops, restaurants, and clubs that line the resort's ¼-mile boardwalk, which really heats up after the sun goes down. Rooms are Cape Cod style; some have balconies, and corner units have a bit more space. The priciest rooms overlook the boardwalk or pool; the less expensive ones can't avoid a view of the parking lot but are sheltered from the boardwalk noise. Hang on to your swimsuit if you hit the pool's famous—or infamous, depending on how you look at it—200-foot "keister coaster" water slide. See also the reviews for the **Flying Fish Café** (p. 142) and **Spoodles** (p. 143) restaurants.

2101 N. Epcot Resorts Blvd. (off Buena Vista Dr.; P.O. Box 10000), Lake Buena Vista, FL 32830-1000. ✆ **407/934-7639** or 407/939-5100. Fax 407/934-5150. www.disneyworld.com. 378 units. $289–$675 double;

Tips New Arrival

Disney's new **Beach Club Villas** (✆ **407/934-7639** or 407/934-2175; fax 407/934-3850; www.disneyworld.com) make up a resort inspired by Cape May seaside homes of the early 20th century. The 208-room resort ($289–$449 studios, $390–$1,010 villas) is another member of the Disney Vacation Club that rents studios and 1- and 2-bedroom villas to mainstream guests when their owners are not staying on the property. The villas are close to Epcot's International Gateway.

Walt Disney World & Lake Buena Vista Accommodations

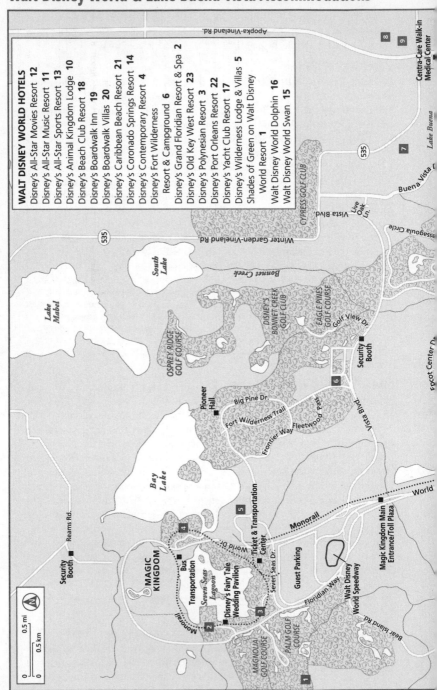

WALT DISNEY WORLD HOTELS

Disney's All-Star Movies Resort **12**
Disney's All-Star Music Resort **11**
Disney's All-Star Sports Resort **13**
Disney's Animal Kingdom Lodge **10**
Disney's Beach Club Resort **18**
Disney's Boardwalk Inn **19**
Disney's Boardwalk Villas **20**
Disney's Caribbean Beach Resort **21**
Disney's Coronado Springs Resort **14**
Disney's Contemporary Resort **4**
Disney's Fort Wilderness
 Resort & Campground **6**
Disney's Grand Floridian Resort & Spa **2**
Disney's Old Key West Resort **23**
Disney's Polynesian Resort **3**
Disney's Port Orleans Resort **22**
Disney's Yacht Club Resort **17**
Disney's Wilderness Lodge & Villas **5**
Shades of Green on Walt Disney
 World Resort **1**
Walt Disney World Dolphin **16**
Walt Disney World Swan **15**

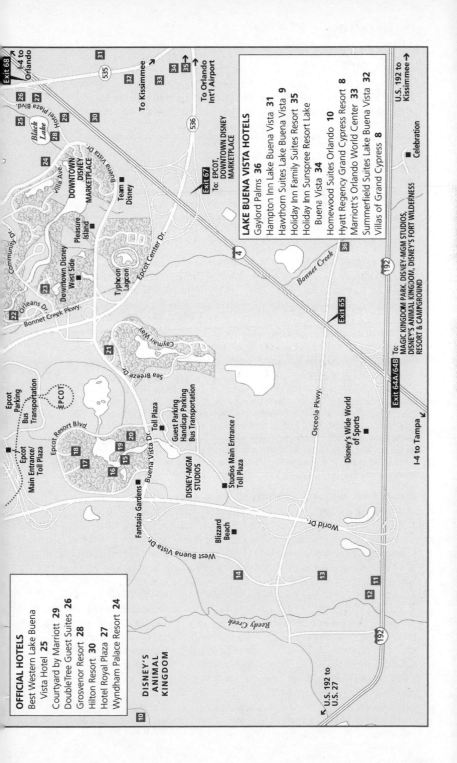

OFFICIAL HOTELS

Best Western Lake Buena Vista Hotel **25**
Courtyard by Marriott **29**
DoubleTree Guest Suites **26**
Grosvenor Resort **28**
Hilton Resort **30**
Hotel Royal Plaza **27**
Wyndham Palace Resort **24**

LAKE BUENA VISTA HOTELS

Gaylord Palms **36**
Hampton Inn Lake Buena Vista **31**
Hawthorn Suites Lake Buena Vista **9**
Holiday Inn Family Suites Resort **35**
Holiday Inn Sunspree Resort Lake Buena Vista **34**
Homewood Suites Orlando **10**
Hyatt Regency Grand Cypress Resort **8**
Marriott's Orlando World Center **33**
Summerfield Suites Lake Buena Vista **32**
Villas of Grand Cypress **8**

Exit 68
I-4 to Orlando

Hotel Plaza Blvd.

Black Lake

To Kissimmee

To Orlando Int'l Airport

Exit 67
To: EPCOT, DOWNTOWN DISNEY MARKETPLACE

DOWNTOWN DISNEY MARKETPLACE

Team Disney

Community Dr.

Villa Ave.

Orleans Dr.

Downtown Disney West Side

Pleasure Island

Typhoon Lagoon

Bonnet Creek Pkwy.

Epcot Center Dr.

Bonnet Creek

Buena Vista Dr.

Epcot Parking Bus Transportation

EPCOT

Epcot Main Entrance/Toll Plaza

Epcot Resort Blvd.

Sea Breeze Dr.

Cayman Way

Fantasia Gardens

DISNEY-MGM STUDIOS

Buena Vista Dr. Toll Plaza

Guest Parking Handicap Parking Bus Transportation

Studios Main Entrance/Toll Plaza

West Buena Vista Dr.

Blizzard Beach

World Dr.

Osceola Pkwy.

Disney's Wide World of Sports

I-4 to Tampa

Exit 64A/64B
To:
MAGIC KINGDOM PARK, DISNEY-MGM STUDIOS, DISNEY'S ANIMAL KINGDOM, DISNEY'S FORT WILDERNESS RESORT & CAMPGROUND

Exit 65

U.S. 192 to Kissimmee →

Celebration

DISNEY'S ANIMAL KINGDOM

Reedy Creek

U.S. 192 to U.S. 27

89

Tips **Sink Space**

Although Disney's resort rooms have notoriously cramped bathrooms, they all sport double sinks, usually set in a small dressing area outside the bathroom. So while you may bang your shin on the shower, at least you won't have to wait in line to brush your teeth.

$545–$2,340 suite. Extra person $25. Children 17 and under stay free in parent's room. AE, DC, DISC, MC, V. Free self-parking, valet $6. Take I-4 east to Exit 67, Hwy. 536/Epcot Center Dr. Follow signs to WDW, then to the resort. Pets $9 a night. **Amenities:** 3 restaurants (steak/seafood, Mediterranean), groceries, grill, 2 lounges, 3 clubs; 2 outdoor heated pools, kids' pool; 2 lighted tennis courts; croquet; health club; Jacuzzi; children's activity center; arcade; concierge; WDW Transportation System, transportation to non-Disney parks for a fee; business center; shopping arcade; 24-hr. room service; babysitting; guest laundry, valet; nonsmoking rooms; concierge-level rooms. *In room:* A/C, TV, dataport, fridge ($10 a night), hair dryer, iron, safe.

Disney's Boardwalk Villas ★★ Located on the same site as the Boardwalk Inn, the villas are an out-of-the-mainstream option that may make sense for those traveling in larger groups. Sold as timeshares, they're also rented to traditional tourists. Rooms range from standard-size studios and villas to 3-bedroom units with 2,100 square feet and beds for 12. Most have a balcony or patio and the same trimmings as the Boardwalk Inn, above. Larger rooms have kitchens or kitchenettes. The service is great, the location near Epcot is convenient, and the spacious rooms are nice for families traveling together.

2101 N. Epcot Resorts Blvd. (off Buena Vista Dr.; P.O. Box 10000), Lake Buena Vista, FL 32830-1000. © 407/934-7639 or 407/939-5100. Fax 407/934-5150. www.disneyworld.com. 520 units. $289–$1,915. Extra person $25. Children 17 and under stay free in parent's room. AE, DC, DISC, MC, V. Free self-parking, $6 valet. Take I-4 east to Exit 67, Hwy. 536/Epcot Center Dr. Follow signs to WDW, then to the resort. Pets $9 a night. **Amenities:** 3 restaurants (steak/seafood, Mediterranean), groceries, grill, 2 lounges, 3 clubs; 2 outdoor heated pools, kids' pool; 2 lighted tennis courts; croquet; health club; Jacuzzi; children's activity center; arcade; concierge; WDW Transportation System, transportation to non-Disney parks for a fee; business center; shopping arcade; 24-hr. room service; babysitting; guest laundry, valet; nonsmoking rooms; concierge-level rooms. *In room:* A/C, TV, dataport, kitchenette, fridge, coffeemaker, hair dryer, iron, safe, microwave.

Disney's Contemporary Resort ★ Real estate agents say three things are critical when buying property: location, Location, LOCATION. If you agree, this hotel is right beside the Magic Kingdom, and one of only three resorts on the monorail system (the Grand Floridian and Polynesian are the others). The Contemporary is also located near Disney golf courses and offers great views of the Magic Kingdom and Bay Lake. On the minus side, the 15-story, 30-year-old A-frame dates to WDW's infancy, and a complete renovation in 1999 didn't fully restore it to the same class as some of the top dogs in this price category. Room decor tends to be a bit dull and the pool is nothing special. Our verdict: It's wiser to ride the monorail through—yes, it goes straight through the resort—and get a better value for your dollars elsewhere. (Do consider sampling the 15th-floor views, though to do that, you'll have to eat at the **California Grill,** reviewed on p. 142.) If you do bunk here, the best views are from upper floors, where the rooms are a tad quieter than those on the lower floors, which are exposed to noisy public areas and the monorail.

4600 N. World Dr. (P.O. Box 10000), Lake Buena Vista, FL 32830-1000. © 407/934-7639 or 407/824-1000. Fax 407/824-3539. www.disneyworld.com. 1,041 units. $239–$545 double; $480–$2,245 suite. Extra person $25. Children 17 and under stay free in parent's room. AE, DC, DISC, MC, V. Free self-parking, $6 valet.

Take I-4 east to Exit 67, Hwy. 536/Epcot Center Dr. Follow signs to WDW, then to the resort. Pets $9 a night. **Amenities:** 3 restaurants (steak, New American, buffet), food court, 2 lounges; 2 outdoor heated pools, kids' pool; 6 lighted tennis courts; fitness center; Jacuzzi; watersports equipment; kids' club; arcade; concierge; WDW Transportation System, transportation to non-Disney parks for a fee; business center; salon; 24-hr. room service; babysitting; guest laundry, valet; nonsmoking rooms; concierge-level rooms. *In room:* A/C, TV, data-port, fridge ($10 a night), hair dryer, iron, safe.

Disney's Grand Floridian Resort & Spa ✿✿✿ *Moments* Ever thought about wandering through an F. Scott Fitzgerald novel without all the oddball personalities? The Grand Floridian may be your ticket. From the moment you step into the opulent 5-story domed lobby, you'll feel as if you've slipped back to an era that started with the late 19th century and lasted through the Roaring '20s, when a guy named Gatsby was at the top of his game. Expect tea to be served in the afternoon (4pm daily) while a piano runs the spectrum from lullabies to ragtime; then, as the evening arrives, a small, '40s-fond band takes the helm upstairs. The Floridian has become the romantic choice for couples, especially honeymooners, who like luxuriating in the first-class spa and health club—the best in WDW. The inviting Victorian-style rooms overlook a garden, pool, courtyard, or the Seven Seas Lagoon. It's one of three resorts on the monorail system and near the Magic Kingdom.

Don't miss our reviews of its top-end restaurants, **Victoria & Albert's** (p. 140) and **Citricos** (p. 140), as well as some **special programs for young aspiring cooks** (see "Pint-Sized Cuisine" on p. 142).

4401 Floridian Way (P.O. Box 10000), Lake Buena Vista, FL 32830-1000. ✆ **407/934-7639** or 407/824-3000. Fax 407/824-3186. www.disneyworld.com. 900 units. $339–$840 double; $900–$2,450 suite. Extra person $25. Children 17 and under stay free in parent's room. AE, DC, DISC, MC, V. Free self-parking, $6 valet. Take I-4 east to Exit 67, Hwy. 536/Epcot Center Dr. Follow signs to WDW, then to the resort. Pets $9 a night. **Amenities:** 5 restaurants (American, seafood), grill, 3 lounges; outdoor heated pool, kids' pool; 2 lighted tennis courts; health club; spa; watersports equipment; children's center; arcade; concierge; car-rental desk; WDW Transportation System, transportation to non-Disney parks for a fee; business center; shopping arcade; salon; 24-hour room service; babysitting; guest laundry, valet; nonsmoking rooms; concierge-level rooms. *In room:* A/C, TV, dataport, minibar, fridge ($10 a night), hair dryer, iron, safe.

Disney's Old Key West Resort ✿ An understated theme (at least by Disney standards) makes the Old Key West a good choice for those not into gingerbread overload. This resort, located between Epcot and Downtown Disney West Side, offers some of the quietest, homiest rooms on WDW property. Architecturally mirroring Key West at the turn of the 20th century, Old Key West is affiliated with the Disney Vacation Club—a timeshare program—but many units are rented when not being used by owners. The 156-acre complex has tree-lined brick walkways edged by white picket fences. Two-bedroom villas have enough beds for eight; grand villas (2,202 sq. ft.) sleep 12. Villas have whirlpool tubs. All of the accommodations sport balconies or patios, and all have kitchens or kitchenettes. *Note:* We have heard complaints about the slowness of Disney transportation to and from this resort.

1510 N. Cove Rd. (off Community Dr.; P.O. Box 10000), Lake Buena Vista, FL 32830-1000. ✆ **407/934-7639** or 407/827-7700. Fax 407/827-7710. www.disneyworld.com. 761 units. $254–$369 studio; $340–$775 1- and 2-bedroom villas; $1,040–$1,460 grand villa. Children 17 and under stay free in parent's room. AE, DC, DISC, MC, V. Free self-parking. Take I-4 east to Exit 67, Hwy. 536/Epcot Center Dr. Follow signs to WDW, then to the resort. Pets $9 a night. **Amenities:** Restaurant (American), groceries; 4 outdoor heated pools, kids' pool; 3 tennis courts (2 lighted); Jacuzzi; sauna; watersports equipment; game room; WDW Transportation System, transportation to non-Disney parks for a fee; massage; babysitting; guest laundry; nonsmoking rooms. *In room:* A/C, TV, kitchen or kitchenette, fridge, coffeemaker, hair dryer, microwave.

Disney's Polynesian Resort ⟨ Just south of the Magic Kingdom, the 25-acre Polynesian Resort bears some similarity to the South Pacific (tropical foliage, luaus, and waterfalls), but there's no denying this is Disney World thanks to Mickey's minions scurrying hither and yon. (And the monorail, which stops here, is a dead giveaway as well.) The resort's extensive play areas and themed swimming pools make it a good choice for those traveling with kids. Public areas have canvas cabanas, hammocks, and big swings overlooking a 200-acre lagoon. Most rooms accommodate five, but the bathrooms are a bit cramped. Many rooms have views of the grounds or Seven Seas Lagoon; some lagoon-view rooms offer great views of Cinderella Castle (for a price, of course), so request your desired view when making your reservation. The main knock: The guest rooms aren't much different than when they opened in the 1970s, making them well located but arguably overpriced for what's inside. See the review of the **'Ohana** restaurant on p. 144 and its **Polynesian Luau Dinner Show** on p. 297.

600 Seven Seas Dr. (P.O. Box 10000), Lake Buena Vista, FL 32830-1000. © 407/934-7639 or 407/824-2000. Fax 407/824-3174. www.disneyworld.com. 853 units. $299–$560 double; $390–$675 concierge level; $495–$2,490 suite. Extra person $25. Children 17 and under stay free in parent's room. AE, DC, DISC, MC, V. Free self-parking, $6 valet. Take I-4 east to Exit 67, Hwy. 536/Epcot Center Dr. Follow signs to WDW, then to the resort. Pets $9 a night. **Amenities:** Restaurant (Pacific Rim), cafe, 2 lounges; 2 outdoor heated pools, kids' pool; watersports equipment; children's club; arcade; concierge; WDW Transportation System, transportation to non-Disney parks for a fee; shopping arcade; 24-hr. room service; babysitting; guest laundry, valet; non-smoking rooms; concierge-level rooms. *In room:* A/C, TV, fridge ($10 a night), hair dryer, iron, safe.

Disney's Yacht Club Resort ⟨⟨ Dennis Connor and Ted Turner wouldn't be impressed, but this Yacht Club is a cut above its sister, the Beach Club (see above), because the rooms, views, service, and atmosphere are a step or so better. It's also geared more toward adults and families with older children, although young kids are catered to (this is Disney after all). The theme is a turn-of-the-20th-century New England yacht club, and the atmosphere is posh. It shares a 25-acre lake, a first-class swimming pool, and magnificent landscaping with the Beach Club. Rooms have beds for up to five and most have balconies; views run from asphalt to Crescent Lake and the gardens; you would, however, have to be a contortionist to see the lake from some of the "water-view" rooms, so if this is a must, make sure that you request one with a direct view. Epcot is a 10- to 15-minute walk from the front door, but you can save a lot of shoe leather by using Disney transports.

The Yacht Club also offers a chance to charter a reproduction of a 1930s mahogany runabout to **cruise Crescent Lake** or see Epcot's IllumiNations fireworks display (from $80.18 plus tax for up to seven people for a 30-minute cruise to $179.24 plus tax for 60 minutes to catch the fireworks show; © **407/824-2621**).

1700 Epcot Resorts Blvd. (off Buena Vista Dr.; P.O. Box 10000), Lake Buena Vista, FL 32830-1000. © 407/934-7639 or 407/934-7000. Fax 407/924-3450. www.disneyworld.com. 630 units. $289–$510 double; $425–$660 concierge level; $525–$2,290 suite. Extra person $25. Children 17 and under stay free in parent's

---

⟨ *Moments*   **A Piece of Yesterday, Today**

The *Grand 1,* the Grand Floridian's 44-foot yacht, is available for hire for groups of 2 to 12. It cruises Seven Seas Lagoon and Bay Lake, where in the evenings you can see the Magic Kingdom's Fantasy in the Sky fireworks or arrange a gourmet-dinner cruise. Voyages are $350 per hour including a captain and deck hand (© **407/824-2439**).

⌐Tips Out with the Old . . .

The **Villas at Disney Institute**—a collection of bungalows, villas, and tree-houses—is another victim of the economy. Disney plans to replace the resort in 2004 with a turn-of-the-20th-century-style timeshare complex called the **Saratoga Springs Resort Spa.** The new property will have 484 rooms, about one-third of which will be new; the others will be remodeled villas from the institute. The resort's pool area will replicate a spring with bubbles escaping from the rocks. Purchase prices for a 1-week share of the units will start at about $12,000 and reach as much as $150,000, plus maintenance fees.

---

room. AE, DC, DISC, MC, V. Free self-parking, $6 valet. Take I-4 east to Exit 67, Hwy. 536/Epcot Center Dr. Follow signs to WDW, then to the resort. Pets $9 a night. **Amenities:** 2 restaurants (steak, seafood), grill, lounge; 2 outdoor heated pools, kids' pool; 2 lighted tennis courts; Jacuzzi; watersports equipment; croquet; children's center; arcade; concierge; WDW Transportation System, transportation to non-Disney parks for a fee; business center; shopping arcade; salon; 24 hr. room service; babysitting; guest laundry, valet, nonsmoking rooms; concierge-level rooms. In room: A/C, TV, dataport, minibar, fridge ($10 a night), coffeemaker, iron, safe.

Walt Disney World Dolphin 🎭🎭   If Antonio Gaudi and Dr. Seuss applied their talents to architectural design, they might have created something like this Sheraton resort, and its sister, the Walt Disney World Swan (see below). Whimsical architect Michael Graves actually designed both hotels. This creation centers on a 27-story pyramid with two 11-story wings that are crowned by 56-foot twin dolphin sculptures that look more like the whale in *Pinocchio*. Because it isn't as theme intensive as the other Disney resorts, it's popular with business travelers and those who prefer their accommodations a little less sugary. Rooms offer views of the grounds and parts of Disney World. Corner rooms have a little more space. A freeform sculpted grotto pool with waterfalls, water slide, rope bridge, and three secluded whirlpools sprawls across 2 acres between the Dolphin and the Swan. They share a beach on Crescent Lake and a Body by Jake health club. Epcot is the nearest park. *Note:* In the fall of 2002, the Dolphin and Swan (see below) announced a multimillion-dollar expansion of the resorts' overall space, mainly an enhancement of convention and exhibition facilities, including ballroom space, but also an upgrade of room furnishings. The work is expected to take place throughout 2003 and may run later than that.

1500 Epcot Resorts Blvd. (off Buena Vista Dr.; P.O. Box 22653), Lake Buena Vista, FL 32830-2653. © 800/ 227-1500 or 407/934-4000. Fax 407/934-4884. www.swandolphin.com or www.disneyworld.com. 1,509 units. $325–$519 double; $485–$3,150 suite. Resort fee $10. Extra person $25. Children 17 and under stay free in parent's room. AE, DC, DISC, MC, V. Free self-parking, valet parking $9. Take I-4 east to Exit 67, Hwy. 536/Epcot Center Dr. Follow signs to WDW, then to the resort. Pets $9 a night. **Amenities:** 4 restaurants (steak, Mexican, American), grill, 2 lounges; 4 outdoor heated pools; 4 lighted tennis courts; health club; watersports equipment; children's center; 2 game rooms; concierge; car-rental desk; WDW Transportation System, transportation to non-Disney parks for a fee; shopping arcade; salon; 24-hr. room service; massage; babysitting; guest laundry, valet; nonsmoking rooms; concierge-level rooms. In room: A/C, TV, Nintendo, dataport, minibar, hair dryer, iron, safe.

Walt Disney World Swan 🎭🎭   Not to be outdone by the huge dolphins at its sister property, this high-rise Westin resort is topped with dual 45-foot swan statues and seashell fountains. It offers a good location—close to Epcot, Fantasia Gardens, and the Boardwalk's nightlife—and a chance to be in the WDW mainstream without being quite so bombarded by mouse decor. It shares a

---

Tips When a WDW Property Is Not a WDW Property

We told you earlier there are nine "official" Disney hotels that aren't owned by Mickey's stockholders. That's true. But there are a couple of asterisks. Walt Disney World Swan and Walt Disney World Dolphin have Uncle Walt's name and they're on mainstream WDW resort property, but they're not Disney-owned resorts, so we consider them "officials."

---

beach, health club, a number of restaurants, and other trimmings with the Dolphin (see above). The best room views are from the 11th and 12th floors' Royal Beach Club, the hotel's concierge level; the beach next to the pool offers a great view of Epcot's IllumiNations fireworks. Note that the guest rooms here are just a tad smaller than those at the Dolphin. (See note about hotel renovations at the Swan in WDW Dolphin review above.)

1200 Epcot Resorts Blvd. (off Buena Vista Dr.; P.O. Box 22786), Lake Buena Vista, FL 32830-2786. © 800/ 248-7926, 800/228-3000, or 407/934-3000. Fax 407/934-4499. www.swandolphin.com or www.disney world.com. 758 units. $325–$519 double; $485–$3,150 suite. Resort fee $10. Extra person $25. Children 17 and under stay free in parent's room. AE, DC, DISC, MC, V. Free self-parking, valet parking $9. Take I-4 east to Exit 67, Hwy. 536/Epcot Center Dr. Follow signs to WDW, then to the resort. Pets $9 a night. **Amenities:** 4 restaurants (American, Italian, Pacific Rim), grill, lounge; 4 outdoor heated pools; 4 lighted tennis courts; health club; watersports equipment; children's center; 2 game rooms; concierge; car-rental desk; WDW Transportation System, transportation to non-Disney parks for a fee; shopping arcade; salon; 24-hr. room service; massage; babysitting; guest laundry, valet; nonsmoking rooms; concierge-level rooms. _In room:_ A/C, TV, Nintendo, dataport, minibar, hair dryer, iron, safe.

EXPENSIVE

Disney's Animal Kingdom Lodge 👺 Disney's mood-setting skills are evident at its newest resort, which has the feel—with a little imagination—of an African game-reserve lodge complete with thatched roofs. The rooms follow a _kraal_ (semicircular) design that gives patient guests a view of 130 bird species and 75 giraffes, gazelles, and other grazing animals on a 30-acre savanna. (Not all rooms have savannah views—you have to pay more for that—though you can get the scenery for nothing through large picture windows in the lobby.) All lodge rooms have a balcony, complete with "mosquito netting" curtains. The rooms are quite comfortable, although the bathrooms are cramped (a problem with many of Disney's properties). Not surprisingly, this is the closest you can stay to Animal Kingdom, but almost everything else on WDW property is quite a distance away. And though families will appreciate the animals and activities for kids, the more relaxed and sedate nature of the resort makes it a good spot for couples as well.

2901 Osceola Pkwy., Bay Lake, FL 32830. © 407/934-7639 or 407/938-3000. Fax 407/939-4799. www. disneyworld.com. 1,293 units. $199–$515 double; $425–$610 concierge level; $635–$2,505 suite. Extra person $25. Children 17 and under stay free in parent's room. AE, DC, DISC, MC, V. Free self-parking, valet parking $9. Take I-4 east to Exit 67, Hwy. 536/Epcot Center Dr. Follow signs to WDW, then to the resort. Pets $9 a night. **Amenities:** 2 restaurants (African, American), lounge; outdoor heated pool; kids' pool; health club; children's center; arcade; concierge; WDW Transportation System, transportation to non-Disney parks for a fee; shopping arcade; limited room service; babysitting; guest laundry; nonsmoking rooms; concierge-level rooms. _In room:_ A/C, TV, dataport, fridge ($10 a night), hair dryer, iron, safe.

Disney's Wilderness Lodge 👺👺👺 The geyser out back, the mammoth stone hearth in the lobby, and bunk beds for the kids are just a few reasons this resort is a favorite of couples and families. The building looks like a rustic national park lodge, in part because it's patterned after the one at Yellowstone. Surrounded by 56 acres of oaks and pines, it offers a woodsy setting and is one of our favorites. If a view is important, ask for a room with a woods view. That geyser we mentioned "blows" periodically throughout the day, and the nightly electric water pageants can be viewed from the shores of Bay Lake (the pageant also passes the Fort Wilderness Resort & Campground, and the Contemporary, Polynesian, and Grand Floridian resorts). The lodge also has an immense serpentine pool. The nearest park is the Magic Kingdom, but the resort is in a remote area. The main drawback of staying: It's more difficult to access other areas via the WDW Transportation System. See our review of its **Artist Point** restaurant on p. 141. *Note:* The lodge offers a free tour touting its architecture, Wednesday through Saturday at 9am.

The 181 units at the **Villas at Disney's Wilderness Lodge** were added in November 2000. This is another Disney Vacation Club timeshare property (the Boardwalk Villas and Old Key West are others) that rents vacant rooms. It offers a more upscale experience, although you get less kitchen space here than in Old Key West. The one- and two-bedroom villas have 727 and 1,080 square feet, respectively.

901 W. Timberline Dr. (on the southwest shore of Bay Lake just east of the Magic Kingdom; P.O. Box 10000), Lake Buena Vista, FL 32830-1000. (C) 407/934-7639 or 407/938-4300. Fax 407/824-3232. www.disney world.com. 909 units. $199 $515 lodge; $279–$955 villas; $350–$475 concierge level; $720–$1,155 suite. Extra person $25. Children 17 and under stay free in parent's room. AE, DC, DISC, MC, V. Free self-parking. Take I-4 east to Exit 67, Hwy. 536/Epcot Center Dr. Follow signs to WDW, then to the resort. Pets $9 a night. **Amenities:** 2 restaurants, 2 lounges; outdoor heated pool; kids' pool; 2 Jacuzzis; watersports equipment; children's center; arcade; WDW Transportation System, transportation to non-Disney parks for a fee; limited room service; babysitting; guest laundry; nonsmoking rooms; concierge-level rooms. *In room:* A/C, TV, fridge ($10 a night), hair dryer, iron, safe.

MODERATE

Disney's Caribbean Beach Resort 𝒦   The Caribbean Beach isn't as bargain basement as the All-Star resorts (a little later in this chapter), but it still offers value for families who don't need a lot of frills or amenities. The units are grouped into five villages around a lake. (This is one of several WDW resorts that share a general layout with slightly different themes.) When booking, ask for a recently refurbished room. Even then, your party had better be into togetherness—the bathrooms are tight. The main swimming pool replicates a Spanish-style fort complete with slide. *Note:* Resort restaurants and shops are in a building quite a hike from most rooms; those in the Martinique and Trinidad North areas are closest. The nearest park is Disney–MGM Studios, but it can take 45 minutes to get there if you use the Disney Transportation System.

900 Cayman Way (off Buena Vista Dr.; P.O. Box 10000), Lake Buena Vista, FL 32830-1000. (C) **407/934-7639** or 407/934-3400. Fax 407/934-3288. www.disneyworld.com. 2,112 units. $133–$219 double. Extra person

---

⸛Tips Sitter Service

Several of the higher-priced Disney resorts—including Animal Kingdom Lodge, Beach Club, Contemporary Resort, Grand Floridian Resort & Spa, and Wilderness Lodge—have supervised kid care, usually from 4 or 4:30 pm to midnight daily ($10 or $11 per child 4–12, dinner and activities included; (C) **407/939-3463**). Disney also offers in-room sitters through **Kid's Night Out** ((C) **407/827-5444**).

$15. Children 17 and under stay free in parent's room. AE, DC, DISC, MC, V. Free self-parking. Take I-4 east to Exit 67, Hwy. 536/Epcot Center Dr. Follow signs to WDW, then to the resort. Pets $9 a night. **Amenities:** Restaurant, grill, lounge; large outdoor heated pool, 6 smaller pools in the villages, kids' pool; Jacuzzi; watersports equipment; arcade; WDW Transportation System, transportation to non-Disney parks for a fee; limited room service; babysitting; guest laundry; nonsmoking rooms. *In room:* A/C, TV, fridge ($10 a night), hair dryer, iron, safe.

Disney's Coronado Springs Resort 🕸

Here's another clone of the Disney moderate class. Were it not for exterior gingerbread and interior decor, it would be hard to tell one from another. The American Southwestern theme carries through four- and five-story hacienda–style buildings with terra-cotta tile roofs and shaded courtyards. As with most WDW properties, it has an above-par pool, in this case inspired by a Mayan temple. The rooms are identical in size to those in the Caribbean Beach Resort; don't expect to fit more than one person into the bathroom at a time. Those nearest the central public area, pool, and lobby tend to be noisier. The nearest park is Animal Kingdom, but the Coronado is at the southwest corner of WDW and a good distance from a lot of the other action.

1000 Buena Vista Dr. (near All-Star resorts and Blizzard Beach), Lake Buena Vista, FL 32830. ⒸⒷ 407/934-7639 or 407/939-1000. Fax 407/939-1003. www.disneyworld.com. 1,967 units. $133–$219 double; $275–$1,105 suite. Extra person $15. Children 17 and under stay free in parent's room. AE, DC, DISC, MC, V. Free self-parking. Take I-4 east to Exit 67, Hwy. 536/Epcot Center Dr. Follow signs to WDW, then to the resort. Pets $9 a night. **Amenities:** Restaurant, grill/food court, 2 lounges; 4 outdoor heated pools, kids' pool; health club; Jacuzzi; sauna; watersports equipment; 2 arcades; WDW Transportation System, transportation to non-Disney parks for a fee; business center; salon; limited room service; massage; babysitting; guest laundry; nonsmoking rooms. *In room:* A/C, TV, dataport, fridge ($10 a night), hair dryer, iron, safe.

Disney's Port Orleans Resort 🕸 ⓥalue

It's one of our favorite resorts based on value, location, and lower-decibel level, and Disney has returned it to being **two resorts in one:** the French Quarter and Riverside. Overall, this New Orleans–style resort offers some romantic spots and is relatively quiet, making it popular with couples. Port Orleans has the best location, landscaping, and, perhaps, the coziest atmosphere of the resorts in this class—but it's still a clone of the others. (The rooms and bathrooms aren't claustrophobia-inducing, but are a tight fit for four people.) Be sure to ask for a recently refurbished room. The Doubloon Lagoon pool is a family favorite, with a water slide that curves out of a dragon's mouth. Port Orleans is just east of Epcot and Disney–MGM Studios.

2201 Orleans Dr. (off Bonnet Creek Pkwy.; P.O. Box 10000), Lake Buena Vista, FL 32830-1000. ⒸⒷ 407/934-7639, 407/934-5000 (French Quarter), or 407/934-6000 (Riverside). Fax 407/934-5353 (French Quarter) or 407/934-5777 (Riverside). www.disneyworld.com. 3,056 units. $133–$219 double. Extra person $15. Children 17 and under stay free in parent's room. AE, DC, DISC, MC, V. Free self-parking. Take I-4 east to Exit 67, Hwy. 536/Epcot Center Dr. Follow signs to WDW, then to the individual resorts. Pets $9 a night. **Amenities:** Restaurant (American), food court, lounge; 2 outdoor heated pools, kids' pools; Jacuzzi; watersports equipment; arcade; WDW Transportation System, transportation to non-Disney parks for a fee; limited room service; babysitting; guest laundry; nonsmoking rooms. *In room:* A/C, TV, fridge ($10 a night), hair dryer, iron, safe.

Shades of Green on Walt Disney World Resort 🕸 ⓥalue

While most resorts were suffering under the 2001 economic downturn, occupancy here was so high that the U.S. Army announced a $50 million expansion that will double its room count by 2003. Shades of Green is open only to folks in the military and their spouses, military retirees and widows, 100% disabled veterans, and Medal of Honor recipients. If you qualify, don't think of staying anywhere else—it's the best bargain on WDW soil. In its past life, this resort was the Disney Inn. It's nestled among three of Disney's golf courses, near the Magic Kingdom. All of the rooms have balconies or patios and offer pool or golf-course views. Transportation—though slow—is available to all of the Disney parks and attractions. *Note:* Shades of Green is scheduled to reopen in fall 2003. In the meantime, guest who'd qualify for a stay at the hotel can get accommodations at the Contemporary Resort in the North Garden Wing for the same price as a room at Shades of Green.

1950 W. Magnolia Dr. (across from the Polynesian Resort). ℭ **888/593-2242** or 407/824-3400. Fax: 407/824-3665. www.shadesofgreen.org. 587 units. $66–$109 double (based on military rank). Extra person $10. Children 17 and under stay free in parent's room. AE, DC, DISC, MC, V. Take I-4 east to Exit 67, Hwy. 536/Epcot Center Dr. Follow signs to WDW, then to the resort. Pets $9 a night. **Amenities:** 2 restaurants (American, Italian), 2 lounges; 2 heated outdoor pools, kids' pool; 2 lighted tennis courts; arcade; activities desk; WDW Transportation System, transportation to non-Disney parks for a fee; babysitting; guest laundry, nonsmoking rooms. *In room:* A/C, TV, coffeemaker, hair dryer, iron, safe.

INEXPENSIVE

Disney's All-Star Movies Resort   Most kids love the larger-than-life themes at the three All-Star resorts, but most adults need dark glasses and Thorazine to combat the visual overload. Still, the themes—in this case, giant cartoon characters such as Buzz Lightyear—serve a designed Disney purpose: They mask a 21st-century rendition of a 1950s Holiday Inn. The rooms are spartan and very small: 260 square feet. (Disney tries to make them look larger by using smaller than normal furniture.) Speaking of small, wait until you step into the bathroom. Don't think about opening the door while one of your roommates is on the commode, or you might break his or her kneecaps. And the soundproofing leaves something to be desired. Like its two siblings (listed next), the All-Star Movies Resort is buried in WDW's southwest corner to avoid frightening the higher-paying guests. If, like the White Rabbit, you're often "late for a very important date," rent a car if you stay in All-Star land.

1991 W. Buena Vista Dr., Lake Buena Vista, FL 32830-1000. ℭ **407/934-7639** or 407/939-7000. Fax 407/939-7111. www.disneyworld.com. 1,900 units. $77–$124 double. Extra person $10. Children 17 and under stay free in parent's room. AE, DC, DISC, MC, V. Free self-parking. Take I-4 east to Exit 67, Hwy. 536/Epcot Center Dr. Follow signs to WDW, then to the resort. Pets $9 a night. **Amenities:** Food court, lounge; 2 outdoor heated pools, kids' pool; arcade; WDW Transportation System, transportation to non-Disney parks for a fee; limited room service; babysitting; guest laundry; nonsmoking rooms. *In room:* A/C, TV, dataport, fridge ($10 a night), safe.

Disney's All-Star Music Resort   Giant trombones and musical themes from jazz to calypso can't hide the fact that this is a clone of the All-Star Movies Resort (see the preceding listing). Tiny rooms and cramped bathrooms, where an opening door can cause injury, are the norm again. But rooms in this class do have perks: They're more than $50 a night (and in some cases hundreds of dollars) cheaper than Disney's other resorts. As for size, a lot of folks don't come to lounge in a room, so if you're only going to be inside to sleep, the cramped quarters may not matter. The closest activities are the Blizzard Beach Water Park and Animal Kingdom, which you can reach (not necessarily in an expedient manner) via the Disney Transportation System.

Tips   **Value in the Eyes of the Beholder**

Disney's All-Star resorts added a "preferred room" rate in 2002, but don't expect much for the top rate of $124—$15 more than the previous high. Guests who book it are paying for location: Preferred rooms are closer to the pools, food court, and/or transportation.

1801 W. Buena Vista Dr. (at World Dr. and Osceola Pkwy.; P.O. Box 10000), Lake Buena Vista, FL 32830-1000. ℂ **407/934-7639** or 407/939-6000. Fax 407/939-7222. www.disneyworld.com. 1,920 units. $77–$124 double. Extra person $10. Children 17 and under stay free in parent's room. AE, DC, DISC, MC, V. Free self-parking. Take I-4 east to Exit 67, Hwy. 536/Epcot Center Dr. Follow signs to WDW, then to the resort. Pets $9 a night. **Amenities:** Food court, lounge; 2 outdoor heated pools, kids' pool; arcade; WDW Transportation System, transportation to non-Disney parks for a fee; limited room service; babysitting; guest laundry; nonsmoking rooms. *In room:* A/C, TV, dataport, fridge ($10 a night), safe.

Disney's All-Star Sports Resort   Yogi Berra said it best: "It's déjà vu all over again." It's a different theme, but the same routine: tight quarters like those in the All-Star Movies and Music resorts, listed above. Rooms here are housed in buildings designed around football, baseball, basketball, tennis, and surfing motifs. For instance, the turquoise surf buildings have waves along the roofs, surfboards mounted on exterior walls, and pink fish swimming along balcony railings. (Again, if your threshold for visual overload is low, you may need to visit a sanatorium once you've left this La-La Land.) *One last warning:* The rates and themes tempt lots of families with little kids and the noise level can get very high, so if you're looking for a quiet vacation or romantic getaway, steer clear of these resorts.

1701 W. Buena Vista Dr. (at World Dr. and Osceola Pkwy.; P.O. Box 10000), Lake Buena Vista, FL 32830-1000. ℂ **407/934-7639** or 407/939-5000. Fax 407/939-7333. www.disneyworld.com. 1,920 units. $77–$124 double. Extra person $10. Children 17 and under stay free in parent's room. AE, DC, DISC, MC, V. Free parking. Take I-4 east to Exit 67, Hwy. 536/Epcot Center Dr. Follow signs to WDW, then to the resort. Pets $9 a night. **Amenities:** Food court, lounge; 2 outdoor heated pools, kids' pool; arcade; WDW Transportation System, transportation to non-Disney parks for a fee; limited room service; babysitting; guest laundry; nonsmoking rooms. *In room:* A/C, TV, dataport, fridge ($10 a night), safe.

A DISNEY CAMPGROUND

Disney's Fort Wilderness Resort & Campground ⍟   Pines, cypress trees, lakes, and streams surround this woodsy 780-acre resort. The biggest knock against it is that it's quite a distance from Epcot, Disney–MGM Studios, and Animal Kingdom. But it's close to the Magic Kingdom, and if you're a true outdoors type, you may want to be sheltered from some of the Mickey madness. There are 784 campsites for RVs, pull-behind campers, and tents (110/220-volt outlets, grills, and comfort areas with showers and restrooms).

Some sites are open to pets—at an additional cost of $3 per site, not per pet, which is cheaper than using the WDW resort kennel, where you pay $9 per pet. The 408 wilderness cabins (actually trailers) offer 504 square feet, enough for six people once you pull down the Murphy beds, and they also have kitchens. Cabins feature an outside deck with grill. Nearby Pioneer Hall is home to the popular **Hoop-Dee-Doo Musical Revue,** which we review on p. 296.

3520 N. Fort Wilderness Trail (P.O. Box 10000), Lake Buena Vista, FL 32830-1000. ℂ **407/934-7639** or 407/824-2900. Fax 407/824-3508. www.disneyworld.com. 784 campsites, 408 wilderness cabins. $35–$82 campsite double; $229–$329 wilderness cabin double. Extra person $2 campsites, $5 cabins. Children 17 and

---

⟨Tips⟩ Getting Away

If you want to be on Disney soil but put some distance between you and the madness, Mickey's timeshare arm, the Disney Vacation Club, offers the option of renting a room 2 hours south at its **Vero Beach Resort** on the Atlantic Ocean. Studios, standard motel-style rooms, one- and two-bedroom villas, and three-bedroom cottages are available ($165–$1,105 per night double), but you'll need to arrange your own transportation (ℂ **407/939-7775**; www.dvcresorts.com).

Tips Coming Soon . . . Maybe

The **Pop Century Resort** was to open in early 2002, but reduced revenues caused by the weak economy froze construction and delayed the opening; half of the resort's 5,760 rooms are now set to open on Dec. 14, 2003. The rooms are classified in Disney's **inexpensive** ($77–$124) category. Much like the All-Star resorts, Pop Century will have themes, in this case decade-long capsules of the 20th century. These will be divided into two half-century categories: The Legendary Years (1900s–40s) and the Classic Years (1950s–90s).

---

under stay free with parent. AE, DC, DISC, MC, V. Free self-parking. Take I-4 east to Exit 67, Hwy. 536/Epcot Center Dr. Follow signs to WDW, then to the resort. **Amenities:** 2 restaurants (American), grill, lounge; 2 outdoor heated pools, kids' pool; 2 lighted tennis courts; watersports equipment; outdoor activities (fishing; horseback, pony, and hay rides; campfire programs); 2 game rooms; WDW Transportation System, transportation to non-Disney parks for a fee; babysitting; guest laundry; nonsmoking homes. _In room (cabins only):_ A/C, TV/VCR, kitchen, fridge, coffeemaker, outdoor grill, hair dryer.

3 "Official" Hotels in Lake Buena Vista

These properties, designated "official" Walt Disney World hotels, are located on and around Hotel Plaza Boulevard, which puts them at the northeast corner of WDW. They're close to Downtown Disney Marketplace, Downtown Disney West Side, and Pleasure Island. The boulevard has been landscaped with enough greenery to make it a contestant for Main Street, U.S.A. (if it weren't for tons of autos spewing exhaust at the joggers and walkers using its sidewalks).

Guests at these hotels enjoy some WDW privileges (see "The Perks of Staying with Mickey," earlier in this chapter), including free bus service to the parks and the ability to purchase discounted length-of-stay passes, but **be sure when booking** to ask which privileges you get, because they vary from hotel to hotel and, sometimes, year to year. Their locations spare you from some of the Mickey mania, but the boulevard's high-speed traffic causes some of its own irritation. Also note that the Walt Disney World Dolphin and Walt Disney World Swan (listed in the previous section) should be considered the eighth and ninth "official" hotels, because they're not Disney-owned. The difference is they're on the mainstream property.

Another perk of the "official" hotels is that they generally have less relentless Disneyesque themes, although some do offer character breakfasts a few days each week (ask the person answering the reservation line for details and schedules). Decide for yourself if that's a plus or a minus.

You can make reservations for all of the below-listed properties through Central Reservations Operations (© **407/934-7639**) or through the hotel numbers included in the listings. However, to ensure you get the best rates, call each hotel or its parent chain to see if there are specials available.

You'll find all of these hotels located on the map "Walt Disney World & Lake Buena Vista Accommodations," earlier in this chapter.

EXPENSIVE

Wyndham Palace Resort 🏰🏰   This hotel is the most upscale of the Hotel Plaza Boulevard–area properties and is popular with leisure travelers, though business people make up 75% of its guests. For that reason, some of the best rates are offered in July and August, contrary to the mainstream tourist resorts. Many of the upscale business-standard rooms have balconies or patios; ask for one above the fifth floor with a "recreation view." That's the side facing the Wyndham's pools, Downtown Disney, Pleasure Island (with its brief midnight fireworks), and, in the distance, Disney–MGM Studios' Tower of Terror. With the exception of the 9pm IllumiNations fireworks, the "Epcot view" offers little to see except the parking lot and distant woodlands. A better place to catch those fireworks is in the lounge at **Arthur's 27,** the resort's signature restaurant (p. 146). The resort is known for its spacious fitness center and full-service European-style spa (massage, wraps, steam room, saunas, salon, fitness center, and more), which are open to the public.

1900 Buena Vista Dr. (just north of Hotel Plaza Blvd.; P.O. Box 22206), Lake Buena Vista, FL 32830. © **800/ 996-3426** or 407/827-2727. Fax 407/827-6034. www.wyndham.com/hotels/MCOPV/main.wnt. 1,014 units. $179–$398 double; $289–$749 suite. Resort fee $8. Extra person $20. Children 17 and under stay free in parent's room. AE, DC, DISC, MC, V. Free self-parking, valet parking $10. From I-4, take Exit 68, Hwy. 535/Apopka–Vineland Rd., north to Hotel Plaza Blvd. and go left. At third stoplight, turn right onto Buena Vista Dr. It's the first hotel on the right. **Amenities:** 2 restaurants (Continental, steak), grill, 4 lounges; 3 outdoor heated pools, kids' pool; 3 lighted tennis courts; half basketball court; sand volleyball court; spa; Jacuzzi; sauna; children's center; arcade; concierge; complimentary bus service to WDW parks, transportation for a fee to non-Disney parks; salon; 24-hr. room service; massage; babysitting; guest laundry, valet; non-smoking rooms; concierge-level rooms. *In room:* A/C, TV w/pay movies, dataport, minibar, coffeemaker, hair dryer, iron.

MODERATE

Best Western Lake Buena Vista Hotel ⭐ *Value* This 12-acre lakefront hotel is reasonably modern, with nicer rooms and public areas than you might find in others within the chain. Rooms are located in an 18-story tower, and all have balconies. The views improve from the 8th floor and up, and those on the west side have a better chance of seeing something Disney, even though the hotel is nearly as far northeast as the DoubleTree (listed below). The hotel's 18th-floor lounge, Toppers, offers an excellent view of the Magic Kingdom's fireworks. Accommodations in this category are usually a step above the "moderates" inside WDW, and this one is not an exception.

You can reserve an oversized room (about 20% larger) or WDW fireworks-view room for $15 more a night. You can also get the same rooms with full American breakfast for up to four people for $20 more per night. If you're in a quartet, it's a reasonably good deal; if not, buy breakfast elsewhere. *Note:* It definitely pays to surf the corporate website at **www.bestwestern.com** if you plan to stay here. It sometimes offers great deals and special rates for this hotel.

2000 Hotel Plaza Blvd. (between Buena Vista Dr. and Apopka–Vineland Rd./Hwy. 535), Lake Buena Vista, FL 32830. © **800/348-3765** or 407/828-2424. Fax 407/828-8933. www.orlandoresorthotel.com. 325 units. $99–$159 standard for 4; $199–$399 suite. Resort fee $5. 5th person $15. AE, DC, DISC, MC, V. Free self-parking. From I-4, take Exit 68, Hwy. 535/Apopka–Vineland Rd., north to Hotel Plaza Blvd. and go left. It's the first hotel on the right. **Amenities:** Restaurant (American), grill; outdoor heated pool, kids' pool; guest

---

⟨Tips **Yet Another Add-On**

Several of the properties in this chapter add resort fees to their daily room rates. That's part of a growing hotel trend of charging for services that used to be included in the rates, such as use of the pool, admission to the health club, or in-room coffee. If it's a concern, ask if your hotel charges such a fee when booking so you don't get blindsided at checkout.

services desk; complimentary bus service to WDW parks, transportation for a fee to non-Disney parks; limited room service; guest laundry; nonsmoking rooms. *In room:* A/C, TV w/pay movies, Nintendo, coffeemaker, hair dryer, iron, safe.

Courtyard by Marriott *Value*   This moderately priced member of the Marriott chain is popular with families. The best things we can say about it: The inner and outer glass elevators provide a free thrill ride, it's in a good location, and the price is pretty—well—decent. That said, we'd stay at several of the other "official" hotels—notably the Wyndham Palace or DoubleTree Guest Suites—first. Furthermore, by this chain's standards, we'd rather be at the Marriott Village at Little Lake Bryan (see "Other Lake Buena Vista Area Hotels," on p. 102). If you come here, ask for a room on floors 8 to 14 on the hotel's west side for a view of the Magic Kingdom and fireworks.

1805 Hotel Plaza Blvd. (between Lake Buena Vista Dr. and Apopka–Vineland Rd./Hwy. 535), Lake Buena Vista, FL 32830. ℂ **800/223-9930** or 407/828-8888. Fax 407/827-4626. www.courtyardorlando.com. 323 units. $99–$229 double. AE, DC, DISC, MC, V. Free self-parking. From I-4, take Exit 68, Hwy. 535/Apopka–Vineland Rd., north to Hotel Plaza Blvd. and go left. It's the third hotel on the left. **Amenities:** Restaurant (American), 2 lounges; 2 outdoor heated pools; kids' pool; Jacuzzi; arcade; guest services desk; complimentary bus service to WDW parks, transportation for a fee to non-Disney parks; car-rental desk; limited room service; guest laundry; nonsmoking rooms. *In room:* A/C, TV w/pay movies, Nintendo, coffeemaker, hair dryer, iron, safe.

DoubleTree Guest Suites *Kids*   Children have their own check-in desk and theater, and they get a gift upon arrival at this hotel, the best of the "official" hotels for families traveling with little ones. Adults may find some of the public areas lacking in personality—this is, after all, Mickeyville. But all of the accommodations in this seven-story hotel are two-room suites that offer 643 square feet—large by most standards—and there's space for up to six to catch some zzzzs. Ask for a recently refurbished room as we've heard reports of uneven quality. This is the easternmost of the "officials," which means it's farthest from the other Disney action, but closest to (even within walking distance of) the free-world (read, moderately priced) shops in the Crossroads Shopping Center on Apopka–Vineland Road. If the idea of a child-oriented resort appeals to you, also check out the Holiday Inn Family Suites and Holiday Inn Sunspree listed later in this chapter. They're off WDW property, but they're comparably priced, or lower, and offer more for kids.

2305 Hotel Plaza Blvd. (just west of Apopka–Vineland Rd./Hwy. 535), Lake Buena Vista, FL 32830. ℂ **800/222-8733** or 407/934-1000. Fax 407/934-1015. www.doubletreeguestsuites.com. 229 units. $119–$249 double. Extra person $20. Children 17 and under stay free in parent's room. AE, DC, DISC, MC, V. Free self-parking. From I-4, take Exit 68, Hwy. 535/Apopka–Vineland Rd., north to Hotel Plaza Blvd. and go left. It's the first hotel on the left. **Amenities:** Restaurant (American), 2 lounges; outdoor heated pool, kids' pool; 2 lighted tennis courts; arcade; concierge; car-rental desk; complimentary bus service to WDW parks, transportation for a fee to non-Disney parks; limited room service; guest laundry; nonsmoking rooms. *In room:* A/C, TV, dataport, fridge, coffeemaker, hair dryer, iron, safe, microwave.

Grosvenor Resort *Overrated*   This lakeside resort is within walking distance of Downtown Disney Marketplace's shops. The high-rise with low-rise wings has a British Colonial look and public areas that make for wonderful "we-stayed-here" snapshots. Unfortunately, the rooms are a hit-or-miss proposition. We've gotten complaints and have seen a couple of examples of rooms in need of refurbishing. Nevertheless, its frequent package deals make it popular with budget travelers, so if you choose to stay here, our best advice is to complain to the front desk if you get a dud. Ask for a Tower Room on the west side (floors 9–19) for a limited view of Lake Buena Vista. A Saturday night mystery dinner theater ($39.95 adults, $10.95 kids 3–9) is held in the Baskerville's restaurant.

1850 Hotel Plaza Blvd. (just east of Buena Vista Dr.), Lake Buena Vista, FL 32830. ✆ 800/624-4109 or 407/828-4444. Fax 407/828-8192. www.grosvenorresort.com. 626 units. $119–$199 double. Extra person $15. Children 17 and under stay free in parent's room. AE, DC, DISC, MC, V. Free self-parking, valet parking $8. From I-4, take Exit 68, Hwy. 535/Apopka–Vineland Rd., north to Hotel Plaza Blvd. and go left. It's the second hotel on the right. **Amenities:** 2 restaurants (American), 3 lounges; 2 outdoor heated pools; 2 lighted tennis courts; fitness center; Jacuzzi; concierge; car-rental desk; complimentary bus service to WDW parks, transportation for a fee to non-Disney parks; babysitting; guest laundry; nonsmoking rooms. *In room:* A/C, TV w/pay movies and VCR, dataport, coffeemaker, safe.

Hilton Resort ⚐

You can't stay any closer to the shops at Downtown Disney Marketplace. Renovations done from 1998 to 2002 modernized this resort's public areas—including the addition of a Disney Store—and many of its rooms. If there is a knock, it's that its rack rates put it at the high end of a category where you can stay comfortably and for less elsewhere on the Boulevard. That said, business travelers are its mainstay. The Hilton is a low-profile landing zone, but from the 6th through 10th floors on the north and west sides, you'll find a view of Downtown Disney and, in the distance, the Magic Kingdom fireworks. All things considered, including value received and location, the Hilton ranks in the middle of the "official" hotel field.

1751 Hotel Plaza Blvd. (just east of Buena Vista Dr.), Lake Buena Vista, FL 32830. ✆ 800/782-4414 or 407/827-4000. Fax 407/827-3890. www.hilton.com/hotels/ORLDWHH/index.html. 814 units. $179–$329 double; $299–$1,500 suite. Resort fee $8. Extra person $20. Children 17 and under stay free in parent's room. AE, DC, DISC, MC, V. Free self-parking, valet parking $8. From I-4, take Exit 68, Hwy. 535/Apopka–Vineland Rd., north to Hotel Plaza Blvd. and go left. It's the fourth hotel on the left. **Amenities:** 3 restaurants (Seafood, Japanese/steak), deli, 3 lounges; 2 outdoor heated pools; kids' pool; fitness center; Jacuzzi; sauna; children's center; arcade; concierge; car-rental desk; complimentary bus to WDW parks, transportation for a fee to non-Disney parks; business center; shopping arcade; salon; 24-hour room service; babysitting; guest laundry; nonsmoking rooms, concierge-level rooms. *In room:* A/C, TV w/pay movies, dataport, minibar, coffeemaker, hair dryer, iron.

Hotel Royal Plaza ⚐

The Plaza is one of the boulevard's originals, but renovations over its 25 years (its most recent makeover was 3 years ago) have kept it in relatively good shape. A favorite with the budget-minded, its hallmark is a friendly staff that provides good service. Poolside rooms have balconies and patios; the tower rooms have separate sitting areas, and some offer whirlpool tubs in the bathrooms. If you want a view from up high, ask for a room facing west and WDW; the south and east sides keep a watchful eye on I-4 traffic.

1905 Hotel Plaza Blvd. (between Buena Vista Dr. and Apopka–Vineland Rd./Hwy. 535), Lake Buena Vista, FL 32830. ✆ 800/248-7890 or 407/828-2828. Fax 407/827-6338. www.royalplaza.com. 394 units. $119–$235 double; $159–$695 suite. Resort fee $7. Extra person $15. Children 17 and under stay free in parent's room. AE, DC, DISC, MC, V. Free self-parking, valet parking $8. From I-4, take Exit 68, Hwy. 535/Apopka–Vineland Rd., north to Hotel Plaza Blvd. and go left. It's the second hotel on the left. **Amenities:** Restaurant (American), lounge; outdoor heated pool; 4 lighted tennis courts; fitness center; Jacuzzi; guest services desk; complimentary bus service to WDW parks, transportation for a fee to non-Disney parks; limited room service; guest laundry; nonsmoking rooms. *In room:* A/C, TV w/pay movies and VCR, dataport, minibar, coffeemaker, hair dryer, iron, safe.

4 Other Lake Buena Vista Area Hotels

The hotels in this section are within a few minutes' drive of the WDW parks. They offer a great location, but not Disney-related privileges given to guests in the "official" hotels, such as Disney bus service and character breakfasts. On the flip side, because you're not paying for those privileges, hotels in this category are generally a shade cheaper for comparable rooms and services.

Note: These hotels are also listed on the "Walt Disney World & Lake Buena Vista Accommodations" map in this chapter.

VERY EXPENSIVE

Gaylord Palms 🎯🎯   Central Florida's newest star is a convention center, but it appeals to vacationers, too. Its entertainment, recreation, dining, and other amenities turn some guests into willing prisoners of this property—with the exception of time pledged to the theme parks. The Gaylord's 4½-acre, 140-foot-high atrium has a glass dome and miniature version of the Castillo de San Marcos, the old fort at St. Augustine. (We know one knowledgeable traveler who likens it to a Vegas resort sans casino. And another wonders, with all that glass, what the atrium's air conditioning bill is in August!)

The resort and its rooms are divided into themes: Emerald Bay, a 362-room hotel within the hotel, has an elegant air; St. Augustine captures the essence of America's oldest city; Key West delivers the laid-back ambience of Florida's southernmost city; and the Everglades uses a misty swamp, snarling faux gator, fiber-optic fireflies, and tin-roofed shanties to muster a wild-and-wooly air. All the guest rooms are business standard—read: comfortable but bland—except for those in Emerald Bay, which offers doggone nice rooms that fall just short of luxurious. The kids' pool has an octopus slide, and cabanas at the adult pool have Internet access. And if you need to unwind further, try the 20,000-square-foot Canyon Ranch Spa Club. Our biggest gripe: Room-to-room and room-to-hall soundproofing should be better in this classy resort.

6000 Osceola Pkwy., Kissimmee, FL 34747. 🕐 877/677-9352 or 407/586-0000. Fax 407/239-4822. www.gaylordpalms.com. 1,406 units. $169–$460. Resort fee $10. Extra adult $20. Children under 18 stay free in parent's room. AE, DC, DISC, MC, V. Free self-parking, valet parking $12. Take I-4 Exit 65/Osceola Pkwy. east to the hotel. **Amenities:** 3 restaurants (steaks, seafood, buffet), 4 lounges; 2 outdoor heated pools; 2 whirlpools; fitness center; spa; children's center; concierge; tour desk; car-rental desk; free transportation to Disney parks, transportation for a fee to non-Disney parks; business center; shopping arcade; salon; room service; massage; babysitting; dry cleaning; nonsmoking rooms; concierge-level rooms. *In room:* A/C, TV w/pay movies and PlayStation, dataport, computer screens and keyboards, coffeemaker, hair dryer, iron, safe.

Hyatt Regency Grand Cypress Resort 🎯🎯🎯 *(Finds* A favorite of those seeking a resort vacation without Mickey Mouse extras, this romantic getaway's lobby has lush foliage and several colorful birds, including a macaw named Lulu that waves to passersby. The 18-story atrium has inner and outer glass elevators (ride the outers to the roof for a panoramic rush). The rooms on the west side, floors seven and up, have a distant view of Disney's Contemporary Resort, Space Mountain, Cinderella Castle, and the Magic Kingdom fireworks. (This vantage point also shows how much of WDW and the surrounding area remains wooded.) The Hyatt shares a golf club and academy, racquet club, and equestrian center with its sister, the Villas of Grand Cypress (see below); both offer excellent packages aimed at the sports set. The Hyatt's half-acre **800,000-gallon pool** is one of the best in Orlando and features caves, grottoes, waterfalls, and a 45-foot water slide. **Hemingway's,** its signature restaurant (p. 147), has a Key West theme and a menu featuring seafood.

1 N. Jacaranda (off Hwy. 535), Orlando, FL 32836. 🕐 800/233-1234 or 407/239-1234. Fax 407/239-3837. www.hyattgrandcypress.com. 750 units. $239–$585 double; $395–$5,750 suite. Optional resort fee (includes health club, free local calls, daily newspaper, and in-room coffee). Extra person $25. Children 18 and under stay free in parent's room. AE, DC, DISC, MC, V. Free self-parking, valet parking $12. Take I-4 Exit 68, Hwy. 535/Apopka–Vineland Rd., north, then left at second traffic light after ramp light onto Hwy. 535. It's on the right. **Amenities:** 4 restaurants (American, seafood, steaks), deli/general store, 4 lounges; large outdoor

heated pool; 45 holes of golf; 12 tennis courts (5 lighted); 2 racquetball courts; spa; health club; watersports equipment; children's center; arcade; concierge; free Disney shuttle, transportation to non-Disney parks for a fee; car-rental desk; salon; 24-hr. room service; massage (in-room); babysitting; guest laundry, valet; nonsmoking rooms; concierge-level rooms. *In room:* A/C, TV, dataport, minibar, hair dryer, iron, safe.

Villas of Grand Cypress 🅐🅐🅐 *(Finds)* Looking for something closer to an upscale, gated community? If money isn't an object, we believe this is *the best place to camp in Orlando.* At its "modest" end, this Mediterranean-inspired resort starts with standard-size rooms with Roman tubs and patios, many of them backing up to ponds whose inhabitants include mallards, soft-shelled turtles, and largemouth bass eager for bread crusts or whatever else you can spare. Floor plans progress to elegant one- to four-bedroom villas that reach about 1,100 square feet on the top end. Some include kitchens, dining rooms, and patios. The resort shares a golf club and academy, racquet club, and equestrian center with the Hyatt Regency Grand Cypress Resort (see above), and its signature eatery, the **Black Swan,** is one of the area's better restaurants (p. 147). Inside the resort, you're almost completely sheltered from the insanity of Disney, which lies only a few hundred yards away. Take some time to wander the lush grounds, which are dotted with lakes, bougainvillea, and hibiscus. There also are walking and jogging trails ranging from .6 to 3.4 miles. Shuttle buses allow you to park your car and get around the resort and the nearby theme parks without driving.

1 N. Jacaranda (off Hwy. 535), Orlando, FL 32836. ℂ 800/835-7377 or 407/239-4700. Fax 407/239-7219. www.grandcypress.com. 146 villas. $215–$500 club suite; $315–$2,000 1- to 4-bedroom villa. Resort fee $10. 1 extra person over the room limit stays free. Children 17 and under stay free in parent's room. AE, DC, DISC, MC, V. Free self-parking. Take I-4 Exit 68, Hwy. 535/Apopka–Vineland Rd., north, then left at second traffic light (after ramp light) onto Hwy. 535. It's on the right. **Amenities:** 2 restaurants (American/Continental), 2 lounges; outdoor heated pool; 45 holes of golf; 12 tennis courts (5 lighted); 2 racquetball courts; spa; health club; watersports equipment; children's center; arcade; concierge; free Disney shuttle, transportation to non-Disney parks for a fee; car-rental desk; salon; 24-hr. room service; massage (in-room); babysitting; guest laundry; nonsmoking rooms; concierge-level rooms. *In room:* A/C, TV, dataport, minibar, hair dryer, iron, safe.

EXPENSIVE

Marriott's Orlando World Center 🅐 Golf, tennis, and spa lovers will find plenty to do at this sprawling 230-acre resort, whose centerpiece is a 28-story

---

Tips **Marriott Montage**

The December 2000 christening of **Marriott Village at Little Lake Bryan,** 8623 Vineland Ave., Orlando, FL 32821 (ℂ 877/682-8552 or 407/938-9001; fax 407/938-9002; www.marriottvillage.com), brought together three of the flagship's properties in a cluster just east of Lake Buena Vista, 3 miles from WDW. The resort includes a 400-room SpringHill Suites ($129–$179 double), a 388-room Fairfield Inn ($119–$169 double), and a 312-room Courtyard by Marriott ($139–$179 double). Children under 17 stay free in parent's room, and an extra person costs an additional $10.

All rooms have fridges. Each property has adult and kids' pools, fitness centers, kids' clubs, whirlpools, and guest services desks. All offer transportation for a fee ($10–$12 per person per day) to Disney parks and non-Disney parks. There are three restaurants within walking distance. To get there, take I-4 Exit 68, Hwy. 535/Apopka–Vineland Rd., then head south to Vineland, and go left a ½ mile to the village. There's free self-parking, and valet parking costs $8.

tower fronted by flowers and fountains. The resort's sports facilities are first class, and the largest of its five pools has water slides and waterfalls. The location, only 2 miles from the Disney parks, is another plus. The rooms are nice but business bland. The poolside rooms on the higher floors offer views of Mickeyville. The **Mikado Japanese Steak House** (p. 158) headlines the Marriott's three restaurants.

8701 World Center Dr. (on Hwy. 536 between I-4 and Hwy. 535), Orlando, FL 32821. © **800/621-0638** or 407/239-4200. Fax 407/238-8777. www.marriott.com. 2,111 units. $189–$410 for up to 5; $425–$2,400 suite. Resort fee $5. Children 17 and under stay free in parent's room. AE, DC, DISC, MC, V. Self-parking $5, valet parking $12. Take I-4 Exit 68, Hwy. 535/Apopka–Vineland Rd., south 1.5 miles, then right/west on Hwy. 536, and go .3 miles. **Amenities:** 4 restaurants (Japanese, steak, Italian, American), 2 lounges; 3 outdoor heated pools, indoor heated pool; kids' pool; 18-hole golf course; 8 lighted tennis courts; health club; spa; Jacuzzi; sauna; concierge; car-rental desk; transportation to all theme parks for a fee; business center; salon; 24-hr. room service; massage; babysitting; guest laundry; nonsmoking rooms. *In room:* A/C, TV w/pay movies, dataport, minibar, coffeemaker, hair dryer, iron, safe.

MODERATE

Hawthorn Suites Lake Buena Vista ⭐ *Value*   One of the things that appeals to us most about this property, which opened in summer 2000, is its floor plan. Its 500-square-foot standard rooms have four areas: a living room with a pullout sofa, chair, and TV; a full kitchen with a dining room table for four; a bathroom with vanity; and a bedroom with a recliner and TV. Two-bedroom units are also available. We think the extras here are a big plus, too. The Hawthorn offers a free American breakfast daily, a social hour (hors d'oeuvres, beer, and wine) Monday through Thursday, and a light meal on Wednesday evenings. The atmosphere is friendly, the service is good, and it's just 3 minutes from Hotel Plaza Boulevard.

8303 Palm Pkwy., Orlando, FL 32836. © **800/936-9417,** 800/527-1133 (forgive the music before the chain identifies itself), or 407/597-5000. Fax 407/597-6000. www.hawthornsuiteslbv.com. 120 units. $99–$179 for 4–6. AE, DC, DISC, MC, V. Free self-parking. From I-4, take Exit 68, Hwy. 535/Apopka–Vineland Rd., east to Palm Pkwy., then right a ¼ mile to hotel. **Amenities:** Outdoor heated pool; basketball court; exercise room; Jacuzzi; free shuttle to Disney parks, transportation for a fee to non-Disney parks; guest laundry; nonsmoking rooms. *In room:* A/C, TV w/pay movies, dataport, kitchen, fridge, coffeemaker, hair dryer, iron, microwave.

Holiday Inn Family Suites Resort ⭐⭐ *Finds*   This all-suite property opened in July 1999 and does a fantastic job catering to a diverse clientele. Families appreciate the two-bedroom Kid Suites that feature a second semiprivate bedroom equipped with bunk beds and changing themes (from Disney to Coke to the comics). In the Classic Suites, the semiprivate bedroom has a queen-size bed. Others cater to honeymooners and romantics (Sweet Heart Suites with a heart-shaped tub) and movie buffs (Cinema Suites with a 60-in. big-screen TV and DVD player). All have kitchenettes. The resort, voted in 2001 as the best Holiday Inn property in North America, has theme nights (movies, magic, and more). The recreational facilities are excellent, and the location—a mile from Disney—is great. And there's also a newly added Sugar & Spice Kids Spa ($10–$99 for manicures, pedicures, and full packages). *Note:* If you have older children or are child free, ask to stay in the West Track Courtyard section, which is much quieter.

14500 Continental Gateway (off Hwy. 536), Lake Buena Vista, FL 328360. © **877/387-5437** or 407/387-5437. Fax 407/387-1489. www.hifamilysuites.com. 800 units. $135–$189 Residential Suite; $146–$199 Kid Suite and Classic Suite; $166–$219 Cinema and Sweet Heart Suite. Rates include a hot breakfast buffet. Kids 12 and under eat free at lunch and dinner with paying adult. AE, DC, DISC, MC, V. Free self-parking. From I-4, take Exit 67, Hwy. 536/International Dr., east 1 mile to the resort. **Amenities:** Restaurant (American), lounge, general store, several fast-food counters; large lap pool, family swimming pool; fitness center;

2 Jacuzzis; 3 outdoor Ping-Pong tables; 2 shuffleboard courts; game room; mini-golf course; complimentary recreation center for ages 4–12; kids' library; free transportation to Disney parks, transportation for a fee to non-Disney parks; coin-op washers and dryers; tour desk. *In room:* A/C, TV w/pay movies and VCR (some with Nintendo), dataport, fridge, coffeemaker, hair dryer, iron, safe, microwave.

Holiday Inn Sunspree Resort Lake Buena Vista 🎯 *Kids* Just a mile from

the Disney parks, this inn caters to kids big time. They get their own check-in desk, a welcome from raccoon mascots Max and Maxine (who will tuck them in at night if you arrange it), and a fun bag with a video game coupon and lollipop. The hotel's 231 Kid Suites have beds for up to six and themes (an igloo, a space capsule, and more). If you like sleeping in, ask for a room that doesn't face the pool area. Kids under 12 eat free in their own restaurant, though it isn't fine dining. The resort has one of the best child activity centers around.

13351 Apopka–Vineland Rd./Hwy. 535 (between Hwy. 536 and I-4), Lake Buena Vista, FL 32821. ℂ 800/ 366-6299 or 407/239-4500. Fax 407/239-7713. www.kidsuites.com. 507 units. $99–$149 standard for up to 4; $119–$179 Kid Suite. Resort fee $2. AE, DISC, MC, V. Free self-parking. Pets under 25 pounds free ($25 refundable deposit required). From I-4, take Exit 68, Hwy. 535/Apopka–Vineland Rd., south a ¼ mile. **Amenities:** Food court; outdoor heated pool, kids' pool; fitness center; Jacuzzi; kids' club; arcade; guest services desk; free shuttle to Disney parks, transportation to non-Disney parks for a fee; guest laundry; limited room service; nonsmoking rooms. *In room:* A/C, TV/VCR, fridge, coffeemaker, hair dryer, iron, microwave.

Homewood Suites Orlando 🎯 These moderately priced family suites are

less than 2 miles from Disney and a good choice if you want a little home-style comfort and the chance to perform do-it-yourself stuff in the kitchen. The hotel is relatively new—it was built in 1998—so everything is in good shape. The two-bedroom suites sleep up to six. A social hour (hors d'oeuvres, beer, and wine) is held Monday through Thursday.

8200 Palm Pkwy. (off S. Apopka–Vineland Rd./Hwy. 535), Orlando, FL 32836. ℂ 800/225-5466 or 407/465-8200. Fax 407/465-0200. www.homewood-suites.com. $109–$259 double. Resort fee $3.50. Extra person $15. Rates include continental breakfast. Children 17 and under stay free in parent's room. AE, DC, DISC, MC, V. Free self-parking. From I-4, take Exit 68, Hwy. 535/Apopka–Vineland Rd., east to Palm Pkwy., then right a ¼ mile to hotel. **Amenities:** Mini-grocery; outdoor heated pool; exercise room; Jacuzzi; concierge; car-rental desk; free shuttle to Disney parks, transportation to non-Disney parks for a fee; business center; babysitting; guest laundry, valet; nonsmoking rooms. *In room:* A/C, TV/VCR w/pay movies, dataport, kitchen, fridge, coffeemaker, hair dryer, iron, microwave.

Summerfield Suites Lake Buena Vista 🎯 An excellent choice for families,

this modern low-rise shares the near-Disney location of all Lake Buena Vista accommodations. Room size, price, and a friendly staff are three reasons to stay here. The hotel's nicely decorated two-bedroom suites measure 550 square feet and have beds for up to eight people.

8751 Suiteside Dr. (off Apopka–Vineland Rd./Hwy. 535), Lake Buena Vista, FL 32836. ℂ 800/833-4353 or 407/238-0777. Fax 407/238-2640. www.summerfield-orlando.com. 150 units. $119–$259 1-bedroom for up to 4; $169–$329 2-bedroom for up to 8. Resort fee $3. Rates include continental breakfast. AE, DC, DISC, MC, V. Free self-parking. Take I-4 Exit 68, Hwy. 535/Apopka–Vineland Rd., right to third light (Vinings Way Rd.), go right, and hotel is on the left. **Amenities:** Deli; outdoor heated pool, kids' pool; exercise room; Jacuzzi; arcade; guest services desk; free Disney shuttle, transportation to non-Disney parks for a fee; guest laundry, valet; nonsmoking rooms. *In room:* A/C, TV/VCR, kitchen, fridge, coffeemaker, iron, safe.

INEXPENSIVE

Hampton Inn Lake Buena Vista Location rules at this modern property,

which is only 1 mile from the entrance to Hotel Plaza Boulevard on the northeast corner of Disney. It's not fancy, but the price is right and there are lots of nearby places to eat, shop, and party. Rooms on the 4th or 5th floors have microwaves and mini-fridges; request one and ask if the rate is higher than for a room on a lower floor.

8150 Palm Pkwy., Orlando, FL. 32836. © **800/370-9259** or 407/465-8150. Fax 407/465-0150. www. hamptoninnlbv.com. 147 units. $69–$129 for up to 4. 5th person $10. Rates include continental breakfast. Children 17 and under stay free in parent's room. AE, DC, DISC, MC, V. Free self-parking. From I-4, take Exit 68, Hwy. 535/Apopka–Vineland Rd., east to Palm Pkwy., then right a ¼ mile to hotel. **Amenities:** Outdoor heated pool; Jacuzzi; guest services desk; free shuttle to Disney parks, transportation to non-Disney parks for a fee; nonsmoking rooms. *In room:* A/C, TV w/pay movies, dataport, coffeemaker, hair dryer, iron.

5 Places to Stay in the Kissimmee Area

This tin-glitz highway is dotted with burger barns and T-shirt shops. It's not what you'd call scenic, and the visuals are further dampened by something that tests motorists' patience: seemingly perpetual road construction that slows traffic to turtle speed. But U.S. 192, also known as Irlo Bronson Memorial Highway— and locally as that *bleeping-bleeper*—has a number of inexpensive motels (don't be surprised if the paper is peeling off the walls) located within 1 to 8 miles of the WDW parks, to which most provide or can arrange transport. Hitching a ride to Universal Orlando and SeaWorld can be trickier, but an always-safe bet is to contact Mears Transportation (see "Getting Around" in chapter 4). The round-trip cost usually runs from $10 to $20 per person per day. You'll find the hotels and motels described on the map "Kissimmee Accommodations" on p. 109.

EXPENSIVE

Celebration Hotel ⚶ Like the yuppie life? Then you'll love this hotel inspired by the same-name Disney-initiated development that surrounds it. Its 3-story wood-frame design is a page from '20s Florida. Rooms have *comfy* beds; some of them four-posters. Ask for a lakefront room for a soothing view. Rooms on the opposite side overlook the gingerbread downtown and homes and apartments beyond it. The biggest perks: its location near Disney, the opportunity to stay in a Main Street, U.S.A.–style community, and a buffer separating you from the Mouse. If those sound appealing, this could be *the* place for you. If not, spend your dollars at a Disney or Lake Buena Vista resort in the "expensive" class. Staying in Celebration means you or your chauffeur will have to battle U.S. 192 traffic and the crowds pouring into the parks from it.

700 Bloom St. © **888/499-3800** or 407/566-6000. Fax 407/566-6001. www.celebrationhotel.com. 115 units. $139–$219 for up to 4; $289–$470 suite. Resort fee $5. AE, DC, DISC, MC, V. Free self-parking, valet parking $10. Take I-4 Exit 64A/U.S. 192 east to second light, then right on Celebration Ave. and follow the signs. **Amenities:** Restaurant (American), lounge; outdoor heated pool; 18-hole golf course; state-of-the-art health-and-fitness center; spa; concierge; free shuttle to Disney parks, transportation to non-Disney parks for a fee; nearby shopping district. *In room:* A/C, TV/Nintendo, dataport, hair dryer, iron, safe.

MODERATE

Holiday Inn Nikki Bird Resort ⚶ *Kids* Here's another family-friendly inn with a roaming mascot (Nikki Bird) and a dedication to kids. The hotel renovated

---

Fun Fact **Not So Magical**

When Disney built the town of Celebration, it planned just over 800 hotel rooms as part of the community. Three years later, in 1997, it raised the ante to 1,039. Now the entertainment and recreation giant wants to add another 1,000 rooms. Enough? The Celebration Patriots, a growing group of residents opposed to the plan, holler, YES! Stay tuned to see which side wins.

its rooms in 1997 and is in good shape. It features standard units as well as Kid Suites that have a separate area for youngsters. Suite themes vary. Kids under 12 eat free at a breakfast buffet next door; they also get entertainment, including puppet shows, songs, and games.

7300 W. Irlo Bronson Memorial Hwy. (U.S. 192), Kissimmee, FL 34747. ℂ 800/206-2747 or 407/396-7300. Fax 407/396-7555. www.hicentralflorida.com. 530 units. $89–$139 for up to 4. AE, DC, DISC, MC, V. Free self-parking. Take I-4 Exit 64B/U.S. 192 west. It's 1½ miles past the Disney entrance on the left. **Amenities:** Restaurant (American), grill, lounge; outdoor heated pool, kids' pool; 3 lighted tennis courts; exercise room; Jacuzzi; kids' club; concierge; free shuttle to Disney parks, transportation to non-Disney parks for a fee; guest laundry, valet. *In room:* A/C, TV w/pay movies, dataport, fridge, coffeemaker, hair dryer, iron.

Renaissance Worldgate   Arguably, this is as close as the Renaissance line gets to a budget hotel. While it's average in comfort and appearance, this converted DoubleTree has a great location, 2 miles west of WDW. The best views are from rooms on the north side of floors six and seven, where you can see the Spaceship Earth geosphere at Epcot, Animal Kingdom's Tree of Life, and, at night, Disney fireworks. The biggest minus: Rooms need some refurbishing and better soundproofing; you can hear your neighbor's phone and, if you're near enough, the thunder of the ice machine.

3011 Maingate Lane (off the north side of U.S. 192), Kissimmee, FL 34747. ℂ 800/468-3571 or 407/396-1400. Fax 407/396-0660. www.renaissanceworldgate.com. 577 units. $109–$159. Resort fee $2.75. Extra person $20. Children under 18 stay free in parent's room. AE, DC, DISC, MC, V. Free self-parking, valet $8. Take I-4 Exit 64B/U.S. 192 west 2 miles past Disney to Maingate (look for Renaissance sign and a mermaid statue on right). **Amenities:** Restaurant (American), deli, lounge; 2 heated outdoor pools; whirlpool; 2 lighted tennis courts; basketball court; exercise room; arcade; concierge; tour desk; car-rental desk; free transportation to Disney parks, transportation for a fee to non-Disney parks; business center; coin-operated laundry; nonsmoking rooms. *In room:* AC, TV w/pay movies and PlayStation, dataport, mini-fridge, coffeemaker, hair dryer, iron, safe.

INEXPENSIVE

In addition to the accommodations described here, there are scores of other inexpensive but serviceable motels, including chains (see appendix B, "Useful Toll-Free Numbers & Websites"). Most are within a few miles of Disney, have rooms in the 300-square-foot range, and arrange transportation to the parks. Many sell attractions tickets, but be careful. Many deeply discounted ticket offers are too good to be true. Some folks land at the parks with *invalid tickets* or waste a half-day or more listening to a timeshare pitch to get 30% to 40% off the regular price (single-day Disney park tickets are $52 for adults, $42 for kids 3–9). If a discount is more than $2 to $5 per ticket, it's probably too good to be true.

⟨Tips⟩ **Coming in 2004 & Beyond**

The 1,200-acre ChampionsGate development southwest of WDW is building a 732-room **Omni Orlando Resort.** Located at I-4 and Highway 532, it will have two golf courses, a spa, and six restaurants and bars. Developers plan to add 3,400 rooms in coming years. Not to be second best, **Reunion Resort & Club** will be a $2 billion, 2,500-acre vacation community. Plans call for 3,000 hotel rooms plus 5,000 homes and timeshares. The project and its three golf courses will be on both sides of I-4, south of Disney in northwest Osceola County. While there isn't a projected opening date yet, **Four Seasons Hotels and Resorts** has purchased 400 acres in Celebration with plans to build a 425-room hotel with an 18-hole golf course. The site also will have single-family homes.

Kissimmee Accommodations

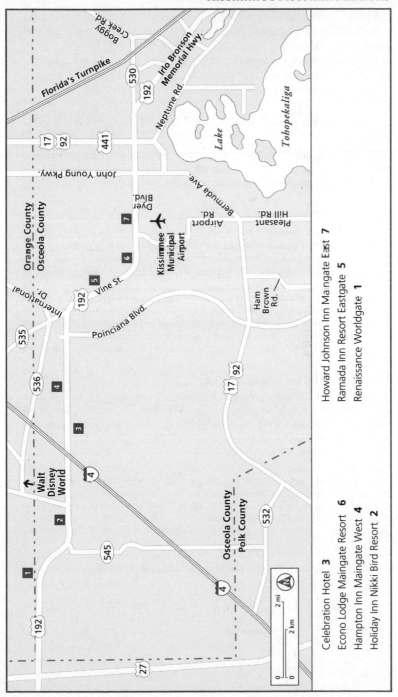

Celebration Hotel **3**
Econo Lodge Maingate Resort **6**
Hampton Inn Maingate West **4**
Holiday Inn Nikki Bird Resort **2**

Howard Johnson Inn Maingate East **7**
Ramada Inn Resort Eastgate **5**
Renaissance Worldgate **1**

Stick to buying tickets through the parks or accept the modest discounts offered by such groups as AAA, AARP, and the visitor information centers listed in chapter 2, "Planning Your Trip to Walt Disney World & Orlando."

Econo Lodge Maingate Resort *(Value*   Location and price are the perks here. The inn is 1.2 miles from the WDW entrance, and its rates are a bargain, though the property lacks any sign of pizzazz. The rooms are clean, but the price means you're not getting any frills.

7514 W. Irlo Bronson Memorial Hwy. (U.S. 192), Kissimmee, FL 34747. © **800/356-6935**, 407/390-9063, or 407/396-2000. Fax 407/390-1226. www.enjoyfloridahotels.com. 445 units. $39–$119 double. Resort fee $2.75. Extra person $10. Children 18 and under stay free in parent's room. AE, DC, DISC, MC, V. Free self-parking. From I-4, take Exit 64B/U.S. 192 west 2.2 miles; hotel is on the left past Reedy Creek Blvd. **Amenities:** Restaurant (steak), lounge; outdoor heated pool; Jacuzzi; arcade; guest services desk; car-rental desk; free shuttle to Disney parks, transportation to non-Disney parks for a fee; limited room service; guest laundry; nonsmoking rooms. *In room:* A/C, TV.

Hampton Inn Maingate West   Just 5½ years old, this inn has a newer, nicer feel because it hasn't been around long enough to earn all of the battle scars usually found in U.S. 192 accommodations. While it's more expensive on the front end than the Econo Lodge, it's also much more modern and upbeat. The inn is located 1½ miles west of the WDW entrance road.

3000 Maingate Lane, Kissimmee, FL. 34747. © **800/936-9417**, 877/428-4782, or 407/396-5457. Fax 407/396-8989. www.hamptoninnmaingatewest.com. 118 units. $69–$119 double. Extra person $10. Rates include a free continental breakfast. Children 17 and under stay free in parent's room. AE, DC, DISC, MC, V. Free self-parking. From I-4, take Exit 64B/U.S. 192 west 3 miles, then right on Maingate Lane (across the street from Celebration). **Amenities:** Outdoor heated pool; guest services desk; free shuttle to Disney parks, transportation to non-Disney parks for a fee; nonsmoking rooms. *In room:* A/C, TV, dataport, fridge, coffeemaker, iron, microwave.

Howard Johnson Inn Maingate East *(Value*   Like most motels fronting U.S. 192, this HoJo offers traffic congestion and noise, but it's only 2 miles from Disney. Rooms are typical of the chain—basic, but a fraction nicer than those in the Econo Lodge, listed earlier in this section. One kid under 12 eats free with each paying adult. Efficiencies and suites with full kitchens offer views of the pool and are probably worth the extra dollars.

6051 W. Irlo Bronson Memorial Hwy. (U.S. 192), Kissimmee, FL 34747. © **800/288-4678** or 407/396-1748. Fax 407/649-8642. www.hojomge.com. 567 units. $45–$95 double; efficiencies $10 more; suites $20 more. Resort fee $2. Extra person $10. Children 18 and under stay free in parent's room. AE, DC, DISC, MC, V. Free self-parking. From I-4, take Exit 64A/U.S. 192 east 1 mile. Motel is on the left. **Amenities:** Restaurant (American); 2 outdoor heated pools; kids' pool; Jacuzzi; arcade; guest services desk; free bus to Disney parks, transportation to non-Disney parks for a fee; guest laundry; nonsmoking rooms. *In room:* A/C, TV w/pay movies and Nintendo, dataport, safe.

Tips Youth Hostel

Hostelling International, 4840 W. Irlo Bronson Memorial Hwy./U.S. 192, Kissimmee, FL 34746, has a nice site on Lake Cecille, about 5 miles east of Walt Disney World (© **800/909-4776** for reservations or 407/396-8282; fax 407/396-9311; www.hiorlando.org or www.hiayh.org). Rooms are $16 to $20 (MasterCard and Visa are accepted) per night including linens. All have bathrooms, air conditioning, and a maximum of six beds. There are also 20 private rooms. The property has a lakefront pool, kitchen, lockers, laundry, Internet access, picnic area with grills, and complimentary paddleboats.

Tips **Homes Away from Home**

Some travelers, especially those who like all the comforts of home or groups of five or more, bypass motels in favor of rental condos or homes. Rates vary widely depending on quality and location, and many require at least a 2- or 3-night minimum. A lot of these properties are 5 to 15 miles from the theme parks and offer no transportation, so having a car is a necessity.

On the plus side, most have two to six bedrooms and a convertible couch, two or more bathrooms, a full kitchen, multiple TVs and phones, and irons. Some have washers and dryers. Homes often have their own pool, while condos have a common one.

On the minus side, they can be sterile. Most don't have daily maid service, and restaurants are often as far away as the parks. (There's another reason you'll need a car.) Unless they're in a gated community, don't expect onsite security. And some don't even offer dinnerware, utensils, or salt-and-pepper shakers—so be sure to ask.

Rates range from about $75 to $350 per night ($300–$1,800 per week).

Windsor Palms Resort (© 888/464-6353; www.WindsorPalmsResort. com) is one of the more popular choices in central Florida. The resort, located about 3 miles southwest of Disney and somewhat out of the tourist frenzy, rents everything from two-bedroom condominiums to six-bedroom houses.

Other popular players include **Blue Tree Resort** at Lake Buena Vista (© 800/688-8733; www.bluetreeresort.com); **Endless Summer Vacation Homes** (© 800/554-4378; www.esvflorida.com); **Holiday Villas** (© 800/344-3959; www.holidayvillas.com); and **Summer Bay Resort** (© 888/742-1100; www.summerbayresort.com).

Ramada Inn Resort Eastgate *Value*   If you're looking for a peer in quality to the HoJo (above), this Ramada is it. Built in 1983 and remodeled in 1998, it's a cut cleaner than many of the chain's standard motels, but no fancier. Standard rooms sport balconies. One kid eats free with each paying adult. The inn is 4 miles from Disney.

5150 W. Irlo Bronson Memorial Hwy. (U.S. 192), Kissimmee, FL 34746. © 888/298-2054 or 407/396-1111. Fax 407/396-1607. www.floridaramada.com. 402 units. $59–$129 double. Resort fee $2.60. Extra person $10. Children 17 and under stay free in parent's room. AE, DC, DISC, MC, V. Free self-parking. From I-4, take Exit 64A/U.S. 192 east 2½ miles to the motel. **Amenities:** Restaurant (American), lounge; outdoor heated pool, kids' pool; Jacuzzi; arcade; car-rental desk; free shuttle to Disney parks, transportation to non-Disney parks for a fee; limited room service; guest laundry, valet; nonsmoking rooms. *In room:* A/C, TV w/pay movies and Nintendo, dataport, coffeemaker, hair dryer, iron, safe.

6 Places to Stay in the International Drive Area

The hotels and resorts listed here are 7 to 10 miles north of Walt Disney World (via I-4) and 1 to 5 miles from Universal Orlando and SeaWorld. Though you won't fully get away from Toon Town anywhere in central Florida, International Drive hotels tend to have few, if any, fur-wearing critters. The advantages of staying on I-Drive: It's a self-supporting place, filled with accommodations, restaurants, and small attractions; it has its own inexpensive trolley service (see "Getting Around" in chapter 4), and it's centrally located for those who want to visit Disney, Universal, SeaWorld, *and* the downtown area. The disadvantages: The north end of I-Drive is badly congested; the shops, motels, eateries, and attractions along this stretch can be as tacky as those on U.S. 192; and many of the motels and hotels don't offer free transportation to the parks (the going rate is $6 to $15 round-trip).

You'll find these places located on the map "International Drive Area Accommodations" in this section.

VERY EXPENSIVE

Peabody Orlando 🐟🐟🐟 *Moments*   Five mallards march through the lobby and into a fountain every morning at 11am, accompanied by John Philip Sousa's "King Cotton March" and their own red-coated duck master (p. 276 for more on the ducks). That's just one of the magnets at a grand hotel that has one of the friendliest staffs in central Florida. The Peabody is primarily a business and convention destination, but it's one of our favorites in O-Town. It's classy without being stuffy, and, if your budget allows the splurge, you won't be disappointed. West-side rooms (6th floor and up) offer a distant view of Disney fireworks. By 2008, the Peabody is expected to add 1,000 rooms. *Tip:* Your best chance at getting bargain rates is in July and August; that's when the convention trade falls flat, and occupancy drops to as little as 20%.

The Peabody's signature restaurant, **Dux,** and two others—**Capriccio** and the **B-Line Diner**—are reviewed in chapter 6, "Where to Dine."

9801 International Dr. (between Bee Line Expressway and Sand Lake Rd.), Orlando, FL 32819. ℂ **800/732-2639** or 407/352-4000. Fax 407/354-1424. www.peabodyorlando.com. 891 units. $380–$480 standard room for up to 3; $520–$1,600 suite. Extra person $20. Children 17 and under stay free in parent's room. AE, DC, DISC, MC, V. Free self-parking; valet parking $8. From I-4, take Exit 74A, Sand Lake Rd./Hwy. 482, east to International Dr., then south. Hotel is on left across from Convention Center. **Amenities:** 3 restaurants (Continental, Northern Italian, American); deli, 3 lounges; outdoor heated pool, kids' pool; 4 lighted tennis courts; fitness center; spa; Jacuzzi; concierge; guest services desk; business center; shopping arcade; transportation to WDW and other parks for a fee; 24-hr. room service; massage; valet; nonsmoking rooms; concierge-level rooms. *In room:* A/C, TV, dataport, minibar, hair dryer.

(Tips Smaller Homes Away from Home

Several area timeshare resorts rent rooms or apartments to tourists when the owners aren't using them. The **Disney Vacation Club** (ℂ **407/939-7775;** www.dvcresorts.com) offers studios and one- to two-bedroom apartments at the Villas at Disney's Wilderness Lodge, Disney's Boardwalk Villas, Disney's Beach Club, and Disney's Old Key West. Some have small fridges and microwaves; others have full kitchens. Rates start at about $250 per night. Outside Disney World, per-night rates begin at $200 to $250 per night for one- and two-bedroom apartments with kitchens. As with hotel rooms, you can get major discounts off the rack rates (as low as $70 a night) for these properties if you do your homework. An especially nice choice is **Sheraton's Vistana Resort** (ℂ **866/208-0003;** www.starwoodvo.com). Another good place to look is the **Marriott Vacation Club** (ℂ **800/845-5279;** www.vacationclub.com).

International Drive Area Accommodations

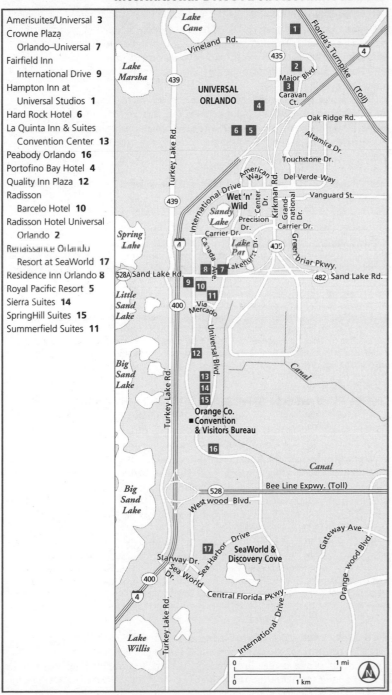

Portofino Bay Hotel ★★★ *(Finds* Universal Orlando's first hotel is as grand as Disney's Grand Floridian (p. 91). This 4-year-old property is a replica of the village of Portofino, Italy, with a harbor and canals on which boats travel to the theme parks. The Old World ambience is carried throughout the public areas, restaurants, and rooms by a staff that tries hard to match the Peabody's friendliness.

The luxurious rooms are large (with sleep space for five), and the beds have Egyptian-woven sheets. The pillows are so soft that you'll want to take them home. (Alas, they're too big for your suitcase, so ask the resort how to order one.) Ask for a view overlooking the piazza and "bay" area. Like many of the Disney properties, the Portofino doesn't just have swimming pools; its beach pool has a fort with a water slide (the villa pool offers several cabanas). One of the biggest pluses: Guests get no-line access to most rides at Universal Studios Florida and Islands of Adventure as well as seating privileges at shows and restaurants. The resort's privately run Greenhouse Spa features a state-of-the-art fitness center and full-service spa. Look for a review of the Portofino's signature restaurant, **Delfino Riviera,** on p. 148.

5601 Universal Blvd., Orlando FL. 32819. © **888/322-5541** or 407/503-1000. Fax 407/224-7118. www. loewshotels.com/hotels/orlando. 750 units. $275–$390 double; $450–$2,100 villas and suite. Extra person $25. Children 17 and under stay free in parent's room. AE, DC, DISC, MC, V. Self-parking $6, valet parking $12. From I-4, take Exit 75B, Kirkman Rd./Hwy. 435, and follow the signs to Universal. **Amenities:** 3 restaurants (Northern Italian), deli, 3 lounges; 2 outdoor heated pools (1 for concierge and suite guests only), kids' pool; bocce courts (concierge and suite guests only); fitness center; spa; watersports equipment; kids' club; arcade; concierge; tour desk; free water-taxi transportation to Universal Studios, Islands of Adventure, and CityWalk; free shuttle to SeaWorld; transportation for a fee to WDW parks; business center; shopping arcade; 24-hr. room service; babysitting; guest laundry, valet; nonsmoking rooms; concierge-level rooms. *In room:* A/C, TV, hair dryer, iron, safe.

EXPENSIVE

Crowne Plaza Orlando-Universal ★ This sleek new high-rise—it opened in summer 2002—towers 15 floors above the intersection of Sand Lake Road and Universal Boulevard (1 block east of I-Drive). Although it's closer to Universal Orlando and SeaWorld (about midway between them), getting to Disney is no problem because the hotel offers free shuttles to the major parks. It's also close to the I-Ride Trolley, which saves shoe leather for those interested in exploring International Drive. The rooms are subdued but well appointed and offer floor-to-ceiling windows. Some of the pricier rooms are in the circular Atrium Tower, where you can climb to the top in glass elevators. The bulk of the rooms are in the Crowne Wing.

7800 Universal Blvd., Orlando, FL 32819. © **866/864-8627** or 407/355-0550. Fax 407/355-0504. www. crowneplazauniversal.com. 400 units. $99–$249 double; presidential suites $450–$600. Extra person $20. Children 17 and under stay free in parent's room. AE, DISC, MC, V. Free self-parking. From I-4, take Exit 74A, Sand Lake Rd./Hwy. 482, east to Universal, then left. **Amenities:** Restaurant (International), cafe, lounge; heated pool; fitness center; game room; concierge; tour desk; free transportation to Disney, Universal, and SeaWorld; gift shop; business center; limited room service; babysitting; guest laundry, valet; nonsmoking rooms. *In room:* A/C, TV w/ Nintendo, dataport, coffeemaker, hair dryer, iron, safe.

Hard Rock Hotel ★★ When it comes to location, you can't get any closer to CityWalk or Universal Studios Florida. This California mission–style resort with a rock 'n' roll theme opened in January 2001 with rates a level cheaper than its Universal sister, the Portofino (see above).

The Hard Rock is a notch above some of Disney's comparable properties, including Animal Kingdom Lodge. All rooms here are very comfortable and, though the bathrooms aren't big, there is (like at the Disney resorts) a separate dressing area that has a sink. Like the Portofino, the best views here are on the "bay" side, overlooking the piazza. Unfortunately, though the rooms are pretty soundproof, a few notes seep through some walls, so ask for a room that's situated away from the lobby area. There is a Hard Rock Cafe several hundred yards from the hotel, but the resort has two of its own restaurants on the property (see our review of **The Palm** on p. 149). One of the biggest perks of staying on Universal property is that guests get no-line access to almost every ride at Universal Studios Florida and Islands of Adventure, and seating privileges for shows and restaurants.

5000 Universal Blvd., Orlando, FL 32819. ℂ **800/232-7827** or 407/363-8000. Fax 407/224-7118. www. loewshotels.com/hotels/orlando. 654 units. $199–$359 double; $345–$1,575 suite. Extra person $20. Children 17 and under stay free in parent's room. AE, DC, DISC, MC, V. Self-parking $6, valet parking $12. From I-4, take Exit 75B, Kirkman Rd./Hwy. 435, and follow the signs to Universal. **Amenities:** 2 restaurants (American), grill; 2 lounges; outdoor heated pool, kids' pool; fitness center; kids' club; arcade; concierge; free water-taxi transportation to Universal Studios, Islands of Adventure, and CityWalk; free shuttle to SeaWorld; transportation for a fee to WDW parks; shopping arcade; 24-hr. room service; babysitting; guest laundry, valet; nonsmoking rooms. In room: A/C, TV, hair dryer, iron, safe.

Renaissance Orlando Resort at SeaWorld 🏰🏰   This stylish hotel, the classiest in this I-Drive price category, offers large rooms and a great location for theme-park nomads: It's across from SeaWorld and about 10 to 15 minutes from Universal Orlando and Walt Disney World. The lobby charms guests with a 10-story atrium, koi pond (at up to 25 lb., they're huge!), free-flight aviary, and six glass elevators that overlook the atrium. East-side rooms, especially from the 6th floor up, have a nice view of SeaWorld, which is within walking distance (but watch the traffic). North- and south-side rooms have balconies overlooking the atrium.

6677 Sea Harbour Dr., Orlando, FL 32821. ℂ **800/327-6677** or 407/351-5555. Fax 407/351-1991. www. renaissancehotels.com. 778 units. $149–$249 double. Extra person $20. Children 17 and under stay free in parent's room. AE, DC, DISC, MC, V. Free self-parking, valet parking $9. From I-4, take Exit 72, Hwy. 528/Beeline Expressway, east to International Dr., then go south to Sea Harbour Dr. and turn right. **Amenities:** 2 restaurants (seafood, American), grill, 3 lounges; outdoor heated pool, kids' pool; 4 lighted tennis courts; health club; spa; 2 Jacuzzis; sauna; arcade; concierge; tour desk; car-rental desk; transportation for a fee to all the parks; business center; shopping arcade; 24-hr. room service; massage; babysitting; guest laundry, valet; nonsmoking rooms. In room: A/C, TV w/pay movies and PlayStation, dataport, safe.

Royal Pacific Resort 🏰 Value   This sister property to the Portofino Bay and Hard Rock resorts (see above) has an open-air courtyard with an exquisite orchid garden, palm trees, waterfalls, and lagoons, including one in which a float plane with a 90-foot wingspan is docked. The Royal Pacific doesn't quite succeed at

---

⌐Tips Coming in July 2003

Ritz-Carlton (ℂ **800/241-3333** or 407/529-2255; www.ritzcarlton.com) finally has plans to enter the Orlando market. Its 584-room luxury hotel ($350–$400 a night) is part of the Grande Lakes Resort complex that also includes a 1,000-room J. W. Marriott hotel, an 18-hole golf course, and a 40,000-square-foot, three-level spa with 40 treatment rooms. The site is well out of the main tourist areas. It's on John Young Parkway near Central Florida Parkway, a 7- or 8-mile drive southeast of SeaWorld and about the same distance east of Walt Disney World.

Tips Stay Tuned

Not long after the new **Royal Pacific Resort** opened in 2002, Universal reiterated an earlier pledge to open at least two more resorts—bringing to five the number of hotels on its south-of-Orlando property. But so far, there hasn't been word about the builder or the theme of the resorts.

---

creating a Polynesian paradise (you can hear the screams of riders on the Hulk Coaster from the pool area), but it's definitely the best Universal resort in the theme department. Its rooms, though smaller than those at other Universal resorts, are attractively decorated with lovely wood accents and carvings; they are far better than those at comparable Disney resorts. And the lagoon pool area—the largest in Orlando—is lovely. The big plus: Guests get no-line access to almost every ride at Universal Studios Florida and Islands of Adventure, and seating privileges for shows and restaurants. The big minus: The self-parking lot is a very long hike from the hotel, and you have to pay $6 for that privilege.

6300 Hollywood Way, Orlando, FL 32819. ✆ 800/232-7827 or 407/503-3000. Fax 407/503-3202. www. loewshotels.com/hotels/orlando. 1,000 units. $159–$299 double; $279–$1,200 suite. Extra person $20. Children 17 and under stay free in parent's room. AE, DC, DISC, MC, V. Self-parking $5, valet parking $10. From I-4, take Exit 75B, Kirkman Rd./Hwy. 435, and follow the signs to Universal. **Amenities:** 2 restaurants (Asian-Polynesian, American), 3 lounges; outdoor heated pool; kids' pool; kids' club; sauna; Jacuzzi; free water-taxi transportation to Universal Studios, Islands of Adventure, and CityWalk; free shuttle to SeaWorld; transportation for a fee to WDW parks; arcade; concierge; babysitting; valet; nonsmoking rooms. _In room:_ A/C, TV, dataport, hairdryer, iron, safe.

Summerfield Suites _Like its Lake Buena Vista cousin (reviewed on p. 106), this hotel is friendly, well run, and neat as a pin. Price and spacious one- and two-bedroom suites (the latter 550 sq. ft., with beds for eight) are two of its biggest pluses. The hotel attracts leisure and business travelers. Courtyard rooms have balconies. The property is across the street from the Mercado shopping village and its restaurants.

8480 International Dr. (between Bee Line Expressway and Sand Lake Rd.), Orlando, FL 32819. ✆ 800/833-4353 or 407/352-2400. Fax 407/352-4631. www.summerfield-orlando.com. 146 units. $119–$259 1-bedroom for up to 4; $189–$329 2-bedroom for up to 8. Resort fee $2. Rates include continental breakfast. AE, DC, DISC, MC, V. Free self-parking. From I-4, take Exit 74A, Sand Lake Rd./Hwy. 482, to International Dr., turn right; hotel is a ½ mile on right. **Amenities:** Deli; outdoor heated pool; kids' pool; exercise room; Jacuzzi; arcade; guest services desk; transportation to all theme parks for a fee; guest laundry; valet; nonsmoking rooms. _In room:_ A/C, TV/VCR, kitchen, fridge, coffeemaker, iron, safe.

MODERATE

AmeriSuites Universal   It's tough to beat the value and roominess of these kitchenette-equipped suites, especially if your goal is to be very close to the Universal theme parks without having to pay the heftier rates that come with staying on park property. The modern, spacious rooms allow you to stretch out more than in standard hotel/motel accommodations, and the location is especially convenient if Universal Orlando is your target.

5895 Caravan Court, Orlando, FL 32819. ✆ 800/833-1516 or 407/351-0627. Fax 407/331-3317. www. amerisuites.com. 151 units. $89–$179 for up to 4. Rates include free buffet breakfast. Children 17 and under stay free in parent's room. AE, DC, DISC, MC, V. Free self-parking. From I-4, take Exit 75B Kirkman Rd., then turn right at the first light, Major Blvd., and the next right, Caravan Court. The hotel is on the right. **Amenities:** Outdoor heated pool; exercise room; tour desk; free transportation to all theme parks; guest laundry; valet; nonsmoking rooms. _In room:_ A/C, TV w/ VCR, dataport, kitchenette w/microwave, fridge, coffeemaker, hairdryer, iron, safe.

Tips **So You Didn't Book a Room . . .**

As we mentioned earlier, coming to Orlando without a reservation isn't a good idea. But if you do and you're looking for a basic room, try these chain properties (see also appendix B, "Useful Toll-Free Numbers & Websites"). They're moderate or inexpensive in price and located in the budget motel corridors. All are relatively convenient to the attractions. While we can't vouch for them personally, their brand names generally mean reliability:

IN KISSIMMEE:

- **Best Western Eastgate,** 5565 W. Irlo Bronson Memorial Hwy., Kissimmee (© **407/396-0707**).
- **Best Western Kissimmee,** 2261 E. Irlo Bronson Memorial Hwy., Kissimmee (© **407/846-2221**).
- **Comfort Suites Maingate Hotel,** 7888 W. Irlo Bronson Memorial Hwy., Kissimmee (© **407/390-9888**).
- **Comfort Suites Resort Maingate East,** 2775 Florida Plaza Blvd., Kissimmee (© **407/397-7848**).
- **Days Inn Maingate East,** 5840 W. Irlo Bronson Memorial Hwy., Kissimmee (© **407/396-7969**).
- **Days Inn Maingate West,** 7980 W. Irlo Bronson Memorial Hwy., Kissimmee (© **407/997-1000**).
- **DoubleTree Villas Maingate,** 4787 W. Irlo Bronson Memorial Hwy., Kissimmee (© **407/397-0555**).
- **Howard Johnson Maingate West,** 8660 W. Irlo Bronson Memorial Hwy., Kissimmee (© **407/396-4500**).
- **Quality Suites Maingate East,** 5876 W. Irlo Bronson Memorial Hwy., Kissimmee (© **407/396-8040**).

IN THE INTERNATIONAL DRIVE AREA:

- **Days Inn Convention Center/SeaWorld,** 9990 International Dr., Orlando (© **407/352-8700**).
- **Days Inn East of Universal Studios,** 5827 Caravan Court, Orlando (© **407/351-3800**).
- **Days Inn International Drive,** 7200 International Dr., Orlando (© **407/351-1200**).
- **Holiday Inn Express International Drive,** 6323 International Dr., Orlando (© **407/351-4430**).
- **Sheraton Studio City Hotel,** 5905 International Dr., Orlando (© **407/351-2100**).
- **Travelodge International Drive,** 5859 American Way, Orlando (© **407/345-8880**).

You also can try **Central Reservation Service** (© **407/740-6442;** www.reservation-services.com) and **Discount Hotels of America** (© **407/294-9600;** www.discounthotelsamerica.com).

Hampton Inn at Universal Studios There's nothing fancy about this simple hotel, but it's in a good location if you plan to spend most of your time at Universal Orlando, which is only 2 blocks away. It's also relatively close to SeaWorld and downtown Orlando and about 10 miles from Disney. Some rooms have microwaves and refrigerators. Although there's no restaurant on the premises, there are several within walking distance.

5621 Windhover Dr., Orlando, FL 32819. ✆ **800/426-7866**, 800/231-8395, or 407/351-6716. Fax 407/363-1711. www.hamptoninn.com. 120 units. $69–$119 double. Extra person $10. Rates include continental breakfast. Children 17 and under stay free in parent's room. AE, DC, DISC, MC, V. Free self-parking. From I-4, take Exit 75B, Kirkman Rd./Hwy. 435, go through 2 traffic lights; turn right at Shoney's Restaurant. It's a 5-story white building. **Amenities:** Outdoor heated pool; exercise room; free transportation to Universal and SeaWorld, transportation for a fee to Disney; guest laundry, valet; nonsmoking rooms. *In room:* A/C, TV, dataport, coffeemaker, iron.

La Quinta Inn & Suites Convention Center Opened in 1998, this is one of a handful of upscale, moderately priced motels on Universal Boulevard, which runs parallel to (but isn't as congested as) I-Drive. The hotel is aimed at business travelers, but this is Orlando, so families traveling with kids are welcomed with open arms. King rooms are designed for extended stays and have a fridge and microwave. A limited number of two-room suites offering separate living and sleeping areas are available.

8504 Universal Blvd., Orlando, FL 32819. ✆ **800/531-5900** or 407/345-1365. Fax 407/345-5586. www.laquinta.com. 185 units. $90–$150 double. Extra person $10. Rates include continental breakfast. Children 18 and under stay free in parent's room. AE, DC, DISC, MC, V. Free self-parking. Take I-4 to Exit 74A, Sand Lake Rd./Hwy. 482, go east toward Universal, then right. **Amenities:** Outdoor heated pool; exercise room; Jacuzzi; transportation for a fee to all theme parks; guest laundry; nonsmoking rooms. *In room:* A/C, TV w/pay movies and Nintendo, dataport, coffeemaker, hair dryer, iron.

Radisson Barcelo Hotel ✦ Like many I-Drive properties, the Radisson offers a good location for people whose vacations center on Universal Orlando or SeaWorld, and a central location for travelers who plan to visit Disney and downtown, too. Rooms are brightly decorated, but views are basic. The 7th floor (the highest) will give you a look at SeaWorld to the south. Otherwise, you'll be watching traffic on I-4 or I-Drive.

8444 International Dr., Orlando, FL 32819. ✆ **888/380-9696** or 407/345-0505. Fax 407/352-5894. www.radisson-orlando.com. 520 units. $79–$199 double. Extra person $15. Children 17 and under stay free in parent's room. AE, DC, DISC, MC, V. Free self-parking. From I-4, take Exit 74A, Sand Lake Rd/Hwy. 482, turn right on International Dr., go a ½ mile, and hotel is on the right. **Amenities:** Restaurant (Florida/regional), grill, lounge; outdoor heated pool; lighted tennis court; bocce court; guest services desk; free shuttle to Universal Orlando and SeaWorld, transportation for a fee to Disney parks; guest laundry, valet; nonsmoking rooms. *In room:* A/C, TV w/pay movies and Nintendo, dataport, fridge, coffeemaker, hair dryer, iron, safe.

Radisson Hotel Universal Orlando ✦ Location alone earns this hotel a star. Built for the convention trade, the former Radisson Twin Towers got a name change in the mid-1990s when people started flocking to Universal Orlando, which is right across the street. Stay here and save over the Portofino Bay, Hard Rock, and Royal Pacific hotels (reviewed earlier). The rooms are reasonably nice and fit for a property that is 2 decades old (the last renovation was in 1997). Rooms on the west side, floors 6 through 18, offer views of the Universal parks and CityWalk.

5780 Major Blvd., Orlando, FL 32819. ✆ **800/333-3333** or 407/351-1000. Fax 407/363-0106. www.radissonuniversal.com. 760 units. $99–$199 double. Extra person $15. Children 17 and under stay free in parent's room. AE, DC, DISC, MC, V. Free self-parking. From I-4, take Exit 75B, Kirkman Rd./Hwy. 435, go north to Major, then right. **Amenities:** Restaurant (American), food court, lounge; outdoor heated pool, kids' pool; exercise room; Jacuzzi; arcade; free transportation to Universal and SeaWorld parks, transportation for a fee to Disney; salon; limited room service. *In room:* A/C, TV, dataport, coffeemaker, hair dryer, iron.

Plan your vacation

- flights, hotels, car rentals
- cruises & vacation packages
- destination guides
- fare alerts
- go to yahoo.com, click travel

DO YOU YAHOO!?

Tips Late Arrival, Early Departure?

The hotels at and near Orlando International Airport are normally used by touch-and-go business passengers. They're not for those of you coming here on vacation (poor location, miserable transportation options, and little to do) unless:

A. You have a late-arriving flight and are too pooped to endure a 15- to 30-minute ride to your regular hotel (that's almost inconceivable), or

B. The flight taking you home is so early that you're afraid you won't make it to the airport in time.

If either scenario fits you, try one of these:

- **AmeriSuites International Airport** (© 800/833-1516 or 407/240-3939; fax 407/240-3920; www.amerisuites.com).
- **Comfort Suites Orlando Airport** (© 800/936-9417 or 407/581-7900; fax 407/581-7901; www.avistahotels.com).
- **Crowne Plaza Hotel** (© 800/227-6963 or 407/856-0100; fax 407/855-7991; www.sixcontinentshotels.com/crowneplaza).
- **Embassy Suites Orlando Airport** (© 800/362-2779 or 407/888-9339; fax 407/856-5956; www.embassysuites.com).
- **Hyatt Regency Orlando International Airport** (© 800/233-1234 or 407/825-1234; fax 407/856-1672; www.hyatt.com).

Residence Inn Orlando ⊛ Marriott's Residence Inns were designed to offer home-away-from-home comfort for business travelers, but the concept works just as well for families. The all-suite hotel is well kept and is situated within a mile of many of International Drive's attractions, shops, and restaurants. The attractive one-bedroom suites are a roomy 500 square feet and sleep four. Some two-bedroom suites are available. An evening social hour is held Monday through Thursday.

7975 Canada Ave. (just off Sand Lake Rd., a block east of International Dr.), Orlando, FL 32819. © 800/227-3978 or 407/345-0117. Fax 407/352-2689. www.marriott.com. 176 units. $89–$159 double; $129–$189 studio suite. Extra person $15. Rates include breakfast. Children 17 and under stay free in parent's room. AE, DC, DISC, MC, V. Free self-parking. From I-4, take Exit 74A, Sand Lake Rd./Hwy. 482, go east to Canada, then left. Pets welcome for $100 deposit (half nonrefundable) plus $10 per day. **Amenities:** Outdoor heated pool; exercise room; Jacuzzi; free bus service to Disney, transportation for a fee to the non-Disney theme parks; guest laundry, valet. *In room:* A/C, TV w/pay movies, dataport, kitchen, fridge, coffeemaker, iron, safe.

Sierra Suites Another respite from I-Drive on the less-than-congested Universal Boulevard, this one's a few blocks north of where the boulevard spills into International Drive at the Convention Center and Peabody Orlando (reviewed earlier in this chapter). You can walk to some minor attractions, and if you take the footpath west a few hundred feet, you can catch the I-Ride Trolley (see "Getting Around" in chapter 4). Size-wise, the rooms are standard motel fare (yes, they're rooms despite the kitchens and the name the property calls itself). The view? Sorry. This mountain ain't tall enough, and the eastward view over a near-nonexistent tree line melts into the next hotel.

8750 Universal Blvd. © 800/474-3772 or 407/903-1500. Fax 407/903-1555. www.sierra-orlando.com. 137 units. $99–$159 for up to 4. AE, DC, DISC, MC, V. Free self-parking. From I-4, take Exit 74A, Sand Lake Rd./

Hwy. 482, go east to the third light (Universal), go right/south, and hotel is a ½ mile on the right. **Amenities:** Outdoor heated pool; exercise room; Jacuzzi; arcade; guest services desk; free shuttle to Disney, Universal, and SeaWorld; guest laundry, valet; nonsmoking rooms. *In room:* A/C, TV, dataport, kitchen, coffeemaker, hair dryer, iron, safe.

SpringHill Suites Orlando Convention Center
Like the Sierra Suites (see the review above), this property offers another chance to stay near but not in the middle of the I-Drive crowds and traffic. Clean, very spacious suites (about 700 sq. ft., with beds for five and a separate living area) and reasonable rates make this all-suite property worth considering.

8840 Universal Blvd., Orlando, FL 32819. 🄲 **888/287-9400** or 407/345-9073. Fax 407/345-9075. www. springhillsuites.com. 167 units. $99–$159 double. Extra person $10. Rates include continental breakfast. Children 17 and under stay free in parent's room. AE, DC, DISC, MC, V. Free self-parking. From I-4, take Exit 74A, Sand Lake Rd./Hwy. 482, go east to the third light (Universal), then go south; hotel is a ½ mile on the right. **Amenities:** Outdoor heated pool; exercise room; Jacuzzi; concierge; transportation for a fee to the theme parks; business center; guest laundry, valet; nonsmoking rooms. *In room:* A/C, TV, dataport, mini-fridge, coffeemaker, hair dryer, iron, microwave.

INEXPENSIVE
Fairfield Inn International Drive 🄰 ⟨Value⟩
If you're looking for I-Drive's best value, it's hard to beat this one. This Fairfield combines a quiet location off the main drag, down-to-earth rates, and a clean, modern motel in one package. It's not only the best in this category, but arguably a half step ahead of the Hampton, La Quinta, and Sierra Suites in the previous one. The rooms are very comfortable, and there are a number of restaurants within walking distance of the hotel.

8342 Jamaican Court (off International Dr. between the Bee Line Expressway and Sand Lake Rd.), Orlando, FL 32819. 🄲 **800/228-2800** or 407/363-1944. Fax 407/363-1944. www.fairfieldinn.com. 135 units. $69–$99 for up to 4. Rates include continental breakfast. AE, DC, DISC, MC, V. Free self-parking. From I-4, take Exit 74A, Sand Lake Rd./Hwy. 482, go east 1 block, turn right on I-Drive, then right on Jamaican Court. Hotel is on the right. **Amenities:** Outdoor heated pool; guest services desk; transportation for a fee to the parks; guest laundry, valet; nonsmoking rooms. *In room:* A/C, TV w/pay movies, dataport, safe.

Quality Inn Plaza
The rooms at this property—across from the Pointe Orlando shopping plaza—are spread through 5-, 6-, and 7-story buildings. The biggest advantage in staying here is the proximity to I-Drive nightlife, restaurants, and shops. The executive rooms have dataports and a king-size bed upon request. Kids under 12 eat free in the hotel's restaurant. Ask for a quiet room away from I-Drive to avoid the morning traffic noise.

9000 International Dr., Orlando, FL 32819. 🄲 **800/999-8585** or 407/996-8585. Fax 407/996-6839. www. qualityinn-orlando.com. 1,020 units. $59–$109 for up to 4. Resort fee $1.50. AE, DC, DISC, MC, V. Free self-parking. From I-4, take Exit 74A, Sand Lake Rd./Hwy. 482, turn east at bottom of ramp. Turn at first intersection, International Dr. The property is 1 mile on the right. Pets $10 a night. **Amenities:** Restaurant (American), deli, lounge; 3 outdoor heated pools; 2 arcades; guest services desk; free transportation to Universal and SeaWorld, transportation for a fee to Disney; limited room service; guest laundry, valet; nonsmoking rooms. *In room:* A/C, TV w/pay movies, fridge, coffeemaker, safe, microwave.

7 Orlando Bed & Breakfasts

Although most of the properties in Orlando are resorts or chains, there are a few good bed-and-breakfast options. These properties offer a respite from the crowded, run-and-gun world of theme parks, and they're ideal for couples looking for a little quiet time or romance. Note that most of the inns and B&Bs in Orlando do not accept children—a major selling point for some visitors. If you choose to stay at one of these properties, you'll need a car or some other kind of transportation, because these inns do not provide it. Unless otherwise noted, all B&Bs in this section can be found on the "Accommodations & Dining Elsewhere in Orlando" map on p. 159. You can find other options in the area through Florida Bed and Breakfast Inns (© **800/524-1880;** www.florida-inns.com).

EXPENSIVE

Courtyard at Lake Lucerne ★ (Finds) Speaking of romance, you might feel the sting of Cupid's arrows in this downtown hideaway. Each of the Courtyard's buildings is historic. The Art Deco Wellborn, a late-bloomer that arrived in 1946, offers 14 one-bedroom apartments and a honeymoon suite (styles range from Thai to the Fab '50s). The Norment–Parry Inn is an 1883 Victorian-style home with six rooms decorated with English and American antiques; four have sitting rooms, all have private baths. It, too, has a honeymoon suite highlighted by a walnut bed and a Victorian fireplace. The I. W. Phillips House, built in 1919, is reminiscent of old Southern homes with large verandas. Upstairs, there are three suites, one with a whirlpool, all with verandas overlooking the gardens and fountain. Finally, the Dr. Phillip Phillips House, built in 1893, made its bed-and-breakfast debut on Valentine's Day 1999 with six rooms.

211 N. Lucerne Circle E., Orlando, FL 32801. © **800/444-5289** or 407/648-5188. Fax 407/246-1368. www. orlandohistoricinn.com. 30 units. $89–$225 double. Rates include continental breakfast. AE, DC, MC, V. Free self-parking. Take Orange Ave. south; immediately following City Hall (dome building with fountains and glass sculpture), turn left onto Anderson. After 2 lights, at Delaney Ave., turn right. Take first right onto Lucerne Circle. Be aware of one-way streets. Follow the brown "historic inn" signs. Children are permitted. **Amenities:** Restaurant (American/Southern); nonsmoking rooms. *In room:* A/C, TV, fridge, coffeemaker, microwave.

MODERATE

Thurston House This Queen Anne–and Victorian-style inn was built on the banks of Lake Eulalia in 1885 by a wealthy businessman. Today, it serves as a quiet getaway on 5 wooded acres. The two-story house has four individually decorated rooms with queen-size beds (one room has a four-poster bed) and private bathrooms (one room has a shower only). Rooms are smoke free and not accessible to travelers with disabilities. An afternoon drink and cheese plate are included in the price.

851 Lake Ave., Maitland, FL 32751. © **800/843-2721** or 407/539-1911. Fax 407/539-0365. www.thurston house.com. 4 units. $140–$150 double. Rates include breakfast and afternoon refreshments. AE, MC, V. Free self-parking. Take I-4 north to Exit 88/Lee Rd., then go east to Wymore and turn north/left; go right on East Kennedy/Hwy. 438A, which becomes Lake Ave. Children under 12 are not permitted. **Amenities:** Nonsmoking rooms. *In room:* A/C, dataport.

Veranda Bed & Breakfast (Finds) Located in Thornton Park, this inn near scenic Lake Eola is another option if you want to stay near downtown. Its four buildings date back to the early 1900s. All units (studios to suites) include private baths and entrances; some have garden tubs, balconies, kitchenettes, and four-poster beds. A few of the nicer options include the Washington Suite, which sports a four-poster bed and a Jacuzzi, and the romantic Carriage Suite, which has a four-poster bed and antique claw-foot tub. The two-bedroom, two-bathroom Keylime Cottage ($199) sleeps four and has a full kitchen.

115 N. Summerlin Ave., Orlando, FL 32801. © **800/420-6822** or 407/849-0321. Fax 407/849-0321, ext. 24. www.theverandabandb.com. 12 units. $99–$199 double. Rates include continental breakfast. AE, DC, DISC, MC, V. From I-4, take Exit 84, Hwy. 50/Colonial Dr., left 1 mile to Summerlin, turn right, and go 1 mile, crossing Robinson St. The inn is 1 block on the left. Children are not permitted. **Amenities:** Outdoor pool, Jacuzzi. *In room:* A/C, TV.

8 Places to Stay Elsewhere in Orlando

There are two good reasons to stay away from the hustle and hassle of the attractions: crowds and, to a lesser degree, prices.

If you're traveling in the middle of the peak season, including summer or around the December holidays, you'll likely find yourself bumping into other people no matter where you go. The closer you are to the attractions, the higher the cost of just about everything, from rooms to soda and film.

There are, of course, disadvantages to staying on the fringes. In most cases, you'll have to travel along I-4 to get to and from the parks. But if you avoid traveling from 7 to 9am and 4 to 6pm, you'll encounter less traffic and the drive may take 20 to 30 minutes or so, barring any accidents on the Interstate. It will also be harder to escape back to your hotel for an afternoon swim or a nap.

The biggest determining factor when choosing a hotel location should be the type of vacation you have planned. If you're the kind of person who will explore the Disney parks all day and then spend the night dancing at Pleasure Island, it makes more sense to stay on Disney property or at least close to it. The same goes for International Drive if you're going to camp in the Universal or Sea-World parks. But if you'd like to get away from it all, take a quiet stroll along a city sidewalk, see a museum, or experience life in the "real" Orlando, consider staying in Downtown Orlando or Winter Park.

You'll find the places described here on the map "Accommodations & Dining Elsewhere in Orlando" on p. 159.

IN DOWNTOWN ORLANDO

All of the following fall within the "Moderate" price category. None of these properties provide free transportation to the theme parks.

Radisson Plaza Hotel Orlando ⚡ This 15-story hotel, built in 1985, is just off I-4, only a few blocks from downtown Orlando and 15 minutes from the airport. It's in a great location for business travelers or others who will spend a lot of time downtown, but presents quite a hoof for anyone wanting to get to the theme parks. If you don't have a car, you'll have to pay for and arrange your own shuttle. Some rooms overlook Lake Ivanhoe and/or the Orlando skyline.

60 S. Ivanhoe Blvd., Orlando, FL 32804. ⓒ 800/333-3333 or 407/425-4455. Fax 407/425-7440. www.radissonorlando.com. 364 units. $105–$300 double. Extra person $15. Children 17 and under stay free in parent's room. AE, DISC, MC, V. Self-parking $4–$6, valet parking $10. Take I-4 to Exit 84/Ivanhoe Blvd. and follow it to the hotel. **Amenities:** Restaurant (American), lounge; outdoor heated pool; 2 tennis courts; fitness center; Jacuzzi; sauna; limited room service; nonsmoking rooms; concierge-level rooms. *In room:* A/C, TV w/pay movies, hair dryer.

Westin Grand Bohemian ⚡⚡ *Finds* Downtown's newest jewel opened in spring 2001 with an early-20th-century Euro-Bohemian theme. It caters almost exclusively to the business and romance crowds, which means—much to the satisfaction of the adult guests here—you'll find almost no children on the premises. The comfortable and plush rooms have an Art Deco look with plenty of chrome and reds or purples. The "Heavenly Beds" (firm mattresses, down blankets and comforters, and five pillows) are among the best in Orlando. (You can buy one for $2,200!) The upper floors on the east side overlook the pool; those on the north side face downtown. The classy hotel, which is smoke free, has more than 100 pieces of 19th- and 20th-century American fine art, and its lounge features a rare Imperial Grand Bösendorfer Piano—one of only two in the world and valued at a cool quarter of a million.

325 S. Orange Ave. (across from City Hall). ℭ **866/663-0024** or 407/313-9000. Fax 407/313-6001. www. grandbohemianhotel.com or www.grandthemehotels.com. 250 units. $159–$189 for up to 4; $225 and up suites. AE, DC, DISC, MC, V. Valet $18. Take I-4 Exit 82C, then left on Magnolia Ave. and go 2 blocks to Jackson St. Left on Jackson. The garage is 2 blocks west on Jackson. **Amenities:** Restaurant (International), lounge, coffee shop; heated outdoor pool and spa; fitness center; concierge; business center; 24-hr. room service, guest laundry and dry cleaning; concierge-level rooms. *In room:* A/C, TV/Nintendo and pay movies, dataport, minibar, coffeemaker, hair dryer, iron, safe.

IN WINTER PARK

Best Western Mt. Vernon Inn *Value*   This is one of the best bargains in town—a place where guests get comfortable rooms and a shield from Mickey Mania. But you had better be sure you want that shield, because this is even farther from the parks (20–25 miles) than the downtown O-Town hotels and inns. The Colonial-style Mount Vernon isn't fancy by resort standards, but its rooms are cozy and the staff is as friendly as kin. Some rooms overlook the pool, and a few have refrigerators. Deluxe rooms feature a small sitting area and offer a choice of one king or two queen beds. Families love visiting the city park across the street.

110 S. Orlando Ave., Winter Park, FL 32789 ℭ **800/992-3379** or 407/647-1166. Fax 407/647-8011. www. bestwestern.com. 147 units. $79–$119 double. Extra person $6. Children 17 and under stay free in parent's room. AE, DC, DISC, MC, V. Free self-parking. The inn is on U.S. 17–92, between Fairbanks Ave. and Lee Rd. **Amenities:** Restaurant (American), lounge; outdoor heated pool; guest laundry, valet; nonsmoking rooms. *In room:* A/C, TV, dataport.

6

Where to Dine

Orlando's fast-food joints arrived en masse in the early 1980s, 5 minutes or so after the city's coronation as a family destination. Theme restaurants—representing everything from hot rods to superheroes—weren't far behind. That's why local cuisine is usually regarded as sub par when compared to that of foodie havens such as New York, San Francisco, and Las Vegas, which in recent years has escaped its blue-plate image. In fairness, though, some of Orlando's 4,000 restaurants can go head-to-head with the competition. (Disbelievers should grab a chair at **Emeril's** at CityWalk, **Victoria & Albert's** at Disney's Grand Floridian Resort & Spa, or **Manuel's on the 28th** in downtown Orlando.)

Because most central Florida visitors spend much of their time at Disney, we're going to focus a lot of our energy there, but we won't leave out worthwhile restaurants beyond Mickey's real estate. We're going to stop at some of the new kids under the Universal Orlando umbrella, sample what's cooking along International Drive, and then visit a fair share of other dining rooms that have benefited from the culinary infusion created by the attractions.

Note to parents: Keep in mind that most moderate to inexpensive restaurants have kids' menus ($4–$6), and many offer distractions, such as coloring books and mazes, to keep your two-footed critters busy until the chow arrives.

If you go to a place catering to children, expect the noise level to be high. They don't take a vacation from squeals of joy or fits of temper, so you won't either.

If kids really get your goat, steer clear of any restaurant that offers "character meals" (see the listings later in this chapter). Also note that the more the meal costs, the less likely you'll be in the same dining room as a lot of little ones. So if you want peace—and can afford it—consider a meal in the more expensive restaurants in the resorts, on International Drive, or around Orlando proper. (Even if the howling kids belong to you, take advantage of the many in-hotel babysitting services for a night and discover the romance again.)

For additional online information about area restaurants, visit **www.disneyworld.com**, **www.universalorlando.com**, **www.orlandoinfo.com**, or the websites in the listings that follow.

PRIORITY SEATING AT WDW RESTAURANTS

Walt Disney World's priority seating is similar to a reservation, but it's less rigid. It means you get the next table available *after* you arrive at a restaurant, but a table isn't kept empty while the eatery waits for you. Therefore, you probably will end up waiting 15 to 30 minutes, even if you arrive at the time you scheduled your meal. You can arrange priority seating 60 days or more in advance at most full-service restaurants in the Magic Kingdom, Epcot, Disney–MGM Studios, Animal Kingdom, Disney resorts, and Downtown Disney. Priority seating also can be arranged for character meals (later in this chapter) and shows throughout the

---

> ## Tips How Early Can You Book It?
>
> At the time this book went to press, priority-seating arrangements could be made 120 days in advance at Disney resorts, Epcot, Animal Kingdom, and for breakfast and lunch at Disney–MGM Studios; 2 years in advance at Disney dinner shows; and 60 days in advance at Magic Kingdom and for MGM dinners. For arrangements, call © **407/939-3463.**

World. To make arrangements, call © **407/939-3463.** Nighttime dinner-theater shows (see chapter 10, "Walt Disney World & Orlando After Dark") can be booked 2 months or more in advance. *Note:* Since the priority seating phone number was instituted in 1994, it has become much more difficult to obtain a table as a walk-in. So we *strongly* advise you to call ahead.

If, however, you don't reserve in advance, you can take your chances by making reservations once you have arrived in the parks.

- **At Epcot:** Make reservations at the Worldkey interactive terminals at Guest Relations in Innoventions East, at Worldkey Information Service satellites located on the main concourse to World Showcase and at Germany in World Showcase, or at the restaurants.
- **At Magic Kingdom:** Make reservations via the telephones at several locations including the Walt Disney World Railroad station just inside the entrance (others are marked on your guide map) or at the restaurants.
- **At Disney–MGM Studios:** Make reservations via the telephones just inside the entrance or at the restaurants.
- **At Animal Kingdom:** Make reservations by visiting Guest Relations near the entrance. You can get priority seating at the Rainforest Cafe at Animal Kingdom. Because this is a *verrry* popular place, the sooner you call the better.

Also, keep these restaurant facts in mind:

- All park restaurants are **nonsmoking.** (As of July 1, 2003, *all Florida restaurants* and bars that serve food are smoke free.)
- The Magic Kingdom (including its restaurants) serves no alcoholic beverages, but liquor is available at Animal Kingdom, Epcot, and Disney–MGM Studios restaurants and elsewhere in the WDW complex.
- All sit-down restaurants in Walt Disney World take American Express, Diners Club, Discover, MasterCard, Visa, and the Disney Visa Card.
- Unless otherwise noted, restaurants in the parks **require park admission.**
- Guests at Disney resorts and official properties can make restaurant reservations through guest services or concierge desks.
- Nearly all WDW restaurants with sit-down or counter service offer children's menus with items ranging from $4 to $6, though in a few cases they're $9 to $10.

1 Restaurants by Cuisine

AFRICAN

Boma (Animal Kingdom Lodge, $$$, p. 141)

Jiko—The Cooking Place ✿ (Animal Kingdom Lodge, $$$, p. 143)

AMERICAN

B-Line Diner (International Drive Area, $$, p. 154)

Cinderella's Royal Table ✿ (Magic Kingdom, $$$, p. 135)

Key to Abbreviations: $$$$ = Very Expensive $$$ = Expensive $$ = Moderate $ = Inexpensive

Cosmic Ray's Starlight Café
(Magic Kingdom, $, p. 135)

50's Prime Time Café
(Disney–MGM Studios, $$,
p. 138)

Hard Rock Cafe (Universal
Orlando, $$, p. 150)

Hollywood Brown Derby (Disney–
MGM Studios, $$$, p. 138)

Liberty Tree Tavern (Magic
Kingdom, $$, p. 135)

Panera Bread (Downtown and
elsewhere, $$, p. 160)

Planet Hollywood (Pleasure Island,
$$, p. 145)

Plaza Restaurant (Magic Kingdom,
$, p. 138)

Sci-Fi Dine-In Theater Restaurant
(Disney–MGM Studios, $$,
p. 139)

Tusker House (Animal Kingdom,
$, p. 139)

BARBECUE

Bubbalou's Bodacious BBQ
(Winter Park, $, p. 161)

Wild Jacks (International Drive,
$$, p. 156)

BRITISH

Rose & Crown Pub & Dining
Room (Epcot, $$, p. 133)

CALIFORNIA

California Grill (Disney's
Contemporary Resort, $$$,
p. 142)

Pebbles (Lake Buena Vista,
$$, p. 147)

Rainforest Cafe (Animal King-
dom & Downtown Disney
Marketplace, $$, p. 139 and
145)

Wolfgang Puck Grand Café
(Disney's West Side, $$, p. 146)

CANADIAN

Le Cellier Steakhouse (Epcot, $$,
p. 132)

CARIBBEAN

Bob Marley—A Tribute to Freedom
(Universal's CityWalk, $$, p. 151)

Jimmy Buffett's Margaritaville
(Universal's CityWalk, $$,
p. 150)

CHARACTER MEALS

Cape May Café (Disney's Beach
Club Resort, $$, p. 162)

Chef Mickey's (Disney's Con-
temporary Resort, $$, p. 163)

Cinderella's Royal Table (Magic
Kingdom, $$, p. 163)

Crystal Palace Buffet (Magic
Kingdom, $$, p. 163)

Donald's Prehistoric Breakfastosaurus (Animal Kingdom,
$$, p. 163)

Garden Grill (Epcot, $$,
p. 163)

Hollywood & Vine Character
Dining (Disney MGM–
Studios, p. 163)

Liberty Tree Tavern (Magic
Kingdom, $$, p. 163)

1900 Park Fare (Disney's Grand
Floridian Resort & Spa, $$,
p. 163)

'Ohana Character Breakfast
(Disney Polynesian Resort, $$,
p. 164)

Princess Storybook Breakfast
(Epcot, $$, p. 164)

CHINESE

Lotus Blossom Café (Epcot, $,
p. 134)

Ming Court (International
Drive, $$, p. 155)

Nine Dragons (Epcot, $$, p. 132)

CUBAN

Bongo's Cuban Cafe (Disney's
West Side, $$, p. 145)

Rolando's (Casselberry, $$,
p. 160)

The Samba Room (International
Drive, $$, p. 155)

FOOD COURT

Sunshine Season Food Fair
(Epcot, $, p. 134)

FRENCH

Chefs de France (Epcot, $$$,
p. 130)

Citricos ✪ (Disney's Grand Floridian Resort & Spa, $$$$, p. 140)

Le Provence ✪ (Downtown Orlando, $$$, p. 157)

Maison & Jardin ✪ (Altamonte Springs, $$$, p. 158)

GERMAN

Biergarten (Epcot, $$, p. 132)

Sommerfest (Epcot, $, p. 134)

INTERNATIONAL

Arthur's 27 (Lake Buena Vista, $$$$, p. 146)

Black Swan (Lake Buena Vista, $$$$, p. 147)

The Boheme (Downtown Orlando, $$$$, p. 156)

Dexter's at Thornton Park (Downtown Orlando, $$, p. 160)

Dux ✪✪ (International Drive, $$$$, p. 152)

La Coquina ✪ (Lake Buena Vista, $$$$, p. 147)

Manuel's on the 28th ✪✪✪ (Downtown Orlando, $$$$, p. 157)

Park Plaza Gardens (Winter Park, $$$, p. 158)

Victoria & Albert's ✪✪✪ (Disney's Grand Floridian Resort & Spa, $$$$, p. 140)

White Wolf Cafe (Downtown Orlando, $$, p. 161)

ITALIAN

Capriccio ✪ (International Drive, $$, p. 155)

Christini's ✪ (International Drive, $$$, p. 152)

Delfino Riviera ✪ (Universal's Portofino Bay Hotel, $$$$, p. 148)

Enzo's on the Lake ✪✪ (Longwood, $$$$, p. 157)

L'Originale Alfredo di Roma (Epcot, $$$, p. 131)

Mama Della's (Universal's Portofino Bay Hotel, $$$, p. 149)

Mama Melrose's Ristorante Italiano (Disney–MGM Studios, $$, p. 139)

Pacino's Italian Ristorante ✪ (Kissimmee, $$, p. 160)

Pastamore Ristorante (Universal's CityWalk, $$, p. 151)

Portobello Yacht Club ✪ (Pleasure Island, $$$, p. 144)

Romano's Macaroni Grill ✪ (Lake Buena Vista, $, p. 148)

Tony's Town Square Restaurant (Magic Kingdom, $$$, p. 135)

Toy Story Pizza Planet (Disney–MGM Studios, $, p. 139)

JAPANESE

Mikado Japanese Steak House ✪ (Lake Buena Vista, $$$, p. 158)

Ran-Getsu of Tokyo (International Drive, $$$, p. 152)

Tempura Kiku (Epcot, $$$, p. 131)

Teppanyaki Dining Room (Epcot, $$$, p. 131)

Yakitori House (Epcot, $, p. 134)

MEXICAN

Cantina de San Angel (Epcot, $, p. 133)

San Angel Inn ✪ (Epcot, $$, p. 133)

MISSISSIPPI DELTA

House of Blues (Disney's West Side, $$, p. 146)

MOROCCAN

Marrakesh ✪ (Epcot, $$$, p. 131)

NEW ORLEANS

Boatwright's Dining Hall (Disney's Port Orleans Resort, $$, p. 143)

Emeril's ✪✪ (Universal's CityWalk, $$$$, p. 149)

NORWEGIAN

Akershus (Epcot, $$, p. 132)

Kringla Bakeri og Kafe (Epcot, $, p. 133)

PACIFIC RIM

'Ohana (Disney's Polynesian Resort, $$, p. 144)

Roy's Restaurant (International Drive, $$$, p. 154)

Tchoup Chop 🍴🍴 (Universal's
Royal Pacific Resort, $$$,
p. 150)

SEAFOOD/STEAKS/CHOPS

Artist Point 🍴 (Disney's
Wilderness Lodge, $$$, p. 141)
Atlantis 🍴 (International Drive
Area, $$$$, p. 151)
Blackfin Seafood Grill & Bar 🍴
(Winter Park, $$$, p. 157)
Cape May Café (Disney's Beach
Club Resort, $$, p. 143)
Charlie's Lobster House (International Drive, $$$$, p. 152)
Coral Reef (Epcot, $$$, p. 130)
Flying Fish Café (Disney's
Boardwalk, $$$, p. 142)
Fulton's Crab House 🍴 (Pleasure
Island, $$$$, p. 144)
Hemingway's (Lake Buena Vista,
$$$, p. 147)

The Palm (Universal's Hard Rock
Hotel, $$$$, p. 149)
Plantation Room (Celebration,
$$$, p. 158)
Yachtsman Steakhouse 🍴 (Disney's
Yacht Club Resort, $$$$,
p. 141)

TAPAS

Cafe Tu Tu Tango 🍴 (International
Drive, $$, p. 154)
Spoodles (Disney's Boardwalk,
$$$, p. 143)

THAI

Siam Orchid 🍴 (International
Drive Area, $$, p. 156)

VIETNAMESE

Little Saigon 🍴 (Downtown
Orlando, $, p. 161)

---

2 Places to Dine in Walt Disney World

From hot-dog stands to posh restaurants, there are nearly 350 places to eat in the WDW theme parks (Epcot, Magic Kingdom, Disney–MGM Studios, and Animal Kingdom), resorts, and "official" hotels. That doesn't include eateries located in entertainment and shopping areas (Pleasure Island, Downtown Disney West Side, and Downtown Disney Marketplace), some of which are listed in the Lake Buena Vista section. Yet, with only a few exceptions, you won't find them winning accolades from *Bon Appétit*. The food in most Disney restaurants is on par with the food at Universal Orlando—filling and palatable, but overpriced for the quality received. The exception: kids' menus. Most sit-down and counter-service eateries in the theme parks offer wee-one meals in the $4 to $6 range.

The prices for adult meals at Orlando restaurants—except at theme parks and other attractions—are no more exorbitant than you'd find anywhere else. Restaurants have been categorized by **the price of an average entree** per person. In this chapter, restaurants in the Inexpensive category charge under $10 for an entree; those in the Moderate category charge anywhere from $11 to $20. Expensive restaurants will set you back $21 to $30, and Very Expensive restaurants will top that, sometimes by a large margin.

One last note: The restaurants we list in this chapter occasionally change menus (and sometimes more than just occasionally). So items we feature here may not be on the menu when you visit. And, as entrees vary, so do prices.

That said, it's time to divide and conquer.

IN EPCOT

Though an ethnic meal at one of the World Showcase pavilions is a traditional part of the Epcot experience, we remind you that many of the following establishments are overpriced for the quality received. Unless money is no object, you may want to consider the lower-priced walk-in places located throughout the park. They

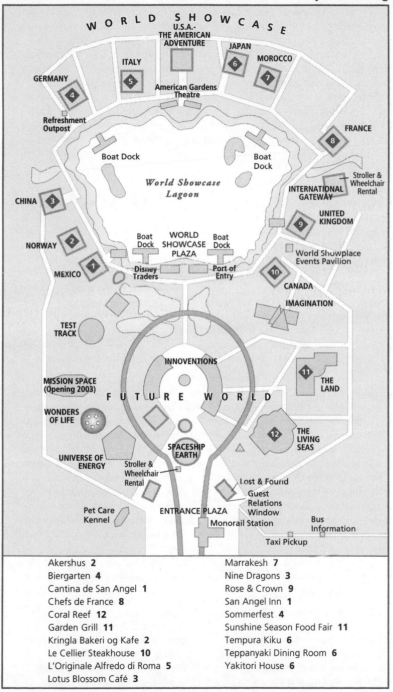

don't require reservations (for details, check the Epcot guide map you'll receive upon entering). Or eat at one of the full-service restaurants at lunch, when entree prices are lower. Almost all of the establishments listed here serve lunch and dinner daily (hours vary with park hours), and, unless otherwise noted, they offer children's meals. All but one or two require theme-park admission and the $7 parking fee, too. These restaurants are located on the "Epcot Dining" map on p. 129.

Note: Because the clientele at even the fanciest Epcot World Showcase restaurant comes directly from the park, you don't have to dress up for dinner. **Priority seating,** which reserves your place but not a specific table, is available at all WDW sit-down restaurants and is strongly recommended. Otherwise, the chances of getting a table without a wait—often a long wait—are pretty slim. Call © **407/939-3463** for priority seating.

EXPENSIVE

Chefs de France TRADITIONAL FRENCH   Three famous chefs—Paul Bocuse, Roger Verge, and Gaston LeNotre—designed the menu, which is respectable by theme-park standards but doesn't threaten better French restaurants in Orlando's free world. The dinner entrees include Mediterranean seafood casserole (grouper, scallops, and shrimp dusted with saffron, then allowed to swim in a mild garlic sauce) and a garlicky braised lamb shank with onion potato au gratin. There's a substantial wine list to complement the menu, and the desserts are among the better ones in the World. Dining areas have an intimate, Art Nouveau feel thanks to candelabras and glass-and-brass dividers, but the service, at times lacking, can chill the fun.

France Pavilion, World Showcase. © **407/939-3463** or 407/827-8709. www.disneyworld.com. Priority seating. Main courses $10–$18 lunch, $14–$30 dinner. AE, DC, DISC, MC, V. Daily noon–3:30pm and 5pm–1 hr. before park closes. Parking $7.

Coral Reef SEAFOOD   Mood is half the fun at the Reef, where you seem to dine under the sea at tables circling a 5.6-million-gallon aquarium. Some of Disney's denizens swim by as songs such as Debussy's "La Mer" and Handel's "Water Music" softly bathe the background. Tiered seats, mainly in semicircular booths, give everyone a good view. Diners get fish-identifier sheets with labeled pictures so they can put names on the faces swimming by their tables. This is one of the most popular restaurants in all of the parks. Nevertheless, it still suffers the theme-park curse: The food is good, but the menu lacks imagination and the prices are a bit overboard. Highlights include pan-seared salmon with garlic-pesto mashed potatoes and candied carrots, grilled mahimahi with wasabi mashed potatoes and collard greens, and Caribbean lobster with summer squash and potatoes. The Reef serves wine by the glass.

Tips Special Tastes

Looking for kosher food? Worried WDW can't entertain your vegetarian taste buds? Disney usually can handle those diets and other special ones (people who need fat-free or sugar-free meals, folks who have allergies or a lactose intolerance, for instance) as long as guests give Disney advance notice—usually no more than 24 hours. You can do that when you make priority-seating arrangements (© **407/939-3463**) or, if you're staying at a Disney resort, at its Guest Relations desk.

> **Fun Fact Fast Food**
>
> Disney guests eat more than 9.7 million burgers, 7.7 million hot dogs, and 9.3 million pounds of french fries every year. That's enough fries to circle the planet three times. And it takes 1.7 million pounds of ketchup to accompany all that fast food.

Living Seas Pavilion, Future World. © 407/939-3463. www.disneyworld.com. Priority seating recommended. Main courses $14–$21 lunch; $16–$32 dinner. AE, DC, DISC, MC, V. Daily 11:30am–3pm and 4:30pm–park closing. Parking $7.

L'Originale Alfredo di Roma *(Overrated)* SOUTHERN ITALIAN   It may be the most popular restaurant in Epcot, but we've heard diners say the overpriced pasta here is matched only by servers who can be too carefree. L'Originale is actually L'Replica of Alfredo De Lelio's eatery in Rome, and the menu includes his celebrated fettuccine dished out in an exhibition kitchen. On the meatier side, a smallish veal chop is grilled and served with Chianti and truffle sauce, mushrooms, asparagus, and roasted potatoes. The *zuppa di pesce* is a medley of grouper, scallops, mussels, shrimp, and calamari in a white wine, garlic, and tomato sauce served on fettuccine. The wine list is reasonably extensive. The dining room noise level can be quite high, so if you want a quieter meal, ask for a seat on the veranda.

Italy Pavilion World Showcase. © 407/939-3463 or 407/827-8418. www.disneyworld.com. Priority seating. Main courses $10–$25 lunch, $17–$38 (most under $25) dinner. AE, DC, DISC, MC, V. Daily noon–park closing. Parking $7.

Marrakesh *(Finds)* MOROCCAN   This dining spot exemplifies the spirit of Epcot more than any other restaurant, yet a lot of guests ignore it because they're worried the menu is too exotic. Speaking of exotic, belly dancers entertain while your eyes feast on options such as marinated beef shish kabob; braised chicken with green olives, garlic, and lemon; and a medley of seafood, chicken, and lamb. Most entrees come with the national dish, couscous (steamed semolina with veggies and sometimes other embellishments). The restaurant's hand-set mosaic tiles, latticed shutters, and painted ceiling represent some 12 centuries of Arabic design. Exquisitely carved faux ivory archways frame the dining area. There's a small selection of wine and beer.

Morocco Pavilion, World Showcase. © 407/939-3463. www.disneyworld.com. Priority seating. Main courses $12–$18 lunch, $17–$26 dinner; $28–$30 prix fixe. AE, DC, DISC, MC, V. Daily noon–park closing. Parking $7.

Tempura Kiku *(Overrated)* JAPANESE   Tempura batter can hide the flaws of almost anything inside—but in this case it can't hide the puny size of the shrimp, chicken, and other morsels within. It's usually a tasty meal, but one can't help but think of Long John Silver's. Tempura Kiku also serves sushi, sashimi, Kirin beer, plum wine, and sake along with specialty drinks.

Japan Pavilion, World Showcase. © 407/939-3463. www.disneyworld.com. Priority seating for teppanyaki; reservations not accepted at tempura counter. Main courses $9.50–$13 lunch, $13–$25 dinner. AE, DC, DISC, MC, V. Daily 11am–1 hr. before park closes. Parking $7.

Teppanyaki Dining Room JAPANESE   If you've been to any of the Japanese steakhouse chains (*teppanyakis*), you know the drill: Diners sit around grill tables while white-hatted chefs rapidly dice, slice, stir-fry, and sometimes launch the food onto your plate with amazing skill. Unfortunately, the culinary acrobatics here are better than the cuisine. (For a real treat, try the Mikado Japanese Steak House reviewed on p. 158.) Expect entrees to have chicken, steak, shrimp, scallops, lobster, or a combination. Like Tempura Kiku (see above), Kirin beer, plum wine, and sake are served. Diners here sit at communal tables, making this a good bet for people traveling alone.

Japan Pavilion, World Showcase. ℂ **407/939-3463**. www.disneyworld.com. Priority seating. Main courses $12–$22 lunch, $13–$32 dinner. AE, DC, DISC, MC, V. Daily 11am–1 hr. before park closes. Parking $7.

MODERATE

Akershus NORWEGIAN   Akershus is a re-created 14th-century castle where you can sample a 40-item smorgasbord of hot and cold dishes, making it a bargain for big eaters. Sure it's cheesy. But it's also reasonably good chow, though some diners will find it difficult to adapt to the Scandinavian taste. Entrees change but usually include venison stew, roast pork, gravlax, smoked mackerel, mustard herring, an array of Norwegian breads and cheeses, smashed rutabaga, and more. The staff is friendly, and the white-stone interior, beamed ceilings, leaded-glass windows, and archways add to the authentic atmosphere. Norwegian beer and aquavit complement a list of French and California wines.

Norway Pavilion, World Showcase. ℂ **407/939-3463**. www.disneyworld.com. Priority seating. Lunch buffet $14 adults, $6 children 3–9; dinner buffet $20 adults, $9 children. AE, DC, DISC, MC, V. Daily noon–park closing. Parking $7.

Biergarten *(Overrated* GERMAN   The Biergarten simulates a Bavarian village at Oktoberfest with a working waterwheel and geranium-filled flower boxes adorning Tudor-style houses. Unfortunately, the festive atmosphere hardly makes up for the bland, methane-producing food. Entertainment might be an oompah band or a strolling accordionist, and guests are encouraged to dance and sing along. The all-you-can-gobble buffet is filled with Bavarian fare (assorted sausages, pork schnitzel, sauerbraten, spaetzle, and sauerkraut). Beck's and Kirschwasser are the featured adult beverages.

Germany Pavilion, World Showcase. ℂ **407/939-3463**. www.disneyworld.com. Priority seating. Lunch buffet $15 adults, $7 children 3–11; dinner buffet $20 adults, $8 children. AE, DC, DISC, MC, V. Daily noon–3:45pm and 4pm–park closing. Parking $7.

Le Cellier Steakhouse CANADIAN   If you're hankering for steak and you're already in Epcot, the convenience of Le Cellier is a plus, but it doesn't compare to the area's better steakhouses (see the Yachtsman Steakhouse on p. 141). The restaurant's French Gothic facade and steeply pitched copper roofs lend a castle-like ambience. The dining room resembles a wine cellar, and you'll sit in tapestry-upholstered chairs under vaulted stone arches. Red-meat main events include the usual range of cuts—including filet, veal chop, and prime rib. Other options include cast-iron seared trout, barbecued duck and confit, pork Porterhouse, and maple- and ginger-glazed salmon. Wash down your meal with a Canadian wine or choose from a selection of Canadian beers.

Canadian Pavilion, World Showcase. ℂ **407/939-3463**. www.disneyworld.com. Priority seating. Main courses $9–$18 lunch, $14–$26 dinner. AE, DC, DISC, MC, V. Daily noon–park closing. Parking $7.

Nine Dragons REGIONAL CHINESE   When it comes to decor, Nine Dragons shines with carved rosewood furnishings and a dragon-motif ceiling. Some windows overlook a lagoon. But (is there an echo?) the food doesn't match its surroundings. Main courses feature Mandarin, Shanghai, Cantonese, and Szechuan cuisines, but portions are small. The dishes include spicy beef stir-fried with squash in sha cha sauce; lightly breaded lemon chicken; and a casserole of lobster, shrimp, and scallops sautéed with ginger and scallions. You can order Chinese or California wines with your meal.

China Pavilion, World Showcase. ☎ 407/939-3463. www.disneyworld.com. Priority seating. Main courses $9.50–$19 lunch, $12.50–$30 dinner; $42.50 sampler for 2. AE, DC, DISC, MC, V. Daily 11:30am–park closing. Parking $7.

Rose & Crown Pub & Dining Room ENGLISH PUB GRUB   Visitors from the U.K. flock to this spot, where English folk music and the occasionally saucy server entertain you as you feast your eyes and palate on a short but traditional menu. It beckons with fish (cod) and chips wrapped in newspaper, bangers and mash, prime rib with Yorkshire pudding, and, the best of the bunch, an English pie sampler (pork and cottage, and chicken and leek). The interior has dark oak wainscoting, beamed Tudor ceilings, and a belly-up bar. Speaking of the bar, it features lighter fare such as sausage rolls, Cornish pasties, and a Stilton cheese and fruit plate. Wash it down with a pint of Irish lager, Bass Ale, or Guinness Stout. By the way, the pub has an ale warmer to make sure Guinness is served at 55 degrees, just like its British guests prefer.

Note: The outdoor tables (weather permitting) offer a fantastic view of Illumi-Nations (p. 210). You can request one when making priority-seating arrangements, and if you can, make the request *at least* 30 days in advance and ask for a 7:30pm seating. Also, if you only want to grab a pint or a snack at the bar, you don't need priority seating.

United Kingdom Pavilion, World Showcase. ☎ 407/939-3463. www.disneyworld.com. Priority seating for dining room, not for pub. Main courses $10–$14 lunch, $15–$19 dinner. AE, DC, DISC, MC, V. Daily 11am–1 hr. before park closes. Parking $7.

San Angel Inn ✮ MEXICAN   It's always night at the San Angel, where you can feast on some of the best South-of-the-Border cuisine in all of the theme parks—not that there's a lot of competition. Candlelit tables set the mood, and the menu delivers reasonably authentic food (unless you're used to the real McCoy in places like Southern Texas and Southern California). *Mole poblano* (chicken brought to life with more than 20 spices, carrots, and a hint of chocolate) is one top seller. Another favorite: *filete motuleño* (grilled beef tenderloin served over black beans, melted cheese, pepper strips, and fried plantains—a sweet, banana-like fruit). Before your edibles arrive, enjoy the sounds of the distant songbirds—heck, join them if you've had multiple margaritas or more than your limit of Dos Equis.

Mexico Pavilion, World Showcase. ☎ 407/939-3463 or 407/842-1130. www.disneyworld.com. Priority seating. Main courses $9.25–$17.50 lunch; $17.75–$23.50 dinner. AE, DC, DISC, MC, V. Daily 11:30am–park closing. Parking $7.

INEXPENSIVE

Cantina de San Angel MEXICAN   Counter-service eateries are the most common places to grab a bite in the parks. This one is a notch above Taco Bell. Come here only if you want a palatable burrito, taco, or churro on the fly. You can also grab a Dos Equis or frozen margarita.

Mexico Pavilion, World Showcase. ☎ 407/939-3463. www.disneyworld.com. No priority seating. Meals $4–$8. AE, DC, DISC, MC, V. Daily 11:30am–1 hr. before park closes. Parking $7.

Kringla Bakeri og Kafe NORWEGIAN   The lunch-pail crowd loves this combination cafe-bakery. Grab-and-go options include a plate of smoked salmon and scrambled eggs, smoked ham and Jarlsberg cheese sandwiches, pastries, and waffles with strawberry preserves. Wine is sold by the glass.

Tips **Flamed Out**

If you're a smoker, **don't plan on lighting up** over dinner. Effective July 1, 2003, a state constitutional amendment bans smoking in Florida's public work places, including restaurants and bars that serve food. Stand-alone bars that serve virtually no food are exempt, as are designated smoking rooms in hotels and motels.

Norway Pavilion, World Showcase. ✆ **407/939-3463**. www.disneyworld.com. No priority seating. Sandwiches and salads $4–$6. AE, DC, DISC, MC, V. Daily 11am–park closing. Parking $7.

Lotus Blossom Café CHINESE   If you've tried one of those Oriental walk-up joints in mall food courts, you know what to expect. It's an inexpensive self-service outlet that won't make a gourmet's wish list. Expect slightly above fast-food quality stir-fry, hot-and-sour, lo mein, and pork-fried rice. You can buy Chinese beer and wine to make you forget Mickey.

China Pavilion, World Showcase. ✆ **407/939-3463**. www.disneyworld.com. No priority seating. Meals $4–$6.50. AE, DC, DISC, MC, V. Daily 11am–park closing. Parking $7.

Sommerfest GERMAN   The quick-bite menu includes bratwurst and frankfurter sandwiches (one is still a hot dog) with sauerkraut. They also serve a chef's surprise (don't ask), apple strudel, wine, and Beck's beer.

Germany Pavilion, World Showcase. ✆ **407/939-3463**. No priority seating. All meals under $7. AE, DC, DISC, MC, V. Daily 11am–park closing. Parking $7.

Sunshine Season Food Fair *Value* FOOD COURT   The food isn't gourmet, but of all cafeterias or counter-service stops in the World, Sunshine Season has the most diversity because it has six walk-ups in one. There's a sandwich shop (subs and more), a barbecue joint (ribs, chicken, pork), a potato place (with stir-fry, chili, and veggies), and a pasta counter (fettuccine, vegetable lasagna, and chicken Alfredo). There's also a small bakery and an ice-cream stand. Colorful umbrella tables under a tent ring a splashing fountain, and hot-air balloons add to the festive decor. Its real value is that family members with different tastes can dine at the same time under one roof. It can get very crowded at mealtimes, but wine by the glass, a frosty draft, or bottled beer dim the din.

Land Pavilion, Future World. ✆ **407/939-3463**. www.disneyworld.com. Reservations not accepted. Meals $5–$7. AE, DC, DISC, MC, V. 11am–park closing. Parking $7.

Yakitori House JAPANESE   While it sounds exotic, the food in this cafeteria is the same quality as that in the Lotus Blossom Café, above: mall caliber. Main events include teriyaki shrimp, chicken, and beef skewers; beef curry; sushi; and shrimp tempura. Liquid relaxants include Kirin beer, plum wine, and sake. Umbrella tables on a terrace overlook a rock waterfall.

Japan Pavilion, World Showcase. ✆ **407/939-3463**. www.disneyworld.com. Reservations not accepted. Meals $5–$8. AE, DC, DISC, MC, V. 11am–park closing. Parking $7.

IN THE MAGIC KINGDOM

In addition to the places mentioned here, there are plenty of fast-food outlets located throughout the park. You may find, however, that a quiet sit-down meal is an essential but all-too-brief way to get away from the forced-march madness. These restaurants are located on the "Walt Disney World & Lake Buena Vista

Dining" map on p. 136 and (more specifically) "The Magic Kingdom" map on p. 178. And remember—Magic Kingdom restaurants *don't serve alcohol.*

EXPENSIVE

Cinderella's Royal Table ⚝ AMERICAN   Can you pass up the chance to eat in Cinderella Castle, the Magic Kingdom's icon? Those who enter are usually swept off their feet by the Gothic interior, which includes leaded-glass windows and a spiral staircase that overlooks commoners in the lobby. (There's also an elevator to the dining area.) The servers treat you like a lord or lady (we're not kidding, that's how they'll address you) and the menu has fetching names, but the fine print reveals traditional entrees. The Earl's Poulet, plainly speaking, is roasted chicken, the Loyal Knight is spice-crusted salmon, and the Grand Duke is a New York strip. As we mentioned earlier, this isn't New York or San Fran, but the food is reasonably good by theme-park standards.

Cinderella Castle, Fantasyland. ℂ **407/939-3463.** www.disneyworld.com. Priority seating. Main courses $11–$16 lunch, $20–$26 dinner. AE, DC, DISC, MC, V. Daily 11:30am–2:45pm and 4pm–1 hr. before park closing. Parking $7.

Tony's Town Square Restaurant ITALIAN   Inspired by the cafe in *Lady and the Tramp,* Tony's dishes out nondescript (sometimes cardboard-quality) lunches and dinners in a pleasant if somewhat harried dining room. Evening fare includes scallops, mussels, rock shrimp, clams, and calamari in a lobster broth; sautéed veal medallions with wild mushrooms; and breaded eggplant with tomato sauce and mozzarella cheese. The original movie cells on the walls may inspire some couples to reenact the film's famous spaghetti smooch. There's additional seating in a sunny, plant-filled solarium.

Main Street. ℂ **407/939-3463.** www.disneyworld.com. Priority seating. Main courses $9.50–$16 lunch, $18.50–$24 dinner. AE, DC, DISC, MC, V. Daily 8:30–10:45am, noon–2:45pm, and 4pm–park closing. Parking $7.

MODERATE

Liberty Tree Tavern AMERICAN   Step into a replica of an 18th-century Colonial pub and its historic atmosphere, including oak-plank floors, pewter ware-stocked hutches, and a big brick fireplace hung with copper pots. The background music suits the period, but the nightly character dinner isn't particularly compelling: roasted turkey, marinated flank steak, and honey mustard ham with trimmings (see "Only in Orlando: Dining with Disney Characters," later in this chapter). If your heart is set on a buffet, you might be happier at Epcot's Akershus (p. 132) or Animal Kingdom's Boma (p. 141), but if you're stuck in the Magic Kingdom, well, this is pretty much the franchise. The food at lunch is similarly decent, although you can order only from an a la carte menu.

Liberty Square. ℂ **407/939-3463.** www.disneyworld.com. Priority seating. Main courses $12–$15 lunch; $21 adults, $10 children 3–11 (character dinner). AE, DC, DISC, MC, V. Daily 11:30am–3pm and 4pm–park closing. Parking $7.

INEXPENSIVE

Cosmic Ray's Starlight Café AMERICAN   The low-budget, high-fat menu includes chicken (whole or half rotisserie, dark meat, white meat, fried or grilled) and sandwiches (burgers, hot dogs, cheese steak). Ray's is typical theme-park on-the-fly cuisine. Bring plenty of antacid.

Main Street. ℂ **407/939-3463.** www.disneyworld.com. Priority seating. All items $6–$8. AE, DC, DISC, MC, V. Daily 11am–park closing. Parking $7.

Walt Disney World & Lake Buena Vista Dining

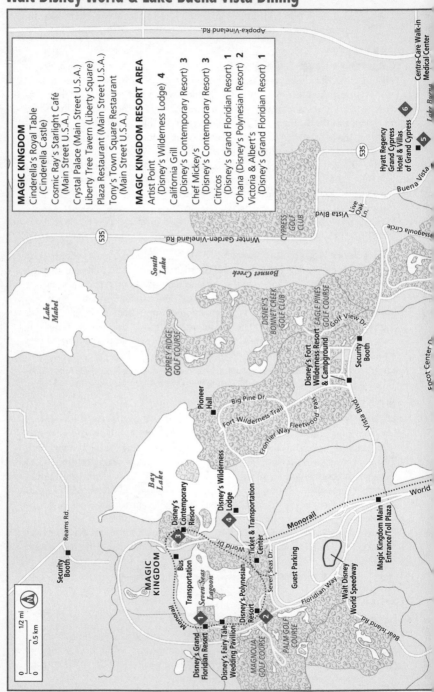

MAGIC KINGDOM

Cinderella's Royal Table (Cinderella Castle)

Cosmic Ray's Starlight Café (Main Street U.S.A.)

Crystal Palace (Main Street U.S.A.)

Liberty Tree Tavern (Liberty Square)

Plaza Restaurant (Main Street U.S.A.)

Tony's Town Square Restaurant (Main Street U.S.A.)

MAGIC KINGDOM RESORT AREA

Artist Point (Disney's Wilderness Lodge) **4**

California Grill (Disney's Contemporary Resort) **3**

Chef Mickey's (Disney's Contemporary Resort) **3**

Citricos (Disney's Grand Floridian Resort) **1**

'Ohana (Disney's Polynesian Resort) **2**

Victoria & Albert's (Disney's Grand Floridian Resort) **1**

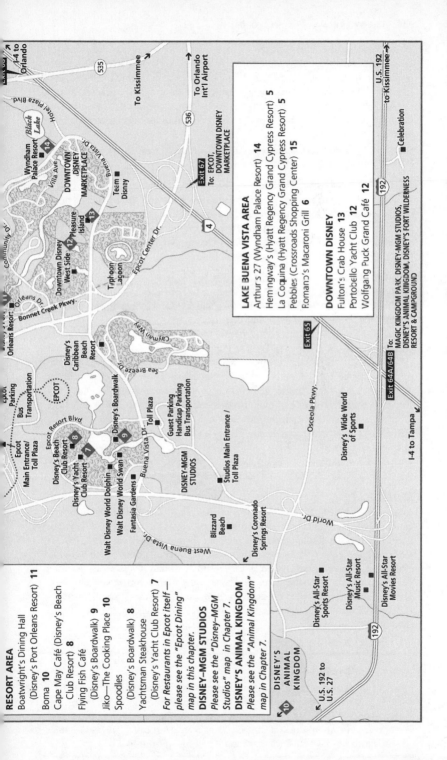

RESORT AREA

Boatwright's Dining Hall
(Disney's Port Orleans Resort) **11**
Boma **10**
Cape May Café (Disney's Beach
Club Resort) **8**
Flying Fish Café
(Disney's Boardwalk) **9**
Jiko—The Cooking Place **10**
Spoodles
(Disney's Boardwalk) **8**
Yachtsman Steakhouse
(Disney's Yacht Club Resort) **7**
*For Restaurants in Epcot itself —
please see the "Epcot Dining"
map in this chapter.*

DISNEY-MGM STUDIOS

*Please see the "Disney-MGM
Studios" map in Chapter 7.*

DISNEY'S ANIMAL KINGDOM

*Please see the "Animal Kingdom"
map in Chapter 7.*

LAKE BUENA VISTA AREA

Arthur's 27 (Wyndham Palace Resort) **14**
Hemingway's (Hyatt Regency Grand Cypress Resort) **5**
La Coquina (Hyatt Regency Grand Cypress Resort) **5**
Pebbles (Crossroads Shopping Center) **6**
Forman's Macaroni Grill **15**

DOWNTOWN DISNEY

Fulton's Crab House **13**
Portobello Yacht Club **12**
Wolfgang Puck Grand Café **12**

Plaza Restaurant AMERICAN   The sundaes, banana splits, and other ice-cream creations—arguably the best in WDW—at this 19th-century inspired restaurant draw more folks than anywhere else, especially during the dog days of summer. The Plaza also has tasty if expensive sandwiches (turkey, Reuben, cheese steak, chicken, and burgers) that come with an order of fries or potato salad. You can eat inside in an Art Nouveau dining room or on a veranda overlooking Cinderella Castle.

Main Street. ☎ 407/939-3463. www.disneyworld.com. Priority seating. Meals $8–$11; ice cream $3.25–$10. AE, DC, DISC, MC, V. Daily 11am–park closing. Parking $7.

AT DISNEY–MGM STUDIOS

There are more than a dozen places to eat in this park, and some have movie-lot names such as Studio Commissary and Starring Rolls Bakery. Those listed below are the best of the bunch. They're located on two maps, "Walt Disney World & Lake Buena Vista Dining" (p. 136) and "Disney–MGM Studios Theme Park" (p. 211).

EXPENSIVE

Hollywood Brown Derby AMERICAN   Modeled after the famed Los Angeles celebrity haunt where Louella Parsons and Hedda Hopper held court, this Derby offers a good-time meal, but one that's pretty pricey. Owner Bob Cobb invented the original restaurant's signature Cobb salad in the 1930s. (It's popular enough that this Derby serves 31,000 a year.) Dinner entrees at Disney's version include pan-seared grouper with balsamic roasted asparagus and mustard-crusted rack of lamb with acorn squash and sweet-and-sour cabbage. The Derby's signature dessert, grapefruit cake with cream-cheese icing, is a perfect meal capper. Among the dining-room visuals: more than 1,500 caricatures of the major stars who patronized the California restaurant—everyone from Bette Davis to Sammy Davis Jr. The Derby has a full bar and a modest selection of California wines.

Hollywood Blvd. ☎ 407/939-3463. www.disneyworld.com. Priority seating. Main courses $14–$22 lunch, $17–$26 dinner. AE, DC, DISC, MC, V. Daily 11:30am–park closing. Parking $7.

MODERATE

50's Prime Time Café *(Kids* *Overrated* AMERICAN   The concept is intriguing: Build a restaurant based on a 1950s time warp/sitcom psychodrama. The atmosphere includes black-and-white TVs showing clips from such classics as *My Little Margie* and *Topper.* The servers add to the fun, greeting diners with lines like, "Hi Sis, I'll go tell Mom you're home," and they may threaten to withhold dessert if you don't eat all your food. We won't blame you if you choose to abstain. The entrees—fried chicken, meat loaf, and pot roast, among others—simply don't deliver on the taste front, although the desserts aren't bad. Beer is the only alcohol served.

(*Tips* **Express Lane**

To get preferred seating at the end-of-the-day spectacular Fantasmic (p. 213)! at no cost above your meal, make priority seating reservations at Hollywood Brown Derby, Mama Melrose's Ristorante Italiano, or Hollywood & Vine, and request a Fantasmic! package. *But call* ☎ **407/939-3463** in advance to make sure the package is still being offered.

Near the Indiana Jones Stunt Spectacular. © 407/939-3463. www.disneyworld.com. Priority seating. Main courses $13–$18.50 lunch and dinner. AE, DC, DISC, MC, V. Daily 11am–park closing. Parking $7.

Mama Melrose's Ristorante Italiano *Overrated* ITALIAN The best (and safest) bets here are the wood-fired flatbreads (grilled pepperoni, four-cheese, Portobello mushroom, and others). The menu is fleshed out with some Italian pretenders, including veal osso bucco and oak-grilled salmon. *Our advice:* Unless you plan to suck down a lot of sangria, find another place to eat.

Near the Backlot Tour. © 407/939-3463. www.disneyworld.com. Priority seating. Main courses $13–$18 lunch, $15–$21 dinner. AE, DC, DISC, MC, V. Daily 11:30am–park closing. Parking $7.

Sci-Fi Dine-In Theater Restaurant *Overrated* AMERICAN Ho-hum. If you read the 50's Prime Time listing above and give it a science-fiction spin, you'll know what to expect. The Sci-Fi is meant to look like a 1950s Los Angeles drive-in movie emporium. Diners sit in chrome convertibles under a starlit sky and are treated to zany newsreels, cartoons, and B horror-movie clips, such as *Frankenstein Meets the Space Monster.* Fun-loving carhops deliver free popcorn and your meal. Unfortunately, the latter needs CPR. Forget adjectives such as smoked, marinated, and pan-seared; the bottom lines are still your basic, overpriced beef, pork, poultry, fish, and pasta. It takes a few too many specialty drinks to kill the taste.

Near Indiana Jones Epic Stunt Spectacular. © 407/939-3463. www.disneyworld.com. Priority seating. Main courses $11–$17 lunch; $14–$19 dinner. AE, DC, DISC, MC, V. Daily 10:30am–park closing. Parking $7.

INEXPENSIVE

Toy Story Pizza Planet PIZZA There's no joy or originality here. Come if you want pizza, salad, or a cup of java on the fly. You can also order a faux Greek salad, but nothing of a mind-altering nature.

In the Muppet's Courtyard. © 407/939-3463. www.disneyworld.com. Priority seating not accepted. All meals $5–$9. AE, DC, DISC, MC, V. Daily 10:30am–park closing. Parking $7.

IN THE ANIMAL KINGDOM

There are few restaurants in the newest of Disney's parks, and most that exist are counter-service or grab-and-go places. In our opinion only two are worth listing.

MODERATE

Rainforest Cafe *Kids* CALIFORNIA Expect California fare with an island spin at this Rainforest, and its cousin, listed later in this chapter on p. 145. Menu offerings tend to be tasty and sometimes creative, but the cafe, like other Disney restaurants, charges more than the outside world. Fun dishes include Mogambo Shrimp (sautéed in olive oil and served with penne pasta), Rumble in the Jungle Turkey Wrap (with romaine, tomatoes, and bacon), and Maya's Mixed Grill (ribs, chicken breast, and shrimp). Tables situated among the dining room's vines and generally inanimate animals are usually packed, a barometer of the lack of options at Animal Kingdom as much as the popularity of this restaurant. Beer, wine, and other intoxicants are served.

Just outside Animal Kingdom entrance. *Admission not required.* (There's an entrance inside, too.) © 407/938-9100. www.rainforestcafe.com. Reservations recommended. Main courses $10–$40 (most under $25) lunch and dinner. AE, DC, DISC, MC, V. Daily 8am–11pm. Parking $7.

INEXPENSIVE

Tusker House AMERICAN Taste is there, even if quantity and quality aren't. The menu includes grilled chicken salad with focaccia bread, rotisserie or fried chicken, and a grilled chicken, ham, and turkey wrap. Beer and wine are served.

Tips **Dining Plans**

Disney's **Dream Maker Silver** package plan allows you to choose meals from its flex features. The **Dream Maker Gold** plan includes three meals a day. Call 𝄞 **407/934-7639** or visit www.disneyworld.com (click "Reservations & Tickets") for details.

In Africa, near entrance. 𝄞 **407/939-3463**. www.disneyworld.com. No priority seating. Main courses $7–$8. AE, DC, DISC, MC, V. Daily 10:30am–4:30pm. Parking $7.

IN THE WALT DISNEY WORLD RESORTS

Most restaurants listed in this category continue the Disney trend of being above market price. On the flip side, many offer food that's a notch or two better than what you find in the theme parks. These restaurants are located on the "Walt Disney World & Lake Buena Vista Dining" map on p. 136.

VERY EXPENSIVE

Citricos 𝄴 NEW FRENCH　The Grand Floridian's No. 2 restaurant (Victoria & Albert's is No. 1) offers a menu featuring what the resort calls French, Alsatian, and Provençal cuisine with California and Florida touches. Items change regularly, but you might find a yummy basil-crusted rack of lamb, sautéed halibut with asparagus and shiitake mushrooms, or grilled salmon with roasted fennel and potatoes. The Old World decor includes plenty of wrought-iron railings, mosaic-tile floors, flickering lights, a show kitchen, and a view of the Seven Seas Lagoon and Magic Kingdom fireworks. Add a three-course wine pairing for $25. The Chef's Domain offers an experience similar to the Chef's Table at Victoria & Albert's, *but beware:* Citricos won't piece together a group. You have to pay the full $650 sticker price (ouch!) for the table whether there are 2 or 12 in your party.

4401 Floridian Way, in Disney's Grand Floridian Resort & Spa. 𝄞 **407/939-3463**. www.disneyworld.com. Priority seating. Main courses $22–$45. AE, DC, DISC, MC, V. Wed–Sun 5:30–10pm; Chef's Domain Tues–Sat 6 and 8:30pm.

Victoria & Albert's 𝄴𝄴𝄴 *Finds* INTERNATIONAL　It's not often we can describe dinner as "an event," but Disney's most elegant restaurant deserves that distinction. Dinner is next to perfect—if the portions seem small, we dare you to make it through all six courses—and the setting is exceptionally romantic. This luxurious experience begins with a personalized menu and a rose for the lady in your party. The fare changes nightly, but expect a feast fit for royalty (and costing a royal fortune). You might begin with Kobe beef carpaccio, followed by Monterey abalone with lemon and baby spinach. Then, pheasant consommé might precede an entree such as Tamari-glazed blue fin tuna over bok choy stir fry or Colorado lamb with corn risotto. English Stilton served with a burgundy-poached pear sets up desserts such as vanilla bean crème brûlée and Kona chocolate soufflé. The dining room is crowned by a domed, chapel-style ceiling; Victorian lamps softly light 20 exquisitely appointed tables; and your servers (always named Victoria and Albert) provide service that will have you begging to take them home. There's an extensive wine list. We suggest a pairing, which provides a wine with most courses for an extra $42 per person.

4401 Floridian Way, in Disney's Grand Floridian Resort & Spa. 𝄞 **407/939-3463**. www.disneyworld.com. Reservations required. Jackets required for men. Not recommended for children. Prix fixe $85 per person, $127 with wine pairing; $115 Chef's Table, $162 with wine. AE, DC, DISC, MC, V. 2 dinner seatings daily

Sept–June, 5:45–6:30pm and 9–9:45pm; 1 dinner seating July–Aug, 6:45–8pm. Chef's Table 6pm only. Free self- and validated valet parking.

Yachtsman Steakhouse ☒ SEAFOOD/STEAKS/CHOPS   We're giving it a backhanded compliment by saying this is the best steakhouse in Disney—there are only two true ones. But even by outside-the-park standards, the Yachtsman earns a B+. Its grain-fed western beef is aged, cured, and cut here. You can see the cuts in a glass-enclosed aging room, and the exhibition kitchen provides a tantalizing glimpse of steaks, chops, and seafood being grilled over oak and hickory. Steak options range from an 8-ounce filet to a 12-ounce strip to a belly-busting 24-ounce T-bone. A filet and warm-water lobster tail combo tops the price chart. If you're not in the mood for beef, the Yachtsman also serves salmon, snapper, chicken, and rack of lamb. The decor includes knotty-pine beams, plank floors, and leather-and-oak chairs. The staff is very cordial. The Yachtsman has an extensive wine list, though it's not in the same league as the other two contestants in this category.

1700 Epcot Resorts Blvd., in Disney's Yacht Club Resort. ℂ 407/939-3463. Priority seating recommended. Main courses $19–$50. AE, DC, DISC, MC, V. Daily 5:30–10pm. Free self- and valet parking.

EXPENSIVE

Artist Point ☒ *Finds* SEAFOOD/STEAKS/CHOPS   Enjoy a grand view of Disney's Wilderness Lodge while you select from a menu that changes seasonally. You might discover a mixed grill of venison, a lamb chop, and rabbit sausage with a root vegetable mash; a spicy Asian-style shrimp and noodle bowl; or cedar-plank roasted Silver Bay salmon with maple-whiskey glaze. The dining room's interior is dotted with western-theme murals (look for Hidden Mickeys; see p. 214), and large windows offer a view of a lake and waterfall. There's terrace seating for fair weather. Expect a reasonably extensive wine list and a wine pairing (three 2½-ounce portions for $16). *Note:* Artist Point has a more relaxed atmosphere than some of the busier WDW resort restaurants.

901 W. Timberline Dr., in Disney's Wilderness Lodge. ℂ 407/939-3463 or 407/824-1081. www.disney world.com. Priority seating recommended. Main courses $23–$34. AE, DC, DISC, MC, V. Daily 5:30–10pm. Free self- and valet parking.

Boma AFRICAN   One of two restaurants in the Animal Kingdom Lodge, this one is themed after an African marketplace. Its show kitchen and wood-burning

---

Finds **The Chef's Table: The Best Seat in the World**

There's a special dining option at **Victoria & Albert's.** Reserve the **Chef's Table** (far, far in advance) and dine in a charming alcove hung with copper pots and dried flower wreaths at an elegantly appointed candlelit table in the heart of the kitchen! Begin by sipping bubbly with the chef while discussing your food preferences for a seven-course menu created especially for you. There's a cooking seminar element to this experience: Diners get to tour the kitchen and observe the artistry of the chefs at work. The Chef's Table can accommodate up to 10 people a night. It's a leisurely affair, lasting 3 or 4 hours. The price is $115 per person without wine, $162 including five wines. This is so popular that Disney takes reservations 120 days in advance, so reserve *early* by calling **407/939-3463.**

Kids Pint-Sized Cuisine

Disney's Grand Floridian Resort & Spa offers two special cooking programs for children. **Great Adventures in Cooking** invites up to 12 youngsters, 3 to 10 years old, to make dessert in a 2-hour cooking class, then share it with guests ($19.95 per child). The **Wonderland Tea Party** gives kids the same age a 1-hour primer in cupcake decorating—with their fingers! They also feast on heart-shaped PB&Js and sip apple juice "tea" while they play with Alice and the Mad Hatter ($24.95 per child). Call © **407/824-3000** or 407/939-3463 for details on both programs.

grill crank out a dinner buffet that has delicacies even more diverse than those at the buffet at Akershus in the Norway pavilion (p. 132). Expect treats such as Moroccan seafood or fennel smoked fish salads, curried coconut seafood stew, chicken pepper pot soup, West African red beans, and much more. The restaurant is set up in "pods," each with a chef who can answer your questions about the cuisine. There's also a breakfast buffet.

2901 Osceola Pkwy., at Disney's Animal Kingdom Lodge. © **407/939-3463**. www.disneyworld.com. Priority seating. Breakfast buffet: $14.99 adults, $7.99 children 3–11. Dinner buffet: $23.99 adults, $9.99 children. AE, DC, DISC, MC, V. Daily 7–11am and 5–10pm. Free self-parking.

California Grill ₰₰₰ CALIFORNIA   Located on the Contemporary Resort's 15th floor, this stunning restaurant offers views of the Magic Kingdom and lagoon below while your eyes and mouth feast on an eclectic menu. A Wolfgang Puckish interior incorporates Art Deco elements (curved pear-wood walls, vivid splashes of color, polished black granite surfaces), but the central focus is an exhibition kitchen with a wood-burning oven and rotisserie. The menu's headliners change to take advantage of fresh market fare but may include seared yellowfin tuna served rare with shiitake mushrooms and scallions, roasted pumpkin ravioli, or grilled pork tenderloin with polenta and balsamic-smothered mushrooms. The Grill also has a nice sushi and sashimi menu (tuna, crab, and shrimp, among others) ranging from appetizers to large platters. This is one of the few spots in WDW that isn't crawling with kids. The list of California wines helps complement the meal and views.

Note: It can be tough to get a table at the Grill, especially on weekends and during Disney fireworks hours, so make a reservation as early as possible.

4600 N. World Dr., at Disney's Contemporary Resort. © **407/939-3463** or 407/824-1576. www.disney world.com. Reservations recommended. Main courses $18–$32; sushi and sashimi $10–$30. AE, DC, DISC, MC, V. Daily 5:30–10pm. Free self-parking.

Flying Fish Café SEAFOOD   Chefs at this Coney Island–inspired restaurant take the stage in a show kitchen that turns out entrees such as potato-wrapped red snapper with a creamy leek fondue, coriander-crusted yellowfin tuna with shiitake mushrooms, and oak-grilled salmon with bread salad, arugula, eggplant, and roasted peppers. The food is better than what you'll find at the Coral Reef (p. 130) and Cape May Café (p. 143), but not in the same league as Artist Point or some of O-Town's other quality seafood restaurants. Considering the show kitchen and vibrant colors inside, this is a nice escape from the Mickey madness.

Note: If you can't get a table here, ask about sitting at the counter—you get a great view of the kitchen.

2101 N. Epcot Resorts Blvd., at Disney's Boardwalk. © **407/939-3463** or 407/939-2359. www.disney world.com. Priority seating. Main courses $18–$29. AE, DC, DISC, MC, V. Daily 5:30–10pm. Free self-parking.

Jiko—The Cooking Place 🦒 AFRICAN   The Animal Kingdom Lodge's signature restaurant is a nice diversion from the normal Disney restaurants and a complementary addition to the multicultural dining rooms at Epcot's World Showcase. Jiko's show kitchen, sporting two wood-burning ovens, turns out a unique menu of international cuisine with African overtones. Dishes, depending on the season, include grilled buttermilk-curry shrimp, pan-roasted monkfish, grilled salmon with heirloom potatoes and spinach in a horseradish vinaigrette, and spicy steamed bass. The wine list features a number of South African vintages. The muted atmosphere makes this a good place for a relaxing dinner.

2901 Osceola Pkwy., at Disney's Animal Kingdom Lodge. ✆ 407/939-3463. www.disneyworld.com. Priority seating. Main courses $18–$29. AE, DC, DISC, MC, V. Daily 5:30–10pm. Free self-parking.

Spoodles TAPAS/MEDITERRANEAN   This lively family restaurant features an open kitchen. The enterprising tapas menu encourages food sharing, which increases the fun factor. The treats include sautéed chili garlic shrimp, fried calamari, and a sampler platter. Entrees include Moroccan-spiced tuna and a grilled pork Porterhouse with goat-cheese polenta. Spoodles has added a respectable wine list, including tableside sangria presentations. *Note:* Although popular, the quality here doesn't rival Cafe Tu Tu Tango, another tapas favorite (p. 154). During the peak summer tourist season, thanks to its location at the Boardwalk, the wait can be long, even with priority seating, so this may not be the best option for famished families.

2101 N. Epcot Resorts Blvd., at Disney's Boardwalk. ✆ **407/939-3463** or 407/939-2380. www.disney world.com. Priority seating. Main courses $15–$25; tapas $5–$20 AE, DC, DISC, MC. V. Daily 7–11am, noon–2pm, and 5–10pm. Free self-parking.

MODERATE

Boatwright's Dining Hall 🄺ids NEW ORLEANS   A family atmosphere (noisy), good food (by Disney standards), and reasonable prices (ditto) make Boatwright's a hit with Port Orleans Resort guests, if not outsiders. Most entrees have a Cajun/Creole spin. The jambalaya is sans seafood, unless you pay $3 more for shrimp, but it's spicy and has chicken and sausage, ruling it out for vegetarians. There really isn't anything French about the "French Quarter" filet; ditto for the pot roast, but they are tasty. Boatwright's is modeled after a 19th-century boat factory, complete with the wooden hull of a Louisiana fishing boat suspended from its lofty beamed ceiling. Most kids like the wooden toolboxes on every table; each contains a saltshaker that doubles as a level, a wood-clamp sugar dispenser, a pepper-grinder-cum-ruler, a jar of unmatched utensils, shop rags (to be used as napkins), and a little metal pail of crayons.

2201 Orleans Dr., in Disney's Port Orleans Resort. ✆ **407/939-3463**. www.disneyworld.com. Priority seating recommended. Main courses $7–$9 breakfast; $16–$28 dinner. AE, DC, DISC, MC, V. Daily 7–11:30am and 5–10pm. Free self-parking.

Cape May Café 🄾verrated SEAFOOD   As a rule, all-you-can-eat marine feasts tend to promise more than they deliver, and this is no exception. Yes, there's an honest seafood selection (clams, mussels, baked fish, and microscopic peel-and-eat shrimp). But seafood served buffet style—allowed to sit out where it collects all sorts of airborne bacteria—isn't an ideal meal in our book, especially inland. If you're still inclined, the nautically themed restaurant has a full bar, and it's said that enough alcohol kills any germ. If you're inclined but not willing to take the risk, the buffet also has chicken, ribs, and flank steak. Cape May Café also offers a character breakfast (p. 162).

1800 Epcot Resorts Blvd., at Disney's Beach Club Resort. ℂ 407/939-3463. www.disneyworld.com. Priority seating. Dinner buffet $24 adults, $10 children 3–11. AE, DC, DISC, MC, V. Daily 5:30–9:30pm. Free self- and valet parking.

'Ohana ⟨R⟩ ⟨Kids⟩ PACIFIC RIM   Its star is earned on the fun front, but the decibel level here turns some folks off, especially those looking for intimacy. Inside, you're welcomed as a "cousin," which fits because *'Ohana* means "family" in Hawaiian. As your food is being prepared over an 18-foot fire pit, the staff keeps your eyes and ears filled with all sorts of shenanigans. The blowing of a conch shell summons a storyteller, coconut races get under way in the center aisle, and you can shed your inhibitions and shake it in the hula lessons. When it starts, the meal is served rapid fire (ask your waiter to slow the pace if it's too fast). The edibles include a variety of skewers (think shish kabob), including turkey, shrimp, steak, and pork. You'll also find lots of trimmings and a full bar with limited wine selections. *Note:* Ask for a seat in the main dining room, or you won't get a good view of the entertainment.

1600 Seven Seas Dr., at Disney's Polynesian Resort. ℂ 407/939-3463 or 407/824-2000. www.disney world.com. Priority seating strongly encouraged. $24 adults, $10 children 3–11. (See p. 164 for more details.) AE, DC, DISC, MC, V. Daily 7:30–11am and 5–10pm. Free self- and valet parking.

3 Places to Dine in Lake Buena Vista

In this section, we've listed restaurants located in Downtown Disney and the Lake Buena Vista area. Many eateries listed below can be found on the "Walt Disney World & Lake Buena Vista Dining" map on p. 136. Downtown Disney is located 2½ miles from Epcot off Buena Vista Drive. It encompasses the Downtown Disney Marketplace, a very pleasant complex of cedar-shingled shops and restaurants overlooking a scenic lagoon; the adjoining Pleasure Island, a nighttime entertainment venue; and Downtown Disney West Side, a slightly more upscale collection of shops, restaurants, Cirque du Soleil (p. 310), and a movie theater. The restaurants below have kids' menus, usually in the $4 to $6 range, unless otherwise noted.

Note: Pleasure Island's restaurants don't require admission.

AT PLEASURE ISLAND
VERY EXPENSIVE
Fulton's Crab House ⟨R⟩ SEAFOOD   Lobster (Maine and Australian) and crab (stone, king, and Dungeness) dominate the menu in this fun and fashionable eatery, which is housed in a replica of a (permanently moored) 19th-century Mississippi riverboat. It's one of the area's best seafood houses, but you might want to bring your banker along for the ride. One popular meal for two combines Alaskan king crab, snow crab, and lobster with potatoes and creamed spinach. The tuna mignon (served rare) and Dungeness crab cakes are delicious. And there's a scattering of Florida seafood, including black grouper, cobia, and red snapper. In mild weather, consider dining on the deck. Fulton's has one of Lake Buena Vista's better wine lists.

1670 Buena Vista Dr., aboard the riverboat docked at Downtown Disney. ℂ 407/934-2628. www.levyrestaurants.com. Priority seating. Main courses $12–$45 lunch, $17–$45 dinner. AE, DC, DISC, MC, V. Daily 11:30am–4pm and 5–11pm. Free self-parking.

EXPENSIVE
Portobello Yacht Club ⟨R⟩ SOUTHERN ITALIAN/MEDITERRANEAN The pizzas here go beyond the routine to *quattro formaggio* (mozzarella and

provolone with sun-dried tomatoes) and *margherita* (Italian sausage, plum tomatoes, and mozzarella). But it's the less casual entrees that pack people into this place. The menu changes from time to time. You may find a nice *costoletta di vitello alla griglia* (a grilled 14-oz. veal chop with garlic whipped potatoes and asparagus) or *spaghettini alla portobello* (pasta with pieces of Alaskan king crab, scallops, shrimp, and clams in light olive oil, wine, and herbs). Situated in a gabled Bermuda-style house, the Portobello's awning-covered patio overlooks Lake Buena Vista. Its cellar is small, but there's a nice selection of wine to match the meals.

1650 Buena Vista Dr., at Pleasure Island. (C) 407/934-8888. www.levyrestaurants.com. Priority seating. Main courses $15–$50; pizzas $9. AE, DC, DISC, MC, V. Daily 5–11pm. Free self-parking.

MODERATE

Planet Hollywood *(Overrated* AMERICAN   Some folks come for a first look, but most diners are fans that flock here for the scenery (including a planetarium-like ceiling and Peter O'Toole's *Lawrence of Arabia* duds). The compulsion is much like that of Hard Rock Cafe fans (p. 150), who go for the tunes. The Planet's servers can cop an attitude, and the food is blasé. If you must, you'll find the usual suspects: wings, pot stickers, sandwiches, big burgers, ribs, fajitas, pizzas, pasta, and questionable steaks. Lines can get long during special events and in peak season.

1506 Buena Vista Dr., at Pleasure Island (look for the big globe). (C) 407/827-7827. www.planetholly wood.com. Limited priority seating. Main courses $8–$21 (most under $15). AE, DC, DISC, MC, V. Daily 11am–1am. Free self-parking.

AT DOWNTOWN DISNEY MARKETPLACE
MODERATE

Rainforest Cafe *(★ (Kids* CALIFORNIA   Don't arrive starving unless you have priority seating. Without it, waits average 2 hours, although even with it you'll wait longer than at Animal Kingdom's Rainforest Cafe (p. 139). Expect fare with an island spin at this Rainforest and its cousin. The menu can be tasty and creative, though somewhat overpriced. Fun dishes include Mogambo Shrimp (sautéed in olive oil and served with penne pasta), Rumble in the Jungle Turkey Wrap (with romaine lettuce, tomatoes, and bacon), and Maya's Mixed Grill (ribs, chicken breast, and shrimp). Beer, wine, and other hallucinogens tend to make adults see things like the hundreds of kids running around—a jungle-like setting where you can call the wild like Tarzan. Go on—no one knows you here.

Downtown Disney Marketplace; near the smoking volcano. (C) 407/827-8500. www.rainforest.com. Priority seating. Main courses $11–$40 lunch and dinner (most under $25). AE, DISC, MC, V. Sun–Thurs 10:30am–11pm; Fri–Sat 10:30am–midnight. Free self-parking.

DISNEY'S WEST SIDE
MODERATE

Bongo's Cuban Cafe *(Overrated* CUBAN   Singer Gloria Estefan and her husband, Emilio, created this eatery with high expectations. Alas, the food isn't great, though the prices say it ought to be. The *palomilla* (a thin, tenderized steak) can't match what you find in Rolando's (see later in this chapter) or some other Cuban eateries in Miami, Bongo's home. The *ropa vieja* (shredded beef) is tasty but on the dry side, and the *arroz con pollo* (chicken with yellow rice, something of a national dish) would be a highlight if the portion matched the price. The best bet: the Cuban sandwich—thinly toasted bread with ham, pork, and cheese—is safe and sanely priced. If you don't mind loud Latin music and groupies, park it inside and enjoy a cold beer or glass of sangria. For quieter times, try the patio or upstairs lounge.

1498 Buena Vista Dr., in Disney's West Side. ✆ 407/828-0999. www.bongoscubancafe.com. Reservations not accepted. Main courses $13–$28 (many under $20). AE, DC, DISC, MC, V. Daily 11am–2am. Free self-parking.

House of Blues MISSISSIPPI DELTA   Most folks come for the blues bands and Sunday's gospel brunch, a foot-tapping, thigh-slapping music affair worth high marks on the entertainment side. The food, however, is so-so. The roast beef is tough, the fish is dry, and the jambalaya is loaded with rice and noticeably absent of the good stuff. (The omelets are good, and there are enough fillers—bacon, salads, dessert, and bread—to do the job. Few leave hungry.) Dinners are a notch better. Features range from a meatier jambalaya (shrimp, chicken, and andouille sausage) to Louisiana crawfish and shrimp étouffée to Cajun meat loaf. Do check out the restrooms. They're decorated with that diamond plating seen on the beds of some pickup trucks, especially in the South.

1490 Buena Vista Dr., at Disney's West Side, beneath water tower. ✆ 407/934-2583. www.hob.com. Reservations not accepted (except brunch). Main courses $14–$25; pizza and sandwiches $9–$11; brunch $30 adults, $15 children 3–9. AE, DISC, MC, V. Daily 11am–2am; brunch 10:30am and 1pm. Free self-parking.

Wolfgang Puck Grand Café ✿ CALIFORNIA   Our favorite stop is the sushi bar, an artistic copper-and-terrazzo masterpiece that delivers some of the best sushi in Orlando. You can also eat gourmet pizza, with thin crusts and exotic toppings, inside or on an outdoor patio. Upstairs, the main dining room offers a seasonally changing menu that might feature rack of lamb with wasabi-infused mashed potatoes, rare yellowfin tuna with tempura-style Bon Secour oysters, or smoked tropical duck with Boursin cheese, mango, and papaya between veggie wontons. The lower level can be noisy, so conversation is difficult, and the downstairs *wait for a table is excruciatingly long.* Puck's also has a grab-and-go express restaurant that has sandwiches, pizzas, desserts, and more.

1482 Buena Vista Dr., at Disney's West Side. ✆ 407/938-9653; www.wolfgangpuck.com/myrestaurants. Reservations for dining room; priority seating in lower level. Main courses upstairs $26–$38, pizza and sushi $8–$25. AE, DC, DISC, MC, V. Daily 11am–1am. Free self-parking.

ELSEWHERE IN LAKE BUENA VISTA
VERY EXPENSIVE
Arthur's 27 *Overrated* INTERNATIONAL   Insiders come here for the 27th-floor views of central Florida sunsets and the Wizard of Disney's fireworks. Those who can afford the high-altitude prices are rewarded with a romantic restaurant that has the feel of a 1930s supper club minus the cigarette smoke. Most tables are set in intimate alcoves facing picture windows. Book an 8pm reservation (well in advance) for a table facing the 9pm Disney fireworks. The cuisine, unfortunately, doesn't live up to the view and prices. The herb-crusted rack of lamb, ordered medium rare, is sufficient to please the eye and taste, but the Chilean sea bass sometimes arrives brittle and liquid. Overall, portions lean toward the small size. The wine list is commendable but priced well above retail. Dinner for two including appetizer, salad, entree, modest wine, dessert, and tip easily can climb to above $200.

Tip: Skip the meal and go for the fireworks view in the Top of the Palace Lounge, also on the 27th floor. But arrive early. It gets crowded.

1900 Lake Buena Vista Dr., in the Wyndham Palace Resort, just north of Hotel Plaza Blvd. ✆ 407/827-3450. Reservations recommended. Jackets suggested for men. Main courses $31–$51; $62–$72 prix fixe; no kids' menu. AE, DC, DISC, MC, V. Daily 6–10pm. Free self-parking. Take I-4 Exit 68, Hwy. 535/Apopka–Vineland Rd., north to Hotel Plaza Blvd., then left to the Wyndham.

Black Swan ⚘ INTERNATIONAL   This is a very sophisticated and elegant restaurant in a Gatsbyian sense (if Fitzgerald were here to give it more of a modern tilt). A pianist plays softly in the entryway, and many tables overlook the lush Villas of Grand Cypress resort. Service is formal and attentive. It's a great place for a nice dinner, although not necessarily a romantic one. One of our favorite temptations is an herb-roasted veal chop (insist on medium rare) with exotic mushrooms and a red-wine demi-glacé. The duck is presented in a trifecta: confit leg, grilled breast, and pan-seared foie gras with a pear-chutney marmalade. Seafood fans can choose baked halibut wrapped in hearts of palm with charred-mango chutney and coconut rice. There also are nightly specials. Note that the Swan adds an 18% gratuity to all bills. *Tip:* Seating is on two levels, but you should skip the second level, which has more of a golf-and-grab atmosphere.

1 N. Jacaranda (off Hwy. 535), in the Villas of Grand Cypress. ℂ **800/835-7377** or 407/239-1999. www.grand cypress.com. Reservations required for non-guests, recommended for others. Main courses $32–$40. AE, DC, DISC, MC, V. Tue–Sat 6–10pm. Free self-parking. Take I-4 Exit 68, Hwy. 535/Apopka–Vineland Rd., north, then left at second traffic light (after ramp light) onto Hwy. 535. It's on the right.

La Coquina ⚘ INTERNATIONAL   Expect an imaginative menu from the most acclaimed of the Hyatt Regency's five restaurants. La Coquina is an upscale but casual eatery that is well appointed with marine life and seashell themes and has a color scheme that includes lots of soft pinks and whites. The veal tenderloin with sake-glazed prawns is a real winner. Ditto for the sugarcane-seared scallops, which arrive with rice grits and artichokes. As for the mango-glazed duck breast, it's introduced with a shiitake-risotto cake. When making your reservation, request a table that has a view of Lake Windsong.

1 Grand Cypress Blvd., in the Hyatt Regency Grand Cypress Resort. ℂ **407/239-1234.** www.grand cypress.com. Reservations recommended. Jackets suggested for men. Main courses $20–$40; no kids' menu. AE, DC, DISC, MC, V. Daily 6:30–10pm. Free self- and validated valet parking. Take I-4 Exit 68, Hwy. 535/Apopka–Vineland Rd., north to Winter Garden–Vineland Rd./Hwy. 535, then left.

EXPENSIVE

Hemingway's SEAFOOD   The interior of Hemingway's has a Key West air, and the walls are hung with sepia photos of the author and his fishing trophies. The restaurant has a romantic indoor dining room lighted by hurricane lamps, and there's a wooden deck near a waterfall. If Papa were to eat here, he might dive into the beer-battered coconut shrimp with horseradish sauce and orange marmalade or the blackened swordfish with Cajun tartar sauce. No doubt, he would skip the wine list (there is a decent one) and opt for a few *Papa Dobles,* a potent rum concoction invented by Hemingway, who, according to legend, once downed 16 at one sitting! It's usually child free, though there is a kids' menu.

1 Grand Cypress Blvd., in the Hyatt Regency Grand Cypress Resort. ℂ **407/239-3854.** www.hyattgrand cypress.com. Reservations recommended. Main courses $21–$36. AE, DC, DISC, MC, V. Daily 6–10pm. Free self- and validated valet parking. Take I-4 Exit 68, Hwy. 535/Apopka–Vineland Rd., north to Winter Garden–Vineland Rd./Hwy. 535, then left.

MODERATE

Pebbles ⚘⚘ *(finds)* CALIFORNIA   If you want to dine like a gourmet without paying a heavy price, here's your meal ticket. Pebbles is a local chain that has earned a reputation for great food, a sexy though small wine list, and creative appetizers. Its Ybor Gold twin filets are seared, then bathed in the namesake lager and delivered with caramelized onions and three-cheese spuds. A sautéed double breast of chicken has a jacket of sour-orange sauce and sliced avocados. And the roast duck arrives in a glaze of strawberries, pistachios, and Triple Sec.

There's also a small selection of sandwiches ($7–$10). Pebbles is popular among a crowd ranging from young yuppies to aging baby boomers.

Note: Pebbles also has locations downtown: 17 W. Church St. (© 407/839-0892); in Longwood, 2110 W. Hwy. 434 (© 407/774-7111); and in Winter Park, 2516 Aloma Ave. (© 407/678-7001).

12551 Apopka–Vineland Rd., in the Crossroads Shopping Center. © **407/827-1111.** www.pebblesworld wide.com. Reservations not accepted. Main courses $10–$18. AE, DC, DISC, MC, V. Sun–Thurs noon–11pm; Fri–Sat 11am–11pm; *sometimes closed Sun.* Free self-parking. Take I-4 Exit 68, Hwy. 535/Apopka–Vineland Rd., north to the Crossroads Shopping Center on the right.

INEXPENSIVE
Romano's Macaroni Grill 🎯 *Value* NORTHERN ITALIAN   Though it's part of a multi-state chain, Romano's has the down-to-earth cheerfulness of a mom-and-pop joint. The laidback atmosphere makes it a good place for families or those looking for a casual dinner. The menu offers thin-crust pizzas made in a wood-burning oven and topped with such items as barbecued chicken. The grilled chicken Portobello (simmering between smoked mozzarella and spinach orzo pasta) is worth the visit. Equally good is an entree of grilled salmon with a teriyaki glaze, also with spinach orzo pasta. Premium wines are served by the glass.

12148 Apopka–Vineland Rd. (just north of County Rd. 535/Palm Pkwy.). © **407/239-6676.** www.macaroni grill.com. Main courses $6–$9 at lunch; $8–$17 at dinner (most under $12). AE, DC, DISC, MC, V. Sun–Thurs 11:30am–10pm; Fri–Sat 11:30am–11pm. Free self-parking. Take I-4 Exit 68, Hwy. 535/Apopka–Vineland Rd. north and continue straight when Hwy. 535 goes to the right. Romano's is about 2 blocks on the left.

4 Places to Dine in Universal Orlando

Universal Orlando stormed onto the restaurant scene with the mid-1999 opening of its dining and entertainment venue, CityWalk, which is between and in front of its two parks, Universal Studios Florida and Islands of Adventure. But Universal's sudden entry onto the food front doesn't mean quality was lost in the rush. Two of its restaurants (Emeril's and Delfino Riviera at the Portofino Bay Hotel) make our all-star team, and several others offer cuisine ranging from respectable light bites to dependable dinners.

Note: Most of the restaurants below can be found on the "CityWalk" map on p. 303. All of the hotel restaurants listed can be found on the "International Drive Area Dining" map on p. 153.

VERY EXPENSIVE
Delfino Riviera 🎯 NORTHERN ITALIAN   The signature ristorante in Universal Orlando's Portofino Bay Hotel overlooks the Harbor Piazza and delivers a romantic mood reminiscent of the Italian Riviera—complete with strolling musicians and crooners. It has a chef's table for eight (there's no extra charge, but you need to reserve at least 2–3 months in advance), in addition to indoor and terrace dining. The menu changes quarterly, but on the pasta side it might feature a savory lobster-champagne risotto, black olive pasta with monkfish, and pesto-stuffed ravioli. Carnivores might find veal roasted with porcini mushrooms or braised breast of veal, while fish fans might reel in a sea bass with mushrooms and potatoes in Chianti sauce. Delfino's service is snappy, and the dining areas are quiet enough to allow intimate conversation. Next to Emeril's, its wine list is one of the best in the I-Drive/Universal Orlando corridor.

5601 Universal Studios Blvd., in the Portofino Bay Hotel. © **407/503-3463** or 407/503-1000. Reservations recommended. Main courses $23–$49. AE, MC, V. Tues–Sat 5–10pm. Free 3-hr. validated self-parking, valet parking $10. From I-4, take Exit 75B, Kirkman Rd./Hwy. 435, and follow the signs to Universal.

Emeril's ⋆⋆ NEW ORLEANS   It's next to impossible to get short-term reservations for dinner (less than 6–8 weeks in advance) at Emeril's unless your stars are aligned or you come at the opening bell and take your chances with no-shows. If you do get in, you'll find the dynamic, Creole-inspired cuisine is worth the struggle. Best bets include the andouille-crusted redfish (an extremely moist white fish with roasted pecan-vegetable relish and meunière sauce) and kosher-salt-and-cracked-black pepper-dusted rib-eye steak with wild mushroom bread pudding and grilled vegetables. If you want some vino with your meal, no problem; the back half of the building is a glass-walled 12,000-bottle above-ground wine cellar. Prices at Emeril's are high enough that the restaurant can afford tons of legroom between tables and an assortment of pricey abstract paintings on the walls. If you want a show, we highly recommend you try for one of eight counter seats where you can watch chefs working their magic, but to get one, reservations are required *excruciatingly* early (2–3 months in advance, especially during holidays, in summer, and on weekends).

Note: Lunch costs about half what you'll spend on dinner, and the menu has many of the same entrees. It's also easier to get a reservation, and the dress code is more casual—jackets are recommended for gents at dinner, although that goes against the grain after a long day in the parks. No matter when you come, leave the kids at home—this restaurant caters to adults.

6000 Universal Studios Blvd., in CityWalk. © 407/224-2424. www.emerils.com/restaurants/index_orlando.htm. Reservations necessary. Main courses $18–$28 lunch, $18–$45 dinner. Daily 11:30am–2:30pm; Sun–Thurs 5:30–10pm; Fri–Sat 5:30–11pm. AE, DISC, MC, V. Parking $8 (free after 6pm). From I-4, take Exit 75B, Kirkman Rd./Hwy. 435, and follow the signs to Universal.

The Palm STEAKS/SEAFOOD   This upscale restaurant is the 23rd member of a chain started more than 75 years ago in New York. The food is good, though, as is the case with most Disney and Universal restaurants, somewhat overpriced for the value received. Beef and seafood rule a menu headlined by a 36-ounce New York strip steak for two ($60) and a 3-pound Nova Scotia lobster (market price). Smaller appetites and budgets can feast on broiled crab cakes, veal piccata, and lamb or veal chops. The decor leans toward the upscale supper club of the '30s and '40s, and the walls are lined with caricatures of celebrities and other famous people.

5800 Universal Blvd., in the Hard Rock Hotel. © 407/503-7256. www.thepalm.com. Reservations recommended. Main courses $9–$31 lunch, $15–$45 dinner (many under $25). AE, DC, DISC, MC, V. Mon–Fri 11:30am–11pm; Sat 5–11pm; Sun 5–10pm. Free 3-hr. validated self-parking, valet $10. From I-4, take Exit 75B, Kirkman Rd./Hwy. 435, and follow the signs to Universal.

EXPENSIVE

Mama Della's *Overrated* NORTHERN ITALIAN   This trattoria is an alternative to Delfino Riviera (above) if you're at the Portofino Bay Hotel and don't want to move. Alas, it's not in the same league as some of central Florida's better Italian restaurants, including Capriccio (p. 155), Pacino's (p. 160), or the Portobello

---

Tips No Reservation?

If you must have dinner at Emeril's and can't get a reservation, try dropping by around 3:15pm. Those who make a date have to confirm by 3pm on the day of their reservations, and there always are a few who don't show. If you're lucky, you may be able to pick up their slack.

Yacht Club (p. 144). Expect marginal comfort food. The beef can be stringy and the *frutti di mare* is somewhat meager (two shrimp, four scallops, and a small hunk of red snapper), especially for this price group. The veal Marsala is a safe bet. Appointments include family portraits, waiters who promise to get mama if you're not happy, tacky ceramics, wood floors, and an accordion player who plays "Amore" a little too often. The wine list, like the menu, could stand some improvement.

5601 Universal Blvd., in Portofino Bay Hotel. ℂ 407/503-1432. Reservations recommended. Main courses $17–$29. AE, MC, V. Daily 6–10pm. Free 3-hr. validated self-parking, valet $10. From I-4, take Exit 75B, Kirkman Rd./Hwy. 435, and follow the signs to Universal.

Tchoup Chop ⭐⭐ PACIFIC RIM   Pronounced "chop chop," the Royal Pacific Hotel's headline restaurant and Emeril Lagasse's second in Orlando is named for the location of his original restaurant—Tchoupitoulous Street in New Orleans. The interior blends colorful flowers, sculpted gardens, and mini waterfalls with Batik fabrics, carved wood grilles, and glass chandeliers. The exhibition kitchen offers a look at the chefs making your meal in woks or on wood-burning grills. Tchoup Chop's January 2003 coming out introduced a Polynesian and Asian influenced menu with temptations such as Kona coffee glazed duck breast with duck and vegetable chow mein; slow-roasted pork and noodles sautéed with spices and seasonal vegetables; and grilled rib-eye steak with garlic mashed potatoes, fried Maui onions, teriyaki sauce, and stir-fried vegetables. *Note:* The dress code here is more casual than at Emeril's (listed earlier), but forget about showing up in a tank top.

6300 Hollywood Way, in Universal's Royal Pacific Hotel. ℂ 407/503-2467. www.emerils.com. Reservations strongly recommended. Main courses $15–$24. AE, DISC, MC, V. Daily 11:30am–2pm; Sun–Thurs 5:30–10pm; Fri-Sat 5:30–11pm. Valet parking $4. From I-4, take Exit 75B, Kirkman Rd./Hwy. 435, and follow the signs to Universal.

MODERATE

Hard Rock Cafe *Overrated* AMERICAN   Cut from the same cloth as Planet Hollywood (see earlier in this chapter), this is rock 'n' roll's entry in the too-much-noise, plenty-of-memorabilia sweepstakes. Kids love it, but don't even think about having a conversation here. Expect the same chain-style bar food (burgers, chicken, marginal steaks, and fried this-and-that) and souvenir shop as at the Planet. *Note:* The adjacent Hard Rock Live! is a huge venue for concerts.

6000 Universal Studios Blvd., near Universal CityWalk. ℂ 407/351-7625. www.hardrock.com. Reservations not accepted. Main courses $9–$23. AE, MC, V. Daily 11am–1am. Parking $8 (free after 6pm). From I-4, take Exit 75B, Kirkman Rd./Hwy. 435, and follow the signs to Universal.

Jimmy Buffett's Margaritaville CARIBBEAN   As soon as the parrotheads have enough to drink (no later than 4pm on weekends, 4:05pm the rest of the week), the noise makes it futile to try to talk with your table mates, but most folks come to Margaritaville to sing and get stupid, not to gab. You might as well join them at one of three watering holes—the Landshark, 12-Volt, and . . . drum roll, *s'il vous plait . . .* Volcano bars, the latter with a margarita-spewing fountain (we'll return to them on p. 304). Despite the cheeseburgers in paradise (yes, they're on the menu at $7.95), Jimmy's vittles have Caribbean leanings. And, while it's not contending for a critic's choice award, it's fairly tasty grub. But watch the tab. At $6 to $8 a pop for margaritas, the bill can climb to $50 or more per person for a routine meal that includes jerk chicken, jambalaya, or a Cuban meat loaf survival sandwich that's a cheeseburger of another kind. If you don't hanker for margaritas, there's a long list of domestic and imported beer.

1000 Universal Studios Plaza, in CityWalk. ℂ 407/224-2155. www.universalorlando.com. Reservations not accepted. Main courses $8–$22 (most under $15). AE, DISC, MC, V. Daily 11am–midnight. Parking $8 (free after 6pm). From I-4, take Exit 75B, Kirkman Rd./Hwy. 435, and follow the signs to Universal.

Pastamore Ristorante SOUTHERN ITALIAN   This family-style restaurant greets you with display cases brimming with mozzarella and other goodies lurking on the menu. The antipasto primo is a meal unto itself. The mound includes bruschetta, eggplant Caponata, melon con prosciutto, grilled Portobello mushrooms, olives, a medley of Italian cold cuts, olives, plum tomatoes, fresh mozzarella, and more. The menu also features such traditional offerings as veal Marsala, chicken piccata, shrimp scampi, fettuccine Alfredo, lasagna, and pizza. The food is actually pretty interesting, and the presentation isn't bad either. There's an open kitchen allowing a view of the chefs. Pastamore has a basic beer and wine menu. You can also eat in a cafe where a lighter menu—breakfast fare and sandwiches—is served from 8am to 2am.

1000 Universal Studios Plaza, in CityWalk. ℂ 407/363-8000. www.universalorlando.com. Reservations accepted. Main courses $7–$18. AE, DISC, MC, V. Daily 5pm–midnight. Parking $8 (free after 6pm). From I-4, take Exit 75B, Kirkman Rd./Hwy. 435, and follow the signs to Universal.

INEXPENSIVE

Bob Marley—A Tribute to Freedom CARIBBEAN   Part club and part restaurant, Marley's is a replica of the late reggae singer's home in Kingston, complete with tile roof and green-shuttered windows. There's nightly music that can get loud, but the decibel level doesn't reach Margaritaville's (see above). The menu has nothing but modestly priced Jamaican fare, including a jerk snapper sandwich on coca bread with yucca fries, a tomato-based fish chowder, and grouper fingers lightly breaded, fried, and topped with red and green peppers. Of course, most folks don't leave without sipping at least one Red Stripe—Jamaica's national beer.

1000 Universal Studios Plaza, in CityWalk. ℂ 407/224-2262. www.universalorlando.com. Reservations not accepted. Main courses $6–$9. AE, DISC, MC, V. Daily 4pm–2am. Parking $8 (free after 6pm). From I-4, take Exit 75B, Kirkman Rd./Hwy. 435, and follow the signs to Universal.

5 Places to Dine in the International Drive Area

International Drive has one of the area's larger collections of fast-food joints, but the midsection and southern third also have some of this region's better restaurants. South I-Drive is 10 minutes by auto from the Walt Disney World parks. Most of the restaurants listed here are located on the "International Drive Area Dining" map on p. 153.

VERY EXPENSIVE

Atlantis ⓕ SEAFOOD/STEAKS/CHOPS   The relatively small dining room of this hotel restaurant has a warm, woody feel, especially if you ask for one of the intimate booths separated by etched-glass panels. Chef's specials such as a Mediterranean seafood medley (Florida lobster, black grouper, shrimp, and scallops) frequently complement menu standards such as grilled sea bass or pan-seared duck and rock shrimp. Sunday's champagne brunch is served in the resort's huge atrium. Themes change monthly, but the 100-item menu often has treats such as quail, duck, lamb chops, Cornish hen, clams, mussels, sea bass, sushi, and more. Although pricey, it's one of Orlando's most popular brunches.

6677 Sea Harbour Dr., in the Renaissance Orlando Resort. ℂ 407/351-5555. www.renaissancehotels.com. Reservations recommended. Main courses $24–$36; Sunday brunch $32 adults, $16 children. AE, DC, DISC, MC, V. Daily 6–10pm; Sun brunch 10:30am–2pm. Free self-parking, valet parking $9. From I-4, take Exit 71/Central Florida Pkwy. east and follow the signs to SeaWorld.

Charlie's Lobster House SEAFOOD   This 17-year-old, good-time eatery cranks out a menu bursting with treats from the Gulf of Mexico, Pacific, and Atlantic. Fish and shellfish specialties include pan-roasted Maine lobster, grilled or blackened yellowfin tuna, Alaskan king crab legs, Maryland-style crab cakes, and broiled shrimp with lump crab stuffing. Landlubbers can choose from a handful of steaks, including filets and strips. Although the atmosphere is kid-friendly, the higher prices discourage most families from coming here.

8845 International Dr., in the Mercado Shopping Plaza. © 407/352-6929. www.charlieslobsterhouse.com. Reservations suggested. Main courses $19–$40; lobster market price. AE, DC, DISC, MC, V. Daily 5–10pm. Free self-parking. From I-4, take Exit 74A, Sand Lake Rd./Hwy. 528, east to International Dr., then south.

Dux ⋆⋆ *(Finds* INTERNATIONAL   The name is a tribute to the Peabody Orlando's resident ducks, who parade ceremoniously in and out of the lobby every day (p. 112), while the food is a tribute to chefs who create a menu that changes quarterly. It might include succulent oven-roasted grouper with bok choy, mushrooms, and ginger sauce. At other times, hope for a tender veal chop marinated in apple cider and honey and served medium rare; steamed red snapper in tomato fricassee and fennel; or sautéed salmon on a bed of couscous with black olives, tomatoes, and chives.

Dux is best reserved for a very special night out or a meal on an expense account. Candlelit tables surround a large chandelier, and textured gold walls are hung with watercolors of the various duck species. (Speaking of ducks, you won't find any on the menu—staffers say that would be sacrilege.) The impeccable service that's a signature of the hotel carries into the restaurant, and Dux has one of the best wine lists in Orlando. *Note:* Because the convention trade slows in August, it's one of the best times to try Dux and avoid crowds. Early birds sometimes have the dining room to themselves.

9801 International Dr., in the Peabody Orlando. © 407/345-4550. www.peabodyorlando.com. Reservations recommended. Main courses $26–$45. AE, DC, DISC, MC, V. Mon–Sat 6–10pm. Free self- and validated valet parking. From I-4, take Exit 74A, Sand Lake Rd./Hwy. 528, east to International Dr., then south. Hotel is on the left across from the Convention Center.

EXPENSIVE

Christini's ⋆ NORTHERN ITALIAN   Insiders from the Universal Orlando/Hollywood set like to hang out in this "survivor" restaurant, which had its coming out in 1984. A tender broiled veal chop seasoned with sage and served with applesauce is one of the headliners. Other acts include pan-seared Chilean sea bass over shrimp-and-lobster risotto; jumbo shrimp flamed with brandy and vodka, then simmered in a spicy sauce and served with linguine; and a prosciutto-wrapped tuna filet sautéed in butter with shiitake and oyster mushrooms. The food is quite good, and the wine list is definitely a winner. Christini's is a little more formal than some tourists like. It's also a little pricey, and some diners feel the restaurant and its staff put on airs because of the studio crowd. But on a good night, you may see the stars.

7600 Dr. Phillips Blvd. © 407/345-8770. www.christinis.com. Reservations recommended. Jackets suggested for men. Main courses $18–$45 (many under $27). AE, DC, DISC, MC, V. Daily 6–11pm. Free self-parking. From I-4, take Exit 74A, Sand Lake Rd./Hwy. 528, west to Dr. Phillips Blvd., turn right, then left into the Marketplace Shopping Plaza.

Ran-Getsu of Tokyo JAPANESE   Authentic cuisine, including a sushi bar, has made Ran-Getsu a popular haunt for moneyed Asian tourists, though some travelers find the prices too high for its menu. *Tekka-don*, tender slices of tuna that are mild enough for first-timers, is a refreshing choice on the sushi side; so

International Drive Area Dining

Atlantis (in the Renaissance Orlando Resort) **13**

B-Line Diner (in the Peabody Orlando) **12**

Cafe Tu Tu Tango **8**

Capriccio (in the Peabody Orlando) **12**

Charlie's Lobster House **9**

Christini's **4**

Delfino Riviera (in the Portofino Bay Hotel) **1**

Dux (in the Peabody Orlando) **12**

Mama Della's (in the Portofino Bay Hotel) **1**

Ming Court **11**

The Palm (in the Hard Rock Hotel) **3**

Ran-Getsu of Tokyo **10**

Roy's Restaurant **7**

The Samba Room **7**

Siam Orchid **6**

Tchoup Chop **2**

Wild Jacks **5**

For restaurants in Universal Orlando's CityWalk, please see the "CityWalk" map in Chapter 10.

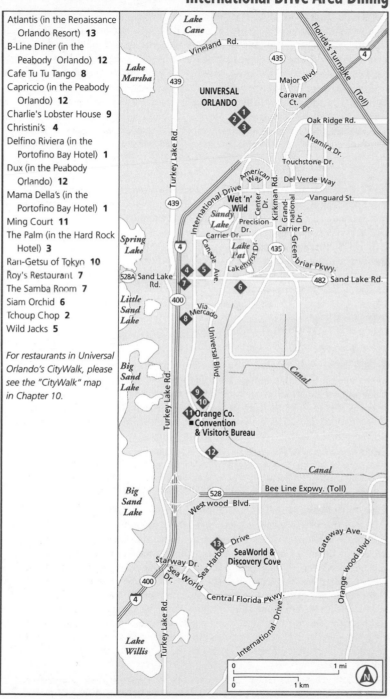

are platters, such as sashimi, maki rolls, and thinly sliced *chirashi* (rice topped with assorted seafood). *Yosenabe* is a bouillabaisse with an unconventional though savory twist—duck and chicken are added to the seafood mix; lobster is available at an added cost. Speaking of seafood, *una-ju* delights eel lovers; the filets are grilled in kabayaki sauce. Less adventurous palates may prefer shrimp tempura or a steak served in teriyaki sauce. A Japanese drum team usually performs at 7:30 and 9pm, Thursday through Saturday. Ran-Getsu has a small wine list as well as sake and plum wine.

8400 International Dr., near Orlando Convention Center. © 407/345-0044. www.rangetsu.com. Reservations recommended. Main courses $14–$35 (most under $25); sushi entrees $14–$41 (most under $25). AE, DC, DISC, MC, V. Daily 5–11pm. From I-4, take Exit 74A, Sand Lake Rd./Hwy. 528, east to International Dr., then south. Restaurant is on right.

Roy's Restaurant PACIFIC RIM   Created in Hawaii in 1988 by chef Roy Yamaguchi, this small chain had its Orlando coming out in 2001. The restaurant has an island theme and, unlike the nearby Samba Room, an atmosphere that allows for intimate conversation. Menus change occasionally, but entrees might include wood-roasted lemongrass shrimp with black-rice risotto, seared mahimahi with macadamia-lobster sauce, Korean-style barbecue beef with shiitake mushrooms, or Mongolian-style pork tenderloin in a sake, soy, and pineapple sauce. Roy's also has a reasonably deep wine list.

7760 W. Sand Lake Road. © 407/352-4844. www.roysrestaurant.com. Reservations suggested. Main courses $17–$34. AE, DC, DISC, MC, V. Daily 5:30–10pm. Take I-4 Exit 74A, Sand Lake Rd./Hwy. 528, and go west 1 mile. Restaurant is on left.

MODERATE

B-Line Diner AMERICAN   You can sink into upholstered booths or belly up to the counter on a stool in this '50s-style diner. The round-the-clock menu features comfort foods such as a chicken pot pie that's up to what mom made; a ham and cheese sandwich on a baguette; and roast pork with grilled apples, sun-dried cherry stuffing, and brandy-honey sauce. The portions are hearty, but so are the prices for diner fare.

9801 International Dr., in the Peabody Orlando. © 407/345-4460. www.peabodyorlando.com. Reservations not accepted. Main courses $4–$14 at breakfast; $7–$17 at lunch; $9–$26 (most under $17) at dinner. AE, DC, DISC, MC, V. Daily 24 hr. Free self- and validated valet parking. From I-4, take Exit 74A, Sand Lake Rd./Hwy. 528, east to International Dr., then south. Hotel is on the left across from the Convention Center.

Cafe Tu Tu Tango ⚜ INTERNATIONAL/TAPAS   Another theme restaurant? Sure, but this eclectic eatery is a respite from the usual suspects. Designed like a Spanish artist's loft, it offers performance or art experiences while you munch on any of dozens of tapas or appetizer-size mini-meals. Some of our favorites include the Cajun egg rolls filled with blackened chicken, corn, and cheddar and goat cheeses, served with chunky tomato salsa and Creole mustard; cracked black pepper-crusted, seared tuna sashimi with rice noodles and cold spinach in a sesame-soy vinaigrette; and alligator bites in pepper sauce. Sampling can be quite expensive, but the larger your party, the more dishes you can sample without going bust (usually two or three per person does the trick). There frequently is an artist bringing a canvas to life. Wine is available by the glass or bottle.

8625 International Dr. (just west of the Mercado). © 407/248-2222. www.cafetututango.com. Reservations not required. Tapas (small plates) $4–$11. AE, DC, DISC, MC, V. Sun–Thurs 11:30am–11pm; Fri–Sat 11:30am–midnight. Free self-parking. From I-4, take Exit 74A, Sand Lake Rd./Hwy. 528, east to International Dr., then south. It's on the left.

Value **Self-Service Suppers**

If you're on a tight budget and your room has a kitchen or a spot to sit and grab a bite, consider dining in a night or two and saving a few bucks. Area grocers, many with delis that turn out ready-to-eat treats, include **Albertson's** near I-Drive (7524 Dr. Phillips Blvd., *©* **407/352-1552**; www.albertsons.com) and **Gooding's** in Lake Buena Vista (Crossroads Shopping Plaza, 12521 Hwy. 535/Apopka–Vineland Ave., *©* **407/827-1200**; www.goodings.com). You can find more options in the Orlando Yellow Pages under "Grocers."

Capriccio *©* NORTHERN ITALIAN   Like its upscale Peabody sister, Dux, Capriccio virtually ensures something different from visit to visit as its menu changes seasonally. The entrees might include bucatini tossed with chunks of mesquite-grilled chicken and mushrooms in a slightly garlicky white-wine/pesto sauce or pan-seared tuna with braised fennel and radicchio served with lentil flan and a buttery citrus sauce. Chefs in the exhibition kitchen also make pizzas and fresh breads in mesquite-burning ovens. There's an extensive wine list. The warm decor and the large amounts of natural wood in the dining room give the restaurant a somewhat refined atmosphere, although it's still more casual than Dux. Capriccio also serves a champagne Sunday brunch (leg of lamb, prime rib, you-peel shrimp, smoked salmon, mussels, crepes, eggs benedict, omelets, and unlimited champagne).

9801 International Dr., in the Peabody Orlando. *©* 407/345-4540. www.peabodyorlando.com. Reservations recommended. Main courses $18–$38 (most pizza and pasta dishes priced below $15); Sun champagne brunch buffet $35 adults, $15 children 5–12. AE, DC, DISC, MC, V. Tues–Sun 6:30–11pm; Sun brunch 11am–2pm. Free self- and validated valet parking. From I-4, take Exit 74A, Sand Lake Rd./Hwy. 528, east to International Dr., then south. Hotel is on the left across from the Convention Center.

Ming Court *©* CHINESE   Local patronage and the diverse menu make this one of O-Town's most popular Chinese restaurants. The lightly battered, deep-fried chicken breast gets plenty of zip from a delicate lemon-tangerine sauce. If you're in the mood for beef, there's a grilled filet mignon that's seasoned Szechuan style (the topping has toasted onions, garlic, and chili). Portions are sufficient, there's a moderate wine list, and the service is good. The candlelit interior is decorated in soft earth tones and creates a romantic atmosphere. Glass-walled terrace rooms overlook lotus ponds, filled with colorful koi, and a plant-filled area under a lofty skylight ceiling. A musician plays classical Chinese music on a *zheng* (a long zither) at dinner.

9188 International Dr., between Sand Lake Rd. and Bee Line Expressway. *©* 407/351-9988. www.ming-court.com. Reservations recommended. Main courses $7–$13 lunch, $13–$36 dinner; dim sum mostly $3–$5. AE, DC, DISC, MC, V. Daily 11am–2:30pm and 4:30–10:30pm. Free self-parking. From I-4, take Exit 74A, Sand Lake Rd./Hwy. 528, east to International Dr., then south. It's on the right.

The Samba Room CUBAN   Don't count on intimate conversation, because the music here is loud, Loud, LOUD. It's also one of the things that attracts regulars, so don't ask your server to have it turned down. (He or she won't, even if you say please.) This small chain has branches in Miami, Dallas, and Chicago. The kitchen turns out an enterprising menu that includes rum-raisin, plantain-crusted mahimahi on coconut rice with mango mojo; paella (chicken, mussels, fish, and sausage over rice); and sugarcane beef tenderloin with chipotle mashed potatoes and spiced mushrooms. There's a patio for mild-weather al fresco dining.

7468 W. Sand Lake Rd. (℃ 407/226-0550. Reservations recommended. Main courses $11–$26. AE, DC, DISC, MC, V. Sun–Thurs 11:30am–11pm; Fri–Sat 11:30am–midnight. Free self-parking. Take I-4 Exit 74A, Sand Lake Rd./Hwy. 528, west 1 mile. Restaurant is on left.

Siam Orchid *★ Finds* THAI   Owners Tim and Krissnee Martsching grow chilies, mint, cilantro, lemongrass, wild lime, and other ingredients in their garden, and the quality of their entrees is consistently high. Pad Thai (soft rice noodles tossed with ground pork, minced garlic, shrimp, crab claws, crabmeat, crushed peanuts, and bean sprouts in a tongue-twanging sweet sauce) is one of our favorites. Royal Thai (chicken chunks, potato, and onion in a yellow curry sauce) is another crowd pleaser. For intimate dining, request a *khun toke,* a private enclosure that's the Thai answer to Japanese *tatami* rooms. The split-level dining room has cushioned booths and banquettes and bamboo chairs; some tables overlook a lake. Siam Orchid serves sake and Thai beers from a full bar.

7575 Universal Dr. (between Sand Lake Rd. and Carrier Dr.). (℃ 407/351-0821. Reservations recommended. Main courses $12–$24. AE, DC, DISC, MC, V. Mon–Fri 11am–2pm; daily 5–10:30pm. Free self-parking. From I-4, take Exit 74A, Sand Lake Rd./Hwy. 528, east to Universal, then go north to the restaurant (on the left).

Wild Jacks BARBECUE/STEAKS   Come hankering red meat or don't come at all to this chuck wagon–style eatery. Jacks serves Texas-size (and sometimes Texas tough) hunks of cow grilled on an open pit and served with jalapeño smashed potatoes and corn on the cob. The ribs are generally moist and tender, but at crowded times, when the kitchen gets backed up, they may be dry and chewy. The menu also has chicken, salmon, and pork, but it's not a good idea to experiment in a beef house, even a marginal one. To add to the mood, you'll be treated to mounted buffalo heads, long-stuffed jack-a-lopes, and more dying-calf-in-a-hailstorm, twitch-and-twang country-western music than a city slicker can endure in a lifetime. Wash the meal down with an icy longneck (there is a wine list, but it's very basic).

7364 International Dr. (between Sand Lake Rd. and Carrier Dr.). (℃ 407/352-4407. Reservations accepted. AE, DC, DISC, MC, V. Main courses $11–$21. Daily 4–10pm. Free self-parking. From I-4, take Exit 74A, Sand Lake Rd./Hwy. 528, east to International Dr., then go south. It's on the right.

6 Places to Dine Elsewhere in Orlando

There's life beyond the main tourist areas, as a lot of locals and some enterprising visitors discover. The restaurants in this part of the chapter are located on the map "Accommodations & Dining Elsewhere in Orlando" on p. 159.

VERY EXPENSIVE

The Boheme INTERNATIONAL *★*   This stylish 2001 arrival has wonderful abstract artwork, as well as an enterprising menu that's a cut above many hotel restaurants. Although it caters to a business crowd, it offers an intimate adult atmosphere that's fine for travelers. Again, the menu changes with the wind, but it might feature peppercorn-seared breast of duck with grilled polenta, roasted Chilean sea bass with sweet corn custard and tomato ceriche, or venison chops with root vegetables and baked yams. The Boheme has a 2,000-bottle wine cellar with vintages from all over the world. The restaurant also has a Sunday jazz brunch (smoked salmon and other seafood, sushi, game, and chicken).

325 S. Orange Ave., across from City Hall in Westin Grand Bohemian Hotel. (℃ **888/472-6312,** 800/937-8461, or 407/313-9000. www.grandbohemianhotel.com. Reservations recommended. Main courses $7–$15 breakfast, $10–$17 lunch, $23–$35 dinner; Sun brunch $35. AE, DC, DISC, MC, V. Sun–Thurs 6am–10:30pm; Fri–Sat 6am–11:30pm. Validated valet parking. Take I-4 Exit 83A, West Robinson/Hwy. 526, then south on Orange. The garage is 2 blocks west on Jackson.

Enzo's on the Lake ★★ *(Finds* SOUTHERN ITALIAN   You'll love the lake-front view and the mood inside this restaurant, which evokes the atmosphere of a Mediterranean villa. But the kitchen creations are what pack people in. Enzo Perlini offers a menu from and beyond his native Rome. For the pasta course, try penne soaked in tomato sauce and cream (then given a kick with vodka-injected peppers) or fettuccine with lobster and shrimp in a light saffron salsa. We also recommend *sogliola al limone* (Dover sole sautéed in olive oil and lemon) and *abbacchio del ducca* (rack of lamb baked with shiitake mushrooms and herbs in a lightly spicy sauce). Enzo's dining room has a view of sculpted gardens and sunsets on Lake Fairy. In addition to the main dining room, there are a limited number of seats on a patio overlooking the lake. The menu is complemented by a good wine list, and the bar stocks most of the grappas on planet Earth.

1130 S. U.S. 17/92, Longwood. ⓒ **407/834-9872.** www.enzos.com. Reservations recommended. Main courses $19–$46. AE, DC, DISC, MC, V. Mon–Sat 6–11pm; Fri 11:30am–2pm. Free self-parking. Take I-4 north to Exit 94/Hwy. 434, go east to U.S. 17/92, then right. Enzo's is on the right.

Manuel's on the 28th ★★★ *(Moments* INTERNATIONAL   The 28th floor of a downtown bank provides part of the name and all of the view, which is no less than beautiful after dark. You can see the city and the distant theme parks (fireworks, too) while fueling your tanks in a restaurant where the food matches the visuals. Despite a smallish kitchen, the chefs work wonders with a changing menu. When available, we can't resist the miso-marinated Chilean sea bass with seaweed salad. Seafood lovers also might encounter asparagus-seared ahi tuna with rice risotto and lump crab hollandaise. And the five peppercorn Angus filet with smoked gouda potatoes wows the red-meat crowd. To make sure you don't miss out on the view, the dining room has floor-to-ceiling windows. Expect very professional service and a far-above-par wine cellar.

390 N. Orange Ave., in the NationsBank Building. ⓒ **407/246-6580.** www.manuelsonthe28th.com. Reservations required. Jackets suggested for men. Main courses $26–$45. AE, DC, DISC, MC, V. Tues–Sat 6–9:45pm. Free self-parking. From I-4 take Exit 82C/Anderson St. east to Orange Ave., then left/north to NationsBank Building.

EXPENSIVE

Blackfin Seafood Grill & Bar ★ SEAFOOD   One of Orlando's best marine cuisineries, Blackfin is a classy and casual eatery for those flexible enough to get to the region's north end. Menu headliners include oak-grilled pompano or orange swordfish in lemon butter, delicately blackened wahoo with pan-seared sesame mayonnaise, and red snapper with a Parmesan crust. Landlubbers find an oak-grilled veal chop with a shiraz demi-glacé and herb-roasted chicken breasts delivered with wild rice.

460 N. Orlando Ave., Winter Park. ⓒ **407/691-4653.** www.blackfinseafood.com. Reservations recommended. Main courses $25–$40 (most under $30). AE, DC, DISC, MC, V. Sun–Wed 5–10pm; Thurs–Sat 5–11pm. Free self-parking. From I-4 Exit 88, go east on Lee Rd.; turn south on US 17-92/N. Orlando Ave. It's located on the east side.

Le Provence ★ NEW FRENCH   This upscale local favorite serves dishes that feature duck, veal, lobster, scallops, and tuna. If you're in the mood for creative seafood, try the snapper stuffed with shrimp mousse, then wrapped in phyllo with smoked tomato compote and braised cabbage. Wow! Duck lovers can drool over a combo plate: breast meat grilled in a subtle citrus marinade and a leg with natural juices and pineapple salsa. Few restaurants in town offer rabbit, and none do it better than Le Provence, where the loin is stuffed with paté and vegetables and served in cognac sauce. There are eight fixed-price menus that range from three to six courses. You can enjoy a martini or an after-dinner drink and a cigar next door at Monaco's, which also serves lunch.

Note: In addition to the valet parking noted below, early birds have a shot at a small amount of metered street parking.

50 E. Pine St., in downtown Orlando. © 407/843-1320. www.cenfla.com/res/leprovence. Reservations recommended. Main courses $7–$13 lunch, $16–$36 dinner (most under $25); $28–$62 prix fixe. AE, DC, MC, V. Mon–Fri 11:30am–2pm and 5:30–9:30pm; Sat 5:30–10:30pm. Valet parking $6. From I-4 take Exit 82C/Anderson St. east to Church St., then left/north on Court Ave. It's near the corner of Court and Pine.

Maison & Jardin ☆ TRADITIONAL FRENCH   This restaurant is a great choice for a romantic evening out, even though the atmosphere is a trifle stuffy. If you're game (sorry!), try the venison chops (but they're small and usually chewy) or the seared quail and ostrich combo (ditto). For slightly tamer palates, there's veal tenderloin with Maine lobster meat and morel sauce, rack of lamb in an awakening mustard tarragon sauce, and shrimp and scallops sautéed with spicy tomato cream and served over pasta. The menu has fixed-price options (five or six courses). Maison & Jardin has one of the best wine cellars around; it's been honored by *Wine Spectator* magazine for an outstanding selection (1,200 varieties).

430 S. Wymore Rd., Altamonte Springs. © 407/862-4410. www.maison-jardin.com. Reservations recommended. Main courses $20–$30 dinner; $44.50–$59.50 prix fixe, $63.75–$82.25 with wine. AE, DC, DISC, MC, V. Tue–Sat 6–10pm. Free self-parking. Take I-4 Exit 92, Hwy. 436/Semoran Blvd., make a left at top of exit ramp, go to 2nd light, and turn left onto Wymore. It's a ½ mile on the right.

Mikado Japanese Steak House ☆ JAPANESE   If you're hungry for sushi, consider an evening at the Mikado, which has one of the area's better menus in that department. Ditto for its teppanyaki, where chefs slice, dice, and hurl chicken, seafood, and beef from their grill to your plate. The latter is certainly better than the Teppanyaki Dining Room at Epcot (p. 131). So is the mood. Shoji screens lend intimacy to a dining area where windows overlook rock gardens, reflecting pools, and a palm-fringed pond. Sake, from the restaurant lounge, is the recommended mood enhancer.

8701 World Center Dr. (off Hwy. 536), in Marriott's Orlando World Center. © 407/239-4200. Reservations recommended. Main courses $16–$35 adults, $8–$10 children. AE, DC, DISC, MC, V. Daily 6–10pm. Free self-and validated valet parking. Take I-4 Exit 67/Hwy. 536 east to the Marriott World Center.

Park Plaza Gardens INTERNATIONAL   The decor of this Winter Park restaurant can best be described as EuroFloridian (imagine Art Deco colliding with black and white), and that description matches the cuisine as well. The inventive menu offers such treats as pan-seared ahi tuna with baby bok choy and shiitake mushrooms; spice-crusted double lamb chops in a pine nut–ginger–carrot sauce; and Maryland crab cakes with mashed potatoes, asparagus, and spicy mayonnaise. The house has an extensive selection of domestic, French, and Italian wines, and its staff is one of the best north of Orlando.

319 Park Ave. S., Winter Park. © 407/645-2475. www.parkplazagardens.com. Reservations recommended. Main courses $8–$19 lunch (sandwiches $8–$9), $21–$29 dinner. AE, DC, DISC, MC, V. Tue–Sat 11:30am–2:30pm and 6–9:30pm; Sun 11am–3pm and 6–9:30pm. Free self-parking. Take I-4 Exit 87, Fairbanks Ave./Hwy. 426, east past U.S. 17/92, and, as you pass Rollins College, turn left on Park. It's on the left.

Plantation Room SEAFOOD/STEAKS   New to the dinner scene, this restaurant (in the Celebration hotel, reviewed on p. 107) delivers a nice menu for a rookie. The seafood selections include sea bass with sweet potato grits and fried leeks as well as a medley of scallops, shrimp, and salmon seared, then comforted with grilled polenta and lobster reduction. Meat-lovers can dig into a New York

Accommodations & Dining Elsewhere in Orlando

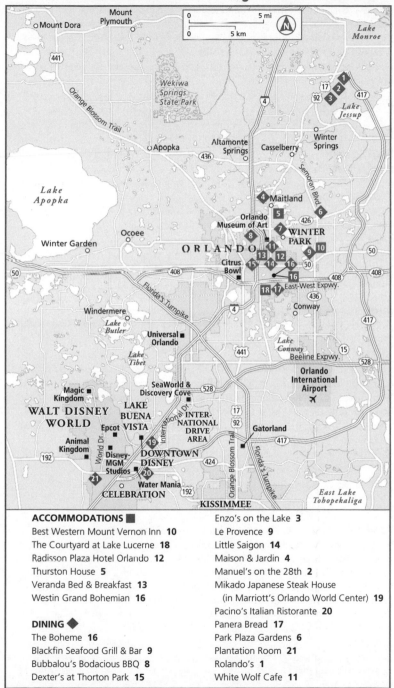

ACCOMMODATIONS ■

Best Western Mount Vernon Inn **10**
The Courtyard at Lake Lucerne **18**
Radisson Plaza Hotel Orlando **12**
Thurston House **5**
Veranda Bed & Breakfast **13**
Westin Grand Bohemian **16**

DINING ◆

The Boheme **16**
Blackfin Seafood Grill & Bar **9**
Bubbalou's Bodacious BBQ **8**
Dexter's at Thorton Park **15**

Enzo's on the Lake **3**
Le Provence **9**
Little Saigon **14**
Maison & Jardin **4**
Manuel's on the 28th **2**
Mikado Japanese Steak House
  (in Marriott's Orlando World Center) **19**
Pacino's Italian Ristorante **20**
Panera Bread **17**
Park Plaza Gardens **6**
Plantation Room **21**
Rolando's **1**
White Wolf Cafe **11**

strip that comes with roasted red potatoes and orange-glazed carrots, while vegetarians might consider the grilled Portobello mushroom with roasted red-pepper coulis over wild mushroom risotto. Sunday's champagne brunch features smoked salmon, omelets, breakfast meats, pancakes, Belgian waffles, and fresh fruit. The plantation-style dining room is cheerful, and there's also al fresco seating on a brick patio.

700 Bloom St., Celebration. 📞 407/566-6000. www.celebrationhotel.com. Reservations recommended. Main courses $15–$36; brunch $29 adults, $15 children. AE, DC, DISC, MC, V. Tue–Sat 5:30–10pm; Sun 11am–2pm. Free self-parking, valet parking $5 for dinner. Take I-4 Exit 64A/U.S. 192, go east to second light, then right on Celebration Ave. and follow the signs.

MODERATE

Dexter's at Thornton Park INTERNATIONAL   This popular cafe and neighborhood bar is just a few blocks from Lake Eola in the center of downtown. The creative fare features such fun foods as crispy duck breast pan seared and glazed with bourbon and maple syrup (talk about a taste explosion); mahimahi wrapped in parchment paper with spinach, tomatoes, capers, garlic, onions, and olives, then baked and served with capellini; and white spinach lasagna that arrives with an herbed focaccia bread to sop up the tangy sauce. Many of the seats are stools at high tables; if that's not for you, you may have a long wait. This is an upbeat, noisy crowd filled with regulars. There's a modest wine list.

808 E. Washington St., near downtown Orlando. 📞 407/648-2777. www.dexwine.com. Reservations not accepted. Main courses $5–$12 lunch ($5–$9 salads and sandwiches), $13–$19 dinner. AE, DC, DISC, MC, V. Mon–Sat 11am–midnight; Sun 5–10pm. Free self-parking. From I-4, take Exit 82C/Anderson St., go to Mills Ave. and take a left. Turn left again on Central Blvd., and continue on Central to Hyer St. Turn left on Hyer; the restaurant is at the corner of Hyer and Washington.

Pacino's Italian Ristorante 👍 NORTHERN ITALIAN   The house specialty, veal osso bucco, is a delicious collision of veal shank, mushrooms, Barolo wine, herbs, and mushrooms. At 32 ounces, the Porterhouse steak is a belly-buster, and the house's *fruitti di mare* has shrimp, calamari, clams, and scallops sautéed with white wine and herbs and heaped onto a mound of linguine. The ceiling's fiber optics help create an illusion of dining under the stars; there's a patio if you want the real thing. Some servers can be a little aloof, but the price and taste make up for it.

5795 W. Irlo Bronson Memorial Hwy./U.S. 192, Kissimmee. 📞 407/396-8022. www.pacinos.com. Reservations accepted. Main courses $13–$27 (most under $20); pizza $9–$11. AE, MC, V. Daily 4–10pm. Free self-parking. From I-4, take Exit 64A/U.S. 192 east 1 mile.

Panera Bread 👍 AMERICAN   This trendy cafe/bakery is a great place for a light meal, and its quick growth in the area (there are several locations) attests to its popularity among locals and tourists. The cafe menu offers a variety of delicious soups (broccoli cheddar, black bean, vegetable sirloin, and others) and salads (Asian sesame chicken, Caesar, and more). But the real main events are sandwiches such as turkey with chipotle mayonnaise, roast beef with creamy horseradish sauce, Portobello and mozzarella panini, and a dozen others. The menu also includes an assortment of fresh bakery items (bagels, brownies, croissants, pastries, and such).

296 E. Michigan St., Orlando. 📞 407/481-9880. www.panerabread.com. Reservations not accepted. Main courses $7–$14; baked goods $1–$5. AE, DISC, MC, V. Mon–Sat 6:30am–9:30pm; Sun 7am–8:30pm. Free self-parking. From I-4, take Exit 80B, U.S. 17/92, and go north to Michigan, then right 1½ miles.

Rolando's 👍 *Finds* CUBAN   If you like neighborhood-style Cuban cuisine, you won't be disappointed here. This mom-and-pop restaurant serves large portions of traditional Cuban fare, such as *arroz con pollo* (chicken with yellow rice), *ropa vieja* (shredded beef), and, if you call a few hours or a day in advance, *paella* (fish and shellfish served on a bed of rice). We also recommend Rolando's roast chicken, which is brushed with crushed garlic, white-wine vinegar, cumin, and oregano, then briefly deep-fried. Entrees are served with yucca (a chewy root) or plantains (a cooked banana-like fruit). The plain dining room has Formica tables, old photographs of Cuba, and potted philodendrons suspended from the ceiling. Soft lighting adds a smidgen of ambience, and there's a very limited beer and wine list.

870 E. Hwy. 436/Semoran Blvd., Casselberry. © 407/767-9677. Reservations accepted. Main courses $4–$6 lunch, $8–$18 dinner. AE, DC, DISC, MC, V. Mon–Fri 11am–9:30pm; Sat noon–10pm; Sun noon–8:30pm. Free self-parking. From I-4, take Exit 82A, Hwy. 408/East–West Expressway, head east, and make a left on Hwy. 436.

White Wolf Cafe INTERNATIONAL   Even the notoriously slow waiters can't dampen our enthusiasm for the food prepared in this restaurant's tiny, deli-style kitchen. But do note the slow service probably rules out firm after-dinner plans unless you eat early. The three-cheese lasagna topped with marinara is always reliable, as is shrimp focaccia—a homemade bread with basil pesto and mozzarella. We also recommend the spinach and ricotta brioche topped with marinara (there goes the cholesterol). Diners rest elbows on marble tables and order from a handwritten menu. Eating at White Wolf evokes the sensation of going to a party at a slightly pretentious loft. There's a small wine and beer menu, the latter including microbrews.

1829 N. Orange Ave. (about 1 mile from Loch Haven Park), Orlando. © 407/895-9911. www.whitewolf cafe.com. Reservations accepted for dinner. Main courses $6–$10 lunch, $9–$17 dinner. AE, MC, V. Mon 11am–4pm; Tues–Thurs 11am–10pm; Fri–Sat 10am–11pm. Free self-parking. Take I-4 Exit 85/Princeton St. and turn right at Orange Ave. Look for striped awnings on the left.

INEXPENSIVE

Bubbalou's Bodacious BBQ *Value* BARBECUE   You can smell the hickory smoke emerging from this restaurant for blocks, the tangy scent cutting through the humid Florida air. This is, hands down, some of the best barbecue you'll find anywhere. And, if nothing else, you have to love the name. There are other things on the menu. If you can eat the night or day away, go for "The Big-Big Pig" platter (beef, sliced pork, and turkey with fixin's). There also are several barbecue baskets, combos, dinners, and sandwiches, as well as side orders ranging from fried pickles and okra to collard greens and black-eyed peas. The uninitiated should stay away from the "Killer" sauce, which produces a tongue buzz that's likely to last for hours; you might even taste-test the mild before moving up to the hot. The beans are the perfect side dish. Only the sometimes-soggy garlic bread brings the meal down, but not too far. Beer is available.

1471 Lee Rd., Winter Park (about 5 min. from downtown Orlando). © 407/628-1212. www.bubbalous.com. Reservations not accepted. Main courses $4–$13. AE, MC, V. Mon–Thurs 10am–9pm; Fri–Sat 10am–10pm. Free self-parking. Take I-4 Exit 88, Lee Rd./Hwy. 423, and follow your nose; Bubbalou's is on the left next to a dry cleaner.

Little Saigon *Finds* VIETNAMESE   Asian immigrants created the demand for Viet cuisine, and this little eatery is one of the best. Better yet, it doesn't attract many tourists. Try the summer rolls—a soft wrap filled with rice, shrimp, and pork served with a delicious peanut sauce. Head next for the grilled pork and egg over rice and noodles or barbecued beef with fried egg and rice. If your appetite is larger than average, try one of the traditional soups with noodles, rice, vegetables, and either chicken, beef, or seafood. The numbered menu isn't translated well, so you may need to ask your server exactly what goes

---

Value **Bargain Buffets**

We won't list them all, but if you spend time on International Drive or U.S. 192/Irlo Bronson Memorial Highway between Kissimmee and Disney, you'll see billboards peddling all-you-can-eat breakfast buffets for $3.99 to $5.99. This is a good way to fill your tanks early and skip or at least go easy on lunch, especially if your day is in the theme parks, where lunches are overpriced. Breakfast buffets are served by **Golden Corral,** 8033 International Dr. (© **407/352-6606**); **Ponderosa Steak House,** 6362 International Dr. (© **407/352-9343**) and 7598 U.S. 192 W. (© 407/396-7721); and **Sizzler Restaurant,** 9142 International Dr. (© **407/351-5369**) and 7602 U.S. 192 W. (© 407/397-0997).

---

into No. 86. (Some don't speak English, so ask to speak to a manager.) As a testament to the restaurant's authenticity, tables here are usually filled with members of the local Vietnamese community. There are very limited wine and beer choices.

1106 E. Colonial Dr./Hwy. 50 (near downtown Orlando). © 407/423-8539. Reservations not accepted. Main courses under $5 lunch, $5–$9 dinner. AE, DISC, MC, V. Daily 10am–9pm. Free self-parking. Take Exit 83B, Colonial Dr./Hwy. 50, off I-4 and head east. Turn right on Thorton Ave. The parking lot is immediately to the left.

7 Only in Orlando: Dining with Disney Characters

Dining with costumed characters is a treat for many Disney fans, but it's a special occasion for those under 10. Some of their favorite cartoon characters show up to greet them, sign autographs, pose for family photos, and interact. These aren't low-turnout events—it's not uncommon for Chef Mickey's, listed below, to have **1,600 or more guests on a weekend morning**—so make reservations as far in advance as possible (when you book your room, if not earlier) and don't expect a lot of one-on-one. The crowds can dampen the event.

The prices for character meals are much the same, no matter where you're dining. Breakfast (most serve it) runs $17 to $20 for adults and $9 to $10 for children 3 to 11; those that serve dinner charge $21 to $24 for adults and $10 to $11 for kids. The prices vary a bit, though, from location to location.

To make reservations for WDW character meals, call © **407/939-3463.** American Express, Diners Club, Discover, MasterCard, Visa, and the Disney Visa Card are accepted at all character meals.

You'll find all of the restaurants mentioned in this section on the map, "Walt Disney World & Lake Buena Vista Dining," earlier in this chapter. For Internet information, go to **www.disneyworld.com**.

Note: Although the character appearances below were accurate when this book went to press, line-ups and booking requirements change frequently (as do menus and prices). We strongly recommend against promising children they will meet a specific character at a meal. If you have your heart set on meeting a certain character, call to confirm his or her appearance when making your priority seating arrangement.

Cape May Café   The Cape May Café, a delightful New England–themed dining room, serves lavish buffet breakfasts (eggs, pancakes, bacon, pastries) hosted by **Admiral Goofy** and his crew—**Chip 'n' Dale** and **Pluto** (characters may vary).

1800 Epcot Resorts Blvd., at Disney's Beach Club Resort. $16.99 adults, $8.99 children. Daily 7:30–11am.

Chef Mickey's 🍴🍴   The whimsical Chef Mickey's offers buffet breakfasts (eggs, bacon, sausage, pancakes, fruit) and dinners (entrees change daily; salad bar, soups, vegetables, ice cream with toppings). **Mickey and various pals** are there to meet and mingle.

4600 N. World Dr., at Disney's Contemporary Resort. Breakfast $16.99 adults, $8.99 children; dinner $23.99 adults, $10.99 children. Daily 7:30–11:30am and 5–9:30pm.

Cinderella's Royal Table 🍴   Cinderella Castle—the focal point of the park—serves character breakfast buffets daily (eggs, bacon, Danish). Hosts vary, but **Cinderella** always puts in an appearance. This is one of the most popular character meals in the park and the hardest to get into, so **reserve far, far in advance** (reservations are taken 60 days in advance, and you must make them with a guaranteed credit card payment that will *cost you $10 for adults and $5 for kids if you cancel them*).

In Cinderella Castle, at the Magic Kingdom. $19.99 adults, $9.99 children. Daily 8–10am. Theme park admission required.

Crystal Palace Buffet 🍴   **Winnie the Pooh** and pals hold court throughout the day. The restaurant serves breakfast (eggs, French toast, pancakes, bacon), lunch, and dinner (hot and cold entrees, peel-and-eat shrimp, and more).

At Crystal Palace, in the Magic Kingdom. Breakfast $15.99 adults, $8.99 children; lunch $16.99 adults, $9.29 children; dinner $20.99 adults, $9.99 children. Daily 8–10:30am, 11:30am–2:45pm, 4pm–park closing. Theme park admission required.

Donald's Prehistoric Breakfastosaurus   **Donald, Goofy,** and **Pluto** host a buffet breakfast (eggs, bacon, French toast) in DinoLand U.S.A.'s Restaurantosaurus.

In DinoLand U.S.A., at Disney's Animal Kingdom. $16.99 adults, $8 children. Daily park opening–10am. Theme park admission required.

Garden Grill 🍴   There's a "Momma's-in-the-kitchen" theme at this revolving restaurant, where hearty, family-style meals are hosted by **Mickey** and **Chip 'n' Dale.** (Mickey sure gets around, eh?) Lunch and dinner (chicken, fish, steak, vegetables, potatoes) are served. The Grill also has an ice-cream social that can be booked at 3, 3:10, or 3:20pm.

In the Land Pavilion at Epcot. Lunch $19.99 adults, $9.99 children; dinner $21.99 adults, $9.99 children. Ice-cream social $6.99 per person. Daily 11am–8pm. Theme park admission required.

Hollywood & Vine Character Dining 🍴   **Minnie, Goofy, Pluto,** and **Chip 'n' Dale** host buffet breakfasts (eggs, pancakes, French toast, bacon, sausage, ham) and lunches (turkey, flank steak, chicken, fish, vegetables).

At Hollywood & Vine, in Disney MGM–Studios. Breakfast $16.99 adults, $8.99 children; lunch $17.99 adults, $9.99 children. Daily 8–3pm. Theme park admission required.

Liberty Tree Tavern 🍴   This Colonial-style 18th-century pub offers character dinners hosted by **Minnie, Goofy, Pluto,** and **Chip 'n' Dale.** The family-style meals include salad, roast turkey, ham, flank steak, cornbread, and apple crisp with vanilla ice cream.

In Liberty Square, in the Magic Kingdom. $20.99 adults, $9.99 children. Daily 4pm–park closing. Theme park admission required.

1900 Park Fare 🍴   The elegant Grand Floridian offers breakfast (eggs, French toast, bacon, pancakes) and dinner buffets (steak, pork, fish) at the exposition-themed 1900 Park Fare. Big Bertha—a French band organ that plays pipes, drums, bells, cymbals, castanets, and xylophone—provides music. **Mary Poppins, Alice in Wonderland,** and friends appear at breakfast; **Cinderella** and friends show up for Cinderella's Gala Feast at dinner.

4401 Floridian Way, at Disney's Grand Floridian Resort & Spa. Breakfast $16.99 adults, $9.99 children; dinner $23.99 adults, $10.99 children. Daily 7:30–11am and 5–9pm.

'Ohana Character Breakfast   Traditional breakfasts (eggs, pancakes, bacon) are prepared in an 18-foot fire pit and served family style. **Mickey** and friends appear, and children are given the chance to parade around with Polynesian musical instruments.

1600 Seven Seas Dr., in 'Ohana at Disney's Polynesian Resort. $16.99 adults, $8.99 children. Daily 7:30–11am.

Princess Storybook Breakfast   **Snow White, Mary Poppins, Princess Aurora, Pocahontas,** or **Belle** might show up at this new character meal buffet (scrambled eggs, French toast, sausage, bacon, and potatoes).

At Akershus Castle in Epcot's Norway Pavilion. Breakfast $19.99 adults, $9.99 children. Daily 8:30–10:20 am. Theme park admission required.

7

Exploring Walt Disney World

You're savvy enough to know the big attraction here is the one that put Orlando on the map—Disney's Magic Kingdom, which opened in 1971. After all these years, it's still the fairest in the land—by far the most popular theme park in the United States—but it's now just part of the Mega Mouse's magic.

The Walt Disney World stable has resorts, restaurants, nightclub venues, smaller attractions, and four theme parks: the Magic Kingdom, Epcot, Disney–MGM Studios, and Animal Kingdom. Even in 2002's sour economy, those parks attracted nearly 38 million paying customers, according to estimates by *Amusement Business* magazine. All four make the country's top five in attendance (the other is Disneyland in California). It's no wonder. They offer a star-spangled, self-sufficient vacation where wonderment, human progress, and old-fashioned family fun are the key themes. They strut their stuff with spectacular parades and fireworks displays, 3-D and CircleVision films, nerve-racking thrill rides, and adventurous journeys through time and space. Though they're expensive, you'll seldom hear people complain about failing to get their money's worth. Most leave saying Disney delivers.

One reason is that rides and shows are periodically updated. And if something doesn't quite work, Disney usually fixes it. As part of this process, the company interviews some of its park-goers to decide how well, or poorly, things are working.

There have been changes and additions as the Magic Kingdom has matured, although not as many as in the other parks. The oldest of its "lands," Tomorrowland, was more than a bit weary when it underwent a late 1990s upgrade. The redecorating has slowed after 1999's torrid pace, which brought new thrill rides to Epcot and Disney–MGM Studios, a new "land" (Asia) in Animal Kingdom, the addition of Fantasmic! at Disney–MGM Studios, and the opening of Cirque du Soleil in Downtown Disney West Side. Still, new things periodically enter the mix, including **Primeval Whirl,** the twin, carnival-style roller coaster at Animal Kingdom. Also, Epcot's **Mission: Space,** a NASA-caliber motion simulator, and the 3-D show **Mickey's Philhar-Magic Orchestra** are scheduled to open in the second half of 2003.

But before we dive into the action, giving you details of these and other fun generators, let's take care of some basic business.

1 Essentials

GETTING INFORMATION IN ADVANCE

Before leaving home, call or write to the Walt Disney World Co., Box 10000, Lake Buena Vista, FL 32830-1000 (© **407/934-7639**) for a vacation video and the *Walt Disney World Vacations* brochure; both are valuable planning aids. When you call, also ask about special events that will be going on during your

---

Tips Tighter Security

Guards at the gates at all Disney parks check a variety of carry-ins, including backpacks and large purses. They also have been known to check guests' IDs, so be sure to bring a government-issued photo identification card. All this, of course, means it takes a little longer to get to the action.

---

visit. While we list big-time events under "When to Go" in chapter 2, there are many other events that may be of interest to you.

Once you've arrived in town, Guest Services and the concierge desks in hotels (especially Disney properties and "official" hotels) have up-to-the-minute information about happenings in the parks. Stop by to ask questions and get literature, including a schedule of park hours and events. If you have questions your hotel's personnel can't answer, call Disney at © **407/824-4321.**

American Express cardholders staying at Disney resorts can get a free booklet with modest discounts (on meals, merchandise, tours, and more) at the resorts' Guest Services desks.

There also are information areas at City Hall in the Magic Kingdom and Guest Relations at Epcot, Disney–MGM Studios, and Animal Kingdom.

If you're hooked into the Internet or have a local library with Internet access, try **www.disneyworld.com**, which features entertaining and regularly updated information on the parks.

Also try the Orlando/Orange County Convention & Visitors Bureau site (**www.orlandoinfo.com**). Once there, click on Attractions in the menu on the left, then use the search function at the bottom of the next screen. Another good site, **www.floridakiss.com**, is sponsored by the Kissimmee–St. Cloud Convention & Visitors Bureau. It, too, has an attractions link.

GETTING TO WDW BY CAR

The interstate exits to all Disney parks and resorts are well marked. Once you're off I-4, there are signs directing you to individual destinations. If you miss your exit, *don't panic.* Simply get off at the next one and turn around. It may take a little more time, but it's safer than cutting across five lanes of traffic to make the off-ramp, or worse—to risk a fender bender. Drive with extra caution in the attractions area. Disney drivers are divided into two categories: workers in a hurry to make their shift and tourists in a hurry to get to the fun (and trying to drive while looking at a map).

Upon entering WDW grounds, you can tune your radio to 1030 AM when you're approaching the Magic Kingdom, or 850 AM when approaching Epcot, for park information. Tune to 1200 AM when departing the Magic Kingdom, or 910 AM when departing Epcot. TVs in all Disney resorts and "official" hotels also have park information channels.

PARKING

All WDW lots are tightly controlled; the Disney folks have parking down to a science. You park where they tell you to park—or here comes security. *Remember to write your parking place (lot and row number) on something so you can find your vehicle later.* Parking attendants won't be there to direct you to it when you leave the park, and, at the end of the day, you'd be surprised at how many autos look alike through tired eyes.

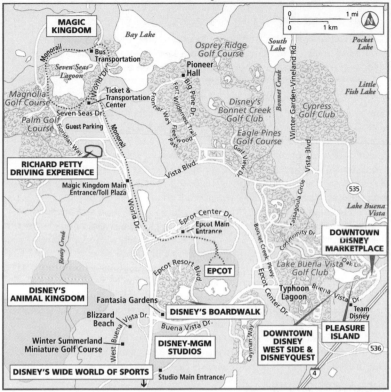

Visitors should ride the free trams in the massive Magic Kingdom lots, but some folks decide to skip them and walk to the gates at Epcot, Disney–MGM Studios, and Animal Kingdom. *Some also don't have a choice. Disney has cut service to some parking areas near the entrances to its parks. Guests who can't make the hike have to park in handicapped areas or have a driver drop them at special unloading areas outside the entrances.* If you're walking, be careful! These lots aren't designed for pedestrians, and you don't want to become road kill.

Parking costs $7 at the four major WDW attractions ($8 for RVs). We expect the fees eventually will go up to $8 and $9, respectively, to match Universal Orlando's. There are special lots for travelers with disabilities (© 407/824-4321 for details).

TICKETS

There are several options, from single- to multiday tickets. Most people find the best bargains to be 4- and 5-day passes. All offer unlimited use of the WDW transportation system. (*Note:* The prices below **don't include 6% sales tax.**)

The **4-Day Park Hopper Passes** provide unlimited admission to the Magic Kingdom, Epcot, Animal Kingdom, and Disney–MGM Studios. The cost is just a few dollars a day less than the cost of single-park tickets, but you also get the option of returning to the parks as many times as you want and your unused days don't expire, so you can use them on a later visit. For a 4-day pass, adults pay $208; kids 3 to 9 pay $167. A **5-Day Park Hopper Plus Pass** also includes

---

Tips **Price Alert**

Single-day and multiday admission prices don't include Florida's 6% sales tax and are subject to change. Annual price increases are normal, so when you visit, prices may be higher than those listed on these pages.

---

your choice of two 1-day admissions to Typhoon Lagoon, Blizzard Beach, Pleasure Island, or Disney's Wide World of Sports. The 5-day pass is $269 for adults and $216 for kids. Park Hopper Plus Passes for 6 and 7 days are available; call © 407/824-4321 or on the Internet go to www.disneyworld.com for details. (*Note:* You can save a few dollars on multiday tickets if you buy them online at the WDW website.) Disney also offers length-of-stay passes, called **Ultimate Park Hopper Passes,** for WDW resort and "official" hotel guests.

A **1-day, 1-park ticket** for Magic Kingdom, Epcot, Animal Kingdom, or Disney–MGM Studios is $52 for adults, $42 for children 3 to 9.

A **1-day ticket to Typhoon Lagoon or Blizzard Beach** is $31 for adults, $25 for children.

A **1-day ticket** to **Pleasure Island** is $19.95. Because this is primarily an 18-and-over entertainment complex, there's no child's ticket.

If you're planning to stay at any WDW resort or "official" hotel (see chapter 5, "Where to Stay"), you're also eligible for money-saving Disney room-and-ticket packages priced according to the length of your stay.

If your stay is long enough or you're going to return within the year, annual passes ($369–$489 adults, $314–$416 children) can be a cheaper way to go than the longer Park Hopper Plus or Unlimited Magic tickets.

OPERATING HOURS

Hours of operation vary throughout the year and can be influenced by special events, so it's a good idea to call to check opening/closing times.

The **Magic Kingdom** and **Disney–MGM Studios** are generally open from 9am to 6 or 7pm, with hours often extended to 9pm and sometimes as late as midnight during major holidays and summer. **Animal Kingdom** usually is open from 8 or 9am to 5 or 6pm, but sometimes closes as late as 7pm.

Epcot's Future World is generally open from 9 or 10am to 7pm and occasionally later. **Epcot's World Showcase** usually opens at 11am or noon and closes at 9pm. Once again, there are extended holiday and summer hours.

Typhoon Lagoon and **Blizzard Beach** are open from 10am to 5pm most of the year (with extended hours during summer and some holidays). Both are closed on a rotating basis part of the winter for maintenance.

2 Making Your Visit More Enjoyable

HOW WE'VE MADE THIS CHAPTER USEFUL TO PARENTS

Before every listing in the major parks, you'll note the **"Recommended Ages"** entry that tells which ages will most appreciate that ride or show. Though most families want to do everything, this guideline is helpful in planning your daily itinerary. In our ride ratings, we've indicated whether a ride will be more enjoyable for kids than for adults. Many, even a couple in the Magic Kingdom, are too intense for young kids, and one bad experience can spook them for a long time. You'll also find any **height and health restrictions** noted in the listings.

BEST TIME OF YEAR TO VISIT

Because of the large number of international visitors, there's really no "off sea-son" at Disney, but during the winter months, usually mid-January through March, crowds are smaller (except weekends), and the weather can be mild. The crowds also thin from mid-September until the week before Thanksgiving, and in May, before Memorial Day weekend. (Again, weekends tend to get clogged with locals.) Summer is when the masses throng to the parks. It's also humid and hot, *Hot,* **HOT.** If you can skip a summer visit, you also won't have to worry much about the possibility of a hurricane (admittedly rare) or an electrical storm (an almost daily occurrence).

BEST DAYS TO VISIT

The busiest days at all parks are generally Saturday and Sunday. Seven-day guests usually arrive and depart on one of these days, so fewer of them turn the turn-stiles; but weekends are when locals and Florida commuters invade. Beyond that: Monday, Thursday, and Saturday are pretty frantic in the Magic Kingdom; Tuesday and Friday are hectic at Epcot; Sunday and Wednesday are crazy at Dis-ney–MGM Studios; and Monday, Tuesday, and Wednesday are a zoo at Animal Kingdom. Periods around major holidays also attract throngs—mid-December through the first weekend in January is very busy. Crowds tend to thin later in the day, so if you're going to visit during the busy season and have the luxury of the park hopper or park hopper plus passes, you'll bump into fewer guests the later you visit. This also applies to the water parks.

The big attractions at Animal Kingdom are, obviously, the animals, and the best time to see them is at the opening bell or late in the day, when things are cooler. You'll also get a decent midday glimpse of some of them during the cooler months.

PLAN YOUR VISIT

How you plan your time at Walt Disney World will depend on a number of fac-tors. These include the ages of any children in your party, what, if anything, you've seen on previous visits, your interests, and whether you're traveling at peak time or off season. Preplanning is always essential. So is choosing age-appropriate activities.

Nothing can spoil a day in the parks more than a child devastated because he or she can't do something that was promised. Before you get to the park, review this book and the suggested ages for children, including *height restrictions.* The WDW staff won't bend the rules despite the pitiful wails of your little ones. *Note:* Many rides that have minimum heights also have enough turbulence to make them unsuitable for folks with neck, back, or heart problems, those prone to motion sickness, or pregnant women.

⟨*Tips* Shorter Days, Fewer Shows

The economic fallout of 2001 and 2002 has included a drop in theme-park attendance, a setback still plaguing Disney. To help combat the problem and reduce overhead, Disney parks in many cases **close earlier** than at sim-ilar times in previous years, and some areas **open later.** Additionally, some shows are closed some days or altogether. The hours and shows listed in this chapter generally apply, but in order to avoid being disappointed, call ℭ **407/824-4321** or go to **www.disneyworld.com** for up-to-the-minute information.

Unless you're staying for more than a week, you can't experience all of the rides, shows, or attractions included in this chapter. A ride may last only 5 minutes, but you may have to wait an hour or so, even with FASTPASS (detailed shortly). You'll wear yourself to a frazzle trying to hit everything. It's better to follow a relaxed itinerary, including leisurely meals and some recreational activities, than to make a demanding job out of trying to see everything.

CREATE AN ITINERARY FOR EACH DAY

Read the previously mentioned *Walt Disney World Vacations* brochure and the detailed descriptions in this book, and then plan your trip to include those shows and attractions that pique your interest and excitement.

Consider your loyalties. Winnie the Pooh doesn't move us the same way he moves our grandsons, Jake and Andy. Put the ride featuring your favorite character, or theirs, at the top of your list. It's a good idea to make a daily itinerary, putting your choices in some kind of sensible geographical sequence, so you're not zigzagging all over the place. Familiarize yourself in advance with the layout of each park. Also recognize that rides or exhibits nearest an entrance may be the busiest when the gates open. That's because a lot of people visit the first thing they see, even if the more popular attractions are deeper into the park.

We repeat this advice: Schedule sit-down shows, recreational activities (a boat ride or a refreshing swim late in the afternoon), and at least some unhurried meals if time permits. This will save you from exhaustion and aggravation. Our

---

Tips FASTPASS

Don't want to stand in line as long as the other guests, yet not flush enough to hire a stand-in? Disney parks use a reservation system where you go to the primo rides, feed your theme-park ticket into a small ticket taker, and get an assigned 1-hour period in which to return. When you do, you get into a short line and climb aboard. Here's the drill:

Hang onto your ticket stub when you enter and head to the hottest ride on your list. If it's a FASTPASS attraction (they're noted in the guide map you get when you enter), feed your stub into the waist-level ticket taker. Retrieve your ticket stub and the FASTPASS stub that comes with it. Look at the two times stamped on the latter. You can return during that 1-hour window and enter the ride with almost no wait. In the meantime, you can do something else until the appointed time.

Note: Early in the day, your 1-hour window may begin 40 minutes after you feed the FASTPASS machine, but later in the day it may be hours later. Initially, Disney only allowed you to do this on one ride at a time. Now, your FASTPASS ticket has a time when you can get a second FASTPASS, usually 2 hours later, even if you haven't yet used the first pass.

Note II: Don't try to feed your ticket stub in multiple times, figuring you can hit the jackpot for multiple rides or help others in your group who lost their tickets. These "smart" stubs will reject your pitiful attempt by spitting out a coupon that says "Not A Valid FASTPASS."

suggested itineraries that follow allow you to see a great deal of the parks as effi-
ciently as possible. And if you have the luxury of a multiday pass, you can divide
and conquer at a slower pace and even repeat some favorites.

SUGGESTED ITINERARIES

Our suggested itineraries will allow you to cover most of the ground in each park in as effi-
cient a manner as possible. Do note, though, that using FASTPASS may require you to double back to a land you've already covered.

There are a ton of ways to see the parks, and we feel, time and budget permitting, it's
often better to do it in limited doses—those where you spend 2 or more days in a park at
a casual pace. We're offering suggested itineraries as options for those on a tighter schedule. The following itineraries are organized to get the most out of the least amount of time.
Where appropriate, we break things into one game plan for families with kids and another
for teenagers and adults. With few exceptions (we'll note them later), Disney World doesn't
have enough true stomach-turning thrill rides to warrant a special itinerary for teens or take-
no-prisoners adults. Frankly, the only Orlando park in that class is Universal's Islands of
Adventure, which we'll tackle in chapter 8, "Exploring Beyond Disney: Universal Orlando,
SeaWorld & Other Attractions."

A Day in the Magic Kingdom with Kids

Consider making a priority seating dinner reservation at **Cinderella's Royal Table** (© **407/939-3463**), located inside Cinderella Castle.

If you have very young kids, go right to the **Walt Disney World Railroad** station on Main Street and take the next train. Get off at **Mickey's Toontown Fair,** where tots are wowed by Mickey, Minnie, and the gang. They can ride the **Barnstormer at Goofy's Wiseacre Farm,** a mini–roller coaster, and explore **Mickey's** and **Minnie's Country Houses.**

If your kids are 8 or older, start the day at **Tomorrowland** and brave the **ExtraTERRORestrial Alien Encounter, Buzz Lightyear's Space Ranger Spin,** and **Space Mountain.** (Little ones like the **Tomorrowland Indy Speedway,** but there's not much else for them here, so skip this part of the park if time is limited.)

Most preteens will find something that's fun in **Fantasyland.** Ride **Dumbo the Flying Elephant** and **Peter Pan's Flight.** Catch **Mickey's PhilharMagic Orchestra** (opening in 2003), then climb aboard **It's a Small World, The Many Adventures of Winnie the**

Pooh, and **Cinderella's Golden Carousel.**

Then grab lunch at **Cosmic Ray's Starlight Café.**

Next, head west to **Liberty Square.** Most kids 10 and older will like the Animatronic history lesson in the **Hall of Presidents** show. Before leaving, visit the **Haunted Mansion,** then move to **Frontierland. Splash Mountain** and **Big Thunder Mountain Railroad** are best suited for those 8 and older, while the **Country Bear Jamboree** and **Tom Sawyer Island** are fun for the younger set and parents looking for a sit-down.

Go to **Adventureland** next. Ride **The Magic Carpets of Aladdin, Pirates of the Caribbean,** and **Jungle Cruise,** then let the kids burn some energy in the **Swiss Family Treehouse.**

Consult the guide map available as you enter the park, and if **Fantasy in the Sky Fireworks** and **SpectroMagic** are scheduled, be sure to watch them.

A Day in the Magic Kingdom for Teenagers & Adults

As we mentioned earlier, consider making a priority seating reservation at **Cinderella's Royal Table** (© **407/939-3463**) if you want a sit-down dinner.

From Main Street, cut through the center of the park to Frontierland and challenge **Splash Mountain,** then ride **Big Thunder Mountain Railroad.** If you need to rest your feet or escape the heat, the **Country Bear Jamboree** is the place for it.

Next, go to Liberty Square and visit the **Haunted Mansion** and **Hall of Presidents.**

Have lunch at the **Liberty Tree Tavern.**

Now cut diagonally through the park, past Cinderella Castle, and into Tomorrowland to ride **Space Mountain, Buzz Lightyear's Space Ranger Spin,** and the **ExtraTERRORestrial Alien Encounter.**

If time permits, head to Adventureland for the **Jungle Cruise** and **Pirates of the Caribbean,** then, if they're scheduled, end the day with **Fantasy in the Sky Fireworks.**

If You Can Spend Only 1 Day at Epcot

Epcot deserves at least 2 days, so this is a barnstorming highlight tour. Remember to get a **Priority Seating** reservation if you want to eat in the park (call © **407/939-3463** before you arrive or make your first stop at the WorldKey terminals in Innoventions East). We suggest the **Coral Reef** restaurant in the Living Seas or the **San Angel Inn** in the World Showcase's Mexico exhibit for lunch, and **Marrakesh** in Morocco or **Akershus** in Norway for dinner. See other options in chapter 6, "Where to Dine."

This is the **least desirable of the parks for young kids.** Even some older ones and teens may not enjoy the heavy learning and technology themes, but there are a few fun rides.

As you enter, go to any of your favorite rides that have FASTPASS (they're noted in the handout guide map). If the lines are short, don't bother with the pass. If the fast track isn't in your itinerary, take the *other* strategic approach:

Future World, near the front of the park, is the first of Epcot's two areas to open, so start there. Skip **Spaceship Earth,** at least for now. It's nearest the entrance, and that big golf ball and its boring show attract most guests as they enter. Go straight to **Body Wars,** which is in the **Wonders of Life** pavilion to the left of Spaceship Earth. Next is **Mission: Space** (opening in 2003) where you can train as the astronauts do. Follow up with next-door-neighbor **Test Track.** Then cut to the west to **Imagination** for *Honey, I Shrunk the Audience.*

If time permits before a 1:30 or 2pm lunch, visit **Innoventions.** On its East Side, all but the smallest kids will like seeing some of today's and tomorrow's high-tech gadgets at the **House of Innoventions** and kicking the tires at **Future Cars.** Over on the West Side, kids and adults find it hard to leave **Video Games of Tomorrow.**

Unless you're eager for the **Spaceship Earth** snoozer, proceed to the **World Showcase** in mid afternoon. To us, this is the best part of Epcot—the pavilions of 11 nations surround a big lagoon that you can cross by boat. But, again, kids and teens may get the itch to leave.

Norway delivers a history lesson and boat ride called *Maelstrom,* **China** and **Canada** have fabulous 360-degree movies, and **Germany's Biergarten** is filled with oompah music. Also, take in the show and concerts at **U.S.A.—The American Adventure.**

After dinner, be sure to watch **IllumiNations.**

If You Can Spend 2 Days at Epcot

Ignore the 1-day itinerary, but consider our earlier advice about priority seating reservations and choice of restaurants.

The basic plan of attack here is to hit Future World and all of its rides and exhibits on your first day, then cruise to World Showcase the next. (Because the showcase opens later, you can hit any missed areas or go back for seconds in Future World early on Day 2.) Remember to go straight to FASTPASS rides that appeal to you (check your guide map).

Day 1 If you want to eat in the park, book **Priority Seating** for lunch and dinner if you haven't already. Skip **Spaceship Earth** because that's where a lot of the park's visitors go first. Head instead to **Test Track,** the park's newest thrill ride, which is in the southeast corner of Future World. If it's crowded, use FASTPASS and come back later. Then blast off to train as the astronauts do on **Mission: Space** (opening in 2003). Next, ride **Body Wars,** which is in the **Wonders of Life** pavilion to the left of Spaceship Earth, then visit the **Cranium Command** and **The Making of Me** shows in the same area. Then double back to **Ellen's Energy Adventure** in the Universe of Energy before grabbing lunch.

Next, spend time in **Innoventions East,** where most older kids and adults will love the household gizmos in the **House of Innoventions** and a look at tomorrow in **Future Cars.** At **Innoventions West,** try your luck at the **Video Games of Tomorrow** exhibit. Before you call it a day, enjoy the peaceful exhibits in the **Living Seas** and **The Land,** then cut to **Imagination** for the *Honey, I Shrunk the Audience* show.

Day 2 If you arrive when the park opens, go to any **Future World** rides or shows that you missed or want to repeat. Or sleep a little later and arrive for the opening of **World Showcase.**

Start in **Canada,** to the far right of the entrance. The movie there is uplifting and entertaining. Then continue counterclockwise to the **United Kingdom** for street shows, people watching, and a real pub. **France** has a captivating film and a wonderful pastry shop; **Morocco** has a colorful casbah with merchants, Moorish tile and art, and little passages that put you in Bogartville. (For some, this is better than the real Casablanca, which is dirty.) **Japan** has a store packed with enticements and grand architecture, but move quickly to **U.S.A.—The American Adventure,** a patriotic triumph of audio-animated characters. This is a large theater, so waits are rarely long. Next, head to **Italy** and St. Mark's Square, which comes complete with a 105-foot bell tower. **Germany's Biergarten** has oompah bands, beer, and wursts. Don't miss the model railway and the Bavarian-looking shops. Then steer yourself to **China,** which offers food, bargain buys, gardens and ponds, and a 360-degree movie. Continuing counterclockwise, **Norway** features the **Maelstrom** ride. **Mexico** completes the World Showcase semicircle with a boat ride into its history.

End things with the **Illumi-Nations** fireworks display.

A Day at Disney–MGM Studios Theme Park

Here's a park that's easier to manage in 1 day.

Remember our advice on making **Priority Seating** (© 407/939-3463) reservations in advance if you want to eat in the park. The **Hollywood Brown Derby** is a decent sit-down option (see chapter 6, "Where to Dine," for more information on dining options in the park).

Head directly to the **Twilight Zone Tower of Terror.** It's a high-voltage ride that's not for the young or faint of heart. The same goes for the new **Rock 'n' Roller Coaster,** which blends incredible take-off speed with three inversions.

The park is small, so backtracking isn't as much of a concern here. Consider passing up attractions that have long lines, or use FAST-PASS where you can. Lines also can be long at **Star Tours** and the **Indiana Jones Epic Stunt Spectacular.**

Voyage of the Little Mermaid is a must for the young (in years or yearnings); the same goes for **Jim Henson's Muppet*Vision 3-D,** a truly fun show for all ages.

With luck, you'll make it through most of the above before a late lunch at the **50's Prime Time Café.** Afterward, watch (and maybe get lucky enough to win at) **Who Wants to Be a Millionaire—Play It!** and go on the ton-of-fun **Backlot Tour.**

Check your show schedule for favorites such as **Playhouse Disney—Live on Stage!** (which is great for little kids) and **Beauty and the Beast,** and, at night, *don't miss* **Fantasmic!**

A Day at Animal Kingdom

Be here when the gates open, usually around 8 or 9am. (Call Disney information at © **407/824-4321** to check the time.) This will give you the best chance of seeing animals, because they're most active in the morning air (the next best is late in the afternoon, although some can be seen throughout the day in cooler months). If you want to eat at the **Rainforest Cafe,** make reservations by calling © **407/939-3463.**

The size of the park (500 acres) means a lot of travel once you pass through the gates. Don't linger in the **Oasis** area or around the **Tree of Life;** instead, head directly to the back of the park to be first in line for **Kilimanjaro Safaris.** This will allow you to see animals before it gets hot and the lines become monstrous. Work your way back through Africa, visiting **Pangani Forest Exploration Trail** and its lowland gorillas. Then head to the **Tree of Life** on Discovery Island for **It's Tough to Be a Bug.** (Older kids, teens, and adults might prefer **Dinosaur** in Dinoland U.S.A., a good choice if you get there before lines form or if you use FASTPASS.) Younger kids deserve some time at the **Boneyard** and on **TriceraTop Spin** in Dinoland as well as **Camp Minnie-Mickey,** on the other side of the park.

Restaurantosaurus is a fair lunch stop in Dinoland.

Then see the park's two best shows, **Tarzan Rocks!** in Dinoland and **Festival of the Lion King** in Camp Minnie-Mickey. If your time allows only one, Lion King is the best choice.

If you want a bird-show fix, park yourself at **Flights of Wonder** in Asia, and don't miss the **Kali River Rapids** and **Maharajah Jungle Trek** in that part of the park.

SERVICES & FACILITIES IN THE PARKS

ATMs   Money machines are available near the entrances to all parks and usually at least one other place inside (see the handout guide map as you enter the park). They honor cards from banks using the Cirrus, Honor, and PLUS systems.

Baby Care   All parks have a Baby Care Center equipped with rocking chairs and selling baby-care basics, which are also available at Guest Relations. All women's restrooms, and some men's, are equipped with changing tables.

Cameras & Film   Film and Kodak disposable cameras are sold at various locations in all parks (at much higher prices than those in the free world).

Tips Smoking Alert

Disney prohibits smoking in shops, attractions, restaurants, and ride lines. All WDW parks stopped selling cigarettes in 1999, and beginning in 2000, smokers were allowed to light up only in designated outdoor areas. Next: Well, we aren't predicting, but could WDW go smoke-free?

Car Assistance If you need a battery jump or other assistance, raise the hood of your vehicle and wait for security to arrive.

First Aid All parks have stations marked on the handout guide maps.

Internet Access Walt Disney World has installed phones with large touch-screens and Internet access capabilities at several locations in the theme parks, resorts, and other locations. You can use them to find a variety of information or make dining reservations and, for 25¢ a minute with a 4-minute minimum, you can access the Internet or check your e-mail.

Lost Children Every park has a designated spot for lost children to be reunited with families. In Magic Kingdom, it's City Hall or the Baby Care Center; in Epcot, the Earth Center or the Baby Care Center; in Disney–MGM Studios, Guest Relations; and in Animal Kingdom, Discovery Island. _Children under 7 should wear nametags; older children and adults should have a prearranged meeting place in case your group gets separated. If that happens, tell the first park employee you see—many wear the same type of clothing and all have nametags._

Package Pickup Clerks at nearly all WDW stores can arrange for large packages to be sent to the front of the park. Allow at least 3 hours for delivery. If you're staying at a Disney resort, you also can have them sent to your hotel.

Parking Disney currently charges $7 for car, light truck, and van parking; it charges $8 for RVs.

Pets Don't leave yours in a parked car, even with a window cracked open. Cars become oven-like death traps in Florida's sun. Only service animals are permitted in the parks, but there are five kennels in the WDW complex (© **407/824-6568**). The ones at the Transportation and Ticket Center in the Magic Kingdom and near the entrance to Fort Wilderness board animals overnight. Day accommodations are offered at kennels just outside the Entrance Plaza at Epcot and at the entrances to Disney–MGM Studios and Animal Kingdom. Proof of vaccination is required. For more information, see "Fast Facts" in chapter 4.

Shops In addition to the ones listed in the following pages, many of Disney's primo rides have small gift shops featuring souvenirs based on that ride's theme.

Stroller Rental Strollers are available near all of the park entrances. The cost is $8 for a single and $15 for a double, including a $1 Disney dollar refund on return.

Wheelchair Rental A wheelchair is $7, including a $1 deposit. Electric wheelchairs rent for $30 plus a $10 refundable deposit.

FOR TRAVELERS WITH SPECIAL NEEDS

WDW does a lot to assist guests with disabilities. Its services are detailed in the _Guidebook for Guests with Disabilities._ You can get one from Guest Relations in the parks, other information areas, at Disney resorts, or **online** at **www.disney world.com** (click "FAQ" on the left side of the home page, then "Guests with

---

(*Moments*   **Hidden Treasure**

If you're looking for something to do on Disney property that's out of the mainstream, consider becoming a monorail pilot (basically, you get to ride up front with the monorail pilot). It requires a little patience, because no more than four or five people can do it per ride, so ask a cast member at the monorail stations at the Grand Floridian, Polynesian, or Contemporary resorts if there's room for you in the cockpit. You won't have much luck in peak seasons or times of day (such as when the parks open and close), during foul weather, or if there's a pilot trainee on board. But at other times, especially if you're patient enough to wait for the next train, it may be your lucky day. And you may be doubly rewarded with a monorail co-pilot's license. Best of all: it's free.

Disabilities FAQ"). You can also call © **407/824-4321** with questions regarding other special needs. Some examples of other services: Almost all Disney resorts have rooms for those with disabilities, and there are Braille directories inside the Magic Kingdom, in the front of the Main Street train station, and in a gazebo in front of the Crystal Palace restaurant. There are special parking lots at all parks. Complimentary guided-tour audiocassette tapes and players are available at Guest Relations to assist visually impaired guests, and personal translator units are available to amplify the audio at some Epcot Attractions (inquire at Earth Station). For information about Telecommunications Devices for the Deaf (TDDs), call © **407/827-5141.**

3 The Magic Kingdom

Attendance in 2002 was down 5%, to 14 million, but this is still America's most popular theme park, and it's second in the world to Tokyo Disneyland, according to *Amusement Business,* a trade magazine that estimates annual attendance. The Magic Kingdom offers 40 attractions, plus shops and restaurants, in a 107-acre package. Its centerpiece and symbol, Cinderella Castle, forms the hub of a wheel whose spokes reach to **seven themed lands.**

ARRIVING   From the parking lot, you have to walk to a tram that will take you to the ticket windows, then wait for a ferry or monorail to take you to the entrance, where you meet post-September 11, 2001, security. Most of the year it **takes at least 35 to 45 minutes** and usually longer to get from your auto to the fun (unless you arrive late), and that doesn't count time spent in lines if you have to stop at Guest Relations or rent a stroller. You'll face the same agony minus security on the way out, so relax. While rides are short, the wait isn't during peak times. This is the worst park for crowds, so plan to arrive an hour before the opening bell or an hour or two later. Parking-lot sectors are named for Disney characters (Goofy, Pluto, Minnie, and so on) and aisles are numbered. *Be sure to write down where you left your sedan.*

Upon entering the park, get a Magic Kingdom guide map (if you can't find one at the turnstiles, go to the nearest shop). It details restaurants and attractions. Also consult its entertainment schedule to see what's cooking during your visit. There are parades, musical performances, fireworks, character appearances, and more, but the days they're available sometimes are staggered.

If you have questions, all park employees are very knowledgeable, and City Hall, on your left as you enter, is an information center—and, like Mickey's Toontown Fair, a great place to meet costumed characters. Character greeting places are also featured on the map.

HOURS   The park is open from at least 9am to 6 or 7pm, sometimes later—as late as midnight during major holidays and summer.

TICKET PRICES   Ticket prices for adults are $52, $42 for children 3 to 9. Kids under 3 get in free. See "Tickets," on p. 167, for information on multiday passes.

SERVICES & FACILITIES IN THE MAGIC KINGDOM

Most of the following are noted on the handout guide maps in the park:

ATMs   Machines inside the park honor cards from banks using the Cirrus, Honor, and PLUS systems. They're near the main entrance, in Adventureland, and in Tomorrowland.

Baby Care   Located next to the Crystal Palace at the end of Main Street, the Baby Care Center is furnished with rocking chairs and toddler-size toilets. Disposable diapers, formula, baby food, and pacifiers are sold at a premium (read–bring your own or pay the price). There are changing tables here as well as in all women's restrooms and some men's.

Cameras & Film   Film and Kodak disposable cameras are available throughout the park.

First Aid   It's located beside the Crystal Palace next to Baby Care and staffed by registered nurses.

Lockers   Lockers are located in the arcade below the Main Street Railroad Station. The cost is $7, including a $2 refundable deposit.

Lost Children   Lost children in the Magic Kingdom are usually taken to City Hall or the Baby Care Center. *Children under 7 should wear nametags.*

Package Pickup   Any large package can be sent by a shop clerk to Guest Relations in the Entrance Plaza. Allow 3 hours for delivery.

 Frommer's Rates the Rides

Because there's so much to do, we're shifting from the star-rating system used for rooms and restaurants to one that has a little more range. You'll notice most of the grades below are As, Bs, and Cs. That's because Disney designers have done a reasonably good job on the attractions front. But occasionally our ratings show Ds for Duds.

Here's what **Frommer's Ratings** mean:

A+	=	Your trip wouldn't be complete without it.
A	=	Put it at the top of your "to-do" list.
B+	=	Make a real effort to see or do it.
B	=	It's fun but not a "must see."
C+	=	A nice diversion; see it if you have time.
C	=	Go if there's no wait and you can walk right in.
D	=	Don't waste your time.

The Magic Kingdom

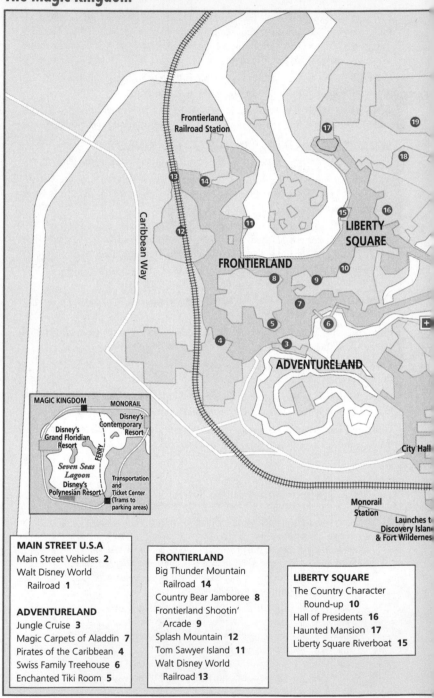

Frontierland
Railroad Station

Caribbean Way

FRONTIERLAND

LIBERTY
SQUARE

ADVENTURELAND

City Hall

MAGIC KINGDOM   MONORAIL

Disney's
Contemporary
Resort

Disney's
Grand Floridian
Resort

FERRY

*Seven Seas
Lagoon*

Disney's
Polynesian Resort

Transportation
and
Ticket Center
(Trams to
parking areas)

Monorail
Station

Launches t
Discovery Islan
& Fort Wilderness

MAIN STREET U.S.A

Main Street Vehicles **2**

Walt Disney World
   Railroad **1**

ADVENTURELAND

Jungle Cruise **3**

Magic Carpets of Aladdin **7**

Pirates of the Caribbean **4**

Swiss Family Treehouse **6**

Enchanted Tiki Room **5**

FRONTIERLAND

Big Thunder Mountain
   Railroad **14**

Country Bear Jamboree **8**

Frontierland Shootin'
   Arcade **9**

Splash Mountain **12**

Tom Sawyer Island **11**

Walt Disney World
   Railroad **13**

LIBERTY SQUARE

The Country Character
   Round-up **10**

Hall of Presidents **16**

Haunted Mansion **17**

Liberty Square Riverboat **15**

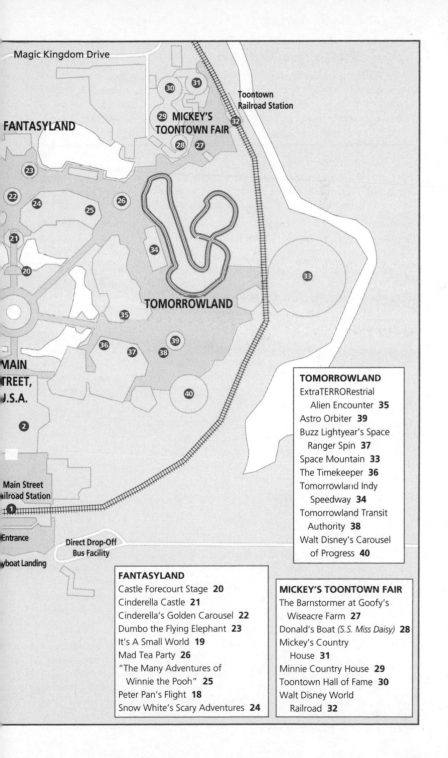

Magic Kingdom Drive

FANTASYLAND

Toontown
Railroad Station

MICKEY'S
TOONTOWN FAIR

TOMORROWLAND

MAIN
STREET,
U.S.A.

Main Street
Railroad Station

Entrance

Boat Landing

Direct Drop-Off
Bus Facility

TOMORROWLAND
ExtraTERRORestrial
    Alien Encounter **35**
Astro Orbiter **39**
Buzz Lightyear's Space
    Ranger Spin **37**
Space Mountain **33**
The Timekeeper **36**
Tomorrowland Indy
    Speedway **34**
Tomorrowland Transit
    Authority **38**
Walt Disney's Carousel
    of Progress **40**

FANTASYLAND
Castle Forecourt Stage **20**
Cinderella Castle **21**
Cinderella's Golden Carousel **22**
Dumbo the Flying Elephant **23**
It's A Small World **19**
Mad Tea Party **26**
"The Many Adventures of
    Winnie the Pooh" **25**
Peter Pan's Flight **18**
Snow White's Scary Adventures **24**

MICKEY'S TOONTOWN FAIR
The Barnstormer at Goofy's
    Wiseacre Farm **27**
Donald's Boat *(S.S. Miss Daisy)* **28**
Mickey's Country
    House **31**
Minnie Country House **29**
Toontown Hall of Fame **30**
Walt Disney World
    Railroad **32**

Tips Mickey's Favorite Barber

The Harmony Barber Shop on Main Street is a real scissor shop where you can get your hair cut from 9am to 5pm daily. Adult haircuts are $15; kids' are $12. If it's your child's first haircut, Disney barbers will cut his or her hair free and throw in a certificate and set of mouse ears. The shop is on Main Street near the firehouse.

Pet Care   Day boarding is available at the Transportation and Ticket Center for $6 (© **407/824-6568**). The center also boards animals overnight ($9 for hotel guests, $11 for others). Proof of vaccination is required.

Strollers   They can be rented at the Stroller Shop near the entrance to the Magic Kingdom. The cost is $8 for a single and $15 for a double, including a $1 deposit.

Wheelchair Rental   For wheelchairs, go to the gift shop to the left of the ticket booths at the Transportation and Ticket Center, or to the Stroller and Wheelchair Shop inside the main entrance to your right. The cost is $7, with a $1 deposit; $30 plus a $10 deposit for electric ones.

MAIN STREET, U.S.A

Designed to model a turn-of-the-20th-century American street (though it ends in a 13th-century European castle), this is the gateway to the Kingdom. Don't dawdle on Main Street when you enter; leave it for the end of the day when you're heading back to your hotel.

Main Street Vehicles

Frommer's Rating: C
Recommended Ages: Mainly nostalgic adults
Ride a horse-drawn trolley, jitney, vintage fire engine, or horseless carriage *only* if you don't mind waiting around. Otherwise, there are far, far better things to see and do throughout the realm.

Walt Disney World Railroad

Frommer's Rating: B
Recommended Ages: All ages
You can board an authentic 1928 steam-powered train for a 15-minute trip clockwise around the perimeter of the park. This is a good way to save wear and tear on your feet *if* you're headed from one of its three stations—the park entrance, Frontierland, and Mickey's Toontown Fair—to another.

And while you're cruising Main Street, be on the lookout for **The Dapper Dans,** a lively barbershop quartet that performs up and down the boulevard.

SHOPPING ON MAIN STREET

Through the years, the Magic Mickey has earned a cult following, and his souvenirs have gone uptown. The **Emporium,** in Town Square, has the park's largest selection of Disneyana, everything from Mickey golf balls to Dumbo cookie jars.

Disney Clothiers sells a reasonably large line of Mickey and other character clothing. And, at the end of Main Street, the **Main Street Gallery** inside Cinderella Castle has family crests, tapestries, suits of armor, and other medieval wares, as well as miniature carousels.

ADVENTURELAND

Cross a bridge and stroll through an exotic jungle of lush foliage, thatched roofs, and totems. Amid dense vines and stands of palm and bamboo, drums are beating and swashbuckling adventures await.

Jungle Cruise

Frommer's Rating: C (B for the foot-weary)
Recommended Ages: 4–adult

This is a yawner for many older kids and teens, but it's a nice break from the madness if the line isn't long or you use FASTPASS. In the course of 10 minutes, your boat sails through an African veldt in the Congo, an Amazon rainforest, and along the Nile in Egypt. There are dozens of Animatronic birds, elephants, zebras, lions, giraffes, crocodiles, and tigers in the scenery, which includes tropical and subtropical foliage (most of it real). You'll pass a Cambodian temple guarded by snakes, a rhino chasing terrified African beaters, and a jungle camp taken over by apes. Most boat captains keep up an amusing banter. While you're waiting to board, read the prop menu. It includes fricassee of giant stag beetle and barbecued three-toed skink.

Magic Carpets of Aladdin

Frommer's Rating: B+ for tykes and parents
Recommended Ages: 2–7

The first major ride added to Adventureland since 1971 delights wee ones and some older kids. Its 16 four-passenger carpets circle a giant genie's bottle while camels spit water at riders (in much the same way riders are spritzed at One Fish, Two Fish at Universal Orlando's Islands of Adventure, see p. 256). The fiberglass carpets spin and move up, down, forward, and back.

Pirates of the Caribbean

Frommer's Rating: B
Recommended Ages: 6–adult

Although the Disneyland version of this ride has been sanitized in the name of political correctness, the pirates in Florida still chase "wenches." You'll proceed through a long grotto to board a boat in a dark cave, which may frighten young kids. Therein, hundreds of audio-Animatronic figures (including lifelike dogs, cats, chickens, pigs, and donkeys) populate a faux Caribbean town. To a background of yo-ho-ho music, passengers pass into the line of fire as some fierce-looking pirates swig rum while they loot and plunder. This sentimental favorite is a good spot to cool off during the heat of the day. Alas, if you've been before, you've seen it all, as it hasn't changed in more than a decade.

⌜Fun Fact Separate Skivvies

Your mother may have always warned you about the importance of having clean underwear, but Mickey Mouse's may have skipped that particular piece of advice. Magic Kingdom cast members who play the roles of Mickey Mouse, Cinderella, and others are issued athletic supporters, tights, and other undergarments so their own "bunched-up" underwear can't be seen through their costumes. The issued clothing used to be turned in at the end of a shift, but employees complained that the Magic Kingdom laundry didn't always do a good job. As a result, the union, as part of the 2001 employee contract negotiations, asked for a provision that allowed workers to take their WDW-issued undergarments home to clean them themselves.

> ### Tips A (Baker's) Dozen Suggestions for Fewer Headaches
>
> 1. **Go Where the Crowds Aren't:** If you have time and aren't a slave to the compressed itinerary of a 1-day visit, go to the left when the masses go to the right. Try to get to one major attraction early, but save the others for later in the day or go the FASTPASS route. Eat a little earlier or later than others. That means 11am or 2pm for lunch and 4 or 7pm for dinner. A few minutes can make a big difference in restaurant lines.
> 2. **Note Your Car's Location:** That purple minivan in the next space may not be there when you get out. Write your lot and row number on something with ink that won't run if it gets wet.
> 3. **Avoid Rush Hour:** I-4 is woefully over capacity, so be ready for bumper-to-bumper traffic from 7 to 9am and 4 to 6pm, and often in between. This happens in both directions, 7 days a week.
> 4. **Don't Overplan:** You aren't going to be able to do everything in every park. As a group, list three or four "must-do" things each day. If your group is large enough, consider splitting up, with each adult taking one or more kids if you come as a family. You can compare notes later, and, if you're on a multiday pass, you can go where the others went the day before.
> 5. **Pace Yourself:** It's common to see people running across the parking lot to the trams, then to and through the turnstiles. Relax—the park isn't going anywhere, and they're just rushing to lines and exhaustion. Once inside, stagger those lines with indoor shows or even breaks on a shady bench.
> 6. **Make Dining Reservations:** If a sit-down dinner is important, make sure to get Priority Seating reservations (© **407/939-3463**) either before your visit or when you enter the park.

Swiss Family Treehouse
Frommer's Rating: C+
Recommended Ages: 4–12

This attraction, based on the 1960 Disney movie version of *Swiss Family Robinson*, was renovated in 1998, but die-hard fans needn't worry—it's still an adult-size house in a sprawling banyan tree. Visitors can walk a rope-suspended bridge and ascend the 50-foot tree for a close-up look into the rooms. The "tree," designed by Disney Imagineers, has 330,000 polyethylene leaves sprouting from a 90-foot span of branches; although it isn't real, it's draped with actual Spanish moss. It's a good place for kids to work off some excess energy. *Note:* People with limited mobility beware—this attraction requires a lot of climbing.

The Enchanted Tiki Room
Frommer's Rating: C+
Recommended Ages: 2–10 and older adults

Once called the Tropical Serenade, this attraction's newer hosts include Iago of *Aladdin* fame. It's still in a large, hexagonal, Polynesian-style building with a

7. **Set a Spending Limit:** Kids should know they have a set amount to spend on take-home trinkets. You should, too. But build in a small contingency "fun" fund.

8. **Take a Break:** If you're staying at a WDW property, spend the mid-afternoon napping or unwinding in the pool. Return to the parks for a few more attractions and the closing shows. (Get your hand stamped when you leave, and you'll be readmitted without charge.)

9. **Dress Comfortably:** This may seem like a no-brainer, but judging by the limping, blistered crowds, some people don't understand they'll be walking—a lot! This isn't the place to break in clogs. Comfortable walking shoes are a must.

10. **Sunscreen, Sunscreen, Sunscreen:** Locals spot tourists by their bright-red glow. The Florida sun can bake you, even in the shade and in the cooler months, and a bad 1st-day burn can ruin your trip. Bring hats for toddlers and infants, even if they'll stay in a stroller. Also, drink plenty of water in summer to avoid dehydration. This is especially important for children. Bringing a pair of sunglasses is a smart move, too.

11. **Travel Light:** Don't carry large amounts of cash. The Pirates of the Caribbean aren't the only thieves in WDW. There are ATMs in the parks if you run short.

12. **Get a Little Goofy:** Relax, put on those mouse ears, eat that extra piece of fudge, and sing along at the shows. Don't worry about what the staff thinks; they've seen it all.

13. **If You Have Kids, Measure Their Heights Before You Arrive:** This guide, park maps, and information boards outside the more adventurous rides list minimum heights. If you know the restrictions early, you can avoid disappointment in the parks. Trust us—WDW plays hardball on this one.

thatched roof, bamboo beams, and tapa-bark murals. It's also still home to 250 tropical birds, chanting totem poles, and singing flowers that whistle, warble, and tweet. It's cute but corny.

SHOPPING IN ADVENTURELAND
Look for hats, Captain Hook T-shirts, ships in bottles, toy muskets, all sorts of toy swords, and loads of other pirate and nonpirate booty at the **House of Treasure** outside Pirates of the Caribbean.

FRONTIERLAND
From Adventureland, step into the wild and woolly past of the American frontier, where Disney employees (they're called "cast members") are clad in denim and calico, sidewalks are wooden, rough-and-tumble architecture runs to log cabins and rustic saloons, and the landscape is Southwestern scrubby with mesquite, cactus, yucca, and prickly pear. Tom Sawyer Island, reachable via log rafts, is across the river.

Tips Ride the Rails

Although it's an oldie, Big Thunder Mountain Railroad is still a magnet to the masses. If you don't want to use FASTPASS, try riding it late in the day (coaster veterans swear the ride is even better after dark) or during one of the scheduled parades that frequently pull visitors away from the attractions.

Big Thunder Mountain Railroad
Frommer's Rating: A
Recommended Ages: 8–adult

This roller coaster earns high marks for what it is—a ride designed for those not quite up to the lunch-losing thrills of Rock 'n' Roller Coaster at Disney–MGM Studios (p. 217) or Dueling Dragons and Incredible Hulk Coaster at Islands of Adventure, listed in chapter 8. Think of Big Thunder as *Roller Coasters 101.* (Survive and graduate to the next level.) It sports fun hairpin turns and dark descents rather than sudden, steep drops and near collisions. Your runaway train covers 2,780 feet of track and careens through the ribs of a dinosaur, under a thundering waterfall, past spewing geysers, and over a bottomless volcanic pool. Animatronic characters (such as a long john–clad fellow in a bathtub) and critters (goats, chickens, donkeys) enhance the scenic backdrop, along with several hundred thousand dollars' worth of authentic antique mining equipment. ***Note:*** You must be at least 40 inches tall to ride, and Disney discourages expectant mothers and people prone to motion sickness or those with heart, neck, or back problems from riding.

Country Bear Jamboree (Finds
Frommer's Rating: A
Recommended Ages: 4–adult

This is a foot-stomping hoot! (Middle and older teens, though, may hate it.) Like many of the shows and rides in the Magic Kingdom, it doesn't have a companion in the other parks because it dates to a time when entertainment was more low-tech but still fun. But if you saw the Country Bear movie released in 2002, you get the picture. This Bears actually opened when the park did (in 1971!), but it has the power to bridge the generations. The 15-minute show stars a troupe of fiddlin', strummin', harmonica-playin' bears (audio-Animatronic, of course) belting out lively tunes and woeful love songs. The chubby Trixie, decked out in a satiny skirt, laments lost love as she sings "Tears Will Be the Chaser for Your Wine." Teddi Barra descends from the ceiling in a swing to perform "Heart, We Did All That We Could." Big Al moans "Blood in the Saddle." In the finale, the cast joins in a rousing sing-along. *Blue-light bonus:* The jamboree is a great summertime place to cool your heels in the A/C.

The Country Character Round-Up
Frommer's Rating: B
Recommended Ages: 6–adult

Here's another summer cooler. The Diamond Horseshoe Saloon Revue that was here for years is scheduled to be replaced about the time this guide hits bookstores. The new attraction will be an interactive character meet and greet with a rotating cast of Disney favorites. It has the tentative name of The Country Character Round-Up, but that could change by the time you visit. You can eat deli or peanut-butter-and-jelly sandwiches at lunchtime.

Frontierland Shootin' Arcade
Frommer's Rating: C
Recommended Ages: 8–adult
Combining state-of-the-art electronics with a traditional shooting-gallery format, this arcade presents an array of targets (slow-moving ore cars, buzzards, and gravediggers) in an 1850s boomtown scenario. Fog creeps across the graveyard, and the setting changes as a calm, starlit night turns stormy with flashes of lightning and claps of thunder. Coyotes howl, bridges creak, and skeletal arms reach out from the grave. If you hit a tombstone, it might spin around and mysteriously change its epitaph. To keep things authentic, newfangled electronic firing mechanisms loaded with infrared bullets are concealed in vintage buffalo rifles. Fifty cents buys you 25 shots.

Splash Mountain
Frommer's Rating: A+
Recommended Ages: 8–adult
If you need a quick cooling off, this is the place to go—because you will get wet! Based on Disney's 1946 film *Song of the South,* Splash Mountain takes you flume-style down a flooded mountain, past 26 colorful scenes that include backwoods swamps, bayous, spooky caves, and waterfalls. Riders are caught in the bumbling schemes of Brer Fox and Brer Bear as they chase the ever-wily Brer Rabbit, who, against the advice of Mr. Bluebird, leaves his briar-patch home in search of fortune and the "laughing place." The music from the film forms a delightful audio backdrop. Your hollow-log vehicle twists, turns, and splashes, sometimes plummeting in darkness as the ride leads to a 52-foot, 45-degree, 40-mph splashdown in a briar-filled pond. And that's not the end. The ride keeps going until it's a Zip-A-Dee-Do-Da kind of day. *Note:* You must be at least 40 inches tall to ride. Also, expectant mothers and people prone to motion sickness or those with heart, neck, or back problems shouldn't climb aboard.

Tom Sawyer Island
Frommer's Rating: C for most, B+ for kids who need an energy burner
Recommended Ages: 4–12
Board Huck Finn's raft for a 2-minute float across a river to the densely forested Tom Sawyer Island, where kids can explore the narrow passages of Injun Joe's cave (complete with such scary sound effects as whistling wind), a walk-through windmill, a serpentine abandoned mine, and Fort Sam Clemens, where an audio-Animatronic drunk is snoring off a bender. Maintaining one's balance while crossing rickety swing and barrel bridges is part of the fun for some, but not for those with mobility impairments. Narrow, winding dirt paths lined with oaks, pines, and sycamores create an authentic backwoods atmosphere. It's easy to get briefly lost and stumble upon some unexpected adventure. You can combine this attraction with lunch at Aunt Polly's Dockside Inn, which serves sandwiches and such, and has outdoor tables on a porch overlooking the river. Adults can rest while the kids explore.

⌒Tips Best Protein Snack in the Parks

For our money, you can't beat the smoked turkey drumsticks sold for about $5 in WDW parks, including at The Lunching Pad in Tomorrowland. How popular are they? Each year, Disney guests gobble-gobble 1.6 million of them.

(*Fun Fact*   **It's a Dirty Job . . .**

The Disney parks are usually fairly clean, but there's one notable spot in the Magic Kingdom that takes pride in its dreary image. In order to maintain the Haunted Mansion's worn appearance, employees spread large amounts of dust over the home's interior and also string up plenty of real-looking cobwebs. It takes a lot of effort to keep the place looking bedraggled, which may explain why your haunted hosts are only a handful of Disney cast members without smiles plastered on their faces.

SHOPPING IN FRONTIERLAND

Mosey into the **Frontier Trading Post** for cowboy boots and hats, western shirts, coonskin caps, turquoise jewelry, belts, and toy rifles.

LIBERTY SQUARE

This transition zone between Frontierland and Fantasyland has an 18th-century-America feel, complete with Federal and Georgian architecture, Colonial Williamsburg–type shops, and flowerbeds bordering manicured lawns. Thirteen lanterns, symbolizing the first colonies, are suspended from the Liberty Tree, an immense live oak. You might encounter a fife-and-drum corps marching along the cobblestone streets. The Liberty Tree Tavern (p. 135) is one of the better Magic Kingdom restaurants.

Hall of Presidents

Frommer's Rating: B+

Recommended Ages: 8–adult

American presidents from George Washington to George W. Bush (who made his debut in the fall of 2001, when the exhibit was reopened following several months of renovations) are represented by lifelike audio-Animatronic figures. If you look closely, you'll see them fidget and whisper during the performance. The show begins with a film projected on a 180-degree, 70mm screen. It talks about the importance of the Constitution, then the curtain rises on America's leaders, and, as each comes into the spotlight, he nods or waves with presidential dignity. Lincoln then rises and speaks, occasionally referring to his notes. In a tribute to Disney thoroughness, painstaking research was done in creating the figures and scenery, with each president's costume reflecting period fashion, fabrics, and tailoring techniques.

Haunted Mansion

Frommer's Rating: B, A+ for faithful followers

Recommended Ages: 6–adult

What better way to show off Disney's special effects than through a decades-old ride in which ghostly attendants harry groups of visitors. They escort you, voluntarily or not, past a graveyard (be sure to look at the epitaphs on the tombstones) and then turn you over to a ghostly host, who encloses you in a windowless portrait gallery (Are those eyes following you?) where the floor seems to descend. Darkness, spooky music, eerie howling, and mysterious screams and rappings enhance its ambience. Your vehicle takes you past bizarre scenes and objects: a ghostly banquet and ball, a graveyard band, a suit of armor that comes alive, cobweb-draped chandeliers, luminous spiders, a talking head in a crystal ball, weird flying objects, and more. At the end of the ride, a ghost joins you in your car. The experience is more amusing than terrifying, so you can take most children 6 and older inside. This ride has changed little over the years and may be stale for some, but it continues to draw long lines and a cult following.

Liberty Square Riverboat *Overrated*
Frommer's Rating: C
Recommended Ages: all ages
A steam-powered sternwheeler called the *Liberty Belle* departs for cruises along the Rivers of America. The passing landscape sort of looks like the Wild West. It makes a restful interlude for foot-weary park-stompers.

SHOPPING IN LIBERTY SQUARE
The **Yankee Trader** is a charming country store where the shelves are stocked with Lion King and Winnie the Pooh cookie jars, Mickey cookie cutters, and fancy food items.

Ye Olde Christmas Shoppe offers ideas to help celebrate long before and after the season.

FANTASYLAND
The attractions in this happy land are themed along Disney classics such as *Snow White, Peter Pan,* and *Dumbo.* They're especially popular with young visitors. If your kids are under 8, you may want to make this and Mickey's Toontown Fair (details later in this section) your first stops in the Magic Kingdom.

Cinderella Castle *Moments*
Frommer's Rating: A (for visuals)
Recommended Ages: All ages
There's not a lot to do here, but its status as the Magic Kingdom's icon makes it a must. It's at the end of Main Street, in the center of the park, a fairyland castle with Gothic spires 185 feet high. Inside, there's a restaurant, Cinderella's Royal Table (p. 135), and shops. Mosaic murals depict the Cinderella story, and Disney family coats of arms are displayed over a fireplace. An actress portraying Cinderella, dressed for the ball, often makes appearances in the lobby. You can see live shows on the Castle Forecourt Stage; check the guide-map schedule for **Cinderella's Surprise Celebration,** a character show starring Cinderella and several other cartoon heroes (from Prince Charming to Donald and Goofy) and villains (including Captain Hook). After the show, several of the characters come down from the stage to greet guests.

Cinderella's Golden Carousel *Moments*
Frommer's Rating: B+, A for carousel fans
Recommended Ages: All ages
This beauty was built by the Philadelphia Toboggan Co. in 1917 and served tours of duty at amusement parks in Michigan and Illinois before Walt Disney bought it and brought it to Orlando 5 years before the Magic Kingdom opened. Disney

---

Fun Fact Behind the Scenes
Ever wonder why you never catch a glimpse of, say, Mickey relaxing with his head off, or Pluto taking a candy bar break? The people inside the characters, and other cast members, take breaks as well as travel around the park through an intricate system of underground tunnels that are off-limits to the public, unless you pay a premium for a behind-the-scenes tour that we'll tell you about in the "Epcot" section.

artisans refurbished it and added 18 hand-painted scenes from Cinderella on a wooden canopy above the horses. Its organ plays Disney classics such as "When You Wish Upon a Star." Children and their parents adore riding it, and older adults like reminiscing about past carousel rides. But here they often have to wait in long lines.

Dumbo the Flying Elephant
Frommer's Rating: B+ for young kids and parents
Recommended Ages: 2–7
This kiddie ride is very much like Magic Carpets of Aladdin (earlier in this chapter) except it features Dumbo cars that go around in a circle, gently rising and dipping. If you can stand the brutal lines, it's a favorite of the preschool set, although older children will probably want to run the other way.

It's a Small World
Frommer's Rating: B+ for youngsters and first-timers
Recommended Ages: 2–8
It rates a B+ (rather than a lower grade) because the very young love it, and adults ought to have to endure it at least once. If you don't know the song, you will by the end of the ride (and probably ever after). It'll crawl into your mind like a brain-eating mite, playing continually as you sail around this world, built for the 1964 New York World's Fair and later bought by Disney. In each country, appropriately costumed audio-Animatronic dolls greet you by singing "It's a Small World" in Munchkin-like voices (if you've ever talked after sucking on a helium balloon, you know the pitch). The cast of thousands includes Chinese acrobats, Russian kazatski dancers, Indian snake charmers, French cancan girls, and, well, you get the picture. Anyway, pay your dues—*ride* the ride.

Mad Tea Party
Frommer's Rating: C+
Recommended Ages: 4–adult
This is a traditional amusement park ride a la Disney, with an Alice in Wonderland theme. Riders sit in big pastel-hued teacups on saucers that careen around a circular platform while tilting and spinning. A woozy mouse pops out of a big teapot in the center of the platform. Believe it or not, this can be a pretty active or nauseating ride, depending on how much you spin your teacup's wheel. Adolescents seem to consider it a badge of honor if they can turn the unsuspecting adults in their cup green—you have been warned!

The Many Adventures of Winnie the Pooh
Frommer's Rating: B
Recommended Ages: 2–8 and their parents
When this replaced Mr. Toad's Wild Ride in 1999, it drew a small storm of protest from Toad lovers, but things have quieted since then. This fun ride features the cute and cuddly little fellow along with Eeyore, Piglet, and Tigger. You board a golden

---

Tips New Show in Town
Legend of the Lion King had been a popular show at the Magic Kingdom for years (though not as popular as Animal Kingdom's Festival of the Lion King, listed later in this chapter). The Magic Kingdom version closed in the fall of 2002 to make way for **Mickey's PhilharMagic Orchestra.** The new show, set to open in fall 2003, stars Mickey, Donald, Ariel, Aladdin, and others in an animated 3-D adventure projected on a 150-foot screen.

honey pot and ride through a storybook version of the Hundred-Acre Wood, keeping an eye out for Heffulumps, Woozles, Blustery Days, and the Floody Place. Kids love it, but be prepared to brave *very* long lines if you don't use FASTPASS.

Peter Pan's Flight

Frommer's Rating: B+ for kids and parents
Recommended Ages: 3–8
Riding in airborne versions of Captain Hook's ship, passengers glide through dark passages while experiencing the story of Peter Pan. The adventure begins in the Darlings' nursery and includes a flight over nighttime London (the major draw for adults) to Never-Never Land. There, you encounter mermaids, Indians, Tick Tock the Croc, the Lost Boys, Princess Tiger Lilly, Tinker Bell, Hook, and Smee, all while listening to the theme, "You Can Fly, You Can Fly, You Can Fly." It's *very* tame fun for the young. The technology is also very past its prime.

Snow White's Scary Adventures

Frommer's Rating: B for young kids and parents
Recommended Ages: 4–8
Disney had to change the original incarnation of this ride to actually include Snow White and eliminate the way-too-scary-for-youngsters encounter with the wicked witch. The attraction once focused only on the more sinister elements of Grimm's fairy tale, most notably the evil queen and the cackling, toothless witch, leaving some small children terrorized. It's been toned down, with Snow White appearing in a number of pleasant scenes, such as at the wishing well and riding away with the prince to live happily ever after. There are new audio-Animatronic dwarfs, and the colors have been brightened and made less menacing. Even so, this ride could be scary for kids under 4.

SHOPPING IN FANTASYLAND

It's always the holiday season at **Sir Mickey's,** supply central for a variety of Disney-motif trinkets.

Little girls adore **Tinker Bell's Treasures,** its wares comprising Peter Pan merchandise, costumes (Tinker Bell, Snow White, Cinderella, Pocahontas, and others), and collector dolls.

Boys and girls alike get the *"Mommy-I-Want-Its"* in **Pooh's Thotful Shop.**

MICKEY'S TOONTOWN FAIR

Head off those cries of "Where's Mickey?" by taking young kids to this 2-acre site. Toontown provides a chance to meet kids' favorite Disney characters, including Mickey, Minnie, Donald, Goofy, and Pluto. The Kingdom's smallest land is set in a whimsical collection of cottages and the candy-striped **Judge's** and **Toontown Hall of Fame tents,** home to several characters.

The Barnstormer at Goofy's Wiseacre Farm *(finds*

Frommer's Rating: A+ for kids and parents, B+ for others, except coaster crazies, who may find it a D
Recommended Ages: 4 and up
This mini–roller coaster is the twin of Woody Woodpecker's Nuthouse Coaster (which it likely inspired) at Universal Studios Florida (p. 248). It's designed to look and feel like a crop duster that flies slightly off course and right through the Goofmeister's barn. The ride has very little in the dip-and-drop department, but a little zip on the spin-and-spiral front. It even gets squeals of joy from some adults. *Note:* The 60-second ride has a 35-inch height minimum and expectant mothers are warned not to ride it.

Tips It Ain't Fair, But . . .

Disney rides sometimes break down or need routine maintenance (called ride rehab) that can take them out of commission for a few hours, a day, a week, or a lot longer. Test Track at Epcot, for example, frequently had mechanical problems that shut it down during its first year, and occasionally it still experiences technical difficulties. The Hall of Presidents, at Magic Kingdom, was shut down for several months in 2001 for maintenance and the addition of the audio-Animatronic likeness of President George W. Bush. Some, but not all, of the ride rehabs get listed on the Disney website (**www.disneyworld.com**; click "Parks & More," then "Parks & More FAQ" and go to "Which Attractions Are Currently Closed?"). By the way, don't expect Disney—or Universal—to discount tickets when such shutdowns occur. You still get hit with the full price.

Mickey's & Minnie's Country Houses
Frommer's Rating: B+ for kids and parents
Recommended Ages: 2–8
These separate cottages offer a lot of visual fun and some marginal interactive areas for youngsters, but they're usually crowded and the lines flow like molasses. Mickey's place features garden and garage playgrounds. Minnie's lets kids play in her kitchen, where popcorn goes wild in a microwave and the utensils strike up a symphony of their own.

Donald's Boat (S.S. Miss Daisy)
Frommer's Rating: B+ for kids
Recommended Ages: 2–12
The good ship offers a lot of interactive fun, and the "waters" around it feature fountains of water snakes and other wet things that earn squeals of joy (and relief on hot days).

SHOPPING IN MICKEY'S TOONTOWN FAIR
The **Toontown Hall of Fame Tent** has continuous meetings with Disney characters as well as a large assortment of Disney souvenirs.

TOMORROWLAND
This land attempts to focus on the future, but in 1994, the WDW folks decided Tomorrowland (originally designed in the 1970s) was beginning to look a lot like "Yesteryear." So it was revamped to show the future as a galactic, science fiction–inspired community inhabited by humans, aliens, and robots. A video-game arcade also was added.

ExtraTERRORestrial Alien Encounter
Frommer's Rating: A+
Recommended Ages: 10–adult
Star Wars director George Lucas earned a tidy paycheck when he added his space-age vision to this attraction. It begins with a mysterious corporation called X-S Tech selling transporter services to Earthlings like you. When it's working properly, the service can beam you between planets light-years apart. But when a sinister corporate robot named S.I.R. tries to demonstrate on Skippy, a cute and fuzzy alien, the subject gets singed a little and disfigured a lot. Despite that dubious beginning, X-S technicians try to transport their corporate head, Chairman

Clench, to Earth. But the machine malfunctions, sending him to a distant planet and sending a fearsome extraterrestrial to your backyard. This sensory show carries a legitimate child warning about being dark, scary, and confining (a shoulder plate locks you in, but you can force it up with a little muscle). It delivers special effects such as the alien's breath on your neck and a mist of alien slime. *Note:* Riders must be at least 44 inches tall.

Astro Orbiter (Overrated

Frommer's Rating: B for the younger set
Recommended Ages: 8 and under
This tame ride is like the ones you might have ridden when you were a child and the carnivals came to town. Its "rockets" are on arms attached to "the center of the galaxy," and they move up and down while orbiting planets, which are on top of a tower. (Think of an elevated version of Magic Carpets of Aladdin, which was reviewed on p. 181.) The line tends to move at the pace of a snail, so unless it's short, skip this one.

Buzz Lightyear's Space Ranger Spin

Frommer's Rating: B+
Recommended Ages: 5 and up
Join Buzz and try to save the universe, flying your cruiser through a world you'll recognize from the original *Toy Story* movie. Kids enjoy using the dashboard-mounted laser cannons as they spin through the sky (filled with gigantic toys instead of stars). If they're good shots (and they'll have to be—the trigger mechanisms are hard to use), they can set off sight and sound gags with their lasers. A display in the car keeps score, so take multiple cars if you have more than one child. This is one of the newer additions to Tomorrowland. It uses the same technology as Universal Studios Florida's Men in Black: Alien Attack (p. 246), but it's aimed at a younger audience, and, therefore, it's lamer and tamer.

Space Mountain

Frommer's Rating: B+
Recommended Ages: 10–adult
This cosmic roller coaster usually has *long* lines (but it has FASTPASS), and most guests find only marginal entertainment value in the pre-ride space-age music and exhibits (meteorites, shooting stars, and space debris whizzing past overhead). Once aboard your rocket, you'll climb and dive through the inky, starlit blackness of outer space. The hairpin turns and plunges make it seem as

---

(*Value* Touring Tip

The Magic Kingdom's **E-Ride Nights** are a bargain for Disney hotel guests persistent enough to track them down. Only offered a few times during the off season and with little advance notice, E-Ride tickets cost $12 for adults and $10 for kids 3 to 9. They give resort guests 3 hours to ride the nine most popular rides—Big Thunder Mountain Railroad, Space Mountain, and ExtraTERRORestrial Alien Encounter, to name a few—as many times as they can. Better still, Disney only lets 5,000 guests into the park on these nights. Tickets are sold on a first-come, first-served basis at the **Guest Services** desks in the Disney hotels and at the **Magic Kingdom** ticket window (you will be required to show a Disney Resort Guest ID and a valid multiday admission pass). Call (*C*) **407/824-4321** for details.

⌒Tips Parental Touring Tip

Many of the attractions at Walt Disney World offer a **Ride-Share program** for parents traveling with small children. One parent can ride an attraction while the other stays with the kids; then the adults can switch places without the second one having to stand in line again. Notify a cast member if you wish to participate when you get in line. Many other Orlando theme parks offer this option, too.

---

if you're going at breakneck speed, but your car doesn't go any faster than 28 mph. The front seat of the train offers the best bang, but Space Mountain is one of the first generation of modern, dark-side coasters, and, therefore, somewhat outdated. If you like dark or semidark thrill rides, you'll be much happier with Rock 'n' Roller Coaster at Disney–MGM Studios. *Note:* Riders must be at least 44 inches tall. Also, expectant moms and people prone to motion sickness or those with heart, neck, or back problems shouldn't climb aboard.

The Timekeeper
Frommer's Rating: C
Recommended Ages: 8–adult
This Jules Verne/H. G. Wells–inspired multimedia show combines CircleVision and IMAX footage with audio-Animatronics. It's hosted by a robot/mad scientist (Robin Williams) and his assistant, 9-EYE, a flying, camera-headed 'droid that moonlights as a time-machine test pilot. In this escapade, the audience hears Mozart as a young prodigy playing for French royalty, visits medieval battlefields in Scotland, watches da Vinci work, and floats in a hot-air balloon over Moscow's Red Square. Voices include Jeremy Irons and Rhea Perlman. *Note:* Don't plan on resting your feet; you have to stand. Also, this ride in the past has been closed in the off season.

Tomorrowland Indy Speedway
Frommer's Rating: B+ for kids, D for most teens and childless adults
Recommended Ages: 4–12
Younger kids love this ride, especially if their adult companion lets them drive (there's a 52-inch height minimum to take a lap without a big person), but teens and other fast starters hate it. The cars are *incredibly* slow (think of pine sap), the steering is atrocious, and the vehicles are on a loose track even though they're actual gas-powered, mini sports cars. Warp speed on this 4-minute spin around the track is 7 mph. The long lines for this ride move even slower than that. *Note:* It carries Disney's warning that expectant mothers and people with heart, neck, or back problems shouldn't climb aboard, likely because of the potential for getting bumped as you try to board or disembark.

Tomorrowland Transit Authority
Frommer's Rating: C, B+ for tired adults
Recommended Ages: All ages
A futuristic means of transportation, these small five-car trains are engineless. They work by electromagnets, belch no pollution, and use little power. Narrated by a computer guide named Horack I, TTA offers an overhead view of Tomorrowland, including an interior look at Space Mountain. Lines are often nonexistent. If you're in the Magic Kingdom for only 1 day, skip this. If you're looking for a little snooze cruise or a chance to rest your feet, it's a must.

Walt Disney's Carousel of Progress *Overrated*
Frommer's Rating: D
Recommended Ages: Only the comatose

Here's another *now-you-see-it, now-you-don't* attraction that's open seasonally. It debuted at the 1964 World's Fair and was "updated" a few years ago, but it still comes up way short. We apologize to the few park veterans who like this ride, but it's a complete waste of 22 minutes unless: (a) you need the break from the insanity rampant through the rest of the park, (b) you have no clue what's happened technologically since the 1930s, or (c) you are a sentimentalist looking for any attraction that Uncle Walt actually designed.

SHOPPING IN TOMORROWLAND
Mickey's Star Traders, a large Disneyana shop, is your best bet.

PARADES, FIREWORKS & MORE
You can pick up a guide map when you enter the park. It includes an **entertainment schedule** that lists all kinds of special goings-on for the day. These include concerts, encounters with characters, holiday events, and the major happenings listed next.

Fantasy in the Sky Fireworks
Frommer's Rating: A+
Recommended Ages: All ages

It feels like the 4th of July when you attend **Fantasy in the Sky Fireworks,** one of the most explosive displays in Orlando. Disney has pyrotechnics down to an art form, and this is clearly the best way to end your day in the Magic Kingdom. Tinker Bell begins things with her flight from Cinderella Castle. The fireworks go off nightly during summer and holidays and on selected nights (usually Mon and Wed–Sat) the rest of the year. See your entertainment schedule for details. Suggested viewing areas are Liberty Square, Frontierland, and Mickey's Toontown Fair. Disney hotels close to the park (Grand Floridian, Polynesian, Contemporary, and Wilderness Lodge) also offer excellent views.

SpectroMagic *Moments*
Frommer's Rating: A
Recommended Ages: All ages

In April 2001, this after-dark display returned for a second engagement at WDW, replacing the **Main Street Electrical Parade,** a Disney classic that ran from 1976 to 1991, and again from 1996 to 2001 at the Magic Kingdom. *SpectroMagic is only held on a limited number of nights.* The 20-minute production combines fiber optics, holographic images, clouds of liquid nitrogen, old-fashioned twinkling lights, and a soundtrack featuring classic Disney tunes. Mickey,

---

Moments Where to Find Characters

Mickey's Toontown Fair was designed as a place where kids can meet and mingle with their favorite characters all day at the Judge's Tent and Toontown Hall of Fame Tent. Mickey and others are stars in residence. In **Fantasyland,** look for Ariel's Grotto and Fantasyland Character Festival for daily greetings. **Main Street** (Town Square) and **Adventureland** (at Pirates of the Caribbean and near Magic Carpets of Aladdin) are other hot spots.

dressed in an amber and purple grand magician's cape, makes an appearance in a confetti of light. You'll also see the SpectroMen atop the title float, and Chernabog, *Fantasia's* monstrous demon, who unfolds his 38-foot wingspan. It takes the electrical equivalent of seven lightning bolts (enough to power a fleet of 2,000 over-the-road trucks) to bring the show to life. See your entertainment schedule for availability.

Share a Dream Come True Parade
Frommer's Rating: B
Recommended Ages: All ages
Replacing Magical Moments, this is the Magic Kingdom's parade honoring the 100th anniversary of Uncle Walt's birth. Giant gloves and loads of Disney characters march up Main Street and into Frontierland daily.

4 Epcot

Epcot is an acronym for *Experimental Prototype Community of Tomorrow,* and it was Walt Disney's dream for a planned city. (For an idea of what he wanted, visit **www.waltopia.com** on the Internet.) Alas, after his death, it became a theme park—central Florida's second major one, which opened in 1982. Its aims are described in a dedication plaque: "May Epcot entertain, inform, and inspire. And, above all . . . instill a new sense of belief and pride in man's ability to shape a world that offers hope to people everywhere."

Ever growing and changing, Epcot occupies 300 vibrantly landscaped acres. If you can spare it, take a little time to stop and smell the roses on your way to and through the two major sections: Future World and World Showcase.

Epcot is so big that hiking the World Showcase end to end (1.3 miles from the Canada pavilion on one side to Mexico on the other) can be an exhausting experience. That's why some folks are certain Epcot stands for "Every Person Comes Out Tired." Depending on how long you intend to linger at each country in World Showcase, this part of the park can be experienced in 1 day. One way to conserve energy is to take the launches across the lagoon from the edge of Future World to Germany or Morocco. But most visitors simply make a leisurely loop, working clockwise or counterclockwise from one side of the Showcase to the other.

Unlike Magic Kingdom, much of Epcot's parking lot is close to the gate. Parking sections are named for themes (Harvest, Energy, and so forth) and the aisles are numbered. While some guests are happy to walk to the gate from nearer areas, trams are available, but these days mainly to and from the outer areas.

Be sure to pick up a guide map and entertainment schedule as you enter the park. Folks with children can grab a copy of the ***Epcot Kids' Guide.*** (The regular guide uses a yellow K in a red square to note "Kidcot" stops.) These play and learning stations are for the younger set. They open at 1pm daily.

If you plan to eat lunch or dinner here and haven't already made reservations (© **407/939-3463**), you can make them at the WorldKey terminals behind Spaceship Earth. Many Epcot restaurants are described in chapter 6, "Where to Dine."

Before you get under way, check the map's schedule and incorporate any shows you want to see into your itinerary.

HOURS Future World is usually open from 9 or 10am to 7pm but sometimes as late as midnight during major holidays and the summer. World Showcase doesn't open until 11am or noon, and it usually closes at 9pm but sometimes later.

Epcot

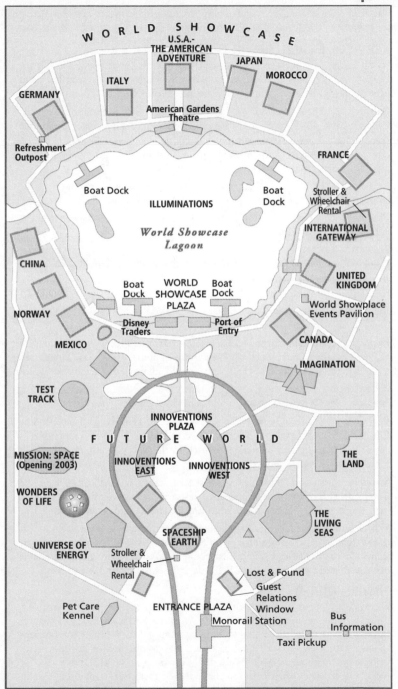

WORLD SHOWCASE

U.S.A.-
THE AMERICAN
ADVENTURE

ITALY

JAPAN

MOROCCO

GERMANY

American Gardens
Theatre

Refreshment
Outpost

FRANCE

Boat Dock

Boat
Dock

ILLUMINATIONS

Stroller &
Wheelchair
Rental

World Showcase
Lagoon

INTERNATIONAL
GATEWAY

CHINA

UNITED
KINGDOM

Boat
Dock

WORLD
SHOWCASE
PLAZA

Boat
Dock

NORWAY

World Showplace
Events Pavilion

Disney
Traders

Port of
Entry

MEXICO

CANADA

IMAGINATION

TEST
TRACK

INNOVENTIONS
PLAZA

FUTURE   WORLD

MISSION: SPACE
(Opening 2003)

INNOVENTIONS
EAST

INNOVENTIONS
WEST

THE
LAND

WONDERS
OF LIFE

THE
LIVING
SEAS

SPACESHIP
EARTH

UNIVERSE OF
ENERGY

Stroller &
Wheelchair
Rental

Lost & Found

Guest
Relations
Window

Pet Care
Kennel

ENTRANCE PLAZA

Monorail Station

Bus
Information

Taxi Pickup

TICKET PRICES Ticket prices are $52 for adults, $42 for children 3 to 9, free for children under 3. See "Tickets," earlier in this chapter, for 4- and 5-day passes.

SERVICES & FACILITIES IN EPCOT

ATMs The machines here accept cards issued by banks using the Cirrus, Honor, and PLUS systems and are located at the front of the park, in Italy, and near the bridge between World Showcase and Future World.

Baby Care Epcot's Baby Care Center is by the First Aid station near the Odyssey Center in Future World. It's furnished with rocking chairs; disposable diapers, formula, baby food, and pacifiers are for sale. There are also changing tables in all women's restrooms, as well as in some of the men's restrooms. Disposable diapers are also available at Guest Relations.

Cameras & Film Kodak disposable cameras are available throughout the park, including at the Kodak Camera Center at the Entrance Plaza.

First Aid The First Aid Center, staffed by registered nurses, is located near the Odyssey Center in Future World.

Lockers Lockers are to the west of Spaceship Earth, outside the Entrance Plaza, and in the Bus Information Center by the bus parking lot. The cost is $7 a day, including a $2 deposit.

Lost Children Lost children in Epcot are usually taken to Earth Center or the Baby Care Center, where lost children logbooks are kept. *Children under 7 should wear nametags.*

Package Pickup Any large package you purchase can be sent by the shop clerk to Guest Relations in the Entrance Plaza. Allow 3 hours for delivery. There's also a package pickup location at the International Gateway entrance in the World Showcase.

Parking It's $7 for cars, pickups, and vans; $8 for RVs.

Pet Care Day accommodations are offered at kennels just outside the Entrance Plaza at Epcot for $6 (② **407/824-6568**). Proof of vaccination is required. There are also four other kennels in the WDW complex. (See "Fast Facts" in chapter 4 for more details.)

Strollers These can be rented from special stands on the east side of the Entrance Plaza and at World Showcase's International Gateway. The cost is $8 for a single and $15 for a double, including a $1 refundable deposit.

Wheelchair Rental Rent wheelchairs inside the Entrance Plaza to your left, to the right of ticket booths at the Gift Shop, and at World Showcase's International Gateway. The cost for regular chairs is $7, including a $1 refundable deposit. Electric wheelchairs cost $30 a day, plus a $10 refundable deposit.

FUTURE WORLD

Future World is in the northern section of Epcot, the first area mainstream guests see after entering the park. Its icon is a huge geosphere known as Spaceship Earth—aka, that thing that looks like a giant golf ball. Major corporations sponsor Future World's 10 themed areas (that means they're making pricey investments, such as the $60 million that GM dropped on the Test Track ride you'll read about a little later in this chapter). The focus here is on discovery, scientific achievements, and tomorrow's technologies in areas running from energy to undersea exploration.

Top 10 Orlando-Area Activities for Grown-Ups

1. **Spa Treatments**   First-rate spas such as those at Disney's Grand Floridian Resort & Spa, the Wyndham Palace Resort, Portofino Bay Hotel, and Gaylord Palms hotel provide heavenly pampering and relief for the sore muscles and tired feet caused by the parks (see chapters 1 and 5).
2. **World Showcase Pavilions**   Experience a 'round-the-world journey, visiting 11 "nations" with authentically reproduced architectural highlights, restaurants, shops, and cultural performances (later in this chapter).
3. **Cirque du Soleil**   This no-animals circus (p. 301) is compelling for most anyone over the age of 6, but its intensity and choreography make it a real winner for adults.
4. **Pleasure Island and CityWalk**   These entertainment and restaurant districts are located at WDW and Universal Orlando, respectively (see chapter 10). They provide nonstop fun for the wine-dine-and-dance set.
5. **A Romantic Dinner at Victoria & Albert's**   Loving couples cherish the intimate evening and scrumptious seven-course dinner at the headline restaurant in Disney's Grand Floridian Resort & Spa (p. 140).
6. **Discovery Cove**   Few who can afford the $229 sticker shock come away disappointed with their swim with the dolphins at this theme park, which is a sister of SeaWorld (see chapter 8).
7. **Richard Petty Driving Experience**   *Vrrrooooommmmmm!* If you're 18 or older and have the courage, try driving or at least riding in a real NASCAR rocket at speeds significantly above the legal limit (p. 234).
8. **The *Grand 1***   Take another break from the Mickey madness and cruise Disney's Seven Seas Lagoon (perhaps catching a glimpse of Fantasy in the Sky Fireworks) aboard this vintage, 44-foot yacht (p. 92).
9. **Innoventions**   Epcot is generally geared more to adults than the other WDW parks, and this display of future technologies is especially intriguing, providing a preview of life well into the 21st century (see below).
10. **Tee Time**   Orlando is home to some of the country's best golf courses—Walt Disney World alone offers 99 holes, including one with a sandtrap shaped like Mickey Mouse—so enthusiasts will find plenty of places to tee up (see "Hitting the Links" in chapter 8).

Here are the main attractions.

Innoventions East and West
Frommer's Rating: A for hungry minds
Recommended Ages: 8–adult
Innoventions East, behind Spaceship Earth and to the left as you enter the park, features the **House of Innoventions.** It's a preview of tomorrow's smart house, but

Behind the Scenes: Special Tours in Walt Disney World

In addition to the greenhouse tour in Epcot's The Land pavilion (p. 200), the Disney parks offer a number of walking tours and learning programs. The tours are subject to change. These tours represent the most recent ones available at press time. Times, days, and prices also change. It's best to call ahead to Disney's tour line, ✆ **407/939-8687,** to make reservations or get additional information.

- Epcot's new **Aqua Seas Tour** lends you a wetsuit, and then takes you on a 2½-hour journey that includes a 30-minute swim in the 5.7-million gallon Living Seas Aquarium, home to some 65 marine species. The tour includes a souvenir T-shirt and group photo. The cost is $100, plus park admission, and it's open to guests 8 and older (those under 18 must be accompanied by an adult). It's offered daily at 12:30pm.
- The **Family Magic Tour** explores the nooks and crannies of the Magic Kingdom in the form of a 2-hour scavenger hunt. You meet and greet characters at the end. Children and adults, $25. You must also buy admission tickets to the park and book in advance. It begins daily at 11:30am outside City Hall. It's sometimes held at 9:30am, too.
- The **Magic Behind Our Steam Trains** tour (ages 10 and up) is a fun one for locomotive buffs. A pair of inveterate conductors give you insight other guests don't get into the history and present operations of the little engines that could. Monday, Thursday, and Saturday at 7:30am, $30 per person, plus park admission.

The following tours are for those 16 and older:

- The 3-hour **Hidden Treasures of World Showcase** explores the architectural and entertainment offerings of Epcot's 11 "nations." The $59 tours (plus admission) are at 9:45am on Tuesday and Thursday.
- **Gardens of the World,** a 3-hour tour of the extraordinary landscaping at Epcot, is held Tuesday and Thursday at 9:45am and is led by a Disney horticulturist ($59 per person, again, plus admission).

many of its products are already on the market (at astronomical prices). Its refrigerator has an Internet-savvy computer that can make your grocery list and place the order. A smart picture frame can store and send photos to other smart frames. And its toilet has a seat warmer, automatic lid opener and closer, and a sprayer and blow dryer that eliminate the need for toilet paper if you're worldly. **Future Cars** shows off autos run by fuel cells, an all-electric vehicle, and other GM visions of the future, while **Internet Zone** profiles tomorrow's online games for kids, including laser tag with Disney characters. Across the plaza at **Innoventions West,** crowds flock to **Video Games of Tomorrow,** which has nearly three dozen game stations, and **Medicine's New Vision** showcases things like radiology's 3-D body images.

Note: A new Underwriters Laboratories exhibit at Innoventions East, the **Test the Limits Lab,** has six kiosks that let kids and fun-loving adults try out a variety of products. In one, you can pull a rope attached to a hammer that crashes into a TV screen to see if it's shatter resistant. In another, you can push a button that releases a magnet that falls onto a firefighter's helmet.

- The 4½-hour **Keys to the Kingdom** tour provides an orientation to the Magic Kingdom and a glimpse into the high-tech systems behind the magic. It's $58 (lunch is included, but mandatory park admission isn't) and is held daily at 8:30, 9:30, and 10am.
- At the top of the price chain ($199 per person) is **Backstage Magic,** a 7-hour, self-propelled bus tour through areas of Epcot, the Magic Kingdom, and Disney–MGM Studios that aren't seen by mainstream guests. The 10am weekday tour is limited to 20 adults, and you might have trouble getting a date unless you book early. Some will find this one isn't worth the price, but if you have a brain that must know how things work or simply want to know more than your family or friends, you might find it's worth the cost. You'll see WDW mechanics and engineers repairing and building Animatronic beings from "It's a Small World" and other attractions. You'll peek over the shoulders of cast members who watch close-circuit TVs to make sure other visitors are surviving the harrowing rides. And at the Magic Kingdom, you'll venture into the tunnels used for work areas as well as corridors for the cast to get from one area to the others without fighting tourist crowds. It's not unusual for tour takers to see Snow White enjoying a Snickers bar, find Cinderella having her locks touched up at an underground salon, or view woodworkers as they restore the hard maple muscles of the carousel horses. Park admission *isn't* required.
- **Backstage Safari** at Animal Kingdom ($65 per person plus park admission) offers a 3-hour look at the park's veterinary hospital as well as lessons in conservation, animal nutrition, and medicine (Mon, Wed, and Fri). *Note:* You won't see animals.
- **Yuletide Fantasy,** available November 30 to December 24 each year, gives visitors a front-row look at how Disney creates a winter wonderland to get visitors in the holiday spirit. It costs $59 per person, and theme park admission *isn't* required.

Imagination
Frommer's Rating: B+
Recommended Ages: 6–adult

In this pavilion, even the fountains are magical. "Water snakes" arc in the air, offering kids a chance to dare them to "bite." This pavilion was upgraded in 2001 to include more high-tech gadgets, and a year later Figment, the pavilion's much-loved mascot, returned (see below).

The 3-D **Honey, I Shrunk the Audience** ride is the big attraction here, deserving an **"A" rating** by itself. Based on the Disney hit *Honey, I Shrunk the Kids* film, you're terrorized by mice and, once you're shrunk, by a large cat; then you're given a good shaking by a gigantic 5-year-old. Vibrating seats and creepy tactile effects enhance dramatic 3-D action. Finally, everyone returns to proper size—except the family dog, which creates the final surprise.

Figment, the crazy-but-lovable dragon, was resurrected in a new **Journey into Your Imagination** ride in June 2002. Things begin with an open house at the

Tips Blast Off!

In mid August 2003, Epcot, with an assist from Compaq and NASA, opened a new out-of-this-world, $150 million attraction called **Mission: Space.** Located in the former Horizons pavilion, its headliner is a motion simulator like those used by astronauts training for space. (Think g-force and weightlessness.) As the launch begins, the rocket rumbles under you, white clouds of steam billow around you and you shoot into the galaxy. Of course, there are some unexpected twists and turns that require you to react pronto in order to complete the mission successfully. In the pre-ride show, you go to the futuristic **International Space Training Center,** then proceed to the **Ready Room** where you learn your role as commander, pilot, navigator or engineer. The post-ride area offers interactive experiences such as **Space Race,** where as many as 60 people compete on teams to get their rockets back from Mars; **Space Base,** a fun crawl space for kids; and **Expedition: Mars,** where you can use a joy stick and button to explore the surface of Mars. Check for updates at **www.disney.go.com/vacations/ missionspace/index.html** or at the official WDW website, **www.disney world.com.**

Imagination Institute, with Dr. Nigel Channing taking you on a tour of labs that demonstrate how the five senses capture and control one's imagination, except you never get to touch and taste once Figment arrives to prove it's far, far better to set your imagination free. He invites you to his upside-down house, where a new perspective enhances your imagination. "One Little Spark," an upbeat ditty that debuted when the attraction opened in 1983, has also been brought back.

The Land
Frommer's Rating: B+ for environmentalists, gardeners; B for others
Recommended Ages: 8–adult
The largest of Future World's pavilions highlights food and nature.

Living with the Land is a 13-minute boat ride through three ecological environments (a rainforest, an African desert, and the windswept American plains), each populated by appropriate audio-Animatronic denizens. New farming methods and experiments ranging from hydroponics to plants growing in simulated Martian soil are showcased in real gardens. If you'd like a more serious overview, take the 45-minute **Behind the Seeds** guided walking tour of the growing areas, offered daily. Sign up at the Green Thumb Emporium shop near the entrance to Food Rocks. The cost is $7 for adults, $5 for children 3 to 9. *Note:* It's really geared to children.

Circle of Life combines spectacular live-action footage with animation in a 15-minute motion picture based on *The Lion King.* In this cautionary environmental tale, Timon and Pumbaa are building a monument to the good life called Hakuna Matata Lakeside Village, but their project, as Simba points out, is damaging the savanna for other animals. The message: Everything is connected in the great circle of life.

In **Food Rocks,** audio-Animatronic mock rock performers deliver an entertaining message about nutrition. Neil Moussaka sings "Don't Take My Squash Away from Me," the Refrigerator Police perform "Every Bite You Take," and the Peach Boys harmonize a rendition of "Good Vibrations" ("Good, good, good,

good nutrition . . . "), while Excess, a trio of disheveled, obnoxious hard rockers, counters by extolling the virtues of junk food. Chubby Checker, Neil Sedaka, Little Richard, and the Pointer Sisters perform the actual voice-over parodies of their music. The recommended age group for this one is 6 to 14, but all ages will have a good time.

The Living Seas
Frommer's Rating: B
Recommended Ages: 8–adult
This pavilion contains a 5.7-million-gallon saltwater aquarium including coral reefs inhabited by some 4,000 sharks, barracudas, parrot fish, rays, dolphins, and other critters. While waiting in line, visitors pass exhibits tracing the history of undersea exploration, including a diving barrel used by Alexander the Great in 332 B.C. and Sir Edmund Halley's first diving bell (1697).

A 2½-minute multimedia preshow about today's ocean technology is followed by a 7-minute film demonstrating the formation of the earth and seas as a means to support life.

After the films, you enter "hydolators" for a hokey "descent" to the simulated ocean floor. Upon arrival, you can journey through a tunnel for close-up views through acrylic windows of the denizens, including manatees in all-too-tight quarters. *Note:* A program called **Epcot DiveQuest** enables certified adult divers to participate in a 3-hour program that includes a 30-minute dive in the Living Seas aquarium. The program costs $140. Call ✆ **407/939-8687** for more information. Keep in mind, however, that you get more for your money at Discovery Cove (p. 271) if you want to swim with the dolphins.

Spaceship Earth *(Overrated*
Frommer's Rating: C
Recommended Ages: All ages
This massive, silvery geosphere symbolizes Epcot. That makes it a must-do for many, though it's something of a yawner—another slow-track journey back in time to trace the progress of communications. Long lines can be avoided by saving it until late in the day when you might be able to just walk in. The 15-minute show/ride takes visitors to the distant past where an audio-Animatronic Cro-Magnon shaman recounts the story of a hunt while others record it on cave walls. You advance thousands of years to ancient Egypt, where hieroglyphics adorn temple walls and writing is recorded on papyrus scrolls. You'll progress through the Phoenician and Greek alphabets, the Gutenberg printing press, and the Renaissance, trying not to notice that several of these guys look an awful lot like Barbie's dream date, Ken. Technologies develop at a rapid pace, through the telegraph, telephone, radio, movies, and TV. It's but a short step to the age of electronic communications. You're catapulted into outer space to see Spaceship Earth from a new perspective, returning for a finale that places the audience amid interactive global networks. *Note:* Sharp-eyed or just plain bored riders may notice at least two green "exit" lights peeking through the heavens, one near the very end of the ride.

Tips **Stay Tuned**
Local media scuttlebutt says Spaceship Earth will be shut down in 2005 so a new moving ride can be built in time for Epcot's 25th anniversary in 2007. At publication time, Disney wasn't commenting.

(Fun Fact It Costs How Much?

Single-day theme park admission at Disney costs an adult $52 plus tax. That's staggering, but so was the then-asking price when Disney opened its Magic Kingdom in 1971. Guests paid $2 general admission plus $4.75 for a 7-ticket book or $5.75 for an 11-ticket one. The tickets were marked in an A to E code with E being the primo rides. If you ran out of tickets (most of us did), you bought more individually.

Test Track
Frommer's Rating: A
Recommended Ages: 8–adult

Test Track is a long-time-coming marvel that combines GM engineering and Disney Imagineering. It might leave some of you believing GM is making too much profit if it blew $60 million to build a ride, but most of you will have a blast. The line can be more than an hour long in peak periods, so consider the FASTPASS option. The last part of the line snakes through displays about corrosion, crash tests, and other things from the GM proving grounds (you can linger long enough to see them even with FASTPASS). The 5-minute ride follows what looks to be an actual highway. It includes braking tests, a hill climb, and tight S-curves in a 6-passenger convertible. The left front seat offers the most thrills as the vehicle moves through the curves. There's also a 12-second burst of speed that reaches 65 mph on the straightaway. *Note:* Riders must be at least 40 inches tall. Also, expectant mothers and people prone to motion sickness or those with heart, neck, or back problems shouldn't test the track.

Note II: This is the only attraction in Epcot that has a single-rider line, which allows singles to fill in vacant spots in select cars. If you're part of a party that doesn't mind splitting up and riding in singles, you can shave off some major waiting time by taking advantage of this option. But FASTPASS offers the same time savings without the break up.

Universe of Energy
Frommer's Rating: B
Recommended Ages: 8–adult

Sponsored by Exxon, this pavilion has a roof full of solar panels and a goal of bettering your understanding of America's energy problems and potential solutions. Its 32-minute ride, **Ellen's Energy Adventure,** features comedian Ellen DeGeneres being tutored (by Bill Nye the Science Guy) to be a *Jeopardy!* contestant. On a massive screen in Theater I, an animated motion picture depicts the Earth's molten beginnings, its cooling process, and the formation of fossil fuels. You move back in time 275 million years into an eerie, storm-wracked landscape of the Mesozoic Era, a time of violent geological activity. Here, giant audio-Animatronic dragonflies, earthquakes, and streams of molten lava threaten you before you enter a steam-filled tunnel deep in the bowels of a volcano. When you emerge, you're in Theater II and the present. In this new setting, which looks like a NASA Mission Control room, a 70mm film projected on a massive 210-foot wraparound screen depicts the challenges of the world's increasing energy demands and the emerging technologies that will help meet them. Your moving seats now return to Theater I, where swirling special effects herald a film about how energy impacts our lives. It ends on an upbeat note, with a vision of an energy-abundant future, and Ellen as a new *Jeopardy!* champion. (Speaking of the end, thanks to hard-plastic seats, your keister may be sore by the end of this journey unless you have plenty of padding.)

Wonders of Life
Frommer's Rating: A
Recommended Ages: 10–adult
Housed in a vast geodesic dome fronted by a 75-foot replica of a DNA strand, this pavilion offers some of Future World's most engaging shows and attractions.

The *Making of Me,* starring Martin Short, is a captivating 15-minute motion picture combining live action with animation and spectacular *in utero* photography to create a sweet introduction to the facts of life. Don't miss it, although the presentation may prompt some questions from young children; therefore, we recommend it for ages 10 and up. Short travels back in time to witness his parents as children, their meeting at a college dance, their wedding, and their decision to have a baby. Along with him, we view his development inside his mother's womb and witness his birth.

During the very popular **Body Wars** ride, you're reduced to the size of a cell for a medical rescue mission inside the immune system of a human body. Your objective: Save a miniaturized immunologist who has been accidentally swept into the bloodstream. This motion-simulator ride takes you on a wild journey through gale-force winds in the lungs and pounding heart chambers. Engineers designed this ride from the last row of a car, so that's where to sit to get the most bang for your buck. Although you know they're part of the Disney show, it's a little eerie passing through dermatopic purification stations in order to undergo miniaturization. It's not as good as the similarly built **Star Tours** at Disney–MGM studios, but it definitely has its moments. This one isn't a smart choice for those prone to motion sickness or who generally prefer to be stirred rather than shaken. *Note:* Riders must be at least 40 inches tall. Also, steer clear if you're an expectant mother, or have heart, neck, or back problems.

In the hilarious, multimedia **Cranium Command,** Buzzy, an audio-Animatronic brain-pilot-in-training, is charged with the seemingly impossible task of controlling the brain of an average 12-year-old boy. The boy's body parts are played by Charles Grodin, Jon Lovitz, Bob Goldthwait, George Wendt, and Kevin Nealon and Dana Carvey (as Hans and Franz). It's another must-see attraction (recommended for ages 8 and up) and has a loyal following among Disney veterans. The audience is seemingly seated inside Bobby's head as Buzzy guides him through a day of typical preadolescent traumas such as running for the school bus, meeting a girl, fighting bullies, and a run-in with the school principal.

There are large areas filled with fitness-related shows, exhibits, and participatory activities, including a film called *Goofy About Health.*

SHOPPING IN FUTURE WORLD
Most of the shopping fun lies ahead in World Showcase, but there are a few places in this part of the park that offer special souvenirs. You can browse through cells and other collectibles at the **Art of Disney** in Innoventions West (how about an $8,800, 5-ft. wooden Mickey watch?), purchase modern merchandise at **MouseGear** in Innoventions East, and find gardening and other gifts in **The Land.**

(Fun Fact **Eat, Drink, and Be Merry**

In mid-October, Epcot's month-long International Food & Wine Festival adds 25 booths to the park's 1.3-mile World Showcase promenade. Here's your chance to walk off some calories while you sip and savor the food and beverages of several of the world's cultures. On the food front, the appetizer-size temptations might include burgundy escargot, seared alligator medallions, green mussels, shrimp on the Barbie, octopus on purple potato salad, chicken sha cha, and much more ($1–$5). You also can sample wine and beer from more than 60 wineries and breweries. Tickets for the dinner-and-concert series or a special wine tasting are $79 to $125 including gratuity, but you also can cruise the festival for standard park admission ($52 adults, $42 kids 3–9), which all must pay. Call © 407/824-4321 for details or on the Internet go to **www.disneyworld.com**.

WORLD SHOWCASE

This community of 11 miniaturized nations surrounds the 40-acre World Showcase Lagoon on the park's southern side. All of the showcase's countries have authentically indigenous architecture, landscaping, background music, restaurants, and shops. The nations' cultural facets are explored in art exhibits, song and dance performances, and innovative rides, films, and attractions. And all of the employees in each pavilion are natives of the country represented.

All pavilions offer some kind of live entertainment throughout the day. Times and performances change, but they're listed in the guide map. World Showcase opens between 11am and noon daily, so there's time for a Future World excursion if you arrive earlier.

Canada

Frommer's Rating: A

Recommended Ages: 8–adult

Our neighbors to the north are represented by architecture ranging from a mansard-roofed replica of Ottawa's 19th-century French–style Château Laurier (here called Hôtel du Canada) to a British-influenced stone building modeled after a famous landmark near Niagara Falls.

An Indian village complete with a rough-hewn log trading post and 30-foot replicas of Ojibwa totem poles signifies the culture of the Northwest. The Canadian wilderness is reflected by a rocky mountain, a waterfall cascading into a whitewater stream, and a mini forest of evergreens, stately cedars, maples, and birch trees. Don't miss the stunning floral displays of azaleas, roses, zinnias, chrysanthemums, petunias, and patches of wildflowers inspired by the Butchart Gardens in Victoria, British Columbia.

The pavilion's highlight attraction is **O Canada!**—a dazzling 18-minute, 360-degree CircleVision film that shows Canada's scenic splendor, from a dogsled race to the thundering flight of thousands of snow geese departing an autumn stopover near the St. Lawrence River. If you're looking for foot-tapping live entertainment, **Off Kilter** raises the roof with New Age Celtic music as well as some get-down country music. Days and times vary.

Northwest Mercantile carries sandstone and soapstone carvings, fringed leather vests, duck decoys, moccasins, an array of stuffed animals, Native American dolls, Native American spirit stones, rabbit-skin caps, heavy knitted sweaters, and, of course, maple syrup.

China
Frommer's Rating: A
Recommended Ages: 10–adult

Bounded by a serpentine wall that snakes around its perimeter, the China pavilion is entered via a triple-arched ceremonial gate inspired by the Temple of Heaven in Beijing, a summer retreat for Chinese emperors. Passing through the gate, you'll see a half-size replica of this ornately embellished red-and-gold circular temple, built in 1420 during the Ming dynasty. Gardens simulate those in Suzhou, with miniature waterfalls, fragrant lotus ponds, and groves of bamboo, corkscrew willows, and weeping mulberry trees.

Reflections of China 🎞🎞 is a new 20-minute movie that explores the culture and landscapes in and around seven Chinese cities. Shot over a 2-month period in 2002, it visits Beijing, Shanghai, and the Great Wall (begun 24 centuries ago!), among other places. **Land of Many Faces** is an exhibit that introduces China's ethnic peoples, and entertainment is provided daily by the amazing **Dragon Legend Acrobats.**

The **Yong Feng Shangdian Shopping Gallery** features silk robes, lacquer and inlaid mother-of-pearl furniture, jade figures, cloisonné vases, Yixing teapots, brocade pajamas, silk rugs and embroideries, wind chimes, and Chinese clothing. Artisans occasionally demonstrate calligraphy.

France
Frommer's Rating: B
Recommended Ages: 8–adult

This pavilion focuses on La Belle Epoque, a period from 1870 to 1910 in which French art, literature, and architecture flourished. It's entered via a replica of the beautiful cast-iron Pont des Arts footbridge over the Seine. It leads to a park with bleached sycamores, Bradford pear trees, flowering crape myrtle, and sculptured parterre flower gardens inspired by Seurat's painting *A Sunday Afternoon on the Island of La Grande Jatte.* A one-tenth-scale replica of the Eiffel Tower constructed from Gustave Eiffel's original blueprints looms above *les grands boulevards.*

The highlight is **Impressions de France.** Shown in a palatial sit-down theater à la Fontainebleau, this 18-minute film is a scenic journey through diverse French landscapes projected on a vast 200-degree wraparound screen and enhanced by the music of French composers. The seemingly lifeless forms of **Imaginum, A Statue Act,** delight visitors daily, as do the yummy pastries at *Boulangerie Patisserie.*

The covered arcade has shops selling French prints and original art, cookbooks, wines (there's a tasting counter), French food, Babar books, perfumes, and original letters of famous Frenchmen ranging from Jean Cocteau to Napoléon. Another marketplace/tourism center revives the defunct Les Halles, where Parisians used to sip onion soup in the wee hours.

Germany
Frommer's Rating: C+
Recommended Ages: 8–adult

Enclosed by castle walls and towers, this festive pavilion is centered on a cobblestone *platz* (square) with pots of colorful flowers girding a fountain statue of St. George and the Dragon. An adjacent clock tower is embellished with whimsical glockenspiel figures that herald each hour with quaint melodies. The pavilion's **Biergarten** (p. 132) was inspired by medieval Rothenberg and features a year-round Oktoberfest and its music. And 16th-century facades replicate a merchant's hall in the Black Forest and the town hall in Römerberg Square.

The shops here carry Hummel figurines, crystal, glassware, cookware, Anton Schneider cuckoos, cowbells, Alpine hats, German wines (there's a tasting counter) and specialty foods, toys (German Disneyana, teddy bears, dolls, and puppets), and books. An artisan demonstrates molding and painting Hummel figures; another paints detailed scenes on eggs. Background music runs from oompah bands to Mozart symphonies.

Model train enthusiasts and kids enjoy the exquisitely detailed miniature version of a small Bavarian town, complete with working train station.

Italy
Frommer's Rating: C+
Recommended Ages: 10–adult
One of the prettiest World Showcase pavilions, Italy lures visitors over an arched stone footbridge to a replica of Venice's intricately ornamented pink-and-white Doge's Palace. Other architectural highlights include the 83-foot Campanile (bell tower) of St. Mark's Square, Venetian bridges, and a piazza enclosing a version of Bernini's Neptune Fountain. A garden wall suggests a backdrop of provincial countryside, and citrus, cypress, pine, and olive trees frame a formal garden. Gondolas are moored on the lagoon.

Shops carry cameo and filigree jewelry, Armani figurines, kitchenware, Italian wines and foods, Murano and other Venetian glass, alabaster figurines, and inlaid wooden music boxes.

Japan
Frommer's Rating: A
Recommended Ages: 8–adult
A flaming red *torii* (gate of honor) on the banks of the lagoon and the graceful blue-roofed Goju No To pagoda, inspired by a shrine built at Nara in A.D. 700, welcome you to this pavilion, which focuses on Japan's ancient culture. In a traditional Japanese garden, cedars, yews, bamboo, "cloud-pruned" evergreens, willows, and flowering shrubs frame a contemplative setting of pebbled footpaths, rustic bridges, waterfalls, exquisite rock landscaping, and a pond of golden koi. It's a haven of tranquility in a park that's anything but. The **Yakitori House** is based on the renowned 16th-century Katsura Imperial Villa in Kyoto, designed as a royal summer residence and considered by many to be the crowning achievement of Japanese architecture. Exhibits ranging from 18th-century Bunraki puppets to samurai armor take place in the moated **White Heron Castle,** a replica of the Shirasagi-Jo, a 17th-century fortress overlooking the city of Himeji. There's also a gallery exhibit on **Japanese baseball.**

The drums of **Matsuriza**—one of the best performances in the World Showcase—entertain guests daily, and the **Mitsukoshi Department Store** (Japan's answer to Macy's) is housed in a replica of the Shishinden (Hall of Ceremonies) of the Gosho Imperial Palace, built in Kyoto in A.D. 794. It sells lacquerware, kimonos, kites, fans, dolls in traditional costumes, origami books, samurai swords, Japanese Disneyana, bonsai trees, Japanese foods, Netsuke carvings, pottery, and modern electronics.

Mexico
Frommer's Rating: B+
Recommended Ages: 8–adult
You'll hear the music of marimbas and mariachi bands as you approach the festive showcase of Mexico, fronted by a towering Mayan pyramid modeled on the

Aztec temple of Quetzalcoatl (God of Life) and surrounded by dense Yucatán jungle landscaping. Upon entering the pavilion, you'll be in a museum of pre-Columbian art and artifacts.

Down a ramp, a small lagoon is the setting for **El Rio del Tiempo** (River of Time), where visitors board boats for an 8-minute cruise through Mexico's past and present. Passengers get a close-up look at the Mayan pyramid. **Mariachi Cobre,** a 12-piece band, plays Tuesday to Saturday.

Shops in and around the **Plaza de Los Amigos** (a "moonlit" Mexican *mercado* with a tiered fountain and street lamps) display an array of leather goods, baskets, sombreros, piñatas, pottery, embroidered dresses and blouses, maracas, jewelry, serapes, colorful papier-mâché birds, and blown-glass objects (an artisan occasionally gives demonstrations). The Mexican Tourist Office also provides travel information.

Finds Great Things to Buy at Epcot

Sure, *you* want to be educated about the cultures of the world, but for most of us the two big attractions at the World Showcase are eating and shopping. Dining options are explained in chapter 6. This list gives you an idea of additional items available for purchase.

If you'd like to check out the amazing scope of Disney merchandise at home, everything from furniture to bath toys, you can order a catalog by calling © **800/237-5751** or surfing the Web to **www.disney store.com.**

- The silver jewelry at the Mexico pavilion is beautiful. Choose from a range of merchandise that goes from a simple flowered hair clip to a kidney-shaped stone and silver bracelet.
- There are lots of great sweaters available in the shops of Norway, and it's really tough to resist the Scandinavian trolls. They're so ugly, you have to love them.
- Forget about all those knock-off products stamped "Made in China." The merchandise in this country is among the more expensive to be found in Epcot, from jade teardrop earrings to multicolored bracelets to Disney art.
- Porcelain and cuckoo clocks are the things to look at in Germany. You might find a Goebel Collectible Winnie the Pooh or a hand-crafted Pooh cuckoo clock. Of course, Hummel figurines are big sellers, too.
- In Italy, look for 100% silk scarves in a variety of patterns as well as fine silk ties and crystal.
- Your funky teenager might like the Taquia knit cap, a colorful fez-like chapeau, that's available in Morocco. There's also a variety of celestial-patterned pottery available in vases and platters.
- Tennis fans may be interested in the Wimbledon shirts, shorts, and skirts available in the United Kingdom. There's also a nice assortment of rose-patterned tea accessories, Shetland sweaters, tartans, pub accessories, and loads of other stuff from the U.K.

Tips **Stay Tuned**

There have been many wannabes, but Disney hasn't added a new "nation" to World Showcase since Norway became the 11th in 1988. But the latest buzz has Spain possibly becoming the 12th, a blend of the city of Toledo with some architectural highlights of Madrid and Barcelona. Call it another (potential) cash cow: Disney didn't pay to build the other countries, which ranged from $50 million up. Disney also doesn't pay any of the operating costs. But the Magic Mick collects rent and a share of all merchandise sales.

Morocco
Frommer's Rating: A
Recommended Ages: 10–adult

This exotic pavilion has architecture embellished with geometrically patterned tile work, minarets, hand-painted wood ceilings, and brass lighting fixtures. It's headlined by a replica of the Koutoubia Minaret, the prayer tower of a 12th-century mosque in Marrakesh. Note the imperfections in each mosaic tile; they were put there on purpose in accordance with the Muslim belief that only Allah is perfect. The Medina (old city), entered via a replica of an arched gateway in Fez, leads to **Fez House** (a traditional Moroccan home) and the narrow, winding streets of the *souk,* a bustling marketplace where all manner of authentic handcrafted merchandise is on display. Here, you can browse or purchase pottery, brassware, hand-knotted Berber or colorful Rabat carpets, ornate silver and camel-bone boxes, straw baskets, and prayer rugs. There are weaving demonstrations in the souk periodically during the day. The Medina's rectangular courtyard centers on a replica of the ornately tiled Najjarine Fountain in Fez, the setting for musical entertainment.

Treasures of Morocco is a three-times-per-day 35-minute guided tour (1–5pm) that highlights this country's culture, architecture, and history. The pavilion's **Gallery of Arts and History** contains an ever-changing exhibit of Moroccan art, and the Center of Tourism offers a continuous three-screen slide show. Morocco's landscaping includes a formal garden, citrus and olive trees, date palms, and banana plants. On the entertainment side, **Mo'Rockin'** kicks things up Tuesday through Saturday.

Norway
Frommer's Rating: B+
Recommended Ages: 10–adult

This pavilion is centered on a picturesque cobblestone courtyard. A *stavekirke* (stave church), styled after the 13th-century Gol Church of Hallingdal, has changing exhibits. A replica of Oslo's 14th-century **Akershus Castle,** next to a cascading woodland waterfall, is the setting for the featured restaurant (p. 132). Other buildings simulate the red-roofed cottages of Bergen and the timber-sided farm buildings of the Nordic woodlands.

There's a two-part attraction here. **Maelstrom,** a boat ride in a dragon-headed Viking vessel, traverses Norway's fjords and mythical forests to the music of Peer Gynt. (It's the only attraction in World Showcase that offers FASTPASS.) Along the way, you'll see images of polar bears prowling the shore, then trolls cast a spell on the boat. The watercraft crashes through a narrow gorge and spins into the

North Sea, where a storm is in progress. (This is a relatively calm ride, though it's not recommended for expectant mothers or folks with heart, neck, or back problems.) The storm abates, and passengers disembark safely to a 10th-century Viking village to view the 5-minute 70mm film *Norway,* which documents 1,000 years of history. **Spelmanns Gledje** entertains with Norwegian folk music.

Shops sell hand-knit wool hats and sweaters, troll dolls, toys (there's a Lego table where kids can play), woodcarvings, Scandinavian foods, pewterware, and jewelry.

United Kingdom
Frommer's Rating: B
Recommended Ages: 8–adult

The U.K. pavilion takes you to Merry Olde England through **Britannia Square,** a formal London-style park complete with a copper-roof gazebo bandstand, a stereotypical red phone booth, and a statue of the Bard. Four centuries of architecture are represented along quaint cobblestone streets; there's a traditional British pub; and a formal garden with low box hedges in geometric patterns, flagstone paths, and a stone fountain replicates the landscaping of 16th- and 17th-century palaces.

The **British Invasion,** a group that impersonates the Beatles daily except Sunday, and pub pianist **Pam Brody** (Tues, Thurs, Fri, and Sun) provide entertainment. High Street and Tudor Lane shops display a broad sampling of British merchandise, including toy soldiers, Paddington bears, personalized coats of arms, Scottish clothing (cashmere and Shetland sweaters, golf wear, tams, and tartans), English china, Waterford crystal, and pub items such as tankards, dartboards, and the like. A tea shop occupies a replica of Anne Hathaway's thatched-roof 16th-century cottage in Stratford-on-Avon. Other emporia represent the Georgian, Victorian, Queen Anne, and Tudor periods. Background music ranges from "Greensleeves" to the Beatles.

U.S.A.—The American Adventure
Frommer's Rating: A
Recommended Ages: 8–adult

Housed in a vast Georgian-style structure, **The American Adventure** is a 29-minute dramatization of U.S. history, utilizing a 72-foot rear-projection screen, rousing music, and a large cast of lifelike audio-Animatronic figures, including narrators Mark Twain and Ben Franklin. The adventure begins with the voyage of the *Mayflower* and encompasses major historic events. You'll view Jefferson writing the Declaration of Independence, Matthew Brady photographing a family about to be divided by the Civil War, the stock market crash of 1929 (but not the crash of Disney stock in 1999 and 2000), Pearl Harbor, and the *Eagle* heading toward the moon. Teddy Roosevelt discusses the need for national parks. Susan B. Anthony speaks out on women's rights; Frederick Douglass, on slavery; and Chief Joseph, on the plight of Native Americans. It's one of Disney's best historical productions. Entertainment includes the **Spirit of America Fife & Drum Corps** and **Voices of Liberty,** an a cappella group that sings patriotic songs.

Formal gardens shaded by live oaks, sycamores, elms, and holly complement the 18th-century architecture. **Heritage Manor Gifts** sells autographed presidential photographs, needlepoint samplers, quilts, pottery, candles, Davy Crockett hats, books on American history, historically costumed dolls, classic political campaign buttons, and vintage newspapers with banner headlines such as "Nixon Resigns!"

Tips Cruise Control

There are two cruise-style options for watching Epcot's IllumiNations fire-works display (below) from World Showcase Lagoon. You can charter the 1930s vintage speedboat *Breathless* ($180, up to seven people) or catch the show aboard a less romantic but cheaper pontoon boat ($120, up to 12 people). Both last about an hour and can be arranged by Disney's Sports and Recreation telephone line, © **407/939-7529.**

OTHER SHOWS

IllumiNations *Moments*
Frommer's Rating: A+
Recommended Ages: 3–adult

Little has changed since Epcot's millennium version of IllumiNations ended on January 1, 2001. This grand nightcap continues to be a blend of fireworks, lasers, and fountains in a display that's signature Disney. The show is worth the crowds that flock to the parking lot when it's over. *Tip:* Stake your claim to your favorite viewing area a half-hour before show time (listed in your entertainment schedule). The ones near Showcase Plaza have a head start for the exits.

Epcot's entertaining **Tapestry of Dreams Parade** was scrapped in the spring of 2003 after a 17-month run; at press time, there was no word about a replacement.

5 Disney–MGM Studios

You'll probably see the Tower of Terror and the Earrfel Tower, a water tank with mouse ears, before you enter this park, which Disney bills as "the Hollywood that never was and always will be." Once inside, you'll find pulse-quickening rides such as **Rock 'n' Roller Coaster,** movie- and TV-themed shows such as **Who Wants to Be a Millionaire—Play It!,** and a spectacular laser-light show called **Fantasmic!** The main streets include Hollywood and Sunset boulevards, where Art Deco movie sets remember the golden age of Hollywood. New York Street is lined with miniature renditions of Gotham's landmarks (the Empire State, Flatiron, and Chrysler buildings) and characters peddling knock-off watches. You'll find some of the best street performing in the Disney parks here. More importantly, it's a working movie and TV studio where shows are occasionally in production.

Arrive at the park early. Unlike Epcot, MGM's 154 acres of attractions can pretty much be seen in 1 day. The parking lot reaches to the gate, but trams serve some areas. Pay attention to your parking location; this lot isn't as well marked as the Magic Kingdom's. Again, write your lot and row number on something you'll be able to find at the end of the day.

If you don't get a *Disney–MGM Studios Guide Map* and entertainment schedule as you enter the park, you can pick one up at Guest Relations or most shops. Straight off, check show times and work out an entertainment schedule based on highlight attractions and geographical proximity. Our favorite MGM restaurants are described in chapter 6, "Where to Dine."

There's a Guest Information Board listing the day's shows, ride closings, and other information at the corner of Hollywood and Sunset.

HOURS   The park is usually open from 9am to at least 6 or 7pm, with extended hours sometimes as late as midnight during holidays and summer.

Disney–MGM Studios Theme Park

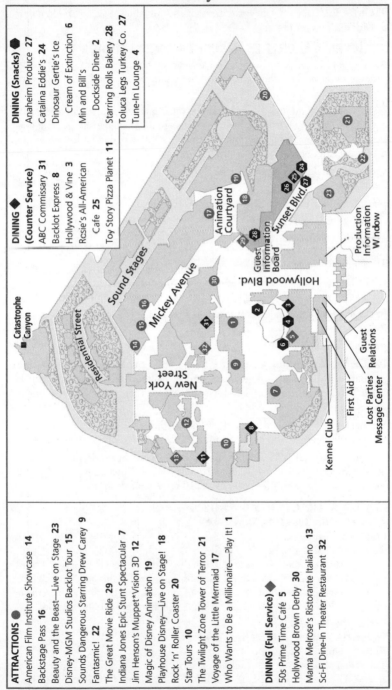

TICKET PRICES   A 1-day park ticket is $52 for adults, $42 for children 3 to 9. Kids under 3 get in free.

SERVICES & FACILITIES IN DISNEY–MGM STUDIOS

ATMs   ATMs accepting cards from banks using the Cirrus, Honor, and PLUS systems are located on the right side of the main entrance and near Toy Story Pizza Planet.

Baby Care   MGM has a small Baby Care Center to the left of the main entrance where you'll find facilities for nursing and changing. Disposable diapers, formula, baby food, and pacifiers are for sale. Changing tables are also in all women's restrooms and some men's restrooms.

Cameras & Film   Film and Kodak disposable cameras are available throughout the park.

First Aid   The First Aid Center, staffed by registered nurses, is in the Entrance Plaza adjoining Guest Relations and the Baby Care Center.

Lockers   Lockers are located alongside Oscar's Classic Car Souvenirs, to the right of the Entrance Plaza after you pass through the turnstiles. The cost is $7, including a $2 deposit.

Lost Children   Lost children at Disney–MGM Studios are taken to Guest Relations, where lost children logbooks are kept. *Children under 7 should wear nametags.*

Package Pickup   Any large purchase can be sent by the shop clerk to Guest Relations in the Entrance Plaza. Allow 3 hours for delivery.

Parking   It's $7 a day for cars, light trucks, and vans; $8 for RVs.

Pet Care   Day accommodations for $6 are offered at kennels to the left and just outside the entrance (© **407/824-6568**). There are also four other kennels in the WDW complex. (See "Fast Facts" in chapter 4 for more details.) Proof of vaccinations is required.

Strollers   Strollers can be rented at Oscar's Super Service, inside the main entrance, for $8 for a single and $15 for a double, including a $1 deposit.

Wheelchair Rental   Wheelchairs are rented at Oscar's Super Service inside the main entrance. The cost for regular chairs is $7 a day, including a $1 deposit. Electric wheelchairs rent for $30 plus a $10 refundable deposit.

MAJOR ATTRACTIONS & SHOWS

American Film Institute Showcase
Frommer's Rating: C
Recommended Ages: 10–adult
This is a shop with an exhibit area that looks at the efforts of the editors, cinematographers, producers, and directors whose names roll by in the blur of credits. It also showcases the work of the American Film Institute's Lifetime Achievement Award winners, including Bette Davis, Jack Nicholson, and Elizabeth Taylor.

Backstage Pass *(Overrated*
Frommer's Rating: D, C for backstage fans
Recommended Ages: Adults
The actual set from the ABC Television show *Home Improvement* is one of the areas you'll see on this (ho-hum) 25-minute walking tour of a working television production facility. (There's also a periodically changing movie featured.) How lame is it? So lame you may not find it on park guide maps, but there is a walk-in gate at the Backlot Tour (see below).

Disney–MGM Studios Backlot Tour
Frommer's Rating: B+
Recommended Ages: 6–adult

There's a world of difference between *backlot* and *backstage*. This 35-minute tram tour takes you behind the scenes for a close-up look at the vehicles, props, costumes, sets, and special effects used in your favorite movies and TV shows. On many days, you'll see costume makers at work in the wardrobe department (Disney has around 2 million garments here). But the real fun begins when the tram heads for **Catastrophe Canyon,** where an earthquake in the heart of oil country causes canyon walls to rumble. A raging oil fire, massive explosions, torrents of rain, and flash floods threaten you and other riders before you're taken behind the scenes to see how filmmakers use special effects to make such disasters. The preshow is almost as interesting. While waiting in line, you can watch entertaining videos hosted by several TV and movie stars. The Backlot Tour is a solid ride that's of the same type as Universal Studios Florida's Earthquake—The Big One (p. 246).

Beauty and the Beast Live on Stage
Frommer's Rating: B+
Recommended Ages: All ages

A 1,500-seat covered amphitheater is the home of this 30-minute live Broadway-style production of *Beauty and the Beast* that's adapted from the movie. Musical highlights from the show include the rousing "Be Our Guest" opening number and the poignant title song featured in the romantic waltz scene finale. The sets and costumes are lavish, and the production numbers are pretty spectacular. There are usually four or five shows a day.

Fantasmic! *Moments*
Frommer's Rating: A+
Recommended Ages: All ages

Disney mixes heroes, villains, stunt performers, choreography, laser lights, and fireworks into a spectacular end-of-the-day extravaganza. This is a 25-minute visual feast where the Magic Mickey comes to life in a show featuring shooting comets, great balls of fire (our apologies to Jerry Lee), and animated fountains that really charge the audience. The cast includes 50 performers, a giant dragon, a king cobra, and 1 million gallons of water, just about all of which are orchestrated by a sorcerer mouse that looks more than remotely familiar. You'll probably recognize other characters as well as musical scores from Disney movie classics such as *Fantasia, Pinocchio, Snow White and the Seven Dwarfs, The Little Mermaid,* and *The Lion King.* You'll also shudder at the animated villainy of Jafar, Cruella De Vil, and Maleficent in the battle of good versus evil, part of which is projected onto huge, water-mist screens. The amphitheater holds 9,000 souls including standing room, and during busy periods (holidays and summers) it's often standing-room-only, so arrive early.

Tips Front-Row Seat

Make a Priority Seating reservation for the Hollywood Brown Derby, Mama Melrose's Ristorante Italiano, or Hollywood & Vine in Disney–MGM Studios (see chapter 6), and when you do, ask for the Fantasmic! package (no extra charge). After dinner you'll get preferred seating at the show. You can make Priority Seating arrangements in advance by calling © **407/939-3463** or on the Internet by going to **www.disneyworld.com**.

Finds   Find the Hidden Mickeys

Hidden Mickeys started as an inside joke among early Disney Imagineers and soon became a park tradition. Today, dozens of subtle Mickey images—usually silhouettes of his world-famous ears, profile, or full figure—are hidden (more or less) in attractions and resorts throughout the Walt Disney empire. No one knows how many, because sometimes they exist only in the eye of the beholder. But there's a semiofficial, maybe-you-agree-maybe-you-don't list. See how many HMs (Hidden Mickeys) you can locate during your visit. And be sharp-eyed about it. Those bubbles on your souvenir mug might be forming one. Here are a few to get you started:

In the Magic Kingdom
- In the Haunted Mansion banquet scene, check out the arrangement of the plate and adjoining saucers on the table.
- In the Africa scene of It's a Small World, note the purple flowers on a vine on the elephant's left side.
- While riding Splash Mountain, look for Mickey lying on his back in the pink clouds to the right of the *Zip-A-Dee Lady* paddle-wheeler.

At Epcot
- In Imagination, check out the little girl's dress in the lobby film of *Honey, I Shrunk the Audience,* one of five HMs in this pavilion.
- In The Land pavilion, don't miss the small stones in front of the Native American man on a horse and the baseball cap of the man driving a harvester in the *Circle of Life* film.
- As you cruise through the Mexico pavilion on El Rio del Tiempo, notice the arrangement of three clay pots in the marketplace scene.
- In Maelstrom in the Norway pavilion, a Viking wears Mickey ears in the wall mural facing the loading dock.

(There is sometimes an additional show earlier in the evening.) *Note:* The show's loud pyrotechnics may frighten younger children, and earplugs aren't a bad idea for anyone with ears sensitive to very loud noises.

The Great Movie Ride
Frommer's Rating: C for most, B for adults who love classics
Recommended Ages: 8–adult
Film footage and 50 audio-Animatronic replicas of movie stars are used to re-create some of the most famous scenes in filmdom on this 22-minute ride through movie history. You'll relive magic moments from the 1930s through the present: the classic airport farewell scene by Bergman and Bogart in *Casablanca;* Rhett carrying Scarlett up the stairs of Tara for a night of whoopee; Brando bellowing "Stellaaaaa"; Sigourney Weaver fending off slimy aliens; Gene Kelly singin' in the rain; and arguably the best Tarzan, Johnny Weissmuller, giving his

- There are four HMs inside Spaceship Earth, one of them in the Renaissance scene, on the page of a book behind the sleeping monk. Try to find the other three.

At Disney–MGM Studios

- On the Great Movie Ride, there's an HM on the window above the bank in the gangster scene.
- At Jim Henson's Muppet*Vision 3D, take a good look at the top of the sign listing five reasons for turning in your 3-D glasses, and note the balloons in the film's final scene.
- In the Twilight Zone Tower of Terror, note the bell for the elevator behind Rod Serling in the film. There are at least five other HMs in this attraction.
- Outside Rock 'n' Roller Coaster, look for two HMs in the rotunda area's tile floor.
- By the way, the park's least Hidden Mickey is what's called the Ear-rfel Tower, Disney–MGM Studios' tall water tower, which is fitted with a huge pair of Mouseket-EARS.

In Animal Kingdom

- Look at The Boneyard in DinoLand U.S.A., where a fan and two hard hats form an HM.
- There are 25 Hidden Mickeys at Rafiki's Planet Watch, where Mickey lurks in the murals, tree trunks, and paintings of animals.

In the Resort Areas

- HMs are on the weather vane atop the Grand Floridian Resort & Spa's convention center, in the interactive fountains at the entrance to Downtown Disney Marketplace, and one forms a giant sand trap next to the green at the Magnolia Golf Course's 6th hole.

If you're Internet savvy, learn more at **www.hiddenmickeys.org**.

trademark yell while swinging across the jungle. The action is enhanced by special effects, and outlaws hijack your tram en route. So pay attention when the conductor warns, "Fasten your seat belts. It's going to be a bumpy night." The setting is a full-scale reproduction of Hollywood's famous Mann's Chinese Theatre, complete with handprints of the stars out front.

Indiana Jones Epic Stunt Spectacular

Frommer's Rating: A+

Recommended Ages: 6–adult

Visitors get a peek into the world of movie stunts in this dramatic 30-minute show, which re-creates major scenes from the Indiana Jones series. The show opens on an elaborate Mayan temple backdrop. Indy crashes onto the set via a rope, and, as he searches with a torch for the golden idol, he encounters booby traps, fire, and steam. Then a boulder straight out of *Raiders of the Lost Ark*

Fun Fact Ain't All Hugs and Kisses

Not everyone loves the Mouse. Just ask the folks at the **Society of Disney Haters (www.sodh.org)**, where alternative views (expressed in chat, essays, and "rants") tackle everything from Disney labor issues to complaints about the treatment of animals.

---

chases him! The set is dismantled to reveal a colorful Cairo marketplace where a sword fight ensues, and the action includes virtuoso bullwhip maneuvers, gunfire, and a truck bursting into flames. An explosive finale takes place in a desert scenario. Theme music and an entertaining narrative enhance the action. Throughout this, guests get to see how elaborate stunts are pulled off. Arrive early and sit near the stage if you want a shot at being picked as an audience participant. Alas, it's a job for adults only.

Jim Henson's Muppet*Vision 3D
Frommer's Rating: A+
Recommended Ages: All ages
This must-see film stars Kermit and Miss Piggy in a delightful marriage of Jim Henson's puppets and Disney audio-Animatronics, special-effects wizardry, 70mm film, and cutting-edge 3-D technology. The coming-right-at-you action includes flying Muppets, cream pies, and cannonballs, plus high winds, fiber-optic fireworks, bubble showers, even an actual spray of water. Kermit is the host; Miss Piggy sings "Dream a Little Dream of Me"; Statler and Waldorf critique the action (which includes numerous mishaps and disasters) from a balcony; and Nicki Napoleon and his Emperor Penguins (a full Muppet orchestra) provide music from the pit. In the preshow area, guests view an entertaining Muppet video on overhead monitors. Note the cute Muppet fountain out front and the Muppet version of a Rousseau painting inside. The 25-minute show (including the 12-min. video preshow) runs continuously.

Magic of Disney Animation
Frommer's Rating: B
Recommended Ages: 8–adult
Disney characters come alive at the stroke of a brush or pencil as you tour a real, glass-walled animation studio. Walter Cronkite and Robin Williams (guess who plays straight man?) explain what's going on via video monitors, and they also star in a funny 8-minute Peter Pan–themed film about the basics of animation. It's painstaking work: To produce an 80-minute film, the animation team must do more than 1 million drawings of characters and scenery! Original cells (drawings/paintings on celluloid sheets) from Disney movies and some of the many Oscars won by Disney artists are on display. The 35-minute guided tour includes entertaining video talks by animators and a finale of magical moments from Disney classics such as *Pinocchio, Snow White, Bambi,* and *Beauty and the Beast.*

Playhouse Disney—Live on Stage!
Frommer's Rating: B
Recommended Ages: 2–5
Younger audiences love this 20-minute show where they meet characters from Bear in the Big Blue House, The Book of Pooh, and other stories. The show encourages preschoolers to dance, sing, and play along with the cast. It happens several times a day. Check your show schedule.

Rock 'n' Roller Coaster *(Moments*

Frommer's Rating: A+

Recommended Ages: 10–adult

Some say this is one of Disney's attempts to go head to head with Universal Orlando's Islands of Adventure. True or not, this inverted roller coaster is the best thrill ride WDW has to offer. It's a fast-and-furious indoor ride in semi-darkness. You sit in a 24-passenger "stretch limo" outfitted with 120 speakers that blare Aerosmith at 32,000 watts! Flashing lights deliver a variety of messages and warnings, including "prepare to merge as you've never merged before." Then, faster than you can scream "I want to live!" (around 2.8 sec., actually), you shoot from 0 to 60 mph and into the first gut-tightening inversion at 5Gs. It's a real launch (sometimes of lunch) followed by a wild ride through a make-believe California freeway system. One of three inversions cuts through an "O" in the Hollywood sign, but you don't feel you're going to be thrown out. It's too fast for that. So fast, the Disney hype says, it's similar to sitting atop an F-14 Tomcat. (We've never been in an F-14, so we can't argue.) The ride lasts 3 minutes, 12 seconds, the running time of Aerosmith's hit, "Sweet Emotion." Like Space Mountain, all of the ride action takes place indoors. But this one is much better. *Note:* Riders must be at least 48 inches tall, and expectant moms and people prone to motion sickness or those with heart, neck, or back problems shouldn't try to tackle this ride.

Sounds Dangerous Starring Drew Carey

Frommer's Rating: C+

Recommended Ages: All ages

Drew Carey provides laughs while dual audio technology provides some hair-raising effects during this 12-minute show at ABC Sound Studios. You'll feel like you're right in the middle of the action of a TV pilot featuring undercover police work and plenty of mishaps. Even when the picture disappears and the theater is plunged into darkness, you continue on Detective Charlie Foster's chase via headphones that show off "3-D" sound effects.

Star Tours

Frommer's Rating: B

Recommended Ages: 8–adult

Cutting edge when it first opened, this galactic journey based on the original *Star Wars* trilogy (George Lucas collaborated on the ride) is now a couple of rungs below the latest technology, but it's still fun. The preshow, expected to be updated eventually with characters from *Episode II: Attack of the Clones,* now has R2-D2 and C-3PO running an intergalactic travel agency. Once inside, you board a 40-seat spacecraft for an other-worldly journey that greets you with sudden drops, crashes, and oncoming laser blasts as it careens out of control. This is another of those virtual-simulator rides where you go nowhere, but it sure feels like you do. *Note:* Riders must be at least 40 inches tall. Also, expectant mothers

---

Tips Tune Time

Weekdays from noon to 4pm, you can watch B.B. Good broadcast his Radio Disney show live from a studio next to Sounds Dangerous Starring Drew Carey. You can tune into the show and others on Radio Disney at 990 on your AM dial.

and people with neck, back, and heart problems or those prone to motion sickness shouldn't ride.

The Twilight Zone Tower of Terror (Moments)
Frommer's Rating: A+
Recommended Ages: 10–adult
This is a truly stomach-lifting (and dropping) ride, and Disney continues to fine-tune it to make it even better. That includes a January 2003 upgrade that added random drop sequences, meaning you might get a different fright each time you ride. The legend says that during a violent storm on Halloween night 1939, lightning struck the Hollywood Tower Hotel, causing an entire wing and an elevator full of people to disappear. And you're about to meet them as you become the star in a special episode of . . . *The Twilight Zone*. En route to this formerly grand hotel, guests walk past overgrown landscaping and faded signs that once pointed the way to stables and tennis courts; the vines over the entrance trellis are dead; and the hotel is a crumbling ruin. Eerie corridors lead to a dimly lit library, where you can hear a storm raging outside. After various spooky adventures, the ride ends in a dramatic climax: a 13-story free-fall in stages. Some believe this rivals Rock 'n' Roller Coaster in the thrill department. At 199 feet, it's the tallest ride in the World, and it's a grade above Dr. Doom's Fearfall at Islands of Adventure. *Note:* You must be at least 40 inches tall to ride, and expectant moms and people prone to motion sickness or those with heart, neck, or back problems shouldn't try to tackle it.

Voyage of the Little Mermaid
Frommer's Rating: B+
Recommended Ages: 4–adult
Hazy lighting creates an underwater effect in a reef-walled theater and helps set the mood for this charming musical based on the Disney feature film. The show combines live performers with more than 100 puppets, movie clips, and innovative special effects. Sebastian sings the movie's Academy Award–winning song, "Under the Sea"; the ethereal Ariel shares her dream of becoming human in a live performance of "Part of Your World"; and the evil Ursula, 12 feet tall and 10 feet wide, belts out "Poor Unfortunate Soul." It has a happy ending, as most of the young audience knows it will; they've seen the movie. This 17-minute show is a great place to rest your feet on a hot day, and you get misted inside the theater to further cool you off.

Who Wants to Be a Millionaire—Play It!
Frommer's Rating: B+
Recommended Ages: 8–adult
Contestants can't win $1 million, but they can win points used to buy prizes ranging from collectible pins to a leather jacket or a 3-night cruise on one Disney's cruise ships. Based on Disney–owned ABC TV's game show, the theme-park version features lifelines (such as asking the audience or calling a stranger on two phones set up in the park). Contestants get a shot at up to 15 multiple-choice questions in the climb to the top. Games run continuously in the 600-seat studio. Audience members play along on keypads. And unlike the TV show,

---

In the Words of Walt Disney
A family picture is one the kids can take their parents to see and not be embarrassed.

(*Moments* **You Want Characters?**

Characters and hot spots change, but as of this writing, the best bets at Disney–MGM Studios are:

Toy Story Friends   Near Mama Melrose's Ristorante Italiano. See the handout Times Guide for the schedule.

Mickey & Friends   Mickey Avenue between Backlot Tour and Who Wants to Be a Millionaire. See the handout Times Guide.

---

the entire audience competes to get in the hot seat; the fastest to answer qualifying questions become contestants.

PARADES, PLAYGROUNDS & MORE

Disney Stars and Motor Cars is MGM's parade celebrating the 100th anniversary of Uncle Walt's birth in Chicago. The motorcade includes a fun, highly recognizable procession of Disney characters and their chariots. The parade is popular enough that if you decide to skip it, you'll find shorter lines at the park's primo rides (check the parade schedule in your park map).

Discover the Stories Behind the Magic is an exhibit under the giant sorcerer's hat at the end of Hollywood Boulevard. Its interactive kiosks let you explore the magic inspirations of the chapters in Disney's life.

SHOPPING AT DISNEY–MGM STUDIOS

The **Animation Courtyard Shops** carry collectible cells, costumes from Disney classic films, and pins.

Sid Cahuenga's One-of-a-Kind sells autographed photos of the stars, original movie posters, and star-touched items such as canceled checks signed by Judy Garland and others.

Celebrity 5 & 10, modeled after a 1940s Woolworth's, has movie-related merchandise: *Gone with the Wind* memorabilia, MGM Studio T-shirts, movie posters, Elvis mugs, and more.

The major park attractions also have merchandise outlets selling Indiana Jones adventure clothing, Little Mermaid stuffed characters, *Star Wars* souvenirs, and so on.

6 Animal Kingdom

Disney's fourth major park combines animals, elaborate landscapes, and a handful of rides to create yet another reason that many WDW resort-goers don't venture outside this World. The bulk of the $800 million park opened in 1998. Its most recent "land," Asia, opened in 1999. Speaking of Asia, it will be the home of Animal Kingdom's long-awaited first thrill ride. Expected to debut in 2006, **Expedition Everest** will be a high-speed, coaster-like train ride that moves forward and backward through glaciers, waterfalls and canyons, climaxing with an encounter with a yeti. Even with that announcement, some visitors (and we're among them!) believe there isn't enough here to justify this being in the same league as other theme parks that charge $52 per adult.

But don't tell Disney CEO Michael Eisner. He says Animal Kingdom is the next best thing to going to Africa. Even those straddling the fence on this issue might suggest King Mike's losing touch with the real world. Sure, Animal

Kingdom is different as Orlando theme parks go because it has exotic wildlife. There are also a couple of great shows—including Festival of the Lion King. And if the animals are cooperative, you can have an up-close encounter that you aren't likely to find in another theme park.

Animal Kingdom surely ranks as one of the top two critter parks in Florida when it comes to volume and diversity of things to do. Busch Gardens in Tampa (a $51.95 per-adult, $42.95 per-child entry) is the other. While that park will be discussed in depth in chapter 11, "Side Trips from Orlando," we're going to talk about it briefly here for the sake of drawing a few comparisons.

Animal Kingdom is more a park for animals, a conservation venue as much as an attraction. The short of it is that it's not as easy to see the critters here. They've been given a lot more cover than at Busch Gardens, so when they want to, they can escape your probing eyes and the heat. The best bet for animal viewing here is to arrive in time for the park's opening, usually 8 or 9am but sometimes earlier, or try to see them near closing. More animals are likely to be on the prowl then than at midday, especially in the heat of summer. *Note:* Both parks offer some shade for the animals, but the amount of cover given to tourists waiting in line is decidedly unimpressive. Arriving early at both parks, especially in summer, will save you the *very* unpleasant experience of languishing under a blistering sun.

Animal Kingdom wins the battle of shows, with humdingers such as **Tarzan Rocks!** and **Festival of the Lion King.** But Busch Gardens clearly wins the battle of thrill rides. Whereas Animal Kingdom has three (and we're being kind to call two of them "thrill" rides), Busch Gardens has five adult-size roller coasters alone—including Gwazi, a dual wooden coaster.

Animal Kingdom is more centrally located. Busch Gardens is a 90-minute drive from Orlando, and there isn't as much to see and do elsewhere in Tampa. But even if that city is out of the picture geographically, those of you coming with younger kids and limited time will find more fun at other WDW parks, such as the Magic Kingdom and Disney–MGM, than at Animal Kingdom. Critter lovers, on the other hand, should put this one at the top of their list.

Animal Kingdom is divided into areas: The **Oasis,** a shopping area near the entrance that has limited animal viewing; **Discovery Island,** home of the Tree of Life, which is the park's icon; **Camp Minnie-Mickey,** the Animal Kingdom equivalent of Mickey's Toontown Fair in the Magic Kingdom; **Africa,** the main animal-viewing area, which is dedicated to the wildlife in Africa today; **Asia,** which has a river raft ride, animal exhibits (including Bengal tigers and giant fruit bats), and a bird show; and **Dinoland U.S.A.,** which has rides, games, and the show, Tarzan Rocks!

The park covers more than 500 acres (Busch Gardens has 335), and your feet will tell you that you've covered the territory at the end of the day.

⌒Tips Heat Alert!

Orlando is one place where you don't want to go for the burn. The scalding Florida sun can get you in many directions. Slather sunscreen on any exposed skin, including your back, shoulders, the backs of your legs, and anywhere else you leave exposed. And don't think winter is a safe time—you can get a burn on a chilly day, too.

Animal Kingdom

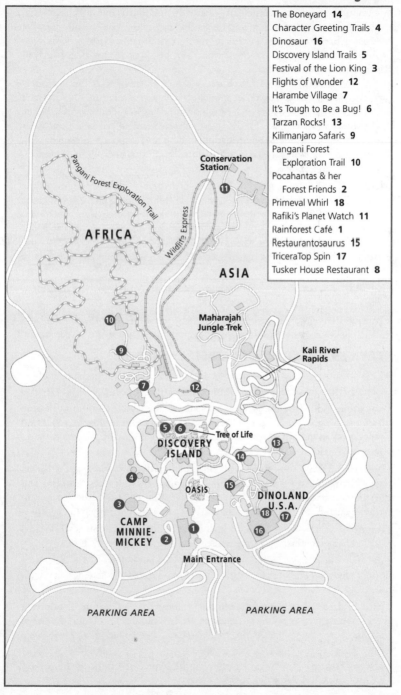

The Boneyard **14**
Character Greeting Trails **4**
Dinosaur **16**
Discovery Island Trails **5**
Festival of the Lion King **3**
Flights of Wonder **12**
Harambe Village **7**
It's Tough to Be a Bug! **6**
Tarzan Rocks! **13**
Kilimanjaro Safaris **9**
Pangani Forest
   Exploration Trail **10**
Pocahantas & her
   Forest Friends **2**
Primeval Whirl **18**
Rafiki's Planet Watch **11**
Rainforest Café **1**
Restaurantosaurus **15**
TriceraTop Spin **17**
Tusker House Restaurant **8**

Conservation Station

Pangani Forest Exploration Trail

AFRICA

Wildlife Express

ASIA

Maharajah Jungle Trek

Kali River Rapids

Tree of Life

DISCOVERY ISLAND

OASIS

DINOLAND U.S.A.

CAMP MINNIE-MICKEY

Main Entrance

PARKING AREA

PARKING AREA

Most of the rides are accessible to guests with disabilities, but the hilly terrain, large crowds, narrow passages, and long hikes can make for a strenuous day if there's a wheelchair-bound person in your party. Anyone with neck or back problems as well as pregnant women may not be able to enjoy rides like **Kali River Rapids** and **Dinosaur.**

The 145-foot-tall **Tree of Life** is in the center of the park. It's an intricately carved free-form representation of animals, handcrafted by a team of artists over the period of a year. It's not nearly as tall or imposing as the silver golf ball–like dome, also known as Spaceship Earth, which has come to symbolize Epcot, or Cinderella Castle in the Magic Kingdom. The tree is impressive, though, with 8,000 limbs, 103,000 leaves, and 325 mammals, reptiles, bugs, birds, dinosaurs, and Mickeys in its trunk, limbs, and roots.

ARRIVING   From the parking lot, walk or (where available) ride one of the trams to the entrance. If you do walk, watch out for the trams and autos, because the lot isn't designed for pedestrians. Also, make certain to note where you parked (section and row). Lot signs aren't as prominent as in the Magic Kingdom, and the rows look alike when you come back out. Upon entering the park, consult the handout guide map for special events or entertainment. If you have questions, ask park staffers.

HOURS   Animal Kingdom is open at least from 8 or 9am to 5pm, but it sometimes stays open an hour or so later.

TICKET PRICES   The ticket prices are $52 for adults, $42 for children 3 to 9. See "Tickets," earlier in this chapter, for information on 4- and 5-day passes.

SERVICES & FACILITIES IN ANIMAL KINGDOM

ATMs   Animal Kingdom has an ATM near Garden Gate Gifts to the right of the entrance. It accepts cards from banks using the Cirrus, Honor, and PLUS systems.

Baby Care   The Baby Care Center is located near Creature Comforts gift shop on the west side of the Tree of Life, but as in the other Disney parks, you'll find changing tables in both restrooms, and you can buy disposable diapers at Guest Relations.

Cameras & Film   You can drop film off for same-day developing at the Kodak Kiosk in Africa and Garden Gate Gifts near the park entrances. Cameras and film are available in Disney Outfitters in Safari Village; at the Kodak Kiosk in Africa, near the entrance to the Kilimanjaro Safari; and in Garden Gate Gifts.

First Aid   The First Aid Center, which is staffed by registered nurses, is located near Creature Comforts gift shop on the west side of the Tree of Life.

Lockers   Lockers ($7, including a $2 deposit) are located in Garden Gate Gifts to your right as you enter the park. They're also located to the left, near Rainforest Cafe.

Lost Children   A center for lost children is located near Creature Comforts at the Baby Care Center on the west side of the Tree of Life. This is also the site of same-day lost and found. At the risk of rehash, *make your younger kids wear nametags.*

Package Pickup   Any large packages can be sent to the front of the park at Garden Gate Gifts. Allow 3 hours for delivery.

Parking   The cost is $7 a day for cars, light trucks, and vans; $8 for RVs.

> ## ⌒*Tips* Animal Kingdom Tip Sheet
>
> 1. Arrive at opening or stay until near closing for the best view of the animals.
> 2. **Kilimanjaro Safaris** is one of the most popular rides and the best place to see a lot of animals in one sitting. But in summer, the animals can be scarce except near park opening and closing times. If you can hoof it there first thing, do it. If not, try late in the day. The same applies to viewing the gorillas on the **Pangani Forest Exploration Trail**.
> 3. The **Festival of the Lion King** show is a must.
> 4. Looking for Disney characters? Go to the Character Greeting Trails in **Camp Minnie-Mickey**.

Pet Care   Pet facilities are located just outside the park entrance ($6 per day; ✆ **407/824-6568**). There are four other kennels located in the WDW complex. (See "Fast Facts" in chapter 4 for more information.) Proof of vaccinations is required.

Strollers   Stroller rentals are available at Garden Gate Gifts to the right as you enter the park ($8 for a single, $15 for a double, including a $1 refundable deposit). There are also satellite locations throughout the park. Ask a Disney employee to steer you.

Wheelchair Rental   You can rent wheelchairs at Garden Gate Gifts to the right as you enter the park. Rentals are $7, including a $1 deposit for a standard wheelchair; $30 for an electric wheelchair plus a $10 deposit (both deposits are refundable). Ask Disney employees for other locations throughout the park.

THE OASIS

This painstakingly designed landscape of streams, grottoes, and mini waterfalls sets the tone for the rest of the park. This is a good place to see wallabies, tiny deer, giant anteaters, sloths, iguanas, tree kangaroos, otters, and macaws (*if*, we remind *ad nauseum,* you get here early or stay late). But thick cover provides a jungle tone and makes seeing the animals sometimes difficult. There are no rides in this area, and, aside from the animals, it's mainly a pass-through zone. Those guests traveling with eager children will probably have more time to enjoy these exhibits on the way out.

DISCOVERY ISLAND

Like Cinderella Castle in the Magic Kingdom and Spaceship Earth in Epcot, the 14-story **Tree of Life** located here has been designed to be the park's central landmark. The manmade tree and its carved animals are the work of Disney artists. Teams of them worked for 1 year creating the various sculptures, and it's worth a stroll on the walks around its roots, but most folks are smart to save it for the end of the day. (Much of it can be seen while you're in line for **It's Tough to Be a Bug!** or on **the Discovery Island Trails**.) The intricate design makes it seem as if a different animal appears from every angle. One of the creators says he expects it to become one of the most photographed works of art in the world. (He's probably a Disney shareholder.) There's a wading pond directly in front of the tree that often features flamingos.

Fun Fact It Costs to Recycle

The animals here deposit more than 1,600 tons of dung a year. Disney pays a company to haul it away, then buys some of it back as compost for landscaping.

It's Tough to Be a Bug!
Frommer's Rating: A
Recommended Ages: 5–adult

This show's cuteness quotient is enough to earn it a B+. But it goes a rung higher thanks to the preshow: To get to the theater, you have to wind around the Tree of Life's 50-foot base, giving you a front-row look at this manmade marvel. After you've passed that, grab your 3-D glasses and settle into a sometimes creepy-crawly seat. Based on the film *A Bug's Life*, the special effects in this multimedia show are pretty impressive. It's not a good one for very young kids (it's dark and loud) or bug haters, but for others it's a fun, sometimes poignant look at life from a smaller perspective. Flick, Hopper, and the rest of the cast—ants, beetles, spiders, and, ugh, a stink bug—awaken your senses with, literally, some in-your-face action. And the show's finale always leaves the crowd buzzing.

Discovery Island Trails
Frommer's Rating: B
Recommended Ages: All ages

The old, pre-FASTPASS queue **for It's Tough to Be a Bug!** provides a leisurely path through the root system of the Tree of Life and a chance to see real, not-so-rare critters, such as axis deer, red kangaroos, otters, flamingos, lemurs, Galapagos tortoises, ducks, storks, and cockatoos. Again, the best viewing times are early or late in the day.

DINOLAND U.S.A

Enter by passing under Olden Gate Bridge, a 40-foot Brachiosaurus reassembled from excavated fossils. Speaking of which, until late summer 1999, this land had three paleontologists working on the very real skeleton of Sue, a monstrously big *Tyrannosaurus rex* unearthed 9 years earlier in the Black Hills of South Dakota. They patched and assembled the bones here because Disney helped pay for the work. Alas, Sue's permanent home is at Chicago's Field Museum, but Dinoland U.S.A. has a replica cast from her 67 million-year-old bones. It's marked as **Dino-Sue** on park guide maps.

The Boneyard
Frommer's Rating: B+ for children, B for parents who need to rest their feet
Recommended Ages: 3–12

Kids love the chance to slip, slither, slide, and slink through this giant playground and dig site where they can discover the real-looking remains of triceratops, *T. rex,* and other vanished giants. Contained within a latticework of metal bars and netting, this area is popular, but not as inviting as the *Honey, I Shrunk the Kids* play area in Disney–MGM Studios.

Dinosaur
Frommer's Rating: B
Recommended Ages: 8–adult

Formerly called Countdown to Extinction, this ride hurls you through darkness in CTX Rover "time machines" that pass an array of snarling (though sometimes hokey) dinosaurs. Young children may find the large lizards and the darkness a bit frightening. For now this is as close as Animal Kingdom gets to a thrill ride. Although we know people who like it better than we do, exceptional it isn't—and some find it jarring. As with most things in this Kingdom, there's a message about the frailty of all life forms, including big carnivores. *Note:* You must be 40 inches or taller to climb aboard. Also, expectant mothers and people with neck, back, and heart problems or those prone to motion sickness shouldn't ride.

Primeval Whirl
Frommer's Rating: B+
Recommended Ages: 8–adult
Disney introduced this spinning, free-style twin roller coaster in 2002. You control the action through its wacky maze of curves, peaks, and dippity-do-dahs, encountering faux asteroids and hokey cutouts of dinosaurs. This is a cross between those old carnival coasters of the '50s and '60s and an expanded version of the Barnstormer at Goofy's Wiseacre Farm (p. 189). *Note:* The ride carries a 48-inch height minimum, and expectant moms as well as those with neck, back, or heart problems and folks prone to motion sickness should stay planted on firm ground.

TriceraTop Spin
Frommer's Rating: B+ for tykes and parents
Recommended Ages: 2–7
Cut from the same cloth as The Magic Carpets of Aladdin at WDW's Magic Kingdom, this is another mini-thrill for youngsters. In this case, cars that look like cartoon dinosaurs are attached to arms that circle a hub while moving up and down and all around. This ride, Primeval Whirl, and an arcade-game area make up a Dinoland U.S.A. mini-land called Chester & Hester's Dino-Rama.

Tarzan Rocks!
Frommer's Rating: A
Recommended Ages: All ages
This 28-minute show pulses with music and occasional aerial theatrics. Phil Collins's movie soundtrack supports a cast of 27, including tumblers, dancers, and in-line skating daredevils who really get the audience into the act. Costumes and music are pretty spectacular, second in Animal Kingdom only to Festival of the Lion King in Camp Minnie-Mickey (see below). Our only criticism: When Tarzan does appear, it's clear by his face, physique, and acting ability that he's there more for eye candy than anything. The show is held in the 1,500-seat Theater in the Wild.

CAMP MINNIE-MICKEY
Disney characters are the main attraction in this land designed in the same vein as an Adirondack resort. Aside from those characters, however, this zone for the younger set isn't as kid-friendly as rivals Mickey's Toontown Fair in the Magic

---

Tips   Pin Mania
Pin buying, collecting, and trading can reach frenzied proportions among Disney fans, including many cast members. All of the theme parks have special locations set aside for the fun, which are marked on the handout guide maps. You can learn more about the madness on the Internet at **www.dizpins.com** and **www.officialdisneypintrading.com**.

Kingdom (reviewed earlier in this chapter) or Woody Woodpecker's KidZone in Universal Studios Florida (see "Universal Studios Florida," in chapter 8).

Character Greeting Trails *Moments*
Frommer's Rating: A for kids, parents, and Disney softies
Recommended Ages: 2–12
This is a must-do for people traveling with children. A variety of Disney characters, from Winnie the Pooh and Pocahontas to Timon and Baloo, have separate trails where you can meet and mingle. Mickey, Minnie, Goofy, and Pluto also make appearances.

Festival of the Lion King *Finds*
Frommer's Rating: A+
Recommended Ages: All ages
Almost everyone in the audience comes alive when the music starts in this rousing 28-minute show in the Lion King Theater. It's one of the top three theme-park shows in central Florida. The production celebrates nature's diversity with a talented, colorfully attired cast of singers, dancers, and life-size critters leading the way to an inspiring sing-along that gets the entire audience caught up in the fun. Based loosely on the animated film, this stage show blends the pageantry of a parade with a tribal celebration. The action is on stage as well as moving around the audience. Even though the pavilion has 1,000 seats, it's best to arrive at least 20 minutes early.

Pocahontas and Her Forest Friends
Frommer's Rating: C
Recommended Ages: All ages
The wait can be nightmarish, and the 15-minute show isn't close to the caliber of Festival of the Lion King and Tarzan Rocks! In this one, Pocahontas, Grandmother Willow, and some forest creatures (a raccoon, turkey, porcupine, snake, and some rats) hammer home the importance of treating with respect. If you must, go early. The theater only has 350 seats, but they allow standing-room crowds.

AFRICA
Enter through the town of Harambe, a run-down representation of an African coastal village poised on the edge of the 21st century. Costumed employees will greet you as you enter the buildings. The whitewashed structures, built of coral stone and thatched with reed by African craftspeople, surround a central marketplace rich with local wares and colors.

Kilimanjaro Safaris
Frommer's Rating: A+ early or late, B+ other times
Recommended Ages: All ages
Animal Kingdom doesn't have many rides, so calling this the best may sound like a qualified endorsement. But the animals you'll see make it a winner as long as

---

Fun Fact Did You Know?

Tobacco products aren't the only things unavailable in the theme parks. You can't buy chewing or bubble gum either. It seems too many guests stuck it under tables, benches, and chairs—or tossed it on sidewalks, where it often hitched a ride on the soles of the unsuspecting.

Tips Coming Soon . . . Maybe

Sometimes criticized for being too passive, Animal Kingdom may be diving a little deeper into the thrill-ride fray with a full-fright roller coaster in the Camp Minnie-Mickey area, but in a new land called **Beastly Kingdom**. While details are pretty scarce, this is a land of mythical creatures, so the coaster should fit the theme. The question is, when? The earliest projections say 2004, but others suggest 2006.

---

your timing is right. They're scarce at midday during most times of year (cooler months are the exception), so we recommend you ride it as close to the park's opening or closing as possible. Also, if you don't make it in time for one of the first or last journeys, the lines can be incredibly long, so consider using FASTPASS.

Your ride vehicle is a very large truck that takes you through what pretends to be an African landscape (just a few years ago it was a cow pasture). The animals usually seen along the way include black rhinos, hippos, antelopes, Nile crocodiles, zebras, wildebeests, cheetahs, and a pair of lions that may offer half-hearted roars toward some gazelles that are safely out of reach. Again, the theme is heavy on conservation. Early on, a shifting bridge gives riders a cheap thrill; later, there's some drama as you help catch some poachers. While everyone has a good view, photographers may get a few more shots when sitting on the left side of their row.

Pangani Forest Exploration Trail *(Finds*
Frommer's Rating: B+, A if you're lucky enough to see the gorillas
Recommended Ages: All ages
The hippos put on quite a display (and draw a riotous crowd reaction) when they do what comes naturally and use their tails to scatter it over everything above and below the surface. There are other animals here, including ever-active mole rats, but the **lowland gorillas** are the main event. The trail has two gorilla-viewing areas: One sports a family, including a 500-pound silverback, his ladies, and his children; the other has bachelors. Guests who are unaware of the treasures that lie herein often skip or rush through it, missing a chance to see some magnificent creatures. That said, they're not always cooperative, especially in hot weather, when they spend most of the day in shady areas out of view. There's also a new Endangered Animal Rehabilitation Centre with Colobus and Mona monkeys.

Rafiki's Planet Watch *(Overrated*
Frommer's Rating: C
Recommended Ages: All ages
Board an open-sided train (the Wildlife Express) near Pangani Forest Exploration Trail for a trip to the back edge of the park, which has three attractions. **Conservation Station** offers a behind-the-scenes look at how Disney cares for animals. You'll pass nurseries and veterinarian stations. But these facilities need to be staffed to be interesting, and that's not always the case. **Habitat Habit!** is a trail with small animals such as cotton-top tamarins. The **Affection Section**'s petting zoo has goats and potbelly pigs.

ASIA
Disney's Imagineers have outdone themselves in creating the kingdom of **Anandapur.** The intricately painted artwork at the front is appealing, and it also seems to make the lines move a tad faster.

Fun Fact **Cool Trivia**

Two things you might hear during your day in the park: Bugs make up 80% of the real animal kingdom, and cheetahs are the only great cats that purr. Both are true.

Flights of Wonder
Frommer's Rating: B
Recommended Ages: All ages
This live-animal action show has undergone several transformations since the park opened. It's a low-key break from the madness and has a few laughs, including Groucho the African yellow-nape, who entertains the audience with his op-*parrot*-ic a cappella solos, and the just-above-your-head soaring of a Harris hawk and a Eurasian eagle owl.

Kali River Rapids
Frommer's Rating: B+
Recommended Ages: 6–adult
Here's a pretty darn good raft ride—slightly better, we think, than Congo River Rapids at Busch Gardens in Tampa, though not quite as good as Popeye & Bluto's Bilge Rat Barges at Islands of Adventure (p. 258). Its churning water mimics real rapids, and optical illusions have you wondering if you're about to go over the falls. The ride begins with a peaceful tour of lush foliage, but soon you're dipping and dripping as your tiny craft is tossed and turned. You *will* get wet. (Bring a plastic garbage bag for your valuables. The rafts' center storage areas alone likely won't keep them dry.) The lines can be long, but keep your head up and enjoy the marvelous art overhead and on beautiful murals. *Note:* There's a 38-inch height minimum, and expectant moms and people with neck, back, and heart problems or those prone to motion sickness shouldn't ride it.

Maharajah Jungle Trek
Frommer's Rating: B
Recommended Ages: 6–adults
Disney keeps its promise to provide up-close views of animals with this exhibit. If you don't show up in the midday heat, you may see Bengal tigers through a wall of thick glass, while nothing but air separates you from dozens of giant fruit bats hanging in what appears to be a courtyard. Some have wingspans of 6 feet. (If you have a phobia, you can bypass this, though the bats are harmless.) Guides are on hand to answer questions, and you can also check a brochure that lists the animals you may spot; it's available on your right as you enter. You'll be asked to "recycle" it as you exit.

PARADES
Mickey's Jammin' Jungle Parade at Animal Kingdom is an interactive street party featuring characters and animals on expedition.

7 Disney Water Parks

Note: All of the attractions mentioned in this section can be found on the "Walt Disney World Parks & Attractions" map on p. 167.

TYPHOON LAGOON

Ahoy swimmers, floaters, run-aground boaters!
A furious storm once roared 'cross the sea
Catching ships in its path, helpless to flee . . .
Instead of a certain and watery doom
The winds swept them here to TYPHOON LAGOON.

Such is the Disney legend relating to **Typhoon Lagoon** ⭐⭐⭐, which you'll see posted on consecutive signs as you enter the park. Located off Buena Vista Drive between the Downtown Disney Marketplace and Disney–MGM Studios, this is the ultimate in water-theme parks. Its fantasy setting is a palm-fringed island village of ramshackle, tin-roofed structures, strewn with cargo, surfboards, and other marine wreckage left by the "great typhoon." A storm-stranded fishing boat (the *Miss Tilly*) dangles precariously atop 95-foot Mount Mayday, the steep setting for several attractions. Every half hour, the boat's smokestack erupts, shooting a 50-foot geyser of water into the air.

ESSENTIALS

HOURS The park is open from at least 10am to 5pm, with extended hours during some holiday periods and summer (📞 **407/560-4141;** www.disneyworld.com).

ENTRANCE FEES A 1-day ticket (without 6% tax) to Typhoon Lagoon is $31 for adults, $25 for kids 3 to 9.

HELPFUL HINTS In summer, arrive no later than 9am to avoid long lines. The park is often filled to capacity by 10am and then closed to later arrivals. Beach towels ($2.50 per towel) and lockers ($5 and $8) can be rented, and beachwear can be purchased at **Singapore Sal's.** Light fare is available at two eateries, **Leaning Palms** and **Typhoon Tillie's.** A beach bar called **Let's Go Slurpin'** sells beer and soft drinks. There are picnic tables (consider bringing picnic fare; you can keep it in your locker until lunch). Guests aren't permitted to bring their own flotation devices, and glass bottles are prohibited.

ATTRACTIONS IN THE PARK

Castaway Creek

Hop onto a raft or an inner tube and meander along this 2,100-foot lazy river that circles most of the park. It tumbles through a misty rainforest, then by caves and secluded grottoes. It has a theme area called **Water Works,** where jets of water spew from shipwrecked boats, and a Rube Goldberg assemblage of broken bamboo pipes and buckets wet you. Tubes are included in the admission price.

Ketchakiddie Creek

Many of the park's other attractions require guests to be older children, teens, or adults, but this section is a **kiddie area** exclusively for 2- to 5-year-olds. An innovative water playground, it has bubbling fountains to frolic in, mini–water

---

Tips Closed for the Winter

Both Disney water parks are refurbished annually. That means if you're traveling in fall or winter, it is likely that one of the parks will be closed for a month or more. So if a water park is on your itinerary, ask in advance about closings.

slides, a pint-size "white-water" tubing run, spouting whales and squirting seals, rubbery crocodiles to climb on, grottoes to explore, and waterfalls to loll under. It's also small enough for you to take good home videos or photographs.

Shark Reef

Guests are given free equipment (and instruction) for a 15-minute swim through this very small snorkeling area that includes a simulated coral reef populated by about 4,000 parrot fish, angelfish, yellowtail damselfish, and other cuties including small rays and sharks. If you don't want to get in, you can observe the fish via portholes in a walk-through viewing area. *Note:* There's also a supplied-air, scuba-assisted program for kids available for an extra $20.

Typhoon Lagoon Surf Pool

This large (2.75 million gal.) and lovely lagoon is the size of two football fields and is surrounded by a white sandy beach. It's the park's main swimming area. The chlorinated water has a turquoise hue much like the Caribbean. **Large waves** roll through the deeper areas every 90 seconds. A foghorn sounds to warn you when one is coming. Young children can wade in the lagoon's more peaceful tidal pools—**Blustery Bay** or **Whitecap Cove.** The lagoon also is home to a **special weekly surfing program** (see "Staying Active" in chapter 8).

Water Slides

Humunga Kowabunga consists of three 214-foot Mount Mayday slides that propel you down the mountain on a serpentine route through waterfalls and bat caves and past nautical wreckage before depositing you into a bubbling catch pool; each offers slightly different views and 30-mph thrills. There's seating for non-Kowabunga folks whose kids have commissioned them to "watch me." Women should wear a one-piece swimsuit on the slides (except those who don't mind putting on a show for gawkers). *Note:* You must be 48 inches or taller to ride this. **Storm Slides** offer a tamer course through the park's manmade caves.

Tips Water Park Dos & Don'ts

1. Go in the afternoons, about 2pm, even in summer, if you can stand the heat that long and want to avoid crowds. The early birds usually are gone by then.

2. Go early in the week when most of the week-long guests are filling the lines at the theme parks.

3. Kids can get lost just as easily at a water park as at the other parks, and the consequences can be tragic. All Disney parks have lifeguards, usually wearing bright red suits, but, to be safe, make yourself the first line of safety for the kids in your crew.

4. Women should remember the one-piece bathing suit rule we mentioned earlier under "Water Slides." And all bathers should remember the "wedgie" rule on the more extreme rides, such as Summit Plummet (at Blizzard Beach, below). What's the "wedgie" rule? It's a principle of physics that says you may start out wearing baggies and end up in a thong.

5. Use a waterproof sunscreen with an SPF of at least 30 and drink plenty of fluids. Despite all that water, it's easy to get dehydrated in summer.

> **(*Fun Fact* Did You Know?**
>
> - Walt Disney World sprawls across 47 square miles, which makes it the size of San Francisco or twice that of Manhattan. Less than a quarter of it is developed and another quarter is a preserve.
> - Mickey Mouse has more than 80 outfits, ranging from scuba gear to formal wear. Minnie has a mere 50.
> - There are enough Mouse ears sold yearly to cover the head of every man, woman, and child living in Pittsburgh.
> - The Liberty Oak, the big tree in Liberty Square, has produced more than 500 offspring, all of which began as acorns.
> - Spaceship Earth, the golf ball–like focal point of Epcot, weighs 16 million pounds.
> - On an average day, 100 pairs of sunglasses are turned in to the Lost and Found at the Magic Kingdom. That's more than 1.1 million since the opening bell in 1971.
> - In that same span, the WDW monorail has logged enough miles to travel 25 times to the moon.
> - Walt Disney World gift shops sell about 500,000 character watches annually. Not surprisingly, most of them are Mickeys.
> - Both Disneyland in California and Walt Disney World were built on former citrus groves in counties named Orange.

White-Water Rides

Mount Mayday is the setting for three white-water rafting adventures—**Keelhaul Falls, Mayday Falls,** and **Gangplank Falls**—all offering steep drops coursing through caves and passing lush scenery. Keelhaul Falls has the most winding route, Mayday Falls has the steepest drops and fastest water, and the slightly tamer Gangplank Falls uses large tubes so that the whole family can pile on.

BLIZZARD BEACH

Blizzard Beach ✯✯✯ is the younger of Disney's water parks, a 66-acre "ski resort" in the midst of a tropical lagoon centering on the 90-foot, uh-oh, Mount Gushmore. There's a legend for this one as well. Apparently a freak snowstorm dumped tons of snow on Walt Disney World, leading to the creation of Florida's first—and, so far, only—mountain ski resort. Naturally, when temperatures returned to their normal broiling range, the snow bunnies prepared to close up shop, when they realized—this is Disney, happy endings are a must—that what remained of their snow resort could be turned into a water park featuring the fastest and tallest waterlogged "ski" runs in the country. The base of Mount Gushmore has a sand beach with several other attractions, including a wave pool and a smaller version of the mount for younger children. The park is located off World Drive, just north of the All-Star Movie, Music, and Sports resorts.

ESSENTIALS

HOURS   It's open from at least 10am to 5pm, with extended hours during holiday periods and summer (© **407/560-3400;** www.disneyworld.com).

ENTRANCE FEES   A 1-day ticket to Blizzard Beach is $31 (without 6% tax) for adults, $25 for children 3 to 9.

HELPFUL HINTS   Arrive at or before opening to avoid long lines and to be sure you get in. Beach towels ($2.50 per towel) and lockers ($5 and $8) are available, and you can buy the beachwear you forgot to bring at the **Beach Haus.** You can grab something to eat at **Avalunch** and **Lottawatta Lodge** (burgers, hot dogs, nachos, pizza, and sandwiches).

MAJOR ATTRACTIONS IN THE PARK
Cross Country Creek
Inner-tubers can float lazily along this park-circling 2,900-foot creek, but beware of the mysterious cave where you'll get splashed with melting ice.

Melt-Away Bay
This 1-acre bobbing wave pool is fed by waterfalls of melting "snow" and features relatively calm waves.

Runoff Rapids
Another tube job, this one lets you careen down any of three twisting-turning runs, one of which sends you through darkness.

Ski-Patrol Training Camp
Designed for preteens, it features a rope swing, a T-bar drop over water, slides like the wet and slippery **Mogul Mania** from the Mount, and a challenging ice-floe walk along slippery floating icebergs.

Slush Gusher
This superspeed slide travels along a snow-banked gully. *Note:* It has a 48-inch height minimum.

Snow Stormers
These three flumes descend from the top of Mount Gushmore and follow a switchback course through ski-type slalom gates.

Summit Plummet
Read *every* speed, motion, vertical-dip, wedgie, and hold-onto-your-breast-plate warning in this guide. Then, test your bravado in a bull ring, a space shuttle, or dozens of other death-defying hobbies as a warm-up. This puppy starts pretty slow, with a lift ride to the 120-foot summit. Then . . . well . . . kiss any kids or religious medal you may be carrying. Because, if you board, you *will enter* the World's fastest body slide, a test of your courage and swimsuit that virtually goes straight down and has you moving *sans* vehicle at 60 mph by the catch pool (aka, stop zone). Even the hardiest rider may find this one hard to handle; a veteran thrill-seeker described the experience to us as "15 seconds of paralyzing fear." *Note:* It has a 48-inch height minimum. Also, expectant mothers and people with neck, back, and heart problems shouldn't ride.

Teamboat Springs
On the World's longest white-water raft ride, your six-passenger raft twists down a 1,200-foot series of rushing waterfalls.

Tike's Peak
This kid-size version of Mount Gushmore offers short water slides, rideable animals, a snow castle, a squirting ice pond, and a fountain play area for young guests.

Toboggan Racers
Here's an eight-lane slide that sends you racing head first over exhilarating dips into a snowy slope.

Tips **River Runs Dry**

As this book goes to press, Disney's River Country water park remains closed for another season, and its future is uncertain. To check on its current status, call ℂ **407/824-4321** or visit **www.disneyworld.com**.

---

8 Other WDW Attractions

Note: All of the attractions mentioned in this section can be found on the "Walt Disney World Parks & Attractions" map on p. 167.

FANTASIA GARDENS & WINTER SUMMERLAND

Fantasia Gardens Miniature Golf ⋆⋆, located off Buena Vista Drive across from Disney–MGM Studios, offers two 18-hole miniature courses drawing inspiration from the Walt Disney classic cartoon of the same name. You'll find hippos, ostriches, and alligators on the **Fantasia Gardens** course, where the Sorcerer's Apprentice presides over the final hole. It's a good bet for beginners and kids. Seasoned minigolfers probably will prefer **Fantasia Fairways,** which is a scaled-down golf course complete with sand traps, water hazards, tricky putting greens, and holes ranging from 40 to 75 feet.

Santa Claus and his elves provide the theme for **Winter Summerland** ⋆⋆, which has two 18-hole miniature golf courses across from Blizzard Beach on Buena Vista Drive. The **Winter** course takes you from an ice castle to a snowman to the North Pole. The **Summer** course is pure Florida, from sandcastles to surfboards to a visit with Santa on the "Winternet."

Tickets at both venues are $9.76 for adults and $7.78 for children 3 to 9. Both are open from 10am to 10 or 11pm daily. For information about Fantasia Gardens, call ℂ **407/560-4582.** For information about Winter Summerland, call ℂ **407/560-3000.** You can find both on the Internet at **www.disneyworld.com**.

DISNEY'S WIDE WORLD OF SPORTS

This 200-acre complex has a 7,500-seat professional baseball stadium, 10 other baseball and softball fields, six basketball courts, 12 lighted tennis courts, a track-and-field complex, a golf driving range, and six sand volleyball courts. It's a haven for sports fans and wannabe athletes.

It's open daily from 10am to 5pm; the cost is $10 adults, $7.50 kids 3 to 9. Organized programs and events include:

- The **Multi-Sports Experience,** which challenges guests with a variety of activities, covering many sports: football, baseball, basketball, hockey, soccer, and volleyball. It's open on select days. *Note:* This replaced the NFL Experience in 2002.
- The **Atlanta Braves** play 16 spring-training games during a 1-month season that begins in early March. Tickets cost $12 to $19.75. For tickets call Ticketmaster (ℂ **407/839-3900**).
- The **NFL, NBA, NCAA, PGA,** and **Harlem Globetrotters** also host events, sometimes annually and sometimes more frequently, at the complex. Admission varies by event.

Disney's Wide World of Sports is located on Victory Way, just north of U.S. 192 (west of I-4; ℂ **407/939-1500;** www.disneyworld.com).

Finds DisneyQuest

The reaction that visitors have upon experiencing this popular attraction is often the same. No matter if it's from kids just reaching the video-game age, teens who are firmly hooked, or adults who never outgrew *Pong*, they leave saying: "Awesome!"

This five-level virtual-video arcade has everything from nearly old-fashioned pinball to virtual games and rides. Want appetizers?

Aladdin's Magic Carpet Ride puts you astride a motorcyclelike seat and flies through the 3-D Cave of Wonders. **Invasion: An Extraterrestrial Alien Encounter** has the same kind of intensity. Your mission is to save colonists from intergalactic bad guys. One player flies the virtual module while others fire weapons.

Pirates of the Caribbean: Battle for Buccaneer Gold puts you and three mates in 3-D helmets so that you can battle pirate ships virtual-reality style. One plays captain, steering your ship, while the others assume positions behind cannons to blast the black hearts into oblivion. Each time you do, you're rewarded with some doubloons, but beware of the sea monsters that can gobble you and your treasure. In the final moments, you come face to face with a ghost ship, which can send you to Davey Jones's Locker.

Songmaker has short lines, perhaps for a reason. It involves karaoke. Step into a phone booth–size recording studio to make your own CD and buy it for $10.

Try the **Mighty Ducks Pinball Slam** if you're a pinball fan. It's an interactive life-size game where you ride platforms and use body English to score points.

If you have an inventive mind, stop in the **Create Zone** 🎯🎯, where Bill Nye the Science-Turned-Roller-Coaster Guy helps you create the ultimate loop-and-dipster, which you can then ride in a simulator. It's a major hit with the coaster-crazy crowd.

Finally, if you need some quiet time, sign up at **Animation Academy** for a minicourse in Disney cartooning. There are also snack and food areas for those who need something more tangible than virtual refreshment.

The concept plays well here because the theme parks are a magnet for cash-laden tourists. But plans for DisneyQuests in 20 other cities fell flat. The only other one built, in Chicago, closed in 2001.

DisneyQuest (☎ **407/828-4600;** www.disneyquest.com) is located in Downtown Disney West Side on Buena Vista Drive. The admission ($31 for adults, $25 for kids 3 to 9; prices don't include 6% sales tax) allows you unlimited play from 11:30am to 11pm (until midnight Fri–Sat). Unfortunately, heavy crowds tend to gather here after 1pm, which can cut into your fun and patience.

RICHARD PETTY DRIVING EXPERIENCE

Test Track is for sissies. The **Richard Petty Driving Experience** at WDW gives you a chance to do the real thing in a 600-horsepower Winston Cup car. How real is it? Expect to sign a two-page waiver that features words like **DANGER-OUS** and **CALCULATED RISK** before you climb in. At one end of the spectrum, you can ride shotgun for a couple of laps at 145 mph ($89). At the other, spend from 3 hours to 2 days learning how to drive the car yourself and race fellow daredevils in 8 to 30 laps of excitement ($349–$1,249). *Note:* You must be 18 years old to do this. Hours and seasons vary. For reservations call ✆ **800/237-3889**; or head on the Web to **www.1800bepetty.com**.

8

Exploring Beyond Disney: Universal Orlando, SeaWorld & Other Attractions

Call it the Great Theme-Park War—the ongoing, "anything-you-can-do-we-can-do-better," knock-down-drag-out battle between the Magic Mickey and top-ranked challenger Universal Orlando, which each year since 1999 has chipped away at what once was WDW's virtual monopoly. Still, make no mistake: Disney is king, leading in theme parks (4–2) and smaller attractions (9–1). It has a 2-to-1 edge in nightclub venues, a huge lead in restaurants, and, when it comes to hotel rooms, its lead is probably insurmountable.

Nevertheless, Universal is trying. It had a substantial growth spurt in 1999, bolstering its original park, **Universal Studios Florida,** with a second theme park, **Islands of Adventure;** a nightclub and restaurant complex, **CityWalk;** and its first resort, **Portofino Bay,** a 750-room Loews hotel. In January 2001, it opened a second resort, the **Hard Rock Hotel,** and, in 2002, its third, the **Royal Pacific Resort.** Universal Orlando has more than 2,000 adjoining acres on which to expand, and, while the company's lips are sealed, it's known there are plans for at least two more hotels, a golf course, and possibly 300 acres of additional rides and attractions.

A few miles south, **SeaWorld** and its sister park, **Discovery Cove,** also grab a share of the Orlando action.

Aside from greater variety, these players mean more multiday packages and special deals for you. To compete with Disney, SeaWorld and Universal Orlando teamed up on multiday pass options a few years back. They offer a **FlexTicket** that also includes admission to **Wet 'n' Wild** (a Universal-owned water park) and **Busch Gardens** in Tampa. (Unfortunately for you, Universal, SeaWorld, and Busch Gardens also match Disney with single-day tickets that, without tax, cost more than $50 for adults and $40 for children 3–9.)

While the wars rage on in the traditional tourist areas, it has finally dawned on the rest of Orlando that central Florida is one of the world's favorite vacation destinations.

Since the early 1990s, downtown Orlando has gotten a makeover that woos hundreds of thousands to its attractions, nightclubs, and restaurants. Recent expansions at the Orlando Museum of Art and the Orlando Science Center show the city is trying to grab its share of the tourist pie. This expansion means visitors can enjoy the spoils: more variety, greater opportunities, and a world beyond the theme parks.

THE FLEXTICKET The most economical way to see the various "other-than-Disney" parks is with these passes, which counter Disney's

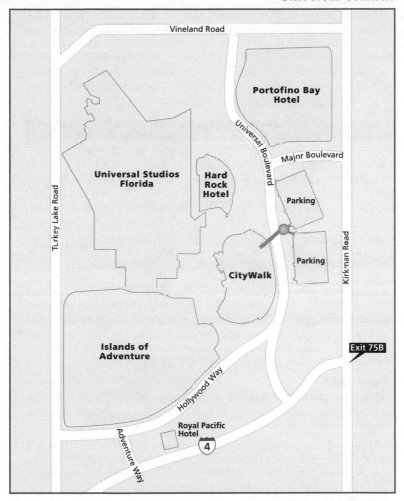

Park Hopper tickets. With the **FlexTicket,** you pay one price to visit any of the participating parks as many times as you want during a 14-day period. A four-park pass to Universal Studios Florida, Islands of Adventure, Wet 'n' Wild, and SeaWorld is $175.95 for adults and $142.95 for children 3 to 9. A five-park pass, which adds Busch Gardens in Tampa, is $209.95 for adults and $175.95 for kids. The **FlexTicket** can be ordered through Universal (© **800/ 711-0080** or 407/363-8000; www. universalorlando.com); SeaWorld

(© **407/351-3600;** www.seaworld. com); or Wet 'n' Wild (© **800/992- 9453** or 407/351-9453; www.wetn wild.com). *Note:* There's a round-trip shuttle available to Busch Gardens (p. 312) that's free for FlexTicket buyers (it's $5 for other guests).

UNIVERSAL EXPRESS This is Universal's answer to Disney's FAST-PASS. Universal Express has two tiers. Guests of the Portofino Bay, Hard Rock, and Royal Pacific hotels (see chapter 5, "Where to Stay") only need to show their room keys to get at or near the front of the line for most rides. Single-day and multiday ticket buyers who don't stay at a Universal resort can make one reservation at a time. Waits are usually 15 minutes or less. Guests can return for more when their reservations are used or expire (and like Disney get a second ticket 2 hr. after the first is issued). The system is available throughout the day. Call ✆ **800/711-0080,** 800/837-2273, or 407/363-8000, or go to **www. universalorlando.com** for more information.

1 Universal Studios Florida

Even with fast-paced grown-up rides based on blockbusters such as *Twister, Terminator,* and *Men in Black,* Universal Studios Florida is a ton of fun for kids. And, as an added plus, it's a working motion picture and TV production studio, so occasionally there's some live filming done at Nickelodeon's sound stages or elsewhere in the park. Even if there isn't a film or show in production, you can see reel history displayed in the form of some 40 actual sets exhibited along Hollywood Boulevard and Rodeo Drive. And there are plenty of action shows and rides including **Twister . . . Ride It Out, Earthquake—The Big One, Back to the Future, Jaws,** and **Terminator.**

While 2001 was quiet on the expansion front, 2002 saw Universal close three attractions with plans to replace them in 2003 with new ones: the Funtastic World of Hanna-Barbera gave way to **Jimmy Neutron's Nicktoon Blast,** Alfred Hitchcock—the Art of Making Movies stepped aside for **Shrek 4-D,** and Kongfrontation closed, to be replaced by a ride based on *The Mummy.* Universal also replaced some stale shows and characters with fresh ones (see, "Universal Has New Characters & Shows" on p. 243).

ESSENTIALS

GETTING TO UNIVERSAL BY CAR   Universal Orlando is a half-mile north of I-4 Exit 75B, Kirkman Road/Highway 435. There may be construction in the area, so follow the signs directing you to the parks.

PARKING   If you park in the multilevel garages, remember the theme and row in your area to help you find your car later. Or, do it the old-fashioned way: Write it down. Parking costs $8 for cars, light trucks, and vans. Valet parking is $14. Universal's garages are connected to its parks and have moving sidewalks, but it's still a long walk.

TICKET PRICES   A **1-day ticket** costs $51.95 (plus 6% sales tax) for adults, $42.95 for children 3 to 9. (That's $2 higher than a year ago, marking the third straight year tickets have been bumped $2.) A 2-day 2-park unlimited-access escape pass is $96.95 for adults, $83.95 for children 3 to 9; a 3-day 2-park pass is $111.95 for adults, $96.95 for children 3 to 9. All multiday passes let you move between Universal Studios Florida and Islands of Adventure. *Multiday passes also give you free access to the CityWalk clubs at night.* Because the parks are within walking distance of each other, you won't lose much time jockeying back and forth, which is not the case at Disney. Nevertheless, it's a long walk for tikes and people with limited mobility, so consider a stroller or wheelchair.

See the beginning of this chapter for information on the **FlexTicket,** which provides multiple-day admission to Universal Studios Florida, Islands of Adventure, SeaWorld, and Wet 'n' Wild.

There are also 5-hour **VIP tours** at Universal Studios Florida or Islands of Adventure, including line-cutting privileges, for $120 per person including

> ### ⌒ *Tips* Shorter Days
>
> Like Disney, Universal juggles park hours to combat the soft economy. The hours listed in this chapter are generally accurate, but sometimes the parks close earlier, or some rides or shows open later. To avoid disappointment, check the park's website at **www.universalorlando.com** or call ⓒ **800/711-0080** or 407/363-8000 for up-to-the-minute schedules.

admission. The passes provide a guided tour with priority entrance to at least eight attractions. For more information on the VIP tour, call ⓒ **800/711-0080.** They start at 10am and noon daily. If you plan on visiting during peak season, money isn't an issue, and you aren't staying at one of the Universal resorts, this is a good way to experience the best of the park without having to spend most of your day in lines.

HOURS   The park is open 365 days a year, usually at least from 9am to 6pm, though it's open as late as 8 or 9pm in summer and around holidays. The best bet is to call before you go so that you're not caught by surprise.

MAKING YOUR VISIT MORE ENJOYABLE
PLANNING YOUR VISIT
You can get information before you leave home by calling **Universal Orlando Guest Services** at ⓒ **800/711-0080,** 800/837-2273, or 407/363-8000. Ask about travel packages as well as theme-park information. Universal sometimes offers a promotion that adds a second-day free or at a deeply discounted price. You can also write to Guest Services, 1000 Universal Studios Plaza, Orlando, FL 32819-7601.

ONLINE   Find information about Universal Orlando at **www.universal orlando.com**. Orlando's daily newspaper, the *Orlando Sentinel,* also produces Orlando Sentinel Online at **www.orlandosentinel.com**. Additionally, there's a lot of information about the parks, hotels, restaurants, and more at the Orlando/Orange County Convention and Visitors Bureau site: **www.orlando info.com**.

INFORMATION FOR VISITORS WITH SPECIAL NEEDS
Guests with disabilities should go to **Guest Services,** located just inside the main entrance, for a *Disabled Guest Guidebook,* a Telecommunications Device for the Deaf (TDD), or other special assistance. You can rent a standard wheelchair for $8 or an electric one for $40 (both require a credit-card imprint, a driver's license, or $50 as a deposit). You can reserve them 24 hours or more in advance by calling ⓒ **407/224-6350.** You can arrange for sign language interpreting services at no charge by calling ⓒ **888/519-4899** (toll-free TDD), 407/224-4414 (local TDD), or 407/224-5929 (voice). Make arrangements for an appointment with an interpreter 1 to 2 weeks in advance.

PETS   You can board your small animals at the shelter located inside the parking garages for $5 a day (no overnight stays). Ask the attendant when you pay for parking to direct you to the kennel.

BEST TIME OF YEAR TO VISIT
As with Walt Disney World, there's really no off-season for Universal, but the week after Labor Day until mid December (excluding Thanksgiving week) and

Universal Studios Florida

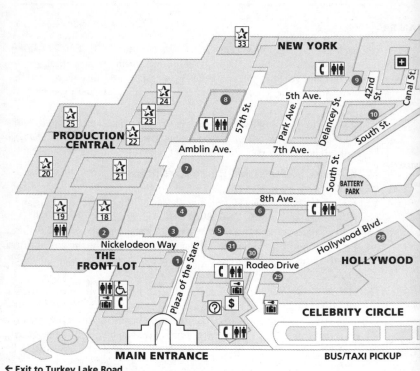

PRODUCTION CENTRAL
The Bates Motel Gift Shop **6**
The Boneyard **7**
Hanna-Barbera Store **4**
Jimmy Neutron's
  Nicktoon Blast **3**
Nickelodeon Studios **2**
Shrek 4-D **5**

NEW YORK
Blues Brothers **10**
Second Hand Rose **9**
Twister...Ride it Out **8**

THE FRONT LOT
Universal Studios Store **1**

HOLLYWOOD
The Universal Horror
  Make-Up Show **28**
Lucy, A Tribute **30**
Silver Screen Collectibles **31**
Terminator 2: 3-D Battle
  Across Time **29**

WORLD EXPO
Back to the Future: The Store **21**
Back to the Future: The Ride **18**
Men in Black Alien Attack **17**

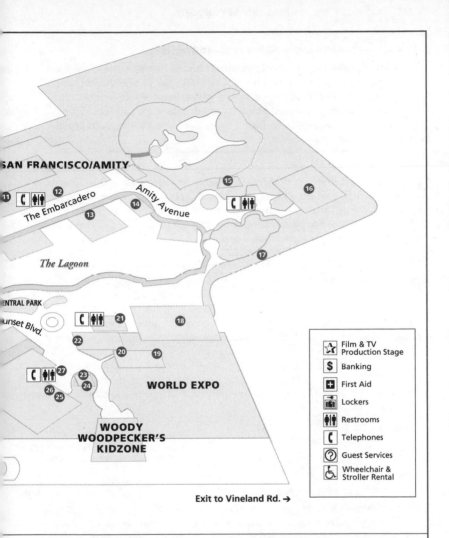

WOODY WOODPECKER'S KIDZONE

Animal Planet Live! **22**
The Barney Store **20**
Curious George Goes to Town **27**
A Day in the Park with Barney **19**
E.T. Adventure **25**
E.T.'s Toy Closet **26**
Fievel's Playland **23**
Woody Woodpecker's
   Nuthouse Coaster **24**

SAN FRANCISCO/AMITY

Beetlejuice's Rock 'n Roll
   Graveyard Revue **11**
Earthquake—The Big One **12**
Jaws **15**
Lombard's Seafood Grille **13**
Quint's Nautical Treasures **14**
Wild, Wild, Wild West
   Stunt Show **16**

(Moments Universal Has a Few 'Toons, Too

While the options pale in comparison to Disney, Universal has character meet-and-greets on a rotating basis. At **Universal Studios Florida,** you may run into Woody Woodpecker, SpongeBob SquarePants, Scooby Doo, Jimmy Neutron, and others. At **Islands of Adventure,** the cast may include Spider-Man, Popeye & Olive, Beetle Bailey, the Cat in the Hat, Betty Boop, or Boris & Natasha.

January to mid-May (excluding spring break) are known for smaller crowds, cooler weather, and less humid air. The summer months, when the masses throng to the parks, are the worst time for crowds and hot, sticky, humid days. During cooler months, you also won't have to worry about daily thunderstorms.

If you're planning a trip from mid-February to mid-April, keep in mind that a raucous Mardi Gras celebration goes on in the evenings (weekends only at first, but daily during the last 2 weeks). It's a very grown-up event with lots of alcohol flowing and a separate ticket price. It's really not suitable for younger children. The park is still open for all during the day, but it closes earlier than usual.

Some of the park's best rides are action-based thrill rides, which means your options are limited if you're pregnant, are prone to motion sickness, or have heart, neck, or back problems. The same applies to smaller children. Review the rides and restrictions on the following pages or when you enter the park so that you don't stand in line for something you're unable to enjoy. (There are stationary areas available at some moving rides. Check your park guide under "expectant mothers," as well as the boards in front of each ride, then ask the attendants for help as you enter.)

THE BEST DAYS TO VISIT

Go near the end of the week, on a Thursday or Friday. The pace is somewhat fast Monday through Wednesday, with the heaviest crowds on weekends and during summers and holidays.

CREATE AN ITINERARY

Pick three or four things that you must see or do and plan your day along a rough geographical guide. Universal Studios Florida is relatively small, so walking from one end of the park to the other isn't as daunting as it is in some of the Disney parks.

CHOOSE AGE-APPROPRIATE RIDES/SHOWS

Here, as in Walt Disney World, height and age restrictions aren't bent to accommodate a screaming child. Even where restrictions don't exist, some shows have loud music and pyrotechnics that can frighten kids. Check the attraction descriptions that follow to make sure your child won't be unduly disappointed or frightened.

SUGGESTED ITINERARIES

A Suggested Itinerary for Families with Young Children

Waste no time: Hoof it to Woody Woodpecker's KidZone, where you and your heirs can spend most of the day. If they're 36 inches or taller, don't miss multiple rides on **Woody Woodpecker's Nuthouse Coaster.**

Try to make an early pit stop at **Fievel's Playland** (especially its water slide, which is slow-moving and has longer lines after 10:30am). Then take a leisurely pace to see **E.T. Adventure, A Day in the Park with Barney,** and **Animal Planet Live!**

If you stick around long enough for lunch, get a hoagie or hot dog at **Animal Crackers** and don't leave before visiting the wet-and-wild **Curious George Goes to Town.** Round out the day with stops at the **Wild, Wild, Wild West Stunt Show** and **Nickelodeon Studios.**

A Suggested Itinerary for Older Children, Teens & Adults

A single day is usually sufficient to see the park if you arrive early and keep a fairly brisk pace. Skip the city sidewalks of the main gate and **Terminator 2: 3-D Battle Across Time** until later. Go to the right and tackle **Men in Black Alien Attack** and **Back to the Future . . .**

The Ride. Then make a counter-clockwise loop, visiting **Jaws, Earthquake—The Big One,** and **Twister . . . Ride It Out.** Break for lunch somewhere in that quartet, then watch the **Wild, Wild, Wild West Stunt Show,** tackle the 'toons in the new **Jimmy Neutron's Nicktoon Blast** and the **Shrek 4-D** adventure, then catch the fun in **Terminator 2: 3-D Battle Across Time.** If your kids are young enough to appreciate the TV channel, catch the 45-minute **Nickelodeon Studios** tour and show (4- to 14-year-olds love it).

A second day lets you revisit some of your favorites or see those you missed. With the pressure to hit all the major rides lessened, you can delay your **Nickelodeon Studios** visit until day 2 (the first tour usually isn't until 10:30am or so). You can also visit the **Universal Horror Makeup Show** and **Beetlejuice's Rock 'n Roll Graveyard Revue.**

SERVICES & FACILITIES IN UNIVERSAL STUDIOS FLORIDA

ATMs Machines accepting cards from banks using the Cirrus, Honor, and Plus systems are to the right of the main entrance (outside and inside the park) and in San Francisco/Amity near Lombard's Landing restaurant.

Baby Care Changing tables are in men's and women's restrooms; there are nursing facilities at Family Services, just inside the main entrance and to the right. Diapers aren't sold on the premises.

⌒Tips Universal Has New Characters & Shows

Universal Studios Florida has replaced some of its old (read—stale, if you've been there a few times) street characters and shows in favor of new ones. The fresh lineup includes: **Extreme Ghostbusters: The Great Fright Way,** a revised show that has Beetlejuice and The Ghostbusters singing and dancing to hits from the '60s through the '90s; **Lucy and Ricky,** in which Lucy pulls guests into an impromptu conga line; **Sarita and Rico,** two Latin characters who get guests singing and dancing to high-energy tunes such as "Hot, Hot, Hot" and "Mambo #5"; and the **Men in Black** show, in which the agents know there are a lot of aliens in the park, and they must put unsuspecting guests through a humorous screening test. *Note:* Characters rotate or appear seasonally.

Cameras & Film   Film and disposable cameras are available at the On Location shop in the Front Lot, just inside the main entrance. One-hour photo developing is available, though we don't recommend paying park prices.

Car Assistance   Battery jumps are provided. If you need assistance with your car, raise the hood and use the call boxes located throughout the garage to call for security.

First Aid   The First Aid Center is located between New York and San Francisco, next to Louie's Italian Restaurant on Canal Street. There's also one just inside the main entrance next to Guest Services.

Lockers   Lockers are across from Guest Services near the main entrance and cost $6 and $9 a day, plus a $2 refundable deposit.

Lost Children   If you lose a child, go to Guest Services near the main entrance or contact any park employee for assistance. Children under 7 should wear nametags.

Pet Care   A kennel is available ($5 a day) near the newest parking lot. Ask the parking attendant for directions upon entering the toll plaza. Overnight boarding is not permitted.

Stroller Rental   Strollers can be rented in Amity and at Guest Services just inside the entrance to the right. The cost is $9 for a single, $15 for a double.

Wheelchair Rental   Regular wheelchairs can be rented for $8 in Amity and at Guest Services just inside the main gate. Electric wheelchairs are $40. Both require a credit-card imprint, driver's license, or $50 as a deposit.

MAJOR ATTRACTIONS AT UNIVERSAL STUDIOS FLORIDA

Rides and attractions have cutting-edge technology such as OMNIMAX 70mm film projected on 7-story screens to create terrific special effects. While waiting in line, you'll be entertained by excellent preshows—better than those at the Disney parks. Universal, as a whole, takes itself less seriously than the Mouse That Roared, and the atmosphere is peppered by subtle reminders that in the competitive theme-park industry, it's not a small world after all.

Animal Planet Live!
Frommer's Rating: B
Recommended Ages: All ages
Get a behind-the-scenes look at the Animal Planet television network through a multimedia show that combines video with live actors. The stars can include Meesha the fox, Sniffles the raccoon, and Spooner the Australian shepherd.

Back to the Future . . . The Ride
Frommer's Rating: A
Recommended Ages: 8–adult
Blast through the space-time continuum in one of 24 flight simulators built to look like the movie's famous DeLorean. Along the way, you'll dive into blazing

---

⎛Value⎞ Money Saver

You can save 10% off your purchase at many Universal Orlando gift shops or eateries by showing your AAA (American Automobile Association) card. This discount isn't available at food and merchandise carts or on tobacco, candy, film, collectibles, and sundry items.

Frommer's Rates the Rides

As we do for the Disney parks in chapter 7, "Exploring Walt Disney World," we're using a grading system to score the Universal Orlando and SeaWorld rides in this chapter. (We'll return to the star-rating system toward the end of the chapter, when we explore some of Orlando's smaller attractions.) Most of the grades below are *A*s, *B*s, and *C*s. That's because the major parks' designers have done a pretty good job on the attractions. But you'll also find a few *D*s for Duds. Here's what the Frommer's ratings mean:

A+	=	Your trip wouldn't be complete without it.
A	=	Put it at the top of your "to-do" list.
B+	=	Make a real effort to see or do it.
B	=	It's fun but not a "must see."
C+	=	A nice diversion; see it if you have time.
C	–	Go if it appeals to you but not if there's a wait.
D	=	Don't waste your time.

volcanic tunnels, collide with Ice Age glaciers, thunder through caves and canyons, and briefly get swallowed by a dinosaur in an eye-crossing multi-sensory adventure. You twist, you turn, you dip, you dive—all the while feeling like you're really flying. Sit in one of the car's back seats to avoid ruining the illusion (in the front seat you can lean forward and see your neighbors careening hydraulically in the next bay). This is similar to, *but more intense than,* the Body Wars ride at Epcot (p. 203). It's bumpy and might not be a good idea if you're prone to dizziness or motion sickness. *Note:* Heed the health warnings displayed at the ride, which has a 40-inch height minimum. Also, Universal recommends that expectant mothers skip this ride.

Beetlejuice's Rock 'n Roll Graveyard Revue
Frommer's Rating: B for classic rock fans, C for others
Recommended Ages: 10–adult
Universal, in 2002, added some new steps and tunes to this rock musical that stars Dracula, Wolfman, the Phantom of the Opera, Frankenstein and his bride, and Beetlejuice. The fun includes pyrotechnic special effects, some adult jokes, and MTV-style choreography. It's loud and lively enough to scare some small children and frazzle some older adults. It carries Universal's PG-13 rating, meaning it may not be suitable for preteens.

A Day in the Park with Barney
Frommer's Rating: A+ for tiny tots and parents, D for almost everyone else
Recommended Ages: 2–6
Set in a park-like theater-in-the-round, this 25-minute musical stars the Purple One, Baby Bop, and BJ. It uses song, dance, and interactive play to deliver an environmental message. This could be the highlight of the day for preschoolers (parents can console themselves with their kids' happiness). The playground adjacent to the theater has chimes to ring, tree houses to explore, and lots to intrigue wee ones. The theater is air-conditioned, but even in the hottest months that's not enough to entice us to spend another instant around Barney.

Earthquake—The Big One

Frommer's Rating: B+

Recommended Ages: 6–adult

You climb on a BART train in San Francisco for a peaceful subway ride, but just as you pull into the Embarcadero Station, there's an earthquake—a big one, 8.3 on the Richter scale! As you sit helplessly trapped, slabs of concrete collapse around you, a propane truck bursts into flames, a runaway train hurtles your way, and the station floods (65,000 gallons of water cascade down the steps). *Note:* Universal says expectant moms should skip this one.

E.T. Adventure

Frommer's Rating: B+ for preteens and their families

Recommended Ages: All ages

You'll soar with E.T. on a mission to save his ailing planet, through the forest and into space aboard a bicycle. You'll also meet some characters created by Steven Spielberg for the ride, including Botanicus, Tickli Moot Moot, Horn Flowers, and Tympani Tremblies. This family favorite is definitely a charmer. If there is a knock, it's that there are two waiting areas—inside and outside. And wait you will.

Jaws

Frommer's Rating: B+

Recommended Ages: 6–adult

As your boat heads into the 7-acre, 5-million-gallon lagoon, a dorsal fin appears on the surface. Then, what goes with the fin—a 3-ton, 32-foot, mechanical great white shark—tries to sink its urethane teeth into your hide (or at least your boat's). A 30-foot wall of flame that surrounds the vessel truly causes you to feel the heat in this $45 million attraction. We won't tell you exactly how it ends, but in spite of a captain who can't hit the broad side of a dock with his grenade launcher, some lucky Orlando restaurant will be serving blackened shark tonight. (*Tip:* The effects of this ride are far more spectacular after dark.) *Note:* While it lacks a height requirement, the shark may be too intense for some kids younger than 6, and Universal recommends that expectant mothers avoid it.

Jimmy Neutron's Nicktoon Blast

Frommer's Rating: A

Recommended Ages: 6–adult

Buckle up for one of the park's two new rides. In this one, you climb aboard Jimmy's Rocket Pod, which hurtles you through hyperspace thanks to a motion simulator, sophisticated computer graphics, state-of-the-art ride technology, animation, and programmable motion-based seats. Your task: Defeat the evil Yokians—egg-shaped aliens bent on taking over our world if you lose. The attraction also features Jimmy's robot dog, Goddard, his nemesis, Cindy Vortex, and popular characters from several other cartoons, including SpongeBob SquarePants, Rugrats, Wild Thornberrys, and Fairly Odd Parents. This attraction replaced the Funtastic World of Hanna-Barbera.

Men in Black Alien Attack

Frommer's Rating: A+

Recommended Ages: 8–adult

Armageddon may be upon us unless you and your mates fly to the rescue and destroy the alien menace. Once on board your six-passenger cruiser, you'll buzz the streets of New York, using your "zapper" to splatter up to 120 bug-eyed targets. You have to contend with return fire and distractions such as light, noise, and clouds of liquid nitrogen (aka fog), any of which can spin you out of control.

Tips   Goodbye Kong, Hello Mummy

Kongfrontation was part of Universal Studios Florida when it opened in 1990, but the ride closed in September 2002 and will be replaced in spring 2004 with **Revenge of the Mummy.** The new $40-million indoor roller coaster will rely on speed, pyrotechnics, and robotics for its thrill factors as riders hurtle through Egyptian sets, passageways, and tombs in cars that move forward and in reverse. The 5-minute journey includes encounters with overhead flames and a skeletal warrior that hops aboard your coaster.

Your laser tag–style gun fires infrared bullets. Earn a bonus by hitting Frank the Pug (to the right, just past the alien shipwreck). The 4-minute ride relies on 360-degree spins rather than speed for its thrill factor. At the conclusion, you're swallowed by a giant roach (it's 30 ft. tall with 8-ft. fangs and 20-ft. claws) that explodes, dousing you with bug guts—okay, it's just warm water—as you blast your way to safety and into the pest-control hall of fame—maybe. When you exit, Will Smith rates you anywhere from galaxy defender to bug bait. (There are 38 possible scores; those assigned to less than full cars suffer the scoring consequences.) Guests must be at least 42 inches tall to climb aboard this $70 million ride.

Note: Men in Black often has a *much* shorter line for single riders. Even if you're not alone but are willing to be split up, get in this line and hop right on a vehicle that has less than six passengers.

Nickelodeon Studios
Frommer's Rating: A for Nick fans, C+ for others
Recommended Ages: 4–14
You'll tour the sound stages where Nick shows are produced, view concept pilots, visit the kitchen where Gak and green slime are made, and try new Sega video games. This 45-minute behind-the-scenes walking tour is a fun escape from the hustle of the midway and there's lots of audience participation. A child volunteer gets slimed, but it's only dessert-food slime, so even if yours is the lucky victim and swallows, green applesauce is as bad as it gets.

Shrek 4-D
Frommer's Rating: B+
Recommended Ages: All ages
Universal Studios' other new ride is a 20-minute show that can be seen, heard, felt, and smelled thanks to film, motion simulators, OgreVision glasses, and other special effects, such as water spritzers. The attraction picks up where the movie left off—allowing you to join Shrek and Princess Fiona on their honeymoon (at least the G-rated portions of it). Once settled in specially designed seats in the main auditorium, you're transported to the fairy-tale realm of Duloc, as the screen comes alive. The theater's seats are pneumatic air propulsion nodules that are capable of turning and tilting. The pre-ride features the ghostly return of the vertically challenged Lord Farquaad.

Terminator 2: 3-D Battle Across Time
Frommer's Rating: A+
Recommended Ages: 10–adult
This is billed as "the quintessential sight and sound experience for the 21st century!" The same director who made the movie, Jim Cameron, supervised this

$60 million production. After a slow start, it builds into an impressive experience featuring the Big Man (on film), along with other original cast members. It combines 70mm 3-D film (utilizing three 23-x-50-foot screens) with thrilling technical effects and live stage action that includes a custom-built Harley Davidson "Fat Boy" and six 8-foot-tall cyberbots. *Note:* The crisp 3-D effects are among the best in any Orlando park, but Universal has given this show a PG-13 rating, meaning the violence and loud noise may be too intense for preteens. That may be a little too cautious, but some kids under 10 may be frightened.

Twister . . . Ride It Out
Frommer's Rating: A
Recommended Ages: 8–adult
Visitors from the twister-prone Midwest may find this re-creation a little too close to the real thing. An ominous funnel cloud, 5 stories tall, is created by swirling 2 million cubic feet of air per minute (that's enough to fill four full-size blimps), and the sound of a freight train fills the theater at rock-concert level as cars, trucks, and a cow fly about while the audience stands just 20 feet away. It's the windy version of *Earthquake* and packs quite a wallop. Crowds have been known to applaud when it's over. *Note:* This show, too, comes with a PG-13 rating. Its loudness and intensity certainly can be too much for children under 8. Also, readers who have visited Universal Studios Hollywood in California will find Twister similar in theme to that park's Backdraft attraction, although (sacrilege!) we think the one in California offers a better overall experience.

Wild, Wild, Wild West Stunt Show
Frommer's Rating: B
Recommended Ages: All ages
Stunt people demonstrate falls from 3-story balconies, gun and bullwhip fights, dynamite explosions, and other Wild West staples in this 18-minute show held at least three times a day. It's well performed, funny, and a big hit among foreign visitors who have celluloid visions of the American West. *Warning:* Heed the splash zone, or you will get very wet.

Woody Woodpecker's Nuthouse Coaster (Kids)
Frommer's Rating: A+ for kids and parents, B+ for others
Recommended Ages: 4–adult
This is the top attraction in Woody Woodpecker's KidZone, an 8-acre concession Universal Studios made a few years ago after being criticized for having too little for young visitors. This ride is a kiddie coaster that will thrill some moms and dads, too. While only 30 feet at its peak, it offers quick, spiraling turns while you sit in a miniature steam train. The ride lasts only 55 seconds and waits can be 30 minutes or more, but few kids will want to miss it. It's very much like the Barnstormer at Goofy's Wiseacre Farm in the Magic Kingdom (p. 186). *Note:* Its height minimum is 36 inches.

ADDITIONAL ATTRACTIONS
The **Boneyard** is an oft-changing area where you can see props used in a number of Universal movies.

The somewhat corny **Universal Horror Makeup Show** gives behind-the-scene looks at what goes into (and oozes out of) some of Hollywood's most frightening monsters (PG-13, shows from 11am). **Lucy, A Tribute** is a remembrance of America's queen of comedy, and the **Blues Brothers** launch their foot-stomping revue several times a day on Delancy Street.

Universal Cuisine

The best restaurants here are just outside the main gates at CityWalk, Universal's restaurant and nightclub venue. But there are more than a dozen places to eat inside the park. Here are our favorites:

Best Sit-Down Meal: Lombard's Seafood Grille has a hearty fried clam basket, as well as lobster, fish, steak, pasta, and burgers ($11–$30). It's located across from Earthquake.

Best Counter Service: Universal Studios' Classic Monsters Cafe is one of the newer park eateries. It serves salads, pizza, pasta, and rotisserie chicken ($6–$12). It's off 7th Avenue near the Boneyard.

Best Place for Hungry Families: Similar to a mall food court, the **International Food and Film Festival** offers a variety of food in one location. With options ranging from stir-fry to fajitas, it's a place where a family can split up and still eat under one roof. There are kid's meals for under $4 at most locations. The food is far from gourmet but a cut above regular fast food ($6–$11). It's located near the back of Animal Planet Live! and the entrance to Back to the Future.

Best Snack: The floats ($3–$5) at **Brody's Ice Cream Shop** are just the thing to refresh you on a hot summer afternoon. Brody's is located near the Wild, Wild, Wild West Stunt Show.

Back at Woody Woodpecker's KidZone, **Fievel's Playland** is a wet, western-themed playground with a house to climb and a water slide for small fry. **Curious George Goes to Town** has water- and ball-shooting cannons.

SHOPPING AT UNIVERSAL STUDIOS FLORIDA

Every major attraction has a theme store attached. Although the prices are high when you consider you're just buying a souvenir, the **Hard Rock Cafe** shop in adjacent CityWalk is extremely popular and has a small but diverse selection of Hard Rock everything (including memorabilia with astronomical sticker prices). If you've often longed for a pair of Fred Flintstone boxer shorts or some Scooby snacks, visit the **Hanna-Barbera Store.**

More than two dozen other shops in the park sell collectibles. Be warned, though, that unlike Walt Disney World, where Mickey is everywhere, Universal's shops are specific to individual attractions. If you see something you like, buy it. You probably won't find it in another store, although those at Orlando International Airport carry some items.

Note: Universal has a service similar to Disney's in which you can have your purchases delivered to the front of the park. Allow 3 hours.

GREAT BUYS AT UNIVERSAL STUDIOS FLORIDA

Here's a sampling of the more unusual gifts available at some of the Universal stores. Of course, in addition to these options, you can find the standard tourist fare with a staggering array of mugs, key chains, T-shirts, and the like. We've tried to include things you wouldn't find (or consider buying) anywhere else.

- **Back to the Future—The Store**   Real fans of the movie series will find lots of intriguing stuff here, but one of the more interesting items is a miniature version of a DeLorean.
- **Second Hand Rose**   There's a wide range of Coca-Cola memorabilia and a ton of sweet gifts inside this shop in the park's New York section.
- **E.T.'s Toy Closet and Photo Spot**   This is the place for plush stuffed animals including a replica of the alien namesake.
- **Hanna-Barbera Store**   Scooby Doo Slippers and Fred Flintstone T-shirts are great gifts for the young and young at heart.
- **Quint's Nautical Treasures**   This is the place to go for a different kind of T-shirt. Tropical colors, with subtle Universal logos, are the thing here.
- **Silver Screen Collectibles**   Fans of *I Love Lucy* will adore the small variety of collectible dolls. There's also a Betty Boop line. For an interesting, practical, and inexpensive little something to take home, check out the Woody Woodpecker back-scratcher.
- **Universal Studios Store**   This store, near the entrance, sells just about everything when it comes to Universal apparel.

2 Islands of Adventure

Universal's second theme park opened in 1999 with a vibrantly colored, cleverly themed collection of fast and sometimes furious rides. At 110 acres, it's the same size as its big brother, Universal Studios Florida, but it seems larger and it's definitely *the* Orlando park for thrill-ride junkies. Roller coasters roar above pedestrian walkways, and water rides slice through the park. The trade-off: There are few shows.

Expect total immersion in the park's various "islands." From the wobbly angles and Day-Glo colors in **Seuss Landing** to the lush foliage of **Jurassic Park,** Universal has done a good job of differentiating various sections of this $1 billion park (unlike Universal Studios Florida, where it's hard to tell if you're in San Francisco or New York). It's also done an outstanding job of differentiating Islands from Disney or any other Orlando park. The closest competitor in Florida is Busch Gardens in Tampa, but this attraction clearly has the edge on the ride front.

The adventure is spread across six islands: the **Port of Entry,** a pass-through zone that has a collection of shops and restaurants, and five themed areas— **Seuss Landing, The Lost Continent, Jurassic Park, Toon Lagoon,** and **Marvel Super Hero Island.** The park offers a concentration of thrill rides and coasters, plus it has generous play areas for kids.

ESSENTIALS
GETTING TO UNIVERSAL BY CAR   Universal Orlando is a half-mile north of I-4 Exit 75B, Kirkman Road/Highway 435. There may be construction in the area, so follow the signs directing you to the park.

PARKING   If you park in the multilevel garage, make a note of the row and theme in your area to help you find your car later. Parking costs $8 for cars, light trucks, and vans. Valet parking is available for $14.

TICKET PRICES   A **1-day ticket** costs $51.95 (plus 6% sales tax) for adults, $42.95 for children 3 to 9. (That's $2 higher than a year ago, marking the third straight year tickets have been bumped $2.) A 2-day 2-park unlimited-access escape pass is $96.95 for adults, $83.95 for children 3 to 9; a 3-day 2-park pass is $111.95 for adults, $96.95 for children 3 to 9. All multiday passes let you move between Universal Studios Florida and Islands of Adventure. *Multiday*

Islands of Adventure

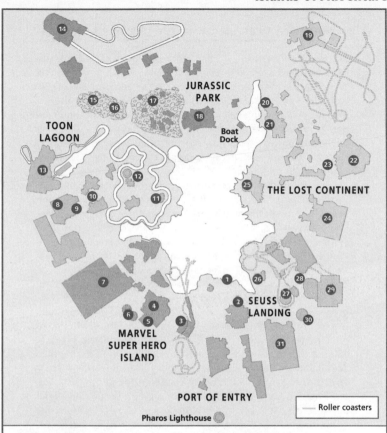

JURASSIC PARK

TOON LAGOON

Boat Dock

THE LOST CONTINENT

SEUSS LANDING

MARVEL SUPER HERO ISLAND

PORT OF ENTRY

Pharos Lighthouse

Roller coasters

PORT OF ENTRY
Island Skipper Tours **1**
Confisco Grille **2**

MARVEL SUPER HERO ISLAND
Incredible Hulk Coaster **3**
Cafe 4 **4**
Storm Force Accelatron **5**
Doctor Doom's Fearfall **6**
The Amazing Adventures of Spider-Man **7**

TOON LAGOON
Comic Strip Café **8**
Toon Lagoon Beach Bash **9**
Comic Strip Lane **10**
Popeye & Bluto's Bilge-Rat Barges **12**
Me Ship, The Olive **11**
Dudley Do-Right's Ripsaw Falls **13**

JURASSIC PARK
Jurassic Park River Adventure **14**
Camp Jurassic **15**

Pteranodon Flyers **16**
Triceratops Discovery Trail **17**
Jurassic Park Discovery Center **18**

THE LOST CONTINENT
Dueling Dragons **19**
Flying Unicorn **20**
The Eighth Voyage of Sindbad **22**
Enchanted Oak Tavern
  (and Alchemy Bar) **21**
Mystic Fountain **23**
Poseidon's Fury **24**
Mythos Restaurant **25**

SEUSS LANDING
Green Eggs and Ham Cafe **26**
Caro-Seuss-El **27**
If I Ran the Zoo **28**
Circus McGurkus Cafe Stoo-pendous **29**
One Fish, Two Fish, Red Fish, Blue Fish **30**
The Cat in the Hat **31**

Tips **Some Practical Advice for Island Adventurers**

1. **The Shorter They Are . . .**   Nine of the 14 major rides at Islands of Adventure have height restrictions. Dueling Dragons and the Incredible Hulk Coaster, for instance, deny access to anyone under 54 inches. For those who want to ride but come with kids, there's a baby or child swap at all of the major attractions, allowing one parent to ride while the other watches the tikes. But sitting in a waiting room isn't much fun for the little ones. So take your child's height into consideration before coming to the park or at least some of the islands.

2. **Cruising the Islands**   If you hauled your stroller with you on your vacation, bring it with you to the park. It's a very long walk from your car, through the massive parking garage and the nighttime entertainment district, CityWalk, before you get to the fun. Carrying a young child and the accompanying paraphernalia, even with a series of moving sidewalks, can make the long trek seem even longer—especially at the end of the day.

3. **The Faint of Heart**   Even if you don't have children, make sure you consider all of the ride restrictions. Expectant mothers, guests prone to motion sickness, and those with heart, neck, or back trouble will be discouraged—with good reason—from riding most primo attractions. There's still plenty to see and do, but without the roller coasters, Islands of Adventure isn't so special.

4. **Beat the Heat**   Several rides require that you wait outside without any cover to protect you from the sizzling Florida sun, so bring some bottled water with you for the long waits (a 50¢ free-world bottle costs $2.50 if you buy it here) or take a sip or two from the fountains placed in the waiting areas. Also, beer, wine, and liquor are more available at the Universal parks than the Disney ones, but booze, roller coasters, and hot weather can make for a messy mix.

5. **Cash in on Your Card**   You can save 10% on your purchases at any gift shop or on a meal at Islands of Adventure by showing your AAA (American Automobile Association) card. This discount isn't available at food or merchandise carts. And tobacco, candy, film, collectibles, and sundry items aren't included.

passes also give you free access to the CityWalk clubs at night. Because the parks are within walking distance of each other, you won't lose much time jockeying back and forth, contrary to the situation at Disney. Nevertheless, it's a long walk for tikes and people with limited mobility, so consider a stroller or wheelchair.

See the beginning of this chapter for information on the **FlexTicket,** which provides multiple-day admission to Universal Studios Florida, Islands of Adventure, SeaWorld, and Wet 'n' Wild.

There are also 5-hour **VIP tours** at Universal Studios Florida or Islands of Adventure, including line-cutting privileges, for $120 per person including admission. The passes provide a guided tour with priority entrance to at least eight attractions. For more information on the VIP tour, call ⟮ **800/711-0080.**

They start at 10am and noon daily. If you plan on visiting during peak season, money isn't an issue, and you aren't staying at one of the Universal resorts, this is a good way to experience the best of the park without having to spend most of your day in a line.

HOURS The park is open 365 days a year, generally from 9am to 6pm, though often later, especially in summer and around holidays, when it's sometimes open until 9pm. Also, during Halloween Horror Nights, the park closes around 5pm, reopens at 7pm (with a new admission), and remains open until at least midnight. The best bet is to call before you go so that you're not caught by surprise.

INFORMATION FOR VISITORS WITH SPECIAL NEEDS
Guests with disabilities should go to **Guest Services,** located just inside the main entrance, for a *Disabled Guest Guidebook,* a Telecommunications Device for the Deaf (TDD), or other special assistance. You can rent a standard wheelchair for $8 or an electric one for $40 (both require a credit-card imprint, a driver's license, or $50 as a deposit). You can reserve them 24 hours or more in advance by calling ✆ **407/224-6350.** You can arrange for sign language interpreting services at no charge by calling ✆ **888/519-4899** (toll-free TDD), 407/224-4414 (local TDD), or 407/224-5929 (voice). Make arrangements for an appointment with an interpreter 1 to 2 weeks in advance.

PLANNING YOUR VISIT
You can get information before you leave by calling ✆ **800/711-0080,** 800/837-2273, or 407/363-8000. Ask for information about travel packages, as well as theme-park information. Universal sometimes offers a second day's ticket free or at a deeply discounted price. You can also write to Guest Services, 1000 Universal Studios Plaza, Orlando, FL 32819-7601.

ONLINE Find information about Universal at **www.universalorlando.com.** Orlando's daily newspaper, the *Orlando Sentinel,* also produces Orlando Sentinel Online at **www.orlandosentinel.com.** Additionally, there's a lot of information about the parks, hotels, restaurants, and more at the Orlando/Orange County Convention & Visitors Bureau's website, **www.orlandoinfo.com.**

THE BEST DAYS TO VISIT
Like Universal Studios Florida, it's best to visit Islands near the end of the week, on a Thursday or Friday. The pace is somewhat fast Monday to Wednesday, with the heaviest crowds on weekends and during summer and holidays.

SERVICES & FACILITIES AT ISLANDS OF ADVENTURE
ATMs Machines accepting cards from banks using the Cirrus, Honor, and Plus systems are located outside and to the right of the main entrance and in the Lost Continent near the bridge to Jurassic Park.

Baby Care There are baby-swap stations at all of the major attractions. This allows one parent to wait while the other rides. Nursing facilities are located in the Guest Services building in the Port of Entry. Look for Family Services.

Cameras & Film Film and disposable cameras are available at De Foto's Expedition Photography, to the right just inside the main entrance.

Car Assistance Battery jumps are provided. If you need assistance with your car, raise the hood and use the call boxes located throughout the garage to call for security.

First Aid   There's one just inside and to the right of the main entrance and another in the Lost Continent, across from Oasis Coolers.

Lockers   Lockers are across from Guest Services near the main entrance and cost $6 and $9 a day, plus a $2 refundable deposit. There are also lockers near the Incredible Hulk Coaster in Marvel Super Hero Island, the Jurassic Park River Adventure in Jurassic Park, and Dueling Dragons in the Lost Continent. The lockers at Dueling Dragons and the Incredible Hulk Coaster are free for the first 45 minutes. Thereafter or at the Jurassic Park River Adventure, they're $2 per hour to a maximum of $14 per day. You're not supposed to—and shouldn't—take things on these rides, so put them in a locker or give them to a nonrider.

Lost Children   If you lose a child, go to Guest Services near the main entrance or go to the first park employee you see. Children under 7 should wear nametags.

Pets   You can board your small animals at the shelter in the parking garages for $5 a day (no overnight stays). Ask the attendant where you pay for parking to direct you to the kennel.

Ride Restrictions   Many of the park's attractions have minimum height requirements (see the listings that follow). Universal also recommends that expectant mothers steer clear of some rides (also noted in the listings).

Stroller Rental   Look to the left as you enter through the turnstiles. The cost is $9 for a single, $15 for a double.

Wheelchair Rental   Regular wheelchairs can be rented for $8 in the center concourse of the parking garage or to your left as you enter the turnstiles of the main entrance. Electric wheelchairs are $40. Both require a credit-card imprint, driver's license, or $50 as a deposit.

SUGGESTED ITINERARIES

For Children & Families

If you have kids under 10, enter and go to the right to **Seuss Landing,** an island where everything is geared to the young and young at heart. You'll easily spend the morning or longer exploring real-life interpretations of the wacky, colorful world of Dr. Seuss. (The wild colors make for some good photographs.) Be sure to ride **The Cat in the Hat; One Fish, Two Fish, Red Fish, Blue Fish;** and **Caro-Seuss-El.** After all that waiting in line, let the little ones burn some energy playing in **If I Ran the Zoo.** Grab lunch at the **Green Eggs and Ham Cafe.** Next, head to the **Lost Continent** to ride the **Flying Unicorn** (36-in. height minimum) and talk to the **Mystic Fountain,** then let them play in **Camp Jurassic** or watch a "hatching" at the **Discovery Center** in **Jurassic Park.** They can have some more interactive fun in **Toon Lagoon** aboard **Me Ship, The Olive** and grab autographs at the **Toon Lagoon Beach Bash.** Those 40 inches or taller can end the day in **Marvel Super Hero Island** by riding the **Amazing Adventures of Spider-Man.**

For Teens & Adults

Head left from Port of Entry to **Marvel Super Hero Island** and ride the **Incredible Hulk Coaster, The Amazing Adventures of Spider-Man,** and **Doctor Doom's Fearfall.** (If you arrive early, the line will be short for your first choice, but you'll have to wait or use Universal Express for the others.) There should be time to squeeze in **Dudley Do-Right's Ripsaw Falls** in **Toon Lagoon** before you break for lunch at **Comic Strip Café** or **Blondie's: Home of the Dagwood.** Now that you're fully refueled, ride **Popeye & Bluto's Bilge-Rat Barges,** then move to **Jurassic Park,** where you can ride **Jurassic Park River Adventure** and visit the **Discovery Center.** End your day in the **Lost Continent,** where you can catch the show in **Poseidon's Fury,** then test your courage aboard **Dueling Dragons.**

PORT OF ENTRY

This "greeting card" to the park has five shops, four places to grab a bite, and **Island Skipper Tours,** which ferries passengers from the port to **Jurassic Park.** If you plan to save shopping for the end of the day, return to **Islands of Adventure Trading Company,** which offers a variety of merchandise linked to attractions throughout the park—from Jurassic T-shirts to stuffed Cat in the Hat dolls.

SEUSS LANDING

This 10-acre island, inspired by the works of the late Theodore Seuss Geisel, is awash in Day-Glo colors, whimsical architecture, and curved trees (the latter were downed and bent by Hurricane Andrew before the park acquired them). Needless to say, the main attractions here are aimed at the younger set, though anyone who loved the good Doctor as a child will enjoy some nostalgic fun on these rides. And those who aren't familiar with his work will enjoy the visuals— Seussian art is like Dalí for kids.

Caro-Seuss-El

Frommer's Rating: A+ for young kids, parents, and carousel lovers
Recommended Ages: All ages
Forget tradition. This not-so-average carousel gives you a chance to ride seven whimsical characters of Dr. Seuss (a total of 54 mounts), including cowfish, elephant birds, and mulligatawnies. They move up and down as well as in and out. Their eyes blink and heads bob as you twirl through the riot of color surrounding the ride. *Note:* A special ride platform lets guests in wheelchairs experience the up-and-down motion of the ride, making this a great stop for visitors with disabilities.

The Cat in the Hat

Frommer's Rating: A for preteens, C+ for teens and adults
Recommended Ages: All ages
Any Seuss fan will recognize the giant candy-striped hat looming over the entrance to this ride and probably the chaotic journey. Comparable to, but spunkier than, It's a Small World at WDW's Magic Kingdom, The Cat in the Hat is among the signature children's experiences at Islands of Adventure. Love or hate the idea, *do it* and earn your stripes. Your couch travels through 18 scenes retelling *The Cat in the Hat*'s tale of a day gone very much awry. You, meanwhile, spin about and meet Thing 1 and Thing 2 in addition to other characters. The highlight is a revolving 24-foot tunnel that alters your perceptions and leaves your head with a feeling oddly reminiscent of a hangover. *Note:* Pop-up

---

Tips Finding Your Way

Other-than-English park maps are available at Guest Services in the Port of Entry in French, German, Japanese, Portuguese, and Spanish.

characters may be scary for riders under 5, and expectant moms are discouraged from riding The Cat.

If I Ran the Zoo *Kids*
Frommer's Rating: A for the very young
Recommended Ages: 2–7
This 19-station interactive playland features flying water snakes and a chance to tickle the toes of a Seussian animal. Kids also can spin wheels, explore caves, fire water cannons, climb, slide, and otherwise burn off some excited energy.

One Fish, Two Fish, Red Fish, Blue Fish
Frommer's Rating: B+ for kids and parents
Recommended Ages: 2–7
This kiddie charmer is similar to the Dumbo and Magic Carpets rides at WDW's Magic Kingdom (including the ridiculously long line), although this one has a few added features. Your controls allow you to move your funky fish up or down 15 feet as you spin around on an arm attached to a hub. All the while, a song belts out rhyming flight instructions. Watch out for "squirt posts," which spray unsuspecting riders who don't follow the rhyme. Actually, even the most careful driver is likely to get wet.

MARVEL SUPER HERO ISLAND
Thrill junkies love the twisting, turning, stomach-churning rides on this island filled with building-tall murals of Marvel Super Heroes. Fans can **Meet the Marvel Super Heroes** in front of The Amazing Adventures of Spider-Man (check your guide map, handed out when you enter, or grab a copy at Guest Services, for times). And the munch crowd can dig into sandwiches and burgers at **Captain America's Diner** (in the $6–$9 range) and **Café 4** for pizza, pasta, and sandwiches ($4–$11).

The Amazing Adventures of Spider-Man *Finds*
Frommer's Rating: A+
Recommended Ages: 8–adult
The original Web Master stars in this exceptional show/ride (arguably, the best in town), which features 3-D action and special effects. The story line: You're on a tour of the *Daily Bugle* when—yikes!—something goes horribly wrong. Peter Parker suddenly encounters evil villains and becomes Spider-Man. This high-tech ride isn't stationary like the Back to the Future ride at Universal Studios Florida. Cars twist and spin, plunge and soar through a comic-book universe. Passengers wearing 3-D glasses squeal as computer-generated objects fly at their 12-person cars. There's a simulated 400-foot drop that feels an awful lot like the real thing. After the September 11, 2001, terrorist attacks, Universal removed pre-show video depicting lower Manhattan under attack by comic-book villains. *Note:* Expectant mothers or those with heart, neck, or back problems shouldn't ride. There's a 40-inch height minimum.

Tip: Waits can be 45 minutes even on an off-day, so use Universal Express if necessary. The ride also offers a single-rider line that can drastically reduce waiting times. So if it's an option on the day you're here and your party doesn't mind splitting up, take advantage of it.

Doctor Doom's Fearfall
Frommer's Rating: A
Recommended Ages: 8–adult
Look! Up in the sky! It's a bird, it's a plane . . . uh, it's you falling 150 feet, if you're courageous enough to climb aboard this towering metal skeleton. The screams

---

Fun Fact **Score One for the Park**

Music at Universal's Islands of Adventure was composed specifically for the theme park, much like a score for a movie. It's the first time such a large-scale musical effort has been mounted for a theme park.

---

that can be heard at the ride's entrance add to the anticipation of a big plunge followed by smaller ones. The plot? You're touring a lab when—are you sensing a recurring theme here?—something goes wrong as Doctor Doom tries to cure you of fear. You're fired to the top, with feet dangling, and dropped in intervals, feet first, leaving your stomach at several levels. The experience isn't quite up to the Tower of Terror's at Disney–MGM Studios, but it's still frightful (and you do get a neat view of the entire park). *Note:* Expectant mothers or those with heart, neck, or back problems shouldn't ride. Minimum height is 52 inches.

Incredible Hulk Coaster *(Finds*

Frommer's Rating: A+

Recommended Ages: 10–adult

Bruce Banner is working in his lab when—yes, again—something goes wrong. But this rocking rocket of a ride makes everything oh, so right, except maybe your heartbeat and stomach. From a dark tunnel, you burst into the sunlight, while accelerating from 0 to 40 mph in 2 seconds. While that's only two-thirds the speed of Disney–MGM's Rock 'n' Roller Coaster, this is in broad daylight, there's a lot more motion still to come, and you can *see* the asphalt! From there you spin upside down 128 feet from the ground, feel weightless, and careen through the center of the park over the heads of other visitors. Coaster-lovers will be pleased to know that this ride, which lasts 2 minutes and 15 seconds, includes seven inversions and two deep drops. Sunglasses, change, and an occasional set of car keys lie in a mesh net beneath the ride—proof of its motion and the fact that most folks don't heed the warnings to stash their stuff in the nearby lockers. As a nice touch, the 32-passenger metal coaster glows green at night (riders who ignore all the warnings occasionally turn green as well). *Note:* Expectant mothers or those with heart, neck, or back problems shouldn't ride it. Riders must be at least 54 inches tall.

Storm Force Accelatron

Frommer's Rating: C

Recommended Ages: 4–adult

Despite the exotic name, this ride is little more than a spin-off of the Magic Kingdom's Mad Tea Party—spinning teacups that, in this case, have a 22nd-century design. While aboard, you and the X-Men's superheroine, Storm, try to defeat the evil Magneto by converting human energy into electrical forces. To do that, you need to spin faster and faster. In addition to some upset stomachs, the spiraling creates a thunderstorm of sound and light that gives Storm all the power she needs to blast Magneto into the ever-after (or until the next riders arrive). This ride is sometimes closed during off-peak periods. *Note:* Expectant moms are advised not to ride this ride.

TOON LAGOON

More than 150 life-size sculpted cartoon images—characters range from Betty Boop and Flash Gordon to Bullwinkle and Cathy—let you know you've entered an island dedicated to your favorites from the Sunday funnies.

Dudley Do-Right's Ripsaw Falls
Frommer's Rating: A
Recommended Ages: 7–adult
The setting and effects at WDW's Splash Mountain are better, but the adrenaline rush here is higher. The staid red hat of the heroic Dudley can be deceiving: The ride that lies under it has a lot more speed and drop than onlookers suspect. Six-passenger logs (they're pretty uncomfortable, especially if you have long legs) take you around a 400,000-gallon lagoon before launching you into a 75-foot drop at 50 mph. At one point, you're 15 feet below the surface. Though the water is contained on either side of you, you *will* get wet. *Note:* Once again, expectant mothers or folks with heart, neck, or back problems should do something else. Riders must be at least 44 inches tall.

Me Ship, The Olive
Frommer's Rating: B+
Recommended Ages: 4–adult
This 3-story boat is a family-friendly playland with dozens of interactive activities from bow to stern. Kids can toot whistles, clang bells, or play the organ. Sweet Pea's Playpen is a favorite of younger guests. Kids 6 and up as well as adults will love Cargo Crane, where they can drench riders on Popeye & Bluto's Bilge-Rat Barges (see below). *Note:* The second and third deck of the good ship offer **great views and photo ops** of the Incredible Hulk Coaster and some of the rest of Islands of Adventure.

Popeye & Bluto's Bilge-Rat Barges
Frommer's Rating: A
Recommended Ages: 6–adult
This is the same kind of ride with the same kind of raft as Kali River Rapids at WDW's Animal Kingdom, but it's a bit faster and bouncier. You'll be squirted by mechanical devices as well as the water cannons fired by guests at Me Ship, The Olive (see above), and the water is *c-c-cold*, a blessing on hot summer days but less so in January. The 12-passenger rafts bump, churn, and dip (14 feet at one point) along a white-water course lined with Bluto, Sea Hag, and other villains. You will get *s-s-soaked*. Yes, once again, expectant mothers or people with heart, neck, or back problems shouldn't ride this one. Riders must be at least 42 inches tall.

Toon Lagoon Beach Bash
Frommer's Rating: C+
Recommended Ages: All ages
Beetle Bailey and other favorites from the Sunday comics will have you rockin' and rollin' in the streets as they sing and make you laugh during this several-times-a-day, surfing-safari-and-limbo show. It's one to skip if you're on a tight schedule, but it's a nice respite from the madness.

JURASSIC PARK
All of the basics and some of the high-tech wizardry from Steven Spielberg's wildly successful films are incorporated in this lushly landscaped tropical locale that includes a replica of the visitor's center from the movie. Expect long lines at the River Adventure and pleasant surprises at the Discovery Center.

Camp Jurassic *(Kids*
Frommer's Rating: A for young children
Recommended Ages: 2–7
This play area, similar in theme to the Boneyard in WDW's Animal Kingdom, has everything from lava pits with dinosaur bones to a rainforest. Watch out for

the spitters that lurk in dark caves. The multilevel play area has plenty of places for kids to crawl, explore, and spend energy. Young kids need close supervision, though. It's easy to get turned around inside the caverns.

Jurassic Park Discovery Center
Frommer's Rating: B
Recommended Ages: All ages

Here's an amusing, educational pit stop that has life-size dinosaur replicas and some interactive games, including a sequencer that pretends to combine your DNA with a dinosaur's. The "Beasaur" exhibit allows you to see and hear as the huge reptiles did. You can play the game show You Bet Jurassic (grin) and scan the walls for fossils. The highlight is watching a velociraptor "hatch" in the lab. Because there are a limited number of interactive stations, this can consume a lot of time on busy days.

Jurassic Park River Adventure
Frommer's Rating: A
Recommended Ages: 7–adult

After a leisurely raft tour along a faux river, some raptors escape and could hop aboard your boat at any moment. The ride lets you literally come face-to-face with "breathing" inhabitants of Jurassic Park. At one point, a *Tyrannosaurus Rex* decides you look like a tasty morsel, and at another point, spitters launch venomous saliva your way. The only way out: an 85-foot plunge in your log-style life raft. It's steep and quick enough to lift your fanny out of the seat. (When Spielberg rode it, he made them stop the ride and let him out before the plunge.) Expect to get wet. If your stomach can take only one flume ride, this one's a lot more comfortable than Dudley Do-Right (see earlier), and the atmosphere is better. *Note:* Expectant mothers or those with heart, neck, or back problems shouldn't ride. Guests must be at least 42 inches tall.

Pteranodon Flyers *Kids*
Frommer's Rating: B
Recommended Ages: All ages

The 10-foot metal frames and simple seats are flimsy, but this quick spin around Jurassic Park offers a great bird's-eye view. The landing is bumpy and you'll swing side to side throughout, which makes some riders queasy. Unlike the traditional gondolas in sky rides, on this one your feet hang free from the two-seat skeletal flyer, and there's little but a restraining belt between you and the ground. *Note:* That said, this is a child's ride—single passengers must be between 36 and 56 inches tall; adults can climb aboard *only* when accompanying someone that size. And, because this ride launches only two passengers every 30 to 40 seconds, it can consume an hour of your day, even in the off-season. So, although it is nice, pass it up if you're pressed for time.

Tips Up, Up, and Away

Strength and fitness folks can get a little extra workout at the small rock-climbing venue ($5 per person) outside the Thunder Falls Terrace restaurant in Jurassic Park. If you or the kids are looking for a more economical and less strenuous option, try walking the elevated trails and climbing the net ladders beneath the Pteranodon Flyers attraction, also in Jurassic Park.

(*Fun Fact* **Coaster Tidbit**

One Dueling Dragon coaster seems to have an obvious advantage over the other. The Fire Dragon can reach speeds up to 60 mph, while the Ice Dragon has a top end of only 55 mph.

Triceratops Discovery Trail
Frommer's Rating: C+
Recommended Ages: All ages
Meet a "living" dinosaur and learn from its "trainers" about the care and feeding of a 24-foot-long, 10-foot-high Triceratops. It responds to touch, and its movements include realistic blinks, breathing, and flinches. Children get a chance to touch this heavyweight dino as it turns its head and groans. *Note:* This is another exhibit that's often closed seasonally and worthy of a visit only if you're not in a hurry.

THE LOST CONTINENT

Although they've mixed their millennia—ancient Greece with a medieval forest—Universal has done a good job creating a foreboding mood in this section of the park, whose entrance is marked by menacing stone griffins.

Dueling Dragons *(Finds*
Frommer's Rating: A+
Recommended Ages: 10–adult
Maniacal minds created this thrill ride—sending two roller coasters right at each other at high speeds. True coaster crazies will love the intertwined set of leg-dangling racers that climb to 125 feet, invert five times, and three times come within 12 inches of each other as the two dragons battle and you prove your bravery by tagging along. A couple of thrill junkies (after riding this one for the third time in a day) revealed to us that this is where they head when they want the ultimate adrenaline rush. For the best ride, try to get one of the two outside seats in each of the eight rows. If you want to get into the front seat, there's a special (yes, longer!) line near the loading dock so that daredevils can claim the first car. *Note:* Expectant mothers or those with heart, neck, or back problems shouldn't ride. (Why aren't you surprised?) Riders must be at least 54 inches tall.

Eighth Voyage of Sindbad *(Overrated*
Frommer's Rating: C
Recommended Ages: 6–adult
The mythical sailor is the star of a stunt demonstration that takes place in a 1,700-seat theater decorated with blue stalagmites and eerie, gloomy shipwrecks. The show has water explosions and dozens of pyrotechnic effects including a 10-foot circle of flames. But it doesn't come close to the quality of the Indiana Jones stunt show in Disney–MGM Studios.

Flying Unicorn
Frommer's Rating: A+ for kids and parents, B+ for others, except coaster crazies, who may find it a D
Recommended Ages: 4–adult
The Flying Unicorn is a small roller coaster that travels through a mythical forest on the Lost Continent, next to Dueling Dragons. It's very much like Woody Woodpecker's Nuthouse Coaster at Universal Studios Florida (p. 248) and the Barnstormer at Goofy's Wiseacre Farm in the Magic Kingdom (p. 186). That

means a fast corkscrew run that is sure to earn squeals, but probably not at the risk of someone losing their lunch. *Note:* Here's another one expectant moms are warned not to ride. The Unicorn has a 36-inch height minimum.

Mystic Fountain
Frommer's Rating: B+ for kids
Recommended Ages: 3–8
Located just outside Sindbad's theater, this interactive "smart" fountain delights younger guests. It can see and hear, leading to a lot of kibitzing with those who stand before it. But if you want to stay dry, don't get too close when it starts "spouting" its wet wisdom. On the other hand, if you need a quick cool-off—go for it.

Poseidon's Fury
Frommer's Rating: B+
Recommended Ages: 6–adult
Clearly, this is the park's best show—though with a lack of competition, that's something of a back-handed compliment. The story line has changed a couple of times, but it still revolves around a battle between the evil Poseidon, god of the sea, and Zeus, king of the gods. Speaking of revolving, you'll pass through a small room that has a 42-foot vortex where 17,500 gallons of water swirl around you, barrel-roll style. (If you wear glasses, note that they will fog up completely when passing through the vortex—take them off if you can.) In the battle royale, the gods hurl 25-foot fireballs at each other. It's more interesting than frightening, but it's not worth the long lines that often plague it, so if you're on a tight schedule, use Universal Express or skip it. *Note:* The fireballs, explosive sounds, and rushing water may be a little too intense for children under 6.

SHOPPING AT ISLANDS OF ADVENTURE
There are more than 20 shops within the park, offering a variety of theme merchandise. You may want to check out **Cats, Hats & Things** and **Dr. Seuss' All**

Tips   Great Things to Buy at Islands of Adventure

Here's a sampling of some of the more unusual wares available at Islands of Adventure. It represents a cross section of tastes.

Jurassic Outfitters   There are plenty of T-shirts with slogans like "I Survived (the whatever ride)."

WossaMotta U   It's probably a good bet that no one at the office will have a Rocky or Bullwinkle ceramic mug, just one of the things you can pick up at this store in Toon Lagoon.

Spider-Man Shop   This stop specializes in its namesake's paraphernalia, including red Spidey caps covered with black webs and denim jackets with logos.

Toon Extra   Where else can you buy a miniature stuffed Mr. Peanut bean bag, an Olive Oyle and Popeye frame, or a stuffed Beetle Bailey? Life doesn't get any better for some of us.

Treasures of Poseidon   Located in the Lost Continent, it carries an array of blue glassware including tumblers, shot glasses, and oversize mugs as well as brass sculptures.

the Books You Can Read for special Seussian material. **Jurassic Outfitters** and **Dinostore** feature a variety of stuffed and plastic dinosaurs, plus safari-themed clothing. Superhero fans should check out **The Marvel Alterniverse Store** and the **Spider-Man Shop,** and the **Betty Boop Store** in Toon Lagoon is fun for her legions. **Islands of Adventure Trading Company** is a good stop on the way out if you're still searching for something that will help you or the folks back home remember your visit.

Note: Universal has a service similar to Disney's in which you can have your purchases delivered to the front of the park. Allow 3 hours.

DINING AT ISLANDS OF ADVENTURE

There are a number of stands where you can get a quick bite to eat, and a handful of full-service restaurants. The park's creators have taken some extra care to tie in restaurant offerings with the theme. The **Green Eggs and Ham Cafe** may be one of the few places on earth where you'd be willing to eat tinted huevos. (They sell as an egg-and-ham sandwich for about $6.) There are dozens of sit-down restaurants, eateries, and snack carts. To save money, look for the kiddie menus, offering a children's meal and a small beverage for $5. Also consider combo meals, which usually offer a slight price break. **Thunder Falls Terrace** in Jurassic Park, for instance, offers a rib-and-chicken combo as well as other options in the $8 to $12 range.

Here are some of our other favorites at Islands:

- **Best Sit-Down Restaurant** At **Mythos** in the Lost Continent, choose from occasionally changing selections such as jerk grouper, lobster-stuffed potato, pepper-painted salmon with lemon couscous, or pan-fried crab cakes with lobster sauce and basil. The atmospheric cavelike setting is pleasant. This is a grown-up dining affair, best suited for older children and adults. Entrees cost $10 to $21 and Mythos is usually open from 11:30am to 3:30pm daily.
- **Best Atmosphere for Adults** The **Enchanted Oak Tavern (and Alchemy Bar),** also in the Lost Continent, also has a cavelike interior, which from the outside looks like a mammoth tree, and is brightened by an azure blue skylight with a celestial theme. The tables and chairs are thick planks, and the servers are clad in "wench wear." Try the chicken/rib combo with waffle fries for $13. The menu offers 45 types of beer.
- **Best Atmosphere for Kids** The fun never stops under the big top at **Circus McGurkus Cafe Stoo-pendous** in Seuss Landing, where animated trapeze artists swing from the ceiling. Kids' meals, including a souvenir cup, are $6 to $7. The adult menu features fried chicken, lasagna, spaghetti, and pizza. Try the fried chicken platter for $8 or the lasagna for $7.
- **Best Vegetarian Fare** **Fire-Eater's Grill,** located in the Lost Continent, is a fast-food stand that offers a tasty veggie falafel for $6. You can also get a tossed salad for $3.
- **Best Diversity** **Comic Strip Café,** located in Toon Lagoon, is a four-in-one counter service–style eatery offering burgers, Chinese food, Mexican food, and pizza and pasta ($6–$8).

Fun Fact **Food for Thought**
Those green eggs get their color from a variety of spices, not food dye.

There are also several restaurants (see chapter 6, "Where to Dine") and clubs (see chapter 10, "Walt Disney World & Orlando After Dark") that are just a short walk from the park in Universal's entertainment complex, CityWalk.

3 SeaWorld

This popular 200-acre marine park explores the mysteries of the deep in a format that combines wildlife conservation awareness with plain old fun. While that's what Disney is attempting with its latest park, Animal Kingdom, the message here is subtle and a more inherent part of the experience.

SeaWorld's beautifully landscaped grounds center on a 17-acre lagoon and include flamingo and pelican ponds and a lush tropical rainforest. Shamu, a killer whale, is the star of the park along with his expanding family, which includes baby whales. The pace is much more laid-back than at either Universal or Disney, and it's a good way to break up a long week trudging through the other parks. Close encounters at feeding pools are among the real attractions (so be sure to budget a few extra dollars to buy fishy handouts for the sea lions and dolphins, which make begging an art form).

SeaWorld manages a few thrills and chills. **Journey to Atlantis** is a high-tech water ride similar to Splash Mountain at Disney's Magic Kingdom and Jurassic Park River Adventure at Universal Orlando's Islands of Adventure. And **Kraken** is a floorless roller coaster that sports seven inversions, much like coasters such as Montu and Kumba at SeaWorld's sister, Busch Gardens in Tampa (p. 312). But this park doesn't try to compete with the wonders of WDW or Universal. Instead it lets you discover the crushed-velvet texture of a stingray or the song of the seals.

ESSENTIALS

GETTING TO SEAWORLD BY CAR   The marine park is south of Orlando and Universal, north of Disney. From I-4, take Exit 72, Beeline Expressway/Highway 528, and follow the signs.

PARKING   Parking costs $7 for cars, light trucks, and vans. The lots aren't huge, and most folks can walk to the entrance. Trams also run. Note the location of your car. SeaWorld characters such as Wally Walrus mark sections, but at the end of a long day it's easy to forget where you parked.

TICKET PRICES   A **1-day ticket** costs $51.95 for ages 10 and over, $42.95 for children 3 to 9, plus 6% sales tax. (That's $2 higher than a year ago, marking the third straight year tickets have been bumped $2.) The park's new online ticketing allows you to go to its website, **www.seaworld.com**, buy your ticket over the Internet, then print it out and take the printout right to the turnstiles. *Note:* SeaWorld sometimes offers promotions for a second day free.

See the ticket information for Universal Orlando at the beginning of this chapter for information on the **FlexTicket,** multiday admission tickets for SeaWorld, Universal Orlando, Wet 'n' Wild, and Busch Gardens.

SeaWorld's **Adventure Express Tour** ($75 adults, $70 kids plus park admission) is a 6-hour guided excursion that includes front-of-the-line access to Journey to Atlantis, Kraken, and Wild Arctic; reserved seating at two animal shows; lunch; and a chance to touch or feed penguins, dolphins, stingrays, and sea lions (© **800/406-2244** or 407/363-2380). It's the only way to dodge park lines, which aren't as long as Disney's or Universal's.

HOURS   The park is usually open from 9am to 6pm and sometimes later, 365 days a year. Call © **800/327-2424** for more information.

Tips Shuttle Service

SeaWorld and Busch Gardens in Tampa, both owned by Anheuser-Busch, have a shuttle service that offers $5 round-trip tickets to get you from Orlando to Tampa and back. The 1½- to 2-hour one-way shuttle runs daily and has five pick-up locations in Orlando, including at Universal and on I-Drive (© 800/221-1339). The schedule allows about 7 hours at Busch Gardens. The service is free if you have a FlexTicket.

TIPS FOR MAKING YOUR VISIT MORE ENJOYABLE
PLAN YOUR VISIT
Get information before you leave by writing to **SeaWorld Guest Services** at 7007 SeaWorld Dr., Orlando, FL 32801, or call © **800/327-2424** or 407/351-3600.

ONLINE SeaWorld information is available at **www.seaworld.com**. The *Orlando Sentinel* newspaper produces *Orlando Sentinel Online* at **www.orlando sentinel.com**. You can get a ton of information from the Orlando/Orange County Convention & Visitors Bureau website, **www.orlandoinfo.com**.

INFORMATION FOR VISITORS WITH SPECIAL NEEDS
The park publishes a guide for guests with disabilities, although most of its attractions are easily accessible to those in wheelchairs. SeaWorld also provides a Braille guide for the visually impaired. For the hearing impaired, there's a very brief synopsis of shows. For information, write to Guest Services at the address above or call © **800/327-2424** or 407/351-3600.

BEST TIME OF YEAR TO VISIT
Because this is a mostly outdoor, water-related park, you may want to keep in mind that even Florida gets a tad nippy during January and February. SeaWorld has smaller crowds from January through April.

BEST DAYS TO VISIT
Weekends, Thursday, and Friday are busy days at this park. Monday through Wednesday are usually better days to visit because tourists coming for a week go to the Disney and Universal parks early in their stays, saving SeaWorld for the end, if at all.

CHOOSE AGE-APPROPRIATE ACTIVITIES
Because it has few thrill rides, SeaWorld has few restrictions, but you may want to check out the special tour programs offered through the education department. SeaWorld lives up to its reputation for making education fun. There are three 1-hour options: **Polar Expedition Tour** (touch a penguin), **Predators** (touch a shark), and **To the Rescue** (see manatees and sea turtles). All cost $10 for adults and $9 for children, plus park admission. Call © **800/406-2244** or 407/351-3600 for information.

BUDGET YOUR TIME
SeaWorld has a leisurely pace, because its biggest attractions are up-close encounters with the animals. Don't be in a rush. This park can easily be enjoyed in a day. Its layout and the many outdoor exhibits give it an open feel. Because of the large capacity and walk-through nature of many of the attractions, crowds generally aren't a concern except at Journey to Atlantis and Kraken. You also

SeaWorld

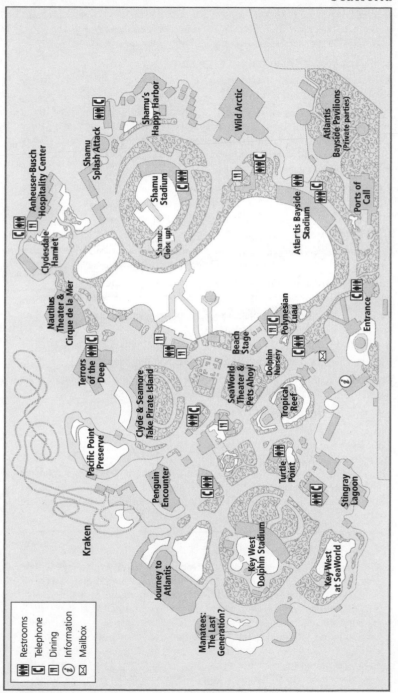

Restrooms
Telephone
Dining
Information
Mailbox

Anheuser-Busch Hospitality Center

Clydesdale Hamlet

Nautilus Theater & Cirque de la Mer

Terrors of the Deep

Clyde & Seamore Take Pirate Island

Pacific Point Preserve

Penguin Encounter

Kraken

Journey to Atlantis

Key West Dolphin Stadium

Key West at SeaWorld

Manatees: The Last Generation?

Shamu Splash Attack

Shamu's Happy Harbor

Shamu Stadium

Shamu: Close up!

Wild Arctic

Atlantis Bayside Pavilions (Private parties)

Ports of Call

Atlartis Bayside Stadium

Polynesian Luau

Beach Stage

SeaWorld Theater & Pets Ahoy!

Dolphin Nursery

Tropical Reef

Turtle Point

Stingray Lagoon

Entrance

need to be in Shamu Stadium in plenty of time for the show. Wild Arctic also draws a sizable crowd. But the lines here don't reach Disney's proportions, so relax. Isn't that what a vacation is supposed to be about?

SERVICES & FACILITIES AT SEAWORLD

ATMs   An ATM machine is located at the front of the park. It accepts Cirrus-, Honor-, and Plus-affiliated cards.

Baby Care   Changing tables are in or near most women's restrooms, and in the men's restroom at the front entrance near Shamu's Emporium. You can buy diapers in machines located near changing areas and at Shamu's Emporium. There's a special area for nursing mothers near the women's restroom at Friends of the Wild gift shop, near the center of the park.

Cameras & Film   Film and disposable cameras are available at stores throughout the park.

First Aid   First Aid Centers staffed with registered nurses are behind Stingray Lagoon and near Shamu's Happy Harbour.

Lockers   Lockers are located next to Shamu's Emporium, just inside the park entrance. The cost is $6 a day, plus a $2 deposit.

Lost Children   Lost children are taken to the Information Center. A parkwide paging system helps reunite guests. *Children under 7 should wear nametags.*

Pet Care   A kennel is available between the parking lot and the main gate. The cost is $6 a day (no overnight stays).

Strollers   Dolphin-shaped strollers can be rented at the Information Center near the entrance. The cost is $10 for a single, $16 for a double.

Wheelchair Rental   Regular wheelchairs are available at the Information Center for $8; electric chairs are $32, with a $25 deposit.

MAJOR ATTRACTIONS

Cirque de la Mer

Frommer's Rating: B

Recommended Ages: All ages

Other than the costumes, there's little aquatic about it, but the show's acrobats, mimes, dancers, musicians, and comics provide a show that's at times artistic and funny (and always entertaining). The sets and costumes focus on Peru's folklore

---

⎛Tips New Dining Programs

SeaWorld is diving deeper into the restaurant game with **Dine with Shamu** (© **800/327-2424** or 407/351-3600 for information and reservations), a reservations-only seafood buffet served poolside with Shamu as a special guest. While eating, guests can mingle and question SeaWorld trainers. The menu also includes chicken, beef, and salads. The cost is $28 for adults and $16 for kids 3 to 9, in addition to park admission. Reserving a spot 2 to 3 weeks in advance is usually more than enough unless you're coming in one of the crunch periods (summer, holidays). Last fall, the park also opened **Sharks Underwater Grill**, where diners can dig into Florida and Caribbean treats while watching denizens swim by in the Terrors of the Deep exhibit.

Tips **Ski No More**

In another sign of the economic cutbacks Central Florida attractions have made since the September 11, 2001, terrorist attacks, SeaWorld has closed its **Intensity Water Ski Show,** arguably the best ski show in the state.

and Incan past, and there's a small amount of audience participation during one of the mime routines.

Clyde & Seamore Take Pirate Island
Frommer's Rating: B+
Recommended Ages: All ages
A lovable sea lion and otter, with a supporting cast of walruses and harbor seals, appear in this fish-breath comedy with a swashbuckling conservation theme. It's corny, but don't hold it against the animal stars. With all those high-tech rides at the other parks, you need a break, and this one delivers some laughs.

Clydesdale Parades and Hitching Barn
Frommer's Rating: B (A for horse lovers)
Recommended Ages: All ages
Twice a day except Fridays, eight equine beefcakes allow themselves to be hitched to a rig for a parade through the park, beginning and ending at their barn area, where visitors can also watch the parade tack going on and off. In late winter and spring, you may get to see a mare and foal that aren't part of the team.

Journey to Atlantis
Frommer's Rating: A
Recommended Ages: 8–adult
Taking a cue from Disney Imagineers, SeaWorld has created a story line to go with this $30 million water coaster. It has to do with a Greek fisherman and ancient Sirens in a battle between good and evil. But what really matters is the drop—a wild plunge from an altitude of 60 feet, in addition to luge-like curves and a shorter drop. Journey to Atlantis breaks from SeaWorld's edu-tainment formula and offers good old-fashioned fun. There's no hidden lesson, just a splashy thrill when you least expect it. It's nearly as good as Jurassic Park River Adventure at Islands of Adventure (p. 259). *Note:* Riders must be at least 42 inches tall. Expectant moms, as well as folks with heart, neck, or back problems, should find some other way to pass the time.

Key West at SeaWorld
Frommer's Rating: B
Recommended Ages: All ages
This Caribbean-style village has island food, entertainers, and street vendors. But the big attractions are the hands-on encounters with harmless Southern diamond and cownose rays; Sea Turtle Point, the home of threatened and endangered species; and Dolphin Cove, where you can feed smelt to the namesakes. *Warning:* If you have a soft heart, it's easy to spend $20 feeding them.

Key West Dolphin Fest
Frommer's Rating: B
Recommended Ages: All ages
At the partially covered, open-air Key West Dolphin Stadium, Atlantic bottlenose dolphins perform flips and high jumps, twirl, swim on their backs, and

give rides to trainers. There's also an appearance by some false killer whales or *pseudocra crassidens* (see Whale Encounter, below, for a special experience). The tricks are impressive, but it's like any other dolphin show. If you go, see this before Shamu. He puts these little mammals to shame.

Kraken
Frommer's Rating: A+
Recommended Ages: 10–adult
SeaWorld's deepest venture onto the field of thrill-ride battle starts slow, like many coasters, but it ends with pure speed. Kraken is named for a massive, mythological, underwater beast kept caged by Poseidon. This 21st-century version offers floorless and open-sided 32-passenger trains that plant you on a pedestal high above the track. When the monster breaks loose, you climb 151 feet, fall 144 feet, hit speeds of 65 mph, go underground three times (spraying bystanders with water), and make seven loops during a 4,177-foot course. It may be the longest 3 minutes, 39 seconds of your life. *Note:* Kraken carries a 54-inch height minimum. Expectant moms, as well as folks with heart, neck, or back problems, should skip this one.

Manatees: The Last Generation?
Frommer's Rating: B+
Recommended Ages: All ages
Today, the West Indian manatee is an endangered species. There are as few as 3,200 remaining in the wild. Underwater viewing stations, innovative cinema techniques, and interactive displays combine here for a tribute to these gentle marine mammals. While this isn't as good as seeing them in the great outdoors, it's as close as most folks get, and it's a much roomier habitat than the tight quarters their kin have at the Living Seas in Epcot.

Penguin Encounter (Overrated)
Frommer's Rating: C
Recommended Ages: All ages
Sadly, this is a very superficial encounter that transports you aboard a 120-foot moving sidewalk through Arctic and Antarctic displays. On the other side of the Plexiglas, you'll get a glimpse of 200 or so polar penguins as they preen, socialize, and swim at bullet speed in their 22°F habitat. You'll also see puffins and murres in a similar, separate area.

Pets Ahoy!
Frommer's Rating: B
Recommended Ages: All ages
Eighteen cats, 12 dogs, three pot-bellied pigs, and a horse are joined by birds and rats to perform comic relief in a 25-minute show held several times a day. Almost all of the stars were rescued from animal shelters.

Tips VIP Privileges
SeaWorld's guided **Adventure Express** tour gets you front-of-the-line access to Kraken, Journey to Atlantis, and Wild Arctic plus reserved seating for shows, a personal introduction to a penguin, a chance to feed dolphins and sting rays, and lunch. It costs $75 for adults and $70 for kids 3 to 9 plus park admission (© **800/406-2244**).

Shamu Adventure *(Moments)*
Frommer's Rating: A+
Recommended Ages: All ages

Everyone comes to SeaWorld to see the big guy. The featured event is a well-choreographed show planned and carried out by very good trainers and very smart Orcas. The whales (reaching 25 ft. and 10,000 lb.) really dive into their work. The fun builds until the video monitor flashes an urgent Weather Watch and one of the trainers utters the fateful warning: "Uh-oh!" Hurricane Shamu is ready to make landfall. At this point, a lot of folks remember the warnings posted throughout the grandstand: *If you want to stay dry, don't sit in the first 14 rows.* Those who didn't pay attention get one last chance to flee. Then the Orcas race around the edge of the pool, creating huge waves of *icy* water and profoundly soaking anything in range. Veteran animal handler Jack Hanna also makes a video appearance on the huge overhead monitors, compliments of ShamuVision. *Note:* Arrive 30 minutes early for a good seat. The stadium is large, but it fills quickly.

Shamu: Close Up! is an adjoining exhibit that lets you get close to killer whales and learn about breeding programs. Don't miss the underwater viewing area. You may get to see a mother with her baby.

Shamu's Happy Harbor *(Kids)*
Frommer's Rating: A for kids
Recommended Ages: 3–12

This 3-acre play area has a 4-story net tower with a 35-foot crow's-nest lookout, water cannons, remote-controlled vehicles, nine slides, a submarine, and a water maze. It's one of the most extensive play areas at any park and a great place for kids to unwind. Bring extra clothes for the kids (and maybe for yourself, too) because it's not designed to keep you dry.

Terrors of the Deep
Frommer's Rating: B
Recommended Ages: 3–adult

Remember Shark Encounter? SeaWorld has added other species—about 220 specimens in all. Pools out front have small sharks and rays (feeding isn't allowed here). The interior aquariums have big eels, beautiful but poisonous lionfish, hauntingly still barracudas, and bug-eyed pufferfish. This isn't a tour for the claustrophobic because you have to walk through an acrylic tube, beneath hundreds of millions of gallons of water. Also, small fry may find the swimming sharks a little too much to handle. *Note:* Part of this exhibit has given way to a new restaurant, Sharks Underwater Grill.

Trainer for a Day
Frommer's Rating: A for trainer wannabes
Recommended Ages: 13–adult

Expect to invest a sizable chunk of your day and budget in this 8-hour program. You work side-by-side with a trainer, preparing meals and feeding the animals, learning basic training techniques, and sharing lunch. It costs $389, which includes park admission, lunch, disposable camera, and T-shirt. *Note:* You must be at least 13 years old, 52 inches tall, and able to climb, as well as able to lift and carry 15 pounds of critter cuisine. Call © **407/370-1382** for reservations.

Whale Encounter
Frommer's Rating: B+ for touchy-feely animal lovers
Recommended Ages: 13–adult

Fun Fact **Shark Encounter**

A new SeaWorld program gives snorkelers and divers a chance to have limited, hands-off contact with the 58 sharks, including a near 9-foot sand tiger, in the Terrors of the Deep area. Two at a time, guests don wetsuits for a 30-minute encounter inside a cage that rides a 125-foot track. Part of the cage is above water, but participants can dive up to 8 feet underwater for a close-up look at the denizens. The cost is $125 per person (certified divers can rent scuba gear for an extra $25). The price includes park admission for 2 days and a T-shirt. Call ℭ **407/370-1382** for reservations.

Keeping with its animal-encounter theme, SeaWorld, in January 2002, added this program that allows four guests per day to get in the water with false killer whales, which are a cousin of Atlantic bottlenose dolphins but at 1,300 pounds, are up to two or three times their size. The $200, 2-hour encounter includes 30 minutes in waist-deep water with one of the park's four critters, lunch, a T-shirt, souvenir photo, and 1 week's admission to SeaWorld. *Note:* This experience lets you touch but not swim with these pseudorcas. It also carries a 52-inch height minimum and requires participants to be at least 13 years of age. Call ℭ **407/370-1382.**

Tip: If you're willing to splurge on only one program, we'd opt for Discovery Cove (see below) over this one because it's much more hands-on, though it is a little more expensive.

Wild Arctic

Frommer's Rating: B+

Recommended Ages: All ages for exhibit; 6–adult for ride

Enveloping guests in the beauty, exhilaration, and danger of a polar expedition, Wild Arctic combines a high-definition adventure film with flight-simulator technology to display breathtaking Arctic panoramas. After a hazardous faux flight over the frozen north, you emerge into an exhibit where you can see a playful polar bear or two, beautiful beluga whales, and walruses performing aquatic ballets (on different levels, you can see them both above and below the surface). Kids and those prone to motion sickness may find the ride bumpy. There's a separate line if you want to skip the flight and just see the critters.

ADDITIONAL ATTRACTIONS

The park's other attractions include **Pacific Point Preserve,** a 2½-acre natural setting that duplicates the rocky home of California sea lions and harbor seals. **Tropical Rain Forest,** a bamboo and banyan tree habitat, is the home of cockatoos and other birds. And the **Anheuser-Busch Hospitality Center** lets you indulge in free samples of Anheuser-Busch beers, then stroll through the stables to watch the famous Budweiser Clydesdale horses being groomed.

The **Aloha! Polynesian Luau Dinner and Show** is a full-scale dinner show featuring South Seas–style food (fish, chicken, and pork) while you're entertained by a dance troupe. It's hardly haute cuisine or Broadway, but is very much on par with Disney's Polynesian Luau (p. 297). It's held daily at 6:30pm. Park admission is not required. The cost is $37.95 for adults, $27.95 for children 8 to 12, $16.95 for kids 3 to 7. Reservations are required and can be made by calling ℭ **800/327-2424** or 407/363-2559.

SHOPPING AT SEAWORLD

SeaWorld doesn't have nearly as many shops as Walt Disney World and Universal Orlando, but there are lots of cuddly toys for sale around the park. Where else can you get a stuffed manatee but at **Manatee Cove?** The **Friends of the Wild** gift shop (it's near Penguin Encounter) is also nice, as is the shop attached to **Wild Arctic.**

And, because of the Anheuser-Busch connection, the gift shop outside the entrance to the park offers a staggering array of Budweiser-related items.

DISCOVERY COVE: A DOLPHIN ENCOUNTER

Speaking of Anheuser-Busch, the company spent $100 million building this park, which debuted in 2000. That's one-tenth the price tag on Universal's Islands of Adventure. But Discovery Cove's gate price is substantially higher than its Universal and Disney rivals. Visitors can choose from two options: $229 per person plus 6% sales tax—ages 6 and up—if you want to swim with a dolphin; $129 if you can skip that luxury. Both choices come with additional perks. We'll tell you more about those in a moment. First, let's dive into the main event.

If you've never gone for a dip with a dolphin, words hardly do it justice. But we'll try. It's exhilarating and exciting—exactly the kind of thing that can make for a most memorable vacation.

The actual dolphin encounter deserves an **"A+" rating.** It's open only to those ages 6 and older (younger guests or those who don't want to participate in the dolphin swim can take part in the other activities, although it's hard to imagine they will get $129 worth of benefit from them).

The park has a cast of more than two-dozen dolphins, and each of them works from 2 to 4 hours a day. Many of them are mature critters that have spent their lives in captivity, around people. They love their bellies, flukes, and backs rubbed. They also have an impressive bag of tricks. Given the proper hand signals, they can make sounds much like a human passing gas, chatter in dolphin talk, and do seemingly effortless 1½ gainers in 12 feet of water. They take willing guests for rides in the piggyback or missionary position. They also wave "hello" and "goodbye" with their flippers and take great pleasure in roaring by guests at top speed, creating waves that drench them.

The dolphin experience lasts 90 minutes, about 35 to 40 minutes of which is spent in the lagoon with one of them. Trainers use the rest of the time to teach visitors about these remarkable mammals.

Unfortunately, the rest of the day isn't nearly as exciting. Discovery Cove doesn't deliver thrill rides, water slides, or acrobatic animal shows. But it has a number of other things to do if you're a member of the sun-and-surf set. Here's what you get even without the dolphin encounter:

(Tips New Arrival

SeaWorld's new 5-acre Waterfront area, which debuted in late spring 2003, added a seaport-themed village to the park's landscape. On High Street, look for a blend of shops, a purebred cat show, and the SeaFire Inn restaurant, where lunch includes a musical revue called Rico and Roza's Family Feast. At Harbor Square, the funny Seaport Symphony orchestra has chefs making music with pots and pans. The park also is adding street performers, including a crusty old captain who tells fish tales and makes music with bottles and brandy glasses.

- A limit of **no more than 1,000 other guests a day,** so you won't get that "crowded" feeling. (The average daily attendance at Disney's Magic Kingdom is 41,000.)
- Lunch, a towel, locker, sunscreen, snorkeling gear including a flotation vest, and free parking. Souvenir photos are about $20 a pop, but if you do the encounter, it's hard to resist one or more of you doing the tango with your dolphin.
- Other 9am-to-5:30pm activities include a chance to swim near (but on the other side of the Plexiglas from) **barracudas and black-tip sharks.** There are no barriers between you and the gentle rays and brightly colored tropical fish in a new 12,000-square-foot lagoon where some of the rays are 4 feet in diameter. The 3,300-foot Tropical River is a great place to swim or float in a mild current—it goes through a cave, two waterfalls, and a large aviary where you can also take a stroll, becoming a human perch for some of the 30 exotic bird species. There are also beach areas for catching a tan.
- Seven consecutive days of **unlimited admission** to SeaWorld (park admission normally costs $51.95 a day for adults and $42.95 for kids 3–9).

One other option is Discovery Cove's trainer for a day ticket, which for $399 allows guests 6 and older to also have a dolphin training encounter, participate in guided snorkeling tours, feed fish, and interact with other critters, including rays. A paying adult must accompany guests ages 6 to 12.

You can drive to Discovery Cove by following the above directions to SeaWorld, then follow the signs. Unlike other parks, Discovery Cove doesn't have a parking charge. For up-to-the-minute information, call © **877/434-7268,** or on the Internet go to **www.discoverycove.com**.

If you're headed for this adventure, we recommend making a reservation far in advance. There may be a lot of other deep-pocketed travelers landing when you do. *Note:* There is a chance of getting in as a walk-up customer. The park reserves a small number of tickets daily for folks whose earlier dolphin sessions were canceled due to bad weather. The best chance for last-minute guests comes during any extended period of good weather.

4 Other Area Attractions

There are—surprise!—a number of cool things in Orlando that don't revolve around Mickey, the Hulk, or Shamu. Now that we've covered the monster parks, we're going to explore some of central Florida's best smaller attractions.

IN KISSIMMEE

Kissimmee's tourist strip is on Walt Disney World's southern border and extends about 2 miles west and 8 to 10 miles east. Irlo Bronson Memorial Highway/U.S. 192, the highway linking the town to WDW and points west, is under perpetual road construction, and the development clutter can make it hard to see some smaller destinations. Check with your hotel's front desk or the attractions for updates that might make finding them a little easier.

Note: The following prices don't include the 6% to 7% sales tax unless otherwise noted.

Florida Splendid China *(Overrated* Crowds are reasonably small at this 76-acre attraction, partly due to a lack of publicity, but mainly because it doesn't deliver the same entertainment pizzazz that the bigger parks do. Splendid China has more than 60 miniature replicas of that country's man-made and natural wonders.

Orlando Attractions

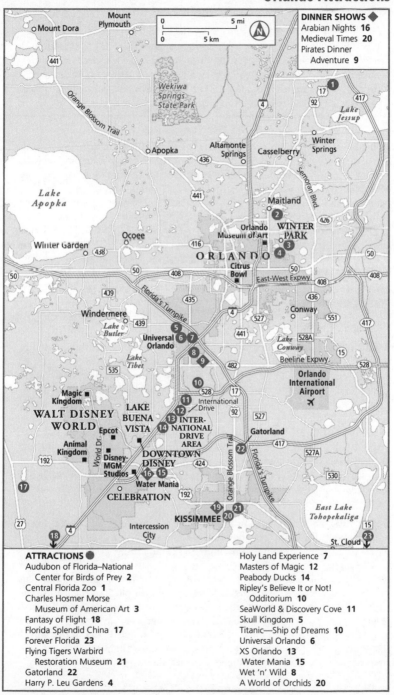

Tips **High-Flying Fun**

If you want to taste the real deal, **Warbird Adventures,** 233 N. Hoagland Blvd., Kissimmee, FL (*C* **800/386-1593** or 407/870-7366; www.warbird adventures.com), will take you skyward in a World War II fighter-trainer for sightseeing or aerobatic flights. The adventures last 15 to 60 minutes and range in price from $160 to $490.

Highlights include replicas of the 4,200-mile Great Wall of China (half-mile long here), the Forbidden City's 9,999-room Imperial Palace, the massive Leshan Buddha originally carved in a mountainside, the Stone Forest of Yunan, and the Mongolian mausoleum of Genghis Khan. The Mysterious Kingdom of the Orient is a 90-minute dance and acrobatic show held Tuesday through Sunday night in the Golden Peacock Theater. It's included in the admission, or, if you don't want to go to the park, a separate ticket is $16 for adults, $10.65 for kids 5 to 12. Trams circle the attraction throughout the day, stopping at the major attractions, shops, and arts and crafts displays for pickup and drop-off. Unless you're an armchair traveler or a miniature lover, we'd skip this spot. Allow 4 to 5 hours.

3000 Splendid China Blvd. (off Irlo Bronson Memorial Hwy./U.S. 192). *C* **800/244-6226** or 407/396-7111. www.floridasplendidchina.com. Admission $28.88 adults, $18 children 5–12 including tax. Daily from 9:30am; closing hours vary seasonally (call ahead). Free parking. From I-4, take Exit 64B/U.S. 192 west and turn left at the Florida Splendid China dragons.

Flying Tigers Warbird Restoration Museum   If you're a fan of vintage flying machines and their restoration, this working museum displays and restores aircraft from the World War II through Vietnam eras. Owner Tom Reilly offers guided tours through a museum full of hands-on exhibits. The outdoor showroom includes changing exhibits of birds that have been or are being restored, such as a 1909 Martin M-1, a 1944 B-17 Flying Fortress, a 1944 P-38 Lightning, and a 1965 MIG 21. Plan on spending 2 hours. It's interesting, and a must for aviation buffs, but the show here is almost entirely visual. Fantasy of Flight (later in this chapter) offers more to do.

231 N. Hoagland Blvd. (south of U.S. 192). *C* **407/933-1942.** www.warbirdmuseum.com. Admission $9 adults, $8 seniors 60 and over and children 8–12. Daily 9am–5pm. Free parking. From I-4, take Exit 64A/U.S. 192 east of Disney to Kissimmee, then turn right on Hoagland.

Gatorland⌕ *Finds*   Founded in 1949 with only a handful of alligators living in huts and pens, Gatorland now houses thousands of alligators and crocodiles on its 70-acre spread. Breeding pens, nurseries, and rearing ponds are situated throughout the park, which also displays toads, insects, turtles, and a Galápagos tortoise. Its 2,000-foot boardwalk winds through a cypress swamp and breeding marsh. There are three shows. **Gator Wrestlin'** uses the old "put-them-to-sleep" trick, but it's more of an environmental awareness program. The **Gator Jumparoo** is a crowd-pleaser in which the big reptiles lunge 4 or 5 feet out of the water to snatch a hunk of meat from a trainer's hand. And **Jungle Crocs of the World** showcases some of the world's toothiest carnivores. While you're here, try the smoked gator ribs or nuggets in the open-air restaurant, or grab a gator-skin souvenir in the gift shop. Allow 4 to 5 hours.

Note: Gatorland's new **Adventure Tours** program lets up to five guests become a Trainer for a Day. The $190 experience puts you side by side with trainers and includes a chance to wrangle and doctor some alligators (minimum age 12). You get a disposable camera to help record your experience. Other Adventure Tours include half-day airboat rides ($55 adults, $45 kids), a night-time airboat ride ($38 adults, $28 kids), and a spring alligator egg-collecting excursion ($49, minimum age 12).

14501 S. Orange Blossom Trail (U.S. 441; between Osceola Pkwy. and Hunter's Creek Blvd.). ℂ 800/393-5297 or 407/855-5496. www.gatorland.com. Admission $19.95 adults, $9.95 children 3–12 including tax. Daily 9am–5 or 6pm usually, but closing times vary by season. Free parking. From I-4, take Exit 65/Osceola Pkwy. east to U.S. 17/92/441 and go left/north. Gatorland is 1½ miles on the right.

Water Mania You'll find a variety of aquatic attractions in this 36-acre water park. You can boogie board or body surf in the wave pools, float lazily along an 850-foot river, enjoy a white-water tube run on **Riptide,** and spiral down the **Twin Tornadoes** water slide. If you dare, ride **The Screamer,** a 72-foot freefall speed slide, or the **Abyss,** an enclosed tube slide that corkscrews through 380 feet of darkness, exiting into a splash pool. There's a rainforest-themed water playground for kids, a miniature golf course, and a picnic area with arcade games, volleyball, and a beach. *Note:* This park has fewer thrill rides than Disney's Typhoon Lagoon and Blizzard Beach (see chapter 7, "Exploring Walt Disney World") or Wet 'n' Wild (listed a bit later), so it has fewer teens and young adults, making it more attractive to older adults or families with younger kids. Allow 4 to 5 hours.

6073 W. Irlo Bronson Memorial Hwy./U.S. 192 (just east of I-4). ℂ 800/527-3092 or 407/396-2626. www.water mania-florida.com. Admission $19.95 adults, $16.95 kids 3–9. Mar–Sept daily 10am–5pm; Oct 10am–5pm Wed–Sat. Parking $6. From I-4, take Exit 64A/U.S. 192 east about ½ mile.

A World of Orchids *Value* Lovers of horticulture will enjoy touring this conservatory and showroom filled with thousands of orchids—many of them rare—that are magnificently abloom at all times and on display as well as for sale. Streams, waterfalls, koi ponds, and birds enhance the grounds. Also on the premises: a nature walk through a wooded area, aquariums of exotic fish, and a small aviary. Allow 1 hour, more if you're gaga over orchids.

2501 Old Lake Wilson Rd./Hwy. 545 (off U.S. 192). ℂ 407/396-1881. www.orchidmall.com/awoo. Free admission. Tues–Sun 9:30am–4:30pm. Free parking. From I-4, take Exit 64B/U.S. 192 west 2 miles, turn left on Old Lake Wilson Rd. (CR 545). The conservatory is 1 mile ahead on the left.

INTERNATIONAL DRIVE AREA

These attractions are a 10- to 15-minute drive from the Disney area and 5 to 10 minutes from Universal Orlando. Most appeal to special interests, but one is free (the Peabody Ducks' show) and another, Wet 'n' Wild, is in a class that includes WDW's top two water parks: Typhoon Lagoon and Blizzard Beach.

Holy Land Experience Failed battles to get tax-exempt church status and smaller-than-expected attendance have caused this tourist attraction to add a parking fee and boost rates by $13 in its 2+-year lifetime. But backers still believe Jesus Christ and John the Baptist can go head to head with (or at least play second harp to) Mickey Mouse and Woody Woodpecker. This $20 million, 15-acre attraction near Universal Orlando is trying to court more believers by offering exhibits focusing on Jerusalem between the years 1450 B.C. and A.D. 66. Instead of thrill rides, visitors get lessons about Noah's Ark, the limestone caves where the Dead Sea Scrolls were discovered, 1st-century Jerusalem, and Jesus' tomb. The trimmings include a display of old Bibles and manuscripts, a Bedouin tent where biblical personalities tell Old and New Testament stories, and a cafe serving Middle Eastern food. The attraction has caused some controversy: Orlando-area rabbis, among others, say they believe it's a ploy to convert Jews to Christianity. Allow 3 to 4 hours.

4655 Vineland Rd. ℂ **866/872-4659** or 407/367-2065. www.theholylandexperience.com. Admission $29.75 adults, $19.75 children 4–12. Mon–Sat 10am–5 or 6pm; Sun noon–6pm; sometimes later. Parking $5. From I-4, take Exit 78/Conroy Rd. west to Vineland Rd. It's on Vineland at Conroy.

Masters of Magic ⋆   U.S. Navy veteran "Typhoon" Lou Maran launched his magic show in spring 2000. It's something of a gamble given the number of International Drive shows that have come and gone in the last decade, but its novelty may give it a small edge (and a niche) over the dearly departed—and also earns it a star. Lou and his friends combine illusions, digital sound, and special effects for a 90-minute performance that is better than several of the tourist trappings on I-Drive. Here's hoping they're not a now-you-see-them, now-you-don't story. Allow 2 hours.

8815 International Dr. (between Sand Lake Rd. and the Beeline Expressway). ℂ **866/624-4233** or 407/345-3456. www.mastersofmagic.net. $29.95 adults, $19.95 kids 4–12. Wed–Sun 6:30 and 9:15pm. Free self parking. Take I-4 Exit 75B, Kirkman Rd./Hwy. 435, southeast to International Dr., then southwest to the show on the left.

Peabody Ducks ⋆ *(Moments*   One of the best shows in town is short but sweet, and, more importantly, *free.* The Peabody Orlando's five mallards march into the lobby each morning, accompanied by John Philip Sousa's "King Cotton March" and their own red-coated duck master. They get to spend the day splashing in a marble fountain. Then, in the afternoon, they march back to the elevator and up to their 4th-floor "penthouse." Donald Duck never had it this good. Allow 1 hour.

9801 International Dr. (between the Bee Line Expressway and Sand Lake Rd.). ℂ **800/732-2639** or 407/352-4000. Free admission. Daily at 11am and 5pm. Free self-parking, valet parking $8. From I-4, take Exit 74A, Sand Lake Rd./Hwy. 528, east to International Dr., then south. Hotel is on the left across from the Convention Center.

Ripley's Believe It or Not! Odditorium *(Overrated*   Do you crave weird science? If you're a fan of the bizarre, here's where you'll find lots of oddities. Among the hundreds of exhibits: a two-headed kitten, a five-legged cow, a three-quarter–scale model of a 1907 Rolls-Royce made of 1 million matchsticks, a mosaic of the *Mona Lisa* created from toast, torture devices from the Spanish Inquisition, a Tibetan flute made of human bones, and Ubangi women with wooden plates in their lips. There are exhibits on Houdini and films of people swallowing coat hangers. Visitors are greeted by a hologram of Robert Ripley. Allow 2 hours.

8201 International Dr. (1½ blocks south of Sand Lake Rd.). ℂ **800/998-4418** or 407/363-4418. www.ripleys.com/orlando2.htm. Admission $14.95 adults, $12.95 seniors, $9.95 children 4–12. Daily 9am–1am. Free parking. From I-4, take Exit 74A, Sand Lake Rd./Hwy. 528, and turn right on International Dr.

Tips **The New Kid in Town**

The **Hard Rock Vault,** a $32 million collection of guitars, rock star costumes, photos, and other memorabilia owned by Hard Rock Cafe International, opened in late 2002. It's in The Mercado, a shopping and entertainment plaza on International Drive (ℂ **407/445-7625, ext. 2420;** www.hardrock.com/Vault). Among the treasures: A pair of Jim Morrison's leather pants, Buddy Holly's signature specs, and an Elvis Presley electric guitar. Speaking of Elvis, he hasn't left this building. In fact, he has his own room—The King's Chamber. Admission costs $14.95 adults, $8.95 kids.

Central Orlando

Lake Eola Park **4**
Orlando Museum of Art **2**
Orlando Science Center **1**
TD Waterhouse Centre **3**

Skull Kingdom   As you wander the stone halls inside the Skull Castle, you'll be taunted and terrified by a cast of ghoulish characters second in central Florida only to the crew at Universal Orlando's Halloween Horror Nights, but this show runs year-round. It's not for children under 8. Allow about 30 minutes to walk through the castle.

5933 American Way (just off the intersection of International Dr. and Universal Blvd., 3 blocks east of Universal Orlando). ② **407/354-1564.** www.skullkingdom.com. Admission $11.79 per person. Free parking. Mon–Thurs 6–11pm; Fri–Sun noon–midnight. From I-4, take Exit 75A/Hwy. 435 South to American Way and look for the giant skull castle.

Titanic—Ship of Dreams *Overrated*   If you didn't get enough of the movie, news clips, and expedition, you will get that *no-more* feeling in this 25,000-square-foot attraction. It has some 200 artifacts (a deck chair, life jacket, stationery, and so on), movie memorabilia, actors, and even a replica of the great ship's grand staircase and re-created rooms. This one is strictly for ardent fans. Allow 1 to 2 hours.

8445 International Dr. (3 blocks south of Sand Lake Rd.). © 407/248-1166. www.titanicshipofdreams.com. Admission $16.95 adults, $11.95 children 6–11. Free parking. Daily 10am–8pm. Take I-4 Exit 74A, Sand Lake Rd./Hwy. 528, and turn left on International Dr., and go three-quarters of a mile. It's in the Mercado.

Wet 'n' Wild 𝕽𝕽   Who knew people came in so many shapes and sizes? Stacked or stubby, terribly tan or not, all kinds come here, so there's no reason to be bashful about squeezing into a bathing suit and going out in public. Wet 'n' Wild is America's third most popular water park (behind Blizzard Beach and Typhoon Lagoon, respectively). It offers 25 acres of fun, including: **The Flyer,** a 6-story four-passenger toboggan run through 450 feet of banked curves; the **Surge,** which is one of the longest (580 ft. of curves) and fastest multipassenger tube rides in the Southeast; and **Black Hole,** a two-person spaceship-style raft that makes a 500-foot twisting, turning voyage through darkness (all three rides require that children 36 to 48 in. be accompanied by an adult). You can also ride **Raging Rapids,** a simulated white-water run with a waterfall plunge; **Blue Niagra,** a 300-foot 6-story loop-and-dipster that also has a plunge (48-in. height minimum); **Knee Ski,** a cable-operated half-mile knee-boarding course that's open in warm-weather months only (56-in. height minimum); **Der Stuka,** a 6-story, free-fall speed slide; and **Mach 5,** which has a trio of twisting, turning flumes. The park also has a large kids' area with mini-versions of the big rides. If you enjoy the water, plan on spending a full day here.

Note: In addition to the admission prices below, Wet 'n' Wild is part of the multiday **FlexTicket package** that includes admission to Universal Orlando (which owns this attraction), SeaWorld, and Busch Gardens in Tampa (see the beginning of this chapter for more information).

6200 International Dr. (at Universal Blvd.). © 800/992-9453 or 407/351-1800. www.wetnwild.com. Admission $31.95 adults, $25.95 children 3–9. Hours vary seasonally, but the park usually is open at least 10am–5pm daily, weather permitting. You can rent tubes ($4), towels ($2), and lockers ($5); all require a $2 deposit. Parking is $6 for cars, light trucks, and vans. From I-4, take Exit 75A/Hwy. 435 South, and follow the signs.

XS Orlando   As the owners say, you can "dine, dance, and defend the world" in this summer 2001 arrival. The attraction's 110 simulators—featuring golf, thoroughbred racing, and NASCAR driving, among others—are the primary calling cards for some. You can win prizes (T-shirts and more) that also are sold in the gift shop. You can buy game cards by time ($20 an hour, $25 for two) or dollar amount. There's also a DJ and restaurant (serving seafood and steaks, with entrees running $17–$27).

9101 International Dr., in Pointe Orlando. © 407/226-8922. www.xsorlando.com. Free admission. Sun–Thurs noon–midnight; Fri–Sat noon–2am. From I-4, take Exit 74A, Sand Lake Rd./Hwy. 528, east to International Dr.; turn south. Pointe Orlando is on the left.

ELSEWHERE IN CENTRAL FLORIDA

The listings that follow are out of the mainstream tourist areas, meaning you won't have to battle heavy crowds. The Central Florida Zoo, Orlando Museum of Art, and Orlando Science Center are close enough to incorporate a visit to Winter Park if you choose to make a day of it.

Central Florida Zoo *Finds*   This community zoo has come a long way since it was born in 1923 when a circus came to town, leaving a monkey and a goat behind. The monkey rode the goat in the earliest show. Today, the animal collection includes beautiful clouded leopards, cheetahs, and black-footed cats, all of which are endangered. You'll also meet a ham of a hippo named Geraldine as well as black howler monkeys, siamangs, American crocodiles, a banded Egyptian cobra, a Gila monster, hyacinth macaws, barred owls, bald eagles, and dozens of other species. The zoo has half-price admission for everyone Thursdays from 9 to 10am and all day Tuesdays for seniors 60 and over. Allow 2 to 3 hours.

3755 NW U.S. 17/92, Sanford. © 407/323-4450. www.centralfloridazoo.org. Admission $8 adults, $5 seniors, $4 children 3–12. Daily 9am–5pm. Free parking. Take I-4 Exit 104 right onto Orange Ave., turn left at the traffic light on Lake Monroe Rd., then right on U.S. 17/92. The zoo is on the right.

Forever Florida   The 4,700-acre Crescent J Ranch is a nature preserve that offers a chance to see native wildlife, Florida flora, and a working cattle ranch by guided tour. Options include touring by horseback, bike, covered wagon, and Cracker coach, a funky buggy that puts riders on a perch 10 feet above sea level. Allow a half day or longer to get here, take the tour, and see the grounds, which also include a pony riding ring, hiking trails, and a petting zoo.

4755 N. Kenansville Rd., St. Cloud (southeast of Kissimmee). © 866/854-3837. www.foreverflorida.com. Tours $18–$28 adults, $15–$18 children 4–11. Mon–Thurs 8am–3pm; Fri–Sat 8am–6pm; first tours at 10am. Free parking. Take I-4 Exit 64A/U.S. 192 east about 15 miles to U.S. 441, then go south 7½ miles to Forever Florida on the left.

Harry P. Leu Gardens ⊛ (Value   This 50-acre botanical garden on the shores of Lake Rowena offers a serene respite from the theme-park razzle-dazzle. Paths lead through giant camphors, moss-draped oaks, palms, cicadas, and camellias—the latter represented by one of the world's largest collections: 50 species and some 2,000 plants that bloom from October through March. There are 75 varieties of roses in the site's formal gardens, as well as orchids, azaleas, desert plants, and colorful annuals and perennials. The attraction also has palm, bamboo, and butterfly gardens. Businessman Harry P. Leu, who donated his 49-acre estate to the city in the 1960s, created the gardens. There are $6 guided tours of his house, built in 1888, on the hour and half hour (advance reservations suggested). The interior has Victorian, Chippendale, and Empire furnishings and pieces of art. Admission is free Mondays from 9am to noon. It takes about 2 hours to see the house and gardens.

1920 N. Forest Ave. (between Nebraska St. and Corrine Dr.). © 407/246-2620. www.leugardens.org. Admission $4 adults, $1 children grades K–12. Daily 9am–5pm; house daily 10am–3:30pm (closed during July). Free parking. Take I-4 Exit 85/Princeton St. and go east, then right on Mills Ave. and left on Virginia Dr. Look for the gardens on your left, just after you go around a curve.

Orlando Museum of Art ⊛   This local heavyweight handles some of the most prestigious traveling exhibits in the nation. The museum, founded in 1924, hosts special exhibits throughout the year, but even if you miss one, it's worth a stop to see its rotating permanent collection of 19th- and 20th-century American art, pre-Columbian art dating from 1200 B.C to A.D. 1500, and African art. Allow 2 to 3 hours.

2416 N. Mills Ave. (in Loch Haven Park). © 407/896-4231. www.omart.org. Admission $6 adults, $5 seniors and students, $3 children 4–11. Tues–Sat 10am–5pm; Sun noon–5pm. Free parking. Take I-4 Exit 85/Princeton St. east and follow signs to Loch Haven Park.

Orlando Science Center ⊛⊛ (Finds   The 4-story center, the largest of its kind in the Southeast, provides 10 exhibit halls that allow visitors to explore everything from Florida swamps to the arid plains of Mars to the human body. One of the big attractions is the **Dr. Phillips CineDome,** a 310-seat theater that presents large-format films, planetarium shows, and laser-light extravaganzas. In **KidsTown,** little folks wander in exhibits representing a miniature version of the big world around them. In one section, there's a pint-sized community that includes a construction site, park, and wellness center. **Science City,** located nearby, includes physics lessons and a power plant, and **123 Math Avenue** uses puzzles and other things to make learning math fun. Allow 3 to 4 hours, more if you have an inquiring mind.

777 E. Princeton St. (between Orange and Mills aves., in Loch Haven Park). ℭ 888/672-4386 or 407/514-2000. www.osc.org. Basic admission (exhibits only) $10 adults, $9 seniors 55 and older, $7.50 children 3–11; additional prices for CineDome film and planetarium show. Tues–Thurs 9am–5pm; Fri–Sat 9am–9pm; Sun noon–5pm. Parking available in a garage across the street for $3.50. Take I-4 Exit 85/Princeton St. east and cross Orange Ave.

5 Staying Active

You will most likely burn more calories than you ever thought possible by simply strolling through the theme parks. Nevertheless, if you want some exercise other than walking the parks, Walt Disney World and the surrounding areas have plenty of recreational options. Most of those that are listed below are open to everyone, no matter where you're staying. The prices listed don't include tax unless otherwise noted. For further information about WDW recreational facilities, call ℭ **407/939-7529,** or on the Internet go to **www.disneyworld.com** and click the "recreation" link.

AIRBOATING

You can giddy-up-and-glide across the surface of local waters at **Boggy Creek Airboat Rides** in Kissimmee (ℭ **407/344-9550;** www.bcairboats.com), where you'll pay $18 per adult and $13 per child for half-hour tours. Another choice is **Old Fashioned Airboat Rides** in Christmas, east of Orlando (ℭ **407/568-4307;** www.airboatrides.com), which charges $35 per adult and $15 per child for 90 minutes.

BALLOONING

There are several places in the area to experience an early-morning hot-air balloon flight, including **Orange Blossom Balloons** in Lake Buena Vista (ℭ **407/239-7677;** www.orangeblossomballoons.com) and **Blue Water Balloons** in Orlando (ℭ **800/586-1884** or 407/894-5040; www.bluewaterballoons.com). Rates run about $165 per person and include a champagne toast at the conclusion of the flight and a breakfast buffet or picnic afterward.

BICYCLING

Bike rentals (single and multispeed bikes for adults, tandems, baby seats, and children's bikes including those equipped with training wheels) are available from the **Bike Barn** (ℭ **407/824-2742**) at Fort Wilderness Resort and Campground. Rates are $8 per hour, $22 per day. Fort Wilderness offers good bike trails.

BOATING

With a ton of manmade lakes and lagoons, WDW owns a navy of pleasure boats. **Capt. Jack's** at Downtown Disney rents Water Sprites and canopy boats ($22–$35 per half hour). For information call ℭ **407/828-2204.**

The **Bike Barn** at Fort Wilderness (ℭ **407/824-2742**) rents canoes and paddleboats ($6.50 per half hour, $12 per hour).

Be sure to see the Grand Floridian, Yacht Club, and Beach Club listings in chapter 5, "Where to Stay," for information on some special cruises.

FISHING

Disney offers a variety of fishing excursions on the various Disney lakes, including Bay Lake and Seven Seas Lagoon. The lakes are stocked, so you may catch

> **_Tips_ Hitting the Links**
>
> Walt Disney World operates five 18-hole, par-72 golf courses and one 9-hole, par-36 walking course. All are open to the public and offer pro shops, equipment rentals, and instruction. The rates are $109 to $175 per 18-hole round for resort guests ($5 more if you're not staying at a WDW property). Twilight specials are available. For tee times and information, call (C) **407/824-2270** up to 7 days in advance (up to 30 days for Disney resort and "official" property guests). Call (C) **407/934-7639** for information about golf packages.
>
> Beyond Mickey's shadow, try **Celebration Golf Club,** which has an 18-hole regulation course (greens fees $35–$115) and a 3-hole junior course for 5 to 9 year olds ((C) **888/275-2918** or 407/566-4653; www. celebrationgolf.com). **Champions Gate** offers 36 holes designed by Greg Norman ((C) **407/787-4653**; www.championsgategolf.com), where greens fees will set you back $82 to $125. **Orange County National** has 36 Phil Ritson–designed holes ((C) **407/656-2626**; www.orangecounty nationalgolf.com); greens fees run $50 to $135.
>
> _Golf_ magazine recognized the 45 holes designed by Jack Nicklaus at the **Villas of Grand Cypress** ⚜⚜⚜ resort as among the best in the nation. Tee times begin at 8am daily. Special rates are available for children under 18. For information call (C) **407/239-1909.** The course is generally restricted to guests or guests of guests (an average of $175 per round), but there's limited play available to those not staying at the resort. Fees begin at $225.
>
> Also consider **Golfpac** ((C) **888/848-8941** or 407/260-2288; www.golf pacinc.com), an organization that packages golf vacations with accommodations and other features and prearranges tee times at more than 40 Orlando-area courses. The earlier you call (months, if possible), the better your options. **Tee Times USA** ((C) **888/465-3356**; www.teetimes usa.com) and **Florida Golfing** ((C) **866/833-2663**; www.floridagolfing. com) are two other reservation services that offer packages and course information.

something, but true anglers probably won't find it much of a challenge. The excursions can be arranged 2 to 90 days in advance by calling (C) **407/824-2621.** A license isn't required. The fee is $165 to $195 for up to five people for 2 hours ($80 for each additional hour), including refreshments, gear, guide, and tax. Bait is purchased separately for $15.

A less-expensive alternative: Rent fishing poles at the **Bike Barn** ((C) **407/ 824-2742**) to fish in the Fort Wilderness canals. Pole rentals cost $6 per hour, $10 per day. Bait is $3.50. A license isn't necessary.

Outside the realm, **A Pro Bass Guide Service** ((C) **800/771-9676** or 407/877-9676; www.probassguideservice.com) offers guided bass fishing trips along some of central Florida's most picturesque rivers and lakes. Hotel pickup is available; the cost is $225 for 2 people per half day, $325 for a full day.

HAYRIDES

The hay wagon departs **Pioneer Hall** at Disney's Fort Wilderness nightly at 7 and 9:30pm for 45-minute old-fashioned hayrides with singing, jokes, and games. The cost is $8 for adults, $4 for children ages 3 to 10. An adult must accompany children under 12. No reservations; it's first-come, first-served. Call ✆ **407/824-2832.**

HIKING

The **Nature Conservancy's Disney Wilderness Preserve** (✆ **407/682-3664;** www.nature.org/florida) is a 12,000-acre, little discovered getaway from the theme-park madness. It has 7 miles of trails at the headwaters of the Everglades ecosystem, just south of Orlando. Admission costs $2 adults, and $1 for kids ages 6 to 17. It's open Monday through Friday in summer from 9am to 5pm; it's open daily from 9am to 5pm the rest of the year. The preserve also features periodic **buggy rides** ($10 adults, $5 kids).

HORSEBACK RIDING

Disney's Fort Wilderness Resort and Campground offers 45-minute guided trail rides several times a day. The cost is $32 per person. Children must be at least 9 years old. Maximum rider weight is 250 pounds. For information and reservations up to 30 days in advance, call ✆ **407/824-2832.**

The **Villas of Grand Cypress** opens its equestrian center to outsiders. You can go on a 45-minute walk-trot trail ride (offered four times daily) for $45. A 30-minute private lesson is $55; an hour's lesson is $100. Call ✆ **407/239-4700** and ask for the equestrian center.

HORSEDRAWN CARRIAGE RIDES

In 2002, Disney added carriage rides at two locations around the World, **Fort Wilderness Resort and Campground** and the **Port Orleans Resort** (✆ **407/ 824-2832**). The 30-minute rides cost $30 for up to four people.

JOGGING

Many of the Disney resorts have scenic jogging trails. For instance, the **Yacht** and **Beach Club** resorts share a 2-mile trail; the **Caribbean Beach Resort's** 1.4-mile promenade circles a lake; **Port Orleans** has a 1.7-mile riverfront trail; and **Fort Wilderness's** tree-shaded 2.3-mile jogging path has exercise stations about every quarter-mile. Pick up a jogging trail map at any Disney property's Guest Services desk.

PARASAILING

The **Sammy Duvall Watersports Centre** (✆ **407/939-0754;** www.sammyduvall. com) at Disney's Contemporary Resort will take you up to 600 feet above Seven Seas Lagoon and Bay Lake on a flight that lasts 8 to 12 minutes. The cost ranges from $85 to $155.

SURFING

It's true. The creative minds at Disney have added a way for you to learn how to catch a wave and "hang ten" at the Typhoon Lagoon water park (p. 229). Tuesdays and Fridays, instructors from **Carroll's Cocoa Beach Surfing School** show up for an early-bird session in the namesake lagoon, which has a wave machine capable of 8-footers. The 2½-hour sessions are held before the park opens to the general public. They're limited to 14 people. Minimum age is 8. The $125 cost

(Finds) Swimming with the Manatees

An organization called **Oceanic Society Expeditions** (© **800/326-7491** or 415/441-1106; www.oceanic-society.org) offers a once-a-year swim-with-the-manatees program (usually in Jan.) in the Crystal River area, 2 hours west of Disney. A biologist leads 5-day trips from Orlando for up to 11 people. Activities include swimming with these gentle, slow-moving marine mammals, snorkeling the area's springs and manatee haunts, and an excursion to a facility for injured and orphaned wildlife. The cost is about $1,100 including excursions, room, and most meals. Reserve as far in advance as possible, but note that the trips can be cancelled if the society doesn't get a full group of takers.

doesn't include park admission, which you have to pay if you want to hang around after the lesson (© **407/939-7529**).

SWIMMING

The **YMCA Aquatic Center** has a full fitness center, racquetball courts, and an indoor Olympic-size pool. Admission is $10 per person, $25 for families. It's at 8422 International Dr. For information call © **407/363-1911.**

TENNIS

There are 22 lighted tennis courts scattered throughout the Disney properties. They're free and open to resort guests on a first-come, first-served basis. Call © **407/824-2270** to make reservations or for more information. The Racquet Club at the Contemporary Resort has six clay courts, all lighted for evening play, and offers lessons ($40–$70; the price depends on the duration of the lesson).

WATER-SKIING & WAKEBOARDING

Water-skiing trips (including boats, drivers, equipment, and instruction) can be arranged Tuesday through Saturday at **Walt Disney World** by calling © **407/824-2621** or 407/939-0754. Make reservations up to 14 days in advance. The cost for skiing is $125 per hour for up to five people. Wakeboarding is $130 for up to four people. You also can wakeboard and ski at the **Sammy Duvall Watersports Centre** at Disney's Contemporary Resort (© **407/939-0754;** www.sammyduvall. com); it costs $80 for 30 minutes, $140 for 60 minutes.

Outside Disney, you can get some time behind a boat or at the end of an overhead cable at the **Orlando Watersports Complex,** which has lights for nighttime thrill seekers. The complex is located close to Orlando International Airport (8615 Florida Rock Rd.). Prices for skiing, including lessons, begin at about $45 an hour for a cable and $75 a half-hour behind a boat. For information call © **407/251-3100** or on the Internet go to **www.orlandowatersports.com.**

6 Spectator Sports

Disney doesn't want to give the competition a sporting chance. In May 1997, it branched out with the multimillion-dollar **Wide World of Sports Complex,** a 200-acre facility. The Mouse hopes to hit a home run with a 7,500-seat baseball stadium—dubbed Cracker Jack Stadium in 2002—that's the spring training home of the Atlanta Braves. In addition, there's a 5,000-seat field house featuring six basketball courts, a fitness center, and training rooms; major-league practice fields and pitching mounds; 4 softball fields; 12 tennis courts, including a 2,000-seat stadium center court; a track-and-field complex; a golf driving range; and more. A variety of events, from tennis tournaments to band competitions, have been held here since the center opened. For information about events taking place during your stay, call ✆ **407/939-1500** or visit **www.disneyworld sports.com**.

Even taking the above into account, Disney isn't the only show in town.

ARENA FOOTBALL

The **Orlando Predators** play from February through mid-May. For the uninitiated, arena football is a wide-open sport played by eight-man teams on a much-abbreviated field. You don't necessarily need to know the rules to enjoy the up-close crunching and beer-fest atmosphere. The Predators have a loyal and rowdy following, not to mention a few championships under their belts. Sold-out games are common, but single tickets ($7.50–$40) are often available the day of the game at the **TD Waterhouse Centre,** formerly the Orlando Arena. Call ✆ **407/447-7337** or surf the Web to **www.orlandopredators.com**.

BASEBALL

The **Atlanta Braves** (✆ **407/828-3267;** www.atlantabraves.com) began spring training at Disney's Wide World of Sports in 1998. There are 18 games during a 1-month season that begins in March. Tickets are $12 to $19.75. You can get tickets through **Ticketmaster** (✆ **407/839-3900**).

From April to September, the **Orlando Rays,** the Tampa Bay Devil Rays' Class AA Southern League affiliate, play their 70 home games at Disney's Wide World of Sports (✆ **407/939-4263**). You can get tickets through **Ticketmaster** (✆ **407/839-3900**). They sell for $5 to $8.

BASKETBALL

The 17,500-seat TD Waterhouse Centre—known in a prior life as the Orlando Arena—is the home court of the NBA's **Orlando Magic** (✆ **407/896-2442;** www.nba.com/magic/), which plays 41 of its regular-season games here from October to April. Single-game tickets ($25–$175) can be hard to acquire. To get there, take I-4 east to Exit 83B, Hwy. 50/U.S. 17/92 (Amelia St.), turn left at the traffic light at the bottom of the off-ramp, and follow the signs. For up-to-the-minute parking information, turn your car radio to 1620 AM.

JAI ALAI

Orlando Jai Alai, 6405 S. U.S. 17/92, at Highway 436 in Fern Park (✆ **407/ 339-6221**), offers what's billed as the world's fastest game. It's like handball but with a much longer court (180 ft.), wicker "gloves" called cestas, and ball speeds that reach 150 mph. This is a pari-mutuel game, which means you can bet on the action.

The program/betting form offers information on how the game is played and how to wager (trust anyone who tells you how to gamble about as much as a chicken farmer would trust a fox).

Note: The fronton also has simulcast wagering, which means you can bet on jai alai and other pari-mutuels such as greyhound and horse racing telecast from other locations. Kids 39 inches and taller are welcome; the minimum betting age is 18. Admission is $1, reserved seats are $2 to $3, restaurant seating is $3 with a $7 minimum order, and box seats are $5. Parking is free; valet parking is $2.

⸨Moments⸩ The Multi-Sports Experience

In 2002, Disney replaced its NFL Experience at the Wide World of Sports complex with an expanded multi-sports venue that not only lets you test your skills at football but also at baseball, basketball, hockey, soccer, and volleyball. Admission is $10 for adults and $7.50 for kids 3 to 9. It's open on select days. For information call ℰ **407/939-1500.**

If you're a true sports fan, your best bet is to write in advance for a package of information about the facilities and a calendar of events at Wide World of Sports. Write to **Disney's Wide World of Sports,** P.O. Box 10,000, Lake Buena Vista, FL 32830-1000, or call ℰ **407/939-1500.**

It's open year-round Wednesday to Sunday. Call for the evening and matinee schedule. From the Walt Disney World area, take I-4 east to Exit 90A, Maitland Blvd./Hwy. 414, turn right at U.S. 17/92, and look for the fronton 2 miles along on your right. It's about a 40-minute drive.

7 Attractions Outside Orlando

Just outside Orlando, you'll find a couple more places to visit. **Fantasy of Flight** offers a look at the yesterday, today, and tomorrow of aviation as well as a simulator. It's a good way for aviation buffs to spend a morning or an afternoon. For a more extended day trip away from the theme-park hubbub, there's a three-pack of attractions in beautiful **Winter Park.**

Fantasy of Flight   Wannabe flyboys and -girls can have all sorts of fantasies in this attraction, which takes guests to the days when earthlings, in this case pilots, went sky diving . . . because they had no other choice. The fun includes flying a fighter simulator outfitted with the sights, sounds, and (hang onto your lunch) motion of a World War II combat plane. Immersion experiences give you the feeling of flying through stratosphere clouds. Exhibits include a P-51C Mustang, an F3F Flying Barrel, a British Spitfire MK9, a Japanese Zero, and a replica of the *Spirit of St. Louis*. You also can tour an airplane restoration shop. Allow 2 to 3 hours.

1400 Broadway Blvd., Polk City. ℰ **863/984-3500.** www.fantasyofflight.com. Admission $24.95 adults, $22.95 seniors 60 and over, $13.95 children 5–12. Daily 9am–5pm. Free parking. Take I-4 south of Orlando to Exit 44/Hwy. 559, turn north to the attraction.

WINTER PARK

This lakeside town—just a 30-minute or so drive from the madness of the theme parks—is a lovely place to spend an afternoon. The upscale community sports some classy museums. Visitors can also cruise the area's lakes or browse in the posh boutiques that line Park Avenue.

To get to Winter Park from downtown Orlando (about a 5-mile drive), head east on I-4 to Fairbanks Avenue, turn right, and proceed about a mile, making a left on Park Avenue.

Audubon of Florida—National Center for Birds of Prey ⸨ ⸩ ⸨Finds⸩   In addition to being a rehabilitation center—one of the biggest and most successful in the Southeast—this is a great place to get to know winged wonders that

Going, Going, Gone

Cypress Gardens, an old-time tourist attraction that opened south of Orlando in 1936, closed its doors in April 2003, the victim of 10 years of declining attendance worsened by the post September 11th economy. The park changed little over the years, wasn't on a main thoroughfare, and appealed mainly to retirees rather than the families and young adults who represent the bulk of central Florida's tourists.

roost here and earn their keep by entertaining the relatively few visitors who come. You can get a close look at hams such as Elvis, the blue suede shoe–wearing American kestrel; Daisy, the polka dancing barn owl; and Trouble, an eagle born with a misaligned beak. *Note:* The center reopened in spring 2002 after a $2 million, 4-year expansion. Allow 2 hours.

1101 Audubon Way, Maitland. © **407/644-0190.** www.adoptabird.org/. Recommended donation $5 adults, $4 children 3–12. Tues–Sun 10am–4pm. From Orlando, go north on I-4 Exit 88, Lee Rd./Hwy. 423, turn right/east, and at the first light (Wymore Rd.) go left, then right/east at the next light (Kennedy Blvd.). Continue a half-mile to East Ave., turn left, and go to the stop sign at Audubon Way. Turn left, and the center is on the right.

Charles Hosmer Morse Museum of American Art ✵ *Value*   Louis Comfort Tiffany is in the spotlight here, and, though it may not be a New York–quality house, if you're a fan, this is a must. This museum, founded in 1942 to display his art collection, has 40 vibrantly colored windows and 21 paintings by the master artist. In addition, there are non-Tiffany windows ranging from creations by Frank Lloyd Wright to 15th-century German masters. Look for leaded lamps by Tiffany and Emile Gallè; paintings by John Singer Sargent, Maxfield Parrish, and others; jewelry designed by Tiffany, Lalique, and Fabergé; photographs by Tiffany and other 19th-century artists; and Art Nouveau furnishings. Allow 2 hours.

445 Park Ave. N. (between Canton and Cole aves.). © **407/645-5311** or 407/645-5324 (for a 24-hr. recorded message). www.inusa.com/tour/fl/orlando/morse.htm. Admission $3 adults, $1 children 12–17. Tues–Sat 9:30am–4pm; Sun 1–4pm. Take I-4 Exit 87, Fairbanks Ave./Hwy. 426, east to Park Ave., and go left for 4 traffic lights.

Scenic Boat Tour ✵   For more than a half-century, tourists have been boarding pontoons for leisurely hour-long cruises on Winter Park's beautiful, natural chain of lakes. The ride winds through canals built by loggers at the turn of the 20th century and tree-shaded fern gullies lined with bamboo and lush tropical foliage. You'll see lakeside mansions, pristine beaches, cypress swamps, dozens of marsh birds, and maybe an American bald eagle. The captain entertains you with stories, some of which are fact and some of which are fable. It's a delightful, laid-back trip and tours are held year-round.

On the lake at the eastern end of Morse Blvd. © **407/644-4056.** www.scenicboattours.com. Admission $8 adults, $4 children 2–11. Weather permitting, tours depart daily every hour on the hour 10am–4pm except Christmas. Call for directions.

9

Shopping

Except for mouse ears and other tourist trinkets, Orlando has few products to call its own. Still, many of you need some kind of a shopping fix, and goofy souvenirs often are among your priorities. But before putting your credit cards into high gear, consider these words to the wise: If you're going to ring registers in the theme parks, you're going to pay top dollar. Alas, most official Disney and Universal merchandise is only available in company stores or websites. But when it comes to other goods, plan a day away from tourist central and be as savvy here as you are back home. You can find a lot of what you want, and at the best possible prices, by knowing what is *and isn't* a bargain. And if you must have officially licensed Mickey merchandise, pay attention to the park opportunities outlined in chapter 7, "Exploring Walt Disney World," and chapter 8, "Exploring Beyond Disney: Universal Orlando, SeaWorld & Other Attractions."

1 The Shopping Scene

For away-from-the-park sorties, explore areas such as Park Avenue in Winter Park, downtown's Antique Row, Orlando's outlet malls, and Mount Dora's quaint shops. No matter whether it's your 1st or 15th visit, these side trips are a fast relief from the attractions, even if you come away empty-handed.

Tourist hot spots such as International Drive and Kissimmee are packed with plenty of 3-for-$10 T-shirt shacks selling *un*durables that shrink to troll size on the first washing. Ditto for seashells that roar like the ocean (more so after a bottle of your favorite screw-cap wine). Every third or fourth storefront sells them. But there also are shops that sell quality merchandise.

If you decide to blow your budget on large items, you face a problem at checkout time: How do you get them home? Few of us want to buy it, haul it around for the entire trip, then try to wedge it into the overhead bin before the carry-on police blow the whistle. Because Orlando is geared for travelers, many retailers offer to ship packages home for a few dollars more. So, if you're pondering an extra-large purchase, ask. If a retailer doesn't offer this service, check with your hotel. Many can arrange a pickup by United Parcel Service, the slow-but-good-old U.S. Postal Service, or another carrier to keep you from dragging a 6-foot stuffed Pluto into the Friendly Skies.

One thing that's no different here than the rest of the country: If you're coming during the holiday season, from the end of November to January 1, it's best to avoid local shopping malls, especially on weekends. They're just as crowded as they are back home—maybe worse. Also, don't leave your good judgment at the door of the outlet malls. Although there are some bargains, the prices on many items, such as athletic shoes, often aren't much lower than you can find at home. (But the selection may be larger than you're used to—especially if you're from outside the United States.)

Many Orlando area stores, particularly those in malls or other shopping centers, are open from 9 or 10am until 9 or 10pm Monday through Saturday and from noon to 6pm on Sunday.

Sales tax in Osceola County, which includes Kissimmee, is 7%. In Orange County, which includes the International Drive area and most of the attractions, it's 6%. In Seminole County, about 40 miles north of Walt Disney World, the rate is 7%.

GREAT SHOPPING AREAS

CELEBRATION   This isn't the place for power shopping, but it is a pleasant look at mid-20th-century mainstream America with a Disney spin and 400% markup. Celebration will eventually be home to about 20,000 people. The downtown includes a dozen shops on or near Market Street, a couple of art galleries, some restaurants, and a three-screen theater. The storefronts, especially the galleries and gift shops, offer interesting but overpriced merchandise. You'll find Market Street Gallery (Swarovski crystal, Disney collectibles, and more), Sherlock's of Celebration (a shop that sells wine and English tearoom goods), an art gallery, a grocer, a post office, a perfumery, and a jeweler. The real plus is the leisurely, very clean atmosphere. The big minus: Again, ridiculous prices. If Celebration reminds you of the movie *The Truman Show,* you won't be alone. The movie was filmed in Seaside, a Florida panhandle community that inspired the builders of this burg (© **407/566-2200**).

DOWNTOWN DISNEY   There are three distinct areas—West Side, Pleasure Island, and Marketplace—in this complex of shops, restaurants, and entertainment venues (**www.downtowndisney.com**). Stars on the shopping front include the **Lego Imagination Center** (© **407/828-0065**), **Virgin Megastore** (© **407/ 828-0222**), **Art of Disney** (© **407/824-4321**), **Once Upon A Toy** (© **407/824- 4321**), and **Guitar Gallery** (© **407/827-0118**).

INTERNATIONAL DRIVE AREA   This tourist mecca extends 7 to 10 miles northeast of the Disney parks between Highway 535 and the Florida Turnpike. (*Note:* Locally, this road is always referred to as **I-Drive.**) From bungee jumping and ice-skating to dozens of themed restaurants and T-shirt shops, this is *the* tourist strip in central Florida. Its main shopping draw is **Pointe Orlando** (© **407/248-2838;** www.pointeorlandofl.com), a worth-your-time collection of restaurants and specialty shops such as **Abercrombie & Fitch, Banana Republic,** and **FAO Schwarz.** You also can find **Orlando Premium Outlets** off south I-Drive (see below).

KISSIMMEE   Skirting the south side of Walt Disney World, Kissimmee centers on U.S. 192/Irlo Bronson Memorial Highway—a somewhat tacky strip, as archetypal of modern American cities as Disney's Main Street is of America's yesteryear. U.S. 192 is lined with budget motels, smaller attractions, and every fast-food restaurant known to humankind. Kissimmee is still, in many ways, true to its cowboy roots, and there are some Western shops to prove it. The shopping

---

⌐Tips   Where Was That Piglet Doll?

If you saw an eye-catching item when you were in the Disney theme parks and aren't sure where, call © **407/363-6200**. Tell the customer service rep the park you were in and describe the item; you'll likely be able to order it by phone.

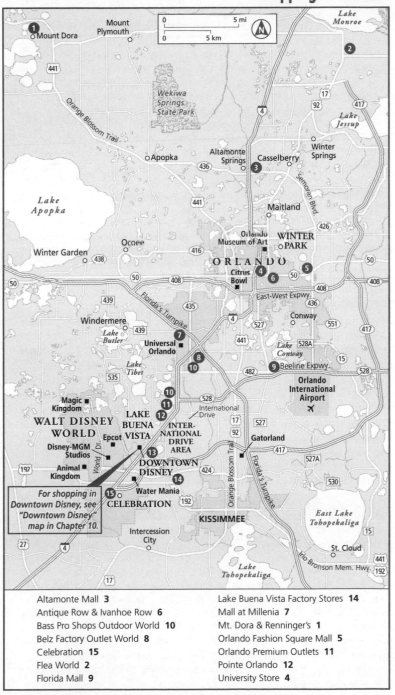

Altamonte Mall **3**
Antique Row & Ivanhoe Row **6**
Bass Pro Shops Outdoor World **10**
Belz Factory Outlet World **8**
Celebration **15**
Flea World **2**
Florida Mall **9**

Lake Buena Vista Factory Stores **14**
Mall at Millenia **7**
Mt. Dora & Renninger's **1**
Orlando Fashion Square Mall **5**
Orlando Premium Outlets **11**
Pointe Orlando **12**
University Store **4**

Value **A Disney Bargain? The World's Best-Kept Secret**

From a pink Cadillac to a 4-foot beer stein, tons of wacky treasures are regularly put on the auction block at Walt Disney World.

In addition to castoffs from the theme parks and WDW resorts, there are more routine items available, from over-the-hill lawn maintenance gear to never-been-used stainless-steel pots and pans. If you're looking for a unique piece of Disney, the auctions are held six times a year. Some of the more unusual items sold in the past include furniture from Miss Piggy's dressing room and a motorized surfboard. The auction takes place on Disney's back lots. Call property control (© **407/824-6878;** www.auctionweb.com/disney) for information, dates, and directions.

Bigger yet are trinkets sold by gavel at **www.disneyauctions.com** on eBay. The mainstream includes stuffed animals, Winnie the Pooh watches, and other modest merchandise. But sometimes things go big time. A dress Glenn Close wore as Cruella De Vil in *102 Dalmatians* sold for $5,000, a Dumbo car from the ride at WDW earned $9,000, and the Porsche from the Disney movie *The Kid* fetched $77,100.

here is notable for the quantity, not necessarily the quality, but it's a good place to pick up some knickknacks or white elephant gifts.

WINTER PARK   Just north of downtown Orlando, Winter Park (© **407/ 644-8281;** www.winterparkcc.org) is the place many of central Florida's old-money families call home. It began as a haven for Yankees trying to escape the cold. Today, its centerpiece is Park Avenue, which has quite a collection of upscale retail shops—Ann Taylor, Restoration Hardware, Bath & Body Works, Crabtree & Evelyn, and Williams-Sonoma—along its cobblestone route. No matter which end of Park Avenue you start at, there are more shops than most can survive, but you're bound to find something here you'll not find anywhere else. Park Avenue also has restaurants and some art galleries. To get here, take I-4 Exit 87, Fairbanks Avenue/Highway 426, east past U.S. 17/92 to Park Avenue and turn left.

2 Orlando Area Outlets & Malls

FACTORY OUTLETS

Belz Factory Outlet World   This is the largest of the Orlando factory outlet centers. It has 170 stores in two enclosed malls and four shopping annexes. It offers a wide range of merchandise, and in a few cases the savings can be 75% off retail prices, but, as is the case with most outlets, *most buys here are no better than what you'll find in discount houses in your town.* There are more than a dozen shoe stores (Bass, Nike, Rockport, and so on); nearly as many housewares shops (Fitz & Floyd, Corning-Revere, Oneida, and Mikasa); and 60-some clothing shops for men, women, and children (London Fog, Van Heusen, Tommy Hilfiger, Danskin, Izod, Liz Claiborne, Guess Jeans, Calvin Klein, and Geoffrey Beane). You can also shop for books, records, electronics, sporting goods, health and beauty aids, jewelry, toys, gifts, accessories, lingerie, hosiery, and parking spaces.

It goes on forever, but don't kill yourself trying to get to every building. Many of the manufacturers have more than one location here, with much the same selections. Also, unless you're from out of the country, most of the brand-name shoe stores don't offer much of a deal. 5401 W. Oak Ridge Rd. ℂ 407/354-0126. www. belz.com. From I-4, take Exit 74B and turn north on I-Drive, continuing to the mall.

Lake Buena Vista Factory Stores *(Overrated* The three dozen or so outlets here include Big Dog Sportswear, Casuals (Ralph Lauren and Tommy Hilfiger), Liz Claiborne, Fossil, Osh Kosh, and Reebok. Savings reach 75%, but most are much more modest, and this is the area's "abandon ship" outlet—more stores have left than are staying aboard. Some of these, in fact, may be gone by the time you arrive. 15591 S. Apopka–Vineland Rd. ℂ 407/238-9301. www.lbvfs.com. From I-4, take Exit 68, Apopka-Vineland Rd./Hwy. 535 south 2 miles and look for the outlet on the left.

Orlando Premium Outlets Opened in June 2000, this 440,000-square-foot center is the new kid in town. It's billed as Orlando's only upscale outlet, which may be true, thanks to a dearth of true outlets, premium or otherwise. It has 110 tenants, including Coach, Donna Karan, Kenneth Cole, Nike, Polo/Ralph Lauren, Timberland, and Tommy Hilfiger. Some of the best buys are at Banana Republic (jeans usually are marked down 50% from retail). 0200 Vineland Ave. ℂ 407/ 238-7787. www.PremiumOutlets.com. From I-4, take Exit 68, Apopka-Vineland Rd./Hwy. 535 right/south to the first light, then go left at the first light to the outlet.

THE MALLS

Altamonte Mall As surely as Disney brought new life to Orlando, this mall and I-4 brought new life (and a ton of traffic) to the then-one stoplight town of Altamonte Springs, north of Orlando. Built in the early 1970s, it got a major renovation in 1989. It's the second largest mall in the area behind the Florida Mall (see below), but it's well north of the tourist mainstream. Its tenants include Burdines, JCPenney, Sears, and 175 specialty shops. 451 E. Altamonte Dr. ℂ 407/830-4422. www.altamontemall.com. From I-4 go 15 miles north of the downtown to Exit 92, Hwy. 436/Semoran Blvd., and go east about a ½ mile.

Florida Mall The exciting news at this popular shopping spot is the expected arrival of Nordstrom and Lord & Taylor to combat the opening of Mall at Millenia (see below). Other anchors include Burdines, Dillard's, JCPenney, Sears, Saks, and Parisian to go along with an Adam's Mark Hotel and more than 250 specialty stores, restaurants (Buca di Beppo, Le Jardin, Pebbles, and Ruby Tuesday), and entertainment venues. 8001 S. Orange Blossom Trail. ℂ 407/851-6255. www.shop simon.com. Take I-4 Exit 74A, Sand Lake Rd./Hwy. 482, and look for it on the corner of Orange Blossom and Sand Lake.

Tips **Homegrown Souvenirs**

Oranges, grapefruit, and other citrus products rank high on the list of local products. **Orange Blossom Indian River Citrus,** 5151 S. Orange Blossom Trail, Orlando (ℂ 800/624-8835 or 407/855-2837; www.orange-blossom.com), is one of the top sellers during the late-fall-to-late-spring season. Alligator-skin leather goods are a specialty in the gift shop at **Gatorland Zoo,** 14501 S. Orange Blossom, Orlando (ℂ 407/855-5496; www.gatorland.com). And manatee dolls and trinkets are featured in several spots, including **Save the Manatee Club** (mail order only; ℂ 800/432-5646 or 407/539-0990; www.save themanatee.org).

Mall at Millenia   This 1.3-million-square-foot upscale center made quite a splash on the mall scene when it debuted in October 2002 with anchors that include Bloomingdale's, Macy's, and Neiman Marcus. The landing caused so much of a stir that former No. 1 Florida Mall (see above) went to work recruiting some new high-profile names. But it may be tough to compete. In addition to the heavyweight anchors, Millenia offers 200 specialty stores that include Cartier, Chanel, Crabtree & Eveyln, Giorgio's of Palm Beach, Gucci, Louis Vitton, Swarovski, and Tiffany & Co. The mall is 5 miles from downtown Orlando. 4200 Conroy Rd. (at I-4 near Universal Orlando). ✆ 407/363-3555. www.mallatmillenia.com. Take I-4 Exit 74A, Sand Lake Rd./Hwy. 482 east to the John Young Pkwy./Hwy. 423, and go north to Conroy, then west to mall.

3 Other Shopping in Orlando

IN DOWNTOWN ORLANDO

If you can think of nothing better than a relaxing afternoon of bargain hunting or scouring thrift and antiques shops, check out **Antique Row** and **Ivanhoe Row** on North Orange Avenue (stretching from Colonial Dr./Hwy. 50 to Lake Ivanhoe) in downtown Orlando. This collection is a long way from the manufactured fun of Disney. The shops are an interesting assortment of the old, the new, and the unusual. **Flo's Attic,** 1800 N. Orange Ave. (✆ **407/895-1800**), and **A.J. Lillun,** 1913 N. Orange Ave. (✆ **407/895-6111**), sell traditional antiques.

Down the road, a handful of places offer less conventional items. **Wildlife Gallery,** 1219 N. Orange Ave. (✆ **407/898-4544**), sells pricey, original works of wildlife art, including sculpture. And the **Fly Fisherman,** 1213 N. Orange Ave. (✆ **407/898-1989**), sells—no surprise here—fly-fishing gear. Sometimes you can spot people taking casting lessons in the park across the street.

Most of these downtown shops are open from 9 or 10am to 5pm, Monday to Saturday; the owners usually run them, so hours can vary. All are spread over 3 miles along Orange Avenue. The heaviest concentration of shops lies between Princeton Street and New Hampshire Avenue, although a few are scattered between New Hampshire and Virginia avenues. The more upscale shops extend a few blocks beyond Virginia. To get there, take I-4 Exit 85/Princeton St. and turn right on Orange Avenue. Parking is limited, so stop wherever you find a space along the street.

Additionally, you can shop for fresh produce, plants, baked goods, and crafts every Saturday from 8am to 2:30pm at a downtown **farmer's market.** It's located at the intersection of North Magnolia and East Central. Get more information at **www.downtownorlando.com/farmersmarket.asp**.

A FLEA MARKET

Flea World *(Overrated)*   You'll find what may be Florida' largest flea market in Sanford, about 45 minutes north of the attractions. Flea World is pretty much exactly what the name implies: a huge, tacky flea market with a twist. It has everything from dentists' and lawyers' offices to lingerie and lamp shops. Although many folks give it an assortment of derogatory names, it's fun for people-watchers as well as those in desperate need of tractor tires, leather chaps, ginsu knives, and other uncommon merchandise. It has some 2,000 booths. Among this babble of not-so-many bargains are many shops selling Florida T-shirts and souvenir-worthy knickknacks. Just in case the merchandise doesn't give you visual overload, sometimes there is entertainment as diverse as live lions

OTHER SHOPPING IN ORLANDO

> ⌐*Tips* **Back in Disneyville**
>
> In you're a POD (Prisoner of Disney) or just want some options in the land of the Magic Mickey, be sure to check out our shopping tips in chapter 7, especially those in Epcot's World Showcase, including **Yong Feng Shang-dian Shopping Gallery** in the China pavilion or the funky gift shop at Gatorland, which you'll find in chapter 8.

---

and tigers, Elvis impersonators, and bingo. It's open from 10am to 6pm, Friday through Sunday. 4311 Orlando Ave., off U.S. 17/92, Sanford. © **407/321-1792.** www.flea world.com. Take I-4 Exit 98/Lake Mary Blvd., go 3 miles to U.S. 17/92 and turn left. Continue 1 mile. Flea World is on the right.

A HOMESPUN ALTERNATIVE

Mount Dora *Finds* This haven for artists and retirees is also an enjoyable day trip, not to mention a wonderful alternative to Disney. The town, established in 1874, has the genuine feel of old Florida, with an authentic Main Street, far less crowded than the one Disney tries to re-create. The 19th-century buildings lining the streets are picture-perfect, leading to the calm, dark green waters of Lake Dora. Unlike most of Florida, this town actually has rolling hills, adding to the charm. Highlights include **Renninger's Antique Center and Farmer's Market** (© **352/383-8393** for the antique center or **352/383-3141** for the farmer's market; www.renningers.com). The hundreds of shops and booths are open Saturday and Sunday. Up to 1,000 dealers attend Renninger's 3-day antique extravaganzas held the third weekends of January, February, and November. After you've worked up an appetite, take a lunch break at the Beauclaire Dining Room at the historic **Lakeside Inn,** 221 E. 4th Ave. (© **800/556-5016** or 352/383-4101; www.lakeside-inn.com). Enjoy lemonade and cookies while rocking on the front porch overlooking the lake. **Mount Dora.** © 352/383-2165. www.mountdora.com. Take I-4 Exit 92, Hwy. 436, go west to U.S. 441, then north and follow the signs to Mount Dora and its "business district."

SPECIALTY STORES

Bass Pro Shops Outdoor World If you're looking for the retail version of fishing and hunting (including archery) heaven, schedule a visit to this store in Belz's Festival Bay shopping center. The store also features areas for water sports equipment, camping gear, and outdoor apparel as well as a golf pro shop and an aquarium. The store is open daily, usually from 9am to 6pm (closed Christmas). 5156 International Dr. © **407/563-5200.** www.basspro.com. Take I-4 Exit 75A and turn north on I-Drive. It's on the left.

University Store Fans will find a collection of souvenirs and memorabilia from those arch rivals, the University of Florida and Florida State University, and, closer to home, from the University of Central Florida Golden Knights. It's open Monday through Saturday. 1406 N. Mills Ave. © **407/896-9391.** Take I-4 Exit 85/Princeton St., turn right on Orange Ave., then left at Virginia Ave. The store is at the corner of Mills and Virginia.

10

Walt Disney World & Orlando After Dark

After their 2-week annual assault on Disney and Orlando, friends of ours from the United Kingdom needed a week to recover (not counting post-partum time). That's true for a lot of visitors, especially first-timers, who burn it on both ends, wear themselves out, and then need a vacation after their vacation.

Some of you know the feeling. You're hardcore partiers who aren't willing to give it up after a long day in the parks. You want after-hours adventure and, in the last decade, Orlando's tourism czars have built a bundle of entertainment to satisfy your cravings.

The success of Universal's **City-Walk,** a food and club venue that opened in 1999, shows that many visitors have the pizzazz to withstand life after a day of schlepping around

Mickeyville. But don't think **Down-town Disney West Side** and **Pleasure Island** are hurting for business. They, too, are typically filled to capacity.

Check the "Calendar" section of Friday's ***Orlando Sentinel*** for up-to-the-minute details on local clubs, visiting performers, concerts, and events. It has hundreds of listings, many of which are online at **www.orlandosentinel.com**. The ***Orlando Weekly*** is a free magazine found in red boxes throughout central Florida. It highlights the more offbeat and often more spur-of-the-moment performances. You can see it online at **www.orlandoweekly.com**. Another good source on the Internet is **www.orlandoinfo.com**, operated by the Orlando/Orange County Convention & Visitors Bureau.

1 The Performing Arts

While Disney occasionally hosts classical music acts, you'll usually have to go downtown to get a taste of the traditional arts.

CONCERT HALLS & AUDITORIUMS

The city continues to dream of getting financing for a multimillion-dollar world-class performing arts center. While you're holding your breath, there are two existing facilities, both of which fall under the wand of Orlando Centroplex.

Florida Citrus Bowl With 70,000 seats, the bowl is the largest venue in the area for rock concerts, which in the past have featured such heavyweights as Elton John and the Rolling Stones. 1610 W. Church St. (at Tampa St.). © **407/849-2001** for event information, **407/849-2020** to get box office information, © **877/803-7073** or 407/839-3900 to charge tickets via Ticketmaster. www.orlandocentroplex.com. Parking $5–$6.

TD Waterhouse Centre Formerly the Orlando Arena, this 17,500-seat venue has a resume that includes the NBA's Orlando Magic (see "Spectator Sports" in chapter 8) as well as big-name concert performers such as Garth Brooks, Elton

---

⌒Tips First-Run Films

Orlando has a number of multi-theater movie houses in the mainstream tourist areas. Some of the top draws include: **AMC 24** at Pleasure Island (📞 **407/298-4488**); **Cinemark 16 Festival Bay** on North International Drive (📞 **407/351-3117**; www.cinemark.com); **Muvico Pointe 21 Theatres** at Pointe Orlando on International Drive (📞 **407/926-6843**; www.muvico.com); and **Universal Cineplex 16** (📞 **407/354-5998**; www.enjoytheshow.com).

John, and Bruce Springsteen. It also features family-oriented entertainment including the Ringling Bros. Barnum & Bailey Circus in January and a slate of cultural offerings such as Broadway-style shows, ballets, plays, and symphony performances. 600 W. Amelia St. (between I-4 and Parramore Ave.). 📞 407/849-2001 for event information, 407/849-2020 to get box office information, 📞 877/803-7073 or 407/839-3900 for tickets through Ticketmaster. www.orlandocentroplex.com. Parking $5–$6.

THEATER

Orlando–UCF Shakespeare Festival *Finds* The company is known for placing traditional plays in contemporary settings and offers special programs throughout the year, such as *Shakespeare Unplugged,* a reading series. Performances are held in three venues: The Ken and Trisha Margeson Theater, which has 300 seats wrapped around three sides of the stage; the Marilyn and Sig Goldman Theater, an intimate 120-seater; and the Lake Eola Amphitheater, where the 936 seats give a view of Shakespeare under the stars. 812 E. Rollins St. 📞 407/447-1700. www.shakespearefest.org. Tickets $10–$35. Call ahead for reservations. Free parking for indoor season; metered parking in fall.

Orlando Youth Theatre *Kids* Here's a nifty way for families to keep the "kid" theme going outside the parks. This theater by the young includes 6- to 18-year-olds presenting drama, dance, music, and improv in fall and spring and during summer camps. 128 W. Church St. 📞 407/254-4930. www.orlandoyouththeatre.com. Tickets $8.

Theatre Downtown These engaging local actors, some reaching to the group's formation in 1984, put on a range of Broadway-style plays from Boy Gets Girl to *Cat on a Hot Tin Roof.* Performances are Thursday through Saturday nights and Sunday matinees. 2113 N. Orange Ave. 📞 407/841-0083 for tickets. www.theatredowntown.com. Tickets $15 or less.

OPERA

Orlando Opera Company Local professionals, joined by guest artists from around the country, perform a repertoire of traditional fare. Standards include *Carmen, Macbeth,* and the *Marriage of Figaro,* among others. Shows held in the October-to-May season seldom sell out. Performances are staged at the Bob Carr Performing Arts Centre. 401 W. Livingston St. 📞 800/336-7372 or 407/426-1700. www.orlandoopera.org. Tickets $20–$60. Parking $5–$6.

DANCE

Orlando Ballet Formerly called Southern Ballet Theatre, this troupe stages traditional shows such as *The Nutcracker* using guest artists to augment local talent. There has been a resurgence of interest in the ballet in recent years, but performances rarely sell out. The season runs from October to May. Performances feature the Orlando Philharmonic Orchestra (see below) and are at the Bob Carr Performing Arts Centre. 401 W. Livingston St. ℂ 407/426-1739 for information, ℂ 877/803-7073 or 407/839-3900 to get tickets via Ticketmaster. www.orlandoballet.org. Tickets $10–$60. Parking $5–$6.

FILM

Enzian Theater   This full-time, not-for-profit alternative cinema features first-run, first-rate independent films in a 250-seat theater outfitted with a 33-foot screen. The Enzian also hosts a variety of special events, including June's 10-day run of the Florida Film Festival. 1300 S. Orlando Ave., Maitland. ℂ 407/629-1088 or 407/629-0054 for tickets and show times. www.enzian.org.

CLASSICAL MUSIC

Florida Symphony Youth Orchestra   Kids get into the main event again in a program with roots reaching to 1956 (yes—when President Eisenhower was in office). Its musicians, from a radius reaching 40 or so miles from Orlando, play at the Bob Carr Performing Arts Centre and include joint performances with the Orlando Philharmonic (see below), Orlando Opera (earlier in this chapter), and Orlando Ballet (also earlier). 401 W. Livingston St. ℂ 407/896-6700. www.fsyo.org. Parking $5–$6.

Orlando Philharmonic Orchestra   The orchestra offers a varied schedule of classics and pop-influenced concerts throughout the year at the Bob Carr Performing Arts Centre. The musicians also accompany the Southern Ballet (see above). 401 W. Livingston St. ℂ 407/896-6700. www.orlandophil.org. Tickets begin at $20. Parking $5–$6.

2 Dinner Theater

IN WALT DISNEY WORLD

The Magic Mickey offers tons of nighttime entertainment, including laser-light shows, fireworks, and IllumiNations (p. 210). There are also two distinctly different dinner shows worthy of special note, the Hoop-Dee-Doo Musical Revue and the Polynesian Luau Dinner Show, and a third show that's an occasional player.

Note: While they offer entertainment, don't expect haute cuisine. The food is edible—some even good—but the emphasis is on the show, not the grub.

Hoop-Dee-Doo Musical Revue *Moments*   This is Disney's most popular show, so make reservations *early.* The reward: You feast on a down-home, all-you-can-eat barbecue (fried chicken, smoked ribs, salad, corn on the cob, baked beans, bread, salad, strawberry shortcake, and your choice of coffee, tea, beer, wine, sangria, or soda). While you stuff yourself silly in Pioneer Hall, performers in 1890s garb lead you in a foot-stomping hand-clapping high-energy show that includes a lot of jokes you haven't heard since second grade. *Note:* Be prepared to join the fun or the singers and the rest of the crowd will humiliate you.

Reservations should be made 30 to 60 days in advance or earlier, especially during peak periods such as summer and holidays. Show times are 5, 7:15, and 9:30pm daily. If you catch one of the early shows, consider sticking around for the Electrical Water Pageant at 9:45pm, which can be viewed from the Fort Wilderness Beach. 3520 N. Fort Wilderness Trail (at Fort Wilderness Resort and Campground). ℂ 407/939-3463. www.disneyworld.com. Reservations required. Adults $49.01, kids 3–11 $24.81, including tax and tip. Free parking.

Tips **If You're Lucky . . .**

Mickey's Backyard BBQ (© 407/939-3463; www.disneyworld.com) is a seasonal offering at Pioneer Hall at Fort Wilderness Resort & Campground, where Tom Sawyer and Huck Finn allow you onto their home turf to have a thigh-slapping time and a feast in a covered, outdoor pavilion. Expect Mickey and his pals to join you for a meal that includes barbecued pork ribs, baked chicken, hot dogs, corn on the cob, baked beans, beer, wine, and a filling supporting cast. Meals take place at 6:30pm and cost $38 for adults, $25 for kids. It only happens on Tuesdays and Thursdays . . . sometimes. So **call.**

Polynesian Luau *(Moments)* While not quite as much in demand as the Hoop-Dee-Doo, the Polynesian Resort's delightful (and new) 2-hour show is like a big neighborhood party. Disney's Spirit of Aloha Dinner Show features Tahitian, Samoan, Hawaiian, and Polynesian singers, drummers, and dancers who entertain you while you feast on a menu that includes tropical appetizers, Lanai roasted chicken, Polynesian wild rice, South Seas vegetables, dessert, wine, beer, and other beverages. It all takes place 5 nights a week in an open-air theater (dress for nighttime weather) with candlelit tables, red-flame lanterns, and tapa-bark paintings on the walls. Reservations should be made 30 to 60 days in advance or earlier, especially during peak periods such as summer and holidays. Show times are 5:15 and 8pm Tuesday through Saturday. 1600 Seven Seas Dr. (at Disney's Polynesian Resort). © 407/939-3463. www.disneyworld.com. Reservations required. Adults $49.01, kids 3–11 $24.81, including tax. Free parking.

ELSEWHERE IN ORLANDO

Outside the Disney zone, Orlando has an active dinner theater scene, but its offerings are not on par with those in major cultural centers such as New York, London, or Paris. Most of the local dinner shows focus on pleasing the kids, so if you're looking for fun, you'll find it; but if you want critically acclaimed entertainment, look elsewhere. You also won't find first-class food; dinner may remind you of your school lunch days, unless you consume enough alcohol to anesthetize your taste buds. Still, attending a show is considered by many to be a quintessential Orlando experience, and if you arrive with the right attitude, you'll most likely have an enjoyable evening.

Note: Discount coupons to the dinner shows below can often be found inside the tourist magazines that are distributed in gas stations and tourist information centers; you'll also find them in many non-Disney hotel lobbies and sometimes on the listed websites.

Arabian Nights If you're a horse fancier, this one's a must. One of the classier dinner-show experiences, it stars many of the most popular breeds, from chiseled Arabians to hard-driving Andalusians to beefcake Belgians. They giddy-up through performances that include Wild West trick riding, chariot races, slapstick comedy, and bareback bravado. Locals rate it No. 1 among Orlando dinner shows. On most nights, the performance opens with a ground trainer working one-on-one with a black stallion. The dinner, served during the 2-hour show, includes salad, prime rib, vegetables, potatoes, dessert, wine, and beer. Special diets can be accommodated with advance notice. Show times vary, but

---

Tips **Coming Soon**

The dinner-show circuit is scheduled to get a new player with the projected mid-2003 arrival of **Dolly Parton's Dixie Stampede** (© **877/782-6733** or 407/238-4455; www.dixiestampede.com). Orlando's Stampede will be similar to the theaters the actress and country singer operates in Pigeon Forge, Tennessee; Branson, Missouri; and Myrtle Beach, South Carolina. The $28 million project has already gone through a facelift and a move to a less congested part of town at 8251 Vineland Ave., off I-4, on the same parcel as Orlando Premium Outlets. Tickets will run about $44 for adults and $29 for kids 3 to 11, including a four-course, Southern-style meal (rotisserie chicken or barbecued pork). The show features 32 horses, 30 riders, singers, and dancers. Alcohol won't be served.

---

there is at least 1 show nightly. 6225 W. Irlo Bronson Memorial Hwy. (U.S. 192), Kissimmee. © **800/553-6116** or 407/239-9223. www.arabian-nights.com. Reservations recommended. $44 adults, $27 children 3–11. Free parking. Take I-4 Exit 64A/U.S. 192 and look for the white-light sign on the left.

Medieval Times   Orlando has one of the eight Medieval Times shows in the United States and Canada. Inside, guests gorge themselves on barbecued spare ribs, herb-roasted chicken, soup, appetizer, potatoes, dessert, and beverages including beer. But because this is the 11th century, you eat with your fingers from metal plates while knights mounted on Andalusian horses run around the arena, jousting and clanging to please the fair ladies. Arrive 90 minutes early for good seats and to see the Medieval Village, a re-created Middle Ages settlement, and the Museum of Torture. Show times vary, but there is at least 1 show nightly. 4510 W. Irlo Bronson Memorial Hwy. (U.S. 192), Kissimmee. © **800/229-8300** or 407/396-1518. www.medievaltimes.com. Reservations recommended. $44 adults, $28 children 3–11. Free parking. Take I-4 Exit 64A/ U.S. 192 5 miles until U.S. 192 makes a big sweeping curve to the right. It's on the right.

Pirates Dinner Adventure   The special-effects show at this theater includes a full-size ship in a 300,000-gallon lagoon, circus-style aerial acts, a lot of music, and a little drama. Dinner includes an appetizer buffet with the pre-show, followed by roast chicken and beef, rice, vegetables, dessert, and coffee. After the show, you're invited to the Buccaneer Bash dance party where you can mingle with cast members. Show times vary, but there is at least 1 show nightly. 6400 Carrier Dr. © **800/866-2469** or 407/248-0590. www.orlandopirates.com. Reservations recommended. $43.95 adults, $26.95 children 3–11. Free parking. Take I-4 Exit 74A, Sand Lake Rd./Hwy. 482, north to Carrier, turn right.

3 At Walt Disney World

The places described here can be located on the map "Downtown Disney" on p. 299. For information about nighttime activities throughout Downtown Disney, call © **407/939-2648**.

PLEASURE ISLAND

This rocking Walt Disney World launch pad is a 6-acre complex of nightclubs, restaurants, shops, and movie theaters where you can enjoy for free some things that are open during the day. At night, for a single admission price ($21.25

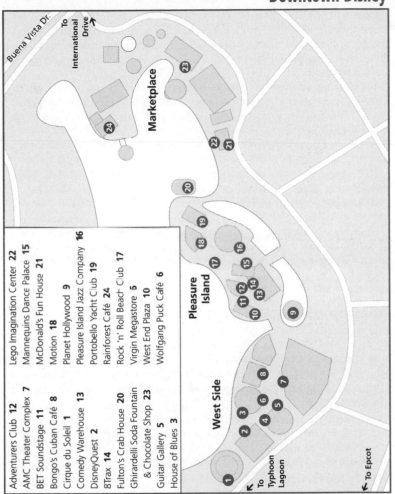

Buena Vista Dr.

To International Drive

Marketplace

Pleasure Island

West Side

To Typhoon Lagoon

To Epcot

Adventurers Club **12**	Lego Imagination Center **22**
AMC Theater Complex **7**	Mannequins Dance Palace **15**
BET Soundstage **11**	McDonald's Fun House **21**
Bongo's Cuban Café **8**	Motion **18**
Cirque du Soleil **1**	Planet Hollywood **9**
Comedy Warehouse **13**	Pleasure Island Jazz Company **16**
DisneyQuest **2**	Portobello Yacht Club **19**
8Trax **14**	Rainforest Café **24**
Fulton's Crab House **20**	Rock 'n' Roll Beach Club **17**
Ghirardelli Soda Fountain & Chocolate Shop **23**	Virgin Megastore **5**
Guitar Gallery **5**	West End Plaza **10**
House of Blues **3**	Wolfgang Puck Café **6**

including tax), you can go club hopping and celebrate New Year's Eve into the wee hours every night of the week. Pay special attention to **Mannequins** (listed a little later). This club is the crème in Pleasure Island and fills quickly, so late arrivals may be left at the door.

Pleasure Island is made to appear like an abandoned waterfront industrial district with clubs in its lofts and warehouses. But the streets are decorated with brightly colored lights and balloons. Dozens of searchlights play overhead and rock music emanates from the bushes. You'll be given a map and show schedule when you enter the park. Take a look at it and plan your evening around the shows that interest you. The mood is always festive, especially at midnight, which is celebrated with a high-energy street party, live entertainment, a barrage of fireworks, and showers of confetti.

Although this is Disney, it's essentially a bar district where liquor is served, so if you're sending your older children, use the same rules you use at home. Also note they must be 19 to get in unless accompanied by a parent or legal guardian.

Pleasure Island has seven regular clubs, plus BET Soundstage, which is included in the ticket on nights it doesn't have a special concert going. In addition to the clubs, there are shops and eateries (with outdoor umbrella tables) on the island. **Planet Hollywood** (p. 145) is adjacent and doesn't require a Pleasure Island ticket.

For more information on Pleasure Island's clubs and events, call © **407/ 934-7781** or surf over to **www.disneyworld.com**. Admission is free before 7pm and $19.95, plus tax, after 7pm. (It's $69 on New Year's Eve.) Admission is included in Disney's 5- to 7-day Park Hopper Plus and Ultimate Park Hopper passes. Clubs are open daily from 7pm to 2am; shops open at 11am and some are open till midnight or later. There's free self-parking; valet parking is $6.

Here's the club lineup:

Adventurers Club   The most unique of Pleasure Island's clubs occupies a multistory building that, according to legend, was designed to house the library and archaeological trophy collection of island founder and compulsive explorer, Merriweather Adam Pleasure, a figment of Disney's imagination. It's also the global headquarters for the Adventurers Club, which Pleasure headed until he vanished at sea in 1941. The plush club is chock-full of artifacts: early aviation photos, hunting trophies, shrunken heads, Buddhas, goddesses, and a mounted "yakoose," a half yak, half moose that occasionally speaks, whether you've been drinking or not. In the eerie Mask Room, more strange sounds are heard and the 100 or so masks move their eyes, jeer, and make odd pronouncements. Also on hand are Pleasure's zany band of globetrotting friends and servants, played by skilled actors who interact with guests while staying in character. Comedy, cabaret, and other shows run in various rooms within the club. We could easily hang out here all night, sipping potent tropical drinks in the library or the bar, where elephant-foot bar stools rise and sink mysteriously.

BET Soundstage   This club grooves—loudly—to the sounds of reggae, the smooth moves of traditional R&B, and the rhyme of hip-hop. If you like the BET Cable Network, you'll love it. You can boogie on an expansive dance floor or kick back on an outdoor terrace. The club also serves Caribbean-style finger food and periodically has concerts for a separate charge (© **407/934-7666**).

Comedy Warehouse   Housed in the island's former power plant, the Comedy Warehouse has a rustic interior with tiered seating. A troupe of comics—the Who, What and Warehouse Players—perform 45-minute improvisational comedy shows based on audience suggestions. This is Disney, so the shows are neither as risqué as those at other improv clubs nor candidates for anyone's top 10. There are several shows nightly and drinks are served. Arrive early.

8Trax   Disco and bell bottoms rule in this 1970s-style club, where some 50 TV monitors air diverse shows and videos over the dance floor. A DJ plays everything from "YMCA" to "The Hustle" while the disco ball spins. All you need to bring is your polyester and patent leather.

Mannequins Dance Palace   Housed in a vast dance hall with a small-town movie-house facade, Mannequins is supposed to be a converted mannequin warehouse (remember, you're still in Disney World). This high-energy club has a big rotating dance floor and it's a local favorite, so much so that it's one of the toughest clubs in Orlando to get into, so arrive early, especially on weekends. Those who get in find three levels of bars and hangout space that are festooned with elaborately costumed mannequins and moving scenery suspended from the

Finds Not Your Ordinary Circus

Lions and tigers and bears?

Oh, no. But you won't feel cheated.

This Disney partnership with the famed no-animals circus is located in Downtown Disney West Side. **Cirque du Soleil,** which translates to "circus of the sun" and flutters off the tongue as *"SAIRK doo so-LAY,"* is nonstop energy. At times it seems all 64 performers are on stage simultaneously, especially during the intricately choreographed trampoline routine. Trapeze artists, high-wire walkers, an airborne gymnast, a posing strongman, mimes, and two zany clowns cement a show called *La Nouba* (it means "live it up") into a five-star performance.

Of all the Cirque du Soleil shows, we think this one may be second only to "O" at the Bellagio in Las Vegas. That said, though *La Nouba* is a ton of fun, it's also one of the priciest shows in town. If you're on a tight or even modest budget, it may be gut-check time: Can you blow your entertainment allowance for a day or two on 90 minutes of fun? There are two ticket categories: $82 for adults and $49 for kids 3 to 9 (plus tax) for center of the theater seats; $72 and $44, respectively, for seats to the right and left of the stage. Shows are at 6 and 9pm 5 nights a week, but times and nights rotate (the show was dark Sun and Mon at press time) and sometimes there's a matinee, so call ahead (© 407/939-7600) or check the show's website (**www.cirquedusoleil. com**) for information and tickets.

overhead rigging. A DJ plays contemporary tunes filtered through speakers powerful enough to blast the hair weave off Burt Reynolds, and there are high-tech lighting effects. You must be 21 to get in, and they're very serious about it. Have your ID ready, even if you learned to dance to the Beatles.

The Pleasure Island Jazz Company   This big barn-like club—purported to be an abandoned waterfront carousel factory—features contemporary and traditional live jazz, with funky coffees and, by club standards, a respectable domestic wine list. Performers are mostly locals, but sometimes there's a big name, such as Kenny Rankin, Lionel Hampton, Maynard Ferguson, the Rippingtons, or Billy Taylor.

Rock 'n' Roll Beach Club   Once the laboratory in which Pleasure developed a unique flying machine, this three-story structure today houses an always-crowded dance club where live bands play classic rock from the '60s through the '90s. There are bars on all three floors, including one that serves international brews. The first level contains the dance floor. The second and third levels offer air hockey, pool tables, basketball machines, pinball, video games, darts, and a pizza and beer stand.

Motion   Pleasure Island's newest dance club is a hyperactive joint that features Top-40 tunes and alternative rock, and appeals to younger or young-at-heart partiers. The club uses moody blue lighting to halfway convey the sensation that you're dancing the night away in space. This club replaced the Wildhorse Saloon, a country-style dance and concert venue that lasted less than 3 years.

DISNEY'S WEST SIDE

This area adjoins Pleasure Island and offers additional shops, restaurants, and a 24-screen AMC Theater. But the two most popular entries are:

Bongo's Cuban Café *(Overrated* Created by Cuban-American singer Gloria Estefan and her husband, Emilio, the cafe is Downtown Disney's version of old Havana. There are leopard spotted chairs and mosaic bar stools shaped like bongo drums. There's no dance floor to speak of, though you could cha-cha on the patio, an upstairs number that overlooks the rest of West Side. It's a great place to sit back and bask in the Latin rhythms. But, while the mood is good, we find the food a little lacking. Open daily from 11am to 2am. © **407/828-0999.** www.bongoscubancafe.com. No reservations. Free self-parking.

House of Blues Several well-known artists have performed here, including Jethro Tull, Blue Oyster Cult, Quiet Riot, Duran Duran, and others. The barn-like building, with three tiers, may be a little difficult for those with disabilities to maneuver, but there really isn't a bad seat in the house. The atmosphere is dark and boozy, perfect for the bluesy sounds that raise the rafters. The dance floor is big enough to boogie without doing the bump with a stranger. You can dine in the adjoining restaurant ($9–$25) on baby-back ribs, Louisiana craw-fish, jambalaya, New Orleans–style shrimp, and Cajun meat loaf. There's also a Sunday gospel brunch (see p. 146 for more about the menu). © **407/934-2583.** www.hob.com. Cover charges vary by event/artist. Free self-parking.

4 CityWalk

Located between the Islands of Adventure and Universal Studios Florida theme parks, this nightclub, restaurant, and shopping district had its coming-out party in 1999 and went nose-to-nose with Disney's Pleasure Island. It opens daily at 11am, but the hours of many clubs and restaurants vary, so call in advance if you're interested in a specific venue. Most clubs stay open until 2am.

At 30 acres, CityWalk (© **407/363-8000** or 407/224-9255; www.citywalk. com or www.universalorlando.com) is five times larger than Pleasure Island. Alcohol is prominently featured here, so an adult should accompany all teens, young children, and party-hearty peers. The nights can get pretty wild.

Unlike Pleasure Island, you can walk the district for free at night or visit indi-vidual clubs and pay an individual cover charge. CityWalk also offers two **party passes.** A pass to all clubs costs $8.95 plus tax. For $12 plus tax, you get a club pass and a movie at Universal Cineplex (© **407/354-5998**). Universal also offers free club access to those who buy 2-, 3-, and other multiday theme-park tickets (see chapter 8, "Exploring Beyond Disney: Universal Orlando, SeaWorld & Other Attractions").

Daytime parking in the Universal Orlando garages costs $8, but parking is free after 6pm. To get to CityWalk, take I-4 Exit 74B (westbound) or 75A (east-bound) and follow the signs to the parks.

Tips Chilling Out

You can grab a margarita to go and "chill" in the brightly colored wooden chairs (think of the Adirondacks) outside Jimmy Buffet's Margaritaville. It's a perfect spot to watch the crowds scurrying to and from the theme parks.

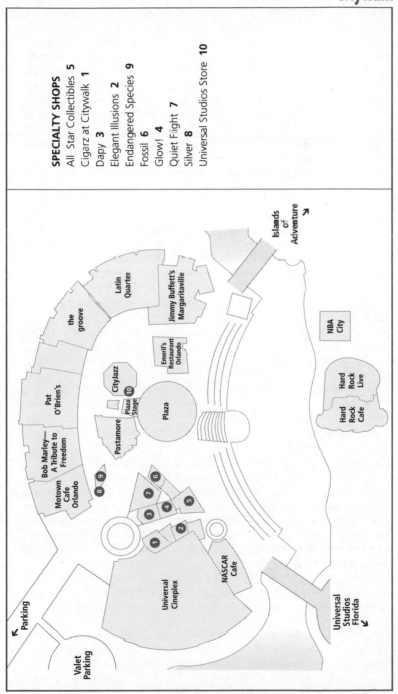

CityWalk

SPECIALTY SHOPS

All Star Collectibles **5**
Cigarz at Citywalk **1**
Dapy **3**
Elegant Illusions **2**
Endangered Species **9**
Fossil **6**
Glow! **4**
Quiet Flight **7**
Silver **8**
Universal Studios Store **10**

Bob Marley—A Tribute to Freedom This hybrid bar/restaurant has a party atmosphere that will make the food more appealing as the night wears on. The clapboard building is said to be a replica of Marley's home in Kingston. Jamaican vittles—such as meat patties, jerk snapper, and, the brew of champions, Red Stripe Beer—are served under patio umbrellas amid portraits of the original Rastamon (p. 151). If you try an Extreme Measure, have a designated driver. Local and national reggae bands perform on a microdot stage. Open daily 4pm to 2am. ✆ **407/224-2262.** www.bobmarley.com. Cover charge $5 after 8pm, more for special acts. Must be 21 or older after 10pm.

CityJazz The cover charge at this club includes the **Downbeat Jazz Hall of Fame** (with memorabilia from Louis Armstrong, Ella Fitzgerald, and other greats) as well as the **Thelonious Monk Institute of Jazz,** a performance venue that's also the site of jazz workshops. The 2-story, 10,500-square-foot building houses more than 500 pieces of memorabilia representing Dixieland, swing, bebop, and modern jazz. It also has a state-of-the-art sound system and stage. Graphic murals and oversize black-and-white photographs set the mood. Acts of national renown perform frequently. It's a real treat for true jazz fans, who can sip cocktails while browsing. On the food side of the equation, expect tapas, sushi, escargot, and such. Open Sunday through Thursday from 8pm to 1am, and Friday and Saturday from 7pm to 2am. ✆ **407/224-2189.** Cover charge $5 (more for special events).

The Groove This is Universal's answer to Mannequin's at Pleasure Island, though it's not as popular, and, therefore, has less of a waiting list. There's a high-tech sound system (read—*LOUD*) and a spacious dance floor in a room gleaming with chrome. Most nights, a DJ plays tunes featuring the latest in hip-hop, jazz-fusion, techno, and alternative rock. Bands occasionally play the house, too. The club features five entertainment eras in as many areas: the 1890s/Vaudeville, the Roaring '20s, the Fabulous '60s, the disco-crazed '70s, and the new millennium. Each spot has a decor, bar, and specialty drink to fit its ambience. Open Sunday through Thursday from 9pm to 2am, and Friday and Saturday from 9pm to 3am. ✆ **407/363-8000.** Cover charge $5. Must be 21 to get in.

Hard Rock Cafe/Hard Rock Live The first concert hall to bear the Hard Rock name is next door to the largest Hard Rock Cafe in the world (p. 150). This building, fashioned to look like an ancient coliseum, has a 2,500-seat concert venue. Call ahead to find out what acts will be featured during your visit. Tickets for big-name performers sell fast. Concerts generally begin about 8pm. The Café is open daily from 11am to midnight. ✆ **407/351-5483.** www.hardrock.com. Tickets $6–$150, depending on concert.

Jimmy Buffett's Margaritaville Flip-flops and flowered shirts are the proper apparel here. Music from the maestro is piped throughout the building, with live music performed on a small stage inside later in the evening. A Jimmy sound-alike strums on the spacious back porch. True parrot-heads know the lyrics at least as well as the singers. Bar-wise, there are three options. The Volcano erupts margarita mix; the Land Shark has fins hanging from the ceiling; and the 12 Volt, is, well, a little electrifying—we'll leave it at that. If you opt for dinner among the palm trees, go for the true Key West experience. Early in the day that means a cheeseburger (in paradise); later it's conch fritters, one of many kinds of fish (pompano, sea bass, dolphin), and key lime pie. Open daily from 11am to 2am. (See p. 150 for more on the food here.) ✆ **407/224-2155.** Cover $5 after 10pm.

Tips Lounging Around

Some of Orlando's best nightlife is located in its hotels. Even locals head to some of these after dark. Consider any of the following and their parent hotels, all of which are listed in chapter 5:

At Disney's Grand Floridian (© **407/824-3000**), a pianist and band alternate playing time from 4 to 11pm outside **Mizner's,** a lounge that has a library look. **Outer Rim** at the Contemporary Resort (© **407/824-1000**) is a trendy nightspot and close to the monorail. **Kimono's** in the Walt Disney World Swan (© **407/934-4000**) turns into a karaoke bar after 8:30pm, while the entertainment is purely visual at the **Dolphin Lobby Bar** in the Renaissance Orlando Resort at SeaWorld (© **407/351-5555**), which overlooks the huge atrium, glass elevators, and koi pond.

The **Laughing Kookaburra Good Time Bar** in the Wyndham Palace Resort (© **407/827-2727**) is open from 7pm to 2am and features dancing and live music or a DJ most nights. The **Top of the Palace Lounge** outside the Wyndham's signature restaurant, Arthur's 27 (© **407/827-2727**), has a great view of Disney's fireworks. **Baskerville's** in the Grosvenor (© **407/827-6534**) offers a solve-it-yourself mystery dinner show on Saturday at 6 and 9pm ($39.95 adults, $10.95 kids 3–9). Nearby, **Moriarty's Pub** features English ales to go along with darts or billiards. And the **Lobby Bar** is a great place to bend an elbow near the piano or watch the world pass through the atrium at the Gaylord Palms ([tel **407/586-0000**).

Latin Quarter   This two-level restaurant/club offers you a chance to absorb the salsa-and-samba culture and cuisine of 21 Latin nations. If you don't know how to move your hips, there's a dance studio to lend a hand. The club features acts ranging from merengue to Latin rock. The sound system is loud enough to blow you into the next county, but before that happens you can leave on your own to see a Latin American art gallery. Open Monday through Friday from 5pm to 2am, and Saturday and Sunday from noon to 2am. © 407/363-5922. Cover $5–$10.

Motown Cafe Orlando   Refuel on finger food and sandwiches ($8–$16) or kick back to the music of Smokey Robinson, the Supremes, the Temptations, and Stevie Wonder (look for their statues, too). Spend time in the indoor/outdoor Big Chill Lounge or browse through memorabilia that includes the light-blue skirts and blouses the Supremes wore in their 1965 Copacabana performance. A live (vs. dead) band frequently plays, giving patrons plenty of incentive to shake their you-know-whats. Open Sunday through Thursday from 11:30am to 11pm, Friday and Saturday from 11am to 2am. © 407/363-8000. Cover charge $5 after 9pm.

NASCAR Café   This one-of-a-kind NASCAR-licensed eatery is a must for gearheads, though its basic vittles (so-so steaks, chicken, pork chops, shrimp, and sandwiches, most under $8) won't win any culinary awards. Race-related souvenirs abound. Open daily from 11am to 11pm or later. © 407/224-3663.

NBA City   This typical theme restaurant and watering hole is an attempt to cash in on fans in a city that has a National Basketball Association team (the Orlando

Magic). The mixed menu ($5–$20) ranges from steaks and chicken to fish, pasta, and sandwiches. The eye candy includes videos and stills of the sport. Fans will like it, but if you're looking for better-than-average food, look elsewhere. Open daily from 11am to midnight or later. © **407/363-5919.**

Pat O'Brien's *Overrated*   It doesn't take a genius to figure out the focus of a place that has a one-page food menu and a booklet filled with drinks. Just like the French Quarter, which is home to the original Patty O's, drinking, drinking, and more drinking are the highlights here. Enjoy the piano bar or the flame-throwing fountain while you suck down the drink of the Big Easy, a Hurricane. Although you can order a soft drink, Pat O'Brien's certainly promotes the hard stuff, and no one under 21 is permitted after 9pm. If your plans for the evening fall anything short of full intoxication (unless you're the designated driver for the aforementioned planners), this may not be the place for you. There's a limited menu of sandwiches and treats like jambalaya and shrimp Creole ($8–$10). Open daily from 4pm to 2am. © **407/363-8000.** Cover charge $5 after 9pm.

5 Hot Spots in Downtown Orlando

Pleasure Island, Downtown Disney, and CityWalk are nighttime magnets for most tourists and some locals. But the dozens of clubs and bars along Orange Avenue and the rest of downtown Orlando attract most home-grown night owls, business travelers who want to stay as far as possible from the Mickey madness, and a small number of enterprising tourists who venture north at night. These places can be located on the map "Downtown Orlando Nightlife" on p. 307.

Cricketers Arms Pub   Regardless of whether you're British or just a sympathizer, this pub is a fun place to party. As the name implies, cricket (and soccer) matches are featured on the telly. Nightly entertainment ranges from karaoke to live bands (usually blues or soft rock). The revelry offers a good excuse to try a pint or two of any of the imports on tap, such as Boddingtons, Fullers ESB, and Old Speckled Hen. There's also a fun menu that offers English standards such as steak-and-ale pie and bangers and mash, among others ($6–$12). Open daily from noon to 2am. 8445 International Dr. © **407/354-0686.** www.cricketersarmspub.com. Cover; $10 for soccer. Free parking.

8 Seconds *Finds*   This honky-tonk has a dark cavernous interior with a huge dance floor. (Ask about free two-step and line-dancing lessons early in the evenings.) There are DJs and live bands. But, what happens outside is what really sets this place apart. A rodeo pen next to the parking lot features "Buckin' Bull Nights" Saturdays with live bulls (there's a mechanical one for novices). Just say, "Yeeehaaaawww" and watch the pros try to hang on. (In order to score, a cowboy needs to stay atop the bull for 8 seconds.) Country stars rising up the charts occasionally hold concerts here. Open Friday and Saturday from 8pm to 2am.

Tips Free Ride

A free public transportation system called **Lymmo** (© **407/841-2279;** www.golynx.com/services/lymmo/index.htm) runs in a designated lane through the downtown area. But because Lymmo stops running at 10pm (midnight on Fri and Sat), it may stop moving before you do. So stash enough cash for a taxi if you're going to party late into the night.

Downtown Orlando Nightlife

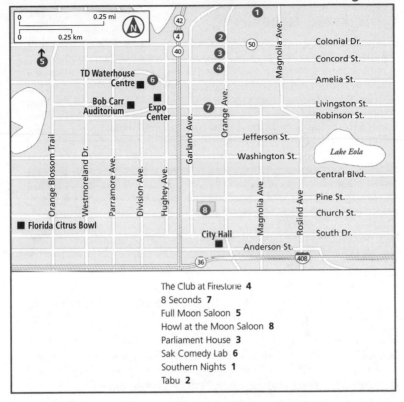

The Club at Firestone **4**
8 Seconds **7**
Full Moon Saloon **5**
Howl at the Moon Saloon **8**
Parliament House **3**
Sak Comedy Lab **6**
Southern Nights **1**
Tabu **2**

100 W. Livingston Ave. ℂ **407/839-4800** or 407/843-5775. www.8-seconds.com/Orlando/html. Cover \$5 for 21 and older; \$7 18–20. Parking in city lot \$3.

Howl at the Moon Saloon   Your best bet is to land on a full moon—even if you're too shy to cock your head back and howllll with the best of them when the club's dueling pianos march through classic rock tunes from the '50s to the '90s. Open daily from 6pm to 2am. 55 W. Church St. ℂ **407/841-9118.** www.howlatthe moon.com. Cover charge Wed–Sat \$2–\$4. Parking in metered lots that run about \$1 an hour.

Sak Comedy Lab   Locals perform at a 200-seat club that has performances several nights of the week. Favorites include the Duel of Fools, where two teams face off in improvised scenes based on suggestions from the audience, and Lab Rats, where students play in improv formats. Shows are usually Tuesday through Wednesday at 9pm, Thursday through Saturday 8 and 10pm. 380 W. Amelia St. ℂ **407/648-0001.** www.sak.com. Admission \$5–\$13. Parking \$5.

Tabu   Once a theater, this downtown club holds a special appeal for members of the under-30 crowd who are on the prowl or older cruisers who want to relive their glory days. DJs and their tunes are the featured attraction on various theme nights. Don't come in flip-flops, denim shorts, or a tank top. Open Tuesday through Sunday from 10pm to 2am. 46 N. Orange Ave., Orlando. ℂ **407/648-8363.** www. tabunightclub.com. Cover \$5–\$10 most nights. Parking \$6.

> ### *Tips* Ghostly Experience
>
> **Orlando Ghost Tours** (© 407/423-5600; www.hauntedorlando.com) puts a different spin on the city's nightlife with 2-hour walking tours that explore the downtown's spookier side. The tours include narratives (some funnier than others) on Florida history and folklore followed by a chance to use "ghost-finding" equipment in a haunted building. It's good fun for those into the supernatural and ghost stories. The cost is $20 adults, $15 kids 6 to 12. Tours run Wednesday through Saturday at 8pm.

---

6 Gay & Lesbian Nightspots

You can get all sorts of useful information on events from **Gay, Lesbian & Bisexual Community Services of Central Florida,** 946 N. Mills Ave., Orlando, FL 32803 (© **407/228-8272;** www.glbcc.org). **GayOrlando Network (www.gay orlando.com)** and the **Gay Guide to Florida (http://gay-guide.com)** also feature a lot of nightlife entries. Travelers interested in sampling some of the city's gay and lesbian hot spots can check out the following places:

The Club at Firestone Go-go boys and drag queens turn Saturday nights into a raucous party. The rest of the week, theme nights (Latin, hip-hop, and more) and other shows keep the dance floor busy. This is a serious club with dark lighting, cavernous rooms, and a high-energy sound. Well-known DJs are sometimes featured. Upstairs, the View Bar offers a good look at the dance floor below. Open daily until 2am; show times vary. 578 N. Orange Ave. (at Concord St. in a converted garage that still bears a Firestone sign). © **407/872-0066.** www.clubatfirestone.com. Cover charge varies, usually from $6–$10. Limited lot parking available for $3–$5.

Full Moon Saloon DJs keep things hopping most nights, but the Moon sometimes offers live entertainment including bands. This club stakes a rightful claim to being Orlando's oldest gay bar. Expect a lot of leather and cowboy duds. The interior is big, but much of the fun happens on the patio and in the expanding backyard. Open daily from noon to 2am; show times vary. 500 N. Orange Blossom Trail (just west of downtown). © **407/648-8725.** www.fullmoonsaloon.com. Cover $5–$10 Fri–Sat, $3 Sun. Free parking.

Parliament House Attached to an aging hotel, this is one of Orlando's wilder, and most popular, gay spots. Not a fancy place, the Parliament House has had years of hard partying and shows it. This is a place to drink, dance, and watch shows that include female impersonators and male revues. There are also DJs. The dance floor is relatively large, but it gets small quickly as the crowd swells. The Parliament has five bars scattered throughout the premises and a 130-room hotel. Open daily from 4pm to 2am; show times vary. 410 N. Orange Blossom Trail (just west of downtown). © **407/425-7571.** www.parliamenthouse.com. Cover $5–$10 Fri–Sat, $3 Sun. Free parking.

Southern Nights Voted "Best Gay Bar" by the readers of a local alternative weekly paper, Southern Nights offers theme nights for women on Saturday and men on Friday. Female-impersonator shows are featured during the week. Open Monday through Friday from 4pm to 3am, Saturday from 8pm to 3am, and Sunday from 7pm to 3am. 375 S. Bumby Ave. (between Anderson St. and Colonial Dr.). © **407/ 898-0424.** www.southern-nights.com. Cover $5 for 21-and-over; $8 for ages 18–20. Free self-parking; valet parking $5.

7 Sports Bars

Champions   The interior is chock-a-block with signed photos, posters, and artifacts. Entertainment includes pool tables, video games, Foosball, darts, and coin-op football and basketball. In addition, sporting events are aired on large-screen TVs and on smaller monitors around the room (a calendar at the entrance lists all game times). Champions offers a fairly extensive bar-food menu.

Note to single women: Men outnumber women about five to one, so this is a good place to meet guys—if you don't mind feeling like a piece of fried chicken at a house-fly convention. Open daily from 4pm to 2am. In Marriott's Orlando World Center, 8701 World Center Dr. ℂ 407/239-4200. Free self-parking; valet parking $15.

ESPN Sports   If you're dying for a sports fix, this is it. Ninety monitors—there are even a few in the bathrooms—broadcast sporting events from around the world. Need we say more? There's a full-service bar, but there's also a restaurant and a small arcade, so you have an excuse to drag your family along. Open daily from 11:30am to 1am. In Walt Disney World at Disney's Boardwalk Resort. ℂ 407/939-3463. www.disneyworld.com. Free parking.

Official All-Star Café   This small chain entry opened at Disney in late 1998. It's just a line drive away from the entrance to the stadium where the Atlanta Braves play their spring training games (see "Spectator Sports" in chapter 8). The interior is dotted with sports memorabilia from Andre Agassi, Wayne Gretzky, Joe Montana, Shaquille O'Neal, and Tiger Woods. There are also a ton of televisions playing your favorite games. Open daily from 11:30am to midnight. At Walt Disney World's Wide World of Sports Complex. ℂ 407/939-3463. Free parking.

Tips **Unsportsmanlike Options**

Disney's Boardwalk has a few options for folks searching for off-the-field nightlife. Street performers sing, dance, and do a little juggling and magic most evenings on the outdoor promenade.

Atlantic Dance (ℂ 407/939-2444 for limited recorded information) features top-40 and '80s dance hits Tuesday through Thursday, and live bands on Friday and Saturday nights. It's open to everyone 21 and over. Hours are from 9pm to 2am and admission is free.

The rustic saloon-style **Jellyrolls** (ℂ 407/939-5100) offers dueling pianos and a boisterous crowd. Strictly for the over-21 set, it's popular with visiting business travelers. There's a $5 cover after 7pm.

If you're looking to hoist a pint, the **Big River Brewery and Grill** (ℂ 407/560-0253) serves micro-brewed beer as well as steaks, ribs, chicken, fish, sandwiches, and salads. Prices range from $7 to $27. It's open Monday through Thursday from 11:30am to 1am; Friday through Sunday from 11:30am to 2am. It's near Atlantic Dance.

Disney's Boardwalk can be a cheap night out if you enjoy strolling and people-watching (and if you stay out of the restaurants and clubs). It has something of a midway atmosphere reminiscent of Atlantic City's heyday.

11

Side Trips from Orlando

Although many visitors to Orlando will never venture outside the city while on vacation, an excursion away from the hubbub of the theme parks can allow you time to recharge your batteries, while still offering a lot of fun and enjoyment. Many families visiting Orlando eventually drive an hour west on I-4 to another major kiddie attraction, Busch Gardens Tampa Bay, but there's a whole lot more to Tampa than a single attraction.

At the head of the bay, the city of Tampa is the commercial center of Florida's west coast—a major seaport and a center of banking, high-tech manufacturing, and cigar making (half a billion drugstore stogies a year). Downtown Tampa may roll up its sidewalks after dark, but a short ride will take you to Ybor City, the historic Cuban enclave, which is now an exciting entertainment and dining venue. You can come here during the day to see the sea life at the Florida Aquarium and stroll through the Henry B. Plant Museum, housed in an ornate Moorish-style hotel built a century ago to lure tourists to Tampa.

Visitors who opt to head southeast usually find their eyes popping open with disbelief at today's Space Coast, where rockets blast off from the Kennedy Space Center at Cape Canaveral. Nearby in Cocoa Beach, they can catch a wave with the surfing crowd. And racing fans sprint toward the deafening roar of the stock cars and motorbikes at Daytona Beach, a town that has earned its designation as the World Center of Racing.

1 Tampa

84 miles W of Orlando

Even if you stay on the beaches 20 miles to the west, you should consider driving into Tampa for a mild taste of metropolis. If you have children in tow, they may *demand* that you go into the city so they can ride the rides and see the animals at Busch Gardens. Once there, you can also educate them (and yourself) at the Florida Aquarium and the city's other fine museums. Additionally, historic Ybor City has the bay area's newest and most contemporary nightlife.

Tampa was a sleepy little port when Cuban immigrants founded Ybor City's cigar industry in the 1880s. A few years later, Henry B. Plant put Tampa on the tourist map by building a railroad that ran into town and constructing the bulbous minarets over his garish Tampa Bay Hotel, now a museum named in his honor. During the Spanish-American War, Teddy Roosevelt trained his Rough Riders here and walked the Ybor City streets with Cuban revolutionary José Martí. A land boom in the 1920s gave the city its charming, Victorian-style Hyde Park suburb, now a gentrified redoubt for the baby boomers just across the Hillsborough River from downtown.

Today's downtown skyline is the product of the 1980s and 1990s booms, when banks built skyscrapers and the city put up an expansive convention center, a performing-arts center, and the St. Pete Times Forum (formerly the Ice Palace), a 20,000-seat bay-front arena that is home to professional hockey's Tampa Bay Lightning. The renaissance hasn't been as rapid as planned, given the recent economic recession, but it is continuing into the 21st century with redevelopment of the seaport area east of downtown. There the existing Florida Aquarium and the Garrison Seaport Center (a major home port for cruise ships bound for Mexico and the Caribbean) are being joined by office buildings, apartment complexes, and a major shopping-and-dining center known as Channelside at Garrison Seaport.

You won't want to spend your entire Florida vacation in Tampa, but everything it offers adds up to a fast-paced, modern city on the go.

ESSENTIALS

GETTING THERE **Tampa International Airport** (© 813/870-8770; www.tampaairport.com), 5 miles northwest of downtown Tampa, is the major air gateway to this area. Most major and many no-frills airlines serve Tampa International, including **Air Canada** (© 800/268-7240 in Canada, 800/776-3000 in the U.S.), **AirTran** (© 800/247-8726), **American** (© 800/433-7300), **America West** (© 800/235-9292), **British Airways** (© 800/247-9297), **Continental** (© 800/525-0280), **Delta** (© 800/221-1212), **JetBlue** (© 800/538-2583), **Lufthansa** (© 800/824-6200), **MetroJet** (© 800/428-4322), **Midway** (© 800/446-4392), **Midwest Express** (© 800/452-2022), **Northwest** (© 800/225-2525), **Southwest** (© 800/435-9792), **Spirit** (© 800/722-7117), **United** (© 800/241-6522), and **US Airways** (© 800/428-4322).

Alamo (© 800/327-9633), **Avis** (© 800/331-1212), **Budget** (© 800/527-0700), **Dollar** (© 800/800-4000), **Enterprise** (© 800/325-8007), **Hertz** (© 800/654-3131), **National** (© 800/227-7368), and **Thrifty** (© 800/367-2277) all have rental-car operations here.

The Limo/SuperShuttle (© 800/282-6817 or 727/527-1111; www.supershuttle.com) operates van services between the airport and hotels throughout the Tampa Bay area. Fares for one person range from $13 to $33 round-trip, depending on your destination. **Taxis** are plentiful at the airport; the ride to downtown Tampa takes about 15 minutes and costs $11 to $19.

Amtrak trains arrive downtown at the **Tampa Amtrak Station,** 601 Nebraska Ave. N. (© **800/872-7245;** www.amtrak.com).

VISITOR INFORMATION Contact the **Tampa Bay Convention & Visitors Bureau,** 400 N. Tampa St., Tampa, FL 33602-4706 (© **800/448-2672,** 800/368-2672, or 813/223-2752; www.visittampabay.com), for advance information. Once you're downtown, head to the bureau's **visitor information center** at 400 N. Tampa St. (Channelside), Suite 2800 (© **813/223-1111**). It's open Monday through Saturday from 9:30am to 5:30pm.

Operated by the Ybor City Chamber of Commerce, the **Centro Ybor Museum and Visitor Information Center,** in Centro Ybor, 1514½ E. 8th Ave. (between 15th and 16th sts. E.), Tampa, FL 33605 (© **813/248-3712;** www.ybor.org), distributes information and has exhibits about the area's history. A 7-minute video will help get you oriented with this area—an 8-block stretch of Seventh Avenue. The center is open Monday through Saturday from 10am to 6pm, Sunday from noon to 6pm.

GETTING AROUND Like most other Florida destinations, it's virtually impossible to see Tampa's major sights and enjoy its best restaurants without a car. You can get around downtown via the free **Uptown-Downtown Connector**

Trolley, which runs north-south between Harbor Island and the city's North Terminal bus station on Marion Street at I-275. The trolleys run every 10 minutes from 6am to 6pm Monday through Friday. Southbound they follow Tampa Street between Tyler and Whiting streets, and Franklin Street between Whiting Street and Harbor Island. Northbound trolleys follow Florida Avenue from the St. Pete Times Forum to Cass Street. It's operated by the Hillsborough Area Regional Transit/HARTline (© **813/254-4278;** www.hartline.org), the area's transportation authority, which also provides scheduled **bus service** ($1.25–$3) between downtown Tampa and the suburbs. Pick up a route map at the visitor information center (see above).

The transportation situation has gotten somewhat better, not to mention nostalgic, with the **TECO Line Street Car System,** a new 2.3-mile old-fashioned streetcar system, complete with overhead power lines, that hauls passengers between downtown and Ybor City via the St. Pete Times Forum, Channelside, Garrison Seaport, and the Florida Aquarium. The cars run every 30 minutes, and one-way fares are $1.25. Check with the visitor center or call HARTline for schedules.

Taxis in Tampa don't normally cruise the streets for fares, but they do line up at public places, such as hotels, the performing-arts center, and bus and train depots. If you need a taxi, call **Tampa Bay Cab** (© **813/251-5555**), **Yellow Cab** (© **813/253-0121**), or **United Cab** (© **813/253-2424**). Fares are $1 at flag fall, plus $1.50 for each mile.

EXPLORING THE THEME & ANIMAL PARKS

Adventure Island *(Kids)*   If the summer heat gets to you before one of Tampa's famous thunderstorms brings late-afternoon relief, you can take a waterlogged break at this 25-acre outdoor water theme park near Busch Gardens Tampa Bay (see below). You can also frolic here during the cooler days of spring and fall, when the water is heated. The Key West Rapids, Tampa Typhoon, Gulf Scream, and other exciting water rides will drench the teens, while other, calmer rides are geared toward younger kids. There are also places to picnic and sunbathe, a games arcade, a volleyball complex, and an outdoor cafe. If you forget to bring your own, a surf shop sells bathing suits, towels, and suntan lotion.

10001 Malcolm McKinley Dr. (between Busch Blvd. and Bougainvillea Ave.). © 813/987-5600. www.4 adventure.com. *Note:* Admission and hours vary from year to year so call ahead, check the website, or get a brochure at the visitor center. Admission at least $29.95 adults, $27.95 children 3–9, plus tax; free for children 2 and under. Combination tickets with Busch Gardens Tampa Bay (1 day each) $64.95 adults, $54.95 children 3–9, free for children under 3. Website sometimes offers discounts. Parking $5. Mid-Mar to Labor Day daily 10am–5pm; Sept–Oct Fri–Sun 10am–5pm (extended hours on holidays). Closed Nov to late Feb. Take Exit 50 off I-275 and go east on Busch Blvd. for 2 miles. Turn left onto McKinley Dr. (N. 40th St.) and entry is on right.

Busch Gardens Tampa Bay *(Kids)*   Although its heart-stopping thrill rides get much of the ink, this venerable theme park (it predates Disney World) ranks among the largest zoos in the country. It had 4.5 million visitors in 2002 (down 2%), according to *Amusement Business,* a trade journal that estimates theme-park attendance. It's a don't-miss attraction for children and adults, who can see, in person, all those wild beasts they've watched on the *Animal Planet*—and they'll get better views of them here than at Disney's Animal Kingdom in Orlando (see chapter 8). Busch Gardens has several thousand animals living in naturalistic environments that help carry out the park's overall African theme. Most authentic is the 80-acre plain, strongly reminiscent of the real Serengeti of Tanzania and

---

<u>**Tips**</u> **If You Need Another Day**

Once you're inside Busch Gardens Tampa Bay and decide you really need more time to see the park, the park frequently offers a **Next-Day Ticket,** which lets you back in the next day for about $16 per person.

Also, if you're going to Orlando, Busch Gardens Tampa Bay is included in the five-park version of the **FlexTicket,** a 14-day pass which also gives admission to Universal Studios Florida, SeaWorld, Islands of Adventure, and Wet 'n' Wild for $209.95 for adults and $175.95 for children 3 to 9.

Kenya, upon which zebras, giraffes, and other animals graze. Unlike the animals on the real Serengeti, however, the grazing animals have nothing to fear from lions, hyenas, crocodiles, and other predators, which are confined to enclosures—as are hippos and elephants.

The park has eight areas, each of which has its own theme, animals, live entertainment, thrill rides, kiddie attractions, dining, and shopping. A Skyride cable car soars over the park, offering a bird's-eye view of it all. Turn left after the main gate and head to **Morocco,** a walled city with exotic architecture, craft demonstrations, a sultan's tent with snake charmers, and an exhibit featuring alligators and turtles. The Moorish-style Moroccan Palace Theater features an ice show, which many families consider to be the park's best entertainment for both adults and children. Here you can also attend a song-and-dance show in the Marrakech Theater. Overlooking it all is the Crown Colony Restaurant, the park's largest.

After watching the snake charmers, walk eastward past Anheuser-Busch's fabled Clydesdale horses to **Egypt,** where you can visit King Tut's tomb with its replicas of the real treasures and listen to comedian Martin Short narrate "Akbar's Adventure Tours," a wacky simulator that "transports" one and all across Egypt via camel, biplane, and mine car. The whole room moves on this ride, which lasts only 5 minutes—much less time than the usual wait to get inside. Youngsters can dig for their own ancient treasures in a sand area. Adults and kids 54 inches or taller can ride Montu, the tallest and longest inverted roller coaster in the world with seven upside-down loops. Your feet dangle loose on Montu, so make sure your shoes are tied tightly and your lunch has had time to digest.

From Egypt, walk to the **Edge of Africa,** the most unique of the park's eight areas, and the home of most of the large animals. Go immediately to the Expedition Africa Gift Shop and see if you can get on one of the park's zoologist-led wildlife tours (see "How to See Busch Gardens," below).

Next stop is **Nairobi,** the most beautiful part of the park, where you can see gorillas and chimpanzees in the Myombe Reserve in a lush area that replicates their natural rainforest habitat. Nairobi also has a baby animal nursery, a petting zoo, turtle and reptile displays, an elephant exhibit (alas, the magnificent creatures seem to be bored to the point of madness), and Curiosity Caverns, where bats, reptiles, and small mammals that are active in the dark are kept in cages (it's the most traditional zoolike area here). The entry to Rhino Rally, the park's safari adventure, is at the western end of Nairobi.

Next, head to **The Congo,** highlighted by rare white Bengal tigers that live on Claw Island. The Congo is also home to two roller coasters: Kumba, the largest and fastest roller coaster in the southeastern United States (54-in. minimum height);

Tampa

 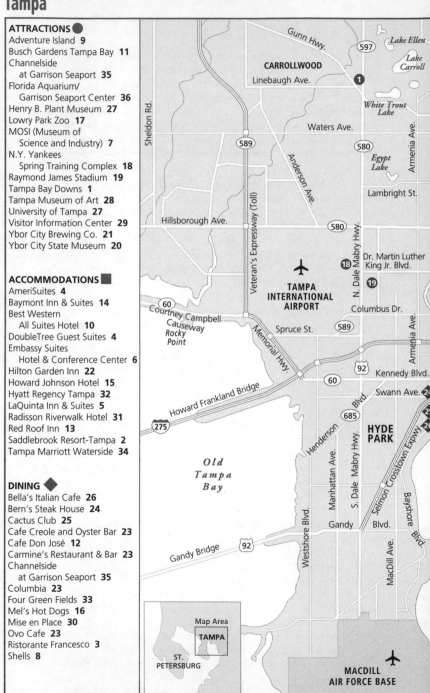

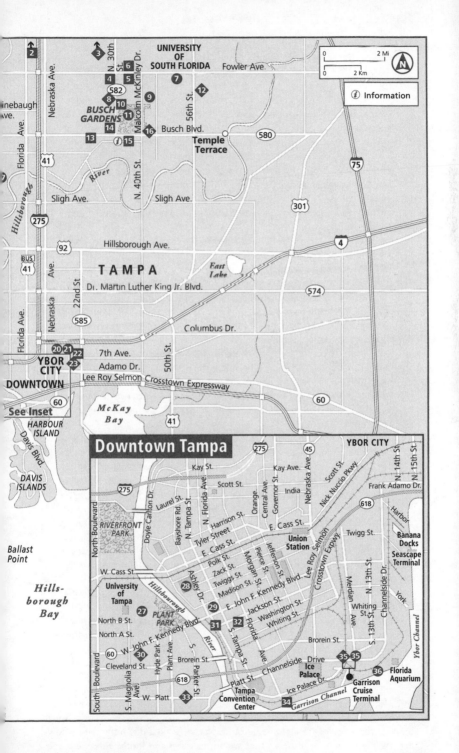

⟨Tips **How to See Busch Gardens**

You can save a few dollars and avoid waiting in long lines by buying your tickets to Busch Gardens Tampa Bay at the privately owned **Tampa Bay Visitor Information Center,** opposite the park at 3601 E. Busch Blvd., at North Ednam Place (℃ **813/985-3601;** www.home town.aol.com\tpabayinfoctr). Owner Jim Boggs worked for the park for 13 years and gives expert advice on how to get the most out of your visit. He sells discounted tickets to Busch Gardens, Adventure Island, and other attractions, and he will book hotel rooms and car rentals for you, often at a discount. The center is open Monday through Saturday from 10am to 5:30pm, Sunday from 10am to 2pm, except Christmas.

Arrive early and allow at least a day to see the park. Try not to come when it's raining, because some rides may not operate. Bring comfortable shoes; and, remember, you will get wet on some of the rides, so wear or bring appropriate clothing (shops near the rides sell plastic ponchos for $5 or $6, but they're cheaper in the outside world). There are lockers throughout the park where you can stash your gear. Don't be surprised if the park's security staff asks to search your bags before they'll let you enter the main gate.

As soon as you're through the turnstiles, pick up a copy of a park map and the day's activity schedule, which tells what's showing and when at the 14 entertainment venues in the park. Then take a few minutes to carefully plan your time—it's a big park with lots to see and do. Busch Gardens continues to grow, so be on the lookout for new attractions.

Although you'll get close to Busch Garden's predators, hippos, and elephants in their glass-walled enclosures, the only way to mingle with the grazers is on a tour. The best is a **VIP Animal Adventure Tour,** on which you'll roam the plains in the company of a zoologist. These 1-hour excursions cost a pricey $75 per person (in addition to the park's entry fee) and usually leave about 1:30pm daily. The tours can fill up fast, and you can't call ahead for reservations, so as soon as you enter the park, go to the Expedition Africa Gift Shop, opposite the Crown Colony Restaurant in the Edge of Africa, to reserve a spot. Another (though less attractive) alternative is the 30-minute, zoologist-led **Serengeti Safari Special Tours,** in which you ride out among the grazers on the back of a flatbed truck. These are worth an extra $30 per person regardless of age. You can make reservations for the morning tour at the Expedition Africa Gift Shop, but the midday and afternoon tours are first-come, first-served. Note that children under 5 are not allowed on either tour.

---

and The Python (48-in. minimum), which twists and turns for 1,200 feet. You will get drenched—and refreshed on a hot day—by riding the Congo River Rapids, where you're turned loose in round boats that float down the swiftly flowing "river" (42-in. minimum). There are bumper cars and kiddie rides here, too.

From The Congo, walk south into **Stanleyville,** a prototype African village, with a shopping bazaar, orangutans living on an island, and the Stanleyville Theater, usually featuring shows for children. Two more water rides are here: the Tanganyika Tidal Wave (48-in. minimum height), where you'll come to a very damp end, and the Stanley Falls Flume (an aqua version of a roller coaster). Serving ribs and chicken, the picnic-style Stanleyville Smokehouse has some of the best chow in the park.

Up next is **Land of the Dragons,** the most entertaining area for small children. They can spend an entire day enjoying a variety of play elements in a fairytale setting, plus just-for-kids rides. The area is dominated by Dumphrey, a whimsical dragon who interacts with visitors and guides children around a three-story treehouse with winding stairways, tall towers, stepping stones, illuminated water geysers, and an echo chamber.

The next stop is **Bird Gardens,** the park's original core, offering rich foliage, lagoons, and a free-flight aviary for hundreds of exotic birds, including golden and American bald eagles. Be sure to see the Florida flamingos and Australian koalas.

Then you're off to take a break at the **Hospitality House,** which offers piano entertainment and free samples of Anheuser-Busch's famous beers. You must be 21 to imbibe (there's a limit of two free mugs per seating), but soft drinks are also available.

If your stomach can take another hair-raising ride, climb aboard **Gwazi** (48-in. minimum), an adrenaline-pumping attraction where a pair of old-fashioned wooden roller coasters (named the Lion and the Tiger) start simultaneously and whiz within a few feet of each other six times as they roar along at 50 mph. The coasters rise to 90 feet. In Gwazi's "Water Wars," participants shoot water-filled balloons at each other with big slingshots. It's a soaking way to end your visit.

If you want to experience the park's fifth and final roller coaster, head to **Timbuktu** and climb aboard the **Scorpion,** a high-speed number with a 60-foot drop and 360-degree loop (42-in. height minimum).

New Fun: In January 2003, Busch joined the interactive animal game by adding a $325, 6-hour zookeeper-for-a-day program. It also devoted 26 acres of its 65-acre Serengeti Plain to free-roaming white rhinos, and debuted a 22-minute multi-sensory *Goosebumps* film in a new 750-seat theater.

You can exchange foreign currency in the park, and interpreters are available.

Note: You can get to Busch Gardens from Orlando via shuttle buses, which pick up at area hotels between 8:00 and 10:15am for the 1½- to 2-hour ride, with return trips starting at 5pm and continuing until the park closes. Round-trip fares are $5 per person. Call ✆ **800/511-2450** for schedules, pickup locations, and reservations.

3000 E. Busch Blvd. (at McKinley Dr./N. 40th St.). ✆ **888/800-5447** or 813/987-5283. www.buschgardens. com. **Note:** Admission and hours vary so call ahead, check the website, or get a brochure at visitor centers. Admission at least $51.95 adults, $42.95 children 3–9, plus tax; free for children 2 and under. Website offers discounts. Daily 10am–6pm (extended hours to 7 and 8pm in summer and on holidays). Parking $8. Take I-275 north of downtown to Busch Blvd. (Exit 50) and go east 2 miles. From I-75, take Fowler Ave. (Exit 54) and follow the signs west.

Florida Aquarium 🐛🐛 *Kids*   See more than 5,000 aquatic animals and plants that call Florida home at this entertaining and informative attraction. The exhibits follow a drop of water from the pristine springs of the Florida Wetlands Gallery, through a mangrove forest in the Bays and Beaches Gallery, and out onto the Coral Reefs, where an impressive 43-foot-wide, 14-foot-tall panoramic window lets you look out to schools of fish and lots of sharks and stingrays. Also worth visiting are the "Explore a Shore" playground to educate the kids, a deep-water exhibit, and a tank housing moray eels. You can also go out on the bay to look for birds and sea life on 90-minute Dolphin Quest cruises in the *Bay Spirit,* a 64-foot diesel-powered catamaran. The aquarium also has added a new **Dive with the Sharks** program (© 813/367-4005) that gives certified scuba divers the chance to swim with blacktip reef, sand tiger, and nurse sharks for 30 minutes. The $150 price tag includes a souvenir photo and T-shirt.

701 Channelside Dr. © 813/273-4000. www.flaquarium.net. Admission $15 adults, $12 seniors, $10 children 5–13, free for children under 5. Dolphin Quest $18 adults, $17 seniors, $13 children 5–13, free for children under 5. Combination aquarium admission and Dolphin Quest $30 adults, $26 seniors, $20 children 5–13, free for children under 5. Website sometimes offers discounts. Parking $4. Daily 9:30am–5pm. Dolphin Quest Mon–Fri 2pm; Sat–Sun 1 and 3pm. Closed Thanksgiving, Christmas.

Lowry Park Zoo *Kids*   The opportunity to watch 3,000-pound manatees, komodo dragons, Persian leopards, and rare red pandas makes this a worthwhile excursion after the kids have seen the plains of Africa at Busch Gardens. With lots of greenery, bubbling brooks, and cascading waterfalls, this 24-acre zoo displays animals in settings similar to their natural habitats. Other major exhibits include a Florida wildlife display, an Asian Domain, a Primate World, an Aquatic Center, a free-flight aviary with a birds-of-prey show, a hands-on Discovery Center, and an endangered-species carousel ride. The new Wallaroo Station has kids' rides, a small water park, a kangaroo walk-about, and a petting zoo. Lowry Park has one of Florida's three manatee hospitals and rehabilitation centers. It's also a sanctuary for Florida panthers and red wolves.

1101 W. Sligh Ave. © 813/935-8552 or 813/932-0245 for recorded information. www.lowryparkzoo.com. Admission $9.50 adults, $8.50 seniors, $5.95 children 3–11, free for children 2 and under. Daily 9:30am–5pm. Closed Thanksgiving, Christmas. Take I-275 to Sligh Ave. (Exit 48) and follow the signs.

VISITING THE MUSEUMS

Henry B. Plant Museum   Originally built in 1891 by railroad tycoon Henry B. Plant as the 511-room Tampa Bay Hotel, this ornate building alone is worth a short trip across the river from downtown to the University of Tampa campus. Its 13 silver minarets and distinctive Moorish architecture, modeled after the Alhambra in Spain, make this National Historic Landmark a focal point of the Tampa skyline. Although the building is the highlight of a visit, don't skip its contents: art and furnishings from Europe and the Orient; and exhibits that explain the history of the original railroad resort, Florida's early tourist industry, and the hotel's role as a staging point for Teddy Roosevelt's Rough Riders during the Spanish-American War.

401 W. Kennedy Blvd. (between Hyde Park and Magnolia aves.). © 813/254-1891. www.plantmuseum.com. Free admission; suggested donation $5 adults, $2 children 12 and under. Tues–Sat 10am–4pm; Sun noon–4pm. Closed Thanksgiving, Christmas Eve, and Christmas Day. Take Kennedy Blvd. (Fla. 60) across the Hillsborough River.

MOSI (Museum of Science and Industry) *Kids*   A great place to take the kids on a rainy day, MOSI is the largest science center in the Southeast and has more than 450 interactive exhibits. You can step into the Gulf Hurricane and experience 74-mile-per-hour winds, defy the laws of gravity in the unique *Challenger* space experience, and explore the human body in The Amazing You. If your heart is up to it, you can ride a bicycle across a 98-foot-long cable suspended 30 feet up in the air above the lobby (don't worry: you'll be harnessed to the bike). You can also watch stunning movies in Florida's first IMAX dome theater or take a 5-minute ride in a flight simulator ($3.50 additional charge). Outside, trails wind through a 47-acre nature preserve with a butterfly garden.

4801 E. Fowler Ave. (at N. 50th St.). (📞 813/987-6100. www.mosi.org. Admission $14.95 adults, $12.95 seniors, $11.95 children 2–12, free for children under 2. Admission includes IMAX movies. Daily 9am–5pm or later. From downtown, take I-275 north to Fowler Ave. E. (Exit 51). Take this 2 miles east to museum on right.

Tampa Museum of Art   Located on the east bank of the Hillsborough River next to the round NationsBank building (locals facetiously call it the "Beer Can"), this fine-arts complex offers eight galleries with changing exhibits ranging from classical antiquities to contemporary Florida art. There's also a 7-acre riverfront park and sculpture garden. Call or check the website for the schedule of temporary exhibits.

600 N. Ashley Dr. (at Twiggs St.), downtown. (📞 813/274-8130. www.tampamuseum.com. Admission $5 adults, $4 seniors, $3 children 6–18 and students with identification cards, free for children under 6, by donation Thurs 5–8pm and Sat 10am–noon. Tues–Wed and Fri–Sat 10am–5pm; Thurs 10am–8pm; Sun 1–5pm. Parking 90¢ per hour. Take I-275 to Exit 44 (Ashley Dr.).

YBOR CITY
Northeast of downtown, the city's historic Latin district takes its name from Don Vicente Martinez Ybor (*Eeee*-bore), a Spanish cigar maker who arrived here in 1886 via Cuba and Key West. Soon his and other Tampa factories were producing more than 300,000 hand-rolled stogies a day.

It may not be the cigar capital of the world anymore, but Ybor is the happening part of Tampa, and it's one of the best places in Florida to buy hand-rolled cigars. It's not on a par with New Orleans's Bourbon Street, Washington's Georgetown, or New York's SoHo, but good food and great music dominate the scene, especially on weekends when the streets bustle until 4am. Live-music offerings run the gamut from jazz and blues to rock.

At the heart of it all is **Centro Ybor,** a dining-shopping-entertainment complex sprawling between 7th and 8th avenues and 16th and 17th streets ((📞 **813/242-4660;** www.thecentroybor.com). Here you'll find a multiscreen cinema, a comedy club, several restaurants, and a large open-air bar. The Ybor City Chamber of Commerce has its visitor center here (see "Essentials," earlier in this chapter), and the Ybor City State Museum's gift shop is here as well (see below).

Check with the visitor center about **walking tours** of the historic district. **Ybor City Ghost Walks** ((📞 **813/242-4660**) will take you to the spookier parts of the area beginning at 4pm Thursday and Saturday. They cost $10 per person, last 75 minutes, and are by reservation only.

Even if you're not a cigar smoker, you'll enjoy a stroll through the **Ybor City State Museum** ⊛, 1818 9th Ave., between 18th and 19th streets ((📞 **813/247-6323;** www.ybormuseum.org), housed in the former Ferlita Bakery (1896–1973). You can take a self-guided tour around the museum to see a collection of cigar labels, cigar memorabilia, and works by local artisans. Admission is $2 per person. Depending on the availability of volunteer docents, admission includes a 15-minute guided tour of **La Casita,** a renovated cigar worker's cottage adjacent to the museum; it's furnished as it was at the turn of the last century. The museum is open daily from 9am to 5pm, but the best time to visit is between 11am and 3pm, when you have the best chance for the guided tour of La Casita. Better yet, plan to catch the cigar-rolling demonstrations Friday through Sunday from 10am to 3pm.

Housed in a 100-year-old, three-story former cigar factory, **Ybor City Brewing Company,** 2205 N. 20th St., facing Palm Avenue ((📞 **813/242-9222**), produces Ybor Gold and other brews, none with preservatives. Admission of $3 per person

Quacking Around

A fun way to tour downtown and Ybor City is with **Duck Tours of Tampa Bay** (© 813/310-3825; www.ducktoursoftampabay.com), which uses refurbished World War II amphibious "Ducks." Now equipped with bench seats under canopies, these bright yellow half-truck, half-boat vehicles pick up at the company's "Quack Shack" at Newk's Cafe, 514 Channelside Dr., opposite the St. Pete Times Forum, Wednesday through Sunday from 11am to 5pm. The narrated 1-hour, 20-minute excursions go on land through Ybor City, then on the river back to downtown. They cost $18.50 for adults, $16.50 for seniors, $9.95 for children 3 to 12, plus tax. Kids under 3 ride free. Call for the schedule and reservations, which are a good idea on weekends and holidays.

includes a tour of the brewery and a taste of the end result. Tours are usually given Monday through Friday at 1pm.

ORGANIZED TOURS

Swiss Chalet Tours, 3601 E. Busch Blvd. (© **813/985-3601;** www.home town.aol.com\tpabayinfoctr), opposite Busch Gardens in the privately run Tampa Bay Visitor Information Center (see "How to See Busch Gardens," above), operates guided bus tours of Tampa, Ybor City, and environs. The 4-hour tours of Tampa are given from 10am to 3pm daily, with a stop for lunch at the Columbia Restaurant in Ybor City. They cost $45 for adults and $40 for children. The full-day tours of both Tampa and St. Petersburg give a good overview of the two cities and the beaches; these cost $70 for adults and $65 for children, 10am to 5pm. Reservations are required at least 24 hours in advance; passengers are picked up at major hotels and various other points in the Tampa/St. Petersburg area. They can also book bus tours to Orlando, Sarasota, Bradenton, and other regional destinations (call for schedules, prices, and reservations).

OUTDOOR ACTIVITIES & SPECTATOR SPORTS

BIKING, IN-LINE SKATING & JOGGING   Bayshore Boulevard, a 7-mile-long promenade, is famous for its sidewalk right on the shores of Hillsborough Bay and is a favorite for runners, joggers, walkers, and in-line skaters. The route goes from the western edge of downtown in a southward direction, passing stately old homes in Hyde Park, a few high-rise condominiums, retirement communities, and houses of worship, ending at Ballast Point Park. The view from the promenade across the bay to the downtown skyline is unmatched here (Bayshore Boulevard also is great for a drive).

FISHING   One of Florida's best guide services, **Light Tackle Fishing Expeditions,** 6105 Memorial Hwy., Suite 4 (© **800/972-1930** or 813/249-5224; www.leftcoastfishing.com), offers private sport-fishing trips for tarpon, redfish, cobia, trout, and snook. Rates are $325–$425 for two anglers. Call for schedule and required reservations.

GOLF   Tampa has three municipal golf courses where you can play for about $30 to $35, a relative pittance when compared with fees at the privately owned courses here and elsewhere in Florida. The **Babe Zaharias Municipal Golf Course,** 11412 Forest Hills Dr., north of Lowry Park (© **813/631-4374**), is an

18-hole, par-70 course with a pro shop, putting greens, and a driving range. It is the shortest of the municipal courses, but its small greens and narrow fairways present ample challenges. Water provides obstacles on 12 of the 18 holes at **Rocky Point Golf Course,** 4151 Dana Shores Dr. (© **813/673-4316**), located between the airport and the bay. It's a par-71 course with a pro shop, a practice range, and putting greens. On the Hillsborough River in north Tampa, the **Rogers Park Golf Course,** 7910 N. 30th St. (© **813/673-4396**), is an 18-hole, par-72 championship course with a lighted driving and practice range. All the courses are open daily from 7am to dusk, and lessons and club rentals are available.

You can book starting times and get information about these and the area's other courses by calling **Tee Times USA** (© **800/374-8633;** www.teetimesusa.com).

If you want to do some serious work on your game, the **Arnold Palmer Golf Academy World Headquarters** is at Saddlebrook Resort, 5700 Saddlebrook Way, Wesley Chapel, 12 miles north of Tampa (© **800/729-8383** or 813/973-1111; www.saddlebrookresort.com). Half-day and hourly instruction is available as well as 2-, 3-, and 5-day programs for adults and juniors. You have to stay at the resort or enroll in the golf program to play at Saddlebrook. See "Where to Stay," below, for more information about the resort.

For course information online, go to **www.golf.com** and **www.floridagolfing. com,** or call the **Florida Sports Foundation** (© **850/488-8347**) or **Florida Golfing** (© **866/833-2663**).

SPECTATOR SPORTS   National Football League fans can catch the Super Bowl champ **Tampa Bay Buccaneers** at the modern, 66,000-seat Raymond James Stadium, 4201 N. Dale Mabry Hwy., at Dr. Martin Luther King Jr. Boulevard (© **813/879-2827;** www.buccaneers.com) August through December. Single-game tickets (starting at $30) are very hard to come by.

The National Hockey League's **Tampa Bay Lightning** play in the St. Pete Times Forum, beginning in October (© **813/301-6500;** www.tampabaylightning. com). You can usually get single-game tickets ($8–$155) on game day.

New York Yankees fans can watch the Bronx Bombers during baseball spring training from mid-February to the end of March at Legends Field (© **813/879-2244** or 813/875-7753; www.yankees.mlb.com), opposite Raymond James Stadium. This scaled-down replica of Yankee Stadium is the largest spring-training facility in Florida, with a 10,000-seat capacity. Tickets are $10 to $16. The club's minor-league team, the **Tampa Yankees** (same phone and website), plays at Legends Field April through August.

The only thoroughbred racecourse on Florida's west coast, **Tampa Bay Downs,** 11225 Racetrack Rd., Oldsmar (© **800/200-4434** in Florida, or 813/855-4401; www.tampadowns.com), is the home of the Tampa Bay Derby. Races are held from December to May ($2 general admission, $3 clubhouse), and the track presents simulcasts year-round. Call for post times.

Cruise Control

The **Port of Tampa** (© 800/741-2297 or 813/905-7678; www.tampaport.com) is home to four cruise lines and a changing cast of ships that travel the Caribbean and Latin America. At press time, the players were Celebrity Cruise Line, Royal Caribbean Cruise Lines, Holland America Cruise Lines, and Carnival Cruise Line.

TENNIS   Players at all levels can sharpen their games at the **Hopman Tennis Program,** at the Saddlebrook Resort (p. 325). You must be a member or a guest to play here.

SHOPPING

Hyde Park and Ybor City are two areas of Tampa worth some window shopping, perhaps sandwiched around lunch at one of their fine restaurants (see "Where to Dine," below).

On the mall front, the newest player in town is the upscale **International Plaza** (© 813/342-3790; www.shopinternationalplaza.com) near Tampa International Airport, where the headliners include Neiman Marcus, Nordstrom, and Lord & Taylor.

CIGARS   Ybor City no longer is a major producer of hand-rolled cigars, but you can still watch artisans making stogies at the **Gonzalez y Martinez Cigar Factory,** 2025 7th Ave., in the Columbia Restaurant building (© 813/247-2469). Gonzalez and Martinez are recent arrivals from Cuba and don't speak English, but the staff does at the adjoining **Columbia Cigar Store** (it's best to enter here). Rollers are on duty Monday through Saturday from 10am to 6pm.

You can stock up on fine domestic and imported cigars at **El Sol,** 1728 E. 7th Ave. (© 813/247-5554), the city's oldest cigar store; **King Corona Cigar Factory,** 1523 E. 7th Ave. (© 813/241-9109); and **Metropolitan Cigars & Wine,** 2014 E. 7th Ave. (© 813/248-3304).

SHOPPING CENTERS   **Old Hyde Park Village,** 1507 W. Swann Ave., at South Dakota Avenue (© 813/251-3500; www.oldhydeparkvillage.com), is a terrific alternative to cookie-cutter suburban malls. Walk around little shops in the sunshine and check out Hyde Park, one of the city's oldest and most historic neighborhoods, at the same time. The cluster of 50 upscale shops and boutiques is set in a village layout. The selection includes Williams-Sonoma, Pottery Barn, Restoration Hardware, Brooks Brothers, Crabtree & Evelyn, and Godiva, to name a few. There's a free parking garage on South Oregon Avenue behind Jacobson's department store. Most shops are open Monday through Saturday from 10am to 7pm, Sunday from noon to 5pm.

The centerpiece of the downtown seaport renovation, the huge new mall known as **Channelside at Garrison Seaport,** on Channelside Drive between the Garrison Seaport and the Florida Aquarium (© 813/223-4250; www.channel side.com), has stores, restaurants, a dance club, a games arcade, and a multiscreen cinema with an IMAX screen. It opened in 2001.

In Ybor City, the new **Centro Ybor,** on 7th Avenue East at 16th Street (© 813/242-4660; www.centroybor.com), is primarily a dining and entertainment complex, but you'll find a few national stores here such as American Eagle, Birkenstock, and Victoria's Secret.

WHERE TO STAY

We've organized the accommodations listings below into three geographic areas: near Busch Gardens, downtown, and Ybor City. If you're going to Busch Gardens, Adventure Island, Lowry Park Zoo, and the Museum of Science and Industry (MOSI), the motels near Busch Gardens are much more convenient than those downtown, about 7 miles to the south. The downtown hotels are geared to business travelers, but staying there will put you near the Florida Aquarium, the Tampa Museum of Art, the Henry B. Plant Museum, the Tampa Bay Performing Arts Center, scenic Bayshore Boulevard, and the dining and

> **(Value Discount Packages**
>
> Many Tampa hotels combine tickets to major attractions such as Busch
> Gardens in their packages, so always ask about special deals.

shopping opportunities in the Channelside and Hyde Park districts. Staying in
Ybor City will put you within walking distance of numerous restaurants and the
city's hottest nightspots.

The Westshore area, near the bay west of downtown and south of Tampa
International Airport, is another commercial center, with a wide range of
national chain hotels catering to business travelers and conventioneers. It's not
far from Raymond James Stadium and the New York Yankees' spring-training
complex. Check with your favorite chain for a Westshore-Airport location.

Room rates at most hotels in Tampa vary little from season to season. This is
especially true downtown, where the hotels do a brisk convention business all
year round. Hillsborough County adds 12% tax to your hotel room bill.

NEAR BUSCH GARDENS

The nearest chain motel to the park is **Howard Johnson Hotel Near Busch
Gardens Maingate,** 4139 E. Busch Blvd. (© **800/4061411** or 813/988-9191),
an older property that was extensively renovated and reopened in 1999. It's 1½
blocks east of the main entrance.

A bit farther away, the 500-room **Embassy Suites Hotel and Conference
Center,** 3705 Spectrum Blvd., facing Fowler Avenue (© **800/362-2779** or
813/977-7066; fax 813/977-7933), is the plushest and most expensive establishment near the park. Almost across the avenue stands **La Quinta Inn & Suites,**
3701 E. Fowler Ave. (© **800/687-6667** or 813/910-7500; fax 813/910-7600).
Side-by-side just south of Fowler Avenue are editions of **AmeriSuites,** 11408 N.
30th St. (© **800/833-1516** or 813/979-1922; fax 813/979-1926), and **Double-
Tree Guest Suites,** 11310 N. 30th St. (© **800/222-8733** or 813/971-7690; fax
813/972-5525).

Baymont Inn & Suites *(Value)*   Fake banana trees and a parrot cage welcome
guests to the terra-cotta–floored lobby of this comfortable and convenient member of the small chain of cost-conscious but amenity-rich motels. All rooms are
spacious and have ceiling fans and desks. Rooms with king beds also have reclin-
ers, business rooms sport dataport phones and extra-large desks, and the suites
have refrigerators and microwave ovens. Outside, a courtyard with an unheated
swimming pool has plenty of space for sunning. There's no restaurant on the
premises, but plenty are within walking distance.

9202 N. 30th St. (at Busch Blvd.), Tampa, FL 33612. © 800/428-3438 or 813/930-6900. Fax 813/930-0563.
www.baymontinns.com. 146 units. Winter $89–$119 double; off-season $79–$99 double. Rates include continental breakfast and local phone calls. AE, DC, DISC, MC, V. **Amenities:** Outdoor pool; game room; coin-op
washers and dryers. *In room:* A/C, TV, dataport, fridge, coffeemaker, hair dryer, iron.

Best Western All Suites Hotel *(Value)*   This three-story all-suites hotel is
the most beachlike vacation venue you'll find close to the park. Whimsical signs
lead you around a lush tropical courtyard with heated pool, hot tub, and a lively,
sports-oriented tiki bar. The bar can get noisy before closing at 9pm, and
ground-level units are musty, so ask for an upstairs suite away from the action.
Suite living rooms are well equipped, and separate bedrooms have narrow

screened patios or balconies. Great for kids, 11 "family suites" have bunk beds in addition to a queen-size bed for parents. Another 28 suites are especially equipped for business travelers (but are great for couples, too) with ergonomic chairs and big writing desks with speakerphones.

Behind Busch Gardens, 3001 University Center Dr. (faces N. 30th St. between Busch Blvd. and Fowler Ave.), Tampa, FL 33612. ℭ 800/786-7446 or 813/971-8930. Fax 813/971-8935. www.thatparrotplace.com. 150 units. Winter $99–$159 suite for 2; off-season $79–$99 suite for 2. Rates include hot and cold breakfast buffet. AE, DC, DISC, MC, V. **Amenities:** Restaurant (breakfast and dinner only); bar; heated outdoor pool; access to nearby health club; Jacuzzi; game room; limited room service; laundry service; coin-op washers and dryers. *In room:* A/C, TV, dataport, fridge, coffeemaker, hair dryer, iron.

Red Roof Inn Less than a mile west of Busch Gardens, this is the best low-budget choice close to the park. Most of the rooms in the pleasant two-story building are away from the busy boulevard, but be sure to request one toward the rear of the building to avoid the road noise. Although in-room amenities are scarce, the units are spacious for the price.

2307 E. Busch Blvd. (between 22nd and 26th sts.), Tampa, FL 33612. ℭ 800/843-7663 or 813/932-0073. Fax 813/933-5689. www.redroof.com. 108 units. Winter $60–$85 double; off-season $40–$76 double. Rates include local phone calls. AE, DC, DISC, MC, V. **Amenities:** Heated outdoor pool; Jacuzzi; sauna. *In room:* A/C, TV, dataport.

DOWNTOWN TAMPA

Hyatt Regency Tampa 𝆑 Just off the Franklin Street pedestrian mall, this Hyatt has lost its place as downtown's premier hotel to the newer Tampa Marriott Waterside (see below), but still attracts the corporate crowd. The spacious, contemporary rooms lack balconies, and the higher office towers that now surround the hotel restrict views from the windows. Office workers congregate at the Avanzare restaurant for inexpensive light lunches.

2 Tampa City Center (corner of Tampa and E. Jackson sts.), Tampa, FL 33602. ℭ 800/233-1234 or 813/225-1234. Fax 813/273-0234. www.tamparegency.hyatt.com. 521 units. $249–$274 double. Weekend packages available in summer. AE, DC, DISC, MC, V. Valet parking $12. **Amenities:** 2 restaurants; bar; heated outdoor pool; exercise room; Jacuzzi; concierge; business center; limited room service; laundry service; coin-op washers and dryers; concierge-level rooms. *In room:* A/C, TV, dataport, coffeemaker, hair dryer, iron.

Radisson Riverwalk Hotel 𝆑 Set on the east bank of the Hillsborough River, this six-story hotel was completely remodeled in 1998. Half the rooms face west and have views from their balconies of the Arabesque minarets atop the Henry B. Plant Museum and University of Tampa across the river—quite a scene at sunset. They cost more but are more preferable to units on the east side of the building, which face downtown's skyscrapers and don't have balconies. Beside the river, the Ashley Drive Grill serves indoor-outdoor breakfasts and lunches, then turns to fine dining in the evenings. The Boulanger bakery and deli, open from 5am to midnight, purveys fresh pastries, soups, sandwiches, and snacks.

200 N. Ashley Dr. (at Jackson St.), Tampa, FL 33602. ℭ 800/333-3333 or 813/223-2222. Fax 813/221-5929. www.radisson.com/tampafl_riverwalk. 282 units. Winter $219–$239 double; off-season $129–$179 double. AE, DC, DISC, MC, V. Valet parking $10, self-parking $7. **Amenities:** 2 restaurants; bar; heated outdoor pool; exercise room; access to nearby health club; sauna; concierge; limited room service; laundry service; coin-op washers and dryers; concierge-level rooms. *In room:* A/C, TV, dataport, coffeemaker, hair dryer, iron.

Tampa Marriott Waterside 𝆑𝆑 This luxurious 22-story hotel occupies downtown's most strategic location—beside the river and between the Tampa Convention Center and the St. Pete Times Forum. Opening onto a riverfront promenade, the towering, three-story lobby is large enough to accommodate the many conventioneers drawn to the two neighboring venues and the hotel's own

50,000 square feet of meeting space. The third floor has a fully equipped spa, modern exercise facility, and outdoor heated pool. About half of the guest quarters have balconies overlooking the bay or city (choice views are high up on the south side). Although spacious, the regular rooms are dwarfed by the 720-square-foot suites. In fall 2002, the Marriott added a 32-slip marina.

700 N. Florida Ave. (at St. Pete Times Forum Dr.), Tampa, FL 33602. ℭ 800/228-9290 or 813/221-4900. Fax 813/221-0923. www.marriott.com. 717 units. $215–$285 double. AE, DC, DISC, MC, V. Weekend rates available. Valet parking $12; no self-parking. **Amenities:** 3 restaurants (American); 3 bars; heated outdoor pool; health club; spa; Jacuzzi; concierge; activities desk; car-rental desk; business center; salon; limited room service; massage; babysitting; laundry service; coin-op washers and dryers; concierge-level rooms. *In room:* A/C, TV, fax, dataport (with high-speed Internet), fridge, coffeemaker, hair dryer, iron.

YBOR CITY

Hilton Garden Inn   This modern, four-story hotel stands just 2 blocks north of the heart of Ybor City's dining and entertainment district. A one-story brick structure in front houses the bright lobby, a comfy relaxation area with fireplace, a dining area providing cooked and continental breakfasts, and a small pantry selling beer, wine, soft drinks, and frozen dinners. You can heat up the dinners in your comfortable guest room's microwave oven or store them in your fridge. Because Hilton's "Garden" hotels are aimed primarily at business travelers (they compete with Marriott's Courtyards), your room will also have a large desk and two phones. If you opt for a suite, you'll have a separate living room and a larger bathroom than in the regular units.

1700 E. 9th Ave. (between 17th and 18th sts.), Tampa, FL 33605. ℭ 800/445-8667 or 813/769-9267. Fax 813/769-3299. www.hiltongardeninn.com. 95 units. $99–$199 double. AE, DC, DISC, MC, V. **Amenities:** Restaurant (breakfast only); heated outdoor pool; exercise room; Jacuzzi; business center; laundry service; coin-op washers and dryers. *In room:* A/C, TV, dataport (with high-speed Internet), fridge, coffeemaker, hair dryer, iron.

A NEARBY SPA & SPORTS RESORT

Saddlebrook Resort–Tampa   Set on 480 rolling acres, Saddlebrook is off the beaten path (30 min. north of Tampa International Airport) and is a landlocked condominium development. If you're interested in spas, tennis, golf, or all of the above, we recommend this resort, which offers complete spa treatments, the Hopman Tennis Program (Jennifer Capriati pitches a tent here), and the Arnold Palmer Golf Academy (see "Outdoor Activities & Spectator Sports," earlier in this chapter). In this condominium development, you'll stay in hotel rooms or one-, two-, or three-bedroom suites. Much more appealing than the rooms, the suites have kitchens and a patio or balcony overlooking lagoons, cypress and palm trees, and the resort's two 18-hole championship golf courses.

5700 Saddlebrook Way, Wesley Chapel, FL 33543. ℭ 800/729-8383 or 813/973-1111. Fax 813/973-4504. www.saddlebrookresort.com. 800 units. Winter $175–$287 per person; off-season $130–$180 per person. Rates include breakfast and dinner. Packages available. AE, DC, DISC, MC, V. Valet parking $10; free self-parking. Take I-75 north to Fla. 54 (Exit 58); go 1 mile east to resort. **Amenities:** 3 restaurants (American); 2 bars; heated outdoor pool; 2 golf courses; 45 tennis courts; health club; spa; Jacuzzi; sauna; massage; bike rental; concierge; activities desk; car-rental desk; business center; limited room service; children's activities program; laundry service; coin-op washers and dryers. *In room:* A/C, TV, dataport, kitchen, minibar, fridge, coffeemaker, hair dryer, iron.

WHERE TO DINE

As with the hotels, we have organized the restaurants that follow by geographic area: near Busch Gardens, in or near Hyde Park (across the Hillsborough River from downtown), and in Ybor City. Although Ybor City is better known, Tampa's trendiest dining scene is along South Howard Avenue—"SoHo" to the locals—between West Kennedy Boulevard and the bay in affluent Hyde Park.

NEAR BUSCH GARDENS

You'll find the national fast food and family restaurants east of I-275 on Busch Boulevard and Fowler Avenue.

Cafe Don José SPANISH/AMERICAN   It's not nearly on a par with the Columbia in Ybor City (see below), but this Spanish-themed restaurant is among the best there is within a short drive of Busch Gardens. High-back chairs, dark wood floors, and Spanish posters and paintings set an appropriate scene for the house specialties of traditional paella (allow 30 min. for preparation) and Valencia-style rice dishes. Don José also offers non-Spanish fare such as red snapper baked in parchment.

11009 N. 56th St. (in Sherwood Forest Shopping Center, ¼ mile south of Fowler Ave.). © 813/985-2392. Main courses $13–$22. AE, DC, MC, V. Mon–Fri 11:30am–4:30pm and 5–10pm; Sat 5–10pm.

Mel's Hot Dogs *Kids* AMERICAN   Catering to everyone from businesspeople on a lunch break to hungry families craving inexpensive all-beef hot dogs, Mel Lohn's red-and-white cottage offers everything from "bagel-dogs" to bacon/cheddar Reuben-style hot dogs. All choices are served on a poppy-seed bun and can be ordered with french fries and a choice of coleslaw or baked beans. Even the decor is dedicated to wieners: The walls and windows are lined with hot-dog memorabilia, and there's usually a wiener-mobile parked out front. And just in case hot-dog mania hasn't won you over, there are a few alternative choices (chicken, beef and veggie burgers, and terrific onion rings).

4136 E. Busch Blvd., at 42nd St. © 813/985-8000. Most items $4–$9. No credit cards. Sun–Thurs 11am–8pm; Fri–Sat 11am–9pm.

Ristorante Francesco *＆* NORTHERN ITALIAN   Gregarious owner Francesco "Frankie" Murchesini patrols the tables in the hottest dining spot in North Tampa (as witnessed by the photos of famous patrons adorning the walls). When not playing his harmonica to celebrate someone's birthday, Frankie's making sure everyone is enjoying his delicious *cernia portofino* (scrumptious grouper in a brandy sauce with shrimp) and other Northern Italian dishes. His sister makes the pasta, which shows up in more traditional fare such as seafood over linguini with a choice of marinara or white-wine sauce. Be sure to start with half a Caesar salad.

In La Place Village Shopping Center, 1441 E. Fletcher Ave. (between 14th and 15th sts.). © 813/971-3649. www.ristorantefrancesco.com. Reservations recommended. Main courses $10–$27. AE, DC, DISC, MC. V. Mon–Fri 11:30am–2:30pm and 5:30–10pm; Sat 5:30–10pm; Sun 5–9pm.

Shells *＆* *Value* SEAFOOD   You'll see Shells restaurants in many parts of the country, and with good reason, for this casual, award-winning chain consistently provides excellent value. They all have virtually identical menus, prices, and hours. Particularly good are the spicy Jack Daniel's buffalo shrimp and scallop appetizers. Main courses range from the usual fried seafood platters to pastas and charcoal-grilled shrimp, fish, steaks, and chicken.

11010 N. 30th St. (between Busch Blvd. and Fowler Ave.). © 813/977-8456. Main courses $9–$20 (most $10–$12). AE, DISC, MC, V. Sun–Thurs 11:30am–10pm; Fri–Sat 11:30am–11pm.

HYDE PARK
Expensive

Bern's Steak House *＆＆* STEAKHOUSE   The exterior of this famous steakhouse looks like a factory. Inside, however, you'll find eight ornate dining rooms with themes such as Rhône, Burgundy, and Irish Rebellion. Their atmospheres are perfect for meat lovers, for here you order and pay for expertly charcoal-grilled steaks of perfectly aged beef according to thickness and weight (the 60-oz., 3-in.-thick Porterhouse can feed four adults). The phone book–size wine list offers more than 7,000 selections, with many available by the glass.

Upstairs, the dessert quarters have 50 romantic booths paneled in aged California redwood, which can privately seat from 2 to 12 guests each. All of these little chambers are equipped with phones for placing your order and closed-circuit TVs for watching and listening to a resident pianist. The dessert menu offers almost 100 selections, plus some 1,400 after-dinner drinks. It's possible to reserve a booth for dessert only, but preference is given to those who dine.

The big secret here is that steak sandwiches are available at the bar but are not mentioned on the menu. Smaller versions of the chargrilled steaks served in the dining rooms, they come with a choice of french fries or crispy onion rings. Add a salad and you have a terrific meal for about half the price of the least-expensive main course.

1208 S. Howard Ave. (at Marjory Ave.). (✆) **813/251-2421.** www.bernssteakhouse.com. Reservations recommended. Main courses $17–$58.50; sandwiches $9–$12. AE, DC, DISC, MC, V. Daily 5–11pm. Closed Christmas. Valet parking $5.

Moderate

Mise en Place 🐛🐛 ECLECTIC   Look around at all those happy, stylish people soaking up the trendy ambience, and you'll know why chef Marty Blitz and his wife, Maryann, have been among the culinary darlings of Tampa since 1986. They present the freshest of ingredients, with a creative menu that changes weekly. Main courses often include fascinating choices such as Creole-style mahimahi served with chili cheese grits and a ragout of black-eyed peas, andouille sausage, and rock shrimp.

In Grand Central Place, 442 W. Kennedy Blvd. (at S. Magnolia Ave., opposite the University of Tampa). ✆ **813/254-5373.** www.miseonline.com. Reservations recommended. Main courses $15–$26; tasting menu $48. AE, DC, DISC, MC, V. Tues–Thurs 11:30am–2:30pm and 5:30–10pm; Fri 11:30am–2:30pm and 5:30–11pm; Sat 5–11pm.

Inexpensive

Bella's Italian Cafe 🐛 *Value* ITALIAN   Creative dishes and very reasonable prices make this sophisticated yet informal cafe one of SoHo's most popular neighborhood hangouts. Although you can order the homemade pasta under traditional Bolognese or Alfredo sauces, the stars here feature the tasty likes of blackened chicken in a creamy tomato sauce over fettuccine, or shrimp and scallops in

---

 Dining on the Bay

One of the newest additions to Tampa's dining scene is the 180-foot-long **StarShip Dining Yacht** (✆ **877/744-7999** or 813/223-7999; www.starshipdining.com), which makes 2-hour lunch and dinner cruises from the Channelside out onto Tampa Bay. The ship's four dining rooms serve exceptional cruise fare. A house band plays during dinner and then moves to the top deck for dancing under the stars. Lunch cruises cost $30 per person with a meal, $16 for sightseers. Dinner cruises range from $50 during the week to $60 on weekends, whether you dine onboard or not. There's also a Sunday brunch for $35. Call for the schedule.

a roasted tomato sauce over bow-tie pasta. Finish with the house version of tiramisu. Local professionals flock to the friendly bar during two-for-one happy hours nightly from 4 to 7pm and from 11pm until closing. The open kitchen provides only appetizers, salads, pizzas, and desserts after 11pm.

1413 S. Howard Ave. (at Mississippi Ave.). *C* 813/254-3355. Reservations not accepted. Main courses $7–$12; pizza $6.50–$8.50. AE, DC, DISC, MC, V. Mon–Tues 11:30am–11:30pm; Wed–Thurs 11:30am–12:30am; Fri 11am–1:30am; Sat 4pm–1:30am; Sun 4–11:30pm.

Cactus Club *Value* AMERICAN SOUTHWEST   You can definitely taste the freshness at this Texas roadhouse–style cantina in the middle of the Old Hyde Park Village shops, because all ingredients except the beans come straight from the market. Our favorite dish is the "fundido"—a spicy casserole of marinated fajita-style chicken strips and sautéed vegetables topped with melted Jack cheese, with beans and rice on the side. Other offerings are more traditional: tacos, enchiladas, chili, sizzling fajitas, hickory-smoked baby-back ribs, Jamaican jerk chicken, burgers, quesadillas, enchiladas (including vegetarian versions), sandwiches, and smoked chicken salad. The lively Cactus Cantina bar is another favorite neighborhood watering hole. Dine inside or outside, but get here early at lunchtime—it's usually packed.

In Old Hyde Park Village shopping complex, 1601 Snow Ave. (south of Swann Ave.). *C* **813/251-4089.** www.cactusclub.com. Reservations not accepted. Main courses $8–$14; burgers and sandwiches $7–$9. AE, DC, MC, V. Sun–Thurs 11:30am–10pm; Fri–Sat 11:30am–11pm.

Four Green Fields IRISH/AMERICAN   Just across the bridge from the downtown convention center, this thatched-roof Irish pub may be surrounded by palm trees instead of potato fields, but it still offers the ambience and tastes of Ireland. Staffed by Irish immigrants, the large room with a square bar in the center smells of Bass and Harp ales. The Gaelic stew is predictably bland, but the salads and sandwiches are passable. The live Irish music Thursday through Saturday nights and on Sunday afternoon draws a crowd ranging from post-college to early retirees.

205 W. Platt St. (between Parker St. and Plant Ave.). *C* **813/254-4444.** www.fourgreenfields.com. Reservations accepted. Main courses $9.50–$15; sandwiches $6–$7. AE, MC, V. Daily 11am–3am.

YBOR CITY
Moderate
Columbia ★★★ SPANISH   Dating from 1905, this hand-painted tile building occupies an entire city block in the heart of Ybor City. Tourists flock here to soak up the ambience, and so do the locals because it's so much fun to clap along during fire-belching Spanish flamenco floor shows Monday through Saturday evenings ($6 per person additional charge). You can't help coming back time after time for the famous Spanish bean soup and original "1905" salad. The *paella a la valenciana* is outstanding, with more than a dozen ingredients from gulf grouper and gulf pink shrimp to calamari, mussels, clams, chicken, and pork. One of our favorites is *boliche* (eye of round stuffed with chorizo) accompanied by plantains and black beans and rice. All entrees come with a crispy hunk of Cuban bread with butter. Lighter appetites can choose from a limited menu of tapas, including "Cuban caviar" (actually a spicy black-bean dip). The decor throughout is graced with hand-painted tiles, wrought-iron chandeliers, dark woods, rich red fabrics, and stained-glass windows. You can breathe your own fumes in the Cigar Bar.

2117 E. 7th Ave. (between 21st and 22nd sts.). *C* **813/248-4961.** www.columbiarestaurant.com. Reservations recommended. Main courses $14–$28. AE, DC, DISC, MC, V. Mon–Thurs 11am–10pm; Fri–Sat 11am–11pm.

Inexpensive

Carmine's Restaurant & Bar CUBAN/ITALIAN/AMERICAN   Bright blue poles hold up an ancient pressed-tin ceiling above this noisy corner cafe. It's not the cleanest joint in town, but a great variety of loyal local patrons gather here for genuine Cuban sandwiches—smoked ham, roast pork, Genoa salami, Swiss cheese, pickles, salad dressing, mustard, lettuce, and tomato on crispy Cuban bread. There's a vegetarian version too, and the combination half-sandwich and choice of black beans and rice or a bowl of Spanish soup made with sausages, potatoes, and garbanzo beans all make a hearty meal for just $7 at lunch, $8 at dinner. Main courses are led by Cuban-style roast pork, thin-cut pork chops with mushroom sauce, spaghetti with a blue-crab tomato sauce, and a few seafood and chicken platters.

1802 E. 7th Ave. (at 18th St.). ℂ 813/248-3834. Reservations not accepted. Main courses $7–$17; sandwiches $4–$8. No credit cards. Mon–Tues 11am–11pm; Wed–Thurs 11am–1am; Fri–Sat 11am–3am; Sun 11am–6pm.

Ovo Cafe ★ INTERNATIONAL   This cafe, popular with the business set by day and the club crowd on weekend nights, features a melange of sophisticated offerings. Pierogies and pasta pillows come with taste-tempting sauces and fillings, and there are several creative salads and unusual individual-size pizzas. Strawberries or blackberries and a splash of liqueur cover the thick waffles. Portions are substantial, but be careful of the strictly a la carte pricing here. The big black bar dispenses a wide variety of martinis, plus some unusual liqueur drinks.

1901 E. 7th Ave. (at 19th St.). ℂ 813/248-6979. Reservations strongly recommended Fri–Sat. Main courses $10–$15; sandwiches $7–$8.50; pizza $8.50–$10. AE, DC, DISC, MC, V. Mon–Tues 11am–3pm; Wed–Thurs 11am–10pm; Fri–Sat 11am–1am.

TAMPA AFTER DARK

The Tampa/Hillsborough Arts Council maintains an **Artsline** (ℂ **813/229-2787**), a 24-hour information service providing the latest on current and upcoming cultural events. Racks in many restaurants and bars have copies of *Weekly Planet* (**www.weeklyplanet.com**), *Focus,* and *Accent on Tampa Bay,* three free publications detailing what's going on in the entire bay area. And you can also check the "BayLife" and "Friday Extra" sections of *The Tampa Tribune* (**www.tampa trib.com**) and the Thursday "Weekend" section of the *St. Petersburg Times* (**www. sptimes.com**). The visitor center usually has copies of the week's newspaper sections (see "Essentials," earlier in this chapter).

THE CLUB & MUSIC SCENE   Ybor City is Tampa's favorite nighttime venue by far. All you have to do is stroll along 7th Avenue East between 15th and 20th streets, and you'll hear music blaring out of the clubs. The avenue is packed with people, a majority of them high schoolers and early 20-somethings, on Friday and Saturday from 9pm to 3am, but you'll also find something going on from Tuesday to Thursday, and even on Sundays. The clubs change names and character frequently, so you don't need names, addresses, or phone numbers;

⟨*Tips* **Careful Where You Park**

Parking can be scarce during nighttime in Ybor City, and the area has seen an occasional robbery late at night. Play it safe and use the municipal parking lots behind the shops on 8th Avenue East or the new parking garages near Centro Ybor, on 7th Avenue East at 16th Street.

your ears will guide you along 7th Avenue East. With all of the sidewalk seating, it is easy to judge what the clientele is like in any given place and make your choice from there.

The center of the action these days is **Centro Ybor,** on 7th Avenue East at 16th Street (© **813/242-4660;** www.thecentroybor.com), the district's large new dining-and-entertainment complex. The restaurants and pubs in this family-oriented center tend to be considerably tamer than many of those along 7th Avenue, at least on non-weekend nights. You don't have to pay to listen to live music in the center's patio on weekend afternoons.

THE PERFORMING ARTS With a prime downtown location on 9 acres along the east bank of the Hillsborough River, the huge **Tampa Bay Performing Arts Center** 𝕗, 1010 N. MacInnes Place next to the Tampa Museum of Art (© **800/955-1045** or 813/229-7827; www.tampacenter.com), is the largest performing-arts venue south of the Kennedy Center in Washington, D.C. Accordingly, this four-theater complex is the focal point of Tampa's performing-arts scene, presenting a wide range of Broadway plays, classical and pop concerts, operas, cabarets, improv, and special events.

A sightseeing attraction in its own right, the restored **Tampa Theatre,** 711 Franklin St. (© **813/274-8286;** www.tampatheatre.org), between Zack and Polk streets, dates from 1926 and is on the National Register of Historic Places. It presents a varied program of classic, foreign, and alternative films, as well as concerts and special events. (And it's said to be haunted!)

The 66,321-seat **Raymond James Stadium,** 4201 N. Dale Mabry Hwy. (© **813/673-4300;** www.raymondjames.com/stadium), is sometimes the site of headliner concerts. The **USF Sun Dome,** 4202 E. Fowler Ave. (© **813/974-3111;** www.sundome.org), on the University of South Florida campus, hosts major concerts by touring pop stars, rock bands, jazz groups, and other contemporary artists.

Ticketmaster (© **813/287-8844**) sells tickets to most events and shows.

2 Cocoa Beach, Cape Canaveral & the Kennedy Space Center 𝕗

46 miles SE of Orlando, 65 miles S of Daytona

The "Space Coast," the area around Cape Canaveral, was once a sleepy place where city dwellers escaped the crowds from the exploding urban centers of Miami and Jacksonville. But then came the NASA space program. Today, the region produces and accommodates its own crowds, especially hordes of tourists who come to visit the Kennedy Space Center and enjoy the area's 72 miles of beaches (this is, after all, the closest beach to Orlando's mega-attractions) and excellent fishing, surfing, and golfing.

Thanks to NASA, this is also a prime destination for nature lovers. The space agency originally took over much more land than it needed to launch rockets. Rather than sell off the unused portions, it turned them over to the Canaveral National Seashore and the Merritt Island National Wildlife Refuge (**www.nbbd.com/godo/minwr**), which have preserved these areas in their pristine natural states.

A handful of Caribbean-bound cruise ships depart from the man-made Port Canaveral, and the number has grown slowly over the years. The south side of the port is lined with seafood restaurants and marinas, which serve as home base for gambling ships and the area's deep-sea charter and group fishing boats.

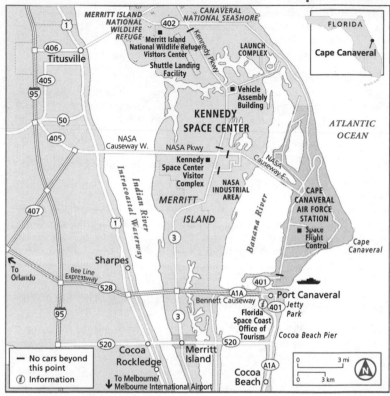

Cape Canaveral

Map labels:

MERRITT ISLAND NATIONAL WILDLIFE REFUGE

CANAVERAL NATIONAL SEASHORE

FLORIDA
Cape Canaveral

402

Kennedy Pkwy

LAUNCH COMPLEX

406
Titusville

Merritt Island National Wildlife Refuge Visitors Center

Shuttle Landing Facility

405
95

50

405

Vehicle Assembly Building

KENNEDY SPACE CENTER

ATLANTIC OCEAN

NASA Causeway W.

NASA Pkwy

Kennedy Space Center Visitor Complex

NASA Causeway E.

NASA INDUSTRIAL AREA

407

Indian River Intracoastal Waterway

MERRITT

ISLAND

1

3

Banana River

CAPE CANAVERAL AIR FORCE STATION

Space Flight Control

Cape Canaveral

Sharpes

To Orlando

Bee Line Expressway

528

95

3

401

Bennett Causeway

A1A
401

Port Canaveral

Jetty Park

Florida Space Coast Office of Tourism

Cocoa Beach Pier

520

Cocoa
Rockledge

Merritt Island

520

Cocoa Beach

A1A

— No cars beyond this point
ⓘ Information

To Melbourne/
Melbourne International Airport

0   3 mi
0   3 km

ESSENTIALS

GETTING THERE   The nearest airport is **Melbourne International Airport** (© 321/723-6227; www.mlbair.com), 22 miles south of Cocoa Beach, which is served by **Continental** (© 800/525-0280; www.continental.com) and **Delta** (© 800/221-1212; www.delta.com). **Orlando International Airport,** about 35 miles to the west, is a much larger hub with many more flight options and generally less expensive fares (see "Getting There," in chapter 2). It's an easy 45-minute drive from the Orlando airport to the beaches via the Bee Line Expressway (Fla. 528, a toll road)—it can take almost that long from the Melbourne airport, where **Avis, Budget, Hertz,** and **National** have car-rental desks. **The Melbourne Airport Shuttle** (© 321/ 724-1600) will take you from the Melbourne airport to most local destinations for about $10 to $20 per person.

VISITOR INFORMATION   For information about the area, contact the **Florida Space Coast Office of Tourism/Brevard County Tourist Development Council,** 8810 Astronaut Blvd., Suite 102, Cape Canaveral, FL 32920 (© 800/872-1969 or 321/868-1126; www.space-coast.com). The office is in the Sheldon Cove building, on Fla. A1A a block north of Central Boulevard and is open Monday through Friday from 8am to 5pm.

The office also operates an information booth at the Kennedy Space Center Visitor Complex (see below).

GETTING AROUND A car is essential in this area. If you're not coming by car, you can rent one at the airport. **Space Coast Area Transit** (© 321/633-1878; www.ridescat.com) operates buses ($1 adults, 50¢ seniors and students), but routes tend to be circuitous and therefore extremely time-consuming.

SEEING THE ATTRACTIONS

In addition to the two attractions below, Brevard College's **Astronaut Memorial Planetarium and Observatory,** 1519 Clearlake Rd., Cocoa Beach (© 321/634-3732; www.brevard.cc.fl.us/~planet), south of Fla. 528, has its own International Hall of Space Explorers, but its big attractions are sound and light shows in the planetarium. Call or check the website for schedules and prices.

Brevard Zoo *Kids* This delightful small-town zoo has more than 500 animals including white rhinos, dingoes, red kangaroos, wallabies, cotton-top tamarins, crocodiles, howler monkeys, bald eagles, red wolves, and river otters. The zoo also offers a 10-minute train tour of the grounds ($2), kayak trips ($3), a new tropical garden inhabited by flying fox bats and muntjac deer, a free-flight aviary, and alligator feedings usually 3 days a week (check the schedule or Internet site below for days and times; they change as the gators' appetites do over the year). There's also a petting zoo where the cute and cuddly critters include fallow deer and Amazon parrots.

8225 N. Wickham Rd., Melbourne (just east of I-95 Exit 73/Wickham Rd.). © 321/254-9453. www.brevard zoo.org. Admission $7 adults, $6 seniors, $5 children 3–12, free for kids under 3. Daily 10am–5pm.

John F. Kennedy Space Center *Kids Kids Kids* Whether you're a space buff or not, you'll appreciate the sheer grandeur of the facilities and technological achievements displayed at NASA's primary space-launch facility. Astronauts departed Earth at this site in 1969 en route to the most famous "small step" in history—humankind's first walk on the moon—and today's space shuttles still regularly lift off from here on their latest missions.

Because all roads other than Fla. 405 and Fla. 3 are closed to the public in the space center, you must begin your visit at the **Kennedy Space Center Visitor Complex.** A bit like a themed amusement park, this privately operated complex has been undergoing an ambitious $130 million renovation and expansion, so check to see that they have not changed their tours and exhibits before going. Call beforehand to see what's happening on the day you intend to be here, and arrive early to plan your visit. You'll need at least 2 hours to see the highlights on the bus tour through the space center, up to 5 hours if you linger at the stops along the way, and a full day to see and do everything here. Buy a copy of the Official Tour Book; it's easier to use than the rental cassette tapes, and you can take it home as a colorful souvenir (though some of our readers think you don't need any extra information because the bus tours are narrated and the exhibits have excellent descriptions).

The visitor complex has real NASA rockets and the actual Mercury Mission Control Room from the 1960s. Exhibits look at early space exploration and where it's going in the new millennium. There are space-related hands-on activities aimed at kids, a daily "Encounter" with a real astronaut, several dining venues, and a shop selling a variety of space memorabilia and souvenirs. IMAX movies shown on 5½-story-high screens are informative and entertaining.

While you could spend your entire day at the visitor complex, you must take a **KSC Tour** to see the actual space center where rockets and shuttles are prepared and launched. Plan to take the bus tour early in your visit and be sure to

---

Tips Out to Launch

If you'd like to see a shuttle launch at the **Kennedy Space Center,** first call
© **321/867-5000** or check NASA's official website (www.ksc.nasa.gov) for
a schedule of upcoming takeoffs. You can buy launch tickets at the
Kennedy Space Center Visitor Complex (*©* **321/449-4444**) or online at
www.ksctickets.com. (*A word of caution:* Shuttle launches are frequently
delayed due to weather, equipment malfunctions, or other factors, so you
might have to make multiple visits to see one. If you don't have that flexibility, the launch window may be delayed beyond your going home
date.)

If you can't get into the space center, other good viewing spots are on
the causeways leading to the islands and on U.S. 1 as it skirts the waterfront in Titusville. The **Holiday Inn Riverside–Kennedy Space Center,** on
Washington Avenue (U.S. 1) in Titusville (*©* **800/465-4329** or 321/269-2121;
www.holidayinnksc.com), also has a clear view of the launch pads across
the Indian River, but area motels raise their rates and often book up during launch periods.

---

hit the restrooms before boarding the bus—there's only one out on the tour. The
buses depart every 10 minutes or so, and you can reboard as you wish. They stop
at the LC-39 Observation Gantry, with a dramatic 360-degree view over launch
pads where space shuttles blast off; the International Space Station Center,
where scientists and engineers prepare additions to the space station now in
orbit; and the impressive Apollo/Saturn V Center, which includes artifacts, photos, interactive exhibits, and the 363-foot-tall Saturn V, the most powerful
rocket ever launched by the United States.

Don't miss the Astronaut Memorial, a moving black-granite monument that
has the names of the U.S. astronauts (the names of those who perished in the
recent Columbia tragedy should be up there by the time this book hits the
shelves) who have died on missions or while in training. The 60-ton structure
rotates on a track that follows the movement of the sun (on clear days, of
course), causing the names to stand out above a brilliant reflection of the sky.

On launch days, the Center is closed at least part of the day. These aren't good
days to see the center, but they're great days to observe history in the making.
For $37.95 adults and $27.95 for kids, you get a **combined ticket** that entitles
you to admission to the center for the shortened operating hours, plus at least a
2-hour excursion to *NASA Parkway* to see the liftoff. You must pick up tickets,
available five days prior to the launch, on site.

Note: The financially troubled **Astronaut Hall of Fame** in Titusville closed
its doors in the fall of 2002. Kennedy Space Center acquired many of its exhibits
and added them as a separate attraction at the KSC visitors center ($13.95 adults
and $9.95 kids 3–11, or $31 adults and $21 kids for a 2-day Maximum Access
Admission to the Center and the Hall of Fame). The new attraction includes
displays, exhibits, and tributes to the heroes of the Mercury, Gemini, and Apollo
space programs. There's also a collection of spacecraft, including a Mercury 7
capsule, a Gemini training capsule, and an Apollo 14 command module. And
in "Simulator Station," guests can experience the pressure of four times the force
of gravity, ride a rover across Mars, and land a Space Shuttle.

NASA Pkwy. (Fla. 405), 6 miles east of Titusville, ½ mile west of Fla. 3. ℂ **321/449-4444** for general information, 321/449-4444 for guided bus tours and launch reservations. www.kennedyspacecenter.com. Admission $26 adults, $16 children 3–11. Annual passes $44 adults, $28 children 3–11. Audio tours $5 per person.
All tours and movies free for children under 3. Daily 9am–5:30pm. Shuttle-bus tours daily 9:45am–2:15pm.
Closed Christmas and some launch days.

BEACHES & WILDLIFE REFUGES

To the north of the Kennedy Space Center, **Canaveral National Seashore**
🦆🦆🦆 is a protected 13-mile stretch of barrier-island beach backed by cabbage
palms, sea grapes, palmettos, marshes, and Mosquito Lagoon. This is a great area
for watching herons, egrets, ibises, willets, sanderlings, turnstones, terns, and
other birds. You might also glimpse dolphins and manatees in Mosquito
Lagoon. Canoeists can paddle along a marked trail through the marshes of Ship-
yard Island, and you can go backcountry camping November through April
(permits required—see below).

The main **visitor center** is at 7611 S. Atlantic Ave., New Smyrna Beach, FL
32169 (ℂ **321/867-4077** or 321/867-0677 for recorded information; www.nps.
gov/cana), on Apollo Beach, at the north end of the island. The southern access
gate to the island is 8 miles east of Titusville on Fla. 402, just east of Fla. 3. A paved
road leads from the gate to undeveloped **Playalinda Beach** 🦆🦆🦆, one of Florida's
most beautiful. While it's illegal, nude sunbathing has long been a tradition here
(at least for those willing to walk a few miles to the more deserted areas). The
beach has toilets but no running water or other amenities, so bring everything you
will need. The seashore is open daily from 6am to 8pm during daylight savings
time, daily from 6am to 6pm during standard time. Admission fees are $5 per
motor vehicle, $3 for pedestrians or bicyclists. National Park Service passports are
accepted. Backcountry camping permits cost $10 for up to six people and must be
obtained from the New Smyrna Beach visitor center (see above). For advance
information, contact the seashore headquarters at 308 Julia St., Titusville, FL
32796 (ℂ **321/867-4077** or 321/267-1110; www.nps.gov/cana).

Its neighbor to the south and west is the 140,000-acre **Merritt Island
National Wildlife Refuge** 🦆🦆, home to hundreds of species of shorebirds,
waterfowl, reptiles, alligators, and mammals, many of them endangered. Stop
and pick up a map and other information at the visitor center, on Fla. 402 about
4 miles east of Titusville (it's on the way to Playalinda Beach). The center has a
quarter-mile-long boardwalk along the edge of the marsh and has displays showing the animals you may see here. You can see them from the 6-mile-long Black
Point Wildlife Drive or one of the nature trails through the hammocks and
marshes. The visitor center is open Monday through Friday from 8am to
4:30pm, Saturday from 9am to 5pm (closed Sun Apr–Oct). Admission is free.
For more information and a schedule of interpretive programs, contact the
refuge at P.O. Box 6504, Titusville, FL 32782 (ℂ **321/861-0667;** www.nbbd.
com/godo/minwr).

Note: Those parts of the national seashore near the Kennedy Space Center
and all of the refuge close 4 days before a shuttle launch and usually reopen the
day after a launch.

Another good beach area is **Lori Wilson Park,** on Atlantic Avenue at Antigua
Drive in Cocoa Beach (ℂ **321/868-1123**), which preserves a stretch of beach
backed by a forest of live oaks. It's home to a small but interesting nature center, and it has restrooms by the beach. The park is open daily from sunrise to
sunset; the nature center is open Monday through Friday from 1 to 4pm.

The beach at **Cocoa Beach Pier,** on Meade Avenue east of Fla. A1A (© **321/ 783-7549**), is a popular spot, especially with surfers, who consider it the East Coast's surfing capital. The rustic pier was built in 1962 and has 842 feet of fishing, shopping, and food and drinks overlooking a wide, sandy beach (see "Where to Dine," below). Because this is not a public park, there are no restrooms other than the ones in the restaurants on the pier.

Jetty Park, 400 E. Jetty Rd. (© **321/783-7111;** www.portcanaveral.org/florida fun/recreation.htm), at the south entry to Port Canaveral, has lifeguards, a fishing pier with bait shop, a children's playground, a volleyball court, a horseshoe pit, picnic tables, a snack bar, a grocery store, restrooms and changing facilities, and the area's only campground. From here you can watch the big cruise ships as they enter and leave the port's narrow passage. The park is open daily from 7am to 10pm, and the pier is open 24 hours for fishing. Admission is $3 per car, $7 for RVs. The 150 tent and RV campsites (some of them shady, most with hookups) cost $17 to $26 a night, depending on location and time of year. No pets are allowed.

OUTDOOR ACTIVITIES

ECOTOURS   Funday Discovery Tours (© 321/725-0796; www.funday tours.com) offers a variety of day trips, including dinner and sunset cruises, airboat and swamp-buggy rides, dolphin-watching cruises, bird-watching expeditions, and personalized tours of the Kennedy Space Center and Merritt Island National Wildlife Refuge. Reservations are required, so call, check the website, or pick up a copy of their list of trips from the visitor center (see "Essentials," above).

FISHING   Head to Port Canaveral for catches such as snapper and grouper. **Jetty Park** (© 321/783-7111), at the south entry to the port, has a fishing pier equipped with a bait shop (see "Beaches & Wildlife Refuges," above). The south bank of the port is lined with charter boats, and you can go deep-sea fishing on the *Miss Cape Canaveral* (© 321/783-5274 or 321/648-2211 in Orlando; www.misscape.com), one of the party boats based here. All-day voyages departing daily at 8am cost $45 to $60 for adults, $40 to $55 for seniors, $35 to $50 for students 11 to 17, and $25 to $40 for kids 6 to 10.

GOLF   You can read about Northeast Florida's best courses in the free *Golfer's Guide,* available at the tourist information offices and in many hotel lobbies.

In Cocoa Beach, the municipal **Cocoa Beach Country Club,** 500 Tom Warringer Blvd. (© **321/868-3351**), has 27 holes of golf and 10 lighted tennis courts set on acres of natural woodland, rivers, and lakes. Greens fees are about $40 in winter, dropping to about $35 in summer, including cart.

On Merritt Island south of the Kennedy Space Center, **The Savannahs at Sykes Creek,** 3915 Savannahs Trail (© **321/455-1377**), has 18 holes over 6,636 yards bordered by hardwood forests, lakes, and savannahs inhabited by a host of wildlife. You'll have to hit over a lake to reach the seventh hole. Fees with cart are about $40 in winter, less in summer.

The best nearby course is the Gary Player–designed **Baytree National Golf Club,** 8010 N. Wickham Rd., a half-mile east of I-95 in Melbourne (© **321/ 259-9060**), where challenging marshy holes are flanked by towering palms. This par-72 course has 7,043 yards with a unique red-shale waste area. Fees are about $90 in winter, dropping to about $50 in summer, including cart.

For course information online, go to **www.golf.com** and **www.floridagolfing. com,** or call the **Florida Sports Foundation** (© **850/488-8347**) or **Florida Golfing** (© **866/833-2663**).

SURFING   Rip through some occasionally awesome waves (by Florida's standards, not California's or Hawaii's) at the **Cocoa Beach Pier** area or down south at **Sebastian Inlet.** Get outfitted at Ron Jon Surf Shop and learn how to hang five or ten with the store's **Cocoa Beach Surfing School** ⟡, 150 E. Columbia Lane (© **321/868-1980;** www.ronjons.com/surfschool). They offer equipment and lessons for beginners or pros at area beaches. Be sure to bring along a towel, flip-flops, sunscreen, and a lot of nerve.

WHERE TO STAY

The hotels listed below are all in Cocoa Beach, the closest resort area to the Kennedy Space Center, about a 30-minute drive to the north. Closest to the space center and Port Canaveral is the **Radisson Resort at the Port,** 8701 Astronaut Blvd. (Fla. A1A) in Cape Canaveral (© **800/333-3333** or 321/784-0000; www.Radisson.com). It isn't on the beach, but you can relax in a landscaped courtyard with a waterfall cascading over fake rocks into an outdoor heated pool. This comfortable, well-equipped hotel caters to business travelers and passengers waiting to board cruise ships departing nearby Port Canaveral.

The newest chain motels in this area are the **Hampton Inn Cocoa Beach,** 3425 Atlantic Blvd. (© **877/492-3224** or 321/799-4099; www.hamptoninncocoa beach.com), and **Courtyard by Marriott,** 3435 Atlantic Blvd. (© **800/321-2211** or 321/784-4800; www.marriott.com). Opened in 2000 and 2001, respectively, they stand side-by-side and have access to the beach via a pathway through a condominium complex.

The **Florida Space Coast Office of Tourism** (see "Essentials," earlier in this chapter) publishes a booklet of the area's Superior Small Lodgings.

The area has a plethora of rental condominiums and cottages. **King Rentals Inc.,** 102 W. Central Blvd., Cape Canaveral, FL 32920 (© **888/295-0934** or 321/784-5046; www.kingrentals.com), has a wide selection in its inventory.

Given the proximity of Orlando, the generally warm weather all year, and business travelers visiting the space complex, there is little if any seasonal fluctuation in room rates here. They are highest weekends, holidays, and during special events, such as space shuttle launches.

Tent and RV camping are available at **Jetty Park** in Port Canaveral (see "Beaches & Wildlife Refuges," above).

You'll pay a 4% hotel tax on top of the Florida 6% sales tax here.

DoubleTree Hotel Cocoa Beach Oceanfront ⟡   This six-story hotel was extensively remodeled and upgraded in 1998, and although not as upscale as the Hilton Cocoa Beach Oceanfront (see below), it's the pick of the full-service beachside hotels here. All rooms have balconies with ocean views and easy chairs, and 10 suites have living rooms with sleeper sofas and separate bedrooms. A charming dining room facing the beach serves decent Mediterranean fare and opens to a bi-level brick patio with water cascading between two heated swimming pools. Conference facilities draw groups.

2080 N. Atlantic Ave., Cocoa Beach, FL 32931. © **800/552-3224** or 321/783-9222. Fax 321/799-3234. www.cocoabeachdoubletree.com. 148 units. $125–$179 double; $185–$275 suite. AE, DC, DISC, MC, V. **Amenities:** Restaurant; bar; 2 heated outdoor pools; exercise room; game room; limited room service; laundry service; coin-op washers and dryers; concierge-level rooms. *In room:* A/C, TV, dataport, coffeemaker, hair dryer, iron.

Econo Lodge of Cocoa Beach (Value   About half of the spacious rooms at this Econo Lodge—more charming than most members of this budget-priced chain—face a tropical courtyard with a V-shaped swimming pool by which stands a sign bearing the names of the seven original astronauts, who built and owned this motel in its original incarnation as the Cape Colony Inn. It was the center of activities in those 1960s days, with helicopters bringing in the likes of anchorman Walter Cronkite and that genie herself, actress Barbara Eden. Today, its comfortable and clean units include standard motel rooms and four suites with living rooms and kitchenettes. Rooms facing the courtyard are preferable to those fronting the surrounding parking lots.

1275 N. Atlantic Ave. (Fla. A1A, at Holiday Lane), Cocoa Beach, FL 32931. ℭ 800/553-2666 or 321/783-2252. Fax 321/783-4485. www.econolodge.com. 128 units. $49–$119 double. AE, DC, DISC, MC, V. Pets accepted in some rooms, no fee. **Amenities:** Restaurant; 2 bars; heated outdoor pool; coin-op washers and dryers. *In room:* A/C, TV, kitchen (suites only), fridge, coffeemaker.

Hilton Cocoa Beach Oceanfront

Instead of balconies or patios from which you can enjoy the fresh air and view down the shore, the rooms at this seven-story Hilton have smallish, sealed-shut windows, and only 16 of them actually face the beach. That and other architectural features make it seem more like a downtown commercial hotel transplanted to a beachside location. Nevertheless, it's one of the few upscale beachfront properties here. No doubt you will run into a crew of name-tagged conventioneers, because it's especially popular with groups. Despite their lack of fresh air, the rooms are spacious and comfortable.

1550 N. Atlantic Ave., Cocoa Beach, FL 32931. ℭ 800/445-8667 or 321/799-0003. Fax 321/799-0344. www.hilton.com. 296 units. $89–$199 double. AE, DC, DISC, MC, V. **Amenities:** Restaurant; 2 bars; heated outdoor pool; exercise room; game room; watersports equipment rentals; business center; limited room service; laundry service; coin-op washers and dryers; concierge-level rooms. *In room:* A/C, TV, dataport, coffeemaker, hair dryer, iron.

Holiday Inn Cocoa Beach Oceanfront Resort *Kids*

Set on 30 beachside acres, this sprawling family-oriented complex offers a wide variety of spacious hotel rooms, efficiencies, and apartments. A few suites are equipped with bunk beds and Nintendo games for the kids. Most are in 1960s-style motel buildings flanking a long central courtyard with tropical foliage surrounding tennis courts. Only those rooms directly facing the beach or pool have patios or balconies; the rest are entered from exterior corridors.

1300 N. Atlantic Ave. (Fla. A1A, at Holiday Lane), Cocoa Beach, FL 32931. ℭ 800/206-2747 or 321/783-2271. www.holidayinnsofcentralflorida.com. Fax 321/783-8878. 500 units. $69–$220 double. AE, DC, DISC, MC, V. **Amenities:** 2 restaurants; 2 bars; heated outdoor pool; 2 tennis courts; exercise room; Jacuzzi; watersports equipment rentals; game room; concierge; limited room service; laundry service; coin-op washers and dryers. *In room:* A/C, TV, dataport, coffeemaker, hair dryer, iron.

The Inn at Cocoa Beach *RR*

Despite having 50 units, an intimate bed-and-breakfast ambience prevails at this seaside inn, far and away the most romantic place to stay in the area (which is why it draws so many couples). The inn began as a beachfront motel but underwent a transformation under current owner Karen Simpler, a skilled interior decorator. She has furnished each unit with an elegant mix of pine, tropical, and French country pieces. Rooms in the three- and four-story buildings are much more spacious and have better sea views from their balconies than the "standard" units in the original two-story motel wing (all but six units here have balconies or patios). The older units open to a courtyard with a swimming pool tucked behind the dunes. Highest on the romance scale are two rooms with Jacuzzi tubs, large showers, and easy chairs facing gas fireplaces. In addition to the complimentary breakfast, guests are treated to evening wine-and-cheese socials and afternoon tea. There's also an honor bar and library.

4300 Ocean Blvd., Cocoa Beach, FL 32932. ℂ **800/343-5307** or 321/799-3460. Fax 321/784-8632. www.the
innatcocoabeach.com. 50 units. $135–$295 double. Rates include continental breakfast and afternoon tea. AE,
DISC, MC, V. No children under 12 accepted. **Amenities:** Bar (guests only); heated outdoor pool; sauna; massage; laundry service. *In room:* A/C, TV, dataport.

WHERE TO DINE

On the **Cocoa Beach Pier,** at the beach end of Meade Avenue, you'll get a fine
view down the coast to accompany the seafood offerings at **Atlantic Ocean
Grill** (ℂ **321/783-7549**) and the mediocre pub fare at adjacent **Marlins Good
Times Bar & Grill** (same phone). The restaurants may not justify spending an
entire evening on the pier, but the outdoor, tin-roofed **Boardwalk Tiki Bar** 𝒦,
where live music plays most nights, is a prime spot to have a cold one while
watching the surfers or a sunset.

Bernard's Surf/Fischer's Seafood Bar & Grill 𝒦 SEAFOOD/STEAKS
Photos on the walls testify that many astronauts—and Russian cosmonauts,
too—come to these adjoining establishments to celebrate their landings. It all
started as Bernard's Surf, which has been serving standard steak-and-seafood fare
in a nautically dressed setting since 1948. Bernard's offers house specials such as
stone crab claws, Florida lobster tails stuffed with crab, char-grilled red snapper,
and a belly-busting platter of shrimp, scallops, grouper, crab cakes, lobster, and
oysters. The fresh seafood also finds its way into Fischer's Seafood Bar & Grill,
a friendly, *Cheers*-like lounge popular with the locals. Fischer's menu features
fried combo platters, shrimp and crab-claw meat sautéed in herb butter, and
mussels with a wine sauce over pasta, to mention a few worthy selections. Fischer's also provides sandwiches, burgers, and other pub fare, and it has the same
25¢ happy-hour oysters and spicy wings as a branch of **Rusty's Seafood & Oyster Bar** (see below), also part of this complex.

2 S. Atlantic Ave. (at Minuteman Causeway Rd.), Cocoa Beach. ℂ **321/783-2401**. Reservations recommended in Bernard's, not accepted in Fischer's. Bernard's main courses $14–$55. Fischer's main courses
$9–$16; sandwiches and salads $4–$9. AE, DC, DISC, MC, V. Bernard's Mon–Fri 4–10pm; Fri–Sat 4–11pm. Fischer's Mon–Thurs 11am–10pm; Fri–Sat 11am–11pm. Closed Christmas.

The Mango Tree 𝒦𝒦 CONTINENTAL   Gourmet seafood, pastas, and
chicken are served in a plantation-home atmosphere with elegant furnishings in
this stucco house, the finest dining venue here. Goldfish ponds inside and a
waterfall splashing into a Japanese koi pond out in the lush tropical gardens provide pleasing backdrops. Start with finely seasoned Indian River crab cakes, then
go on to the chef's expert spin on fresh tuna filets, roast Long Island duckling,
beef tips with peppercorn-mushroom sauce, and other excellent dishes drawing
their inspiration from the continent.

118 N. Atlantic Ave. (Fla. A1A, between N. 1st and N. 2nd sts.), Cocoa Beach. ℂ **321/799-0513**. Reservations recommended. Main courses $15–$39. AE, MC, V. Tues–Sun 6–10pm.

Rusty's Seafood & Oyster Bar *Value* SEAFOOD   This lively sports bar
beside Port Canaveral's man-made harbor offers inexpensive chow ranging from
very spicy seafood gumbo to a pot of seafood that will give two people their fill
of steamed oysters, clams, shrimp, crab legs, potatoes, and corn on the cob. Raw
or steamed fresh oysters and clams from the raw bar are first-rate and a very good
value, as is a lunch buffet on weekdays. Seating is available indoors or out, but
the inside tables have the best view of fishing boats and cruise liners going in and
out of the port. Daily happy hours from 3 to 6pm see beers drafted at 59¢ a
mug, and tons of raw or steamed oysters and spicy Buffalo wings go for 25¢

each. It's a busy and sometimes noisy joint, especially on weekend afternoons, but the clientele tends to be somewhat older and better behaved than at some other pubs along the banks of Port Canaveral. There's another **Rusty's** in the Bernard's Surf/Fischer's Seafood Bar & Grill restaurant complex in Cocoa Beach (see above). It has the same menu.

628 Glen Cheek Dr. (south side of the harbor), Port Canaveral. (℃ 321/783-2033. Main courses $7–$25; sandwiches and salads $4–$7; lunch buffet $6. AE, DC, DISC, MC, V. Sun–Thurs 11am–11:30pm; Fri–Sat 11am–12:30am (lunch buffet Mon–Fri 11am–2pm).

THE SPACE COAST AFTER DARK

For a rundown of current performances and exhibits, call the **Brevard Cultural Alliance's Arts Line** (℃ 321/690-6819). For live music, walk out on the **Cocoa Beach Pier,** on Meade Avenue at the beach, where **Oh Shuck's Seafood Bar & Grill** (℃ 321/783-7549), **Marlins Good Times Bar & Grill** (℃ 321/783-7549), and the alfresco **Boardwalk Tiki Bar** ⟨⟨ (same phone as Marlins) have bands on weekends, more often during the summer season. The tiki bar is a great place to hang out over a cold beer during afternoons and evenings.

3 Daytona Beach ⟨★⟨★

54 miles NE of Orlando, 251 miles N of Miami, 78 miles S of Jacksonville

Daytona Beach is a town with many personalities. It is at once the self-proclaimed "World's Most Famous Beach" and "World Center of Racing," a mecca for tattooed motorcyclists and pierced spring-breakers, *and* the home of a surprisingly good art museum. The city and developers are also spending millions of dollars to turn the somewhat seedy beachfront area (complete with the requisite T-shirt and souvenir shops), around the famous Main Street Pier, into Ocean Walk Village, a redevelopment area of shops, entertainment, and resort facilities.

Daytona Beach has been a destination for racing enthusiasts since the early 1900s when "horseless carriages" raced on the hard-packed sand beach. One thing is for sure: Daytonans still love their cars. Recent debate over the environmental impact of unrestricted driving on the beach caused an uproar from citizens who couldn't imagine it any other way. As it worked out, they can still drive on the sand, but not everywhere, and especially not in areas where sea turtles are nesting.

Today, hundreds of thousands of race enthusiasts come to the home of the National Association for Stock Car Auto Racing (NASCAR) for the Daytona 500, the Pepsi 400, and other races throughout the year. The Speedway is also home to DAYTONA USA, a state-of-the-art motor-sports entertainment attraction worth a visit even by nonracing fans.

Be sure to check the "Florida Calendar of Events," in chapter 2, to know when the town belongs to college students during spring break, hundreds of thousands of leather-clad motorcycle buffs during Bike Week and Biketoberfest, or racing enthusiasts for big competitions. You can't find a hotel room, drive the highways, or enjoy a peaceful vacation when they're in town.

ESSENTIALS

GETTING THERE Continental (℃ 800/525-0280; www.continental.com) and **Delta** (℃ 800/221-1212; www.delta.com) fly into the small, pleasant, and calm **Daytona Beach International Airport** (℃ 386/248-8030; http://flydayton afirst.com), 4 miles inland from the beach on International Speedway Boulevard

(U.S. 92), but you usually can find less expensive fares to **Orlando International Airport,** about an hour's drive away (see "Getting There," in chapter 2). **Daytona-Orlando Transit Service (DOTS)** (© **800/231-1965** or 386/257-5411; www.dots-daytonabeach.com) provides van transportation to and from Orlando International Airport. Fares are about $27 for adults one-way, $49 round-trip; children 11 and under are $14 one-way and $28 round-trip. The service brings passengers to the company's terminal at 1034 N. Nova Rd., between 3rd and 4th Streets, or to beach hotels for an additional fee.

If you fly into the Daytona airport, rates for the **Daytona Shuttle** (© **386/255-2294**) range up to $12 per person, $14 per couple, or $6 per person for parties of three or more. The ride from the airport to most beach hotels via **Yellow Cab Co.** (© **386/255-5555**) is between $7 and $18.

Alamo (© 800/327-9622), **Avis** (© 800/831-2847), **Budget** (© 800/527-0700), **Dollar** (© 800/800-4000), **Enterprise** (© 800/325-8007), **Hertz** (© 800/654-3131), and **National** (© 800/227-7368) have booths at the airport. If it suits you, why not rent a Harley? This is Daytona, after all. Contact **Daytona Harley-Davidson** (© 800/307-4464 or 386/258-0638; www.daytonahd.com). Rates are $125 to $135 daily, $600 to $640 weekly.

Amtrak (© **800/872-7245;** www.amtrak.com) trains stop at Deland, about 15 miles southwest of Daytona Beach, with connecting bus service from Deland to the beach.

VISITOR INFORMATION   The **Daytona Beach Area Convention & Visitors Bureau,** 126 E. Orange Ave. (P.O. Box 910), Daytona Beach, FL 32115 (© **800/544-0415** or 386/255-0415; www.daytonabeach.com), can help you with information on attractions, accommodations, dining, and events. The office is on the mainland just west of the Memorial Bridge. The information area of the lobby is open daily from 9am to 5pm. The bureau also maintains a branch at DAYTONA USA, 1801 W. International Speedway Blvd. (open daily 9am–7pm), and a kiosk at the airport.

GETTING AROUND   Although Daytona is primarily a driver's town, VOTRAN, Volusia County's public transit system (© **386/761-7700;** http://votran.org), runs a **free shuttle** around the Main Street Pier/Ocean Walk Village area and a pay **trolley** along Atlantic Avenue on the beach, Monday through Saturday from noon to midnight. Trolley fares are $1 for adults, 50¢ for seniors and children 6 to 17, and free for kids under 6 riding with an adult. VOTRAN also runs **buses** throughout downtown and the beaches.

For a taxi, call **Yellow Cab** (© **386/255-5555**) or **Southern Komfort Cab** (© **386/252-2222**).

A VISIT TO THE WORLD CENTER OF RACING

Daytona International Speedway/DAYTONA USA 𝕲𝕲   You don't have to be a racing fan to enjoy a visit to the **Daytona International Speedway,** 4 miles west of the beach. Opened in 1959 with the first Daytona 500, this 480-acre complex is one of the keynotes of the city's fame. The track presents about 9 weekends of major racing events annually, featuring stock cars, sports cars, motorcycles, and go-karts, and is used for automobile and motorbike testing and other events many other days of the year. Its grandstands can accommodate more than 150,000 fans. Big events sell out months in advance (tickets to the Daytona 500 in February can be gone a year ahead of time), so get your tickets and hotel reservations as early as possible.

Daytona Beach

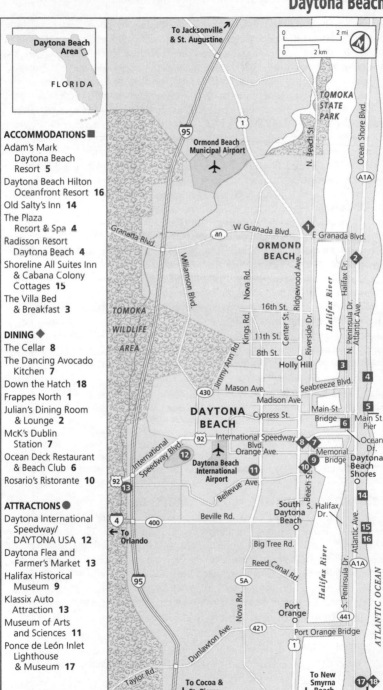

ACCOMMODATIONS ■

Adam's Mark
  Daytona Beach
  Resort **5**

Daytona Beach Hilton
  Oceanfront Resort **16**

Old Salty's Inn **14**

The Plaza
  Resort & Spa **4**

Radisson Resort
  Daytona Beach **4**

Shoreline All Suites Inn
  & Cabana Colony
  Cottages **15**

The Villa Bed
  & Breakfast **3**

DINING ◆

The Cellar **8**

The Dancing Avocado
  Kitchen **7**

Down the Hatch **18**

Frappes North **1**

Julian's Dining Room
  & Lounge **2**

McK's Dublin
  Station **7**

Ocean Deck Restaurant
  & Beach Club **6**

Rosario's Ristorante **10**

ATTRACTIONS ●

Daytona International
  Speedway/
  DAYTONA USA **12**

Daytona Flea and
  Farmer's Market **13**

Halifax Historical
  Museum **9**

Klassix Auto
  Attraction **13**

Museum of Arts
  and Sciences **11**

Ponce de León Inlet
  Lighthouse
  & Museum **17**

Start your visit at the **World Center of Racing Visitors Center,** in the NASCAR office complex at the east end of the speedway. Admission to the center is free, and you can walk out and see the track during nonrace days (there's a small admission to the track during qualifying races leading up to the main events). Entertaining 30-minute guided tram tours of the facility (garage area, pit road, and so on) depart from the visitor center and are well worth taking.

The visitor center houses a large souvenir shop, a snack bar, and the phenomenally popular **DAYTONA USA,** a 60,000-square-foot, state-of-the-art interactive motor-sports entertainment attraction. Here you can learn about the history, color, and excitement of stock car, go-kart, and motorcycle racing in Daytona. In Daytona Dream Laps, one of its newest "rides," you get the feel of what it's like to zoom around the track in a Daytona 500 race from a 32-seat motion simulator. If that doesn't get your stomach churning, hop inside your own 80%-scale NASCAR car in Acceleration Alley, buckle up, and roar up to 200 mph in a spectacular simulator that combines motion, video, projection, and sound for the ultimate virtual reality-like racing experience ($5 per ride above the admission price, below). On the milder side, you can participate in a pit stop on a NASCAR Winston Cup stock car, see an actual winning Daytona 500 car still covered in track dust, talk via video with favorite competitors, and play radio or television announcer by calling the finish of a race. An action-packed IMAX film will put you in the winner's seat of a Daytona 500 race.

To really experience what it's like, you can actually make (for $106) three laps around the track in a stock car from May to October with the **Richard Petty Driving Experience Ride-Along Program** (© **800/237-3889;** www.1800bepetty. com). Professional drivers (sorry, none are named Petty) are at the wheel as you see and feel what it's like to travel an average of 115 mph.

Allow at least 4 hours to see everything and bring your video camera.

1801 W. International Speedway Blvd. (U.S. 92, at Bill France Blvd.). © **386/253-7223** for race tickets, 386/253-7223 for information, or 386/947-6404 or 386/947-6800 for DAYTONA USA. www.daytonaintl speedway.com and www.daytonausa.com. Speedway free admission except on race days; tram rides $7. DAYTONA USA admission $16 adults, $13 seniors, $8 children 6–12. Combination DAYTONA USA–tram tour $20 adults, $17 seniors, $14 children 6–12. Tram rides and DAYTONA USA free admission for children under 6. Speedway daily 9am–7pm; trams depart every 30 min. 9:30am–5pm except during races and special events. DAYTONA USA daily 9am–7pm (later during race events). Closed Christmas.

HITTING THE WORLD'S MOST FAMOUS BEACH

The beautiful and hard-packed beach here runs for 24 miles along a skinny peninsula separated from the mainland by the Halifax River. The bustling hub of activity is at the end of Main Street, near the Adam's Mark Daytona Beach Resort, where you'll find the **Main Street Pier,** which was the longest wooden pier on the East Coast until Hurricane Floyd washed away about a third of its

---

Tips **Driving on the Beach**

You can drive and park directly on sections of the sand along 18 miles of the beach during daylight hours and at low tide (Hurricane Floyd and other recent storms have greatly reduced the beach's width). Watch for signs warning of sea turtles nesting. There's a $5 per vehicle access fee and 10 mph speed limit. *Watch out for the tides.* If you park on an incoming tide and lose track of time, your vehicle may become an inadvertent rust bucket or artificial reef!

1,006 feet in 1999. Out here you'll find a restaurant, bar, bait shop, beach-toy concessions, a chairlift running its length, and views from the 180-foot-tall Space Needle. Admission as far out as the restaurant and bar is free (at about a third of the way, this is far enough for a good view down the beach), but you'll have to pay $1 to walk beyond that point, and more than that if you fish (see "Outdoor Activities," below). Beginning at the pier, the city's famous ocean-side **Boardwalk** is lined with restaurants, bars, and T-shirt shops, as are the 4 blocks of Main Street nearest the beach. The city's Ocean Walk Village redevelopment project begins here and runs several blocks north.

There's another busy beach area at the end of **Seabreeze Boulevard,** which has a multitude of restaurants, bars, and shops.

Couples seeking greater privacy usually prefer the northern or southern extremities of the beach. **Ponce Inlet,** at the very southern tip of the peninsula, is especially peaceful. There is little commerce or traffic to disturb the silence.

OUTDOOR ACTIVITIES

FISHING The easiest and least-expensive way to fish offshore for marlin, sailfish, king mackerel, grouper, red snapper, and more is with the **Critter Fleet,** 4950 S. Peninsula Dr., just past the lighthouse in Ponce Inlet (© **800/338-0850** or 386/767-7676; www.critterfleet.com), which operates two party boats. One goes on all-day trips (about $60 adults, $35 kids under 12), while the other makes morning and afternoon voyages (about $40 adults, $25 kids under 12). The fares include rod, reel, and bait. Call for schedules, prices, and reservations.

Save the cost of a boat and fish with the locals from the **Main Street Pier,** at the ocean end of Main Street near the Adam's Mark Daytona Beach Resort (© **386/253-1212**). Admission for anglers is $3.50 for adults, $2 for kids under 12. Bait and fishing gear are available, and no license is required.

GOLF There are more than 25 courses within 30 minutes of the beach, and most hotels can arrange starting times for you. **Golf Daytona Beach,** 126 E. Orange Ave., Daytona Beach, FL 32114 (© **800/881-7065** or 386/239-7065; fax 386/239-0064), publishes an annual brochure describing the major courses. It's available at the tourist information offices (see "Essentials," above).

For course information online, go to www.golf.com and www.floridagolfing. com, or call the **Florida Sports Foundation** (© **850/488-8347**) or **Florida Golfing** (© **866/833-2663**).

Two of the nation's top-rated links for women golfers are at the **LPGA International** 🏌🏌, 1000 Championship Dr. (© **386/274-5742;** www.lpgainternational.com): Those are the Champions course designed by Rees Jones, and the Legends course designed by Arthur Hills. Both boast 18 outstanding holes. LPGA International is a center for professional and amateur women golfers (workshops and teaching programs), and the pro shop carries a great selection of ladies' equipment and clothing. Greens fees with a cart are usually about $75, less in summer. *Pssst*—They let guys play here, too!

A Lloyd Clifton–designed course, the centrally located 18-hole, par-72 **Indigo Lakes Golf Course,** 2620 W. International Speedway Blvd. (© **386/254-3607;** www.indigolakesgolf.com), has flat fairways and large bunkered Bermuda greens. Fees here are about $65 in winter, including a cart, less in summer.

The semiprivate South Course at **Pelican Bay Country Club,** 550 Sea Duck Dr. (© **386/756-0034;** www.pelicanbaygolfclub.com), is one of the area's favorites, with fast greens to test your putting skills. Fees are about $45 with cart in winter, less in summer (no walking allowed). The North Course is for members only.

The city's prime municipal course is the **Daytona Beach Country Club,** 600 Wilder Blvd. (© **386/258-3119**), which has 36 holes. Winter fees are about $20 to walk, $30 to share a cart. They drop $3 in summer.

HELICOPTER RIDES Take a helicopter ride around the Daytona area to see the city from a different point of view. **Air Florida** (© **386/257-6993;** www.air floridahelicopters.com) offers rides starting at $20 (two-person minimum), leaving from the Daytona Flea & Farmer's Market (see below).

HORSEBACK RIDING **Shenandoah Stables,** 1759 Tomoka Farms Rd., off U.S. 92 (© **386/257-1444**), offers daily trail rides and lessons. Call for prices and schedules.

SPECTATOR SPORTS The **Daytona Cubs** (© **386/872-2827;** www.daytona cubs.com), a Class A minor-league affiliate of the Chicago Cubs, play baseball April through August at Jackie Robinson Ballpark, on City Island downtown. A game here is a treat since the park has been restored to its classic 1914 style by the designers of Baltimore's Camden Yards and Cleveland's Jacobs Field. Tickets are $4 to $7.

WATERSPORTS Watersports equipment, bicycles, beach buggies, and mopeds can be rented along the Boardwalk, at the ocean end of Main Street (see "Hitting the World's Most Famous Beach," above), and in front of major beach-front hotels.

MUSEUMS & ATTRACTIONS

Halifax Historical Museum 🔆
Located on Beach Street, Daytona's original riverfront commercial district on the mainland side of the Halifax River (see "Shopping," below), this local history museum is worth a look just for the 1912 neoclassical architectural details of its home, a former bank (you can see the old vault). A mural of Old Florida wildlife graces one wall, the stained-glass ceiling reflects the sunlight, and across the room an old gold-metal teller's window still stands. The Halifax's eclectic and interesting collection includes tools and house-hold items from the Spanish and British periods, more than 10,000 historic photographs, possessions of past residents (such as a ball gown worn at Lincoln's inauguration), and, of course, model cars. A noteworthy race exhibit opens annually in mid-January as a stage-setter for Race Week.

252 S. Beach St. (just north of Orange Ave.). © 386/255-6976. www.halifaxhistorical.org. Admission $4 adults, $1 children 11 and under, free Sat for children. Tues–Sat 10am–4pm.

Klassix Auto Attraction
True aficionados of the car will enjoy a visit to this attraction, which showcases Corvettes—a model from every year since 1953—and historic vehicles from every motor sport. The rest of us will head to the original "Batmobile" from the 1960s *Batman* TV series, the car from *The Flintstones* series, the "Dragula" owned by the *Munsters,* and "Greased Lightning" from the movie *Grease.* A 1950s-style soda shop and gift shop are also on the premises.

2909 W. International Speedway Blvd., at Tomoka Farms Rd., just west of I-95. © 386/252-3800. www. klassixauto.com. Admission $9 adults, $4.25 children 7–12, free for children under 7. Daily 9am–6pm.

Marine Science Center (Kids)
This new center (opened in June 2002) has interior displays (with exhibits on mangroves, mosquitoes, marine mammal bones, shells, artificial reefs, dune habitats, and pollution solutions), a 5,000-gallon aquarium, and offers educational programs and activities. Though the exhibit area is rather small, there's more than enough information for a child to digest at one time. Perhaps the most interesting part of the center is the space

reserved for the rehabilitation of endangered and threatened sea turtles (once they're "fixed," the healthy turtles are set back into nature).

100 Lighthouse Dr., Ponce Inlet. ℭ 386/304-5545. www.marinesciencecenter.com. $3 adults, $1 children 5–12, free for children under 5. Tues–Sat 10am–4pm; Sun noon–4pm; closed Mon. See directions for Ponce de León Inlet Lighthouse & Museum (below).

Museum of Arts and Sciences ⟨R⟨R⟩ An exceptional institution for a town Daytona's size, this museum is best known for its Cuba: A History of Art exhibit, with paintings acquired in 1956, when Cuban dictator Fulgencio Batista donated his private collection to the city. Among them is a portrait of Eva ("Evita") Perón, said to be the only existing painting completed while she was alive (it hangs near the lobby, not in the Cuban museum). The Dow Gallery displays Smithsonian-quality examples of American decorative arts, and the Bouchelle Study Center for the Decorative Arts contains American and European jewelry, furniture, mirrors, and more. Other rooms worth visiting include the Schulte Gallery of Chinese Art; Africa: Life and Ritual, with the largest collection of Ashante gold ornaments (these are stunning) in the United States, and the Center for Florida history, with the skeleton of a 13-foot-tall, 130,000-year-old giant ground sloth. A recent addition is the unique collection of the late Chapman S. Root, a Daytona philanthropist and a founder of the Coca-Cola empire; among the Root memorabilia is the mold for the original Coke bottle as well as many other changing exhibitions (the collection is very large). The Root family's two private railroad cars are also on display. The planetarium presents 30-minute shows of what the night sky will look like on the date of your visit. Even though this is a first-class art museum, except for the skeleton and the model railroads, children are apt to be bored here.

1040 Museum Blvd. (off Nova Rd./Fla. 5A between International Speedway Blvd. and Bellevue Ave.). ℭ 386/255-0285. www.moas.org. Museum $7 adults, $2 children and students with ID, free for children 5 and under. Planetarium shows $3 adults, $2 children and students. Tues–Fri 9am–4pm; Sat–Sun noon–5pm. Planetarium shows Tues–Fri 2pm; Sat–Sun 1 and 3pm. Closed Thanksgiving, Christmas Eve, Christmas Day. Take International Speedway Blvd. west, make a left on Nova Rd. (Fla. 5A), and look for a sign on your right.

Ponce de León Inlet Lighthouse & Museum ⟨R⟨R⟩ This National Historic Landmark is well worth a stop even if you're not a lighthouse enthusiast. The 175-foot brick-and-granite structure is the second-tallest lighthouse in the United States. (Only the beacon at Cape Hatteras, North Carolina, is taller.) Built in the 1880s, the lighthouse and the graceful Victorian brick buildings surrounding it have been restored (it's one of the only light stations in the United States to have all its original buildings still standing). There are no guided tours, but you can walk through the 12 areas, which feature different exhibits (lighthouse lenses, historical artifacts, and a film of early car racing on the nearby beach), and around the tugboat *F. D. Russell,* now sitting high-and-dry in the sand. Use common sense if you climb the 203 steps to the top of the lighthouse; it's a grinding ascent, but the view from up there is spectacular.

4931 S. Peninsula Dr., Ponce Inlet. ℭ 386/761-1821. www.ponceinlet.org. Admission $5 adults, $1.50 children under 12. Memorial Day–Labor Day daily 10am–9pm; rest of year daily 10am–5pm. Follow Atlantic Ave. south, make a right on Beach St., and follow the signs.

SHOPPING

On the mainland, Daytona Beach's main riverside drag, **Beach Street,** is one of the few areas in town where people actually stroll. The street is wide and inviting, with palms down its median and decorative wrought-iron archways and fancy brickwork overlooking a branch of the Halifax River that separates down-town from City Island, home of municipal offices and the lovingly restored Jackie Robinson Ballpark (see "Spectator Sports," above). Today, Beach Street between Bay Street and Orange Avenue offers antiques and collectibles shops, art galleries, clothiers, a magic shop, the local historical museum (see "Museums & Attractions," above), and several good cafes. 154 S. Beach St. is the home of the **Angell & Phelps Chocolate Factory** (© **386/252-6531;** www.angelland phelps.com), which has been making candy for more than 75 years. Come here to watch the goodies being made (and get a free sample!) or just to buy some of the handmade treats.

"Hog" riders will find several shops to their liking along Beach Street, north of International Speedway Boulevard, including the **Harley Davidson Store,** 290 N. Beach St., at Dr. Mary McLeod Bethune Boulevard (© **386/253-2453**), a 20,000-square-foot retail outlet and diner serving breakfast and lunch. It's one of the nation's largest dealerships. In addition to hundreds of gleaming new and used Hogs, you'll find as much fringed leather as you've ever seen in one place.

The **Daytona Flea & Farmer's Market,** on Tomoka Farms Road at the junc-tion of I-95 and U.S. 92, a mile west of the Speedway (© **386/253-3330;** www.daytonafleamarket.com), is huge, with 1,000 covered outdoor booths plus 100 antiques and collectibles vendors in an air-conditioned building. Most of the booths feature new (though not necessarily first rate) wares along the lines of socks, sunglasses, luggage, handbags, jewelry, tools, and the like. It's open year-round Friday through Sunday from 8am to 5pm. Admission and parking are free.

Ocean Walk Shoppes at Ocean Walk Village (250 N. Atlantic Ave.; © **386/ 257-5077;** www.oceanwalkvillage.com), is a collection of upscale boutiques, restaurants, and theaters.

WHERE TO STAY

Room rates here are among the most affordable in Florida. Some properties have as many as 20 rate periods during the year, but generally they are somewhat higher from the beginning of the races in February all the way to Labor Day. They skyrocket during major events at the Speedway, during bikers' gatherings, and during college spring break (see "Orlando Area Calendar of Events," in chapter 2), when local hotels fill to the bursting point. Even if you can find a room then, there's often a minimum-stay requirement.

Hundreds of hotels and motels line Atlantic Avenue along the beach, many of them family owned and operated. The Daytona Beach Area Convention & Visitors Bureau (see "Essentials," earlier in this chapter) distributes a brochure that lists **Superior Small Lodgings** for Daytona Beach, Deland, and New Smyrna Beach. All of the small motels listed below are members.

If you're going to the races and don't care about staying on the beach, some upper-floor rooms at the new **Hilton Garden Inn Daytona Beach Airport,** 189 Midway Ave. (© **877/944-4001** or 386/944-4000), overlook the interna-tional speedway track. Unlike most members of Hilton's Garden Inn chain, this one has a restaurant.

Thousands of rental condominiums line the beaches here. Among the most luxurious is the new, 150-unit condominium hotel **Ocean Walk Resort,** 300 N. Atlantic Ave., Daytona Beach, FL 32118 (© **800/649-3566** or 386/323-4800; www.oceanwalkresort.com), which is part of the Ocean Walk Village redevelop-ment. Near the Main Street Pier, it's in the center of the action and has one- and two-bedroom apartments with fully equipped kitchens, washers and dryers, and all of the usual hotel amenities, plus a wondrous computer golf simulator, a "lazy river" in the outdoor pool, an island putting green, and much more—including the gaudiest lobby we've ever seen. One of the largest rental agents is **Peck Realty,** 2340 S. Atlantic Ave., Daytona Beach Shores, FL 32118 (© **800/447-3255** or 386/257-5000; www.peckrealty.com).

In addition to the 6% state sales tax, Volusia County levies a 4% tax on hotel bills.

Adam's Mark Daytona Beach Resort 🏖 Daytona's largest beachfront hotel has extensive on-site meeting facilities and the city's Ocean Center convention complex is across the street, meaning lots of big groups stay here. It's also in the middle of the beach action, right on the city's Boardwalk and a block north of the busy Main Street Pier. One of Daytona's best-equipped properties, it's designed so every room has an ocean view.

100 N. Atlantic Ave. (Fla. A1A, between Earl St. and Auditorium Blvd.), Daytona Beach, FL 32118. © 800/444-2326 or 386/254-8200. Fax 386/253-0275. www.adamsmark.com. 746 units. $115–$185 double. AE, DC, DISC, MC, V. Valet parking $9; free self-parking. **Amenities:** 3 restaurants (American); 3 bars; heated outdoor pool; exercise room; Jacuzzis; sauna; watersports equipment rentals; bike rental; game room; concierge; limited room service; massage; babysitting; laundry service; coin-op washers and dryers; concierge-level rooms. In room: A/C, TV, dataport, coffeemaker, hair dryer, iron.

Daytona Beach Hilton Oceanfront Resort 🏖🏖 Far enough south to escape the maddening crowds at Main Street, the Hilton is among the best choices here. It welcomes you in an elegant terra-cotta–tiled lobby with comfortable seating areas, a fountain, and potted palms. The large guest rooms are grouped in pairs and can be joined to form a suite; only one of each pair has a balcony. Oceanfront rooms are preferable, but all have sea and/or river views. A few also have kitchenettes. The surprisingly good Blue Water lobby restaurant is one of Daytona's most beautiful; patio dining is an option.

2637 S. Atlantic Ave. (Fla. A1A, between Florida Shores Blvd. and Richard's Lane), Daytona Beach, FL 32118. © 800/774-1500 or 386/767-7350. Fax 386/760-3651. www.hilton.com. 214 units. $116–$359 double. AE, DC, DISC, MC, V. **Amenities:** Restaurant (American); bar; heated outdoor pool; Jacuzzi; exercise room; watersports equipment rentals; game room; salon; limited room service; babysitting; laundry service; coin-op washers and dryers; concierge-level rooms. In room: A/C, TV, dataport, kitchen, coffeemaker, hair dryer, iron.

Old Salty's Inn The most unusual of the many mom-and-pop beachside motels here, Old Salty's is a lush tropical enclave carrying out a *Gilligan's Island* theme, with old motors, rotting boats, life preservers, and a Jeep lying about. The TV series' main characters are depicted in big murals painted on the buildings. The two-story wings flank a courtyard festooned with palms and banana trees (you can pick one for breakfast). Facing this vista, the bright rooms have microwaves, refrigerators, and front-and-back windows to let in good ventilation. The choice units have picture windows overlooking the beach. There are gas grills and rocking chairs under a gazebo by a heated beachside swimming pool.

1921 S. Atlantic Ave. (Fla. A1A, at Flamingo Ave.), Daytona Beach Shores, FL 32118. © 800/417-1466 or 386/252-8090. Fax 386/947-9980. www.oldsaltys.com. 19 units. $51–$126 (double rooms–efficiencies and suites, depending on the time of year). AE, DISC, MC, V. **Amenities:** Heated outdoor pool; free use of bikes; coin-op washers and dryers. In room: A/C, TV, kitchen, fridge, coffeemaker, hair dryer, iron.

The Plaza Resort & Spa 🏖🏖 Remodeled in 2000 to the tune of $26 million (the original 7-story hotel was built in the early 20th century), these elegant adjoining 7- and 13-story buildings now hold some of Daytona Beach's best rooms (in a much more tasteful atmosphere than many of the neighboring hotels)—provided you don't need a large bathroom. The choice units are the corner suites, which have sitting areas and two balconies overlooking the Atlantic; some even have a Jacuzzi. All units have balconies and microwaves (an on-premises convenience store sells frozen dinners). The renovations also saw the opening of the full-service **Ocean Waters Spa** ⁂ (© **386/267-1660;** www.oceanwatersspa.com). There are 16 treatment rooms and a soothing menu of facials, massages, and wraps.

600 N. Atlantic Ave. (at Seabreeze Ave.), Daytona Beach, FL 32118. © **800/874-7420** or 386/255-4471. Fax 386/238-7984. www.plazaresortandspa.com. 323 units. $69–$449 doubles–suites. AE, DC, DISC, MC, V. **Amenities:** Restaurant (seafood/sushi); bar; heated outdoor pool; exercise room; spa; Jacuzzi; watersports equipment rentals; game room; business center; limited room service; massage; babysitting; laundry service; coin-op washers and dryers; concierge-level rooms. *In room:* A/C, TV, dataport, microwave, fridge, coffeemaker, hair dryer, iron.

Radisson Resort Daytona Beach ⁂

This 11-story, all-modern Radisson sits beachside a half-mile north of the Main Street Pier and around the corner from restaurants and bars on Seabreeze Boulevard. The rooms are among the most spacious on the beach and have angled balconies facing the beach (your neighbor's air conditioner exhausts onto your balcony, however, which can create noise and heat when you're sitting out there). About a third have small additional rooms with wet bars, microwaves, and refrigerators.

640 N. Atlantic Ave. (Fla. A1A, between Seabreeze Blvd. and Glenview Blvd.), Daytona Beach, FL 32118. © **800/333-3333** or 386/239-9800. Fax 386/253-0735. www.daytonaradisson.com. 206 units. $89–$169 double. AE, DC, DISC, MC, V. **Amenities:** Restaurant (American); bar; heated outdoor pool; exercise room; watersports equipment rentals; limited room service; babysitting; coin-op washers and dryers; concierge-level rooms. *In room:* A/C, TV, dataport, fridge, coffeemaker, hair dryer, iron.

Shoreline All Suites Inn & Cabana Colony Cottages (Value)

The Shoreline All Suites Inn, built in 1954 but substantially modernized, features one- and two-bedroom suites that occupy two buildings separated by a walkway leading to the beach. Most have small bathrooms with scant vanity space and—shall we say—intimate shower stalls. Every unit has a full kitchen, plus there are barbecue grills on premises. For a change of scenery, consider the fine little cottage complex at the Shoreline's sister property, the **Cabana Colony Cottages** ⁂. All 12 of the cottages were built in 1927 but have been upgraded by the owners. They aren't much bigger than a motel room with a kitchen, but they're light and airy and are attractively furnished with white wicker pieces. The cottages share a heated beachside swimming pool with the Shoreline.

2435 S. Atlantic Ave. (Fla. A1A, at Dundee Rd.), Daytona Beach Shores, FL 32118. © **800/293-0653** or 386/252-1692. Fax 386/239-7068. www.daytonashoreline.com. 30 units, including 12 cottages. $59–$350 suites–cottages. Rates include continental breakfast. Golf packages available. AE, DISC, MC, V. **Amenities:** Heated outdoor pool; coin-op washers and dryers. *In room:* A/C, TV/VCR, kitchen, coffeemaker.

The Villa Bed & Breakfast ⁂

You'll think you're in Iberia upon entering this Spanish mansion's great room with its fireplace, baby grand piano, terra-cotta floors, and walls hung with Mediterranean paintings. A sunroom equipped with a TV and VCR, a formal dining room, and a breakfast nook are also located downstairs. The lush backyard surrounds a swimming pool and a covered, four-person Jacuzzi. Upstairs, the nautically themed Christopher Columbus room has a vaulted ceiling and a small balcony overlooking the pool. The largest quarter here is the King Carlos suite, the original master bedroom with a four-poster bed, entertainment system, refrigerator, rooftop deck, dressing area, and bathroom equipped with a four-head shower. The Queen Isabella room has a portrait of the queen over a queen-size bed, and the Marco Polo room has Chinese black-lacquer furniture and Oriental rugs evoking the great explorer's adventures.

801 N. Peninsula Dr. (at Riverview Blvd.), Daytona Beach, FL 32118. ✆ and fax **386/248-2020**. www.thevilla bb.com. 4 units (all with bathroom). $125–$250 double. Rates include continental breakfast. AE, MC, V. No children or pets accepted. **Amenities:** Heated outdoor pool; Jacuzzi. *In room:* A/C, TV, hair dryer, no phone.

WHERE TO DINE

Daytona Beach has a few interesting dining venues, but not many are likely to leave an indelible memory. A profusion of fast-food joints line the major thoroughfares, especially along Atlantic Avenue on the beach and International Speedway Boulevard (U.S. 92) near the racetrack. Restaurants come and go in the Beach Street district on the mainland, and along Main Street and Seabreeze Boulevard on the beach. A casual restaurant serves burgers and chicken wings and lots of suds out on the Main Street Pier.

The local **Shells** seafood restaurant is on the beach at 200 S. Atlantic Ave. (✆ **386/258-0007;** www.shellsseafood.com), a block north of International Raceway Boulevard. See p. 326 for details about this inexpensive chain.

There are two other outlets of chain restaurants that are worth a special mention. **Buca di Beppo** (a boisterous, fun, and loud restaurant serving "immigrant southern Italian specialties" family style) is open for dinners only, until 10pm (11pm on Fri and Sat). Expect to take home leftovers, as the portions are huge—but don't worry, you'd want to anyway: The food is surprisingly good, especially for a "theme" restaurant (2514 W. International Speedway Blvd.; ✆ **386/253-6523;** www. bucadibeppo.com). **Stonewood Tavern & Grill** (100 S. Atlantic Ave. in Ormond Beach; ✆ **386/671-1200;** www.stonewoodgrill.com) is a casual but upscale restaurant with a nice but dark mahogany interior, good American food, and excellent service. Also only open for dinner, you won't be disappointed with its menu of steaks, seafood, and the like.

AT THE BEACHES

Down the Hatch 🗣 *Value* SEAFOOD   Occupying a 1940s fish camp on the Halifax River, Down the Hatch serves big portions of fresh fish and seafood (note its shrimp boat docked outside). Inexpensive burgers and sandwiches are available, too. The scenic views include boats and shorebirds visible through the big picture windows—you might even see dolphins frolicking. At night, arrive early to catch the sunset over the river, and also to beat the crowd at this very popular place. In summer, light fare is served outside on an awning-covered deck.

4894 Front St., Ponce Inlet. ✆ 386/761-4831. Call ahead for priority seating. Main courses $9–$25 (most $10–$16); breakfast $2–$5; burgers and sandwiches $3–$6.50; early-bird menu (served 11am–5pm) $6–$8. AE, MC, V. Daily 8am–10pm. Closed 1st week in Dec. Take Atlantic Ave. south, make a right on Beach St., and follow the signs.

Julian's Dining Room & Lounge 🗣 AMERICAN   This family-owned, family-operated restaurant has catered to locals and tourists since 1967, offering a casual atmosphere and friendly service. Unlike most eateries in this area, it specializes in prime Western beef (filets mignons, strip steaks, and T-bones, any of which we recommend). But the seafood is far from second fiddle. Choices include broiled snapper, fried or sautéed softshell crab, and king crab au gratin.

88 S. Atlantic Ave., Ormond Beach. ✆ 386/677-6767. www.juliansrest.com. Reservations suggested. Main courses $9–$26. AE, DC, MC, V. Daily 4–11pm. From Daytona Beach, take Atlantic Ave./Fla. A1A north and look for the large A-frame on the left, 2 blocks before Fla. 40.

Ocean Deck Restaurant & Beach Club *Value* SEAFOOD/PUB FARE Known by spring-breakers, bikers, and other beachgoers as Daytona's best "beach pub" since 1940, the Ocean Deck is also the best restaurant in the busy area around the Main Street Pier. Opening to the sand and surf, the downstairs reggae bar is as sweaty, noisy, and packed as ever (a band plays down there nightly from 9pm–2:30am). The upstairs dining room can be noisy, too, but you can come here for some good food, reasonable prices, and great ocean views. You can choose from a wide range of seafood, chicken, sandwiches, and the best burgers on the beach, but don't pass up the mahimahi (look for "trophy" on the menu), first broiled with peppery Jamaican spices and then finished off on a grill, a bargain at $9. There's valet parking after dark, or you can park free at the lot behind the Ocean Deck's Reggae Republic surf shop, a block away on Atlantic Avenue.

127 S. Ocean Ave. (at Kemp St.). 🕻 386/253-5224. www.oceandeck.com. Main courses $9–$18; salads and sandwiches $5–$8. AE, DISC, MC, V. Daily 11am–2am (bar to 3am).

ON THE MAINLAND

The Cellar AMERICAN   An excellent place for ladies who lunch, this tearoom occupies the basement of a Victorian home built in 1907 as President Warren G. Harding's winter home (he spent election eve here in 1920) and now is listed in the National Register of Historic Places. It couldn't be more charming, with low ceilings, back-lit reproduction Tiffany windows, fresh flowers everywhere, linen tablecloths and napkins, and china teacups. If you can play the piano, help yourself to the baby grand. A wide-ranging lunch menu offers the likes of the house signature chicken salad as a platter or croissant sandwich, a quiche du jour, crab-cake sandwich, vegetarian lasagna, or chicken potpie. In the warm months, there's outdoor seating at umbrella tables on a covered garden patio.

220 Magnolia Ave. (between Palmetto and Ridgewood aves.). 🕻 386/258-0011. Soups, salads, sandwiches $6–$9. AE, DISC, MC, V. Mon–Fri 11am–3pm.

The Dancing Avocado Kitchen 🐨 VEGETARIAN   A healthy place to start your day, or have lunch while touring downtown, this store-front establishment purveys a number of vegetarian omelets, burritos, salads, personal-size pizzas, and hot and cold sandwiches such as an avocado Reuben. A few chicken and turkey items are on the menu, but the only red-meat selection is a hamburger. You can dine outside or inside the store with vegetable drawings on its brick walls and ceiling fans suspended from black rafters.

110 S. Beach St. (between Magnolia St. and International Speedway Blvd.). 🕻 386/947-2022. Breakfast $2.50–$5; sandwiches, salads, pizzas $4–$8. AE, DC, DISC, MC, V. Mon–Sat 8am–4pm.

Frappes North 🐨🐨 CREATIVE AMERICAN/FUSION   It's worth the 6-mile drive north to Bobby and Meryl Frappier's sophisticated, hip establishment, at which they provide this area's most entertaining cuisine. Several chic dining rooms—one has beams extending like spokes from a central pole—set the stage for an inventive, ever-changing "Menu of the Moment" fusing a multitude of styles. Ingredients are always fresh, and the herbs come from the restaurant's garden. You may run into treats such as organically groovy chicken with goat cheese, prosciutto, shiitake mushrooms, and Madeira wine sauce or maple-glazed crispy duck. Bobby and Meryl always have at least one vegetarian (though not necessarily nondairy) main course. Lunch is a steal here, with dinner-size main courses at a fraction of dinnertime prices. The restaurant is in a storefront on the mainland stretch of Granada Boulevard, Ormond Beach's main drag.

123 W. Granada Blvd. (Fla. 40; between Ridgewood Ave. and Washington St.), Ormond Beach. 🕻 386/615-4888. www.frappesnorth.com. Reservations recommended. Main courses $15–$25; lunch $7–$11. AE, MC, V. Mon–Thurs 11:30am–2:30pm and 5–9pm; Fri–Sat 5–10pm. From the beaches, drive 4 miles north on Fla. A1A to left on Granada Blvd. (Fla. 40); cross Halifax River to restaurant on right.

McK's Dublin Station AMERICAN/IRISH   Worth knowing about because it serves food after midnight, this upscale Irish pub has an eclectic menu. The fare includes club sandwiches, burgers, a mahimahi wrap, and a few main courses of steaks, fish, and chicken. The food isn't exceptional, but it's perfectly acceptable after a few Bass ales. The service is sometimes rushed, but usually pleasant.

218 S. Beach St. (between Magnolia St. and Ivy Lane). (C) **386/238-3321.** Reservations not accepted. Main courses $6–$15; salads and sandwiches $5–$8. AE, MC, V. Mon–Wed 11am–9pm; Thurs–Sat 11am–10pm (bar open later).

Rosario's Ristorante ✿ SOUTHERN ITALIAN/TUSCAN   A Victorian boarding house with lace curtains on high windows makes an incongruous setting for a lively restaurant. The menu delivers pastas with Bolognese and marinara sauces, but nightly specials are much more intriguing, drawing inspiration from ancient Tuscan recipes. If the mixed grill of squirrel, pheasant, rabbit, and quail in a hunter's sauce doesn't appeal, you can always opt for grouper Livornese. There's music in the cozy bar Thursday through Saturday nights.

In Live Oak Inn, 448 S. Beach St. (at Loomis Ave.). (C) **386/258-6066.** Reservations recommended. Main courses $12–$24. MC, V. Tues–Sat 5–10pm.

DAYTONA BEACH AFTER DARK

Check the Friday edition of the Daytona Beach *News-Journal* (**www.n-jcenter. com**) for its weekly "Go-Do" and the Sunday edition for the "Master Calendar" section, which list upcoming events. Other good sources are *Happenings Magazine* and *Backstage Pass Magazine,* two tabloids available at the visitor center (see "Essentials," earlier in this chapter) and in many hotel lobbies.

THE PERFORMING ARTS   The city-operated **Peabody Auditorium,** 600 Auditorium Blvd., between Noble Street and Wild Olive Avenue (box office (C) **386/254-4545** or 386/671-3460), is Daytona's major venue for serious performance, including concerts by the local Symphony Society ((C) **386/253-2901**). Professional actors perform Broadway musicals during winter and summer at the **Seaside Music Theater,** 176 N. Beach St., downtown ((C) **800/854-5592** or 386/252-6200; www.seasidemusictheater.org).

Under the city auspices, the **Oceanfront Bandshell** ((C) **386/671-3400**), on the boardwalk next to the Adam's Mark Hotel, hosts a series of free big-name concerts every Sunday night from early June to Labor Day. It's also the scene of raucous spring-break concerts.

THE CLUB & BAR SCENE   In addition to the following, the sophisticated **Clocktower Lounge** at the Adam's Mark Daytona Beach Resort (see "Where to Stay," earlier in this chapter) is worth a visit.

Main Street and **Seabreeze Boulevard** on the beach are happening areas where dozens of bars (and a few topless shows) cater to leather-clad bikers.

A popular beachfront bar for more than 40 years, the **Ocean Deck Restaurant & Beach Club,** 127 S. Ocean Ave. ((C) **386/253-5224;** see "Where to Dine," above), is packed with a mix of locals and tourists, young and old, who come for live music and cheap drinks. Reggae or ska bands play after 9:30pm. There's valet parking after dark, or leave your vehicle at Ocean Deck's Reggae Republic surf shop on Atlantic Avenue.

Appendix A:
Orlando in Depth

1 History 101, or How a Sleepy Southern Town Met (the Other) Mighty Mouse

Outsiders weaned on orange-juice commercials and mouse tales might think the history of the region can be condensed into three sentences: (1) There were orange groves. (2) Walt Disney came. (3) You can now buy three T-shirts for $10. There is, however, considerably more juice to be squeezed from the story. The modern metropolis of Orlando began as a rough-and-tumble Cracker cowboy town, where the promise of a good barbecue dinner and a better shot of whiskey lured early voters to the polls.

SETTLERS VERSUS SEMINOLES: THE ROAD TO STATEHOOD

Florida history dates to 1513—more than a century before the Pilgrims landed at Plymouth Rock—when Ponce de León, a sometimes misguided explorer, spied the shoreline and lush greenery of Florida's Atlantic coast while he was looking for "the fountain of youth." He named it *La Florida*—"the place of flowers." After years of alternating Spanish, French, and British rule, the territory was ceded (by Spain) to the United States in 1821. Lost in the international shuffle were the Seminole Indians. After migrating from Georgia and the Carolinas in the late 18th century to some of Florida's richest farmlands, they were viewed by the *new* Americans as an obstacle to white settlement. A series of compromise treaties and violent clashes between settlers and the Seminoles continued through 1832, when a young warrior named

Dateline

- **1843** Mosquito County in central Florida is renamed Orange County, but the blood-sucking insects stick around.
- **1856** Orlando becomes the seat of Orange County.
- **1875** Orlando is incorporated as a municipality.
- **1880** The South Florida Railroad paves the way for the expansion of Orlando's agricultural markets. Swamp cabbage hits an all-time high on the commodities market.
- **1884** Fire destroys much of Orlando's fledgling business district.
- **1894–95** Freezing temperatures destroy the citrus crops and wreck groves. Many growers lose everything.
- **1910–25** A land boom hits Florida. Fortunes are made overnight.
- **1926** The land boom goes bust. Fortunes are lost overnight.
- **1929** An invasion of Mediterranean fruit flies devastates Orlando's citrus industry. But, who cares? Here comes the stock market crash.
- **1939–45** World War II revives Orlando's ailing economy. There's nothing like a good war to end a depression.
- **1964** Walt Disney begins surreptitiously buying central Florida farmland, purchasing more than 28,000 acres for nearly $5.5 million.
- **1965** Disney announces his plan to build the world's most spectacular theme park, in Orlando.
- **1966** Walt Disney dies of lung cancer.
- **1971** The Magic Kingdom opens its cash drawers. Six new banks, two armored-car companies, and a mint open to handle the loot.

Osceola strode up to the bargaining table, slammed his knife into the papers on it, and, pointing to the quivering blade, proclaimed, "The only treaty I will ever make is this!"

With that dramatic statement, the hostilities worsened. The Seminoles' guerrilla-style warfare thwarted the U.S. Army's attempt to remove them for almost 8 years, during which time many of the resisters drifted south into the interior of central Florida. In what is today the Orlando area, the white settlers built Fort Gatlin in 1838 to offer protection to pioneer homesteaders. The Seminoles kept up a fierce rebellion until 1842, when, undefeated, they accepted a treaty whereby their remaining numbers (about 300) were given land and promised peace. The same year, the Armed Occupation Act offered 160 acres to any pioneer willing to settle here for a minimum of 5 years. The land was fertile: Wild turkeys and deer abounded in the woods, grazing land for cattle was equally plentiful, and dozens of lakes provided fish for settlers and water for livestock. In 1843, what had been Mosquito County was more invitingly renamed Orange County. And with the Seminoles more or less out of the picture (though sporadic uprisings still occurred), the Territorial General Legislature petitioned Congress for statehood. On March 3, 1845, President John Tyler signed a bill making Florida the 27th state.

Settlements and statehood notwithstanding, at the middle of the 19th century, the Orlando area (then named Jernigan for one of its first settlers) consisted largely of pristine lakes and pine-forested wilderness. There were no roads, and you could ride all day (if you could find a trail) without meeting a soul. The Jernigans successfully raised cattle, and their homestead was given a post office in 1850. It became a way stop for travelers and the seat of future development. In

- **1972** A new 1-day attendance mark is set December 27, when 72,328 people visit the Magic Kingdom. It will be broken almost every year thereafter.
- **1973** Shamu swims in on a high tide. SeaWorld opens.
- **1979** Mickey Mouse welcomes the Magic Kingdom's 100 millionth visitor, 8-year-old Kurt Miller from Kingsville, Maryland.
- **1982** Epcot opens with vast hoopla. Participating celebrities include former president Richard Nixon and New York Yankees president George Steinbrenner.
- **1989** WDW launches Disney–MGM Studios (offering a behind-the-scenes look at Tinseltown), Typhoon Lagoon (a 56 acre water theme park), and Pleasure Island (a nightclub district for adults).
- **1990** Universal Studios Florida opens, offering visitors thrilling encounters with ET and King Kong.
- **1993** SeaWorld expands and Universal Studios unleashes the fearsome *Jaws*.
- **1998** Disney starts its own cruise line, and opens most of Animal Kingdom. Universal opens CityWalk, a vast new entertainment complex. Disney's West Side, Pleasure Island, and Disney Village Marketplace become known as Downtown Disney.
- **1999** Islands of Adventure, Universal Orlando's second theme park, opens, featuring stomach-churning thrill rides tied to baby-boomer faves such as Dr. Seuss and Spider-Man. The final section of Animal Kingdom, Asia, opens. The Disney Cruise Line launches Good Ship No. 2, the *Wonder*.
- **2000** SeaWorld opens its second park, Discovery Cove, a wallet-busting chance to swim with the fishes, er, dolphins. SeaWorld also delivers its first roller coaster, Kraken. In December, Universal opens its second resort, the Hard Rock Hotel.
- **2001** A faltering economy closes Church Street Station's doors. The industry takes an even heavier blow due to the September 11, 2001, terrorist attacks.
- **2002–03** Universal opens its third resort, the Royal Pacific.
- **2003** Cypress Gardens closes after 67 years in operation because of poor attendance.

1856, the boundaries of Orange County were revised, and, thanks to the manipulations of resident James Gamble Speer, a member of the Indian Removal Commission, Fort Gatlin (Jernigan) became its official seat.

How the fledgling town came to be named Orlando is a matter of some speculation. Some say Speer renamed the town after a dearly loved friend, whereas other sources say it was named after a Shakespearean character in *As You Like It*. But the most accepted version is that the town was named for plantation owner Orlando Reeves (or Rees), whose homestead had been burned out in a skirmish. For years, it was thought a marker discovered near the shores of Lake Eola, in what is now downtown, marked his grave. But Reeves died later, in South Carolina. It's assumed the name carved in the tree was a marker for others who were on the Indians' trail. Whatever the origin, Orlando was officially recognized by the U.S. Postmaster in 1857.

THE 1860s: CIVIL WAR/CATTLE WARS Throughout the early 1860s, cotton plantations and cattle ranches became the hallmarks of central Florida. A cotton empire ringed Orlando. Log cabins went up along the lakes and the pioneers eked out a somewhat lonely existence, separated from each other by miles of farmland. But there were troubles brewing in the 31-state nation that soon devastated Orlando's planters. By 1859, it was obvious that only a war would resolve the slavery issue. In 1861, Florida became the third state to secede from the Union, and the modest progress it had achieved came to a standstill. The Stars and Bars flew from every flagpole and local men enlisted in the Confederate army, leaving the fledgling town in poverty. A federal blockade made it difficult to obtain necessities and many slaves fled. In 1866, the Confederate troops of Florida surrendered, the remaining slaves were freed, and a ragtag group of defeated soldiers returned to Orlando. They found a dying cotton industry, unable to function without slave labor. In 1868, Florida was readmitted to the Union.

Its untended cotton fields having gone to seed, Orlando concentrated on cattle ranching, a business heavily taxed by the government, and one that ushered in an era of lawlessness and violence. A famous battle involving two families, the Barbers and the Mizells, left at least nine men dead in 2 months in a Florida version of the Hatfields and McCoys.

Like frontier cattle towns out West, post–Civil War Orlando was short on civilized behavior. Gunfights, brawls, and murders were commonplace. But as the 1860s came to an end, large-herd owners from other parts of the state moved into the area and began organizing the industry in a less chaotic fashion. Branding and penning greatly reduced rustling, though they didn't totally eliminate the problem. Even a century later—as recently as 1973—soaring beef prices caused a rash of cattle thievery. Some traditions die hard. Even today, there are a number of rustling complaints each year.

AN ORANGE TREE GROWS IN ORLANDO In the 1870s, articles in national magazines began luring large numbers of Americans to central Florida

---

Fun Fact **A Fountain of Fruit**

Legend has it that Florida's citrus industry has its roots in seeds spit onto the ground by Ponce de León and his followers as they traversed the state searching for the fountain of youth. The seeds supposedly germinated in the rich Florida soil.

with promises of fertile land and a warm climate. In Orlando, public roads, schools, and churches sprang up to serve the newcomers, many of whom replanted defunct cotton fields with citrus groves. Orlando was incorporated under state law in 1875, and boundaries and a city government were established.

New settlers poured in from all over the country, businesses flourished, and by the end of the year the town had its first newspaper, the *Orange County Reporter*. The first locomotive of the South Florida Railroad chugged into town in 1880, sparking a building and land boom—the first of many. Orlando got sidewalks and its first bank in 1883, the same year the town voted itself "dry" in hopes of averting the fist fights and brawls that ensued when cowboys crowded into local saloons every Saturday night for some rowdy R&R. For many years, the city continued to vote itself alternately wet and dry, but it made little difference. Legal or not, liquor was always readily available.

FIRE & ICE   In January 1884, a grocery fire that started at 4am wiped out blocks of businesses, including the *Orange County Reporter*. But 19th-century Orlando was a bit like a Frank Capra movie. The town rallied around, providing a new location for the paper and presenting its publisher, Mahlon Gore, with $1,200 in cash to help defray losses, and $300 in new subscriptions. The paper not only survived, it flourished. And the city, realizing the need, created its first fire brigade. By August 1884, a census revealed a population of 1,666. That same year, 600,000 boxes of oranges were shipped from Florida to points north—most of those boxes originating in Orlando. By 1885, Orlando was a viable town, boasting as many as 50 businesses. This isn't to say it was New York. Razorback hogs roamed the streets and alligator wrestling was major entertainment.

Disaster struck a week after Christmas in 1894, when the temperature plummeted to an unseasonable 24°F. Water pipes burst and orange blossoms froze, blackened, and died. The freeze continued for 3 days, wrecking the citrus crop for the year.

Many grove owners went bust, and those who remained were hit with a second devastating freeze the following year. Tens of thousands of trees died in the killing frost. Small growers were wiped out, but large conglomerates that could afford to buy up the small growers' properties at bargain prices and wait for new groves to mature assured the survival of the industry.

SPECULATION FEVER: GOOD DEALS, BAD DEALS . . .   As Orlando entered the 20th century, citrus and agriculture surpassed cattle ranching as the mainstays of the local economy. Stray cows no longer had to be shooed from the railway tracks. Streets were being paved and electricity and telephone service installed. The population at the turn of the 20th century was 2,481. In 1902, the city passed its first automobile laws, which included an in-town speed limit of 5 mph. In 1904, the city flooded. And in 1905, it suffered a drought that ended—miraculously or coincidentally—on a day when all faiths united at the local First Baptist Church to pray for rain. By 1910, prosperity returned, and Orlando, with a population of nearly 4,000, was in a small way becoming a tourism and convention center. World War I brought further industrial growth and a real-estate boom, not just to Orlando, but to all of Florida. Millions of immigrants, speculators, and builders descended on the state in search of a quick buck. As land speculation reached a fever pitch and property was bought and resold almost overnight, many citrus groves gave way to urbanization. Preeminent Orlando builder and promoter Carl Dann described the action: "It finally became nothing more than a gambling machine, each man buying on a shoestring, betting dollars a bigger fool would come along and buy his option."

(*Fun Fact* **Liquor Ain't Quicker**

The "Wet/Dry" battle in Orlando continued until 1998, when the city removed "Blue Laws" that restricted the sale of liquor on Sunday within the city limits.

Quite suddenly, the bubble burst. A July 1926 issue of the *Nation* provided the obituary for the Florida land boom: "The world's greatest poker game, played with lots instead of chips, is over. And the players are now . . . paying up." Construction slowed to a trickle, and many newcomers who came to Florida to jump on the bandwagon fled to their homes in the North. Though Orlando wasn't quite as hard hit as Miami—scene of the greediest land grabs—some belt-tightening was in order. Nevertheless, the city managed to build a municipal airport in 1928. Then came a Mediterranean fruit-fly infestation that crippled the citrus industry. Hundreds of thousands of acres of land in quarantined areas had to be cleared of fruit and vast quantities of boxed fruit were destroyed. The 1929 stock market crash that precipitated the Great Depression added an exclamation point to Florida's ruined economy.

. . . & NEW DEALS   President Franklin D. Roosevelt's New Deal helped the state climb back on its feet. The Works Progress Administration (WPA) put 40,000 unemployed Floridians back to work—work that included hundreds of public projects in Orlando. Of these, the most important was the expansion and resurfacing of the city's airport. By 1936, the tourist trade had revived somewhat; construction was up once again, and the state began attracting a broader range of visitors. But the event that finally lifted Florida—and the nation—out of the Depression was World War II.

Orlando had weathered the Great Depression. Now it prepared for war with the construction of army bases, housing for servicemen, and training facilities. Enlisted men poured into the city. The airport was again enlarged and equipped with barracks, a military hospital, administration buildings, and mess halls. By 1944, Orlando had a second airport and was known as "Florida's Air Capital," home to major aircraft and aviation-parts manufacturers. Thousands of servicemen did part of their hitch in Orlando, and, when the war ended, many returned to settle here.

POSTWAR PROSPERITY   By 1950, Orlando, with a population of 51,826, was the financial and transportation hub of central Florida. The city shared the bullish economy of the 1950s with the rest of the nation. In the face of the Cold War, the Orlando air base remained and grew, funneling millions of dollars into the local economy. Florida's population increased by a whopping 78.7% during the decade—making it America's 10th most populated state—and tourists came in droves, nearly 4.5 million in 1950.

One reason for the influx was the advent of the air-conditioner, which made life in Florida *infinitely* more pleasant. Also fueling Orlando's economy was a brand-new industry arriving in nearby Cape Canaveral in 1955—the government-run space program. Cape Canaveral became NASA's headquarters, including the Apollo rocket program that eventually blasted Neil Armstrong toward his "giant leap for mankind." During the same decade, the Glenn L. Martin Company (later Martin Marietta), builder of the Matador Missile, purchased 10 square miles for a plant 4 miles south of Orlando. Its advent sparked further industrial growth and property values soared. More than 60 new industries moved to the area in 1959. But even the most optimistic Orlando boosters couldn't foresee the glorious future that was the city's ultimate destiny.

THE DISNEY DECADES In 1964, Walt Disney began secretly buying millions of dollars worth of central Florida farmland. As vast areas of land were purchased in lots of 5,000 acres here, 20,000 there—at remarkably high prices—rumors flew as to who needed so much land and had the money to acquire it. Some thought it was Howard Hughes; others, the space program. Speculation was rife almost to the very day, November 15, 1965 ("D" Day for Orlando), when Uncle Walt arrived in town and announced his plans to build the world's most spectacular theme park ("bigger and better than Disneyland"). In a 2-year construction effort, Disney employed 9,000 people. Land speculation reached unprecedented heights, as hotel chains and restaurateurs grabbed up property near the proposed park. Mere swampland sold for millions. The total cost of the project by its October 1971 opening was $400 million. Mickey Mouse escorted the first visitor into the Magic Kingdom, and numerous celebrities, from Bob Hope to Julie Andrews, took part in the opening ceremonies. In Walt Disney World's first 2 years, the attraction drew 20 million visitors and employed 13,000 people. The sleepy citrus-growing town of Orlando had become the "Action Center of Florida," and the fastest-growing city in the state.

Additional attractions multiplied faster than fruit flies, and hundreds of firms relocated their businesses to the area. SeaWorld, a major theme park, came to town in 1973. All the while, Walt Disney World continued to grow and expand, adding Epcot in 1982 and Disney–MGM Studios in 1989, along with water parks, over a dozen "official" resorts, a shopping/restaurant village, campgrounds, a vast array of recreational facilities, and several other adjuncts that are thoroughly described in this book. In 1998, Disney opened yet another theme park, this one dedicated to zoological entertainment and aptly called Animal Kingdom.

Universal Orlando, whose Universal Studios Florida park opened in 1990, continues to expand and keep the stakes high. In late 1998, it unveiled a new entertainment district, CityWalk, and in 1999, it opened Islands of Adventure, a second theme park including attractions dedicated to Dr. Seuss, Marvel Comics, and Jurassic Park. Also in 1999, it opened the Portofino Bay Hotel, a 750-room Loews property. In 2001, the curtain went up on the Hard Rock Hotel, and in summer 2002, the Royal Pacific resort opened as Universal announced plans to add two more hotels to the property in the next decade.

While the tourist economy suffered for more than a year after the September 11, 2001, terrorist attacks, it has slowly rebounded. One unfortunate casualty of the economic slowdown following the attacks: Cypress Gardens, the first major park in Orlando, which closed its doors in the spring of 2003. Disney and Universal, however, seem to be back in a building mode, albeit not as enthusiastically as during the late 1990s. But by 2004, the Orlando area is expected to lead the nation in the growth of office employment, adding some 65,900 jobs.

(Fun Fact **In the Words of Walt Disney**

Why be a governor or a senator when you can be king of Disneyland? You can dream, create, design, and build the most wonderful place in the world . . . but it requires people to make the dream a reality.

Appendix B:
Useful Toll-Free Numbers & Websites

AIRLINES

Aer Lingus
✆ 800/474-7424 in the U.S.
✆ 01/886-8888 in Ireland
www.aerlingus.com

Air Canada
✆ 888/247-2262
www.aircanada.ca

Air New Zealand
✆ 800/262-1234 or 800/262-2468 in the U.S.
✆ 800/663-5494 in Canada
✆ 0800/737-767 in New Zealand
www.airnewzealand.com

Airtran Airlines
✆ 800/247-8726
www.airtran.com

Alaska Airlines
✆ 800/426-0333
www.alaskaair.com

American Airlines
✆ 800/433-7300
www.aa.com

American Trans Air
✆ 800/225-2995
www.ata.com

America West Airlines
✆ 800/235-9292
www.americawest.com

British Airways
✆ 800/247-9297
✆ 0345/222-111 or 0845/77-333-77 in Britain
www.british-airways.com

Continental Airlines
✆ 800/525-0280
www.continental.com

Delta Air Lines
✆ 800/221-1212
www.delta.com

Frontier Airlines
✆ 800/432-1359
www.frontierairlines.com

Hawaiian Airlines
✆ 800/367-5320
www.hawaiianair.com

JetBlue Airways
✆ 800/538-2583
www.jetblue.com

Midwest Express
✆ 800/452-2022
www.midwestexpress.com

Northwest Airlines
✆ 800/225-2525
www.nwa.com

Qantas
✆ 800/227-4500 in the U.S.
✆ 612/9691-3636 in Australia
www.qantas.com

Southwest Airlines
✆ 800/435-9792
www.southwest.com

United Airlines
✆ 800/241-6522
www.united.com

US Airways
✆ 800/428-4322
www.usairways.com

Virgin Atlantic Airways
✆ 800/862-8621 in Continental U.S.
✆ 0293/747-747 in Britain
www.virgin-atlantic.com

CAR-RENTAL AGENCIES

Advantage
℡ 800/777-5500
www.advantagerentacar.com

Alamo
℡ 800/327-9633
www.goalamo.com

Avis
℡ 800/331-1212 in Continental U.S.
℡ 800/TRY-AVIS in Canada
www.avis.com

Budget
℡ 800/527-0700
https://rent.drivebudget.com

Dollar
℡ 800/800-4000
www.dollar.com

Enterprise
℡ 800/325-8007
www.enterprise.com

Hertz
℡ 800/654-3131
www.hertz.com

National
℡ 800/CAR-RENT
www.nationalcar.com

Payless
℡ 800/PAYLESS
www.paylesscarrental.com

Rent-A-Wreck
℡ 800/535-1391
www.rentawreck.com

Thrifty
℡ 800/367-2277
www.thrifty.com

MAJOR HOTEL & MOTEL CHAINS

Baymont Inns & Suites
℡ 800/301-0200
www.baymontinns.com

Best Western International
℡ 800/528-1234
www.bestwestern.com

Clarion Hotels
℡ 800/CLARION
www.clarionhotel.com or
www.hotelchoice.com

Comfort Inns
℡ 800/228-5150
www.hotelchoice.com

Courtyard by Marriott
℡ 800/321-2211
www.courtyard.com or
www.marriott.com

Days Inn
℡ 800/325-2525
www.daysinn.com

Doubletree Hotels
℡ 800/222-TREE
www.doubletree.com

Econo Lodges
℡ 800/55-ECONO
www.hotelchoice.com

Fairfield Inn by Marriott
℡ 800/228-2800
www.marriott.com

Hampton Inn
℡ 800/HAMPTON
www.hampton-inn.com

Hilton Hotels
℡ 800/HILTONS
www.hilton.com

Holiday Inn
℡ 800/HOLIDAY
www.basshotels.com

Howard Johnson
℡ 800/654-2000
www.hojo.com

Hyatt Hotels & Resorts
℡ 800/228-9000
www.hyatt.com

Inter-Continental Hotels & Resorts
℡ 888/567-8725
www.interconti.com

ITT Sheraton
✆ 800/325-3535
www.starwood.com

Knights Inn
✆ 800/843-5644
www.knightsinn.com

La Quinta Motor Inns
✆ 800/531-5900
www.laquinta.com

Marriott Hotels
✆ 800/228-9290
www.marriott.com

Motel 6
✆ 800/4-MOTEL6 (800/466-8356)
www.motel6.com

Quality Inns
✆ 800/228-5151
www.hotelchoice.com

Radisson Hotels International
✆ 800/333-3333
www.radisson.com

Ramada Inns
✆ 800/2-RAMADA
www.ramada.com

Red Carpet Inns
✆ 800/251-1962
www.reservahost.com

Red Lion Hotels & Inns
✆ 800/547-8010
www.hilton.com

Red Roof Inns
✆ 800/843-7663
www.redroof.com

Residence Inn by Marriott
✆ 800/331-3131
www.marriott.com

Rodeway Inns
✆ 800/228-2000
www.hotelchoice.com

Sheraton Hotels & Resorts
✆ 800/325-3535
www.sheraton.com

Sleep Inn
✆ 800/753-3746
www.sleepinn.com

Super 8 Motels
✆ 800/800-8000
www.super8.com

Travelodge
✆ 800/255-3050
www.travelodge.com

Vagabond Inns
✆ 800/522-1555
www.vagabondinn.com

Westin Hotels & Resorts
✆ 800/937-8461
www.westin.com

Wyndham Hotels and Resorts
✆ 800/822-4200 in Continental U.S.
and Canada
www.wyndham.com

Index

See also Accommodations and Restaurant indexes, below.

ACCOMMODATIONS

ROMMER'S® COMPLETE TRAVEL GUIDES

laska
laska Cruises & Ports of Call
msterdam
rgentina & Chile
rizona
:lanta
ustralia
ustria
ahamas
arcelona, Madrid & Seville
eijing
elgium, Holland & Luxembourg
ermuda
oston
:azil
:itish Columbia & the Canadian
 Rockies
russels & Bruges
idapest & the Best of Hungary
alifornia
anada
ancún, Cozumel & the Yucatán
ape Cod, Nantucket & Martha's
 Vineyard
aribbean
aribbean Cruises & Ports of Call
aribbean Ports of Call
arolinas & Georgia
hicago
hina
olorado
osta Rica
uba
enmark
enver, Boulder & Colorado Springs
ngland
urope
uropean Cruises & Ports of Call

Florida
France
Germany
Great Britain
Greece
Greek Islands
Hawaii
Hong Kong
Honolulu, Waikiki & Oahu
Ireland
Israel
Italy
Jamaica
Japan
Las Vegas
London
Los Angeles
Maryland & Delaware
Maui
Mexico
Montana & Wyoming
Montréal & Québec City
Munich & the Bavarian Alps
Nashville & Memphis
New England
New Mexico
New Orleans
New York City
New Zealand
Northern Italy
Norway
Nova Scotia, New Brunswick &
 Prince Edward Island
Oregon
Paris
Peru
Philadelphia & the Amish Country
Portugal

Prague & the Best of the Czech
 Republic
Provence & the Riviera
Puerto Rico
Rome
San Antonio & Austin
San Diego
San Francisco
Santa Fe, Taos & Albuquerque
Scandinavia
Scotland
Seattle & Portland
Shanghai
Sicily
Singapore & Malaysia
South Africa
South America
South Florida
South Pacific
Southeast Asia
Spain
Sweden
Switzerland
Texas
Thailand
Tokyo
Toronto
Tuscany & Umbria
USA
Utah
Vancouver & Victoria
Vermont, New Hampshire & Maine
Vienna & the Danube Valley
Virgin Islands
Virginia
Walt Disney World® & Orlando
Washington, D.C.
Washington State

ROMMER'S® DOLLAR-A-DAY GUIDES

ustralia from $50 a Day
alifornia from $70 a Day
ngland from $75 a Day
urope from $70 a Day
orida from $70 a Day
awaii from $80 a Day

Ireland from $60 a Day
Italy from $70 a Day
London from $85 a Day
New York from $90 a Day
Paris from $80 a Day

San Francisco from $70 a Day
Washington, D.C. from $80 a Day
Portable London from $85 a Day
Portable New York City from $90
 a Day

ROMMER'S® PORTABLE GUIDES

capulco, Ixtapa & Zihuatanejo
msterdam
:uba
ustralia's Great Barrier Reef
ahamas
erlin
ig Island of Hawaii
oston
alifornia Wine Country
ancún
ayman Islands
harleston
hicago
isneyland®
ublin
orence

Frankfurt
Hong Kong
Houston
Las Vegas
Las Vegas for Non-Gamblers
London
Los Angeles
Los Cabos & Baja
Maine Coast
Maui
Miami
Nantucket & Martha's Vineyard
New Orleans
New York City
Paris
Phoenix & Scottsdale

Portland
Puerto Rico
Puerto Vallarta, Manzanillo &
 Guadalajara
Rio de Janeiro
San Diego
San Francisco
Savannah
Seattle
Sydney
Tampa & St. Petersburg
Vancouver
Venice
Virgin Islands
Washington, D.C.

ROMMER'S® NATIONAL PARK GUIDES

anff & Jasper
amily Vacations in the National
 Parks

Grand Canyon
National Parks of the American West
Rocky Mountain

Yellowstone & Grand Teton
Yosemite & Sequoia/Kings Canyon
Zion & Bryce Canyon

FROMMER'S® MEMORABLE WALKS

Chicago
London

New York
Paris

San Francisco

FROMMER'S® WITH KIDS GUIDES

Chicago
Las Vegas
New York City

Ottawa
San Francisco
Toronto

Vancouver
Washington, D.C.

SUZY GERSHMAN'S BORN TO SHOP GUIDES

Born to Shop: France
Born to Shop: Hong Kong,
    Shanghai & Beijing

Born to Shop: Italy
Born to Shop: London

Born to Shop: New York
Born to Shop: Paris

FROMMER'S® IRREVERENT GUIDES

Amsterdam
Boston
Chicago
Las Vegas
London

Los Angeles
Manhattan
New Orleans
Paris
Rome

San Francisco
Seattle & Portland
Vancouver
Walt Disney World®
Washington, D.C.

FROMMER'S® BEST-LOVED DRIVING TOURS

Britain
California
Florida
France

Germany
Ireland
Italy
New England

Northern Italy
Scotland
Spain
Tuscany & Umbria

HANGING OUT™ GUIDES

Hanging Out in England
Hanging Out in Europe

Hanging Out in France
Hanging Out in Ireland

Hanging Out in Italy
Hanging Out in Spain

THE UNOFFICIAL GUIDES®

Bed & Breakfasts and Country
    Inns in:
  California
  Great Lakes States
  Mid-Atlantic
  New England
  Northwest
  Rockies
  Southeast
  Southwest
Best RV & Tent Campgrounds in:
  California & the West
  Florida & the Southeast
  Great Lakes States
  Mid-Atlantic
  Northeast
  Northwest & Central Plains

Southwest & South Central
    Plains
  U.S.A.
Beyond Disney
Branson, Missouri
California with Kids
Central Italy
Chicago
Cruises
Disneyland®
Florida with Kids
Golf Vacations in the Eastern U.S.
Great Smoky & Blue Ridge Region
Inside Disney
Hawaii
Las Vegas
London
Maui

Mexio's Best Beach Resorts
Mid-Atlantic with Kids
Mini Las Vegas
Mini-Mickey
New England & New York with
    Kids
New Orleans
New York City
Paris
San Francisco
Skiing & Snowboarding in the Wes
Southeast with Kids
Walt Disney World®
Walt Disney World® for
    Grown-ups
Walt Disney World® with Kids
Washington, D.C.
World's Best Diving Vacations

SPECIAL-INTEREST TITLES

Frommer's Adventure Guide to Australia &
    New Zealand
Frommer's Adventure Guide to Central America
Frommer's Adventure Guide to India & Pakistan
Frommer's Adventure Guide to South America
Frommer's Adventure Guide to Southeast Asia
Frommer's Adventure Guide to Southern Africa
Frommer's Britain's Best Bed & Breakfasts and
    Country Inns
Frommer's Caribbean Hideaways
Frommer's Exploring America by RV
Frommer's Fly Safe, Fly Smart

Frommer's France's Best Bed & Breakfasts and
    Country Inns
Frommer's Gay & Lesbian Europe
Frommer's Italy's Best Bed & Breakfasts and
    Country Inns
Frommer's Road Atlas Britain
Frommer's Road Atlas Europe
Frommer's Road Atlas France
The New York Times' Guide to Unforgettable
    Weekends
Places Rated Almanac
Retirement Places Rated
Rome Past & Present